MANET

MANET

A RETROSPECTIVE

Edited by T. A. Gronberg

Hugh Lauter Levin Associates, Inc., New York

Distributed by Macmillan Publishing Company, New York

For my parents

ISBN 0–88363–173–3

This book was designed and produced by
JOHN CALMANN AND KING LTD, LONDON

Designer Robert Updegraff
Typeset by Composing Operations Ltd, England
Printed and bound in Malaysia

The excerpts in this book are reproduced by kind permission of the copyright owners and publishers, as follows:

Letters from Manet to his Wife, edited and translated by Mina Curtiss. By permission of *Apollo* Magazine, London.

Paul Valéry, The Collected Works, edited by Jackson Matthews, Vol. 12: *Degas, Manet, Morisot*, translated by David Paul, Bollingen Series 45. © 1960 Princeton University Press. Excerpts reprinted with permission of Princeton University Press and Routledge, Kegan Paul, London.

A. Tabarant, *Manet, Histoire Catalographique*, 1931. By permission of Éditions Aubier Montaigne, Paris.

The Correspondence of Berthe Morisot, edited by D. Rouart, 1957. By permission of Lund Humphries Publishers, London.

E. Moreau-Nelaton, *Manet Raconté par Lui-Même*. H. Laurens, Paris, 1926.

Pierre Courthion and Pierre Cailler (editors), *Portrait of Manet by Himself and His Contemporaries*, translated by Michael Ross, 1960. By permission of Macmillan Publishing Co, New York.

G.H. Hamilton, *Manet and his Critics*, 1954. By permission of Yale University Press, New Haven and London, 1986.

Manet, Exhibition Catalogue, 1983, at the Metropolitan Museum of Art, New York. Translation © 1983 Metropolitan Museum of Art, published by Harry N. Abrams, Inc, New York.

Émile Zola, *L'Oeuvre*, translated by Ernest Vizetelly. By permission of the estate of the translator and Chatto and Windus, London.

Julius Meier-Graefe, *Édouard Manet*, 1912. © R. Piper & Co. Verlag, Munich, 1912.

F.W.J. Hemmings and Robert J. Niess, *Émile Zola: Salons*, 1959. By permission of Librairie Droz S.A., Geneva.

Roger Fry, *Manet and the Post-Impressionists*, 1910. By permission of the estate of the author and Chatto and Windus, London.

Roger Fry, *Characteristics of French Art*, 1932. By permission of the estate of the author and Chatto and Windus, London.

Julie Manet, *Journal (1893–1899)*. C. Klincksieck, Paris, 1979.

Ambroise Vollard, *En Écoutant Cézanne, Degas, Renoir*, 1938. By permission of Éditions Bernard Grasset, Paris.

Louisine W. Havemeyer, *Sixteen to Sixty: Memoirs of a Collector*. © 1961 Metropolitan Museum of Art, New York. Reprinted with permission.

Clement Greenberg, "Manet in Philadelphia", © *Artforum*, January 1967.

Hans Haacke, *Unfinished Business*. © 1986 the author, the New Museum of Contemporary Art and Massachusetts Institute of Technology Press.

T.J. Clark, *The Painting of Modern Life: Paris in the Art of Manet and his Followers*, 1985. By permission of Thames and Hudson International Ltd, London.

Sander L. Gilman, "Black Bodies, White Bodies: Toward an Iconography of Female Sexuality in late 19th-Century Art, Medicine and Literature", *Critical Enquiry*, 12, Fall 1985. By permission of the author and the University of Chicago Press.

Full information for each excerpt is given in the Bibliographical Index, page 10.

Jacket: Detail of *Reading*, 1865–73/1868–9. Musée d'Orsay, Paris. See Colourplate 25.

CONTENTS

ACKNOWLEDGEMENTS

The preparation of a book such as this inevitably owes a great debt to the scholars and critics who have produced studies on Manet. Their names are too numerous to mention here, although many appear in the bibliographical index and the notes. I would like to extend personal thanks to Jean Harris, who first awakened my interest in nineteenth-century art and criticism when I was a student at Mount Holyoke College.

I owe a special debt of gratitude to Sylvia Backemeyer, head librarian at the Central School of Art and Design, London, and her staff as well as to the library at St. Martin's School of Art. And I am grateful to Pat Gilmour, Mary Hamer, Paul Overy and Jana Sommerlad for help as well as friendly support.

At Calmann and King, Elisabeth Ingles has been a most conscientious editor, and Susan Dixon has contributed much meticulous work to the compilation of this volume.

T.A. GRONBERG

Bibliographical Index

The complete works of Manet (paintings, pastels and drawings) are discussed and illustrated in Denis Rouart and Daniel Wildenstein's *Édouard Manet: Catalogue raisonné*, 2 volumes, Lausanne, 1975 (referred to in the notes of this book as "Rouart/ Wildenstein"). For Manet's prints see Jean Harris, *Édouard Manet: Graphic Works, a Definitive Catalogue Raisonné*, New York, 1970; Juliet Wilson, *Édouard Manet: Das Graphische Werk: Meisterwerke aus der Bibliothèque Nationale und weiterer Sammlungen* (exhibition catalogue), Ingelheim am Rhein, 1977, and Juliet Wilson, *Manet: Dessins, aquarelles, eaux-fortes, lithographies, correspondance* (exhibition catalogue), Galerie Huguette Berès, Paris, 1978. On Manet and "modernity" see Anne Coffin Hanson, *Manet and the Modern Tradition*, New York, 1977; Theodore Reff, *Manet and Modern Paris* (exhibition catalogue), National Gallery of Art, Washington D.C., 1982, and T.J. Clark, *The Painting of Modern Life: Paris in the Art of Manet and his Followers*, London, 1985. Kathleen Adler's *Manet*, Oxford, 1986, is a recent monograph on the artist. The catalogue to the exhibition commemorating the centenary of Manet's death, *Manet 1832–1883*, Paris and New York, 1983, contains an extensive bibliography.

Full details of each source book are listed at the first reference, and in an abbreviated form of author and date thereafter. Where a later edition has been used, the original date of publication is given first in parentheses. Translations of material previously unpublished in English are by Judith Landry.

p. 35 Antonin Proust, *Édouard Manet: Souvenirs*, H. Laurens, Paris, 1913, pp. 1–2, 4–8.

p. 38 Édouard Manet, *Lettres de Jeunesse 1848–1849: Voyage à Rio*, Louis Rouart, Paris, 1928, pp. 51–57.

p. 40 Proust 1913, pp. 15–16.

p. 47 Proust 1913, pp. 21–22.

p. 48 Proust 1913, pp. 23–24.

p. 49 Proust 1913, pp. 29–30, 39–40.

p. 51 Théodore Duret, *Manet and the French Impressionists*, Grant Richards, London, 1910, pp. 31–32.

p. 52 George Heard Hamilton, *Manet and his Critics* (1954), Yale University Press, New Haven and London, 1986, p. 40.

p. 54 Pierre Courthion and Pierre Cailler (eds.), *Portrait of Manet by Himself and his Contemporaries* (1950), trans. Michael Ross, Cassell, London, 1960, pp. 49–50.

p. 54 Hamilton 1986, pp. 62–63.

p. 55 Courthion and Cailler 1960, pp. 144–47.

p. 57 Hamilton 1986, p. 35.

p. 58 Courthion and Cailler 1960, pp. 14–15.

p. 59 Proust 1913, pp. 36–38.

p. 60 Duret 1910, pp. 28–31.

p. 62 Courthion and Cailler 1960, pp. 113–39.

p. 97 Courthion and Cailler 1960, pp. 60–61.

p. 98 Courthion and Cailler 1960, pp. 140–43.

p. 101 Duret 1910, pp. 54–55.

p. 102 Courthion and Cailler 1960, pp. 16–17.

p. 103 Juliet Wilson Bareau, from *Manet 1832–1883* exhibition catalogue, Metropolitan Museum of Art, New York, 1983, US edition Harry N. Abrams, Inc., Publishers, New York, 1983, pp. 531–34.

p. 105 Hamilton 1986, pp. 137–38.

p. 106 Édmond Bazire, *Manet*, A. Quentin, Paris, 1884, pp. 30–32.

p. 109 D. Rouart (ed.), *The Correspondence of Berthe Morisot* (1957), Camden Press, London, 1986, pp. 40–46, 48, 52.

p. 123 Trans. Mina Curtiss (ed.), Letters of Édouard Manet to his Wife during the Siege of Paris 1870–71, *Apollo*, London, June 1981, pp. 384, 386–87, 389.

p. 126 Bazire 1884, pp. 69–71.

p. 127 Courthion and Cailler 1960, pp. 148–50.

p. 130 E. Moreau-Nelaton, *Manet Raconté par Lui-Même*, H. Laurens, Paris, 1926, II, pp. 8–10.

p. 132 *La Renaissance Littéraire et Artistique*, Paris, April 12, 1874, pp. 19–21.

p. 135 Courthion and Cailler 1960, pp. 77–78, and trans. Judith Landry.

p. 135 Courthion and Cailler 1960, pp. 78–79.

p. 136 Courthion and Cailler 1960, pp. 151–54.

p. 139 Ambroise Vollard, *Recollections of a Picture Dealer*, Constable, London, 1936, pp. 149–58.

p. 143 Adolphe Tabarant, *Manet, Histoire Catalographique*, Éditions Montaigne, Paris, 1931, pp. 276–77.

p. 144 *Art Monthly Review*, no. 9, Edinburgh, September 1876, pp. 11–18.

p. 162 Proust 1913, pp. 73–77.

p. 164 F.W.J. Hemmings and Robert J. Niess (eds.), *Émile Zola: Salons*, Librairie Minard, Paris; E. Droz, Geneva, 1959, pp. 226–28, 230.

p. 165 Hamilton 1986, pp. 216–17.

p. 166 Courthion and Cailler 1960, p. 30.

p. 166 Charles Cros, *Oeuvres Complètes* (1954), Louis Forestier et Pascal Pia, Paris, 1964, p. 19.

p. 167 Moreau-Nelaton 1926, II, p. 75.

p. 168 Proust 1913, pp. 120–23.

p. 169 Courthion and Cailler 1960, pp. 30–36.

p. 170 Hamilton 1986, pp. 242–44.

p. 171 *Le Carillon*, Paris, July 16, 1881.

p. 172 *La Grande Revue*, Paris, August 10, 1907, pp. 849–50, 853–55.

p. 174 J.K. Huysmans, *L'Art Moderne* (1883), Gregg International Publishers, Farnborough, 1969, pp. 271–72.

p. 183 Courthion and Cailler 1960, pp. 157–59.

p. 185 Courthion and Cailler 1960, pp. 103–6.

p. 187 Courthion and Cailler 1960, pp. 160–66.

p. 192 Courthion and Cailler 1960, pp. 167–76.

p. 214 Jacques de Biez, *Conférence Faite à la Salle des Capucines*, Baschet, Paris, January 22, 1884, pp. 60–63.

p. 217 de Biez 1884, pp. 63–68.

p. 220 de Biez 1884, pp. 70–72.

p. 221 Courthion and Cailler 1960, pp. 178–82.

p. 224 Rouart 1986, pp. 135–37.

p. 226 Courthion and Cailler 1960, pp. 183–97.

p. 242 Bazire 1884, pp. 116–20.

p. 243 *La Grande Revue* 1907, pp. 859–60.

p. 243 Émile Zola, *L'Oeuvre* (1886), trans. E. Vizetelly, Chatto & Windus, London 1902, pp. 22–23, 36–40, 104–10, 115–18.

p. 250 *Portraits d'Hier*, Paris, December 15, 1909, pp. 30–31.

p. 251 Julie Manet, *Journal (1893–1899)*, Klincksieck, Paris, 1979, pp. 213–4, 216.

p. 252 George Moore, *Modern Painting* (1893), Walter Scott, London; C. Scribner's Sons, New York, 1898, pp. 31–35.

p. 262 *The Studio*, London, January 1901, pp. 234–36.

p. 264 George Moore, *Reminiscences of the Impressionist Painters*, Maunsel, Dublin, 1906, pp. 14–20, 24–26, 30–31, 34–36.

p. 270 Roger Fry, *Manet and the Post-Impressionists*, November 8, 1910–January 15, 1911, catalogue, Grafton Galleries, London, 1910.

p. 271 A.J. Meier-Graefe, *Édouard Manet*, R. Piper & Co, Munich, 1912, pp. 214–18.

p. 272 Proust 1913, pp. 110–14.

p. 273 *La Renaissance de L'Art Française et des Industries de Luxe* no. 5, Paris, July 1918, pp. 149–53.

p. 276 J.E. Blanche, *Propos de Peintre*, Éditions Émile-Paul Frères, Paris 1919–28, I, pp. 136–38, 142–43.

p. 285 Tabarant 1931, pp. 73–74.

p. 286 Tabarant 1931, pp. 259–62.

p. 289 Tabarant 1931, pp. 416–17.

p. 291 *L'Intransigeant*, Paris, January 25, 1932, p. 51.

p. 292 Paul Valéry, *Degas Manet Morisot*, trans. David Paul, Princeton University Press; Routledge & Kegan Paul, London, pp. 105–14.

p. 296 Roger Fry, *Characteristics of French Art*, Chatto & Windus, London, 1932, pp. 119–22.

p. 297 Paul Jamot and Georges Wildenstein, *Manet*, Les Beaux-Arts, Paris, 1932, I, pp. 52–55.

p. 300 Jamot and Wildenstein 1932, I, pp. 50–51.

p. 309 Vollard 1936, pp. 52–59.

p. 313 Ambroise Vollard, *En Écoutant Cézanne, Degas, Renoir*, B. Grasset, Paris, 1938, pp. 119–20, 161–63, 187–88.

p. 316 Nils Gosta Sandblad, *Manet: Three Studies in Artistic Conception*, G.W.K. Gleerup, Lund, 1954, pp. 159–61.

p. 317 Georges Bataille, *Manet* (1955), Skira, Geneva; Macmillan, London, 1983, pp. 71–84.

p. 320 Louisine W. Havemeyer, *Sixteen to Sixty: Memoirs of a Collector*, Private Printing for the Family of Mrs H.O. Havemeyer and the Metropolitan Museum of Art, New York, 1961, pp. 215–40.

p. 340 *Artforum*, San Francisco, January 1967, pp. 22–23, 26.

p. 343 Hans Haacke, *Unfinished Business December 12, 1986 – February 15, 1987*, catalogue, The New Museum of Contemporary Art, New York, MIT Press, Cambridge, Mass. and London, 1986, pp. 118, 130–33.

p. 365 T.J. Clark, *The Painting of Modern Life: Paris in the Art of Manet and his Followers*, Thames and Hudson, London, 1985, pp. 205, 249–55.

p. 370 *Critical Inquiry*, 12, University of Chicago, Autumn 1985, pp. 206–9, 221–23, 231–37.

CHRONOLOGY

1832

JANUARY 23. Manet is born in Paris, the eldest son of Auguste and Eugénie-Désirée (née Fournier) Manet. His father is an important official at the Ministry of Justice and his mother comes from a diplomatic family.

1833

NOVEMBER 21. Birth of Manet's brother, Eugène.

1835

MARCH 16. Birth of Manet's second brother, Gustave.

1844–48

Studies at the Collège Rollin where he befriends Antonin Proust. He and Proust often visit the Louvre in the company of Manet's uncle, Captain Édouard Fournier, who encourages their interest in drawing.

Upon leaving the Collège Rollin, he makes an unsuccessful application to the École Navale, having refused his father's suggestion that he enter the legal profession. Travels to Rio de Janeiro on a training steamer and spends much of the journey sketching.

1849

Arrives in Rio de Janeiro in February and returns to Le Havre in June.

Meets Suzanne Leenhoff, a young Dutch piano teacher who has been employed by the Manets to give lessons to Édouard and Eugène.

1850

Having been unsuccessful once again in gaining admission to the École Navale, he obtains his family's agreement to study painting under the aegis of Thomas Couture. Registers as a pupil at the Louvre in order to copy paintings, and joins Couture's studio in September together with Proust.

1851

DECEMBER 2. Manet and Proust witness the Coup d'État which brings Napoléon III to power and, according to Proust, Manet makes sketches of corpses at Montmartre cemetery.

1852

JANUARY 29. Suzanne Leenhoff's illegitimate son, Léon-Édouard Koëlla, is born. During his lifetime, Suzanne claimed that he was her younger brother, and he was known as Leenhoff. Today, he is thought to be the son of Manet's father.

JULY. Manet makes first trip to Holland.

1853

Spends time making studies from nature while in Normandy with the Couture studio.

SEPTEMBER–OCTOBER. Visits Italy with Eugène Manet and stays in Venice and Florence, copying old master paintings, then goes on to Rome.

1855(?)

Together with Proust he visits Eugène Delacroix, asking permission to copy his *Dante and Virgil* hung in the collection of the Musée du Luxembourg.

1856

FEBRUARY. Leaves Couture and sets up a studio with the animal painter Albert de Balleroy.

1857

Meets Fantin-Latour who becomes a close friend.

NOVEMBER–DECEMBER. A second journey to Italy, this time accompanied by Eugène Brunet. Spends time copying Andrea del Sarto's frescoes in the cloister at S. Annunziata.

1858

His name appears in the register of the Cabinet des Estampes at the Bibliothèque Impériale.

1859

APRIL. *The Absinthe Drinker* is rejected by the Salon, despite receiving Delacroix' support.

JULY. Moves to a new studio at 58 rue de la Victoire following the suicide of his assistant who had been the model for *The Boy with Cherries*.

Registers as an artist at the Louvre so that he can obtain copying privileges.

At the Louvre, meets Degas who is copying Velazquez' *Infanta Margarita* on to copperplate in order to make a print. Manet executes his own copies based on Velazquez' work.

Photograph of Léon Leenhoff (from Manet's photograph album). Bibliothèque Nationale, Paris.

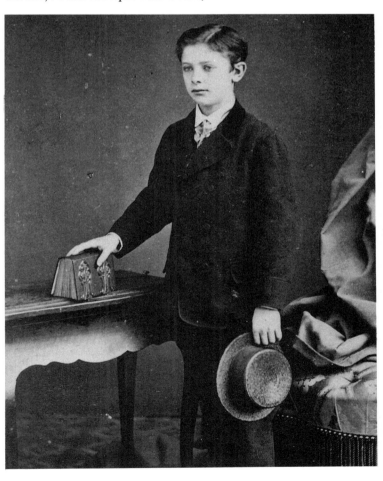

1860

SUMMER. Moves to a new studio on the rue de Douai and rents an apartment in the Batignolles quarter with Suzanne and Léon.

1861

MAY. Exhibits the *Portrait of M and Mme Auguste Manet* and *The Spanish Singer* at the Salon, the latter receiving the *mention honorable*.

On a visit to Manet's studio, the painters Bracquemond, Carolus-Duran, Fantin-Latour and Legros and the writers Baudelaire, Champfleury and Duranty express admiration for *The Spanish Singer*.

Sets up a studio at 81 rue Guyot.

AUGUST–SEPTEMBER. Places *Reading*, a portrait of a neighbour, on sale at the "Permanent Exhibition" of the Galerie Martinet. It is replaced in September by *The Boy with Cherries*.

Shows *The Surprised Nymph* at the Imperial Academy in St Petersburg.

OCTOBER. Exhibits *The Spanish Singer* at Martinet's but does not put it up for sale.

1862

APRIL–MAY. Exhibition of Manet's prints at Cadart's, 66 rue de Richelieu.

Becomes a founding member of the *Société des Aquafortistes* together with Bracquemond, Fantin-Latour, Jongkind, Legros and Ribot, their aim being to revive the popularity of etching. Their first publication includes Manet's *Gypsies*.

Makes *plein air* studies in the Tuileries Gardens. Starts to frequent Café Tortoni, a fashionable meeting-place.

AUGUST–NOVEMBER. The Hippodrome presents a troupe of Spanish dancers who become the subjects for, amongst others, *Lola de Valence* and *Camprubi the Ballet Dancer*, both painted at Alfred Stevens' studio.

Death of Manet's father on September 25. Édouard is left a substantial inheritance.

Victorine Meurent, whom he has just met, starts posing for him.

1863

MARCH. Exhibits fourteen paintings at the Galerie Martinet, including *The Boy with a Sword, Young Woman Reclining in Spanish Costume, Lola de Valence, The Street Singer* and *Music in the Tuileries Gardens* [*Musique aux Tuileries*].

Zacharie Astruc's serenade *Lola de Valence*, illustrated by Manet, is published on March 7.

Manet and Fantin-Latour are introduced to Swinburne by Whistler.

APRIL. Salon jury reject *Luncheon on the Grass* [*Le Déjeuner sur L'Herbe*].

MAY. Opening of the Salon des Refusés. Manet exhibits *Luncheon on the Grass, Portrait of a Young Man in the Costume of a Majo* and *Portrait of Mlle V . . . in the Costume of an Espada* along with three etchings.

AUGUST 17. Together with Baudelaire he attends Delacroix' funeral.

OCTOBER 28. Marries Suzanne Leenhoff at Zaltbommel in Holland.

1864

JANUARY. Manet poses for Fantin-Latour's *Homage to Delacroix*.

MAY. Exhibits *Bullfight* and *Dead Christ with Angels* at the Salon.

JUNE 19. American Civil War naval battle between the ships "Kearsage" and "Alabama" takes place off Cherbourg. Manet executes a number of works based on these events.

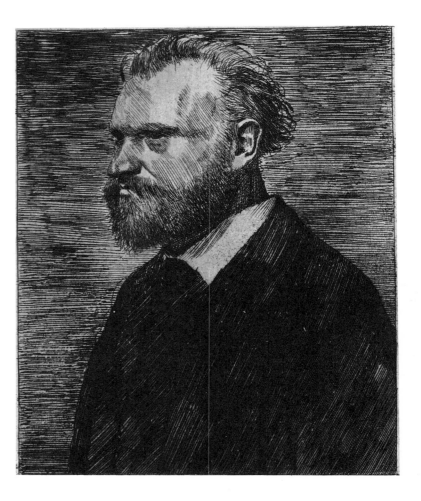

Edgar Degas, *Édouard Manet: Bust-Length Portrait*. 1864–5. Etching and aquatint, 3rd state. Metropolitan Museum of Art, New York (Gift of Mrs Imrie de Vegh, 1949).

NOVEMBER. Moves with his family to 34 boulevard des Batignolles.

1865

In Baudelaire's absence in Brussels, Manet acts as his literary agent.

MAY. Exhibits *Jesus Mocked by the Soldiers* and *Olympia* at the Salon.

His paintings are rejected by the Royal Academy in London.

AUGUST. Goes to Spain on a trip planned by Zacharie Astruc, and has a chance encounter with Théodore Duret at a hotel on the Puerto del Sol.

1866

Meets Cézanne.

MAY. In a review of the Salon, Zola defends Manet. The resulting controversy leads to Zola's resignation from *L'Événement*. Manet asks to meet him.

Zacharie Astruc introduces Manet to Monet.

The Café Guerbois, 11 grande rue des Batignolles, becomes the favourite haunt of Manet and friends such as Astruc, Desboutin, Duranty, Burty and Zola.

AUTUMN. Manet and his family move to Manet's mother's home at 49 rue de Saint Pétersbourg. His mother stays on to live with them.

1867

JANUARY. A biographical and critical study of Manet is published by Zola in *L'Artiste: Revue du XIXe Siècle*.

FEBRUARY. Manet's portrait is painted by Fantin-Latour for exhibition at the next Salon.

MAY. Manet constructs a pavilion at his own expense (with over 18,000 francs advanced from his mother) and opens a one-man exhibition of fifty paintings at the Pont de L'Alma, outside the grounds of the Exposition Universelle. The paintings include *The Tragic Actor*, *Matador Saluting*, *The Fifer*, *Portrait of Zacharie Astruc* and *Young Lady in 1866* (also called *Woman with a Parrot*).

Zola's article of January 1 is re-issued in a newly published brochure, and is accompanied by a portrait of Manet by Bracquemond plus the etching based on *Olympia*.

JUNE 19. Emperor Maximilian is executed in Mexico. Manet undertakes a series of canvases based on this subject.

SEPTEMBER 2. Attends Baudelaire's funeral.

1868

FEBRUARY. Zola sits for his portrait at Manet's studio.

MAY. Exhibits *Portrait of Émile Zola and Young Lady in 1866* at the Salon.

SUMMER. The Manets holiday at Boulogne-sur-Mer. During this time, conceives idea of *Luncheon in the Studio*.

Goes briefly to London with the aim of exhibiting during the following year.

Introduced to Berthe and Edma Morisot at the Louvre by Fantin-Latour.

SEPTEMBER. Works on *The Balcony*. Berthe Morisot is one of the models.

OCTOBER. Manet's lithograph *Cats' Rendezvous* appears on the poster for Champfleury's book *The Cats*.

1869

JANUARY–FEBRUARY. Government opposes both the exhibition of Manet's *Execution of the Emperor Maximilian* painting and the publication of his lithograph on the same theme. Zola writes on his behalf to *La Tribune*.

Introduced to Eva Gonzalès by Alfred Stevens. She becomes Manet's pupil and also poses for him.

MAY. Exhibits *The Balcony*, *Luncheon in the Studio* and five etchings at the Salon.

JULY–SEPTEMBER. Holidays again with his family at Boulogne-sur-Mer. Boulogne forms the subject of several paintings.

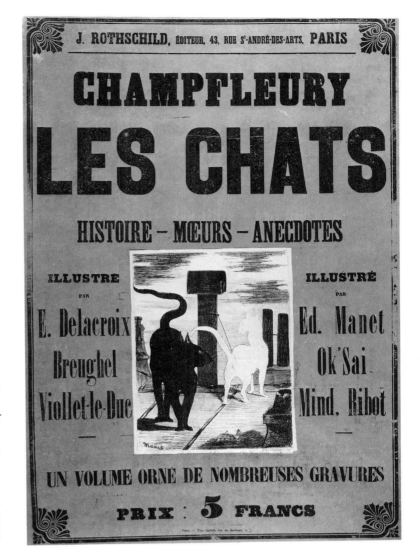

ABOVE Poster for *The Cats* by Champfleury. 1869. Lithograph, 17 × 13″ (43.5 × 33 cm). Bibliothèque Nationale, Paris.

BELOW The new maritime station at Boulogne, for trains between Paris and London. Engraving (Photo Roger-Viollet).

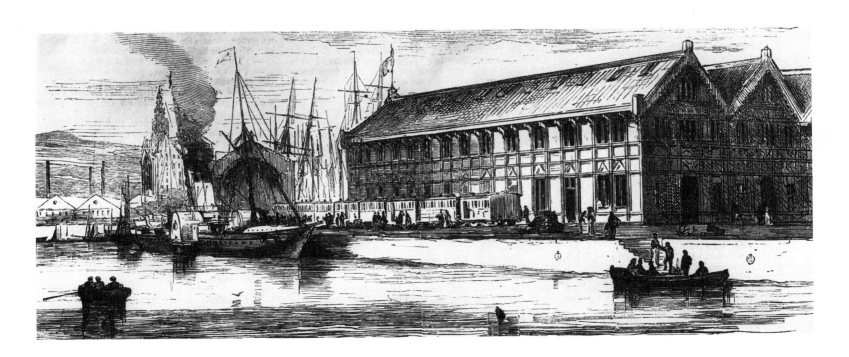

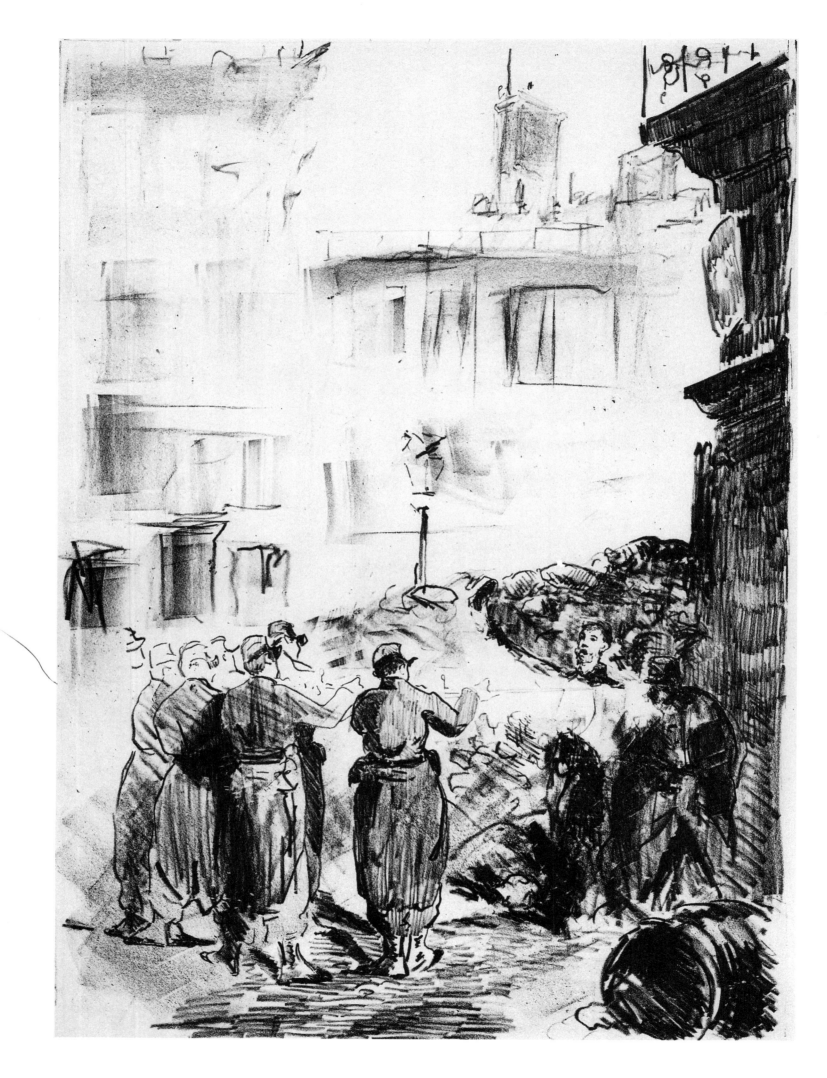

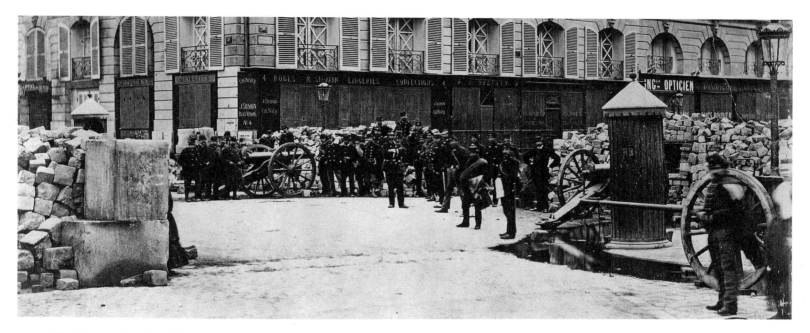

LEFT *The Barricade*. 1871. Lithograph, 18 × 13″ (46 × 33.3 cm).

Photograph of a barricade in the Rue Royale, Paris. May 1871.

1870

FEBRUARY 23. Manet challenges Duranty to a duel, having been provoked by an article in *Paris-Journal*. Duranty is slightly wounded.

MAY. Exhibits *The Music Lesson* and *Portrait of Eva Gonzalès* at the Salon. Fantin-Latour exhibits *The Batignolles Group*.

SEPTEMBER. Owing to the impending threat of the Franco-Prussian war, Manet despatches his family to Oloron-Sainte-Marie in the Pyrenees.

Closes his studio at rue Guyot and stores thirteen paintings with Théodore Duret.

NOVEMBER. Enlists in the National Guard as a lieutenant under the command of the painter Meissonier who is his colonel.

1871

MARCH. Travels to Oloron-Sainte-Marie, Bordeaux and Arcachon. At Arcachon, paints views and interior scenes.

APRIL. In Manet's absence from Paris, he and several other painters and sculptors are elected delegates of a new federation of artists. The manifesto of the federation is published in the *Journal Officiel de la Commune*.

MAY–JUNE. Returns to Paris with his family, probably after the repression of the Commune.

JULY. Visits Versailles frequently and requests permission to paint the portrait of Léon Gambetta, newly elected member of the National Assembly. Gambetta, however, is unable to give Manet sufficient sittings to complete the portrait.

AUGUST. Travels once again with his family to Boulogne-sur-Mer, this time on doctor's orders, having reached a state of nervous exhaustion probably as a result of the strains of war.

1872

JANUARY. Durand-Ruel purchases twenty-four paintings produced by Manet and shows fourteen of them during the year at exhibitions organized by the Society of French Artists in London.

The Café de la Nouvelle-Athènes replaces the Café Guerbois as the meeting-place of Manet and his friends.

Travels again to Holland.

MAY. Exhibits *The Battle of the "Kearsage" and the "Alabama"* at the Salon.

JULY. Moves to a studio at 4 rue de Saint-Pétersbourg near the Gare Saint-Lazare and overlooking the rue Mosnier, later to be depicted in several drawings and paintings.

1873

MAY. Exhibits *A Good Glass of Beer* [*Le Bon Bock*] and *Repose: Portrait of Berthe Morisot* at the Salon. *A Good Glass of Beer* is highly successful.

Meets Stéphane Mallarmé who becomes a close friend.

OCTOBER–DECEMBER. The Old Opéra building on rue Peletier, the site of Manet's *Masked Ball at the Opéra*, is destroyed by fire on October 28.

Sells five paintings to J.B. Faure, the singer, in November.

Makes sketches of the court martial of Marshal Bazaine at the Grand Trianon in Versailles.

1874

APRIL. The Salon jury reject *The Swallows* and *Masked Ball at the Opéra*. As a result, Mallarmé publishes an article entitled *Le Jury de Peinture pour 1874 et M. Manet* [*The Painting Jury for 1874 and Manet*] in *La Renaissance artistique et littéraire*.

MAY. Exhibits *Gare Saint-Lazare* and *Polichinelle* at the Salon. Refuses to exhibit at the first Impressionist exhibition organized by the Société Anonyme des Artistes, Peintres, Sculpteurs et Graveurs.

Having asked friends to write verses as an accompaniment to his lithograph *Polichinelle*, Manet selects the couplet written by Théodore de Banville.

AUGUST. Stays at the family home at Gennevilliers, near Argenteuil. Works on *Argenteuil*, *Boating* and *Claude Monet Painting on his Studio Boat*. Spends time with Renoir and Monet.

DECEMBER 22. Marriage of Manet's brother Eugène and Berthe Morisot.

1875

JANUARY. Illustrates Mallarmé's French translation of Edgar Allan Poe's *The Raven*.

MAY. Exhibits *Argenteuil* at the Salon.

OCTOBER. Visits Venice with his wife and Tissot.

1876

APRIL–MAY. Publication of Mallarmé's poem *L'Après-midi d'un Faune* with wood engravings by Manet.

Doing the Washing [Le Linge] and *The Artist* are rejected by the Salon jury.

Manet's rejected paintings and other works are shown to the public at his studio. These include *Boating* and *The Artist*. The exhibition coincides with the Second Impressionist exhibition. Amongst his visitors is Méry Laurent.

OCTOBER. Mallarmé poses for his portrait at Manet's studio.

1877

APRIL. *Nana* is rejected by the Salon jury but *Portrait of Faure in the Role of Hamlet* is accepted.

MAY 1. *Nana* is exhibited in the window of Giroux's, a shop on the boulevard des Capucines.

1878

Manet and his family move from 49 to 39 rue de Saint-Pétersbourg.

JULY. Manet is forced to leave his studio at rue de Saint-Pétersbourg, and temporarily rents another at 70 rue d'Amsterdam.

AUTUMN. Starts working on *In the Conservatory*.

1879

FEBRUARY. Marriage of Henri Guérard and Manet's pupil and model, Eva Gonzalès.

APRIL. Sets up his final studio at 77 rue d'Amsterdam.

Submits a plan for decorating the Municipal Council Hall in the new Hôtel de Ville to the prefect of the Seine but receives no reply.

SPRING. Meets George Moore.

MAY. Exhibits *Boating* and *In the Conservatory* at the Salon.

JUNE–JULY. Zola's article on contemporary art in Paris is published in St Petersburg (in a Russian translation) in the magazine *Viestnik Europi*.

Le Figaro reports a split between Zola and Manet as a result of criticism in Zola's *Viestnik Europi* article.

SEPTEMBER–OCTOBER. Spends six weeks at Bellevue taking spa treatment for recurring pain in his left leg. Meets the singer Emilie Ambre and paints her portrait.

DECEMBER 1879–JANUARY 1880. Emilie Ambre organizes an exhibition of *The Execution of the Emperor Maximilian* in New York and Boston.

1880

APRIL. The publisher Charpentier organizes an exhibition entitled *New Works by Édouard Manet* at *La Vie Moderne*. Included are *The Plum*, *The Café-Concert*, *Corner in a Café-Concert* and *Portrait of George Moore* (pastel). This exhibition coincides with the fifth Impressionist exhibition.

MAY. Exhibits *Portrait of M. Antonin Proust* and *At Père Lathuille's* at the Salon.

JULY–SEPTEMBER/OCTOBER. Hydrotherapy and rest are prescribed by Manet's doctor. Manet, therefore, rents a house in Bellevue. During his time here, he sends letters and watercolours to his friends.

1881

Works on a project (possibly a commission from Antonin Proust) which is to be a series of four portraits of women forming an allegory of the four seasons.

MAY. Exhibits *Portrait of M. Henri Rochefort*, for which he is awarded a second-class medal, and *Portrait of M. Pertuiset, the Lion Hunter*, at the Salon.

JUNE. Leaves Paris to obtain medical treatment and stays with his family at Versailles for the summer.

OCTOBER–DECEMBER. Returns to Paris in October.

Gambetta appoints Antonin Proust Minister of Fine Arts in November, and Manet is created a *Chévalier de la Légion d'Honneur* in December.

1882

MAY. Exhibits *The Bar at the Folies-Bergère* and *Spring: Jeanne* at the Salon.

JULY–OCTOBER. Stays at Rueil. Works on several landscape paintings.

Makes out will. Suzanne is named sole heir with Léon as residual legatee. Théodore Duret is executor. Manet stipulates that his studio work should either be sold or destroyed.

1883

APRIL. Writes to Francis Defeuille asking for lessons in miniature painting.

Manet's left leg is amputated on April 20.

APRIL 30. Manet dies. He is buried at Passy Cemetery, Paris, on May 3.

1884

JANUARY. Bazire's book *Manet* is published, with illustrations by H. Guerard in the form of reproductions of Manet's work.

The Minister of Fine Arts authorizes a posthumous exhibition of Manet's work at the École des Beaux-Arts (largely as a result of the efforts of Antonin Proust). Included are 116 oil paintings, thirty-one pastels, twelve lithographs and etchings, among them *Boy Blowing Soap Bubbles*, *Portrait of Théodore Duret*, *Portrait of Nina de Callias*, *Masked Ball at the Opéra*, *Blue Venice*, *Portrait of Stéphane Mallarmé*, *Reading L'Illustré* and *Autumn – Méry Laurent*. 13,000 people pay admission to see the exhibition.

FEBRUARY. Sale of Manet's work at Hôtel Drouot.

1886

APRIL–MAY. Works by Manet are shown in New York as part of an exhibition entitled "Impressionists of Paris".

1889

JANUARY. Sargent and Monet start a subscription fund so that *Olympia* will not be acquired by an American collector.

Fifteen works by Manet are exhibited at the Exposition Universelle.

1890

FEBRUARY. Claude Monet writes to the Minister of Public Instruction and Fine Arts offering *Olympia* to the French nation. It is placed in the Musée du Luxembourg.

1894

Caillebotte dies, and leaves his collection of Impressionist works to the Musée du Luxembourg. Manet's *Angelina* and *The Balcony* are accepted but the *Game of Croquet* and *The Races* are rejected.

1905

JANUARY–FEBRUARY. Works by Manet are included in a Durand-Ruel exhibition of Impressionists at the Grafton Galleries, London.

1906

MARCH. Death of Manet's widow, Suzanne.

Five works by Manet, including *Luncheon on the Grass [Le Déjeuner sur L'Herbe]* are presented to the Louvre by Moreau-Nelaton.

1907

Olympia is transferred to the Louvre from the Musée du Luxembourg as a result of Monet's influence on Clemenceau.

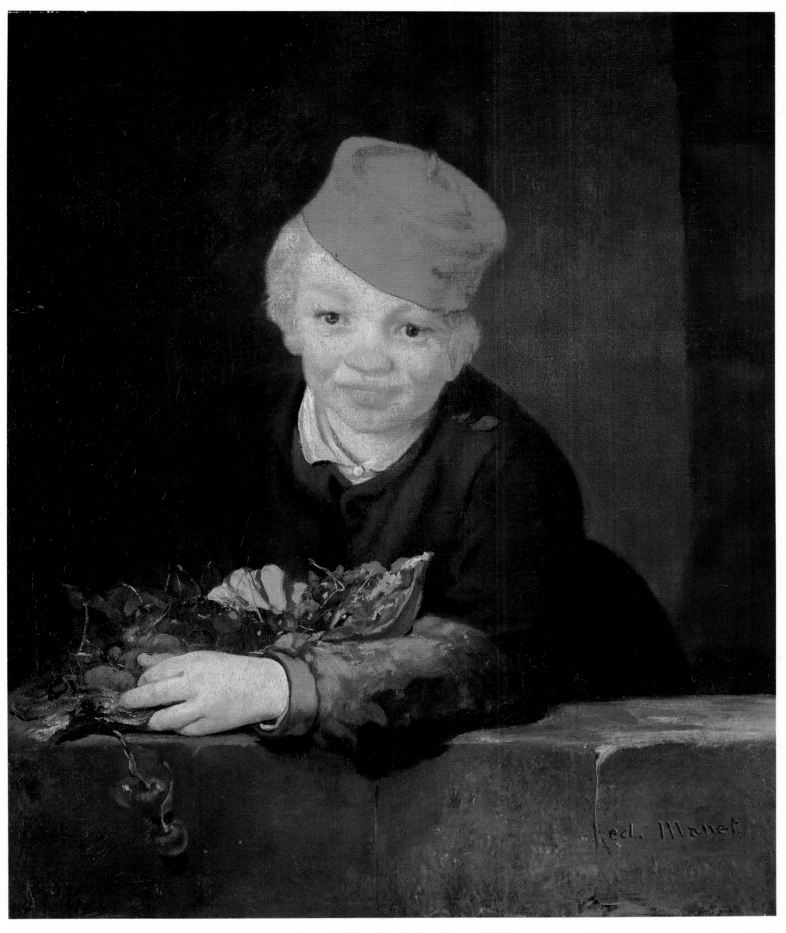

COLOURPLATE 1. *Boy with Cherries*. 1858. 25¾ × 21½″ (65.5 × 54.5 cm).
Calouste Gulbenkian Foundation, Lisbon.

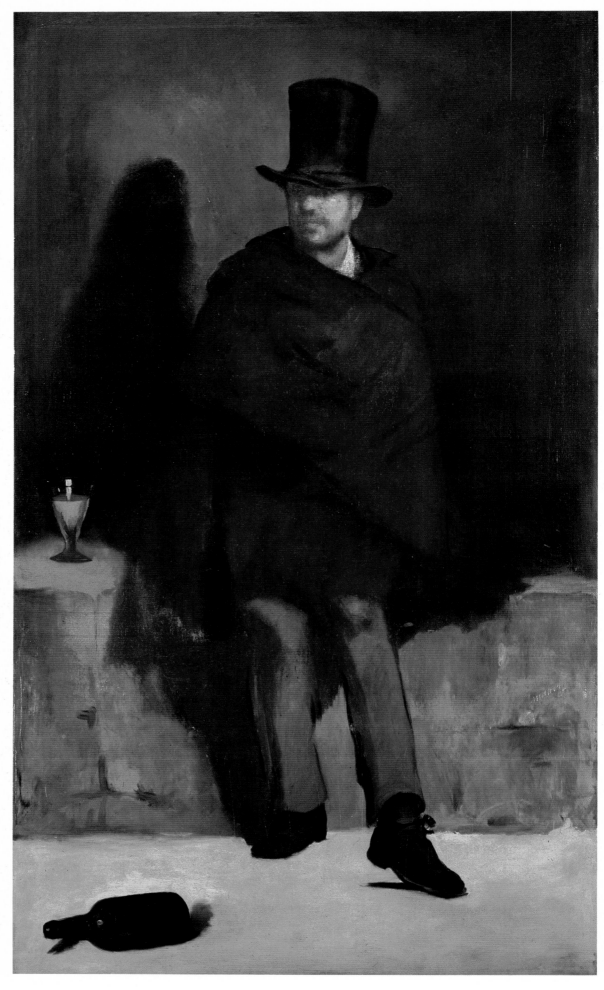

COLOURPLATE 2. *The Absinthe Drinker*. 1858–9. 31¾ × 41¾″ (81 × 106 cm).
Ny Carlsberg Glypotek, Copenhagen.

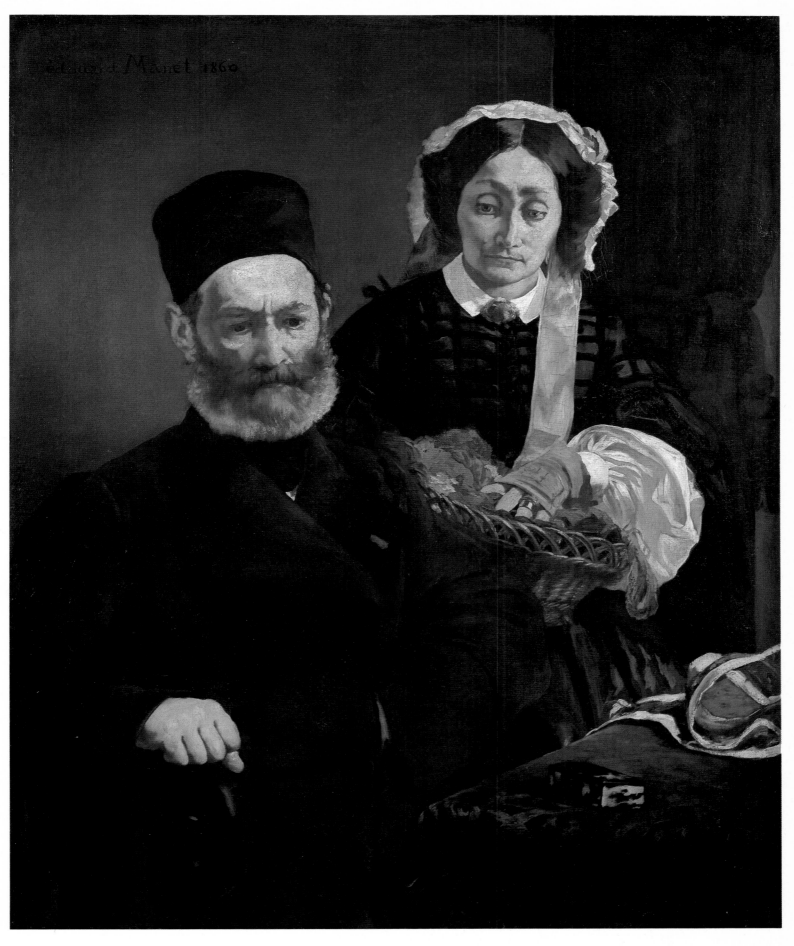

COLOURPLATE 3. *Portrait of M. and Mme Auguste Manet.* 1860. 44 × 35¾″ (111.5 × 91 cm).
Musée d'Orsay, Paris.

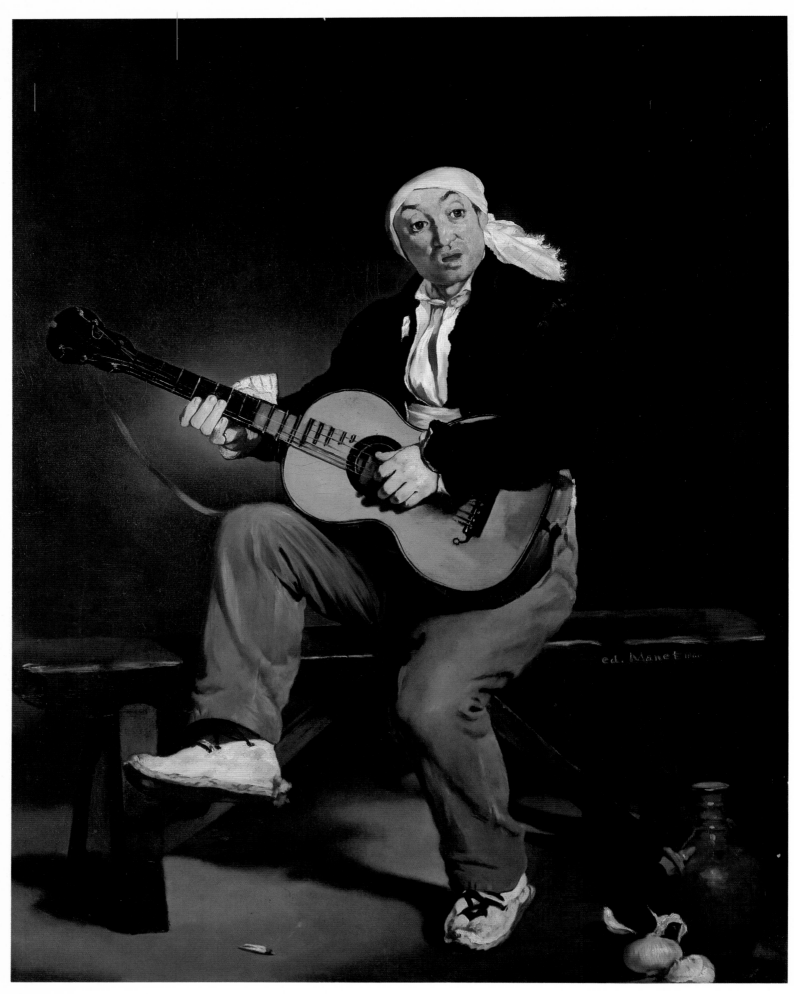

COLOURPLATE 4. *The Spanish Singer*. 1860. 58 × 45″ (147.3 × 114.3 cm).
Metropolitan Museum of Art, New York (Gift of William Church Osborn, 1949).

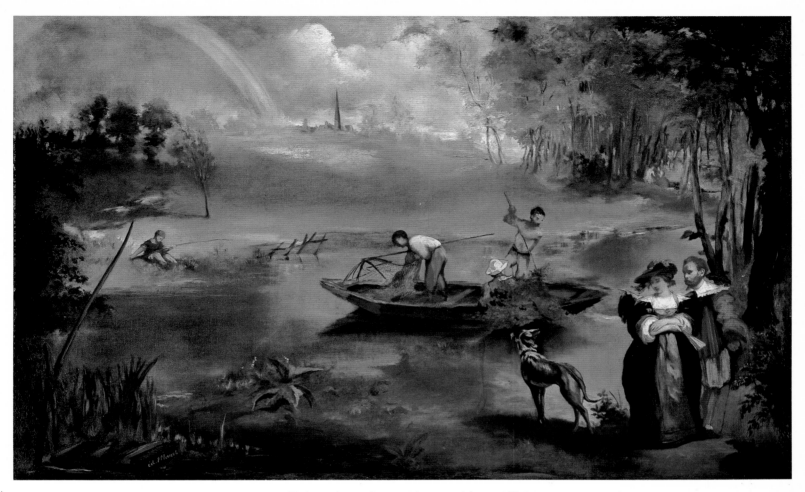

COLOURPLATE 5. *Fishing, Saint-Ouen.* 1861–3. 30¼ × 48½″ (76.8 × 123.2 cm).
Metropolitan Museum of Art, New York (Purchase, Mr and Mrs Richard J. Bernhard Gift, 1957).

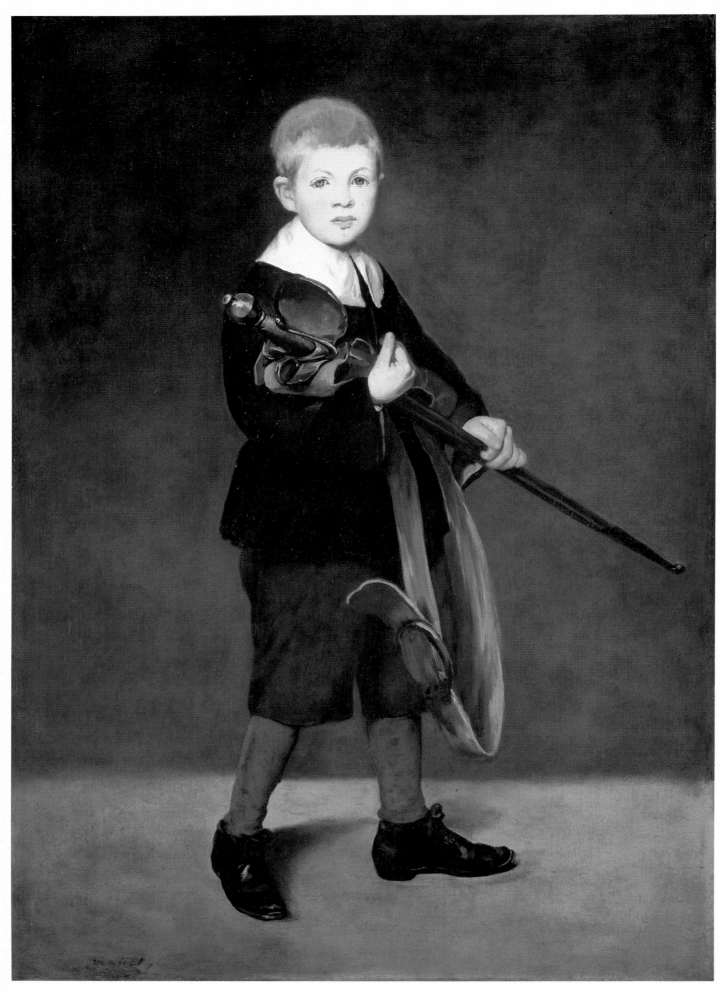

COLOURPLATE 6. *Boy with a Sword*. 1861. 51⅝ × 36¾″ (131.1 × 93.3 cm).
Metropolitan Museum of Art, New York (Gift of Erwin Davis, 1889).

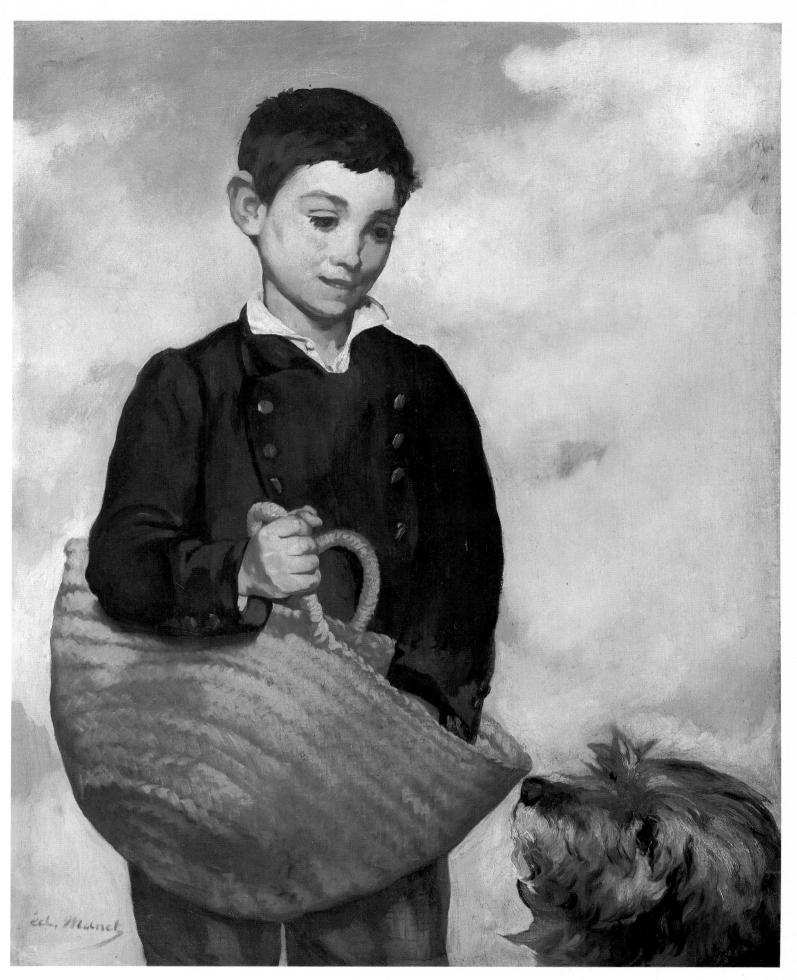

COLOURPLATE 7. *Boy with a Dog*. 1860–1. 36 × 28¼″ (92 × 72 cm).
Private Collection, Paris.

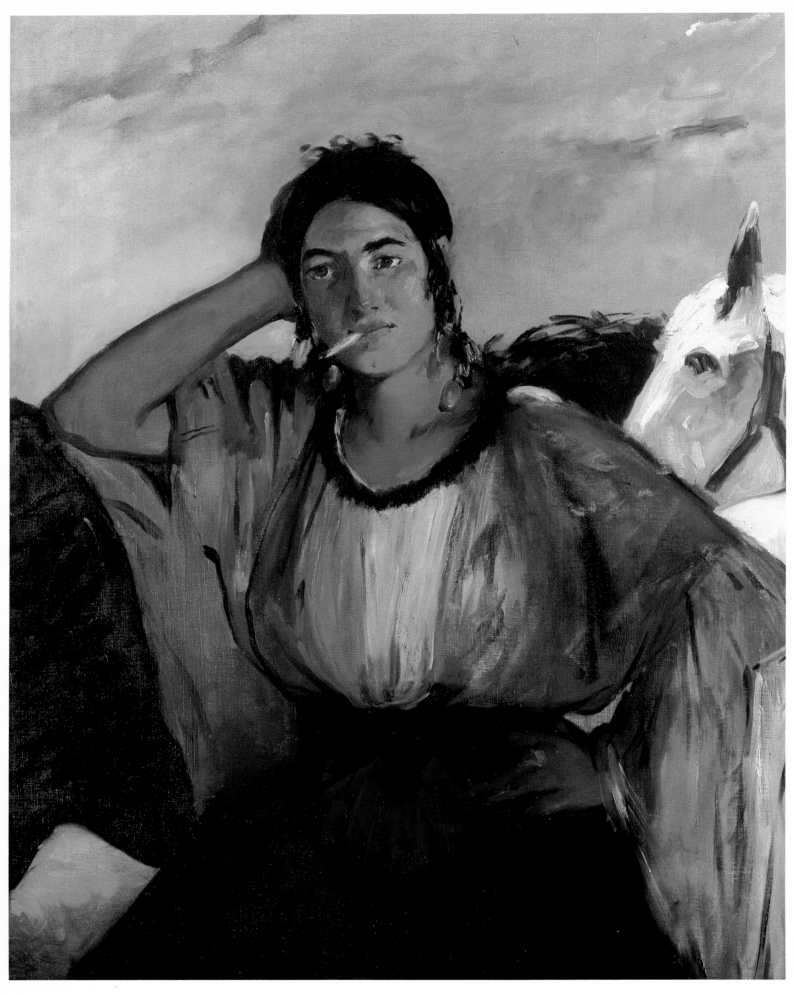

COLOURPLATE 8. *Gypsy with a Cigarette* or *Indian Woman Smoking*. 1861 (1862?). 36 × 29″ (92 × 73.5 cm).
Princeton University Art Museum (Bequest of Archibald S. Alexander).

INTRODUCTION

Of the artists associated with the Impressionist circle, it is Édouard Manet who has emerged as the pivotal figure in histories of nineteenth-century French art. Whether cast as last in the line of the great French masters of realism, following Millet or Courbet,[1] or as the precursor of Impressionism, critics and art historians have repeatedly turned to Manet in attempting to define the history of modern art from the nineteenth century to the present. Modernist art historians and critics have consistently pointed to him as the major inspirational figure for the Impressionists; but in order to appreciate the significance of this interpretation of Manet's work and career, the complexities of the term "Modernism" must be clarified.

The American critic Clement Greenberg and his followers are often cited as having been most influential in defining the terms of Modernist painting, but Modernist interpretations can be found much earlier – in the writings of Roger Fry, for example. This formalist criticism identifies Modernist painting in terms of the characteristics of the medium itself: the qualities of painterliness and flatness or two-dimensionality are valued above content or meaning. And "advanced" art is characterized as that which increasingly concentrates on the medium and technique of its own creation. Modernist art is thus presented as a logical progression towards abstraction: in the case of painting, a development ·from Cubism to European Abstraction and ultimately, American Abstract Expressionism. Modernism does not, however, refer only to a style, or styles, of twentieth-century painting, it implies also the art history which has constructed the precedents for the stylistic march towards abstraction. Manet is thus positioned by, and within, Modernism as the forefather not only of Impressionism but also of all significant art of the twentieth century. The texts included in this book, therefore, allow insights not only into the reasons for the prominence of Manet's oeuvre and career but also into the constitution of Modernism itself.

One of the most influential early judgements of Manet's work has been that of the novelist Émile Zola, published in 1867.[2] In an essay entitled simply *Édouard Manet*, Zola repeatedly asserted that subject matter was merely the pretext for the painter's analytical study of colour and light. For Zola, pictorial representation could be explained primarily in terms of the artist's personal qualities – in Manet's case, sincerity and elegance – which he described as synonymous with the artist's working method. Certain aspects of Manet's technique, to which Zola first drew attention, have been emphasized by Modernist critics and art historians in order to enhance the depiction of Manet as a precursor of twentieth-century art. In particular, the "flatness" of some of Manet's compositions has been stressed. In his *Modernist Painting*, Clement Greenberg stated unequivocally that Manet's paintings "became the first Modernist ones by virtue of the frankness with which they declared the surfaces on which they were painted. The Impressionists, in Manet's wake, abjured underpainting and glazing, to leave the eye under no doubt as to the fact that the colors used were made of real paint that came from pots or tubes."[3]

For Modernist critics, this flatness constitutes the stylistic bridge between Manet's work and what such critics define as the most significant developments in European and American twentieth-century painting. This notion of Manet as a formalist, preoccupied with subject matter solely in terms of pictorial composition, is still the prevalent image not only of Manet himself, but of all artists – and of artistic "creation" itself. That this should be the case is a measure of the continuing dominance of Modernist ideology.

In certain respects, however, the prevailing view of Manet is at odds with Zola's assessment of the artist. For Modernism, it is the individual artistic genius who constitutes the source of creation, and such genius is

[1] *The Manet retrospective of 1983 shown in Paris and New York followed similar shows of the work of Jean-François Millet (1814–75) and Gustave Courbet (1819–77).*

[2] *See pp. 62–96.*

[3] *Reprinted in Francis Frascina and Charles Harrison (editors),* Modern Art and Modernism: a Critical Anthology, *London, 1982, p. 6. For further discussion of Clement Greenberg and Modernism, see Francis Frascina, "Greenberg and the Politics of Modernism",* Art Monthly, *November 1987, No. 111 (pp. 6–11).*

represented as clearly located outside society, concerned only with problems of an "aesthetic" nature. Zola attributed such formalist preoccupations to Manet, but avoided characterizing Manet as an outsider or rebel: "In this orderly police state of ours, an artist's life is the same as that of any quiet bourgeois, he paints his pictures in his studio as others sell pepper over their counters. The long-haired types of 1830, thank heavens, have completely disappeared, and our painters have become what they ought to be – people living the same life as everyone else." He described Manet as "following the same sort of life as most people, but perhaps with this difference, that he is more quiet and cultivated than the majority." Despite Zola's reassuring if ironic view of the artist as a quiet bourgeois, Manet has most often been depicted as a loner in the artistic world of his own day. This has perhaps proved necessary because of the tendency of Modernist writers to represent Manet as a kind of heroic trailblazer for later artistic movements or styles. For such purposes, it is the "notoriety" provoked by the exhibition of works such as the *Luncheon on the Grass* (*Déjeuner sur l'herbe*) in the Salon des Refusés, 1863, and the *Olympia* in the Salon of 1865, which is emphasized, rather than the complex ways in which Manet and his work related to the artistic institutions and practices of his own day. In his introduction to *Manet and the Post-Impressionists* of 1910, the exhibition which claimed to introduce "modern" art to England, Roger Fry referred to Manet as a "hopeless revolutionary". John Rewald's seminal *The History of Impressionism* of 1946, published by the New York Museum of Modern Art, defines Impressionism as a group style, forged by a small number of artists most of whom were friends – an attack on the established academic art of the day. Although Manet never exhibited at any of the eight Impressionist exhibitions, he was on familiar terms with a number of the Impressionist painters and plays a significant role in Rewald's account. Indeed, it is as the isolated but significant "influence" on Impressionism that Manet has been depicted by Modernist art histories such as Rewald's.[4]

COLOURPLATES 18, 14

Having constructed this description of Manet's work as revolutionary yet subject-less, Modernist art history nevertheless has problems in explaining the totality of Manet's *oeuvre*. While such interpretations have depicted Manet as the forerunner of everything from Impressionism to American abstract painting, it is the obsessive focus on Manet's technique which seems, in the end, to short-circuit much Modernist criticism. This is particularly evident in the accusation of "inconsistency" (either of quality or approach) which has been levied against Manet since the nineteenth century; Manet himself claimed to be fed up with hearing this particular criticism of his work. Significantly, Clement Greenberg's article in this book is subtitled "an artist exceptional in his inconsistency". But an art history or a criticism which eschews the historical and institutional context of the production and reception of paintings in order to focus primarily on technique inevitably creates its own blind spots, which will ultimately render even variations in technique inexplicable. Such critics are left with the problem of explaining away apparent contradictions within their own narrative of self-contained artistic development. Equally, Modernist art history has tended to focus attention on certain of Manet's works of the 1860s: those which incorporate the most obvious references to and quotations from earlier art, thus perpetuating the notion that art is principally about art, or those which like the *Olympia* earned the artist notoriety in his own lifetime, thereby reinforcing the idea of Manet as the persecuted rebel.[5] This largely ignores the full significance of, for example, Manet's portraits and fails to investigate how the full range of his "modern life" paintings would have been perceived in their own day. It is not uncommon to find the view expressed by Roger Fry in the 1930s that Manet's works of the 1870s – that is, specifically his modern life subjects – mark a "falling off" from his previous achievements.

* * *

[4] *On John Rewald, see John House, "Impressionism and History: the Rewald Legacy",* Art History, *Vol. 9, No. 3, September 1986 (pp. 369–75).*

[5] *See, for example, Michael Fried, "Manet's Sources: Aspects of his Art",* Artforum 7, *March 1969 (pp. 28–82).*

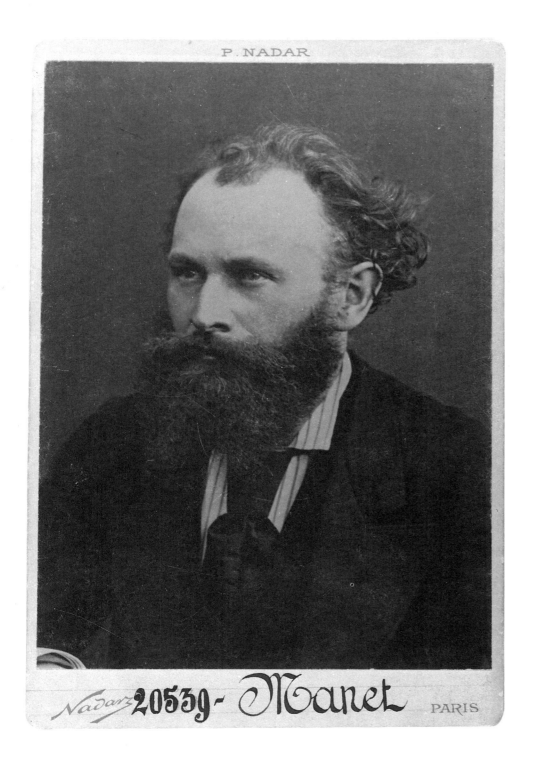

P. NADAR

Nadar 20539 - Manet   PARIS

Photograph of Manet by Nadar.
c. 1865.

Manet's refusal to exhibit with the Impressionists should not be allowed to overshadow his attempts to find alternative, independent venues to the Salon for exhibition, often as a consequence of official rejection. He organized a variety of one-man shows, as in his privately-funded pavilion at the time of the 1867 Exposition Universelle and, in 1876, in his own studio.[6] In addition, his works were exhibited in a number of business premises: the Galerie Martinet on the Boulevard des Italiens in the early 1860s, Giroux's, a shop on the Boulevard des Capucines, where he showed *Nana* in 1877, and the gallery of the offices of the journal *La Vie Moderne* in 1879–80. Because his large-scale *Execution of the Emperor Maximilian* (1867) proved too controversial for Salon exhibition, Manet arranged to tour it privately in North America, and the picture was shown in New York and Boston in 1879–80. Indeed, Manet displayed a shrewd sense of the ways in which his work could be communicated to the public; the many prints executed after, or in relation to, his oil paintings attest to his desire to make his work known to as wide

[6] *See pp. 97 and 143.*

an audience as possible. He seems to have cultivated, too, his relationships with the influential critics of his day, and painted or made printed portraits of the writers who supported his work: Zacharie Astruc, Charles Baudelaire, Émile Zola and Stéphane Mallarmé. However, official recognition in Manet's time consisted of more than favourable reviews in the press, and here too the range of Manet's portraits is revealing of his attempts to cultivate government approval. Antonin Proust, Manet's childhood friend whose portrait he painted in 1880, was briefly Minister of Fine Arts under the prime ministership of Gambetta in 1881–2; it was at this time that Manet's supporters were able to ensure that the artist was awarded the *Légion d'Honneur*. Manet had already approached Gambetta with a request to paint the Republican politician's portrait in 1872, but had been refused. These political and society subjects relate in interesting ways, too, to Manet's own album of photographs, now housed in the Bibliothèque Nationale, in which are collected the photographic "cartes de visite" of many of Manet's friends, acquaintances and professional associates. Both photographs and portraits are revealing of the nineteenth-century preoccupation with the definition of the bourgeois individual and, particularly, the celebrity.

The range of Manet's female portraits is different from that of his male subjects, although superficially there would seem to be many similarities in type of subject. As in the case of Manet's male portraits, his depictions of particular women included those of friends from a similar social position to his own – the many portraits of Isabelle Lemonnier, for example – or wives of friends, as in the case of the pastel portrait of Mme Zola; artistic colleagues such as Berthe Morisot, as well as his pupil Eva Gonzalès. The portraits of male celebrities were of politicians and well-known writers as well as of the opera singer Faure and the composer Chabrier. The female celebrities portrayed by Manet were mainly from the world of entertainment and the popular theatre; these women, from a wide variety of backgrounds, were often categorized in their own times as "demi-mondaines" or "kept" women. A particular instance is represented by Manet's many portraits of Méry Laurent, who had initially made her reputation on the stage, and went on to become a renowned hostess of Parisian writers and artists as well as a close friend of Manet. She was thus a celebrity both in the world of entertainment and of the arts.[7] The portraits of Méry Laurent represent a tribute to friendship; the portrait sittings can themselves perhaps be seen as an aspect of the friendship – many of Manet's sitters commented on the steady flow of witty conversation from the artist while he worked. They are also evidence of Manet's rapturous delight in Méry Laurent's elegant attire.[8] His depiction of Laurent as *Autumn* was an attempt to recast female celebrity as timeless allegory.

The role of evolving and changing notions of femininity in relation to definitions of modernity has not been a concern of Modernist art history. And yet it is clear from many of the illustrations and texts in this book that Manet, like his friend Baudelaire, was fascinated by femininity in the context of the modern city, whether in relation to prostitution, barmaids, his circle of women friends or women's clothing and fashion. Indeed, Modernist art history has obscured many issues around the relation of the male artist to his female subject. Victorine Meurent, for example, has most often gone down in art history as Manet's favourite model – the female subject for *Luncheon on the Grass* and *Olympia*. The fact that Victorine Meurent herself painted and exhibited is generally ignored, as indeed are any facts concerning her life and economic position. Nina de Callias, in contrast to Meurent, was financially independent; accomplished as a musician, active as a composer and writer, she has been immortalized in *Lady with Fans* in her role as salon hostess.[9] Art history has tended to consider the precise historical circumstances of the model as, at most, anecdotal background – irrelevant to the more important "fact" of

[7] *See pp. 289–90.*

[8] *See p. 272.*

[9] *For biographical information concerning Meurent and de Callias, see pp. 285–6, 286–9.*

Manet's role as artistic genius. A similar process of the heroization of the male artist can be detected in discussions of Manet in relation to two contemporary women painters and friends: Berthe Morisot and Eva Gonzalès. The tendency of many contemporaries of Manet's, as well as of later writers, has been to describe Morisot and Gonzalès as followers of Manet. Whether the women's work is praised or disparaged, the net result is the same: an enhancement of Manet's own reputation as a painter.[10] However, not only women artists, but also so-called "feminine" artistic media, have been represented as the necessary foil to male genius. Accounts of Manet working in pastel represent the artist as revitalizing a technique previously considered in terms of a lady's accomplishment.[11]

How, then, can a collection of texts such as those in this book be read? What can we learn about the historical, individual Édouard Manet? Or about the ways in which the works illustrated here have been – and are – interpreted? These documents should not be taken as neutral, transparent accounts of Manet's life and work; although in the main chronologically arranged, they cannot form a seamless narrative biography of the artist. The texts have not only been removed from their original, historically specific contexts (they were produced during a period spanning over 120 years), but are of widely differing types. Some, like Zola's essay "Édouard Manet", were written by professional writers for public consumption; others – Berthe Morisot's letters, for example – were written privately to a close circle of relatives and friends. Many, while claiming to be objective eyewitness accounts of Manet's opinions and working methods, are inevitably written in such a way as to support the author's own views.

It is the very disparate nature of these documents, however, which can enable the reader to formulate alternative views concerning Manet and his work from the prevailing Modernist interpretation outlined above. Rather than sustaining the interpretation of Manet as the isolated artistic hero, both the texts and illustrations in this book suggest that Manet's career and work need to be investigated in relation to the artistic institutions of his own time, as well as in terms of his personal and professional affiliations. Manet consistently refused to exhibit in the Impressionist exhibitions, and categorically stated that it was the official government-run Salon exhibitions in which he wished his work to appear. Nevertheless the Modernist antithesis of "establishment" Salon artists versus "revolutionary" Impressionists is oversimplified: for example, a number of the Impressionist painters also exhibited at the Salon. Nor is the Modernist representation of Manet as the revolutionary single-handedly challenging the Salon an accurate one. That Manet, during his own lifetime, was perceived as a member of artistic and professional circles is evident from Henri Fantin-Latour's two group portraits, *The Homage to Delacroix* (1864) and *The Batignolles Group* (1870). These pictures, which are in effect art-political manifestos, may have been partly intended as depictions of young artists and critics in rebellion against an entrenched art establishment, but they also attest to a need to create alternative artistic groupings. Presumably most of the men represented in these two paintings realized that isolation was not a strong position from which to establish successful careers. *The Homage to Delacroix* shows Manet in the company of painters such as Fantin-Latour, Whistler, Legros, Bracquemond and Balleroy; in *The Batignolles Group*, where Manet is accorded a much more prominent position, the other artists include Renoir, Bazille and Monet. Earlier, in 1862, Manet had joined with Bracquemond, Fantin-Latour, Jongkind, Legros and Ribot in forming the Société des Aquafortistes to promote the revival of etching. Manet's personal circle of friends may have included Impressionist painters such as Berthe Morisot, but he was also on friendly terms with successful Salon artists such as De Nittis, Gervex and Alfred Stevens. A more accurate picture of the artistic context of Manet's work and career should therefore extend far beyond the Impressionist circle.[12]

* * *

[10] *In contrast, see Tamar Garb*, Women Impressionists, *Oxford, 1986; Kathleen Adler and Tamar Garb (introduction and editing)*, The Correspondence of Berthe Morisot, *London, 1986; Kathleen Adler and Tamar Garb*, Berthe Morisot, *Oxford, 1987.*

[11] *See p. 242.*

PAGE 48
PAGE 106

[12] *On Manet and his contemporaries, see Richard Thomson, "Promoting Fantin, Moderating Manet", Art History, Vol. 7, No. 2, June 1984 (pp. 258–62).*

The ultimate accolade, in terms of Manet's reputation, was for his work to be hung in the Louvre. In 1889, six years after his death, fifteen works by Manet were shown at the Exposition Universelle. In that year, J.S. Sargent and Claude Monet started a subscription fund to prevent the *Olympia* from being purchased by an American collector; a total of 19,415 francs was collected. In February 1890 Monet wrote to the Minister of Education offering *Olympia* to the French nation; it was accepted, but placed in the Musée du Luxembourg rather than the Louvre – the usual procedure when an artist had not yet been dead for ten years. Two further paintings, including *The Balcony*, were accepted by the Luxembourg in 1894 as part of the Caillebotte bequest.[13] Monet, however, continued to activate on behalf of the dead artist, and in 1907, largely as the result of his efforts with Georges Clemenceau (then Prime Minister, another politician who had sat for his portrait to Manet) *Olympia* was finally transferred to the Louvre. Étienne Moreau-Nelaton, whose *Manet by Himself* was to appear in 1926, had presented five works by Manet to the Louvre in 1906, including *Luncheon on the Grass*.[14] The *Luncheon* was exhibited along with the rest of Moreau-Nelaton's collection at the Musée des Arts Décoratifs, and only entered the Musée du Louvre in 1934. Thus, by 1906 the two works by Manet which had already achieved both notoriety and canonical status during his own lifetime, *Olympia* and *Luncheon on the Grass*, were in the possession of the French nation and positioned historically as the successors to the great French tradition of Eugène Delacroix and Gustave Courbet. In 1907 the *Olympia* was hung in the Salle des États of the Louvre, next to Ingres' famous nude study, the *Great Odalisque*, and forty-two years after it had first been exhibited at the Salon of 1865 the *Olympia* again aroused controversy. These determined efforts on the part of Claude Monet, and indeed Manet's own strategies for exhibition and self-publicity, reveal the extent to which these artists were aware that posthumous reputation and history are constructed in complex ways, and are never simply the result of a spontaneous recognition of artistic "talent" or achievement.

During his own lifetime, in 1872, Manet had succeeded in selling a certain number of his works to the dealer Paul Durand-Ruel and to some individual collectors, for example to the singer J.B. Faure who was his most important patron.[15] Durand-Ruel had discovered Manet through the artist Alfred Stevens and was instrumental not only in buying works during Manet's life, but in making Manet known after his death through exhibitions in Paris, London and New York. Not long after the artist's death, his works were avidly sought by the American couple Mr and Mrs H.O. Havemeyer, who were adding to their collection often with the advice of the Paris-based American painter Mary Cassatt. (The Havemeyers had bought their first Manet in 1886 – *The Salmon* – from Durand-Ruel's New York exhibition of Impressionist paintings.) American collectors had already shown an interest in Manet's work before the artist's death, for example the New York entrepreneur Erwin Davis, who bought *The Boy with a Sword* in 1881.[16] Thus, by the time of the First World War, a considerable number of major canvases were already held in private North American collections; many of these have subsequently passed into American museums. British collectors were slower than the Americans to show an interest in Manet's work, but his posthumous reputation in that country was established through exhibitions such as Roger Fry's *Manet and the Post-Impressionists* at the Grafton Galleries, London, from 1910 to 1911.

Édouard Manet's status, symbiotically linked to the development of Modernism, has not, therefore, been created solely by nineteenth- and twentieth-century critics and art historians. Modernism has also been institutionalized through the workings of art dealers, private collectors, museums and publishers.[17] All these have operated to maintain the visibility of Manet and his work before an ever-growing international

COLOURPLATE 46
[13] The Balcony *and* Angelina *(Rouart/ Wildenstein I 105) were accepted;* The Game of Croquet *(RW I 105) and* The Races *(RW I 96) were refused. The* Balcony *entered the Louvre in 1929.*

[14] *Étienne Moreau-Nelaton (1859–1927), collector, art historian and donor. Moreau-Nelaton also wrote studies of Corot, Delacroix and Daubigny.*

[15] *See Anthea Callen, "Faure and Manet",* Gazette des Beaux-Arts, *6th series, LXXXIII, March 1974 (pp. 157–78).*

[16] *Other important American collectors who purchased works by Manet include the trolley-car magnate P.A.B. Widener (1834–1915) who owned both* The Dead Toreador *and* At the Races *(National Gallery of Art, Washington D.C.), John G. Johnson (the* Battle of the "Kearsage" *and the* "Alabama", *Philadelphia), Mrs Berthe Honoré Palmer, wife of the Chicago real-estate millionaire, who also bought on the advice of Mary Cassatt (*Races at Longchamp, *The Art Institute of Chicago), Frank Gair Macomber (*The Execution of the Emperor Maximilian, *Boston), George Vanderbilt (*Repose: Portrait of Berthe Morisot, *Museum of Art, Rhode Island School of Design, Providence), Harris Whittemore, Sr. (*The Races in the Bois de Boulogne, *Collection Mrs John Hay Whitney), Ethel Sperry Crocker (*The Grand Canal, Venice), Henry Walters (*Café-Concert, *The Walters Art Gallery, Baltimore) and John Quinn (*Young Woman in a Round Hat, *The Henry and Rose Pearlman Foundation).*

[17] *See Griselda Pollock, "Feminism and Modernism" in Roszika Parker and Griselda*

public. The centenary exhibition of Manet's work organized jointly by the Metropolitan Museum of Art, New York, and the Louvre in France, drew enormous audiences in both countries, and coincided with a fresh spate of research and publications on the artist.

The institutionalization of Modernism may account to a large extent for the prominence accorded to Manet's work. But this alone does not seem adequately to explain the almost obsessive interest which certain canvases – the *Olympia* and the *Bar at the Folies-Bergère*, for example – seem to generate in audiences, scholars and critics, today as much as a hundred years ago.[18] It is perhaps no coincidence that both of these modern life subjects represent, in very different ways, the confrontation of men and women in a modern urban environment. Many of Manet's modern life subjects of the 1870s such as his *café-concert* and *brasserie* scenes were exhibited outside the domain of the Salon: for example, at the offices of the magazine *La Vie Moderne* in 1880. In these paintings, as well as in his final major Salon piece *The Bar at the Folies-Bergère*, working-class women are represented in juxtaposition to bourgeois male customers in ways which construct femininity as visual spectacle for the viewer of the picture as much as for the male customers depicted in the paintings. T.J. Clark's essay discusses how barmaids like the woman represented in the *Bar at the Folies-Bergère* were employed not merely to serve and encourage the purchase of drinks, but were themselves objects of consumption as prostitutes. *The Bar at the Folies-Bergère* is thus a representation of the potential consumption of femininity (the barmaid as prostitute) as well as being itself an object of visual consumption, activating desire in the viewer through the production of woman as spectacle.

Today the reception of Manet's work is no longer limited to Modernist and formalist readings, and recent authors have explored a different range of issues to those mapped out by Modernist critics and historians. The texts reproduced in this book by T.J. Clark and Sander Gilman investigate how art is socially produced by analysing Manet's work in relation to economic and social, as well as artistic and literary, factors.

Manet's work has preoccupied artists as well as historians. Twentieth-century painters such as René Magritte and Larry Rivers have reworked compositions by Manet, aware that references to works such as *The Balcony* or *Olympia* would be easily recognizable to an art-going public. Such

Pollock (editors), Framing Feminism: Art and the Women's Movement 1970– 1985, *London and New York, 1987 (pp. 101–6).*

COLOURPLATE 117

[18] *For a recent discussion among scholars and critics of the* Olympia *see T.J. Clark, "Preliminaries to a Possible Treatment of* Olympia *in 1865", Screen, Spring 1980, Vol. 21, No. 1 (pp. 18–51); Peter Wollen, "Manet: Modernism and Avant-Garde, Timothy Clark's article on Manet's* Olympia, Screen, *Spring 1980", Screen, Vol. 21, No. 2, Summer 1980 (pp. 15–25); T.J. Clark, "A Note in Reply to Peter Wollen", Screen, Vol. 21, No. 3, 1980 (pp. 97–100); C. Harrison, M. Baldwin and M. Ramsden, "Manet's* Olympia *and Contradiction", Block, No. 5, 1981. A revised version of Clark's* Screen *article appears in* The Painting of Modern Life: Paris in the Art of Manet and His Followers, *1985, pp. 79–146 as "Olympia's Choice".*

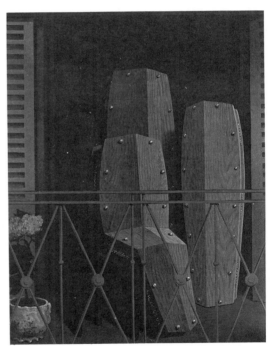

ABOVE René Magritte, *Perspective (Manet's* The Balcony*)*. 1950. 31½ × 23½" (80 × 60 cm). Museum van Hedendaagse Kunst, Gent, Belgium.

LEFT Larry Rivers, *I Like Olympia in Black Face*. 1970. Musée National d'Art Moderne, Paris (© SPADEM/ADAGP).

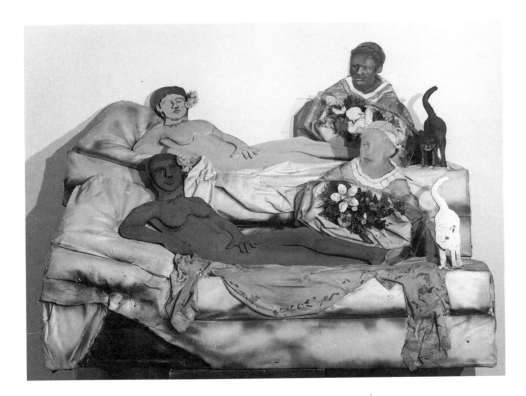

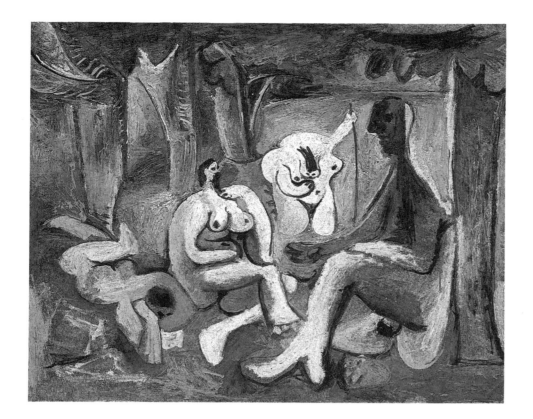

twentieth-century works are themselves indications of the icon-like status achieved by many of Manet's images. Picasso too has paid tribute to Manet, producing paintings and sculpture on the theme of *Luncheon on the Grass*.[19]

In Hans Haacke's "Manet-Projekt '74", however, the artist deflects the spectator's attentions away from the appearance of Manet's painting, the *Bunch of Asparagus* (1880, Wallraf-Richartz-Museum, Cologne) in order to produce a history of ownership.[20] The project begins with Manet, who sold the small canvas to Charles Éphrussi for 1000 francs in 1880, and ends with the acquisition of the work by the Wallraf-Richartz-Museum in 1968. Unlike an exhibition catalogue or *catalogue raisonné* provenance, Haacke lists not only prices at each point of sale, but also detailed economic and social information concerning each owner. He analyses the institutional make-up of the Cologne museum, outlining the official and business affiliations of the Chairman of the Friends of the Museum (responsible for the acquisition of the *Asparagus*) as well as all the donors who contributed to the purchase. "Manet-Projekt '74" thus provides insight not only into Manet's status as an artist on the art market, but also into the consumption of high art over a period spanning almost a century. Like T.J. Clark and Sander Gilman, Haacke has focused on Manet's work in order to challenge the assumption that art is produced and consumed in an aesthetic vacuum, in a world totally separate from the concerns of everyday work, business and politics. These studies are revealing not only of the ways in which Manet's works were produced during the artist's own lifetime, but also of how we understand – or might come to understand – them today.

[19] *For further twentieth-century artistic references to Manet and his work, see the Centre Georges Pompidou exhibition catalogue,* Bonjour Monsieur Manet, *1983.*

[20] *See pp. 343–63.*

MANET

ANTONIN PROUST

ÉDOUARD MANET: SOUVENIRS

Antonin Proust's Friendship with the Young Manet

1913

Édouard Manet was born in Paris on January 23, 1832, in no. 5 rue des Petits Augustins.

His father, Auguste Manet, was a high official at the Ministry of Justice. Later, he was to head the office and staff of M Barthe, the Lord Chancellor in the cabinet of Casimir Périer, then a magistrate at the Paris court of Appeal. On January 18, 1831, Auguste Manet had married Eugénie-Désirée Fournier, the daughter of Joseph-Antoine-Ennemond Fournier and Adelaide-Elisabeth Delanoue, the latter born February 11, 1811.

Through the position he held in Stockholm, Édouard Manet's maternal grandfather, Joseph-Antoine-Ennemond Fournier had been in a position to help put Bernadotte on the throne of Sweden. But if claimants are often most agreeable towards those who can help them in their ascent, they are less outgoing when they are in possession of the coveted position. M Ennemond Fournier had such a low opinion of Charles XIV that he left Sweden.

"My maternal grandfather," Édouard Manet used to say, when talking of the misadventures of M Ennemond Fournier, "was more modest. He had had links with the men of the revolution, and could easily have attained high office, but he preferred simply to remain mayor of Gennevilliers, where his family had owned land for two centuries, and to do a useful job there reclaiming land by damming up the waters of the Seine." Clément Manet died in Gennevilliers in 1814, at the age of 58. It was not until 1899 that the municipality of Gennevilliers, mindful of the benefits of its former mayor, named one of its streets after Clément Manet. . . .

To return to Édouard Manet. We had felt an intense empathy for one another from our earliest childhood. After having placed him in the institution run by the abbé Poiloup, his father had sent him to the Collège Rollin. Mine had sent me to this same school when one of my brothers, Henri, was studying in the special maths class. My oldest brother, Alfred, had left Rollin the year before. My mother and he were with my father in Pisa, where he was to die the following year, carried off by an illness which had caused him to resign as deputy in 1833.

Édouard Manet had attracted me by his open, frank manner. We were seated next to one another in one of those classrooms built as the building regulations required at the time, that is, in one of those ill-lit bunkers, reeking of an evening with the smell of smoky Argand lamps and furnished in a rudimentary fashion with rough screwed-down narrow benches in front of black desks which bit into your chest. We were crammed up against one another like herrings in a barrel. Nothing on the walls, not even a map. The most deprived of primary schools today are more comfortable than the classrooms of Paris's most aristocratic boarding school in 1844.

Édouard Manet was given special treatment by the headmaster, M Defauconpret, the translator of the works of Walter Scott, who had personal ties with his family, in particular with colonel Fournier. He was a man of letters, with a pronounced taste for everything connected with the

Antonin Proust (1832–1905), French journalist, critic and politician. Schoolfriend of Manet. Proust and Manet were to remain lifelong friends. Proust's Édouard Manet, Souvenirs, *published in 1913, is a major source of biographical information about the artist. (See Colourplate 104.)*

Jean-Baptiste-Jules Bernadotte, marshal of France under Napoleon. Became king of Sweden in 1818 and was known as Charles XIV.

Auguste-Jean-Baptiste Defauconpret (1767–1843), French writer and historical novelist. In addition to translating the works of Sir Walter Scott, he also translated Dickens and other British authors.

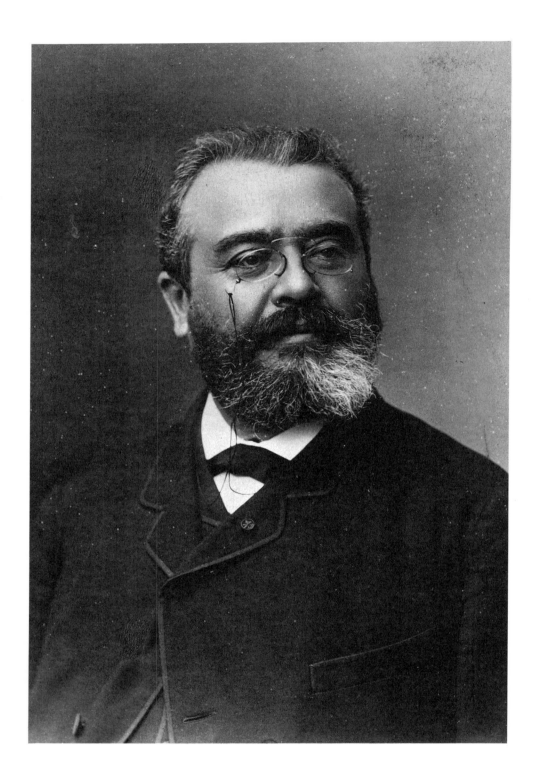

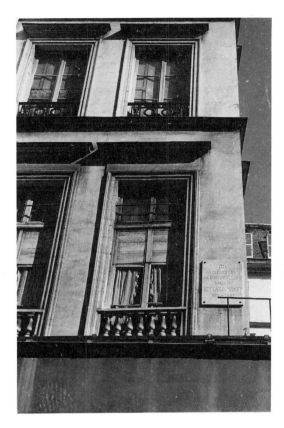

ABOVE Photograph of Manet's birthplace, Rue Bonaparte (formerly Rue des Petits Augustins), Paris.

Photograph of Antonin Proust by Nadar.

arts. He had no greater pleasure than to take us to the Louvre on Sundays, or to Vincennes where he lived. On these outings he noted with relish the facility with which Édouard, pencil and notebook in hand, tried to put down his impressions either from the masters or from nature.

One Sunday evening, he confronted Édouard's father, as they were leaving the dinner table. He advised his brother-in-law to allow his son to follow the optional drawing class available at Rollin. M Manet received this piece of advice very badly. He had three sons, Édouard, Gustave and Eugène, and intended those three sons to perpetuate the family tradition by studying subjects leading to the liberal professions. Colonel Fournier did not press his point, but he went to see M Defauconpret and told him he would pay for the drawing lessons to be given to his nephew.

In this drawing class, which took place next to the gymnasium, the teacher made us draw from Jullien models, rarely from the round. Édouard was so bored that his one desire was to sneak out into the yard where the gymnasium was situated. Was it the promise of physical exercise, at which he was exceptionally skilful, that determined him to apply to join the training ship *Borda*? Or was it rather the desire to leave Rollin as soon as possible? At all events he told his father roundly that since he felt no aptitude for the study of the law and had an actual vocation as a sailor, he had decided to study for Naval School.

The interior of the house on the rue du Mont-Thabor, where the Manet family then lived, was extremely modest. There was no discordant note. The family furniture, their way of dressing revealed that cult of the simple and the measured which is the mark of true French taste. Édouard was as happy at home as he was miserable at the Collège Rollin. There, apart from gym and the drawing course which he followed, (as I said) in a very uneven fashion, the only lessons which interested him were the history classes, given by a young teacher, M Wallon, the future father of the 1875 Constitution. And even then I should say that during M Wallon's lessons, he often read under his desk, immersed in books which he managed to smuggle into the college when he came back on a Sunday.

It was in connection with one of these books that he made an observation one day which already revealed his passion for the direct study of the realities that surrounded him. The book was Diderot's *Salons*. As is well known, in connection with a picture by Roslin, depicting the *King Being Received at the Paris Town Hall*, Diderot spoke of "the banality of our little doublets, our perfect breeches, our hair-nets, our sleeves and our buttonholes. And the absurdity of those enormous magisterial wigs, and the baseness of those bourgeois moon faces." And, further on: "add to the banality of our clothing that of our reverence: our tucked-up sleeves, our tight-fitting trousers, our square-cut pleated coat-tails, our knee garters, our belt buckles with their love-knots, our pointed shoes. I defy a very genius of painting and sculpture to make anything of this mean ensemble. A Frenchman in his buttoned jerkin, his sword and his hat would cut a fine figure in marble or bronze." Finally, in the *Pensées détachées sur la Peinture*, the following thought is expressed: "When the clothing of a people is mean, art must ignore costume;" Manet said to me: "Now that *is* silly; you have to be of your time and paint what you see."

This observation struck me all the more in that we had noticed that during the drawing classes Édouard refused to copy the helmeted models, and drew the heads of his neighbours. And as Joly, Paul de Remusat and I had taken him as our example, there was a positive revolution in the drawing class, a revolution which elicited a report from M Sanval, the vice-principal. As a result of this report, we were barred from the class for a month.

M Defauconpret called us into his study and, after having reprimanded us in a fatherly fashion, he waived the punishment on condition that, from now on, we would faithfully copy the models we were given. Édouard and I had to use black pencil on white paper to reproduce, as exactly as possible three lithographed figures from the picture by the baron Gérard representing the entry of Henri IV into his cherished city of Paris in 1594. . . .

It was on board the ship *Le Havre et Guadeloupe* that Édouard Manet made a trip to Rio de Janeiro, at a salary of 15 francs a month, during which time his taste for painting had an opportunity for expression. The ship had left France with a cargo of Dutch cheeses: the deck was cluttered with them. As the sea air had dulled their colour, captain Besson said one day to Manet, in a bantering tone: "Young man, since you're so fond of painting, here's a pot of red lead and a paintbrush. You can put a layer on these Dutch cheeses for me." Manet did so. "On our arrival in port," he was to say later, "the cheeses were like tomatoes. The natives, the negroes especially, bought them eagerly and devoured them rind and all, sorry that there were not more."

Denis Diderot (1713–84). His Salons *were written between 1759 and 1781 and his* Pensées détachées sur la Peinture *were published in 1777.*
Alexander Roslin (1718–93), Swedish painter who settled in Paris in 1752.

Baron François-Pascal-Simon Gérard (1770–1837), Neoclassical painter; Henri IV (1553–1610), first Bourbon king of France.

ÉDOUARD MANET

LETTRES DE JEUNESSE 1848-49 – VOYAGE À RIO

Letter to his Mother

1928

This is one of the many letters written by the young Manet to his family while on the training ship Havre et Guadeloupe.

Off Rio de Janeiro

Dear Mother,

I told you in my last letter about our arrival in Rio. As I said, the bay is delightful, we had plenty of time to admire it because we didn't go ashore until the following Sunday; it seemed a long wait; the captain, officers and the passenger who is my *bosom friend* kept constantly going ashore, making us long all the more for the moment when we would set foot on dry land. Everyone sent their letter of introduction; I sent the one Reboul had given me, and on Sunday, after mass (for they say mass on board) I went off with Mr Jules Lacarrière, a young man of my own age. He took me to meet his mother, who has a ladies' dress shop in the rue d'Ouvidor and who has a typical little Brazilian house in the country, five miles outside Rio; I lunched and dined with them; the family consists of the oldest son, a little boy, and a girl of thirteen; I was welcomed with open arms, they couldn't have been nicer. After lunch I went with my new friend to look at the whole town. It is quite big, though the streets are very narrow; for a European who has any artistic sense at all it has a very special air to it; the only people you meet in the streets are negroes and negresses; the Brazilian men go out little, and the women even less; you see them only when they go out to mass, or in the evening after dinner, when they sit at their windows; then you may gaze at them to your heart's content, for during the day if they chance to be at their windows and notice you looking at them, they retire immediately. In this country all the negroes are slaves; all these wretched people look brutalized; the power the whites have over them is extraordinary; I saw a slave market, which is a fairly revolting sight for us; the negroes are dressed in trousers, sometimes a loose cloth jacket, but as slaves they are not permitted to wear shoes. The women are mostly naked to the waist, some have a silk scarf round their necks, falling down over their chests, they are mostly ugly, though I saw some quite pretty ones. Some make themselves turbans, others arrange their frizzy hair in a most artistic fashion, and they almost all wear skirts decorated with monstrous flounces.

Most of the Brazilians, however, are very pretty; they have magnificent dark eyes and hair to match; they all wear their hair Chinese style and they always go out bare-headed; they dress in the style of the Spanish colonies, that is, very lightly, in a way that we are not accustomed to; the women never go out alone, they are always followed by their negress or else they are with their children, for in this country people marry at fourteen and earlier. I visited several churches, they are not as fine as ours, all gilded, all lit up, but quite lacking in taste; there are several convents in this town, including an Italian one where the reverend fathers wear monks' robes and long beards. Everything is horribly dear here, they only use paper money and copper coins.

In Rio the Brazilian women have themselves carried on palanquins, and there are carriages too, and omnibuses pulled by mules, for they use them instead of horses.

I forgot to tell you of the emperor's palace, which is modest to the point of being a hovel; in fact he doesn't live there often, he lives some way off in a castle called St Christophe. The Brazilian militia is always very comical, the Brazilians also have a national guard; they have impressment in this country and it is in force at this moment, for there have been troubles in Baia and troops are constantly being sent there.

I'd like you to write a very nice letter to my friend's mother and thank her for the way she received me; they make sure I go out every Sunday; but don't be alarmed at her title of "ladies' dress shop owner," she is quite out of the ordinary and her son is a pupil at the pension Jouffroy, a charming boy and better brought up, I assure you, than many of us at home. I will, however, confess that the first Sunday we went out, I did find it rather odd being in a shop, though I'm used to it now. If you see Reboul, thank him on my behalf and tell him I'll be bringing a letter from his friend on my return.

I haven't heard anything said about M Pinto, though I know his address, he's a Portuguese and I may go and see him one of these days. If by any chance you were to write me a letter to his address – I think father was intending to do so – be careful to address it as follows: *Manuel Ferreira* Pinto 39 via Directa, for all the Portuguese in this town are called Pinto.

We are experiencing the most dreadful rain at the moment, it lasts for four or five days without ceasing, and there is nothing more boring than rain when one is on board ship.

We were not able to find a drawing-master in Rio, the captain has asked me to give lessons to my companions, so lo and behold I am elevated to the rank of drawing-master; I should tell you that during the voyage I had earned myself quite a reputation, that all the officers and teachers asked me to do their caricatures, and the captain himself asked me to do his for his New Year's gift; I was lucky enough to acquit myself throughout so as to please everyone.

Every Thursday we get up at four in the morning and go by boat to the other side of the bay from the town; then we make excursions into the countryside, and bathe; we lunch and dine on the spot; we take with us the cook and head-waiter and provisions of all kinds. These walks are delightful, we have the spectacle of the most beautiful natural scenery possible, and as much fruit as we like; every day a local rowing-boat comes laden with bananas, oranges, pineapples etc., all very cheap.

The Carnival in Rio has a mood all its own. On Quinquagesima Sunday I spent the whole day walking in the town. At three o'clock all the Brazilian women come either to their doors or to their balconies and ply all the passing gentlemen with wax bombs of all colours, filled with water and known as *limes*.

In several streets I was set upon, in accordance with the local custom. I had my pockets full of limes and riposted as best I could, which was very well-received. These goings-on lasted until six in the evening, when order reigns once more and a masqued ball, inspired by the balls at the Opera, takes place, and where only the Frenchman shines. We went to spend Shrove Tuesday in the country. We had a delightful outing deep into the countryside, which I admire more and more; unfortunately there are a lot of snakes; walking in the undergrowth you have to be in a permanent state of alert; I have seen some charming humming-birds.

On Sat. 24th I received your letter, dear Mother, and was delighted by it, it had been so long since I had heard from you.

I have just spent three days in the country with three bachelors and three friends; we had as much fun as it is possible to have; went hunting in virgin forest, and such like.

Good-bye, dearest Mother; I'll stop now, an English packet is just leaving; I embrace you tenderly, as I do father, my brothers, grand-mother, Jules, etc.

Warmest regards to my aunt, Edmond and Marie,

your respectful son,
Édouard Manet

ÉDOUARD MANET: SOUVENIRS

Antonin Proust's Description of Édouard Manet

Compare George Moore's description of Manet on pp. 264–70.

1913

At that time, Édouard Manet was of medium height, and very muscular. He had a rhythmic walk to which his swaying gait gave a particular elegance. Try as he might to exaggerate this swaying motion, and to affect the drawl of the Paris urchin, he could never manage to appear vulgar. One sensed his breeding.

He had a straight, well-defined nose beneath a broad forehead. His mouth, which turned up at the corners, had a mocking expression. He had a limpid gaze. His eyes were small, but very mobile. When he was very

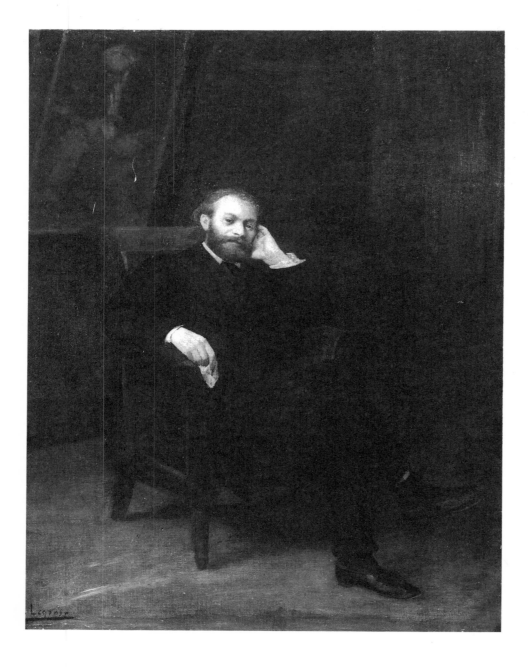

Alphonse Legros, *Portrait of Manet*. 1863. Musée des Beaux-Arts de la Ville de Paris, Petit-Palais, Paris.

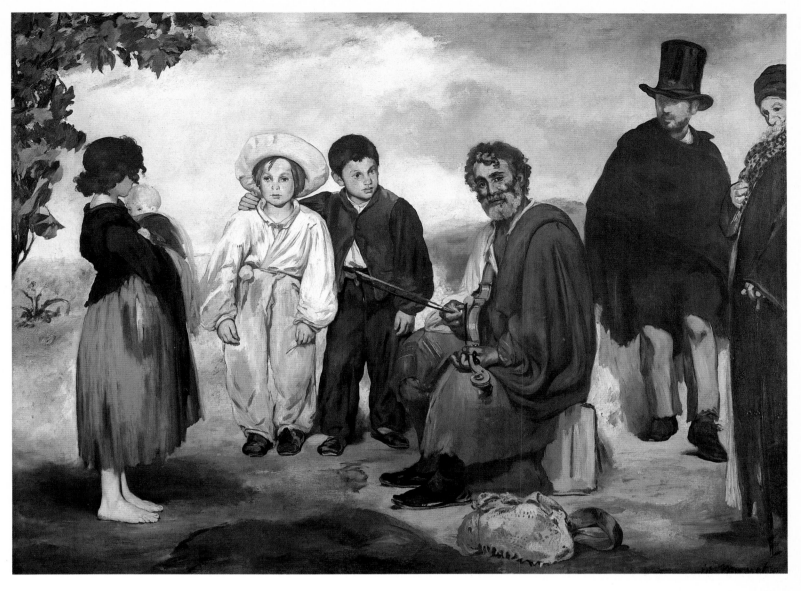

COLOURPLATE 9. *The Old Musician*. 1862. 73¼ × 97¾″ (187.4 × 248.3 cm).
National Gallery of Art, Washington D.C. (Chester Dale Collection).

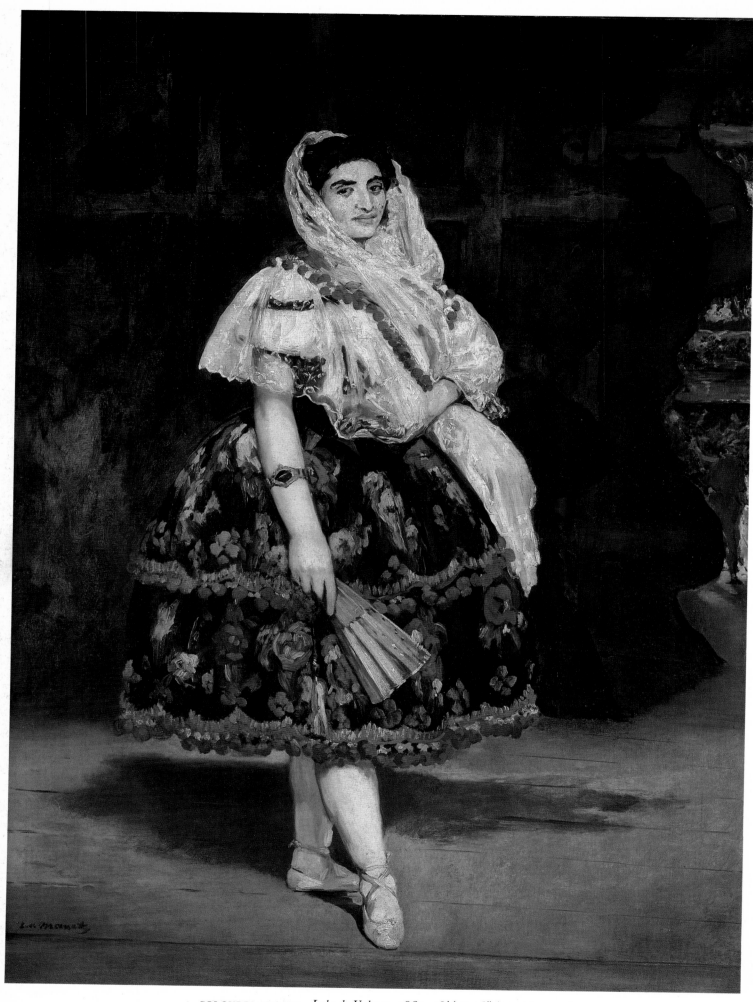

COLOURPLATE 10. *Lola de Valence*. 1862. 48½ × 36″ (123 × 92 cm).
Musée d'Orsay, Paris.

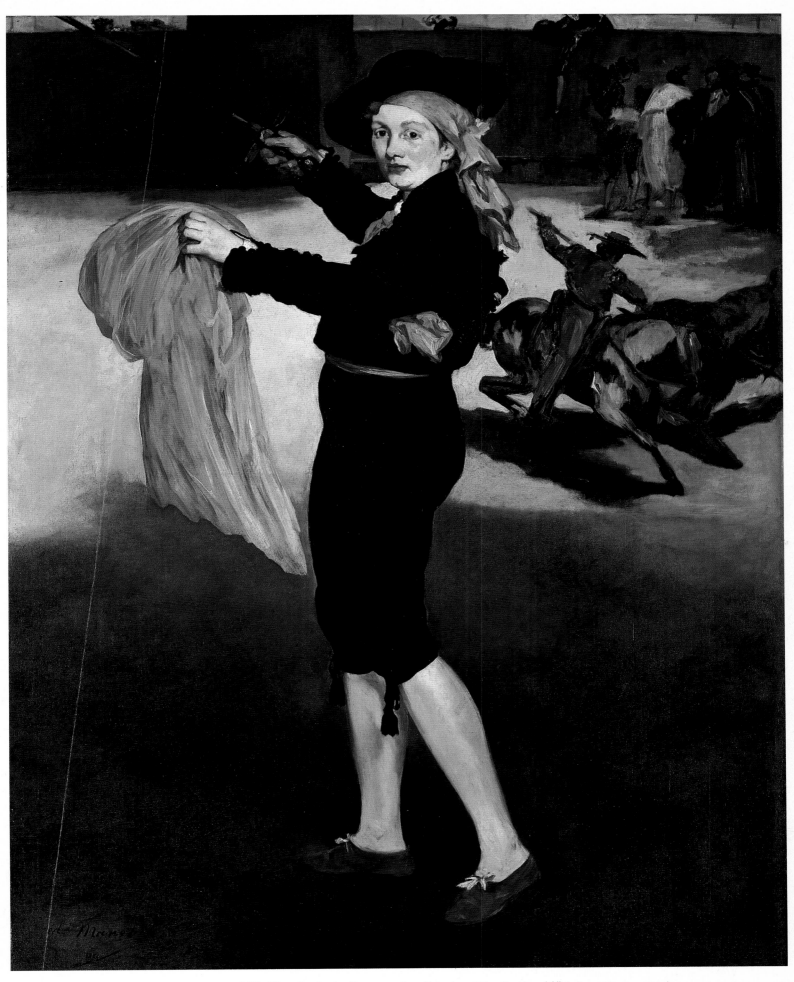

COLOURPLATE 12. *Mlle Victorine in the Costume of an Espada*. 1862. 65 × 50¼″ (165.1 × 127.9cm).
Metropolitan Museum of Art, New York (Bequest of Mrs H.O. Havemeyer, 1929. The H.O.
Havemeyer Collection).

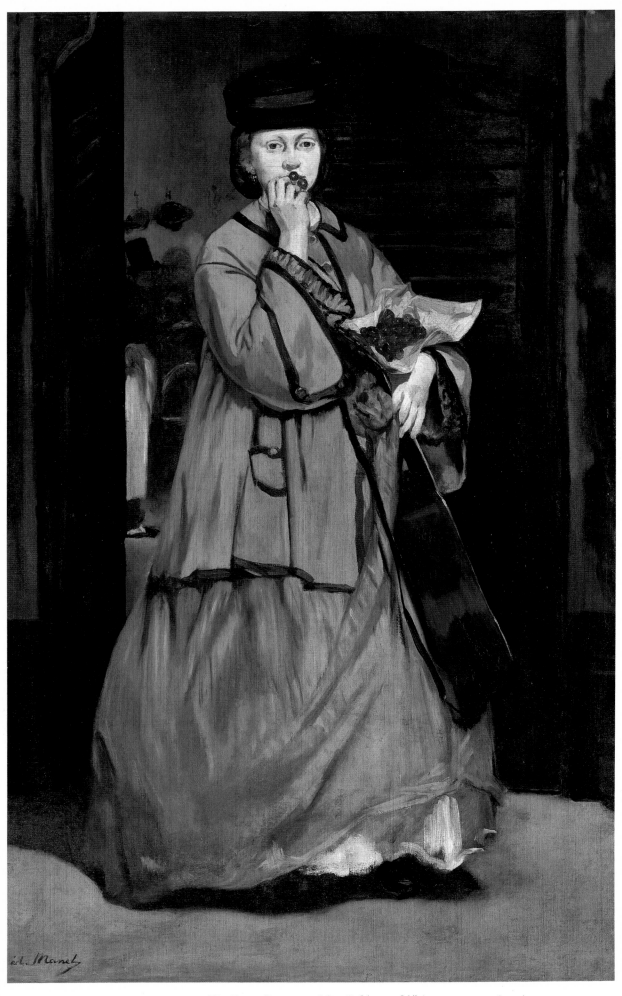

COLOURPLATE 13. *The Street Singer*. c.1862. 67⅜ × 41⅝″ (171.3 × 105.8 cm).
Courtesy, Museum of Fine Arts, Boston (Bequest of Sarah Choate Sears in Memory of her Husband
Joshua Montgomery Sears).

young, he had long, naturally curly hair which he wore thrown back. At eighteen, the hair on his forehead was already slightly thinning, but he had grown a beard. Thus the lower part of his face appeared softer, while his extremely fine hair was a perfect foil for the upper part. Few men have had more allure.

Despite all his wit and his tendency to scepticism, he had remained an innocent. Everything astonished him, the slightest thing amused him. On the other hand, everything connected with art rendered him serious. On this subject, he was uncompromising. His convictions were fixed, unshakeable. He admitted of neither contradiction, nor even discussion. His short sojourn in southern, sunnier countries had inspired him with a conception such that everything appeared to him with a simplicity which Couture did not understand. Given half a chance, he would have done away with halftones. The direct transition from light to shade was his constant preoccupation. He loved Titian's flow of light. He adored the primitives. "I cannot abide anything that is superfluous," he would say to me. "The tricks of the trade have perverted us. What is the answer? Who will give us back the simple and the clear? Who will deliver us from frills and fancies? The thing to do, you know, is to forge straight ahead, without worrying about what people say."

ANTONIN PROUST

ÉDOUARD MANET: SOUVENIRS

Manet and Couture's Models

1913

At the time, people used to say: "Couture is teaching someone called Manet, who does some astonishing things but who is very difficult with the models." And indeed, invariably, every Monday, when they set up the pose for the whole week, Manet would have disagreements with the professional models. Dubosc, Gilbert and Thomas Lours were the most illustrious professionals. Climbing on to the table, they traditionally struck up the most extravagant attitudes.

"Can't you be more natural?" Manet would exclaim. "Do you stand like that when you go to buy a bunch of radishes at the greengrocer's?"

One day Dubosc, who was particularly convinced that he was practising a hallowed profession, took offence at one of Manet's observations.

"M Manet," he said to him, "M Delaroche never had anything but praise for me, and it is hard to be unappreciated by a young man like you."

"I'm not asking for M Delaroche's opinion, I'm giving you mine."

"M Manet," uttered M Dubosc in a voice strangled by emotion, "thanks to me, more than one painter has gone to Rome."

"We are not in Rome and we have no desire to go there. We are in Paris: and that is where we should stay."

Manet went out that day in despair, declaring that there was nothing to be done with such idiots.

Thomas Couture (1815–1879), French painter. Couture had established his reputation at the Salon of 1847 with his Romans of the Decadence *(Musée du Louvre), which won a first-class medal. He opened his own school in the same year. Manet and Proust entered Thomas Couture's studio as pupils in January 1850.*

Paul-Hippolyte Delaroche (1797–1859), French painter.

The prestigious government-sponsored Prix de Rome/Rome Prize was awarded on a competitive basis by the École des Beaux-Arts. The winner was entitled to spend four years in Rome at the French Academy, housed in the Villa Medici.

ANTONIN PROUST

ÉDOUARD MANET: SOUVENIRS

Manet's Visit to the Studio of Eugène Delacroix

Probably around 1855.

1913

"That's all very well," said Manet, when we had taken our leave of the two artists, "but there was one major canvas at the Luxembourg. What if we were to go and see Delacroix? We could say that we had come to ask his permission to make a copy of *Dante and Virgil*."

"Be careful," Murger had said to us, when informed of our plan by Manet, when lunching, "Delacroix is a cold fish."

In fact, Delacroix received us at his studio in Notre-Dame-de-la-Lorette perfectly graciously, questioned us about our preferences and indicated his own. One had to be inspired by Rubens, to copy Rubens. Rubens was God.

His pupil Andrieu, who worked with him, took us to the door. Manet said to me: "It's not Delacroix who is cold: it's his opinions, which are glacial. Anyway, let's copy *Dante and Virgil*."

After *Dante and Virgil*, we went to the Louvre to make a sketch of Velazquez' *The Cavaliers*.

"That," said Manet with a sigh of relief, "is clear-cut. It's enough to put you off stews and brews."

At this date, the Luxembourg Museum was the museum of contemporary art.

Eugène Delacroix's (1798–1863) The Barque of Dante *had been exhibited at the Salon of 1822. Manet made two oil copies of the work during the 1850s.*
Henri Murger (1822–61), novelist. Author of Scènes de la Vie de Bohème, *which was to form the basis of Puccini's opera* La Bohème.

Henri Fantin-Latour, *Homage to Delacroix*. 1864. Musée d'Orsay, Paris. Manet is third from right, Baudelaire bottom right.

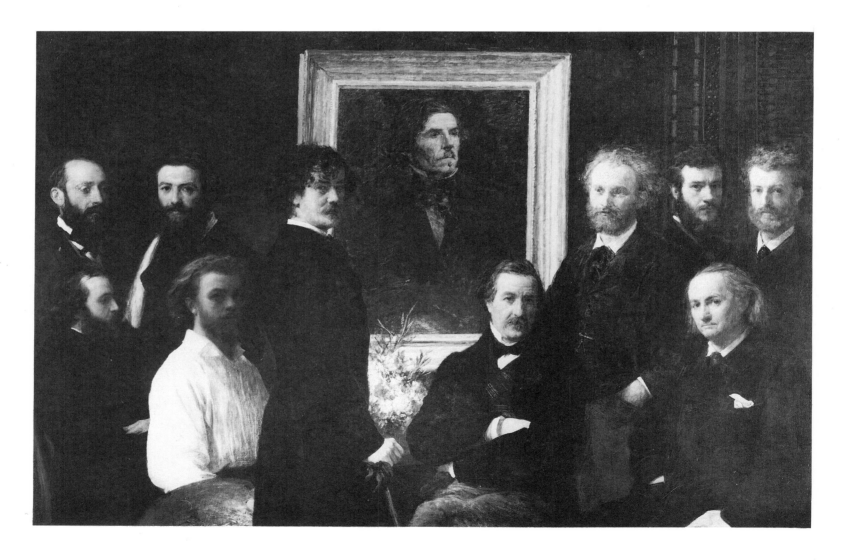

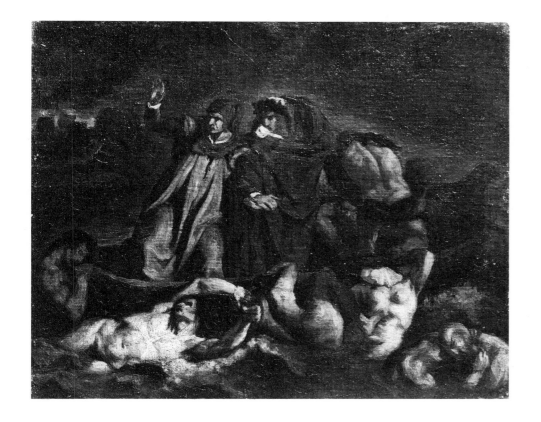

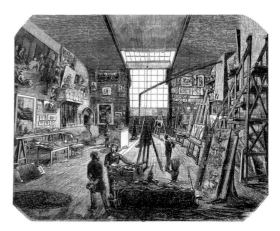

ABOVE *The Studio of Delacroix*, 56 Rue Notre Dame de Lorette, Paris. Engraving by E. Renard, 1852. Bibliothèque Nationale, Paris (Cabinet des Estampes).

LEFT *Dante and Virgil in Hell* (after Delacroix). c. 1854. 15 × 18¼″ (38 × 46 cm). Musée des Beaux-Arts, Lyon (Photo Studio Lontin).

ANTONIN PROUST

ÉDOUARD MANET: SOUVENIRS

Manet and Baudelaire as Parisian *flâneurs*

1913

Manet and Charles Baudelaire had met in 1858 or 1859 and were to remain friends until the poet's death in 1867.

With Manet, the eye played such an important part that Paris has never known a *flâneur* to equal him, nor one who indulged in this "activity" so productively. As soon as the winter days arrived, when the light is muffled by mist from early morning, so that painting in the studio becomes quite impossible, we would decamp straight to the outer boulevards. There, he would draw the slightest thing in his notebook, a profile, a hat, a fleeting impression in short, and when, the following day, a friend would say to him, leafing through: "You ought to finish that," he would double up with laughter: "You must take me for a history painter," he would say.

A flâneur is literally a stroller or lounger; commonly applied to a dandified middle-class idler. Baudelaire gave the term a particular interpretation of the detached intellectual observer. He probably wrote The Painter of Modern Life *shortly after meeting Manet, although it was not published until 1863. This essay, which Baudelaire had based on the artist Constantin Guys, is an evocative description of the modern painter as urban flâneur. (See also p. 316.)*

Those words, from him, were the most cutting insult one could throw at an artist. He professed the greatest scorn for painters who shut themselves up with models, costumes and props, which produce dead paintings when, as he said, there are so many living things to be painted outside.

"And anyway," he would add, "it's quite ridiculous to reconstruct historical figures! Does one paint a man on the basis of his hunting-licence? There is only one right way of going about things: to take down what one sees straight off. When it works, it works. When it doesn't you start again. All else is nonsense." . . .

Manet also had very close ties with Baudelaire, who is credited with great influence over him. It is the reverse that is true. Baudelaire's frequenting of the rôtisserie Pavard and the restaurant Dinocheau (Dinocheau of whom it was said that he and François I shared the honour

François I (1494–1547), king of France from 1515.

of being the "nourishers" of letters and the arts) and the conversations he had with Manet, altered Baudelaire's ways of seeing and judging considerably, and if Manet and Baudelaire were closely attached, it was Manet who retained the influence over his friend.

At a time when the poet used make-up outrageously – "He really lays it on," Manet would exclaim, "but there's so much genius beneath the layer!" – Baudelaire was his constant companion when Manet went to the Tuileries, doing open-air sketches of the children playing beneath the trees and the groups of nurses who had collapsed on to the chairs. The strollers looked with interest at this elegantly clad painter who arranged his canvas, armed himself with his palette and painted with as much serenity as he would have done in his studio.

I have said what a *flâneur* Manet was. One day we walked together up to what has since become the Boulevard Malesherbes, in the midst of the demolition created by the gaping openings of the already flattened sites. The Monceau district had not yet been planned. Manet would stop me at every step. Here a cedar rose in solitude in the midst of a trampled garden. The tree seemed to be seeking the shattered banks of flowers with its long arms. "Do you see its skin?" he would say, "and the purple tones of the shadows?" Further on, the demolition men glimmered whitely against the less white wall collapsing beneath their blows, enveloping them in a cloud of dust. Manet contemplated the sight in absorption. "There it is," he exclaimed, "the symphony in white major Théophile Gautier talks about."

A woman came out of a sleazy cabaret, lifting her dress, clutching her guitar. He went straight up to her and asked her to come and pose for him. She burst out laughing. "I'll get her sometime," he said, "and if she doesn't want to, there's always Victorine." Victorine Meurent, whose portrait he has painted, was his favourite model.

BELOW *Children Playing in the Tuileries Gardens.* 1862. 15 × 18¼" (38 × 46 cm). Museum of Art, Rhode Island School of Design, Providence, Rhode Island (Museum Appropriation).

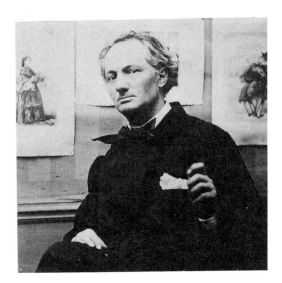

Photograph of Baudelaire by E. Carjat.

This demolition was probably the result of works being carried out in the rebuilding and modernization of Paris as directed by the Prefect of the Seine, Baron Georges-Eugène Haussmann, under the Emperor Napoleon III during the period 1853–70 — the "Haussmannization" of Paris. See The View from Notre-Dame *in T.J. Clark,* The Painting of Modern Life: Paris in the Art of Manet and his Followers, *1985.*
Théophile Gautier (1811–72), poet and critic. His poem "Symphonie en blanc majeur" appears in the collection of short poems Émaux et Camées *(1852).*

Photograph of Manet by E. Carjat.

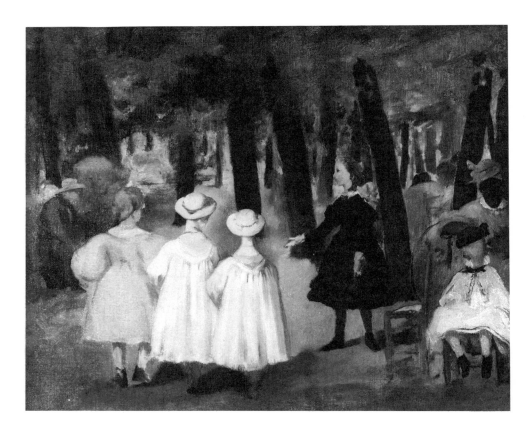

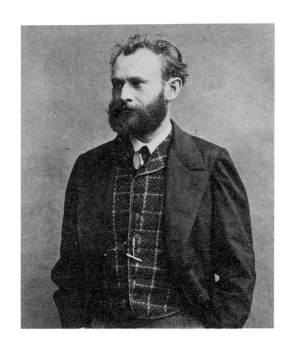

THÉODORE DURET

MANET AND THE FRENCH IMPRESSIONISTS

Manet's Marriage

1910

In 1863 he had married Mlle Suzanne Leenhoff, a Dutch lady born at Delft. She belonged to a family devoted to art. One of her brothers, Ferdinand Leenhoff, was a sculptor and engraver. She herself was a pianist, and although she played only amongst friends, she devoted herself to music with great assiduity. In her Manet found a woman of artistic taste, capable of understanding him and of giving him that strengthening help and encouragement which enabled him better to withstand the attacks from outside. His father had died in 1862, leaving his fortune to be divided among his three sons, enough to support them in comfort. Thus Manet found himself in a privileged position among artists. He was able to live without the necessity of selling his pictures, which nobody in these early days would have bought at any price, and he could set aside a sufficient sum to provide for the necessary expenses of a studio and models.

Leaving the Boulevard des Batignolles, Manet and his wife came to live with his mother in the rue de Saint-Pétersbourg. The flat was furnished with the family furniture of the stiff formal style that had been fashionable in the reign of Louis Philippe. There was no display of bibelots or objects of virtu; only two or three pictures hung on the walls, – the portraits of his father and mother which Manet had painted, and a portrait of himself by Fantin-Latour. His mother possessed the grace and distinction of manner of a woman who had moved much in society. His brothers Eugène and Gustave were constant visitors. Since the death of their father, their chief counsellor and guide had been M de Jouy, an advocate held in high esteem at the Palais de Justice. Manet painted his portrait in 1879. Manet's appearance never clashed with his surroundings. Nothing about him particularly betrayed the artist. He was scrupulously correct in his dress; indeed it was in some measure owing to his example that artists came to exchange the fantastic manner which they had formerly affected for the correctness of dress and bearing of the man of the world.

Nothing was more remarkable than the contrast which existed between Manet's social position and his rôle of revolutionary artist and iconoclast of the venerated traditional aesthetic. On the one hand was the Manet against whom everybody was up in arms, the butt of caricature and witticism, pursued by the mob as a kind of outcast, regarded as a barbarian, the exponent of a brutal and vulgar realism; on the other was the Manet who came of a distinguished family, who lived soberly with his wife and mother, and preserved throughout his life the polished manners of the class to which by birth he belonged.

Théodore Duret (1838–1927), French journalist, art critic and collector. Duret had started work in the cognac trade, but began writing art criticism in 1867. He went on to amass a collection of Impressionist works and wrote two books on Manet: Histoire d'Édouard Manet et de son oeuvre par Théodore Duret, avec un catalogue des peintures et des pastels, *Paris 1902, and* Manet and the French Impressionists, *London 1910. (See Colourplate 41.)*

Suzanne Leenhoff (1830–1906).

Ferdinand Leenhoff (1841–1914).

Louis Philippe (1773–1850) reigned 1830–48.

Eugène (1833–92); Gustave (1835–84) Manet. Jules de Jouy, Manet's cousin who had lived in the same house as the Manets in the rue Bonaparte. He was a lawyer and exécuteur testamentaire *of Manet's will.*

PAUL MANTZ

GAZETTE DES BEAUX-ARTS
Manet, a Parisian Spaniard
April 1, 1863

Paul Mantz (1821–95), art critic, historian and administrator. He became Director General of the Ministry of Fine Arts in 1881. He wrote books on Hans Holbein (1879) and François Boucher (1880).

Manet, who is a Parisian Spaniard, related by some mysterious affinity to the tradition of Goya, exhibited at the Salon of 1861 a *Spanish Singer* which, we must confess, greatly impressed us. It was brutal but it was truthful, and in that rough sketch there was promise of a virile talent. Two years have passed since then, and Manet with his innate bravado has entered the realm of the impossible. We absolutely refuse to follow him. Form is lost in his large portraits of women, and especially in the *Street Singer* where, through a peculiarity which bothers us intensely, the eyebrows have been moved from their horizontal position to a vertical one parallel to the nose, like two dark commas. There is nothing more there than the shattering discord of chalky tones with black ones. The effect is pallid, harsh, ominous. At other times, when Manet is in a good humour, he

COLOURPLATE 4

COLOURPLATE 13

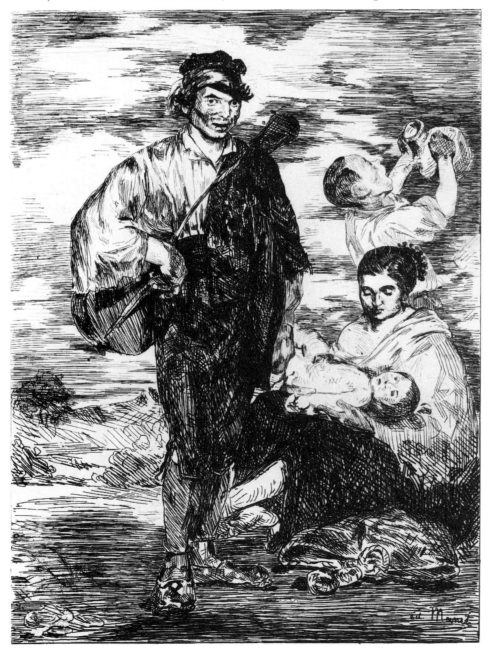

RIGHT *Boy with Pitcher*. c. 1861. 24¼ × 21¼" (61.8 × 54.3 cm). Courtesy, The Art Institute of Chicago (Bequest of Katharine Dexter McCormick). This is a fragment of a large composition, *The Gypsies*, 1862; three fragments have survived. See etching left.

The Gypsies. 1862. Etching, 11 × 8" (28.4 × 20.6 cm).

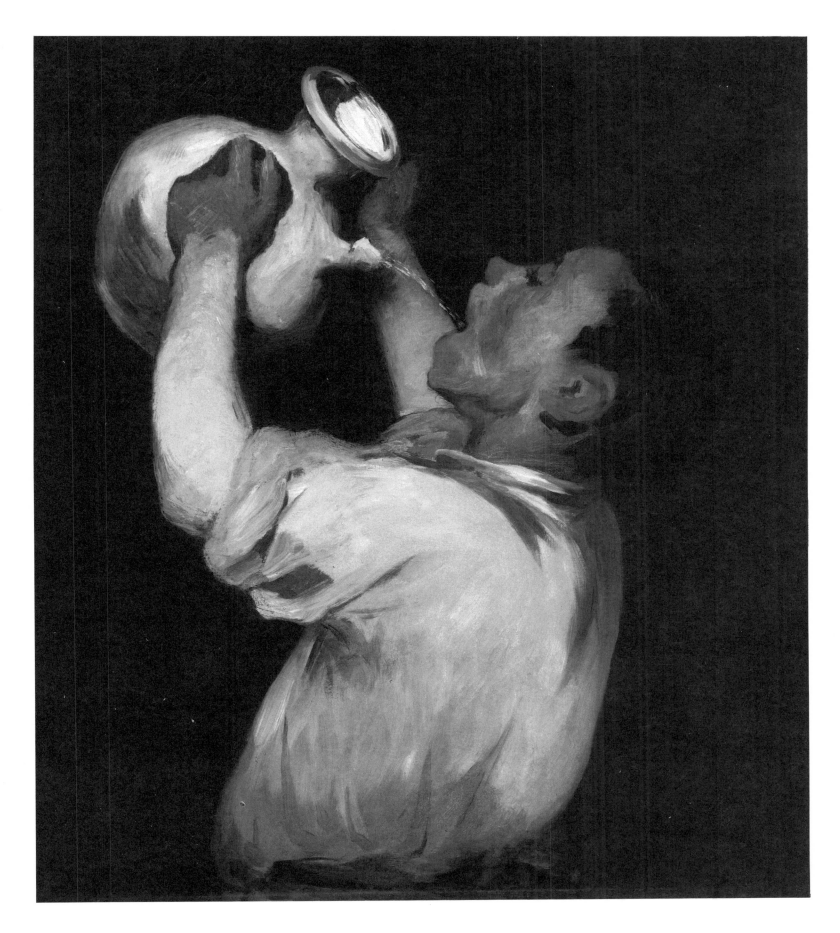

paints the *Music in the Tuileries Gardens*, the *Spanish Ballet* and *Lola de Valence*, paintings which disclose his abundant vigour but which in their medley of red, blue, yellow and black are colour caricatured, not colour itself. In short, this art may be strong and straightforward but it is not healthy, and we feel in no way obliged to plead Manet's cause before the jury of the Salon.

COLOURPLATES 11, 10

THORÉ-BURGER

L'INDÉPENDENCE BELGE

The Influence of Velázquez, Goya and El Greco

June 15, 1864

W. Burger, pseudonym for Théophile Thoré (1807–69), lawyer, political activist, art historian and critic. Burger started writing art criticism in the 1830s and went on to produce important studies of seventeenth-century Dutch art.

Monsieur Manet has the talent of a magician; his colour is luminous and brilliant, like that of his favourite masters, Velazquez and Goya. It is of them that he was thinking when he designed and painted his arena. In his second picture, *The Dead Christ with Angels*, he has imitated with equal force another Spanish master, El Greco, which is a challenge to the bashful lovers of discreet and tidy painting. This Christ, seated like any ordinary person, is seen full face with both arms pressed against his body. It is a terrifying picture to look at. Is he perhaps about to rise from the dead under the wings of the two helping angels? And oh, what strange wings they are – wings from another world, more intensely blue than the deepest sky! No terrestrial birds have such plumage; but maybe angels, the birds of heaven, wear such colours, and a public, which has never seen an angel, has no right to scoff. . . . The colour of angels is not a subject for discussion. But I feel that this awesome Christ and these angels, with wings of Prussian blue, don't care a jot about people who say, "But that's impossible! It's an aberration!" It was a very distinguished lady who thus apostrophized Monsieur Manet's poor Christ, who hangs exposed to the ridicule of the female Pharisees of Paris. But nothing can alter the fact that the white tones of the shroud and the colour of the flesh are extremely accurately observed, and that the broad and free treatment of the modelling, particularly in Christ's right arm, and in the foreshortening of the legs, remind one of some of the greatest masterpieces – Rubens' *Dead Christ* and *Christ on the Straw* in the Antwerp Museum, for example, and even of certain Christs by Annibale Carracci. The comparison is very marked, but it is to El Greco, the student of Titian and the master of Luis Tristan, who in his turn became the master of Velazquez, that Monsieur Manet's *Christ* bears the closest resemblance.

Enough has been said about Manet's eccentricities, which conceal a real painter, whose works, one day perhaps, will be acclaimed by the public. Remember how Eugène Delacroix began his career; remember his success at the Universal Exhibition of 1835, and the sale of his works – after he was dead!

COLOURPLATE 24

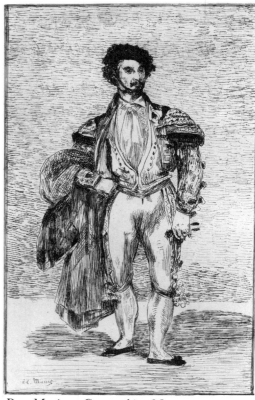

Don Mariano Camprubi. 1862.
Etching, 8¾ × 6″
(22.5 × 15.5 cm). (Photo Philadelphia Museum of Art).

CHARLES BAUDELAIRE

Letter to Thoré-Burger Replying to Comment in *L'Indépendence Belge*

June 1864

Charles Baudelaire (1821–67), poet and critic. Baudelaire's statement on Manet's awareness of Spanish art has been questioned by later historians.

I do not know if you remember me and our discussions of old. So many years pass so quickly! . . . I read your work most assiduously and I want to thank you for the pleasure you have given me in coming to the defence of my friend Édouard Manet, and in dealing him a little bit of justice.

However, there are a few small points to straighten out in the opinions which you have published.

Manet, whom people think wild and insane, is simply a very straightforward, unaffected person, as reasonable as he can be but unfortunately touched by romanticism from birth.

The word "imitation" is unfair. Manet has never seen a Goya; Manet has never seen a Greco; Manet has never seen the Pourtalès Collection. This seems unbelievable to you, but it's true.

I have myself admired, in amazement, these mysterious coincidences.

At the time when we used to enjoy that wonderful Spanish Museum which the stupid French Republic in its excessive respect for private property gave back to the House of Orléans, Manet was a youngster serving in the navy. People have told him so much about his imitations of Goya that now he is trying to see some Goyas.

It is true that he has seen Velazquez, I know not where. You don't believe what I tell you? You doubt that such surprising mathematical parallels can be found in nature? Very well! People have accused me, yes me, of imitating Edgar Poe!

Do you know why I have translated Poe so patiently? *Because he resembled me.* The first time I opened one of his books I saw, with terror and ecstasy, not only subjects I had dreamed of, but *phrases* I had thought of and he had written twenty years earlier.

Et nunc erudimini, vos qui judicatis! . . . Do not be annoyed, but keep in some corner of your mind a kind thought for me. Every time you try to do a good deed for Manet, I shall thank you . . . .

I have the courage, perhaps the complete affrontery, of my convictions. You may quote my letter, or a few lines of it. I have told you the absolute truth.

CHARLES BAUDELAIRE

LE FIGARO

The Rope

February 7, 1864

There are probably as many countless illusions, my friend told me, as there are contacts between man and man, and when the illusion vanishes, that is to say when we see the creature of fact objectively, we experience a strange complicated feeling, which is compounded half of regret for the vanished phantom, and half of agreeable surprise at the novelty of the real thing. If there is anything which is obvious, trite, and always the same, and the nature of which is unmistakable, it is maternal love. It is as difficult to imagine a mother without maternal love as light without warmth. Isn't it then perfectly right to attribute all the actions and words of a mother, concerning her child, to maternal love? But listen, however, to this little story, and how I was singularly mystified by the most natural of illusions.

My profession as a painter obliges me to look at faces attentively, at features which happen to cross my path, and you know what pleasure we draw from this faculty which makes life in our eyes more exciting and significant than for other men. In the backwater in which I live, where vast areas of grass still separate the buildings, I often used to see a child, whose keen roguish expression beguiled me more than any other. He posed more than once for me. Sometimes I turned him into a little

Part of the large collection of Spanish paintings belonging to Louis-Philippe, Duc d'Orléans (1773–1850), on exhibit in the Louvre until 1848. The collection was auctioned off by Christie's in 1853 and dispersed.

Edgar Allan Poe (1809–49) (see pp. 162–3).

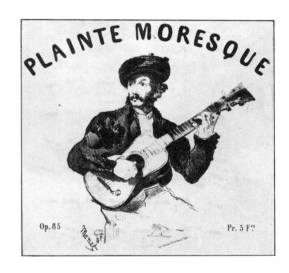

Moorish Lament. 1862. Cover or title-page for sheet music. Lithograph, 7¾ × 7″ (19.7 × 17.8 cm).

Baudelaire's prose poem, which he dedicated to Manet, was based on the tragic story of Manet's fifteen-year-old model, Alexandre, who had hanged himself in Manet's rue Lavoisier studio. (See Colourplate 1.)

vagabond, sometimes an angel, sometimes a mythological *amorino*. I made him carry the vagabond's violin, the crown of thorns and the nails of the Passion, and the torch of Eros. In the end, I got such a lively pleasure out of this urchin's amusing ways, that one day I begged his parents, who were poor people, to be good enough to hand him over to me, promising to clothe him well, to give him some money and not to give him any other job than to wash my brushes and run errands for me.

This child, when cleaned up, looked charming, and the life he led with me seemed to him heaven in comparison with what he would have had in his parents' slum dwelling. Only, I must say, that this little chap astonished me sometimes by his very unusual fits of extraordinary melancholy, and also that he soon began to show an immoderate liking for sugar and liqueurs, so much so that one day when I was aware that, in spite of all my numerous warnings, he had once again committed a petty theft of this sort, I threatened to send him back to his parents. Then I went out and my business kept me quite a long while from home.

Imagine my horror and astonishment when, on coming home, the first thing that caught my eyes was the little lad, the roguish companion of my life hanging from the panel of this cupboard! His feet were nearly touching the floor; a chair, which no doubt he had pushed away with his foot, lay overturned beside him; his head was convulsively twisted on his shoulder; his flushed face and his eyes which were wide open and fixed in a terrifying stare, gave me, to begin with, an illusion of life. To unhook him was not such an easy job as you might imagine. He was already very stiff, and I had an inexplicable repugnance in letting him fall suddenly to the floor. I had to hold him up with one arm and, with the other, cut the rope. But this done, all was not over. The little devil had used a very thin cord, which had cut so deeply into his flesh and had formed such agonizing swellings, that it was difficult to extricate it from his neck.

I have omitted to tell you that I had called loudly for help, but all my neighbours refused to come to my aid, faithful in this respect to the ways of civilized man, who, I don't know why, never wants to get mixed up in a hanging! At last a doctor came who said the child had been dead for several hours. When later we undressed him to prepare him for the burial, the corpse was so stiff that we despaired of flexing his limbs and were obliged to hack and cut away his clothes to take them off. The police inspector, to whom naturally I was obliged to report the accident, looked at me sideways and said, "That's a bit fishy," moved probably by an inveterate wish and force of habit to frighten people at all costs, regardless of whether they are innocent or guilty.

One supreme task remained to be accomplished – even to think of it caused me the most terrible mental agony. It was necessary to warn the parents. My feet refused to take me there, but at last I plucked up courage. However, to my great astonishment, the mother remained quite unmoved, not a tear gleamed in the corner of her eye. I put down this unnatural behaviour to the horror she must be feeling, and I remembered the old saying: "The worst sufferings are silent sufferings." As for the father, he contented himself by saying in a half-stupid, half-pensive way: "After all, perhaps it's for the best. He'd 'ave been sure to come to a bad end!"

In the meantime the body was laid out on my divan and, helped by my servant, I was busy with the final preparations, when the mother came into my studio. She wanted, she said, to see the dead body of her child. In all conscience, I could not stop her indulging her sorrow and refuse her this supreme and sombre consolation. Then she asked me to point out the place where her little boy had hanged himself. "Oh, no, Madam," I answered her, "that would upset you too much!" And as I involuntarily turned my eyes towards the melancholy cupboard, I noticed with a feeling of disgust, mixed with horror and anger, that the nail was still sticking in the inner side of the panel and a long length of cord was still hanging from it. I dashed over to tear out the last traces of the tragedy and, as I was

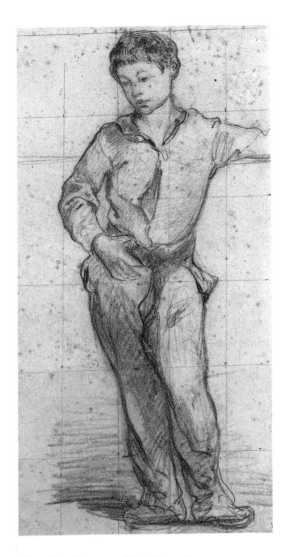

Standing Boy. c. 1865. Conté crayon on buff wove paper, 16 × 8″ (40.7 × 20.6 cm). Courtesy, The Art Institute of Chicago (Helen Regenstein Collection).

Profile Portrait of Charles Baudelaire. 1862. Etching, 5 × 3″ (13 × 7.4 cm).

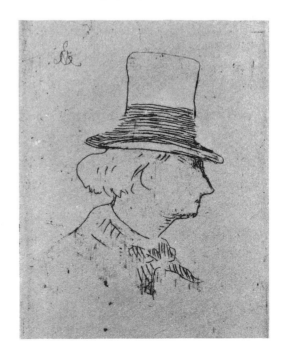

about to throw them out of the window, the poor woman seized my arm and said in a voice which there was no resisting: "Oh, Sir, please leave me that! Please, please!" I imagined her despair must have driven her crazy for her to feel at this moment an affection for the very thing that had served as her son's instrument of death and to want to keep it as a horrible cherished relic.

She went off with nail and cord.

Well, well, all was over. There was nothing left for me but to get down to work again, a little harder than usual, so as to banish the memory of the little corpse which was haunting a corner of my brain, and whose ghost worried me with its big staring eyes.

But on the following day, I received a bundle of letters. Some were from tenants in my house, others from neighbouring houses – one from the first floor, another from the second, another from the third and so on. Some were written in a semi-jocular way, as though the writers were trying to disguise, under an apparent badinage, the sincerity of their request. Others were ill-spelt and completely shameless, but all of them were leading up to the same thing, that is to say, to get hold of a piece of that melancholy and blessed cord. I must say that there were more women among the signatories than men, but not all of them, I assure you, belonged to the lowest common classes. I have kept those letters.

And then, suddenly, I saw the light! I understood now why the mother was so anxious to snatch the cord from me and by what trafficking she intended to console herself.

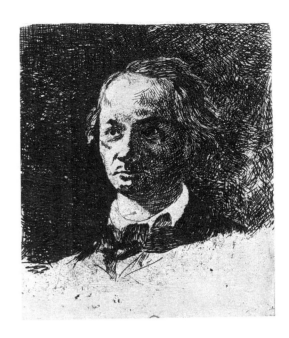

Portrait of Baudelaire, Full Face. 1865/9. Etching. 4 × 3″ (10 × 8 cm).

CHARLES BAUDELAIRE

Letter to Manet

May 11, 1865

I thank you for the good letter which Chorner brought me this morning, as well as for the piece of music . . . . If you see Rops, don't attach too much importance to certain violently provincial mannerisms. Rops likes you, Rops has understood the value of your intelligence, and has confided to me certain observations which he made about the people who hate you (because it seems that you have the honour of inspiring hatred). Rops is *the only real artist* (in the sense in which I, and perhaps I only, understand the word *artist*) that I have found in Belgium.

So I must speak to you of yourself. I must try to show you what you are worth. What you demand is really stupid. *They make fun of you; the jokes aggravate you; no one knows how to do you justice, etc., etc.* . . . . Do you think you are the first man put in this predicament? Are you a greater genius than Chateaubriand or Wagner? Yet they certainly were made fun of. They didn't die of it. And not to give you too much cause for pride, I will tell you that these men are examples, each in his own field and in a very rich world; and that you, *you are only the first in the decrepitude of your art.* I hope you won't be angry with me for treating you so unceremoniously. You are aware of my friendship for you.

I wanted to get a *personal* impression from this Chorner, at least in so far as a Belgian can be considered an *individual*. I must say that he was kind, and what he told me fits in with what I know of you, and with what some imaginative people say of you: *There are some faults, some failings, a lack of balance, but there is an irresistible charm.* I know all that, I was one of the first to understand it. He added that the painting of the nude woman, with the negress and the cat (is it really a cat?), was far superior to the religious painting.

Baudelaire had moved to Brussels in 1864, hoping to earn money by giving lectures. He lived there in financially straitened circumstances for two years.

Félicien Rops (1833–98), Belgian painter and printmaker.

François-Auguste-René, Vicomte de Chateaubriand (1768–1848).

The religious painting was Jesus mocked by the Soldiers *(Rouart/Wildenstein I, 102), painted 1864–5, now in the Art Institute of Chicago.*

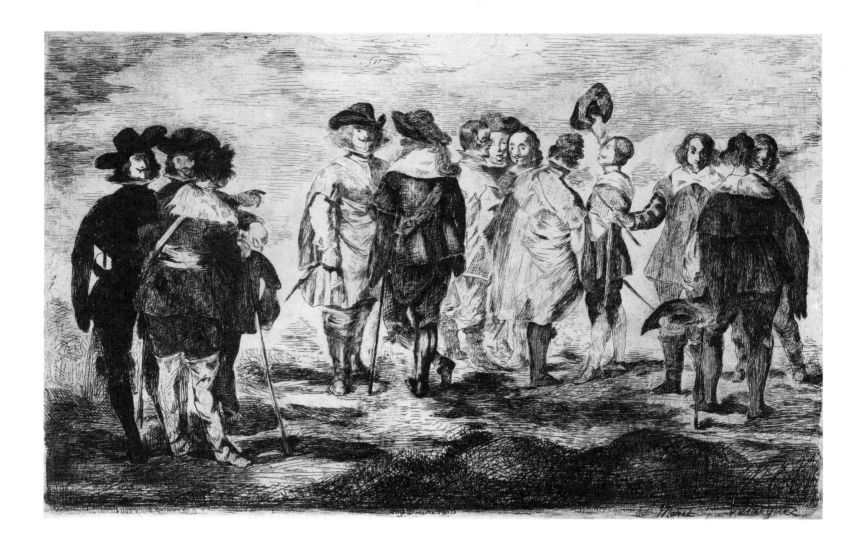

ÉDOUARD MANET

Letter to Fantin-Latour

Madrid, August 1865

Oh, what a pity you are not here; what a pleasure it would have given you to see Velazquez, who alone is worth the whole journey. The painters of every school who surround him in the Madrid Museum, and who are very well represented, all seem second-rate in comparison with him. He is the painter to beat all painters. He didn't astonish me, he enchanted me. The full-length portrait in the Louvre is not by him; only the authenticity of the Infanta can't be doubted. There is an enormous picture here, filled with small figures like those in *The Cavaliers*, in the Louvre, but the figures of the women and men in this one are perhaps better, and all of them are perfectly free from retouching. The background – the landscape – is by a pupil of Velazquez.

The most astonishing work in this splendid collection, and perhaps the most astonishing piece of painting that has ever been done, is the one entitled in the catalogue, *Portrait of a Celebrated Actor in the Time of Philip IV*. The background fades into nothing; the old boy, all in black, so alive, seems to be surrounded by air. And, ah, *The Spinners*; and the beautiful portrait of Alonzo Cano; and *Las Meninas* – another extraordinary picture! The philosophers – what astonishing works! And all the dwarfs too! – one in particular, seated full face with his hands on his hips: a painting for the real connoisseur. And his magnificent portraits! – one would have to include the lot; they are all masterpieces. The well-known portrait of

The Little Cavaliers. 1860. Etching.
$9\frac{1}{2} \times 15\frac{1}{4}$" (24.5 × 38.7 cm).

Henri Fantin-Latour (1836–1904), painter and lithographer. Fantin-Latour had met Manet in the Louvre in 1857. He appears in Manet's Music in the Tuileries Gardens, *Colourplate 11. (See also pages 48, 64 and 106.)*

In Manet's time, The Cavaliers *was thought to be by Velázquez; the painting is now attributed to Mazo. Manet executed a watercolour and an oil copy (c. 1859), as well as an etching (1860), based on this work.*

Charles-Quint by Titian, which certainly deserves to be appreciated and which anywhere else would undoubtedly have seemed to me good, here, in comparison, looks wooden.

And Goya! surely the most curious painter since the Master (whom he imitated too much and in the most servile way). But in spite of this he has great verve. There are two equestrian portraits by him in the museum, painted in the manner of Velazquez; but all the same, they are much inferior in quality. What I have seen of him up to now does not please me enormously. One of these days I must visit a magnificent collection belonging to the Duke de Osuna.

I feel very put out; the weather is very bad this morning and I'm afraid that the bull-fight due to take place this evening, to which I was looking forward to going, will be put off. Until when? Tomorrow I go to Toledo, where I will see El Greco and Goya who, so I'm told, are very well represented there.

Madrid is a pleasant town full of distractions. The Prado, a charming walk, is filled with pretty women, all with mantillas, which makes a very unusual picture. In the streets there are still a lot of costumes to be seen; the toreros have a town costume which is peculiar to themselves.

ANTONIN PROUST

ÉDOUARD MANET: SOUVENIRS

Manet's Impressions of Spanish Artists

1913

I have just spoken of Manet's travels. He went to see the Rubens' in Antwerp, the Rembrandts in Amsterdam, the primitives in Brussels, the Hals' in Harlem, the Albrecht Dürers in Dresden and the Holbeins in Basle. In Italy he was very taken with the Titians and Tintorettos, little attracted by Raphael and Michelangelo. But his obsession was to go to Spain. *The Bullfight* by Alfred Dehodencq, exhibited at the 1851 Salon and

Charles V, *painted between 1532 and 1533, was Titian's second portrait of the Emperor.*

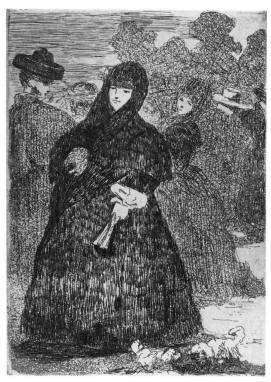

ABOVE *At the Prado.* 1865/8. Etching and aquatint, 8¾ × 6″ (22.1 × 15.5 cm). New York Public Library (Astor, Lenox and Tilden Foundations).

BELOW *Bullfight.* 1864–5. Frick Collection, New York. In 1864 Manet exhibited *Episode from a Bullfight* at the Salon. He subsequently cut up the painting and reworked two fragments, *Dead Toreador* (Colourplate 20) and this one.

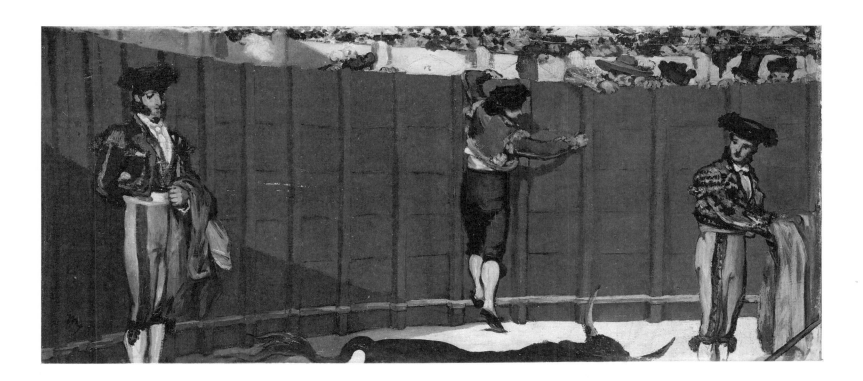

hung in the Luxembourg, filled him with enthusiasm. So he went to Spain. It was then that he made the acquaintance of Théodore Duret in a hotel in the Puerta del Sol, where Manet, who was finicky about food, found everything detestable and where he accosted Duret, who was tucking into the *puchero* like a starving man.

"Ah!" he exclaimed one day, "what good fellows they were, Velazquez, El Greco, Valdès Leal, Herrero el Viejo. I'm not talking about Murillo, I don't much like him, except for certain studies of urchins. Nor the Zurbaráns. But Ribeira and Goya, Goya of whom Reynolds said: 'He's a Spanish painter, but of the school of Gibraltar.' And there are plenty more painters of this calibre! And what streets, what people. Dehodencq took note, and what note. Before going to Spain he was blind. There are people who don't believe in miracles. Well, since Dehodencq, I do."

Alfred Dehodencq (1822–82), painter.

Théodore Duret entered the circle of Manet's friends, in the front rank of whom was Paul Roudier who went everywhere with him, to his father's and mother's Thursday evenings and to the Fridays at the café Guerbois, situated at the entrance to the avenue de Clichy, a stone's throw from Père Lathuille's. In both places the talk was only of art. Oddly enough, Manet's father, who had been the first to berate his son when he complained of his master Couture, now gave himself over to the bitterest sallies against the painters of the *Romans of the Decadence*. The more violent his father became, the calmer Manet seemed.

On Fridays at the café Guerbois there were men of letters and artists. Discussion was lively. Duranty, a novelist and critic, would get carried away, treating Couture as the last of the "image-makers." In the midst of this hubbub, Manet maintained the calm of Olympian Jove.

Louis-Émile-Édmond Duranty (1833–80), novelist and critic, editor of the short-lived review of Le Réalisme *(1856–7). He is best known for his essay written in 1876 in defence of the Impressionists on the occasion of their second group exhibition:* The New Painting: Concerning the Group of Artists exhibiting at the Durand-Ruel Galleries.

THÉODORE DURET

MANET AND THE FRENCH IMPRESSIONISTS

The Meeting of Duret and Manet in Spain

1910

The protests which were called forth by the *Olympia* and the *Jesus Mocked by the Soldiers*, joined to the uproar already provoked by the *Luncheon on the Grass*, gave Manet a greater notoriety than any painter had possessed before. Owing to the persistent preoccupation of caricature in all its forms, and of papers of every shade of opinion, with him and his work, his fame rapidly spread everywhere. It was no exaggeration when Degas said that he was as well known as Garibaldi. When he went out into the street, people turned round to look at him. When he went into any public place a general murmur went round, and he was pointed out as though he had been some curious beast. It might at first have been gratifying to a new painter to find himself the object of general remark, but the marked form which the attention of the public had taken soon destroyed any possible satisfaction which might otherwise have been derived from it. The distinction of being so prominently in the public gaze was due simply to the fact that he was regarded as a madman, a barbarian who committed outrages in the domain of art and trampled under foot the traditions which were the glorious heritage of the nation. Nobody condescended to examine his work with a view to discovering his intention; none of those in authority gave him any credit for his genius as an innovator. The striking reputation which he had acquired only served to brand him as a pariah.

Duret, whom Manet met in Madrid, was to remain a lifelong friend. During the siege of Paris in 1870, Manet entrusted his canvases to Duret, and it was Duret whom Manet named in his will to take charge of the posthumous sale of the artist's work. (See Colourplate 41.) Manet's trip to Spain had been planned by his friend Zacharie Astruc (Colourplate 26).

COLOURPLATE 14
COLOURPLATE 18

Edgar Degas (1834–1917), friend of Manet (see pages 310–12 and 313–15). Giuseppe Garibaldi (1807–88).

When the Salon was closed in the month of August, in order to secure a brief respite from persecution, he carried out his long matured project of a visit to Madrid. It was there that I made his acquaintance. The manner of our meeting was so remarkable and so typical of his impulsive character that I feel bound to relate the incident here.

I was returning from Portugal, through which I had travelled partly on horseback, and had arrived that very morning from Badajoz, after having been in the diligence for forty hours. A new hotel had just been opened in Madrid, in the Puerta del Sol, on the model of the large European hotels, – a thing hitherto unknown in Spain. I arrived worn out with fatigue and literally famishing of hunger. The new hotel where I had put up appeared to me a veritable palace of delight. The lunch to which I had sat down seemed like a feast of Lucullus. I ate with a sensation of luxury. The dining hall was empty except for a gentleman who was sitting some distance away at the same long table as myself. He, however, found the cuisine execrable. Every other minute he ordered some new dish, which immediately afterwards he angrily rejected as inedible. Each time that he sent the waiter away, I on the contrary called him back, and with ravenous appetite partook of all the dishes indifferently. Meanwhile I had paid no attention to my neighbour who was so difficult to please. When, however, I again asked the waiter to bring me a dish which he had refused, he suddenly got up, came near to where I was sitting and exclaimed angrily, "Now, sir, you are doing this simply to insult me, to make a fool of me, – pretending to relish this disgusting cooking and calling back the waiter every time that I send him away!" The profound astonishment that I displayed at this unexpected attack immediately convinced him that he must have made a mistake as to the motive of my behaviour, for he added in a milder tone, "You recognize me; of course, you know who I am?" Still more astonished, I replied, "I don't know who you are. How should I recognize you? I have just arrived from Portugal. I nearly perished of hunger there, and the cuisine of this hotel seems to me to be really excellent." "Ah, you have come from Portugal," he said, "well, I've just come from Paris." This at once explained our divergence of opinion as to the cooking. Realizing the humour of the situation, my friend began to laugh at his fit of anger, and then made his apologies. We drew our chairs nearer to one another and finished our lunch together.

Afterwards he told me his name. He confessed that he had supposed that I was someone who had recognized him and wished to play a vulgar joke upon him. The idea that the persecution which he thought he had escaped by leaving Paris was about to begin again in Madrid had at once exasperated him. The acquaintance thus begun rapidly kindled into intimacy. We explored Madrid together. Naturally we spent a considerable time every day before the paintings of Velazquez in the Prado. At this time Madrid preserved its old picturesque appearance. There was still a number of cafés in the old houses of the Calle di Sevilla, which formed a general rendezvous for people connected with bull-fighting, toreros, aficionados, and for dancers. Large awnings were stretched across the street from the upper storeys of the houses, giving it an agreeable shade and comparative coolness in the afternoon. The Calle di Sevilla with its picturesque life became our favourite haunt. We saw several bullfights, – Manet made sketches of them, which he used later for his paintings. We also went to Toledo to see the Cathedral and Greco's pictures.

There is no need to tell how everything that Manet saw in Spain, which had haunted his dreams for so long, fulfilled his utmost expectations. One thing, however, spoilt his pleasure, – the difficulty which he had experienced from the first, of accommodating himself to the Spanish mode of living. He could not fall in with it. He almost gave up eating. He felt an overpowering repugnance to the odour of the dishes that were set before him. He was in fact a Parisian who could find no comfort out of Paris. At the end of ten days, really starved and ill, he was obliged to return.

Exotic Flower. 1868. Etching and aquatint, 6¼ × 4¼″ (16.1 × 10.7 cm). British Museum.

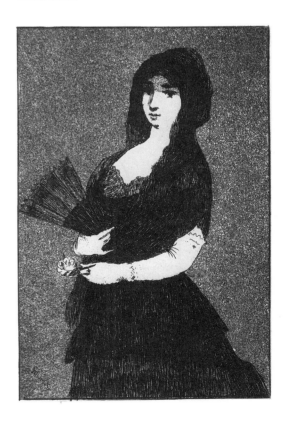

ÉMILE ZOLA

L'ARTISTE: REVUE DU XIXe SIÈCLE

"Édouard Manet"

January 1, 1867

It is a delicate task to establish bit by bit the personality of an artist. Such a labour is always difficult and it is really only possible to give a complete and truthful picture when a man's life work is already achieved – when he has already given all that is expected of his talent. In that case the whole can be analysed; every aspect of his genius can be studied, a precise and exact portrait can be drawn, without fear of losing sight of certain characteristics. In this case the critic gets the most profound pleasure in saying to himself that he can now dissect an individual; that it is a question of the anatomy of an organism; and that later he will be able to reconstruct, as in real life, a man in possession of all his limbs, all his nerves, all his heart, all his dreams and all his senses.

But on studying the painter Manet, today, I cannot taste such joys. The first outstanding works of the artist are not more than six or seven years old. I would not be able to pass a final judgement on him from the thirty or forty canvases which I have been allowed to see and appreciate. Here there is no question of arrested development; the painter has reached that restless age when his talent is developing and growing. Up to now he has no doubt developed only one side of his personality; too much lies ahead of him, too much future; he runs too many risks of all sorts for me to attempt to sum up in these pages his portrait in one definitive stroke.

I certainly would never have undertaken to trace the simple silhouette that I am now allowed to present, if I had not been moved to do so by particular and strong reasons.

Circumstances have made Édouard Manet, who is quite young, into a most unusual and instructive subject for study. The very old place which the public – and even the critics and his artist colleagues – have accorded him in contemporary art, struck me as something which should be carefully studied and explained. And here it is not only the personality of Édouard Manet that I am trying to analyse, but the whole of our artistic movement itself and contemporary opinion on aesthetics.

A curious situation has arisen, and this situation can be summed up in two words. A young painter has obeyed, in a very straightforward manner, his own personal inclinations concerning vision and understanding; he has begun to paint in a way which is contrary to the sacred rules taught in schools. Thus, he has produced original works, strong and bitter in flavour, which have offended the eyes of people accustomed to other points of view. And now you find that these same people, without trying to understand why their eyes have been offended, abuse this painter, insult his integrity and talent; and have turned him into a sort of grotesque lay-figure who sticks out his tongue to amuse fools.

Isn't such a commotion an interesting subject for study? Isn't it a reason for an inquisitive, unbiased man like myself to halt on his way in the presence of the mocking, noisy crowds which surround the young painter and pursue him with their hoots of derision?

I picture myself in the middle of a road where I meet a gang of young ruffians who are throwing brick-bats at Édouard Manet. The art critics – pardon, I mean the police – are not doing their job well. They encourage the row instead of calming it down, and even – may God forgive me! – it looks as though the policemen themselves have enormous brick-bats in their hands. Already, it seems to me, there is something decidedly

Émile Zola (1840–1902), French novelist and critic (Colourplate 40). In 1866, Zola had resigned as art critic of the weekly L'Événement, *refusing to modify his views. His biographical and critical study of Manet was first published in January 1867 in* L'Artiste: Revue du XIXe Siècle, *then again as a brochure in May to coincide with Manet's one-man exhibition at the Exposition Universelle, when it was entitled* Éd. Manet: Étude biographique et critique, accompagnée d'un portrait d'Éd. Manet par Bracquemond et d'une eau-forte d'Éd. Manet, d'après *Olympia.*

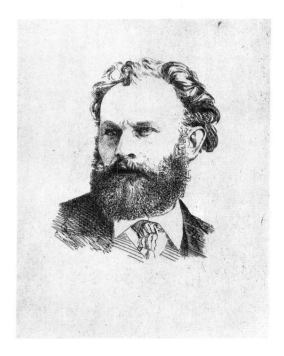

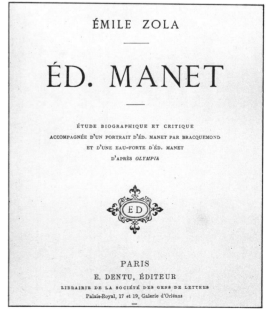

Frontispiece portrait by Félix Bracquemond and title-page to Émile Zola's brochure *Éd. Manet.* 1867. Bibliothèque Nationale, Paris.

unpleasant about this scene which saddens me – me, a disinterested passer-by, calm and unbiased.

I go up to the young ruffians and question them; I question the police, I even question Édouard Manet himself. And I become more and more convinced about something. The reason for the anger of the young ruffians and the weakness of the police is explained to me. I am given to understand what crime it is that this pariah whom they are stoning has committed. I go home and prepare, for the sake of truth, the official evidence which you are about to read.

Obviously, I have only one object in mind – to calm down the blind anger of the rowdies and to try to make them return to a more common-sense point of view, and, at all costs, to stop them making such a din in the street. I ask them not only to criticize Édouard Manet fairly but also *all* original artists who will make their appearance. I extend my plea further – my aim is not only to have one man accepted, but to have all art accepted.

Taking Édouard Manet's case as typical of the way really original personalities are received by the public, I protest against this reception, and from the individual I proceed to a question which touches all real artists.

This article, I repeat, for several reasons, will not be a definitive portrait. It is a simple summary of the existing state of affairs. It is an official account of the regrettable influence – as it seems to me – that centuries of tradition have had on the public as far as art is concerned.

THE MAN AND THE ARTIST

Édouard Manet was born in Paris in 1833. I have only a few biographical details concerning him. In this orderly police state of ours, an artist's life is the same as that of any quiet bourgeois; he paints his pictures in his studio as others sell pepper over their counters. The long-haired types of 1830, thank heavens, have completely disappeared, and our painters have become what they ought to be – people living the same life as everyone else.

Like Manet, Zola was critical of the Imperial régime of Napoleon III. (For Manet's difficulties with government censorship of the arts under Napoleon III, see pages 103–4.)

After spending some years with the Abbé Poiloup at Vaugirard, Édouard Manet finished his education at the Collège Rollin. At the age of seventeen, on leaving college, he fell in love with painting. What a terrible love that is – parents tolerate a mistress, even two; they will close their eyes if necessary to a straying heart and senses. But the Arts! Painting for them is the Scarlet Woman [*la grande impure*], the Courtesan, always hungry for flesh, who must drink the blood of their children, who clutches them, panting, to her insatiable lips. Here is Orgy unforgivable, De-bauchery – the bloody spectre which appears sometimes in the midst of families and upsets the peace of the domestic hearth.

So, of course, at the age of seventeen, Édouard Manet was embarked as a cadet on a ship bound for Rio de Janeiro. Undoubtedly, the Scarlet Woman, that Courtesan, always hungry for fresh blood, embarked with him, and surrounded by the clear, empty vastness of sky and ocean, succeeded in seducing him. She appealed to his flesh, she dangled before his eyes sparkling horizons and spoke to him of passion, in the sweet and compelling language of colour. On his return, Manet was given up entirely to Infamy.

He quit the sea and visited Italy and Holland. But he had not yet found his feet; he wandered around like a young innocent and wasted his time. As evidence of this, he entered the studio of Thomas Couture as a pupil, and stayed there for nearly six years, his hands tied by precepts and counsels, wallowing in complete mediocrity, not knowing how to find his way.

There was a particular trait in his make-up, which prevented him from accepting these first lessons, but the influence of this artistic education, which went against his natural inclination, had an effect on his work, even after he had left the master's studio. For three years, he fought in the dark, he worked without quite understanding what he was seeing, nor what he wanted to do. It was only in 1860 that he painted *The Absinthe Drinker* – a canvas in which there are still traces of the works of Thomas Couture, but which already contains a germ of the artist's own personal manner.

COLOURPLATE 2

His artistic life, after 1860, is known to the public. The strange impression made by several of his canvases in the Martinet Exhibition and in the Salon of Rejected Painters in 1863 will be remembered. It will also be recalled what a hubbub was occasioned by his painting *The Dead Christ with Angels* and *Olympia* in the Salons of 1864 and 1865. In making a study of his works, I will return to that period of his life.

COLOURPLATE 24
COLOURPLATE 14

Édouard Manet is of average height, more short than tall. His hair and beard are pale chestnut; his eyes which are narrow and deep-set are full of life and youthful fire; his mouth is characteristic, thin and mobile and slightly mocking in the corners. The whole of his good-looking, irregular and intelligent features proclaim a character, both subtle and courageous, and a disdain for stupidity and banality. And if we leave his face for his person, we find in Édouard Manet a man of extreme amiability and exquisite politeness, with a distinguished manner and a sympathetic appearance.

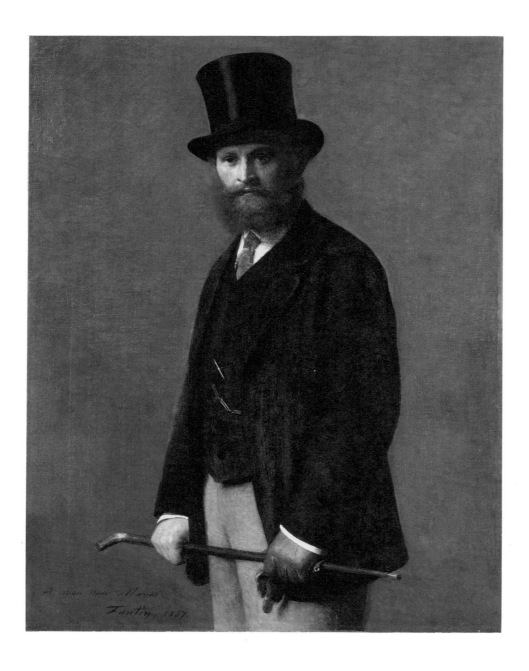

Henri Fantin-Latour, *Portrait of Manet*. 1867. 46¼ × 35½″ (117.5 × 90 cm). Courtesy, The Art Institute of Chicago (Stickney Fund).

I am absolutely obliged to insist on these utterly minor details; because contemporary fools, who earn their living by making the public laugh, have turned Manet into a sort of Bohemian character, a rogue, a ridiculous bogey, and the public has accepted the jokes and the caricatures as so much truth. The truth is far removed from these dummies, created in the imagination of penny-a-line humorists, and it is in order to present the real man that I write these lines.

The artist has confessed to me that he adores society and that he found secret pleasure in the perfumed and glittering refinement of *soirées*. He was drawn to them by his love of bold and vivid colour; but, in his heart of hearts he had an innate need for refinement and elegance which I try hard to find in his works.

Such, then, is his life. He works assiduously and the number of his canvases is already considerable. He paints without getting discouraged; without wearying; marching forward according to his own lights. Then he returns to his home and there tastes the quiet pleasures of the modern bourgeois. He goes out a great deal, following the same sort of life as most people, but perhaps with this difference, that he is more quiet and cultivated than the majority.

I really *had* to write these lines before speaking of Manet as an artist. I feel it is much easier now to tell people who are already prejudiced what I believe to be the truth. I hope that people will cease to treat this man, whose portrait I have attempted to trace in a few lines, as a slovenly dauber, and that they will pay polite attention to the unbiased opinions which I am going to give on a sincere and dedicated artist.

I am certain that the true aspect of the real Manet will surprise many people; he will be judged, henceforth, with less irreverent laughter and with more becoming attention. The question resolves itself on to this: there is no doubt that the painter paints in a completely unaffected and calculated manner, and it is only a question of knowing whether he is producing works of talent or whether he is grossly deceiving himself.

I would not like to lay down the principle, as an argument in favour of Édouard Manet, that because he wasted his time at Thomas Couture's, a student's failure to follow the teaching of his master is a mark of genius. In the career of every artist, there is necessarily a period of groping and hesitation which lasts, more or less, for a long time; it is admitted that each artist must pass through this period in the studio of a professor, and I see no harm in that. The advice received here, even though it may, to begin with, prevent the expression of original talent, does not prevent this talent from eventually manifesting itself; the studio influence will sooner or later be quite forgotten so long as the artist has individuality and perseverance.

But in the present case, it pleases me to regard Édouard Manet's long and difficult apprenticeship as a symptom of originality. It would be a long list if I was to mention here all those artists who were discouraged by their masters and who later became men of the greatest merit. "You will never succeed in doing anything," says the teacher, which no doubt means, "Without me there is no hope, and you are not me." Happy pupils who are not recognized by their masters as their children! They are a race apart, each one adds his word to the great sentence which humanity writes and which will never be complete. They are destined themselves in their own turn to be masters, egoists set in their own opinions.

Édouard Manet tried to find his own way and see for himself.

Thus it was that on leaving the lessons which were quite alien to his character, Édouard Manet tried his hand at exploring and seeing for himself. For three years, I repeat, he remained bruised by the caning he had received. He had the new answer in his mind and it was on the tip of his tongue, as they say, but he was unable to pronounce it. Then, his vision cleared; he was able to see things distinctly; he no longer had an impediment in his speech and he was able to speak.

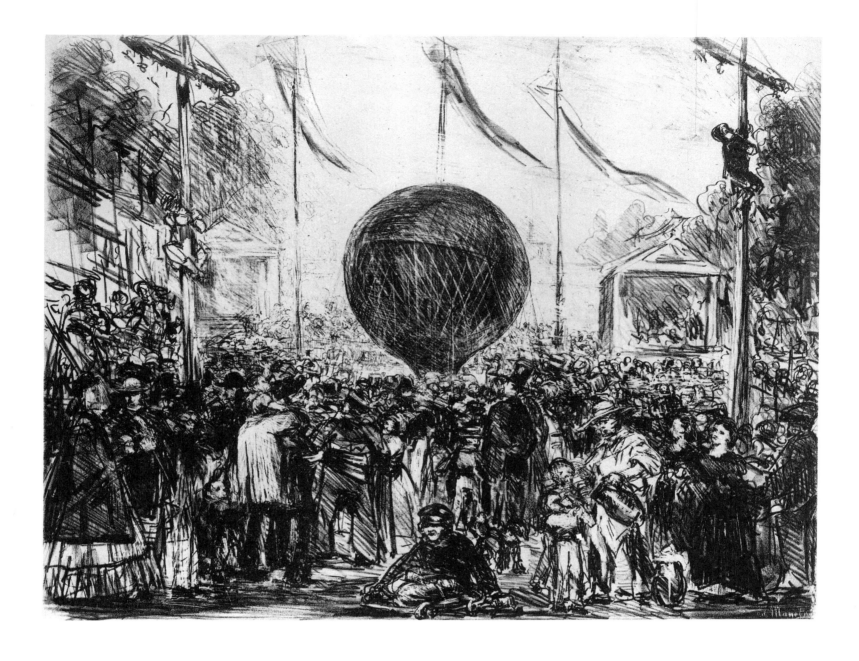

The Balloon. 1862. Lithograph,
15½ × 20" (39.5 × 51 cm). British
Museum.

He spoke in a language full of harshness and grace which thoroughly
alarmed the public. I do not claim that it was an entirely new language
and that it did not contain some Spanish turns of phrase (about which
moreover I will have to make some explanation). But judging by the
forcefulness and truth of certain pictures, it was clear that an artist had
been born to us. He spoke a language which he had made his own, and
which henceforth belonged entirely to him.

This is how I explain the birth of a true artist, Édouard Manet, for
example. Feeling that he was making no progress by copying the masters,
or by painting Nature as seen through the eyes of individuals who differed
in character from himself, he came to understand, quite naturally, one fine
day, that it only remained to him to see Nature as it really is, without
looking at the works or studying the opinions of others. From the moment
he conceived this idea, he took some object, person or thing, placed it at
the end of his studio and began to reproduce it on his canvas in accordance
with his own outlook and understanding. He made an effort to forget
everything he had learned in museums; he tried to forget all the advice
that he had been given and all the paintings that he had ever seen. All that
remained was a singular gifted intelligence in the presence of Nature,
translating it in its own manner.

Thus the artist produced an *oeuvre* which was his own flesh and blood.
Certainly, this work was linked with the great family of works already

created by mankind; it resembled, more or less, certain among them. But it had in a high degree its own beauty – I should say vitality and personal quality. The different components, taken perhaps from here and there, of which it was composed, combined to produce a completely new flavour and personal point of view; and this combination, created for the first time, was an aspect of things hitherto unknown to human genius. From then onwards Manet found his direction; or to put it better, he had found himself. He was seeing things with his own eyes, and in each of his canvases he was able to give us a translation of Nature in that original language which he had just found in himself.

And now, I beg the reader, who has been kind enough to follow me thus far and who is willing to understand me, to look at things from the only logical point of view by which a work of art can be judged properly. Without doing so, we will never understand each other. He would only stick to his prejudices, while I would propound quite different axioms, and so we would go on, becoming more and more separated from each other. On reaching the last line of this article he would regard me as a fool, and I would regard him as a man of little intelligence. We must proceed as the artist himself proceeded; we must forget the treasures of museums, and the necessity of obeying so-called laws; we must banish from our memory the accumulated pictures of dead painters. We must only see Nature face to face, Nature as it really is. We must look, in fact, for nothing more in the works of Édouard Manet than a translation of reality, peculiar to his own outlook and full of human interest.

I am forced here, to my greatest regret, to set forth some general ideas. My aesthetic, or rather the science which I will call "the modern aesthetic," differs too much from the dogma which has been taught up till now, to risk speaking without making myself perfectly clear.

Here is the popular opinion concerning art. There is an "absolute" of beauty which is regarded as something outside the artist or, to express it better, there is a perfect ideal for which every artist reaches out, and which he attains more or less successfully. From this it is assumed that there is a common denominator of beauty. This common denominator is applied to every picture produced, and according to how far the work approaches or recedes from this common denominator, the work is declared good or less good. Circumstances have elected that the Classical Greek should be regarded as the standard of beauty, so that all works of art created by mankind have ever since been judged on their greater or lesser resemblance to Greek works of art.

So here you see the whole output of human genius, which is always in a state of renascence, reduced to terms of the simple flowering of Greek genius. The artists of this country have discovered the "absolute" of beauty and thereafter all has been already said. The common denominator having been fixed, it is only a question of imitating and reproducing the original models as exactly as possible. There are some people who will insist that the artists of the Renaissance are very great because they were imitators. For 2,000 years the world has been constantly changing, civilizations have flourished and crumbled, society has advanced or languished in the midst of ever-changing customs; on the other hand, artists are born here or there, on pale, cold mornings in Holland, or in the warm, voluptuous evenings of Italy and Spain – but what of that! The "absolute" of beauty is there, unchangeable, dominating the centuries. All life, all passions, all that creative energy which has enjoyed itself and suffered for 2,000 years is miserably crushed under this idea.

Here, then, is what I believe concerning art. I embrace all humanity that has ever lived and which at all times, in all climates, under all circumstances, has felt, in the presence of Nature, an imperious need to create and reproduce objects and people by means of the arts. Thus I have a vast panorama, each part of which interests and moves me profoundly. Every great artist who comes to the fore gives us a new and personal vision of Nature. Here "reality" is the fixed element, and it is the differences in outlook of the artists which has given to works of art their individual characteristics. For me, it is the different outlooks, the constantly changing viewpoints, that give works of art their tremendous human interest. I would like all the pictures of all the painters in the world to be assembled in one vast hall where, picture by picture, we would be able to read the epic of human creation. The theme would always be this self-same "nature," this self-same "reality" and the variations on the theme would be achieved by the individual and original methods by which artists depict God's great creation. In order to pronounce fair judgement on works of art, the public should stand in the middle of the vast hall. Here beauty is no longer "absolute" – a ridiculous denominator. Beauty becomes human life itself; the human element, mixed with the fixed element of "reality" giving birth to a creation which belongs to mankind. Beauty lies within us, and not without. What is the use of philosophic abstractions! Of what use is a perfection dreamed up by a little group of men! It is humanity that interests me. What moves me, what gives me exquisite pleasure is to find in each of the creations of man an artist, a brother, who shows me with all his strength and with all his tenderness the face of Nature under a different guise.

A work of art, seen in this way, tells me the story of flesh and blood; it speaks to me of civilizations and of countries. And when in the midst of the vast hall I cast an eye over the immense collection, I see before me the same poem in a thousand different languages, and I never tire of re-reading it in each different picture, enchanted by the delivery or strength of each dialect.

I cannot give you here, in its entirety, the contents of the book which I propose to write on my artistic beliefs, and I content myself with giving only a broad outline. I overthrow no idols – I do not abjure any artist. I accept all works of art under the same title, the title of the manifestation of human genius. They all interest me almost equally; they all possess true beauty and life – life in its thousand different expressions, always changing, always new. The ridiculous common denominator does not exist any more; the critic studies a picture for what it is, and pronounces it a great work when he finds in it a vital and original interpretation of reality. He can then state that to the genesis of human creation another page has been added; that an artist has been born who has given Nature a new soul and new horizons. Our creation stretches from the past into an infinite future. Every society will produce its artists, who will bring with them their own points of view. No systems, no theories can hold back life in these unceasing productions.

Our task then, as judges of art, is limited to establishing the language and the characters; to study the languages and to say what new subtlety and energy they possess. The philosophers, if necessary, will take it on themselves to draw up formulas. I only want to analyse facts, and works of art are nothing but simple facts.

Thus I put the past on one side – I have no rules or standards – I stand in front of Édouard Manet's pictures as if I were standing in front of something quite new which I wish to explain and comment upon.

What first strikes me in these pictures, is how true is the delicate relationship of tone values. Let me explain. . . . Some fruit is placed on a table and stands out against a grey background. Between the fruit, according to whether they are nearer or further away, there are gradations of colour producing a complete scale of tints. If you start with a "note" which is lighter than the real note, you must paint the whole in a lighter key; and the contrary is true if you start with a note which is lower in tone. Here is what I believe is called "the law of values." I know of scarcely anyone of the modern school, with the exception of Corot, Courbet and Édouard Manet, who constantly obeys this law when painting people. Their works gain thereby a singular precision, great truth and an appearance of great charm.

J.-B. Camille Corot (1796–1875), Gustave Courbet (1819–77).

Manet usually paints in a higher key than is actually the case in Nature. His paintings are light in tone, luminous and pale throughout. An abundance of pure light gently illuminates his subjects. There is not the slightest forced effect here; people and landscapes are bathed in a sort of gay translucence which permeates the whole canvas.

What strikes me is due to the exact observation of the law of tone values. The artist, confronted with some subject or other, allows himself to be guided by his eyes which perceive this subject in terms of broad colours which control each other. A head posed against a wall becomes only a patch of something more, or less, grey; and the clothing, in juxtaposition to the head, becomes, for example, a patch of colour which is more, or less, white. Thus a great simplicity is achieved – hardly any details, a combination of accurate and delicate patches of colour, which, from a few paces away, give the picture an impressive sense of relief.

I stress this characteristic of Édouard Manet's works, because it is their dominating feature and makes them what they are. The whole of the artist's personality consists in the way his eye functions: he sees things in terms of light colour and masses.

What strikes me in the third place is his elegance – a little dry but charming. Let us understand each other. I am not referring to the pink and white elegance of the heads of china dolls, I am referring to a penetrating and truly human elegance. Édouard Manet is a man of the world and in his pictures there are certain exquisite lines, certain pretty and graceful *attitudes* which testify to his love for the elegance of the salons. Therein the unconscious element, the true nature of the painter is revealed. And here I take the opportunity to deny the existence of any relationship (as has been claimed) between the paintings of Édouard Manet and Charles Baudelaire. I know that a lively sympathy has brought painter and poet together, but I believe that the former has never had the stupidity, like so many others, to put "ideas" into his painting. The brief analysis of his talent which I have just made, proves with what lack of affectation he confronts Nature.

If he groups together several objects or several figures, he is only guided in his choice by a desire to obtain beautiful touches of colour and contrasts. It is ridiculous to try to turn an artist, obeying such instincts, into a mystical dreamer.

After analysis, synthesis; let us take no matter what picture by the artist, and let us not look for anything other than what is in it – some illuminated objects and living creatures. The general impression, as I have said, is of luminous clarity.

Faces in the diffused light are hewn out of simple bold patches of flesh colour; lips become simple lines; everything is simplified and stands out from the background in strong masses.

The exact interpretation of the tone values imbues the canvas with atmosphere and enhances the value of each object.

It has been said that Édouard Manet's canvases recall the "penny-plain, twopence-coloured" pictures from Épinal. There is a lot of truth in this joke which is in fact a compliment. Here and there the manner of working is the same, the colours are applied in broad patches, but with this difference, that the workmen of Épinal employ primary colours without bothering about values, while Édouard Manet uses many more colours and relates them exactly. It would be much more interesting to compare this simplified style of painting with Japanese engravings, which resemble Manet's work in their strange elegance and magnificent bold patches of colour.

One's first impression of a picture by Édouard Manet is that it is a trifle "hard." One is not accustomed to seeing reproductions of reality so simplified and so sincere. But as I have said, they possess a certain stiff but surprising elegance. To begin with one's eye only notices broad patches of colour, but soon objects become more defined and appear in their correct place.

Épinal, capital of the département *of the Vosges in north-eastern France, had been renowned for its production of cheap, coloured prints since the late eighteenth century.*

After a few moments, the whole composition is apparent as something vigorous; and one experiences a real delight in studying this clear and serious painting which, if I may put it this way, renders Nature in a manner both gentle *and* harsh.

On coming close to the picture, one notices that the technique is more delicate than bold; the artist uses only a brush and that with great caution; there is no heavy impasto, only an even coat of paint. This bold painter, who has been so hounded, works in a very calculated manner, and if his works are in any way odd, this is only due to the very personal way in which he sees and translates objects on to canvas.

In a word, if I were interrogated, if I were asked what new language Manet was speaking, I would answer, "He speaks in a language which is composed of simplicity and truth." The note which he strikes in his pictures is a luminous one which fills his canvas with light. The rendering which he gives us is truthful and simplified, obtained by composing his pictures in large masses.

I cannot repeat too often that, in order to understand and savour his talent, we must forget a thousand things. It is not a question, here, of seeking for an "absolute" of beauty. The artist is neither painting history nor his soul. What is termed "composition" does not exist for him, and he has not set himself the task of representing some abstract idea or some historical episode. And it is because of this that he should neither be judged as a moralist nor as a literary man. He should be judged simply as a painter. He treats figure subjects in just the same way as still-life subjects are treated in art schools; what I mean to say is that he groups figures more or less fortuitously, and after that he has no other thought than to put them down on canvas as he sees them, in strong contrast to each other. Don't expect anything of him except a truthful and literal interpretation. He neither sings nor philosophizes. He knows how to paint and that is all. He has his own personal gift, which is to appreciate the delicacy of the dominant tones and to model objects and people in simplified masses. He is a child of our age. I see him as an analyst painter. All problems have been re-examined; science requires solid foundations and this has been achieved by accurate observation of facts. This approach is not confined to the world of science. In all branches of knowledge and in all the works of mankind, man has tended to find basic and definitive principles in reality.

Compared with our historical and *genre* painters, our modern land-scape artists have achieved much more, because they have studied our countryside, content to interpret the first corner of a forest they came upon. Manet uses this same method in each of his works; while others break their heads trying to compose a new picture of *The Death of Caesar* or *Socrates Drinking Hemlock*, he quietly places some objects or poses some people in a corner of his studio and begins to paint. I repeat, he is merely an analyst. His work is much more interesting than the plagiarisms of his colleagues. Art as practised by him leads to ultimate truth. He is an interpreter of things as they are, and, for me, his works have the great merit of being accurate descriptions, rendered in an original and human language.

He has been reproached for imitating the Spanish Masters. I agree that in his first works, there is a resemblance – one must be somebody's child. But after painting his *Luncheon on the Grass*, he has, it seems to me, established definitely that personality which I have tried to explain and upon which I have briefly commented. Perhaps the truth is that the public, seeing him paint Spanish scenes and costumes, decided that he was taking his models from beyond the Pyrénées, and, this being the case, the accusation of plagiarism soon followed.

But it is as well to know that if Édouard Manet painted his *espada* and *majo*, it was because he had Spanish costumes in his studio and found their colours beautiful. It was only in 1865 that he travelled across Spain; his canvases are too individual in character for him to be taken as nothing more than an illegitimate child of Velazquez or Goya.

The Death of Caesar *was painted by Jean-Léon Gérôme.* Socrates Drinking Hemlock *was painted by Jacques-Louis David (1748–1825).*

COLOURPLATE 18

COLOURPLATES 31, 19

I will now be able, when speaking of the works of Édouard Manet, to make myself better understood. I have described in broad outline the character and talent of the artist, and each picture which I analyse will support the opinion that I have offered. His works are known and it only remains for me to explain the details which make these works what they are. In telling what I feel about each picture, I will re-establish the complete personality of the painter.

The works of Édouard Manet are already considerable. This sincere and hard-working craftsman has employed his last six years well. I would like to see something of his courage and love of work in those great scoffers who treat him as an idle rascal and leg-puller. I saw recently in his studio some thirty canvases, of which the oldest was dated 1860. He had placed them altogether to see what sort of a collection they would make at the Universal Exhibition.

I hope to see them again in the Champ-de-Mars next May, and I consider that they will establish the artist's solid reputation once and for all. It is no longer a question of two or three works, it is a question of thirty at least, and six years of work and talent. It is out of the question to deny the man who has been humiliated by public opinion, a brilliant "return match" from which he will certainly emerge victorious. The Selection Committee must understand, on this forthcoming important occasion, how stupid it would be to hide deliberately some of the most original and sincere examples of contemporary art. Rejection in this case would be veritable murder – an official assassination.

A reference to the Exposition Universelle of 1867.

And therefore I should like to be able to take the sceptics by the hand and lead them to the pictures of Édouard Manet. "Look and judge," I would say. "Behold the grotesque man, the unpopular man. He has worked for six years and here is his work. Do you still laugh at it? Do you still find it an amusing joke? You are beginning to feel, aren't you, that there is more to his talent than just black cats?

"The general effect is completely satisfying. The sincerity of his work is abundantly clear. In each canvas the artist's hand expresses the same simple and precise language. When your eye embraces all the pictures at once, you find that all these different pictures make up one whole; they represent a tremendous sum-total of analysis and vigour. Laugh once more, if you like laughing, but take care! Henceforth you will be laughing at your own blindness."

My first impression on entering Édouard Manet's studio was one of unity and power. One is aware of both harshness and delicacy as one first glances at the walls. Before one's attention is arrested by one particular picture, one's eyes wander from top to bottom, from right to left. These clear tones and graceful shapes, blending together, possess a harmony and a boldness of style which is both simple and extremely powerful.

Then slowly, one by one, I examine minutely each picture. Here in a few lines are my opinions on each. I stress the more important.

As I have said, the oldest is *The Absinthe Drinker* – an emaciated and bewildered-looking man, draped in a cloak and overwhelmed by life. But I don't find here that simplicity and precision, so powerfully and broadly executed, which the artist will practise later.

Next comes *The Spanish Singer* and *Boy with a Sword* which were used as brick-bats to smash the painter's last works. *The Spanish Singer*, a Spaniard seated on a green wooden bench, singing and plucking the strings of his instrument, has obtained an "honourable mention." *Boy with a Sword* is a little boy, standing with an air of innocence and astonishment, holding in his two hands an enormous sword attached to a baldrick. These paintings are firmly and solidly painted but are, at the same time, very delicate and are in no way offensive to the feeble viewpoint of the public. It has been said that Édouard Manet has a certain affinity with the Spanish Masters and he has never acknowledged the fact so potently as in *Boy with a Sword*.

COLOURPLATES 4, 6

The head of the little boy is a marvel of modelling and restrained strength. If the artist had always painted similar heads, he would have been the darling of the public, overwhelmed with praise and money. It is true that he would have remained merely a reflection, and we would never have known his talent for beautiful simplicity. As far as I am concerned I must admit that my sympathies lie elsewhere among the painter's works. I prefer the fresh crispness and the exact and strong masses of his *Olympia*, to the carefully studied niceties of *Boy with a Sword*. But from now onwards I am only going to speak of the pictures which seem to me to be the flesh and blood of Édouard Manet. To begin with there are the pictures of 1863 which, when exhibited at Martinet's in the Boulevard des Italiens, caused a veritable uproar. As usual, hissing and cat-calls announced the fact that a new and original artist had just revealed himself. There were fourteen pictures exhibited; we will find them again at the Universal Exhibition: *The Old Musician, Reading, The Gypsies, Boy with a Dog, Lola de Valence, The Street Singer, The Spanish Ballet* and *Music in the Tuileries Gardens*.

COLOURPLATES 9, 25, 7, 10, 13, 11.

I will content myself with discussing the first four. As far as *Lola de Valence* is concerned, she is extolled in Charles Baudelaire's quatrain which was hissed and treated in much the same way as the picture itself:

> Among so many beauties, everywhere to be seen,
> I can well understand, friends, that desire swings to and fro,
> But in Lola de Valence one sees shining
> The unexpected charm of a jewel, rose-coloured and dark.

Lola de Valence. 1862. Sheet music cover, inscribed to Fantin-Latour. 9 × 8¼″ (23 × 21 cm). Bibliothèque Nationale, Paris.

I don't pretend to defend this verse but, for me, it has the great merit of summing up in rhyme the whole of the artist's individuality. It is perfectly true that *Lola de Valence* is a *bijou rose et noir*. The painter by now is already working only in masses [*taches*] and his Spanish woman is painted largely in bold contrasts. The whole canvas is painted only in two tones.

The picture which I prefer amongst those I have just named is *The Street Singer*. A young woman, well known on the heights of the Panthéon, is making her exit from a brasserie, eating cherries which she holds in a sheet of paper. The whole work is in a soft pale grey. The subject here seems to me to have been analysed with extreme simplicity and accuracy. A work such as this has, apart from its subject, a dignity which makes it appear larger than it really is. One is aware of the search for truth and the conscientiousness of a man who, above all, is setting down honestly what he sees.

It was the two other pictures, *The Spanish Ballet* and *Music in the Tuileries Gardens* which put flame to the powder. An exasperated picture lover went so far as to threaten that if *Music in the Tuileries Gardens* was left any longer in the exhibition hall, he would resort to violence. I can understand why this amateur of the arts was angry. Imagine a crowd, maybe a hundred persons, milling around in the sunshine under the trees of the Tuileries. Each face is just a single blob of paint, barely defined, where details are reduced to lines or black points. Had I been there, I would have asked this amateur of the arts to stand at a respectable distance from the picture; he would have seen that these blobs are alive, that the crowd is talking and that this is one of the artist's characteristic canvases, one in which he has obeyed to the utmost what his eyes and temperament have dictated.

In the Salon des Refusés, in 1863, Édouard Manet exhibited three paintings. I do not know whether it was because he was a persecuted man, but, on this occasion, the artist did find some people to come to his defence and even some admirers. It must be admitted that his contribution to the exhibition was one of the most outstanding; it consisted of *Luncheon on the Grass, Portrait of a Young Man in the Costume of a Mayo*, and a *Portrait of Mademoiselle V . . . in the Costume of an Espada.*

These last two pictures were considered to be quite outrageous, but they were painted with unusual vigour and were extremely strong in tone. I consider that here the painter showed himself more of a colourist than usual. The paint is always fresh – but savagely and startlingly fresh. The separate masses are applied thickly and boldly and stand out from the background with all the vividness of Nature.

Luncheon on the Grass is Édouard Manet's largest picture, in which he has realized the dream of all painters – to pose life-size figures in a landscape. One knows how skilfully he has overcome this problem. There is some foliage, a few tree trunks, and in the background a river in which a woman in a shift is bathing. In the foreground two young men are seated facing a second woman who has just emerged from the water and who is drying her naked body in the open air. This nude woman has shocked the public which has been unable to see anything but her in the picture. Good heavens! How indecent! What! A woman without a stitch of clothing seated between two fully clad men! Such a thing has never been seen before! But this belief is a gross error; in the Musée du Louvre there are more than fifty pictures in which clothed people mix with the naked. But no one goes to the Louvre to be shocked. Besides, the public has taken good care not to judge *Luncheon on the Grass* as a true work of art. The only thing it has noticed is that some people are eating, seated on the grass after bathing. It was considered that the artist's choice of subject was obscene and showy, whereas all that the artist had sought to do was to obtain an effect of strong contrasts and bold masses. Artists, especially Manet, who is an analytical painter, do not have this preoccupation with subject matter which, more than anything else, worries the public. For example the nude woman in *Luncheon on the Grass* is undoubtedly only there to give

The reception to Manet's Déjeuner sur l'herbe *was by no means universally hostile. (See A. Krell,* Manet's "Déjeuner sur l'herbe" in the Salon des Refusés, A Re-Appraisal, Art Bulletin *LXV, June 1983, and pp. 243 ff.)*

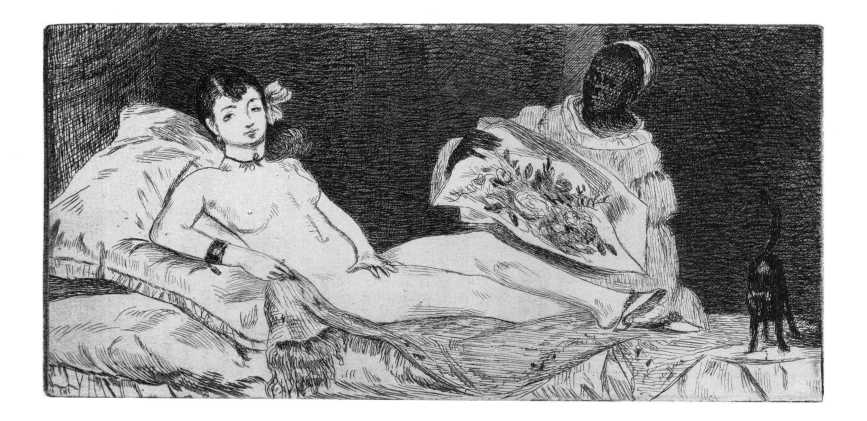

the artist an opportunity of painting flesh. What you have to look for in the picture is not just a picnic on the grass, but the whole landscape, with its bold and subtle passages, its broadly painted solid foreground, its light and delicate background and that firm flesh modelled in broad areas of light, those supple and strong materials, and, particularly that delicate splash of white among the green leaves in the background; in fact to look at the whole of this vast, airy composition, at this attention to Nature, rendered with such accurate simplicity – at the whole of this admirable work, in which the artist has concentrated his unique and rare gifts.

In 1864, Édouard Manet exhibited *The Dead Christ with Angels* and a *Bullfight*. The only portion of this last picture which he has retained is the *espada* in the foreground – *The Dead Man* – which is very akin in manner to *Boy with a Sword*. The painting is tight and detailed, very subtle and solid. I know already that this will be one of the successes of the artist's exhibition, because the public delights to look at pictures closely and does not like to be shocked by the too violent harshness of a sincere originality. For myself, I declare I much prefer *The Dead Christ with Angels*. Here I find again the complete Manet, with his own individualistic direct vision and his bold handling of paint. It has been said that this Christ is no Christ, and I admit that that may be so. For me it is a corpse painted in a full light, boldly and vigorously; and I even like the angels in the background – those children with big blue wings, are so strangely sweet and delicate.

In 1865, Manet was still admitted to the Salon where he exhibited *Jesus Mocked by the Soldiers* and his masterpiece, *Olympia*. I say "masterpiece" and I don't retract the word. I maintain that this painting is the veritable flesh and blood of the painter. It contains everything the artist has in him and nothing but the artist. It will remain as the most characteristic example of his talent, his greatest achievement. In it I decried the personality of Édouard Manet, and when I made an analysis of the artist's character, it was precisely this picture, which incorporates all his characteristics, that I had in my mind's eye. Here we have one of those "penny-plain, twopence-coloured" pictures as the professional humourists say. Olympia, lying on white linen sheets, appears as a large pale mass against a black background. In this black background is seen the head of a Negress carrying a

Olympia. 1867. Etching and aquatint, 3½ × 7″ (8.8 × 17.8 cm). Davison Art Center, Wesleyan University, Conn.

COLOURPLATE 20

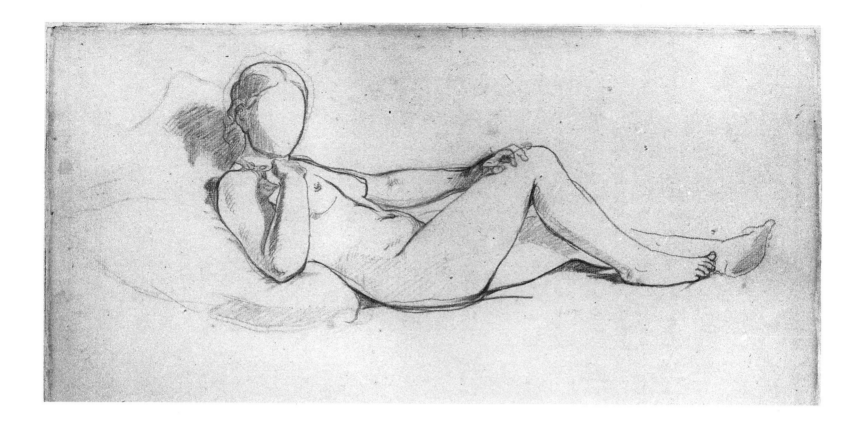

Study for *Olympia*. 1863?
Sanguine. Louvre, Paris (Cabinet
des Dessins).

bouquet of flowers, and that famous cat which so diverted the public. At first sight one is aware of only two tones in the picture – two violently contrasting tones. Moreover, all details have disappeared. Look at the head of the young girl: the lips are just two thin pink lines, the eyes are reduced to a few black strokes. Now look closely at the bouquet, I beg you. Simple masses of rose colour, blue and green. Everything is simplified, and if you want to reconstruct reality, move back a few paces. Then a strange thing happens – each object falls into correct relation, the head of Olympia stands out in astonishing relief from the background, the bouquet becomes a marvel of brilliance and freshness. Accuracy of vision and simplicity of handling has achieved this miracle. The artist has worked in the same manner as Nature, in large, lightly coloured masses, in large areas of light, and his work has the slightly crude and austere look of Nature itself. But the artist has his *partis pris*: for art can only exist by enthusiasm. These *partis pris* consist of precisely that elegant dryness and those violent contrasts which I have pointed out. Here is the personal touch, which gives his works their peculiar flavour. Nothing is more exquisitely delicate than the pale tones of the different white of the linen on which Olympia reclines: in the juxtaposition of these whites an immense difficulty has been overcome. The pale colouring of the child's body is charming. She is a young girl of sixteen, no doubt a model whom Édouard Manet calmly painted just as she was. And yet everybody cried out in protest: the nude body was found to be indecent – but naturally, because here was flesh – a naked girl whose charms are already a little faded, whom the artist had thrown on to canvas. When our artists give us Venus, they "correct" Nature, but Édouard Manet has asked himself, "Why lie, why not tell the truth?" He has made us acquainted with Olympia, a contemporary girl, the sort of girl we meet every day on the pavements, with thin shoulders wrapped in a flimsy faded woollen shawl. The public as usual has taken good care not to understand the painter's intentions. Some people tried to find a philosophic meaning in the picture, others, more light-hearted, were not displeased to attach an obscene significance to it.

Ho there! proclaim out loud to them, *cher Maître*, that you are not at all what they imagine, and a picture for you is simply an excuse for an exercise in analysis. You needed a nude woman and you chose Olympia, the first-comer. You needed some clear and luminous patches of colour, so you added a bouquet of flowers; you found it necessary to have some dark patches so you placed in the corner a Negress and a cat. What does all this amount to – you scarcely know, no more do I. But I know that you have succeeded admirably in doing a painter's job, the job of a great painter; I mean to say you have forcefully reproduced in your own particular idiom the truths of light and shade and the reality of objects and creatures.

I come now to the last works, those which the public does not know. Note the inconstancy of human beings: Édouard Manet, accepted by the Salon twice consecutively, is flatly rejected in 1866. The strangely original *Olympia* is accepted, but neither *The Fifer* nor *The Tragic Actor* is wanted, pictures which, while representing the complete personality of the artist, are not so highly expressive of his art. *The Tragic Actor* (a portrait of Rouvière in the costume of Hamlet) is wearing a black garment which is a marvel of skill. I have rarely seen such subtleties of tone and such apparent ease in the painting of juxtaposed materials of the same colour. On the other hand I prefer *The Fifer* – a fine little fellow – a boy bandsman, who is blowing down his instrument with all his might. One of our great modern landscape painters has said that this picture is a "tailor's shop-sign," and I agree with him if by that he meant that the costume of the young musician is treated with the simplicity of a poster [*image*]. The yellow of the braid, the blue-black of the tunic, the red of the trousers, are here again no more than flat patches of colour. This simplification, produced by the acute and perceptive eye of the artist, has resulted in a picture full of light and *naïveté*, charming to the point of delicacy, yet realistic to the point of ruggedness.

COLOURPLATES 32, 30

Philibert Rouvière (1809–65), painter and actor. Rouvière died before Manet's painting was completed and the hands and arms were posed for by Paul Roudier and Antonin Proust.

Finally there are four canvases, scarcely dry: *Man Smoking a Pipe, Woman Playing the Guitar, Portrait of Madame M . . .* and *Young Lady in 1866.* The *Portrait of Madame M . . .* is one of the best of the artist's productions. I must repeat what I have already said: simplicity and extreme accuracy, clear and delicate observation.

COLOURPLATES 35, 38

In conclusion: that natural elegance which Édouard Manet, the man of the world, has deep within him, is very clearly expressed in his *Young Lady in 1866.* A young woman in a long, pink peignoir is standing with her head graciously inclined, smelling a bouquet of violets which she holds in the right hand. On her left a parrot bends over on its perch. The peignoir is exquisite, pleasing to the eye, very full and rich. The pose of the model has an indefinable charm. This picture could be altogether too pretty, if the composition had not been stamped with the artist's characteristic austerity.

COLOURPLATE 33

I was nearly forgetting four [*sic*] very remarkable marine subjects: *The Steam-Boat, The Battle of the Kearsage and the Alabama, Seaview, Calm Weather, Fishing Boat,* in which the magnificent waves bear witness to the fact that the artist has sailed and loved the ocean. Also seven still-life groups and flower pieces which fortunately are now beginning to be regarded as masterpieces by everybody. The most avowed enemies of Édouard Manet's talent admit that he paints inanimate objects well. That, at least, is a step in the right direction. Amongst the still-life groups, I admired above all a splendid bunch of peonies – *A Vase of Flowers* – and a picture entitled *Luncheon on the Grass* which will always remain in my memory together with *Olympia.*

COLOURPLATE 21

COLOURPLATE 23

But after all, the painter is *obliged* to represent inanimate objects with the greatest cogency, because of the mechanism of his talent, the workings of which I have tried to describe.

Such is the work of Édouard Manet, such is the *ensemble* which, I hope, the public will be invited to see in the galleries of the Universal Exhibition. I cannot believe that the public will remain blind and mocking when they see this harmonious and perfect collection which I have just briefly discussed. There will be such a manifestation of originality and humanity, that truth must be finally victorious. And it is most important that the public should bear in mind that these pictures represent only six years' effort and that the artist is hardly thirty-three years of age. The future lies before him – personally, I dare not confine him to the present.

THE PUBLIC

It now remains to me to study and explain the attitude of the public towards the pictures of Édouard Manet. The man, the artist and his works are already known. There is another element – the public – which must be taken into account if we are to understand entirely the singular artistic state of things which we have seen come to pass. The drama will be complete, we will hold in our hands all the threads connecting the various actors; all the details of this strange adventure.

On the other hand, it would be a mistake to believe that the painter has never met with any sympathy. For the majority, he is a pariah, but for a group of people, which increases in number every day, he is a painter of talent. Latterly, especially, the movement in his favour has increased and become more noticeable. I would astonish the scoffers if I named some of the men who have testified their friendship and admiration for the artist. Certainly there is a tendency to accept him, and I hope that this will be an accomplished fact in the near future.

Among his painter colleagues there are still some who are blind and who thoughtlessly jeer because they see others jeering. But the genuine artists have never denied that Édouard Manet has great qualities as a painter. Obeying their own individual temperaments, they have made reservations, which is as it should be. If they are guilty of anything, it is for having tolerated that one of their colleagues, a young man of merit and sincerity, should have been made game of in the most undignified way. Because they, themselves, were able to see clearly; because they as painters, understood the intentions of this new artist, theirs was the duty, it seems to me, to silence the masses. I have always hoped that one of them would stand up and tell the truth. But in France, in this fickle and courageous country, there exists a terrible fear of ridicule. Thus at some meeting, if three persons laugh at someone, everybody begins to laugh, and if there should be present any who feel constrained to defend the victim of the scoffers, like cowards they humbly lower their eyes, blushing and ill at ease, and smile half-heartedly. I am sure that Édouard Manet must have made some curious observations on the embarrassment experienced by some of his acquaintances in his presence.

Therein lies the whole story of the unpopularity of the artist, and I take it on myself willingly to explain the mockery of some and the cowardice of others.

When the crowd laughs, it is nearly always over a trifle. Take the theatre, for example: an actor falls over and the whole auditorium is convulsed with mirth, and on the following day the spectators will laugh at the recollection of his tumble. Put ten people of average intelligence in front of a new and original picture and these people, all ten, will behave in the most childish way. They will nudge each other and comment on the picture in the drollest way imaginable. Curious idlers, in their turn, will arrive on the scene to swell the group and soon it will turn into a real hubbub – an access of mad folly. I'm not making up anything. The artistic history of our times is there to tell how such purblind fools and scoffers gathered in front of the first paintings by Decamps, Delacroix and Courbet. A writer told me some time ago how once, having had the misfortune to mention in some salon or other that he found Decamps's work not displeasing, he was incontinently shown the door. For jesting is catching, and one fine morning Paris awakes to find it has acquired a new plaything.

Gabriel-Alexandre Decamps (1803–60), French painter and printmaker.

77

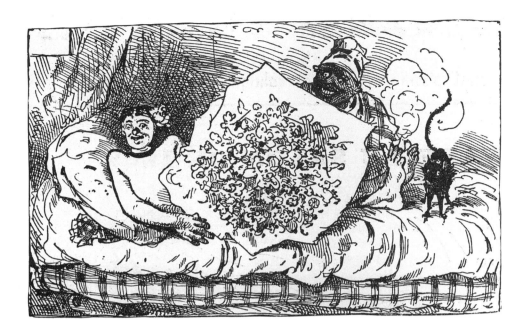

Then the situation becomes delirious. The public has a bone to pick. A whole army exists whose interest is to keep the public amused, and which succeeds very satisfactorily: caricaturists seize on to the man and his work; journalists jeer even louder than the disinterested scoffers. In the main, it is mere mockery which is nothing but hot air – there is not the least conviction, not the slightest consideration for truth. Art is something serious and profoundly boring. One has to laugh at it a bit and some picture must be found in the Salon which can be turned to ridicule, and it is always a fresh work, the ripe fruit of some new personality which is picked for the purpose.

Let us look again at this work. We will see that it is simply the more or less original appearance of the picture which has induced this idiotic mirth. The pose is excruciatingly funny! This colour makes you cry with laughter! This line has made more than a hundred people sick! All that the public has seen is a subject – a subject treated in a certain manner. They look at works of art in the same way as children look at picture books – to amuse themselves, to get some fun out of them. Ignorant people laugh with complete self-assurance; knowledgeable people – those who have studied art in moribund schools – are annoyed, on examining the new work, not to discover in it the qualities in which they believe and to which their eyes have become accustomed. No one thinks of looking at it objectively. The former understands nothing about it, the latter make comparisons. None of them can "see," and hence they are roused to mirth or anger. I repeat, it is simply the superficial way the work presents itself to the eye that is the cause of all this. The public never tries to probe further. They have stuck, as it were, on the surface. What is shocking and irritating to them is not the inner meaning of the work, but the general superficial aspect of it. If it were possible, the public would willingly accept the same subject matter, presented differently.

Originality! That's what shocks. We are all more or less, without knowing it, creatures of habit who obstinately follow the same beaten path to which we are accustomed. Every new path alarms us, we shy at unknown precipices and refuse to go forward. We always want to have the same horizon before us; we laugh at, or are irritated by the things we don't understand. That is why we are quite happy to accept originality when it is watered down but reject violently anything that upsets our preconceived ideas. As soon as someone with individuality appears on the scene, we become defiant and scared; we are like suspicious horses that rear at a

COLOURPLATE 14

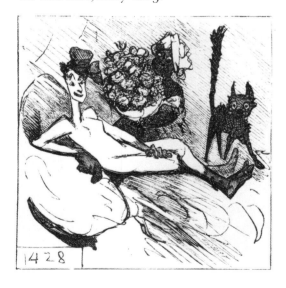

78

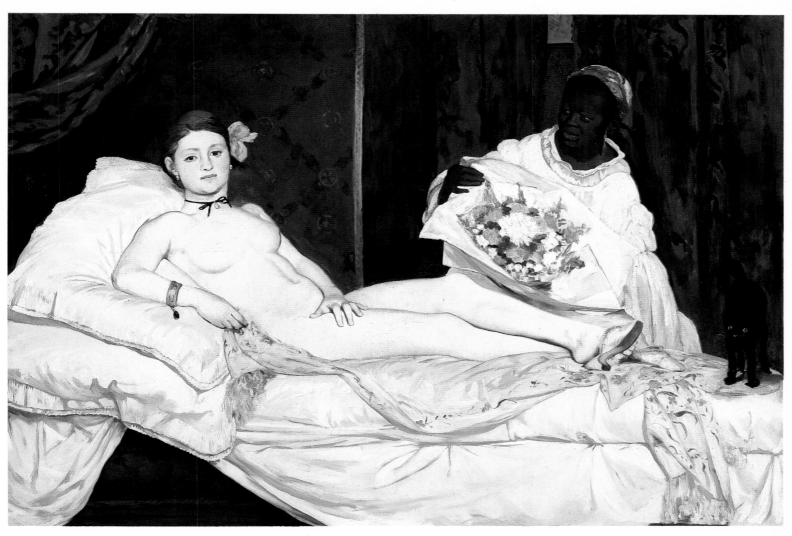

COLOURPLATE 14. *Olympia*. 1863. 51¼ × 74¾″ (130.5 × 190 cm).
Musée d'Orsay, Paris.

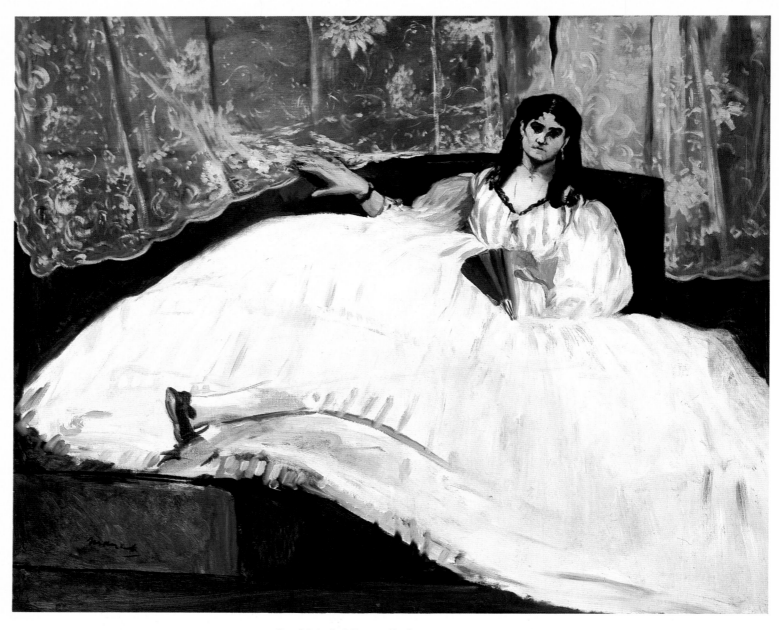

COLOURPLATE 15. *Baudelaire's Mistress Reclining*. 1862. 35 × 44½″ (90 × 113 cm).
Szepmuveszeti Muzeum, Budapest.

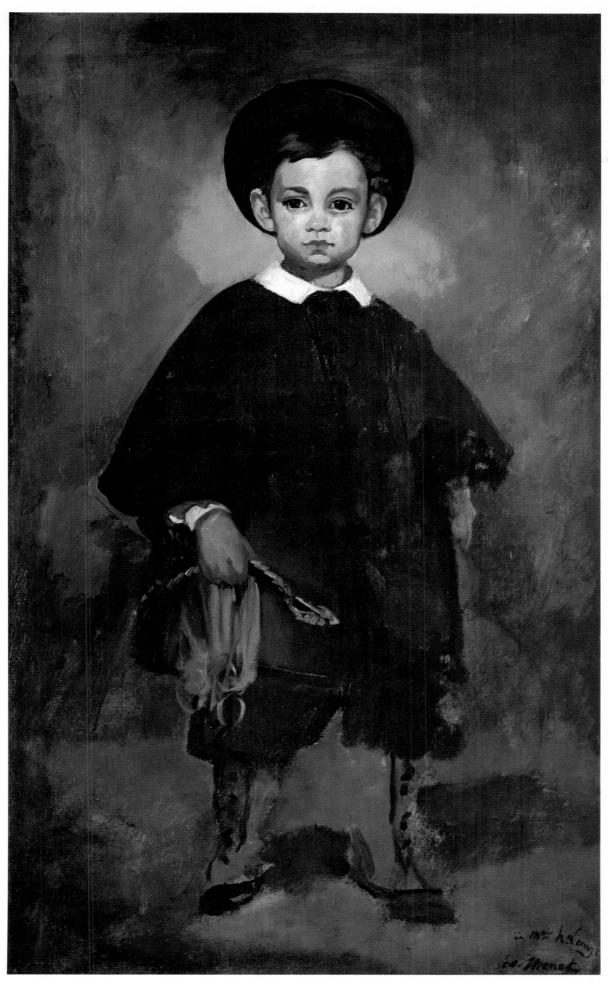

COLOURPLATE 16. *Portrait of the Infant Lange*. 1862. 46 × 28″ (117 × 71 cm).
Staatliche Kunsthalle, Karlsruhe.

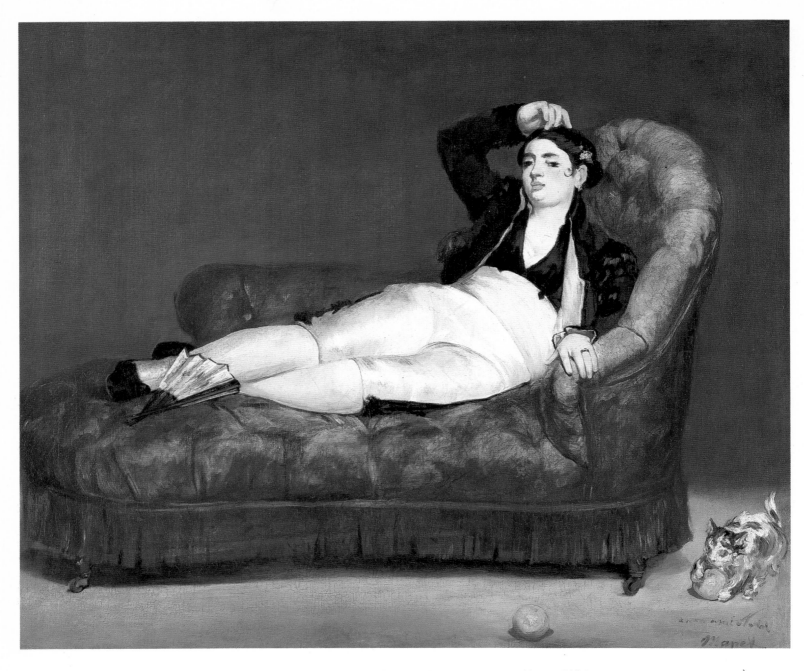

COLOURPLATE 17. *Young Woman Reclining in Spanish Costume.* 1862. 37¼ × 44¾″ (94.7 × 113.7 cm). Yale University Art Gallery, New Haven, Conn. (Bequest of Stephen C. Clark, 1903).

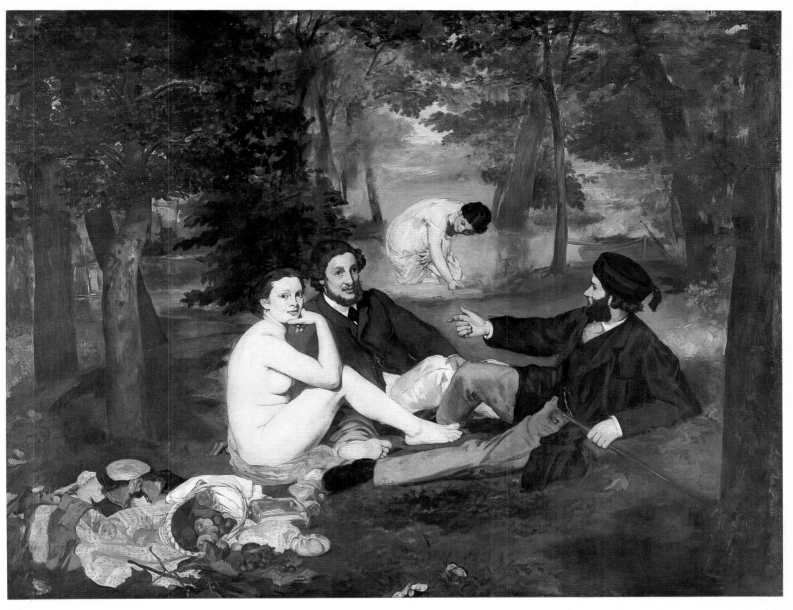

COLOURPLATE 18. *Luncheon on the Grass (Le Déjeuner sur l'herbe)*. 1863. 82 × 104" (208 × 264 cm).
Musée d'Orsay, Paris.

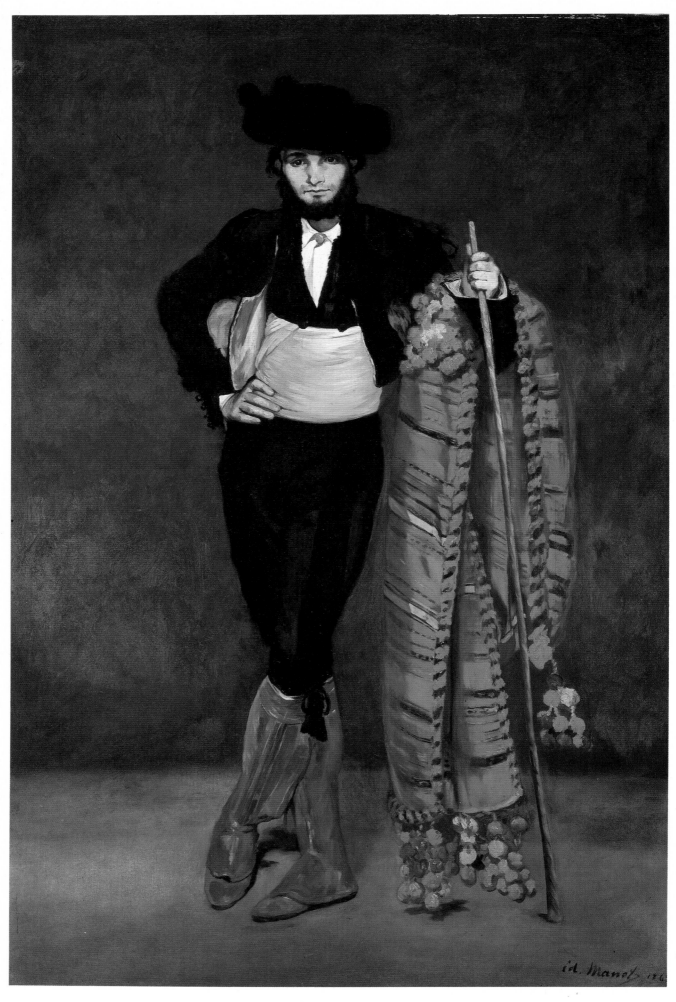

COLOURPLATE 19. *Young Man in the Costume of a Majo.* 1863. 74 × 49⅛″ (188 × 124.8 cm).
Metropolitan Museum of Art, New York (Bequest of Mrs H.O. Havemeyer, 1929. The H.O.
Havemeyer Collection).

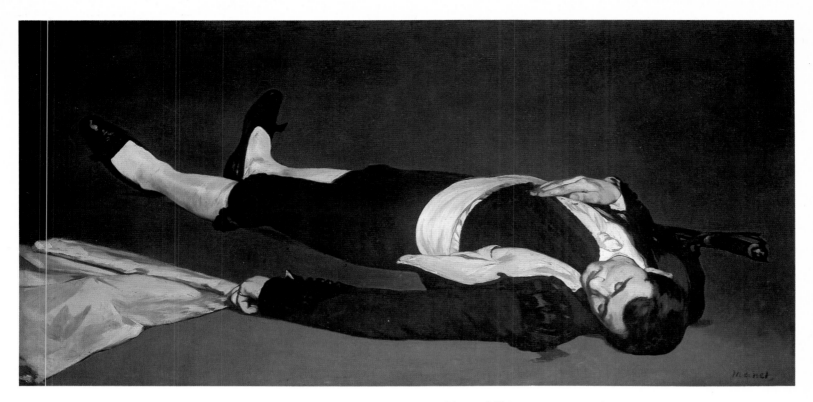

COLOURPLATE 20. *Dead Toreador*. 1863. 29⅞ × 60⅜″ (75.9 × 153.3 cm).
National Gallery of Art, Washington D.C. (Widener Collection).

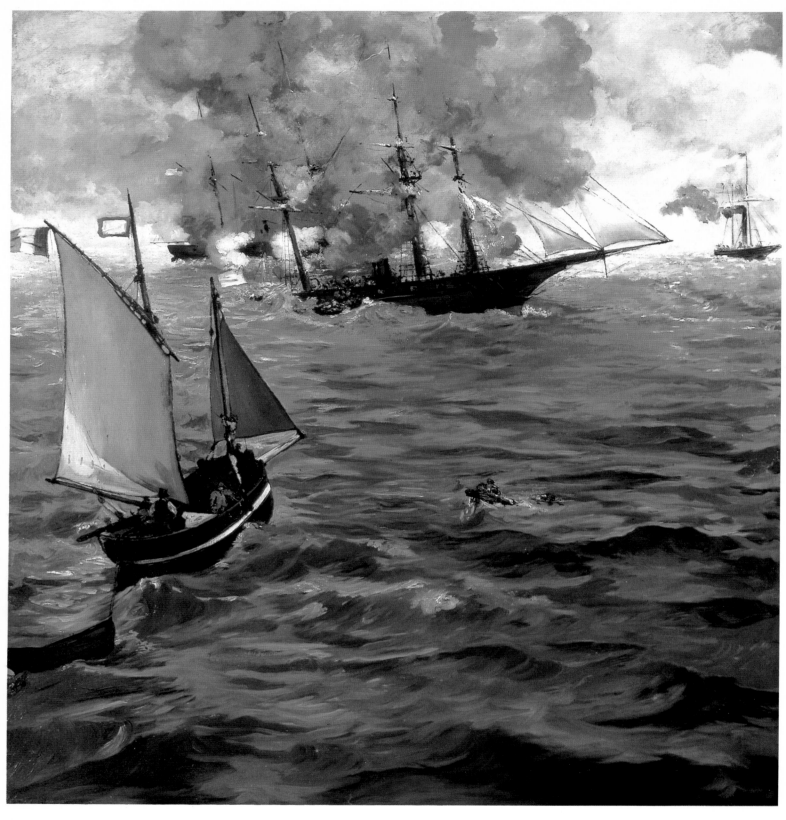

COLOURPLATE 21. *The Battle of the "Kearsage" and the "Alabama".* 1864. 54⅝ × 51⅛" (145 × 130 cm).
John G. Johnson Collection, Philadelphia.

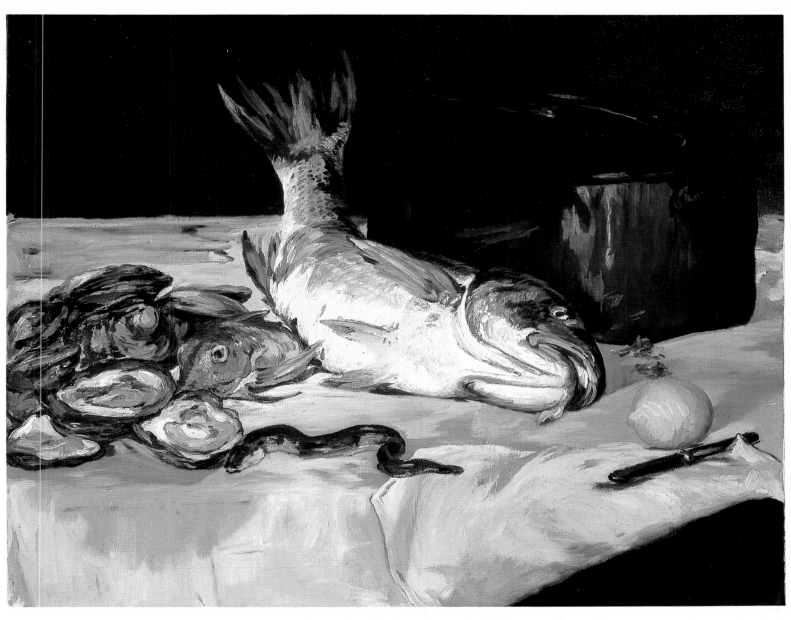

COLOURPLATE 22. *Still Life with Fish*. 1864. 29 × 36¼″ (73.4 × 92.1 cm).
© The Art Institute of Chicago (Mr and Mrs Lewis Larned Coburn Memorial Collection).

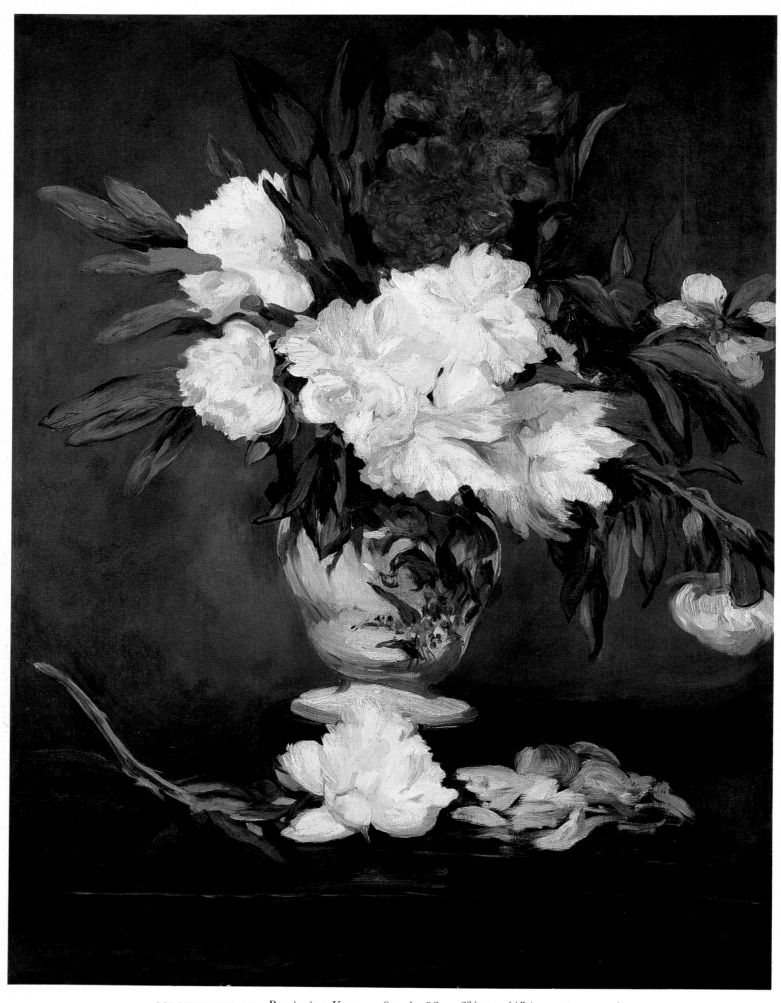

COLOURPLATE 23. *Peonies in a Vase on a Stand.* 1864. 36¾ × 27½″ (93.2 × 70.2 cm).
Musée d'Orsay, Paris.

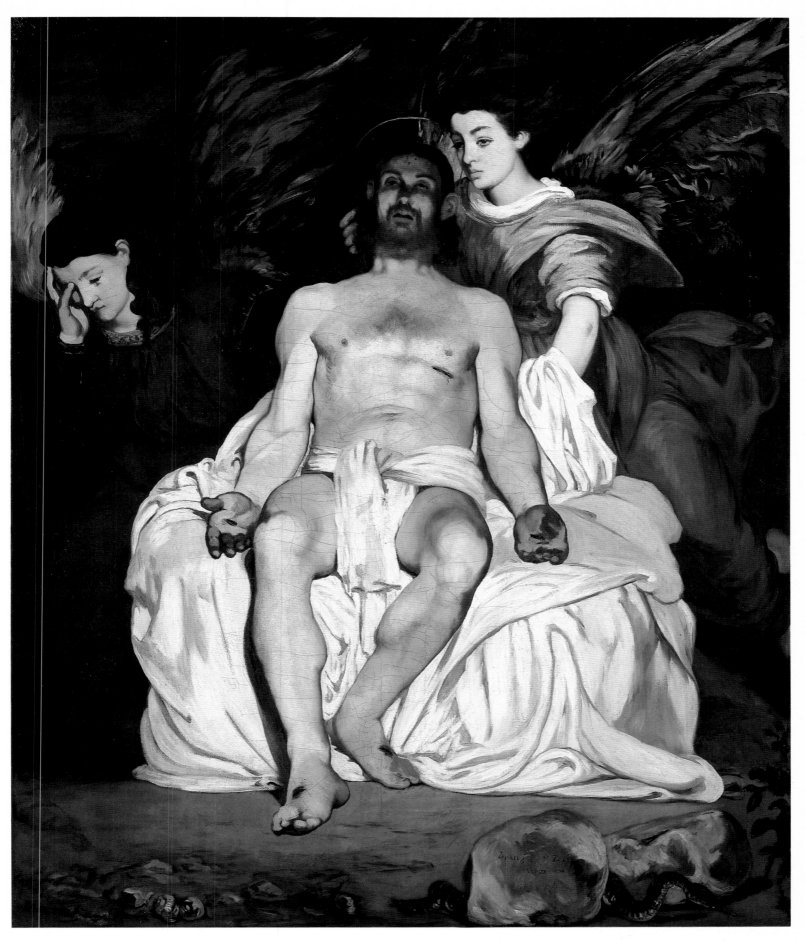

COLOURPLATE 24. *Dead Christ with Angels*. 1864. 70⅝ × 59″ (179.4 × 149.9 cm).
Metropolitan Museum of Art, New York (Bequest of Mrs H.O. Havemeyer, 1929. The H.O.
Havemeyer Collection).

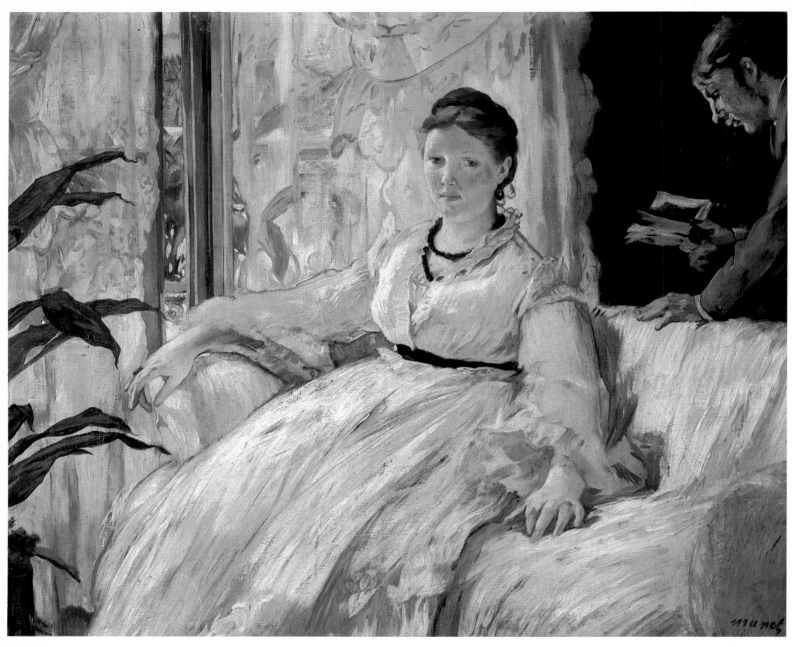

COLOURPLATE 25. *Reading*. 1865–73? (1868–9). 23¾ × 29″ (60.5 × 73.5 cm).
Musée d'Orsay, Paris.

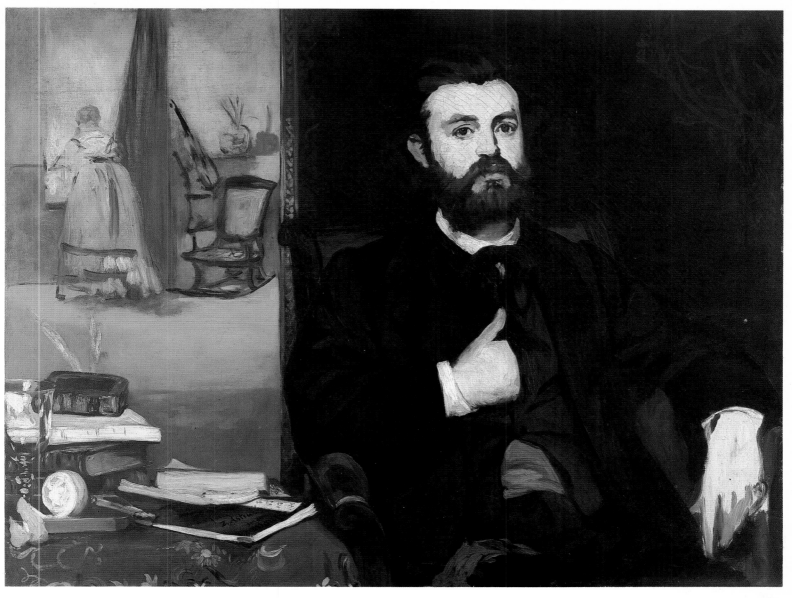

COLOURPLATE 26. *Portrait of Zacharie Astruc*. 1864 (1866). 35½ × 45½″ (90 × 116 cm).
Kunsthalle, Bremen.

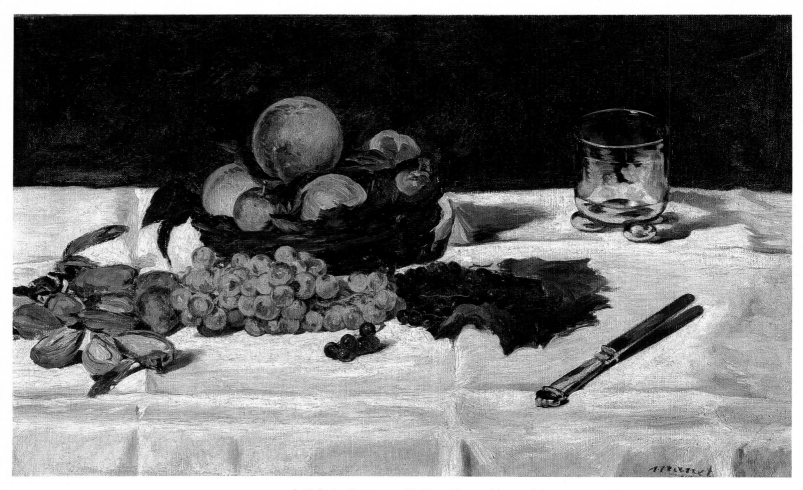

COLOURPLATE 27. *Still Life: Fruits on a Table*. 1864. 17¾ × 29″ (45 × 73.5 cm).
Musée d'Orsay, Paris.

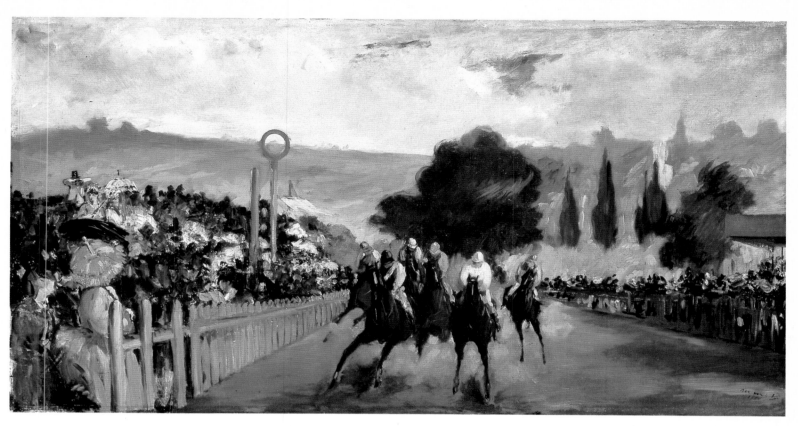

COLOURPLATE 28. *Races at Longchamp.* 1865/7? 17¼ × 33¼″ (43.9 × 84.5 cm).
© The Art Institute of Chicago (Potter Palmer Collection).

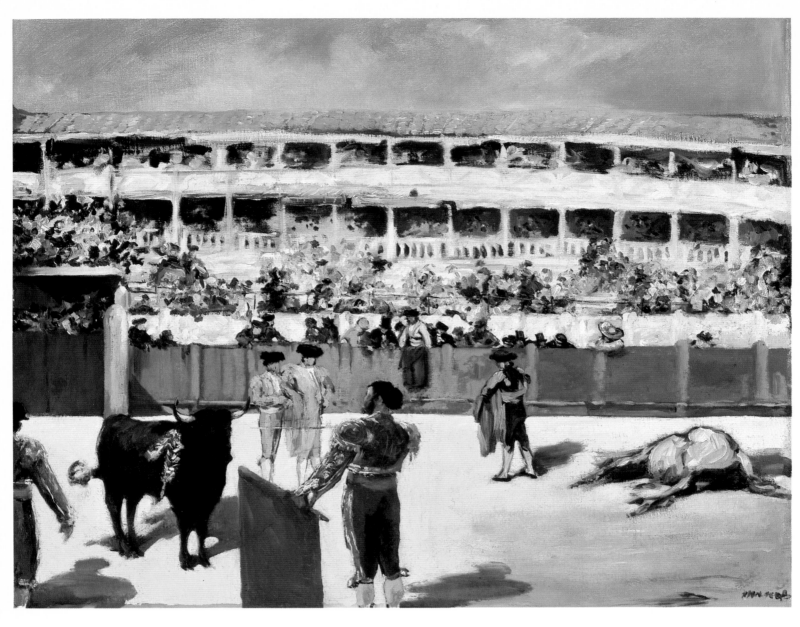

COLOURPLATE 29. *Bullfight*. 1865/6. 19 × 23¾″ (48 × 60.4 cm).
© The Art Institute of Chicago (Mr and Mrs Martin A. Ryerson Collection).

fallen tree across the road because they can't comprehend either the nature or the cause of this obstacle and don't seek any further to explain it to themselves.

It is only a question of what you are used to. By dint of seeing the obstacle, fear and mistrust are diminished. After that there is always some kind passer-by who will make us ashamed of our anger and explain to us the reason for our fear. I want to play the modest role of the passer-by for the benefit of those who, mistrusting the pictures of Édouard Manet, remain cavorting and frightened on the road.

The artist is beginning to get tired of his role of scarecrow. In spite of all his courage, he is beginning to feel that he is losing his strength in the face of the public's exasperation. It is high time that the public drew nigh and recognized the reason for their ridiculous fear.

But we have only to wait. The public, as I have said, is just a great baby without any convictions and always ends up by accepting the people who have minds of their own. The eternal story of neglected talent which is later fanatically admired, will be repeated in the case of Édouard Manet. His fate will be the same as that of Delacroix and Courbet, for example. He has reached that point where the jibes are now beginning to slacken off, where the public is beginning to feel uncomfortable and asks nothing better than to become serious again. Tomorrow, if not today, he will be understood and accepted.

If I lay stress on the public's attitude towards every original painter, it is precisely because the study of this aspect of affairs is my general theme for the next few pages.

The public will never cease to be shocked. In a week's time, Édouard Manet will most likely be forgotten by the mockers, who by then will have found another subject for their mirth. A new energetic individualist will only have to reveal himself for you to hear more cat-calls and hissing. The last-comer is always a monster, the mangy sheep of the flock. The artistic history of our latter days is there to prove the facts of the case, and simple logic is enough to show that it will inevitably be repeated so long as the masses refuse to judge a work of art sensibly.

The public will never be fair towards true artists so long as it fails to regard a work of art solely as a free and original interpretation of Nature. Is it not sad to remember, today, that Delacroix was hissed in his time and that his genius was despised and was triumphant only after his death? What do his detractors think now, and why don't they speak out and admit that they were blind and unintelligent? That should be a lesson to them. Perhaps it would teach them to understand that there is no "common denominator," nor rules, nor obligations of any sort – only living men, bringing with them a liberal expression of life, giving their flesh and blood, becoming more glorious as they become more personal and perfect. In that case one should make straight away for the pictures which are strange and bold – those would be the ones which should be attentively and seriously studied, in order to see if therein human genius is apparent. One would then disdainfully dismiss the copies and stutterings of spurious painters, and all those pictures worth twopence-ha'penny which are merely the products of a skilful hand. What one needs to look for, above all, in a work of art, is the human touch, a living corner of creation, a new manifestation of humanity in the face of the realities of Nature.

But there is nobody to guide the public, and what do you expect the public to do today in the midst of all this hubbub? Art, in a manner of speaking, is split up. The great kingdom, split into pieces, has formed itself into a host of small republics. Each artist has attracted his public, flattering it, giving it what it likes, gilded and decorated toys with rosy favours – this art, with us, has become one vast sweet-shop where there are *bonbons* for all tastes. Painters have merely become pathetic decorators who ornament our terrible modern apartments. The best of them have become antiquaries stealing a bit of this or that from the dead masters, and apart from the landscape painters, these narrow-minded and bourgeois decorators have made the deuce of a noise: each one has his own feeble theory, each tries to please and conquer. The mob, fawned upon, goes from one to the other, enjoying today the whimsies of this painter, and tomorrow the bogus strength of that. And all this disgraceful business, flattery and admiration of trumpery, is carried on in the so-called sacred name of Art. Greece and Italy are staked against chocolate soldiers, beauty is spoken of in the way one speaks of a gentleman acquaintance with whom one is on very friendly terms.

Then come the critics to cast still more trouble into this tumult. Art critics are like musicians who all play their own tunes simultaneously, hearing only their own instruments in the appalling hubbub that they are producing. One wants colour, another drawing, a third intellectual quality. I could name one who polishes his phrases and is only happy when he is able to describe a picture in the most picturesque terms possible, and another, who apropos of a woman lying supine finds occasion to write a discourse on democracy; and yet another who frames his ridiculous opinions in the form of rhyming music-hall couplets. The mob, completely at a loss, doesn't know to whom to turn. Peter says "white," Paul says "black!" If one believes the former, the landscape of this picture should be effaced, if one believes the latter, it is the figures that should be affected, so that in the end nothing remains but the frame, which would be an excellent thing. There is not the slightest analysis in this approach. Truth is not a whole; these are only digressions, more or less. Each looks at the same picture in a different frame of mind, and each one criticizes it according to circumstances or his mood.

So the mob, seeing how little in accord are those who have pretentions of guiding them, allow themselves to admire or jeer as they please. There is no common point of view. A word pleases them, or displeases them – that's all. And note, what pleases them is always the most commonplace, something they have seen every year. Our artists do not spoil them; they have so accustomed them to insipidity, to pretty lies, that they reject the real truth with all their might. It is simply a question of education. When a Delacroix appears on the scene, he is hissed. Why doesn't he look like the others! . . .

Once French wit, that wit which today I would gladly exchange for something a little more serious, becomes involved in these matters, the resulting guffaws are enough to cheer the heart of the saddest. [*L'esprit français, cet esprit que je changerais volontiers aujourd'hui pour un peu de pesanteur, l'esprit français s'en mêle, et ce sont des gorges chaudes à réjouir les plus tristes.*]

And that is how, one day, a gang of urchins met Édouard Manet in the street and started the rumpus which brought me to a halt – me, a fastidious and unbiased passer-by. I laid information against them as well as I could, asserting that the urchins were in the wrong, and sought to snatch the artist from their grasp and lead him to a safe place. There were some policemen – I beg your pardon, I mean art critics – present, who assured me that the man was being stoned because he had outrageously desecrated the Temple of Beauty. I answered them that Destiny had undoubtedly already chosen the future setting in the Louvre for *Olympia* and *Luncheon on the Grass*. No one listened, and I retired as the urchins were now beginning to cast sullen looks at me.

ÉDOUARD MANET

Reasons for Holding a Private Exhibition

1867

Manet's friends Émile Zola and Zacharie Astruc have both been suggested as possible authors or co-authors with Manet of this statement.

Monsieur Manet has been exhibiting or trying to exhibit his pictures since 1861.

This year he has decided to present to the public the whole of his work.

When he first showed in the Salon, Monsieur Manet received a good notice. But later, when he found that he was so often turned down by the jury, he realized that the first stage in an artist's career is a battle, which at least should be fought on equal terms, that is to say that the artist should be able to show the public what he has done. . . . Without this opportunity, the painter would become too easily imprisoned in a circle from which there is no escape. He would be forced to make a pile of his canvases or roll them up in an attic.

Official recognition, encouragements and rewards are in fact regarded as a hallmark of talent; the public have been informed already what to admire and what to avoid, according to whether the works are accepted or rejected. On the other hand an artist is told that it is the public's spontaneous reaction to his pictures which makes them so unwelcome to the various selection committees. In these circumstances the artist has been advised to wait; but wait for what? Until there is no selection committee? He would be much better off if he could thrash the question out directly with the public. The artist today is not saying, Come and see some perfect pictures, but, Come and see some sincere ones.

It is sincerity which gives to works of art a character which makes them appear an act of protest, when in fact the painter has only thought of rendering his own impressions.

Monsieur Manet has never wished to protest. On the contrary, the protest, entirely unexpected on his part, has been directed against himself; this is because there is a traditional way of teaching form, methods and manner of looking at a picture, and because those who have been brought up to believe in these principles will admit no others. It makes them childishly intolerant. Any works which do not conform to these formulas they regard as worthless; they not only provoke criticism, but hostility and even *active* hostility. To be able to exhibit is the vital concern, the *sine qua non* for the artist, because it happens that after looking at something for a while, one becomes familiar with what seemed before to be surprising, or if you will, shocking. Little by little it becomes understood and accepted. Time itself imperceptibly refines and softens the original hardness of a picture.

By exhibiting, an artist finds friends and allies in his struggle for recognition. Monsieur Manet has always recognized talent where he has met it; he had had no pretensions to overthrow old methods of painting or to create new ones. He had simply tried to be himself and no one else.

Further, Monsieur Manet has met with valuable encouragement and recognizes how, day by day, the opinion of men of real discernment is becoming more favourable. It only remains now for the artist to regain the goodwill of a public who have been taught to regard him as an enemy.

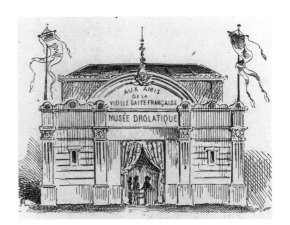

ABOVE *The Temple of Good Taste.* Caricature in *Le Journal Amusant,* 9 June 1867. "Tired of seeing . . . his works rejected by the official exhibition, M. Manet has decided to appeal to the public for adjudication; whatever their decisions, he wants judges, he'll find them."

BELOW Provost, *The Universal Exhibition of 1867, Paris.* The Champ de Mars and surroundings from the Trocadéro. Lithograph, 1867 (Photo Roger-Viollet). (See Colourplate 39.)

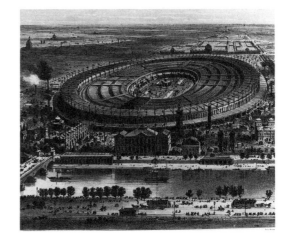

ÉMILE ZOLA

L'ÉVÉNEMENT ILLUSTRÉ

"My Portrait by Édouard Manet"

May 10, 1868

I have just read, in the last edition of *L'Artiste*, these words by Monsieur Arsène Houssaye: "Monsieur Manet could be an outstanding artist if he had 'dexterity'. . . . It is not enough to have a thoughtful brow, or an observant eye: one must have a hand that speaks!"

For me, here is an admission well worth picking on. It is with pleasure that I read this statement by this poet of dainty trifles, this novelist of fine ladies, to the effect that Édouard Manet has a thoughtful brow and an observant eye and could be an outstanding artist. I know that he qualifies his statement, but this reservation is quite understandable. Monsieur Arsène Houssaye, the gallant eighteenth-century epicure, who is misleading us today with his prose and analyses, would like to add a little powder and patches to the artist's sober and precise talent.

I will reply to the poet: "Don't insist too much that the original and very personal master of whom you speak should be more dexterous than he is. Look at those *trompe-l'oeil* pictures . . . in the Salon. Our artists are too clever by half; they play like children with puerile difficulties. If I were a great judge, I would have their wrists cut off and open their minds with pincers."

However, it is not only Monsieur Arsène Houssaye who dares admit today that there *is* talent in the work of Édouard Manet.

Last year, at the time of the artist's private exhibition, I read criticisms in several newspapers, praising a large number of his works. The inevitable reaction which I forecast in 1866 is slowly coming about. The public is becoming used to his work; the critics are calming down and have agreed to open their eyes; success is on its way.

But this year it is especially among his colleagues that Manet has met with increasing understanding. I don't think I have the right to quote here the names of the painters who have so heartily and honestly admired the portrait exhibited by the young master. But these painters are numerous and are amongst the best. As far as the public is concerned, it still does not understand, but it no longer laughs. I was amused last Sunday to study the expressions of the people who stopped to look at the pictures of Édouard Manet. Sunday is the day set aside for the real mob, the uninformed, those whose artistic taste has still to be completely developed.

I saw people arriving who had come with the resolve to be slightly amused. They remained with raised eyes, open-mouthed, completely put out, unable to raise the vestige of a smile. Unknown to them, their outlook had become acclimatized. Manet's originality, which had once seemed to them so prodigiously comic, now occasions them no more astonishment than that experienced by a child confronted by an unknown spectacle.

Others enter the gallery, glance along the walls and are attracted by the strange elegance of the artist's work. They come closer. They open the catalogue. When they see the name Manet, they try to force a laugh. But the canvases are there, clear and luminous, and seem to look down on them proudly and disdainfully. They go away, ill at ease, not knowing any more what to think; moved, in spite of themselves by the sincerity of his talent, prepared to admire it in the years to follow.

From my point of view, the success of Édouard Manet is assured. I never dared dream that it would be so rapid and deserving. It is singularly difficult to make the shrewdest people in the world admit a mistake. In

Manet's portrait of Zola is often interpreted as the artist's expression of thanks for Zola's critical support during 1866 and 1867 (see Colourplate 40).

Arsène Houssaye (1815–96), French novelist, playwright, editor and theatrical producer; editor of L'Artiste. *His* Confessions: Souvenirs d'un Demi-siècle *was published in 1885.*

Paintings whose main purpose is to convince the viewer of the material reality of the subjects represented. Such works are usually highly finished and full of detail. As in this essay by Zola, the term is often used in a derogatory sense.

On 4 and 7 May in L'Événement.

France, a man whom ignorance has made a figure of fun is often condemned to live and die a figure of fun. You will see in the minor newspapers, for a long time to come, that there will still be jokes at the expense of the painter of *Olympia*. But from now on intelligent people have been won over, and as a result the mob will follow.

The artist's two pictures are unfortunately very badly hung in corners, very high, next to the doors. In order to see and judge them satisfactorily they should have been hung "on the line," under the nose of the public which likes to look at pictures close to. I like to think that it is only because of an unfortunate chance that these remarkable pictures have been relegated where they are. However, although they are badly hung you can see them and from a distance; and placed as they are among trifles and surrounded by sentimental trash, they stand out a mile.

I will not speak of the picture entitled *A Young Lady*. It is already known to the public and was seen at the artist's private exhibition. I would only advise those clever gentlemen who dress up their dolls in dresses copied from fashion plates, to go and look at the dress which this young woman is wearing; it's true you cannot tell the grain of the material, nor count the stitches; but it hangs admirably on the living body. It is related to that supple cloth, fatly painted, which the old masters cast over the shoulders of their models. Today, artists provide for themselves at a first-rate dress-maker, like little ladies.

As for the other picture. . . .

One of my friends asked me yesterday if I would talk about this picture which is a portrait of myself. "Why not?" I answered, "I would like to have ten columns of newsprint to proclaim what I quietly thought during

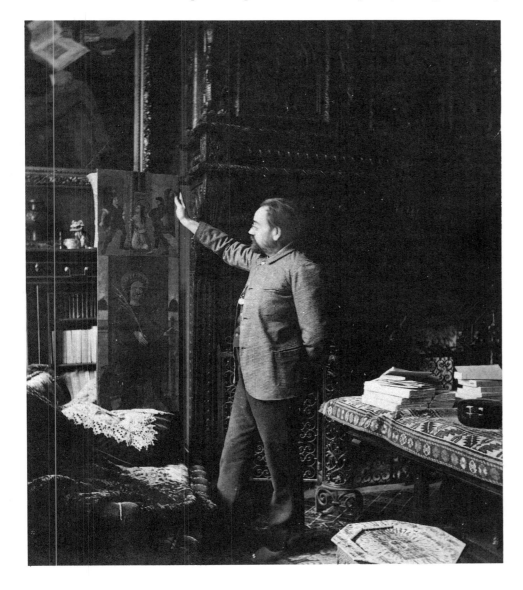

Photograph of Émile Zola at home. Part of Manet's portrait of him is visible in the background, top left.

the sittings, while I watched Édouard Manet struggle foot by foot with Nature. Do you imagine that I have so little dignity that I take pleasure in entertaining people with my own physiognomy? Naturally, I will speak of this picture, and any ill-natured people who find it a subject for witticism are merely fools."

I recall the long hours I sat to him. While my limbs became numbed from not moving, and my eyes were tired from looking straight ahead, the same deep and quiet thoughts continually passed through my mind.

The nonsense that is spread abroad, the lies and platitudes of this and that, all this human hubbub, which flows by uselessly, like so much dirty water, seemed far, far away. It seemed to me that I was outside this world, in an atmosphere of truth and justice and I was filled with a disdainful pity for the poor wretches who were floundering about below.

From time to time, as I posed, half-asleep, I looked at the artist standing at his easel, with features drawn, clear-eyed, engrossed in his work. He had forgotten me, he no longer knew I was there, he simply copied me, as if I were some human beast, with a concentration and artistic integrity that I have seen nowhere else. And then I thought of the slovenly dauber of legend, of this Manet who was a figment of the imagination of the caricaturists, who painted cats as a leg-pull. It must be admitted that wit is often incredibly stupid.

I thought for hours on end of the fate of individual artists which forces them to live apart in the loneliness of their art. Around me, forceful and characteristic canvases, which the public had chosen not to understand, hung on the walls of the studio. It is enough to be different from other people, to think one's own thoughts, to be talented, to be regarded as a monster. You are accused of ignoring your art, of laughing at common sense, simply because your eye and inclinations lead you to individual results. As soon as you no longer follow in the swim of the commonplace, fools stone you, treating you either as mad or arrogant. It was while pondering these ideas that I saw the canvas "fill up." What, personally, astonished me, was the extreme conscientiousness of the artist.

Often, when he was coping with a detail of secondary importance, I wanted to stop posing and gave him the bad advice that he should "invent."

"No," he answered me, "I can do nothing without Nature. I do not know how to invent. As much as I have wanted to paint in accordance with the lessons I have been taught, I have never produced anything worth while. If I am worth something today, it is due to exact interpretation and faithful analysis."

There lies all his talent. Before anything else, he is a naturalist. His eye sees and renders objects with elegant simplicity. I know I won't be able to make the blind like his pictures; but real artists will understand me when I speak of the slightly bitter charm of his works. The colour of it is intense and extremely harmonious. And this, mark you, is the picture by a man who is accused of being able neither to paint nor draw. I defy any other portrait painter to place a figure in an interior so powerfully, and yet avoid making the surrounding still-life objects conflict with the head.

This portrait is a combination of difficulties overcome. From the frames in the background, from the delightful Japanese screen which stands on the left, right up to the very smallest details of the figure, everything holds together in masterly, clear, striking tones, so realistic that the eye forgets the heaps of objects and sees simply one harmonious whole.

I do not speak of the still-life – the accessories and the books scattered on the table. Manet is a past-master where this is concerned. But I particularly draw your attention to the hand resting on the model's knee. It is a marvel of skill. In short, here is skin, but real skin, without ridiculous *trompe l'oeil*. If all parts of the picture had been worked on as much as the hand, the mob itself would have acclaimed it as a masterpiece.

THÉODORE DURET

MANET AND THE FRENCH IMPRESSIONISTS

Manet Paints Duret's Portrait

COLOURPLATE 41

1910

In 1868, in the studio in the rue Guyot, Manet painted my portrait. Here I had an opportunity of observing the actual working of his mind, and the processes by which he built up a picture. The portrait was of a small size and represented me standing up, with the left hand in the waistcoat pocket and the right resting on a cane. The grey frock-coat which I was wearing detached itself from a grey background – the picture thus forming a harmony in grey. When it was finished, quite successfully in my opinion, I saw that Manet was not satisfied with it. He seemed anxious to add something to it. One day when I came in he made me resume the pose in which he had originally placed me, and, moving a stool near to me, he began to paint it with its garnet-coloured cover of woollen stuff. Then the idea occurred to him of taking a book and putting it underneath the stool; this, too, he painted with its cover of bright green. Next he placed on the stool a lacquer tray, with a decanter, a glass and a knife. All these variously coloured objects constituted an addition of still-life in the corner of the picture; the effect was wholly unpremeditated, and came to me as a surprise. Another addition which he made afterwards was still more unexpected – a lemon placed upon the glass on the little tray.

I had watched him make these successive additions with some astonishment. Then, asking myself what was the reason for them, I realized that I had before me a practical instance of his instinctive and, as it were, organic way of seeing and feeling. Evidently the picture painted throughout in a grey monochrome gave him no pleasure. His eye felt the lack of pleasing colours, and, as he had omitted them in his first scheme of the picture, he introduced them afterwards by means of a piece of still-life. Thus the practice of placing bright tones in juxtaposition – the luminous patches contemptuously described as patchwork – which he was accused of having adopted deliberately in order to differentiate his work at all hazards from that of other painters, really proceeded from a perfectly frank and deeply rooted instinct; it was his own natural way of feeling. This portrait had been painted for him and for myself alone; I had no idea of exhibiting it, and in building it up thus by a series of successive additions I can certify that his sole motive was to satisfy himself, without a thought as to what others might say about it.

I have since examined his pictures in the light which came to me through observing the way in which he finished my portrait, and I have discovered in all of them this same method of adding luminous passages, in which he raises the key of the colour scheme by means of a few detached and emphatic tones. Hence in the *Luncheon on the Grass*, the presence of the many-coloured accessories spread on the ground. Hence in the *Olympia*, he introduced the large bouquet of different kinds of flowers, and put the black cat against the white of the bed. Hence in the *Artist*, a picture conceived in just the same scheme of grey as my small portrait, behind the standing figure he painted a dog in bright tones and in the light. This explains his fondness for introducing arrangements of still-life, sometimes as accessory, sometimes as background, into pictures in which probably no one else would have thought of putting them – in the *Portrait of Émile Zola*, in the *Luncheon*, in the *Bar at the Folies-Bergère*.

In 1868, the year in which Manet painted Duret's portrait, Duret had started a republican newspaper, La Tribune française.

COLOURPLATE 18
COLOURPLATE 14

COLOURPLATE 76

COLOURPLATE 40
COLOURPLATE 117

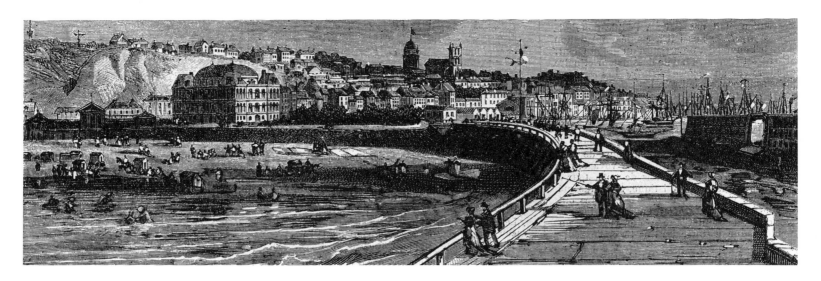

ÉDOUARD MANET
Letter to Fantin-Latour
August 26, 1868

It is quite obvious, my dear Fantin, that you Parisians have all the distractions you need, but I have no one here to chat to and envy your being able to discuss with that great aesthete Degas the inadvisability of bringing art to the poor and allowing pictures to be sold for twopence.

I haven't met anybody with whom I have been able to talk painting since I came here.

Good old Duranty – he will become first-class at billiards if he continues to practise – is greatly mistaken about my "grand projects." He imagines that I am going to paint some large pictures. Certainly not! I have quite enough of those white elephants being left on my hands. What I want to do now is to make some money, and as, like you, I believe there isn't much chance of doing anything in our stupid country, with its population of bureaucrats, I want to try to arrange for an exhibition in London next year.

Millet was quite right not to go chasing after that cheap trinket; it's all very well for children and people like Cassagnac; honestly, I would only admire him if he *didn't* wear it. It seems that Daubigny's son has been very coldly received, which is just as it should be; he has no talent whatsoever and his father is a cad. I believe that if one had any guts and didn't allow oneself to get discouraged, there would be a way of fighting against this strongly united mediocrity.

I am of the same opinion as you: the Morisot girls are charming. It's annoying, however, that they are not men – however, as women, they could further the cause of painting if each was to marry an academician and sow the seeds of discord in the ranks of that rotten lot, but it's asking a lot of their loyalty! In the meanwhile give them my kind regards.

I'm thinking of returning to Paris, because I am doing nothing here. Certainly, two months is a long time. I have received a letter from Bracquemond. He is going to Balleroy to paint a picture. Would it be by any chance the portrait of the countess? The lucky devil is quite capable of it.

Tell Degas to write to me. According to what Duranty tells me, he is becoming the painter of "high life." That's his business and I'm all the more sorry for his sake that he didn't come to London. The sight of well-groomed horses in movement would certainly have inspired him to paint several pictures. Have you heard anything of Stevens? Do they still receive?

Well, my dear Fantin, don't let yourself worship at the feet of *Antiope* too much and give us a rendezvous in London in the coming year.

Hubert Clerget, *General View of Boulogne-sur-Mer.* Engraving for *France Illustrée.* 1880 (Photo Roger-Viollet).

The Manet family holidayed in Boulogne in 1868 and 1869; this letter is from there. (See Colourplates 44, 45.)

Manet had met Degas in the summer of 1859 in the Louvre, where Degas was copying Veláz-quez's Infanta Margarita *directly on to a copperplate in preparation for making a print.*

Manet visited London briefly in 1868. The proposed exhibition never took place. Jean-François Millet (1814–75); the cross of the Légion d'honneur. Manet was to be made a Chevalier in the Légion d'honneur in 1881. Charles-François Daubigny (1817–1879). Yves (1838–93), Edma (1840–1921) and Berthe (1841–95) Morisot were the daughters of Edmé-Tiburce and Marie-Cornélie Morisot. Edma and Berthe studied painting, Berthe practising professionally throughout her life (see pages 109–23, 224–5). Félix Bracquemond (1833–1914), printmaker, thought to have taught Manet etching techniques. Count Albert de Balleroy (1828–72), painter. He and Manet shared a studio in the rue Lavoisier from 1859 to 1860. He appears next to Manet in Music in the Tuileries Gardens *(1862; Colourplate 11) and in Fantin-Latour's 1864* Homage to Delacroix *(page 48). Alfred Stevens (1828–96), Belgian painter, renowned for his fashionable society portraits. A close friend of Manet, he kept works by the artist in his studio in an attempt to help Manet sell to wealthy clients (see page 126).*

Documents Relating to the "Maximilian Affair"

1869

The execution of Emperor Maximilian of Mexico on June 19, 1867 provided Manet with subject-matter for a series of four oil paintings and a large lithograph which he worked on from the summer of 1867 to the winter of 1868–9. Because Napoleon III was directly implicated in the Maximilian affair, the French government blocked the exhibition of Manet's painting at the Salon, as well as the publication of the lithograph. (See Colourplate 36 and page 167.)

LATE JANUARY 1869
UNDATED LETTER FROM MANET TO ZOLA

My dear Zola, have a look at the enclosed letter and return it to me in an envelope along with your opinion.

It seems to me that the authorities are bent on making me take action over my lithograph, which had been causing me considerable worry. I thought they could stop the publication but not the printing. Anyway, it speaks well for the work, since there's no caption of any kind underneath it. I was waiting for a publisher to have the stone inscribed – Death of Max., etc.

I feel that a word about this ridiculously high-handed little act would not be out of place. What do you think?

Yours ever,

The enclosed letter: this no longer survives, but was probably sent from the government department in charge of censorship, in this case, the censorship of prints registered with the Dépôt Légal. It is probable that the letter informed Manet that his Maximilian painting would not be allowed to be exhibited at the Salon and that the printing or publication of the lithograph would be banned.

FEBRUARY 4, 1869 (THURSDAY)

REMARKS BY ZOLA UNDER THE HEADING "COUPS D'ÉPINGLE" ("PINPRICKS"), IN LA TRIBUNE, THURSDAY FEBRUARY 4, 1869, NO. 35

I read in the most recent issue of *La Tribune*, that M Manet has just been refused permission to print a lithograph representing the execution of Maximilian.

This is the sort of measure that can save a government. Is its authority in such a bad way then that those who serve it feel bound to spare it the slightest anoyance?

The censors no doubt thought, "If we allow Maximilian to be shot in public, his shade will go wandering, with ominous cries, in the corridors of the Tuileries. There's a ghost that it is our duty to put behind bars."

I know exactly what kind of lithograph these gentlemen would be delighted to authorize, and if M Manet wants to have a real success in their eyes, I advise him to depict Maximilian alive and well, with his happy, smiling wife at his side. Moreover, the artist would have to make it clear that Mexico has never suffered a bloodbath and that it is living and will long continue to live under the blessed rule of Napoleon III's protégé. Historic truth, thus interpreted, will bring tears of joy to the censor's eyes.

The fact is, I could not at first understand the censor's severity toward M Manet's work. I remember having seen, in all the newspaper vendors' windows, a penny print that came, I believe, from the Epinal workshops, which represented with terrifying naïveté the last moments of Maximilian. Why should an accomplished artist be refused what an industrial artisan was permitted? I believe today that I have found the key to the enigma, and it is truly a gem.

On examining a proof of the condemned lithograph, I noticed that the soldiers shooting Maximilian were wearing a uniform almost identical to that of our own troops. Fanciful artists give the Mexicans costumes from comic opera. M Manet, who truly loves truth, has drawn their real costumes, which closely resemble those of the Vincennes infantrymen.

You can understand the horror and anger of the gentlemen censors. What now! An artist dared to put before their eyes such a cruel irony: France shooting Maximilian!

In M Manet's place, I would regret not having intended to add a biting epigram, an intention with which the censor no doubt credited him.

The Habsburg Archduke Ferdinand-Joseph Maximilian (1832–67), Emperor of Mexico, was the younger brother of the Austrian Emperor Francis-Joseph I. Maximilian's reign had been imposed on the Mexicans by Napoleon III. Maximilian entered Mexico in June 1864, but Napoleon subsequently withdrew the French troops, without whose support Maximilian was unable to govern, in February 1867. The Mexican nationalists under Benito Juárez captured Maximilian and his two generals Tomás Mejía and Miguel Miramón on May 15. The execution of all three took place on June 19 at Cerro de las Campañas, near Querétaro. (See The Department of Art, Brown University, Édouard Manet and the "Execution of Maximilian", Rhode Island, 1981.)

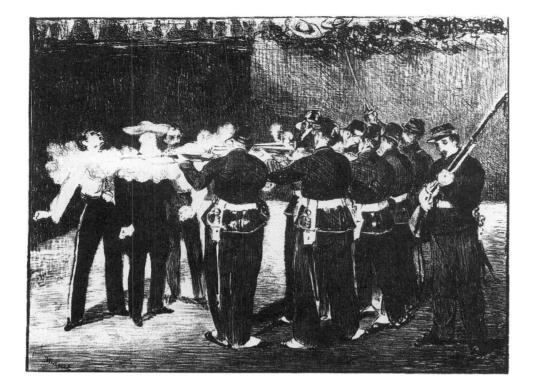

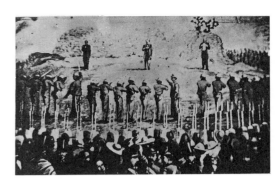

FEBRUARY 21, 1869 (SUNDAY)
AN IMPORTANT QUESTION OF LAW

We have received the following letter:
Sir, "the Maximilian affair," which you have been good enough to bring to the attention of the readers of *La Chronique*, is becoming more complicated.

The printer Lemercier is now refusing to return the lithographic stone to me and is asking for permission to efface it.

I have of course refused, and also refuse to take any steps, as he advises me, to have the ban lifted. And yesterday I sent him an injunction through a process server.

There the matter rests. But it seems to me of some interest to know how it will turn out. One cannot destroy a block, stone, etc., without a court order, it seems to me, and there must at least be a publication to constitute an offence.

I am sending you these details in case you should feel it appropriate to mention this matter again. It is the kind of question that is of the greatest importance to settle in the interest of all artists.

Éd. Manet

The question raised in relation to the seizure of a drawing on lithographic stone is of quite exceptional gravity, and we must be very grateful to M Manet for the firmness he is showing in this affair. It is important for everyone to know what are the legal rights of the prefect of police over the ideas of an author or an artist.

Émile Galichon

FEBRUARY 28, 1869 (SUNDAY)

We learn with pleasure that M Manet's complaints have met with success. The printer Lemercier has advised him that his lithographic stone, representing *The Execution of the Emperor Maximilian* or, if one prefers to remain vague, a *Shooting in Mexico*, is at his disposal.

This letter and that from Galichon, together with the latter's editorial comment, were first published in La Chronique des Arts.

Émile-Léonard Galichon (1829–75), art collector.

Manet was to keep the stone in his studio until his death. Lemercier's firm printed a posthumous edition of the lithograph in 1884.

JULES-ANTOINE CASTAGNARY

LE SIÈCLE

"The Balcony" and "The Luncheon"

June 11, 1869

Jules-Antoine Castagnary (1830–88), French critic and politician. Castagnary was a friend of Charles Baudelaire and a supporter of Courbet and the Impressionists. In 1887 he became Director of the Beaux-Arts.

Manet is a true painter. If he would not prejudice himself too much beforehand, if he would consent to study some more, that is to say to broaden his mind and perfect his technique, I have no doubt that he would leave on contemporary art the mark of genuine originality. Up to now he has been more whimsical than observant, more fantastic than effective. His work is meagre, if one discounts the still-lifes and flowers which he paints masterfully. To what is this sterility due? To the fact that while basing his art on nature he neglects to have as his goal the interpretation of life. He borrows his subjects from the poets or finds them in his imagination; he doesn't bother about discovering them in contemporary life. It follows that much in his compositions is arbitrary. In looking at this *Luncheon*, for example, I see, on a table where coffee has been served, a half-peeled lemon and some fresh oysters; these objects hardly go together. Why were they put there? I know well the reason why. It is because Manet possesses, in the highest degree, a feeling for the coloured spot; because he excels in reproducing what is inanimate, and that, feeling himself superior in still-lifes, he finds himself naturally brought to do as many as possible. This is an explanation but not an excuse. Our minds are more logical, and for this very reason more severe. We need nothing more than what is suitable. I would not have insisted upon this detail if it were not characteristic. Just as Manet assembles, for the mere pleasure of astonishing, objects which should be mutually incompatible, in the same fashion he arranges his people at random without any reason or meaning for the composition. The result is uncertainty and often obscurity in the thought. What is this young man of the *Luncheon* doing, the one who is seated in the foreground and who seems to be looking at the public? He is well painted, it is true, and vigorously brushed, but where is he? In the dining room? If so, having his back to the table, he has the wall between himself and us, and his position is inexplicable. On the *Balcony* I see two women, one of whom is very young. Are they sisters? Is this a mother and daughter? I don't know. And then one has seated herself apparently just to enjoy the view of the street; the other is putting on her gloves as if she were about to leave. This contradictory attitude bewilders me. Certainly, I like the colour, and I freely confess that Manet finds the correct value, often even an agreeable one. I shall add that when he has learned the art of nuances, of half tones, of all those subtle secrets by which objects are modelled and space as well as light developed on canvas, he will rival the most talented of the great colourists. But a feeling for form, for fitness are indispensable. Neither the writer nor the painter can neglect them. Like characters in a comedy, so in a painting each figure must be in its place, play its part and so contribute to the expression of the general idea. Nothing arbitrary and nothing superfluous, such is the law of every artistic composition.

COLOURPLATE 43

COLOURPLATE 46

EDMOND BAZIRE

MANET

The Batignolles Group

1884

This was the opinion of the enthusiasts who gathered around Manet from the time of his earliest work. There were a dozen of them. As can be seen, the three I mentioned had had their imitators. Legros, Whistler and Fantin-Latour had been joined by some writers: Babou, Vignaux, Duranty, Zola; an engraver; Belot, since immortalized in *A Good Glass of Beer*; another engraver: Desboutin, who was also a painter and model, and who carved himself a considerable place among his contemporaries, not as a model, but as a painter and engraver; a sensitive landscapist: Guillemet; an orientalist: Tabar; an all-rounder: Zacharie Astruc, who wields the paintbrush, the stonemason's hammer and the pen with equal ardour. In

Édmond Bazire (1846–93), journalist, republican, syndicalist and author. He was a habitué of Nina de Callias's salon (see pages 286–9) and a friend and collaborator of Henri Rochefort (Colourplate 111). His Manet, *published in 1884, was the first biography of the artist.*

Alphonse Legros (1837–1911), French artist resident in Britain, Slade Professor of Fine Art at University College, London, 1876–92; James Abbott McNeill Whistler (1834–1903); Émile Bellot (see page 170); Marcellin Desboutin (1832–1902), French painter and printmaker. Degas used him as a model for The Absinthe Drinker *(see Manet's portrait of* The Artist, *Colourplate 76); Jean-Baptiste-Antoine Guillemet (1843-*

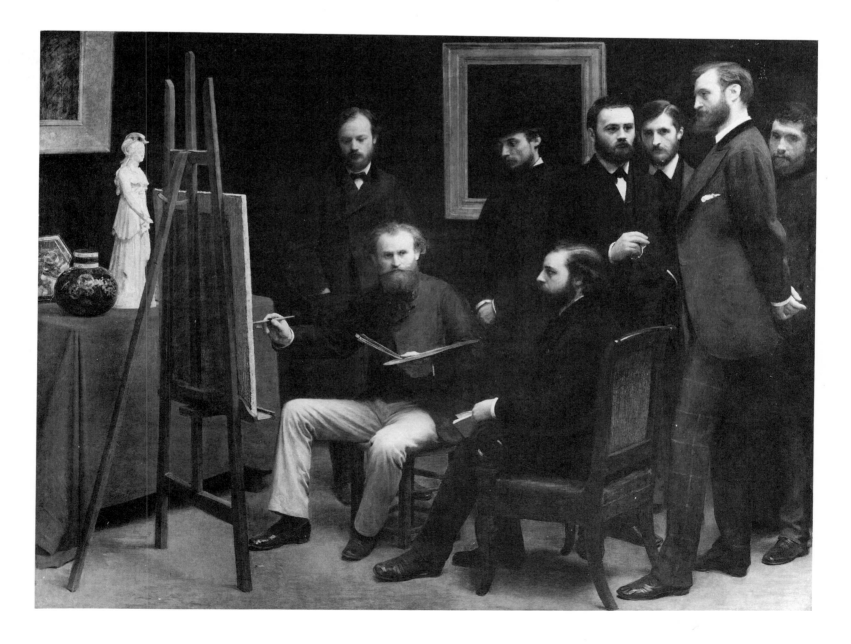

point of fact, you know him. The label accompanying *Olympia*, which I have reproduced, is his, as are many a bronze and many a plaster-cast, not to mention plays and memoirs. Gradually, new names were to be added: Degas, Renoir, Monet, Pissarro.

The meeting place selected was a café in Les Batignolles, the café Guerbois.

Hence the name of the school of Batignolles given to the élite who had made it its centre. Gatherings took place twice a week. There were some irregular attenders: Monginot put in an occasional appearance, Burty would turn up. One evening it would be Antonin Proust; another time, Henri d'Ideville. Henner came sometimes, Stevens more often.

The café is still there. Except that today the Guerbois of those times is a man of independent means, and it is his son who runs the café, which is at the entrance to the Avenue de Clichy, a stone's throw away from Père Lathuille's.

The clients of this group drank little. They talked a lot. They discussed recent exhibitions; they took an interest in new talent; they thought above all of the works they were yet to do, and pettiness, jealousy and envious nit-picking had no part in their conversations. They were artists talking about the arts. They expounded and expatiated upon whole programmes. Where does beauty dwell? That was the question. And debate would ensue, ardent, impassioned, among questors animated and sustained by a single line of thought. From time to time an epigram would whistle by: it was unusual.

But one day a quarrel broke out. Duranty, a prey to some fancy or other, had, in a newspaper article, given proof of a strange ill-humour; he had attacked Manet violently, brutally. What! Duranty! The hitherto faithful friend, for whom no sacrifice had seemed too great! The assiduous visitor to the studio! It was unlikely, and cruel. Manet, who received the impassioned attacks of the serried army of his enemies very patiently, was hurt to the quick, suffered, became indignant and, entering the circle, went straight to the ill-disposed writer, expressed his anger and slapped his face.

People tried to stifle the affair. But it was useless. Seconds were contacted and a duel was decided upon. The report made at the time will give an idea of the heatedness of the affair.

"A duel took place this morning, February 23, 1870, in the forest of St Germain, towards eleven in the morning, between M Manet and M Duranty.

"A single engagement took place, of such violence that the two swords buckled.

"M Duranty was lightly wounded above the right breast, his adversary's sword having slipped to one side.

"In view of this wound, the seconds declared that honour was satisfied and there was no reason to carry on the fight."

1918), French painter; Zacharie Astruc (1835–1907), French critic and artist, friend of Manet. He appears in Music in the Tuileries Gardens *(Colourplate 11) and in Fantin-Latour's* A Studio in the Batignolles Quarter. *Pierre-Auguste Renoir (1841–1919) (see pages 313–15); Claude Monet (1840–1926) (see page 250); Camille Pissarro (1830–1903); Philippe Burty (1830–90), French critic; Jean-Jacques Henner (see page 143).*

Photograph of Marcellin Desboutin (from Manet's photograph album). Bibliothèque Nationale, Paris.

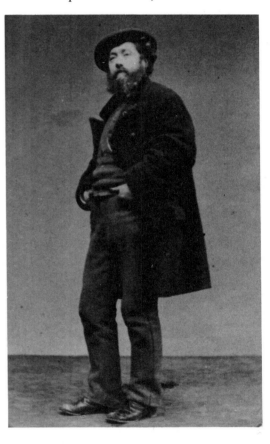

OPPOSITE Henri Fantin-Latour, *A Studio in the Batignolles Quarter.* 1870. 80¼ × 106¼" (204 × 270 cm). Musée d'Orsay, Paris. Manet is in the centre at the easel.

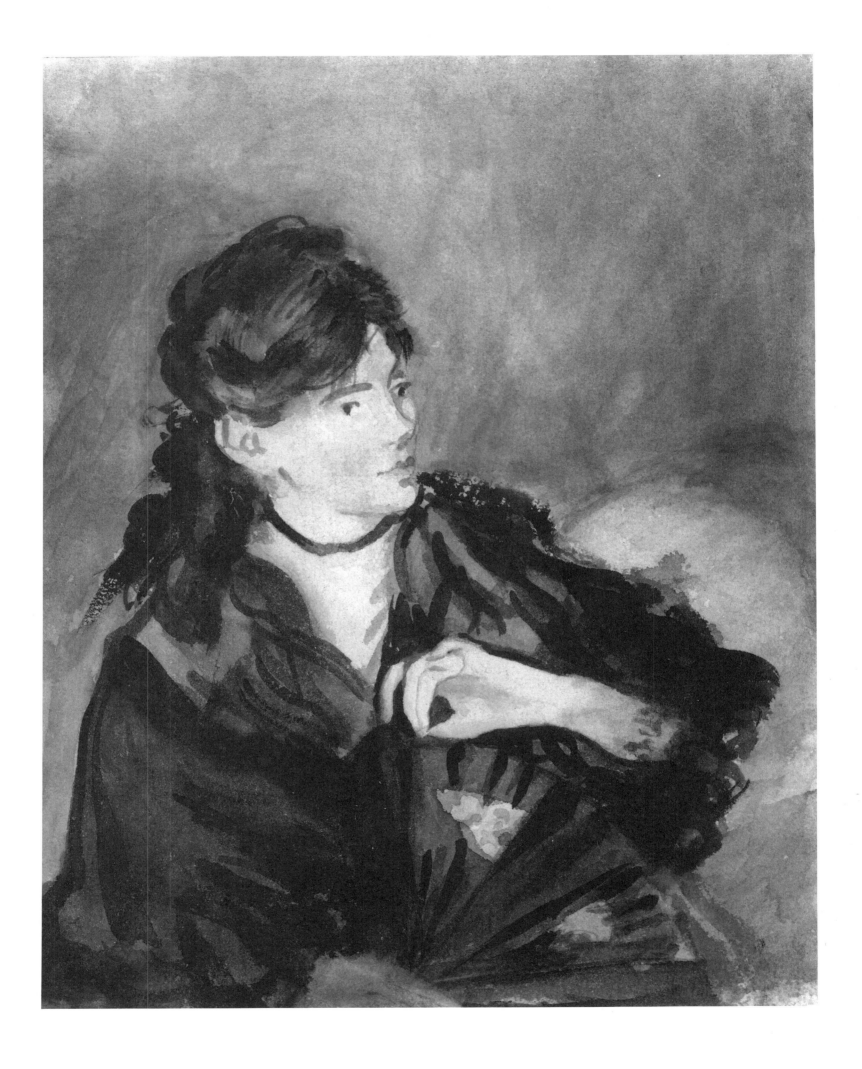

BERTHE MORISOT

Family Letters

1870–71

Mme Morisot: "Manet was laughing heartily. This made him feel better, poor boy, because his lack of success saddens him. He tells you with the most natural air that he meets people who avoid him in order not to have to talk about his painting, and as a result he no longer has the courage to ask anyone to pose for him. He has made indirect overtures to the Gonzalès; as for Madame Stevens, that prospect seems to have fallen through. However, he told me that he had been asked the price of *The Balcony*, it must be someone who wants to make fun of him or perhaps to satisfy his curiosity. He said naïvely that Berthe was bringing him luck. He seems to me very nice because he is interested in Berthe; he also spoke of Tiburce in a tone that shows he likes us.

"Do you know that Monsieur Degas is mad about Yves' face, and that he is doing a sketch of her? He is going back to transfer on to the canvas the drawing that he is doing in his sketchbook. A peculiar way of doing a portrait!" . . . .

* * *

Berthe Morisot (1841–95), French painter. Morisot studied with Camille Corot during the 1860s. She and her sister Edma met Manet in the Louvre in 1867. In 1874 Berthe married Manet's brother Eugène; their daughter Julie was born in 1878. Morisot exhibited in seven of the eight Impressionist exhibitions and was instrumental in organizing the last show in 1886. (See Colourplates 46, 48, 56.)

COLOURPLATE 46

Tiburce Morisot (b.1848), brother of Berthe Morisot.

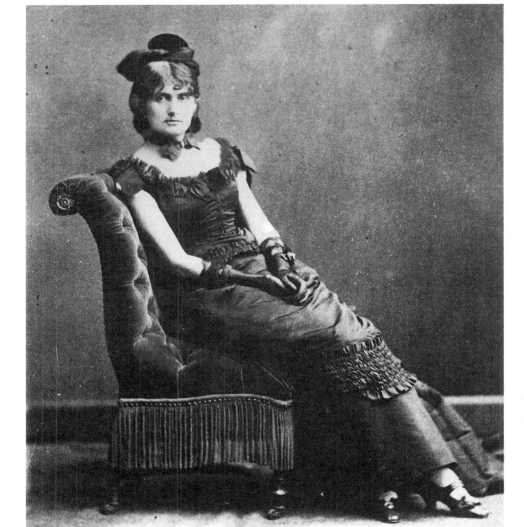

Photograph of Berthe Morisot.

OPPOSITE *Berthe Morisot with a Fan.* 1874. Watercolour, 8 × 6½" (20.5 × 16.5 cm). Courtesy, The Art Institute of Chicago (Joseph and Helen Regenstein Foundation).

Berthe: "As for your friend Degas, I certainly do not find his personality attractive; he has wit, but nothing more. Manet said to me very comically yesterday, 'He lacks spontaneity, he isn't capable of loving a woman, much less of telling her that he does or of doing anything about it.' Poor Manet, he is sad; his exhibition, as usual, does not appeal to the public, which is for him always a source of wonder. Nevertheless he said that I had brought him luck and he had had an offer for *The Balcony.* I wish for his sake that this were true, but I have grave fears that his hopes will once again be disappointed."

* * *

Mme Morisot: "I have taken the books back to Manet, whom I found in greater ecstasies than ever in front of his model Gonzalès. His mother made me touch her daughter-in-law's hands, saying that she was feverish; the latter forced a smile and reminded me that you had promised to write to her. As for Manet, he did not move from his stool. He asked how you were, and I answered that I was going to report to you how unfeeling he is. He has forgotten about you for the time being. Mademoiselle G. has all the virtues, all the charms, she is an accomplished woman – that is what the poor girl whispered into my ear as she showed me to the door. Last Wednesday there was nobody at the Stevenses except Monsieur Degas."

* * *

Berthe: "Manet lectures me, and holds up that eternal Mademoiselle Gonzalès as an example; she has poise, perseverance, she is able to carry an undertaking to a successful issue, whereas I am not capable of anything. In the meantime he has begun her portrait over again for the twenty-fifth time. She poses every day, and every night the head is washed out with soft soap. This will scarcely encourage anyone to pose for him!"

* * *

Edma: "The thought of Mademoiselle Gonzalès irritates me, I do not know why. I imagine that Manet greatly overestimates her, and that we, or rather you, have as much talent as she . . . . To have seen Manet again is already something, it must have helped you recover from the family visits of the day before."

* * *

Berthe: ". . . . We spent Thursday evening at Manet's. He was bubbling over with good spirits, spinning a hundred nonsensical yarns, one funnier than another. As of now, all his admiration is concentrated on Mademoiselle Gonzalès, but her portrait does not progress; he says that he is at the fortieth sitting and that the head is again effaced. He is the first to laugh about it. . . ."

* * *

Berthe: "The Manets came to see us Tuesday evening, and we all went into the studio. To my great surprise and satisfaction, I received the highest praise; it seems that what I do is decidedly better than Eva Gonzalès. Manet is too candid, and there can be no mistake about it. I am sure that he liked these things a great deal; however, I remember what Fantin says, namely, that Manet always approves of the painting of people whom he likes. Then he talked to me about finishing my work, and I must confess that I do not see what I can do. . . . As he exaggerates everything, he predicted success for me in the next exhibition, though he has said many unpleasant things to me. . . ."

* * *

Eva Gonzalès (1849–83), painter, daughter of the novelist Émmanuel Gonzalès. Eva Gonzalès had been introduced to painting by the society portrait-painter Charles Chaplin. She met Manet through Alfred Stevens in 1869 and became his pupil. Gonzalès married Manet's friend Henri Guérard in 1879 (see page 171 and Colourplate 49).

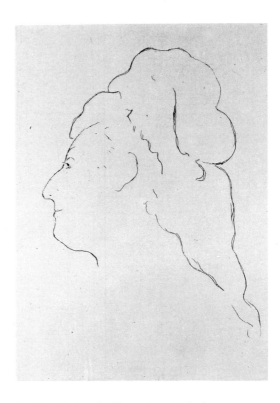

Profile of Eva G. Turned to the Left. 1870. Etching, $9\frac{1}{2} \times 6\frac{1}{4}''$ (24×15.8 cm).

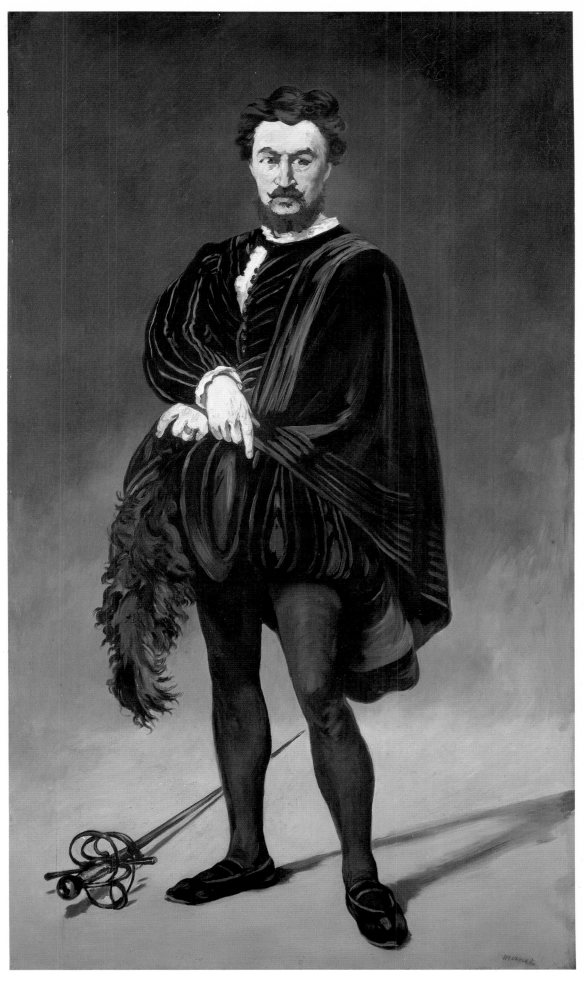

COLOURPLATE 30. *The Tragic Actor: Rouvière as Hamlet.* 1865. 73¾ × 42½″ (187.2 × 108.1 cm).
National Gallery of Art, Washington D.C. (Gift of Edith Stuyvesant Gerry).

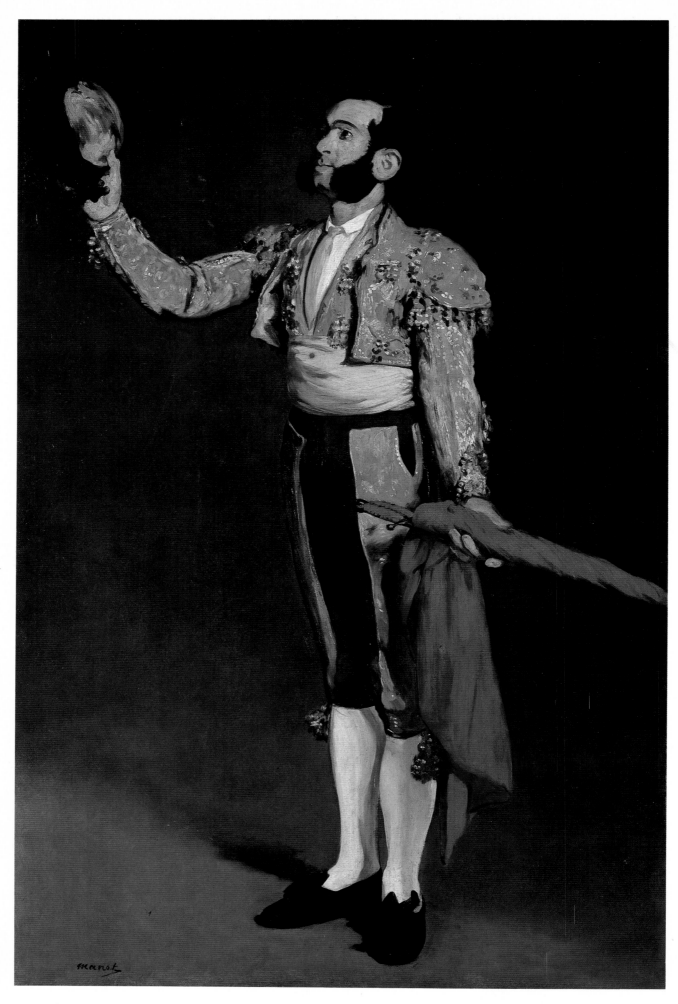

COLOURPLATE 31. *Matador Saluting*. 1866–7. 67⅜ × 44½″ (171.1 × 113 cm).
Metropolitan Museum of Art, New York (Bequest of Mrs H.O. Havemeyer, 1929. The H.O.
Havemeyer Collection).

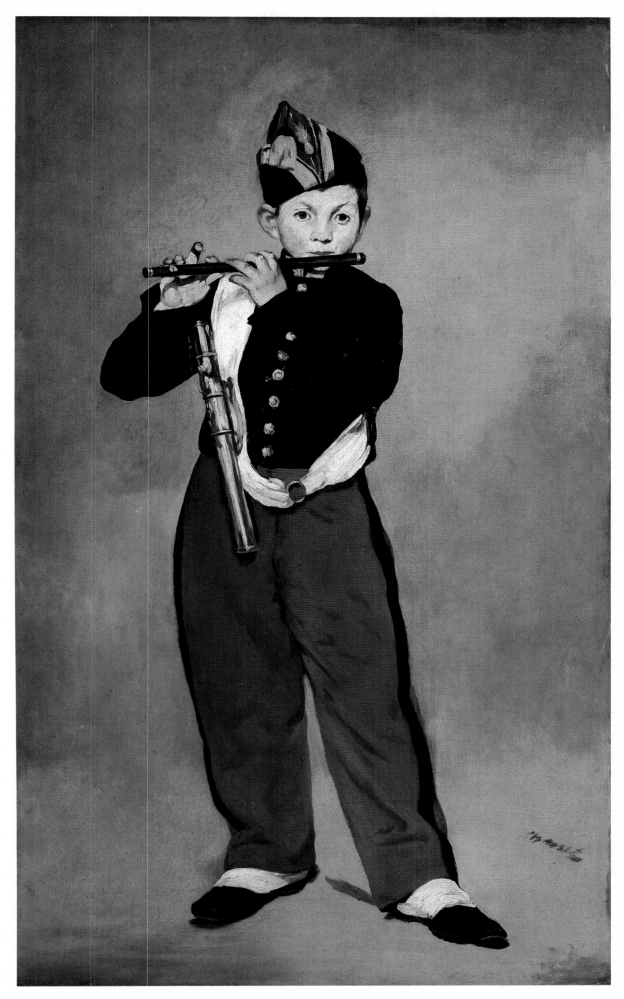

COLOURPLATE 32. *The Fifer*. 1866. 63¼ × 38″ (161 × 97 cm).
Musée d'Orsay, Paris.

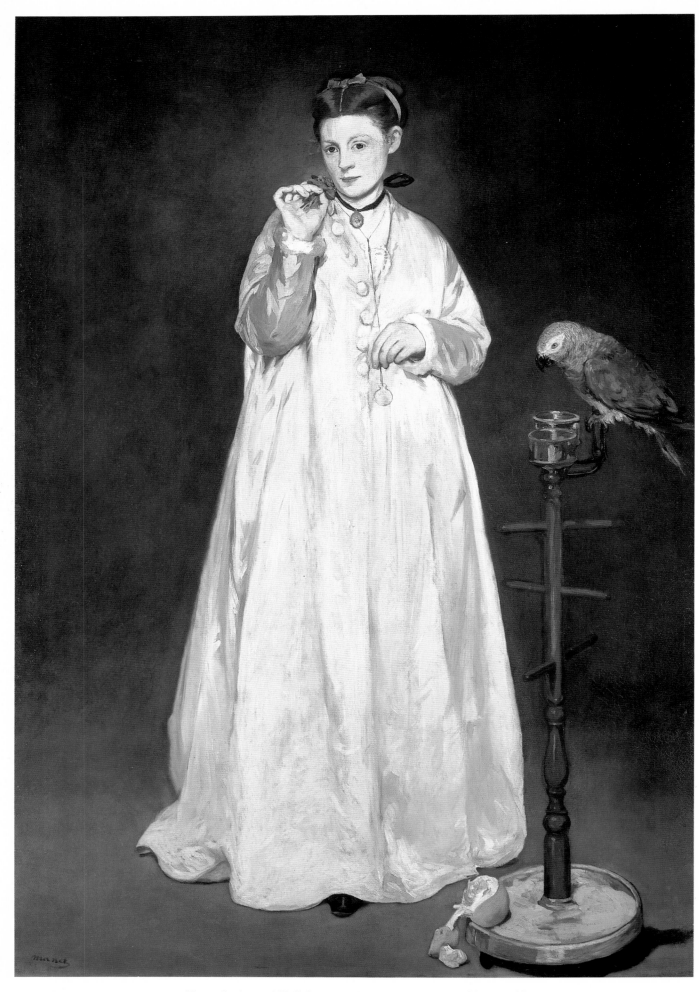

COLOURPLATE 33. *Young Lady in 1866 (Woman with a Parrot)*. 1866. 72⅞ × 50⅝″ (185.1 × 128.6 cm).
Metropolitan Museum of Art, New York (Gift of Erwin Davis, 1889).

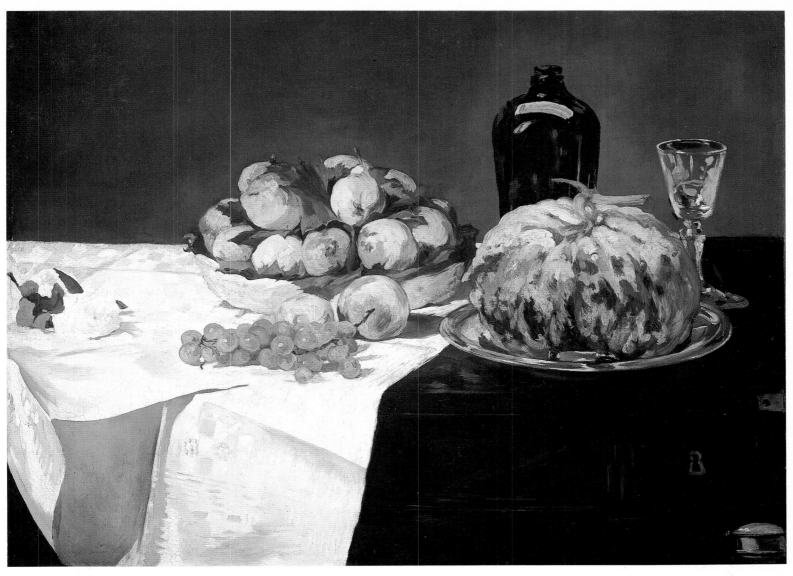

COLOURPLATE 34. *Still Life with Melon and Peaches*. c. 1866. 27⅛ × 36¼″ (69 × 92.2 cm).
National Gallery of Art, Washington D.C. (Gift of Eugene and Agnes Meyer).

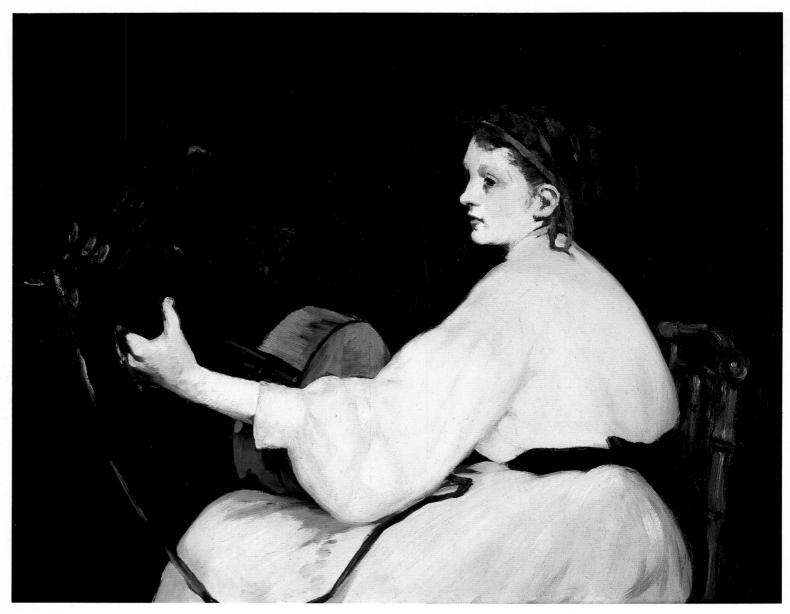

COLOURPLATE 35. *Woman Playing the Guitar*. 1867. 26 × 32¼″ (66 × 82 cm).
Hill-Stead Museum, Farmington, Conn.

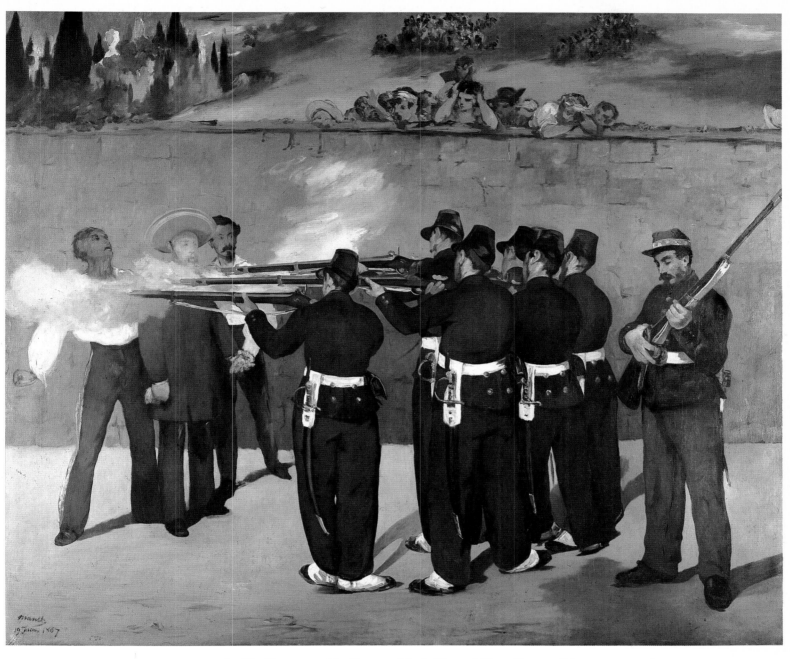

COLOURPLATE 36. *The Execution of the Emperor Maximilian.* 1868. 99¼ × 120" (252 × 305 cm).
Kunsthalle, Mannheim.

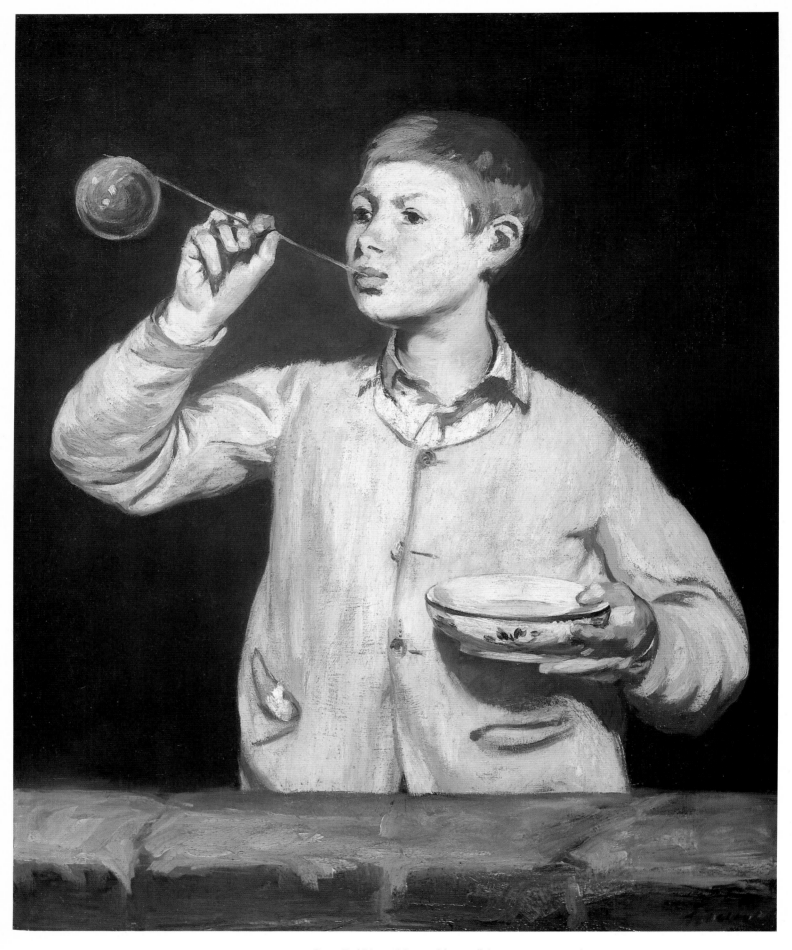

COLOURPLATE 37. *Soap Bubbles*. 1867. 39½ × 32″ (100.5 × 81.4 cm).
Calouste Gulbenkian Foundation, Lisbon.

Berthe: "Manet exhorted me so strongly to do a little retouching on my painting of you, that when you come here I shall ask you to let me draw the head again and add some touches at the bottom of the dress, and that is all. He says that the success of my exhibition is assured and that I do not need to worry; the next instant he adds that I shall be rejected. I wish I were not concerned with all this."

* * *

Berthe: "Tired, unnerved, I went to Manet's studio on Saturday. He asked me how I was getting on, and seeing that I felt dubious, he said to me enthusiastically: 'Tomorrow, after I have sent off my pictures, I shall come to see yours, and you may put yourself in my hands. I shall tell you what needs to be done.'

"The next day, which was yesterday, he came at about one o'clock; he found it very good, except for the lower part of the dress. He took the brushes and put in a few accents that looked very well; mother was in ecstasies. That is where my misfortunes began. Once started, nothing could stop him; from the skirt he went to the bust, from the bust to the head, from the head to the background. He cracked a thousand jokes, laughed like a madman, handed me the palette, took it back; finally by five o'clock in the afternoon we had made the prettiest caricature that was ever seen. The carter was waiting to take it away; he made me put it on the hand-cart, willy-nilly. And now I am left confounded. My only hope is that I shall be rejected. My mother thinks this episode funny, but I find it agonizing."

* * *

Berthe: "One day when I was walking in the salon with that fat Valentine Carré, Manet had a glimpse of her and has been lost in admiration of her ever since. He is pressing me to let him come and do a study of her in the studio. I have only half a mind to do it, but when he takes it into his head to want something, he is like Tiburce – he must have it at once. The best part of it is that this project annoys Puvis, who makes his feelings about it very plain to me.

"I cannot say that Manet has spoiled his paintings. Indeed I saw them in his studio the day before the exhibition, and they enchanted me, but I do not know how to account for the washed-out effect of the portrait of Mademoiselle Gonzalès: the proximity of the other paintings, although execrable, is enormously detrimental. The delicacies of tone, the subtleties that charmed me in the studio, disappear in this full daylight. The head remains weak and is not pretty at all."

* * *

Berthe: "I have made up my mind to stay, because neither father nor mother told me firmly to leave; they want me to leave in the way anyone here wants anything – weakly, and by fits and starts. For my own part I would much rather not leave them, not because I believe that there is any real danger, but because my place is with them, and if by ill luck anything did happen, I should have eternal remorse. I will not presume to say that they take great pleasure in my presence; I feel very sad, and am completely silent. I have heard so much about the perils ahead that I have had nightmares for several nights, in which I lived through all the horrors of war. To tell the truth, I do not believe all these things. I feel perfectly calm, and I have the firm conviction that everything will come out better than expected. The house is dreary, empty, stripped bare; and as a finishing touch father makes inexplicable and interminable removals. He seems to be very much occupied with the preservation of some old pieces of furniture of the First Empire. On the other hand he smiles pityingly when I tell him that the cabinet, the mirror, and the console in the studio are not absolutely worthless. To avoid argument, I refrain from interfering

Pierre Puvis de Chavannes (1824–98), French mural painter. He had met Berthe Morisot in 1868 and become a family friend.

The Paris Commune was provoked partly by the severe terms of the peace negotiated with the Germans following the Franco-Prussian War (July 1870–January 1871) and partly by Parisian reaction to the elections to the Assembly. On March 26 Parisians elected a council that adopted the name Commune of Paris. Louis Adolphe Thiers' (1797–1877) suppression of the Commune by the National Guard occurred May 21 to 28 in what came to be known as "Bloody Week"; the Communards resisted street by street and set fire to numerous public buildings. Many Communards were killed in fighting or by execution.

in anything, and to tell the truth all this interests me very little. Since it is possible to work where you are, why don't you do so? The militia are quartered in the studio, hence there is no way of using it. I do not read the newspapers much any more; one a day is enough for me. The Prussian atrocities upset me, and I want to retain my composure."

* * *

Mme Morisot: "I am sorry that Berthe is not with you. The tales that the Manet brothers have told us about all the horrors that we are liable to experience are almost enough to discourage the most stout-hearted. You know how they always exaggerate, and at present they see everything in the blackest possible light. Their visit has had a bad effect on your father, who is again taking up his favourite theme, trying to persuade us to go away without him. His over-wrought nerves are very trying; he would drive an entire regiment crazy, and at present he is exasperated by my calm. I am accused every minute of being a real doubting Thomas. The fact is, things never turn out as well or as badly as one anticipates. I am not worried, and I think that we shall survive. The Manets said to Berthe: 'You will be in a fine way when you are wounded in the legs or disfigured.' Then Berthe took me to task for refusing to believe such things possible. Nevertheless she does not want to go away."

* * *

Mme Morisot: "Each day we hear the cannonading – and a great deal of it. All the fighting is taking place near us – so far without any important results. It is impossible to keep still; Berthe and I got as wet as water spaniels when we went to see where the fighting was taking place, and we almost fainted when we saw a body on a stretcher, the victim of a fire near the viaduct. There are often disasters of this kind. For instance, two chemical plants across the river blew up only a short time ago.

"Monsieur Degas was so affected by the death of one of his friends, the sculptor Cuvelier, that he was impossible. He and Manet almost came to blows arguing over the methods of defence and the use of the National Guard, although each of them was ready to die to save the country. Stevens had an attack of rheumatism; he did not come. The doctor flirts with Berthe. If the situation were not so serious, these goings-on would be fairly comical. M. Degas has joined the artillery, and by his own account has not yet heard a cannon go off. He is looking for an opportunity to hear that sound because he wants to know whether he can endure the detonation of his guns."

* * *

Berthe: "You are right, my dear Edma, in believing that nothing will be spared us. The Prussians are to enter on Wednesday, and our arrondissement is explicitly mentioned among those to be occupied by them. This news was circulated in the afternoon; it was announced that they would arrive tonight; then the report was denied in the evening, but this only meant that the entry was being delayed. Our Passy, usually so quiet, was animated, the Place de la Mairie and the main street were filled with noisy crowds. The National Guard was against surrendering its arms, and protested loudly. All this is very sad, and the terms are so severe that one cannot bear to think about them. . . .

"Do you know that all our acquaintances have come out of the war without a scratch, except for that poor Bazille, who was killed at Orléans, I think. The brilliant painter Régnault was killed at Buzenval. The others made a great fuss about nothing. Manet spent his time during the siege changing his uniform. His brother writes us today that in Bordeaux he recounted a number of imaginary exploits."

* * *

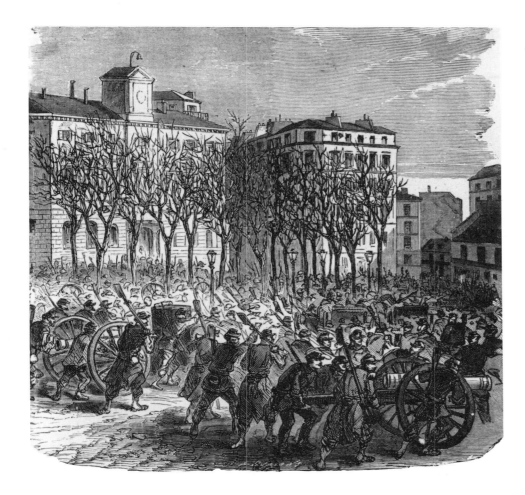

Recaptured cannon are taken back to the Mayor's office at Montmartre, 18 March 1871. Lithograph. Bibliothèque Nationale, Paris.

Mme Morisot: "Paris is far from peaceful; since you are getting newspapers again, you can read in them that the National Guard, under the pretext of salvaging the cannons that had been placed at certain points, kept these pieces, scarcely concealing their intention of using them if need arose. Paris does not want to be tricked out of its republic – it wants the real thing, the republic of the communists and of disorder. Yesterday M. Riesener said something that I think is very true, namely, that the most injurious thing we were able to do to the Prussians was to contaminate their troops, and that the war could not have gone on longer without damage to them in this respect. I think our poor country is rotten to the core. You who are in favour of resistance will admit that the people of the south are not in accord, nor do those of the west make a secret of the fact that they feel the same way. All those fire-eaters of the inland provinces who clamour so loudly for a war to the death took to their heels during our sorties. Nothing is more shameful than the conduct of the men of Belleville and Ménilmontant, who have the courage only to fight their own countrymen, hoping thus to find an opportunity for plunder and for gratifying all their passions."

* * *

Mme Morisot: "Paris on fire! This is beyond any description . . . Throughout the day the wind kept blowing in charred papers; some of them were still legible. A vast column of smoke covered Paris, and at night a luminous red cloud, horrible to behold, made it all look like a volcanic eruption. There were continual explosions and detonations; we were spared nothing. They say the insurrection is crushed; but the shooting has not yet stopped. Hence this is not true . . . Latest official dispatch: the insurrection is now driven back to a very small part of Paris, the Tuileries is reduced to ashes, the Louvre survives, the part of the Finance Ministry building fronting on the Rue de Rivoli is on fire, the Cour des Comptes is burned down, twelve thousand prisoners, Paris strewn with dead . . . Now that the Cour des Comptes has been burned down, my husband has resumed his pet theme more insistently than ever, namely, that this gives good reason for abolishing it. In actual fact all the documents are being scattered to the winds, and this made me say right away that I thought it a good riddance . . . Should M. Degas have got a bit scorched, he will have well deserved it."

* * *

Mme Morisot: "I saw only the Hôtel-de-Ville the day after my arrival . . . What I saw was frightful. To think that this great massive building is ripped open from one end to the other! It was smoking in several places, and the firemen were still pouring water on it. It is a complete ruin. Your father would like all this debris to be preserved as a perpetual reminder of the horrors of popular revolution. It's unbelievable, a nation thus destroying itself! Going down by boat, I saw the remains of the Cour des Comptes, of the Hôtel de la Légion d'Honneur, of the Orsay barracks, of a part of the Tuileries. The poor Louvre has been nicked by projectiles, and there are few streets that do not bear traces of the struggle. I also noticed that half the Rue Royale is demolished, and there are so many ruined houses, it is unbelievable – one rubs one's eyes, wondering whether one is really awake . . .

"Tiburce has met two Communards, at this moment when they are all being shot . . . Manet and Degas! Even at this stage they are condemning the drastic measures used to repress them. I think they are insane, don't you?"

* * *

Mme Morisot: "Guillemet told me yesterday that the Manets have finally managed to return; it was Édouard whom Tiburce met, not his brother. Manet hardly shows much eagerness to come to see me; it is true, of course, that you are not here . . ."

* * *

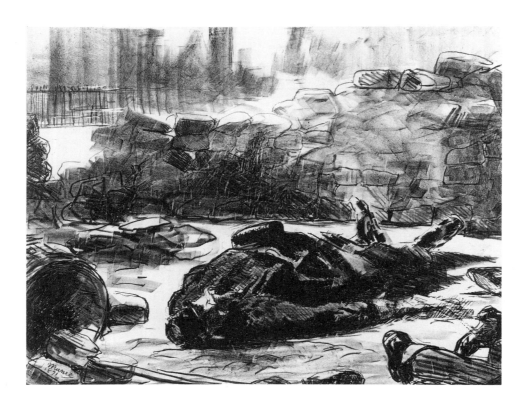

The Civil War. 1871. Lithograph, 15½ × 20″ (39.4 × 50.5 cm). British Museum.

Édouard Manet [*to Berthe*]: "Dear Mademoiselle, we came back to Paris several days ago, and the ladies ask me to send their regards to you and to Madame Pointillon, with whom you are probably staying.

"What terrible events, and how are we going to come out of this? Each one lays the blame on his neighbour, but to tell the truth all of us are responsible for what has happened.

"I met Tiburce a few days ago, and I have been unable to go to see your mother as I had planned. But all of us are just about ruined; we shall have to put our shoulders to the wheel.

"Eugène went to see you at Saint-Germain, but you were out that day. I was pleased to hear that your house in Passy has been spared. Today I saw that poor Oudinot – he too has had his moment of power. What a fall! I hope, Mademoiselle, that you will not stay a long time in Cherbourg. Everybody is returning to Paris; besides, it's impossible to live anywhere else."

ÉDOUARD MANET

Letters to his Wife

1870-71

NOVEMBER 19

My very dear Suzanne,

Time seems interminable, and how cruel it is to have no word from you for so long. We are all fed up, but we don't count on seeing you before the end of December. The outcome of what is happening now will be decisive.

Paris is powerfully defended. You needn't worry about us. I suffer most from having no news of you. The other privations imposed on us by the siege are trivial compared to that.

Paris is mortally sad. The gas is running low. It is being shut off in all the public buildings. Food is becoming impossible. The only thing that consoles me for having you so far away, and no doubt worried, is the thought that you are well and comfortably installed.

Smallpox is very widespread, and particularly hits the refugee peasants. The active life we lead is very good for us. I drill in the park every day for two hours. The men in my battery are very polite and considerate. For the time being I have no night duty, and shan't have until we are sent to a fort.

Advise Mama to order for your return the kind of preserves they make in the country. Life will be horribly expensive in Paris after the siege. The environs of Paris are all mined. Potatoes cost eight francs a bushel and there are now cat, dog and rat butchers in Paris. We no longer eat anything but horsemeat, when we can get it. I wish you could see me in my artillery uniform overcoat, an excellent indispensable garment. My soldier's knapsack serves at the same time to hold everything necessary for painting. I shall soon start to make some sketches from life. They will be souvenirs that will one day have value. I shall be equipped to make some very interesting things.

Dear Suzanne, kiss Mama and Léon for me. Tell him to work hard. Greetings to all, especially to M Lailhacar, who must find that we are taking advantage of his hospitality and whom I thank with all my heart.

Tout à toi,
Édouard M

Manet was in Paris throughout the siege of the city by the Prussian army, from September 1870 to February 1871. He had sent his mother, wife and Léon Leenhoff to Oloron-Sainte-Marie for safety. Many of Manet's letters written during this period were delivered by hot-air balloon.

Queue in Front of the Butcher's Shop. 1870. Etching, 6¾ × 5¾" (16.9 × 14.6 cm). New York Public Library (Astor, Lenox and Tilden Foundations).

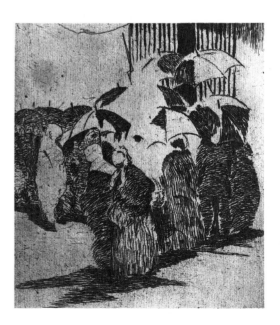

My dear Suzanne, I often find myself regretting having made you go away, but that really is pure selfishness as I knew in advance how hard it would be to be separated from you. But I couldn't believe it would be for such a long time; the only thing I suffer from, I assure you, is our being apart. If at least I knew you were well, that there is nothing you need, for you are so used to my pampering and taking care of you, you must often miss me, even if not all the time. I miss you very much, too. For the past two days I've had to stay in my room. Riding horseback has given me piles, and with the abominable cold we are having here, one must look after one's health. I hope I shan't have them for too long; it's really boring to stay alone in my room, even though I am surrounded by pictures of you. I do hope that you are in fresh air and well-nourished. Here food is more and more of a problem. Don't worry too much.

The bombardment against our forts that began on the 28th has not been very effective. The Prussians have up to this time launched against us something like 7,000 or 8,000 projectiles, which have wounded or killed very few. The news that comes, or rather leaks out, to us from the provinces seems very good; I think we can still hold out here for a long time; at least, we will do it as long as possible. We can't help hating the wretches. They have made us suffer too much; they'd better watch out if they're beaten.

Eugène and Gustave are well. We went with Eugène to see the Morisot ladies; they are not well, and find it hard to bear the hardship of the siege; they would certainly like to be in your place. Do be patient and don't exaggerate the dangers or the hardships we have to bear. If only I had news of you I wouldn't complain; that's all I suffer from. Tell Léon that I say he should be considerate of you and Mama, so that he can't be blamed for anything. I do hope you are getting my letters. At least it's a consolation for you to know that we are all right. When shall we see the end of all this anguish?

Adieu my dear Suzanne. Greetings to all. Kiss Mama for us.

Je t'embrasse comme je t'aime.
your husband
Édouard M

JANUARY 30, 1871 (MONDAY)

My dear Suzanne,

It is over and we are all three alive and functioning. I hope to come and take you in my arms as soon as possible. Probably it will be soon. We shall have to wait until after the elections and then try to adjust the timing of your return. Although I am longing to see you we must wait until there is no danger. Holding out was no longer possible. People were starving to death and there is still great distress here. We are all as thin as rails and I have been unwell for several days as a result of fatigue and bad food.

I have had a carbuncle which forced me to stay in bed for four days. It is over now and I shall be able to get up tomorrow. The good doctor was as always superb but the lancing hurt frightfully. However I am filled with joy at the certainty of seeing you again. I hope to find you in good health.

Alas, there are many dead here in Paris. You would really have had to go through it yourself to know what it is like. To build up my strength I was able to buy several pounds of cow-meat for which I paid seven francs a pound, and tonight we shall treat ourselves to a good *pot-au-feu*, but naturally with no vegetables. You see what we are reduced to.

My relief that we are all intact after the adventures we have had and the unfortunate New Year's gifts has put them out of my mind. Be patient a little longer, it is essential. I will come to fetch you as soon as possible and you may be sure I want to do so.

Manet left Paris to rejoin his family at Oloron-Sainte-Marie on February 12, 1871.

A new government was being elected in order to negotiate peace terms; this had been a condition of the armistice.

Duret, a candidate for the Assembly, is leaving with a safe-conduct and has offered to post this letter outside the Prussian lines. It will not be easy to re-establish communications and the necessary feeding of an exhausted population will come first. Fortunately I have collected some biscuits. The bread they give us is indigestible. As soon as possible send me a dispatch so I can have word of you. I long for details about how you are.

The elections that are about to take place will play an important part in the future of the country. Everyone will have to take part in hoping that they will go off quietly and that we will not again see Parisians shooting each other as they did on January 23. As you know, the Prussians are occupying the ramparts but are not entering Paris. I can't give you any details. There is so much to tell, it would take a whole volume. We are alive and well which is, I believe, more important than anything else at this time.

A bientôt. Love to all of you. Because I long to see you, you can count on my making every effort to get there as soon as possible. I hope Mama is well. We have often said that she could never have borne the hardship of the siege.

A bientôt, my dear Suzanne.
Your husband
Édouard M

This refers to a riot in which the first shot had been fired by a member of the National Guard.

Bazaine Before the Council of War. 1873. Lead pencil on squared paper, 7¼ × 9¼" (18.5 × 23.8 cm). Boymans-Van Beuningen Museum, Rotterdam. Marshal François-Achille Bazaine (1811–88) was courtmartialled in 1873 for his surrender of French troops at Metz, 27 October 1870.

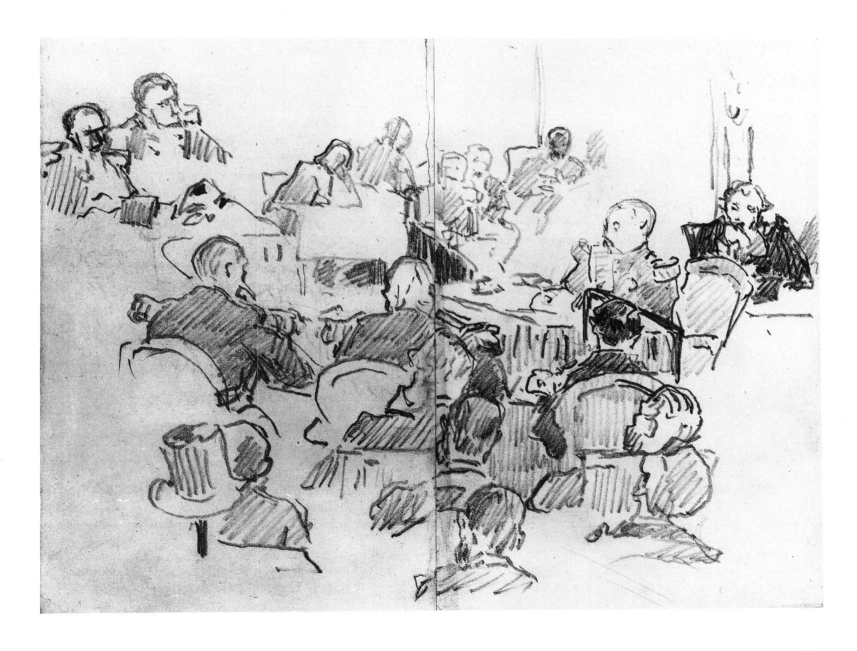

EDMOND BAZIRE

MANET

M. Durand-Ruel's Purchase 1872

1884

"Well! Would you care to tell me who does not sell 50,000 francs worth of paintings a year?"

"You!" the chorus of friends replies.

Well, it wasn't him [Manet]. He had made a sale, and made a sale to a discriminating art dealer, M Durand-Ruel, who had stopped hesitating – after having hesitated several times – to become the owner of a considerable portion of the disparaged works.

M Durand-Ruel was not the first to be divine, nor to understand. Théodore Duret had preceded him and, in agreement with his opinions (sometimes published in controversial papers) he had earmarked for himself one of the studies which best characterize the master's second manner.

M Duret, whose lead M Durand-Ruel had followed, had other imitators: in his wake he had carried M Gérard, who took *Boy with a Dog*, the disarming urchin who, his nose in the air, jauntily carries a basket lusted after by an eager spaniel – plus several still-lifes marked by the luminous tones of the Spanish painters; the *Salmon*, among others, which Velazquez would not have disavowed.

Then there came collectors, far-sighted or enthusiastic, such as M Faure, the incomparable singer, MM Hecht, Deudon, Ephrussi, Bernstein, Charpentier, de Bellio, Gauguin, May, Pertuiset, who sensed the future value and esteem to be accorded to the canvases discredited by the jealous, and resisted by the blind.

In this way the following paintings were scattered far and wide: *The Swallows*, that marvellous landscape sinking beneath a low and endless sky from which the swallows have flown; the *Woman Playing the Guitar*, so elegant in her white tunic, her tapering fingers wandering over the strings, the *Monk at Prayer* . . . the *Dead Man*, the *Spanish Singer*, the *Portrait of Mlle V . . . in the Costume of an Espada*, the *Racing at the Bois de Boulogne*, *Bordeaux Harbour*, the *Beggars*, of which one is at Nancy, the other at Nantes, not to mention the third which is at rue Neuve-les-Mathurins; the *Café-concert* – a pendant of the *Reichshoffen* – which took so many Parisian figures to Marseilles. . . .

Now that buyers were coming, spite became powerless, the cliques were becoming worried. Scenes of modern life, it seemed, were no longer so alarming! Monstrous nature and abominable sincerity were acceptable in a Salon!

Certain "proper" old men covered their heads with sackcloth, and pondered.

In January 1872 the art dealer Paul Durand-Ruel (1831–1922), an early supporter of the Barbizon artists and the Impressionists, purchased over twenty canvases from Manet for 35,000 francs.

Jean-Baptiste Faure (1830–1914), famous baritone. Faure collected (and speculated in) Impressionist paintings. He made his farewell performance at the Opéra on May 13, 1876 as Hamlet (see Colourplate 80). (See also Anthea Callen, "Faure and Manet", Gazette des Beaux-Arts *6th series, LXXXIII, March 1974.) Albert and Henri Hecht, brothers and art collectors; Charles Éphrussi (1849–1905), banker, art collector and art historian (see page 343); Marcel Bernstein, art collector. Manet painted a portrait of his son Henry; Georges de Bellio (1828–94), Rumanian doctor and collector of Impressionist paintings; Paul Gauguin (1848–1903); Eugène Pertuiset, hunter, arms merchant and art collector (Colourplate 110).*

In August 1878 Manet started work on a large canvas entitled Café-Concert of Reichshoffen. *The Reichshoffen was a brasserie situated on either the Boulevard Rochechouart or the Boulevard de Clichy. Before finishing the picture, Manet decided to cut the canvas into two sections. These formed the works now known as* Corner in a Café-Concert (The Waitress), *and* At the Café (Colourplates 90 and 82). *The engraver Henri Guérard (see page 171) and the actress Ellen Andrée posed for the figures in* At the Café. *Méry Laurent took Fernand Baroil to Manet's studio in 1879; he bought the* Corner in a Café-Concert *and took it to Marseilles, but was apparently forced to return the picture as his wife disliked it.*

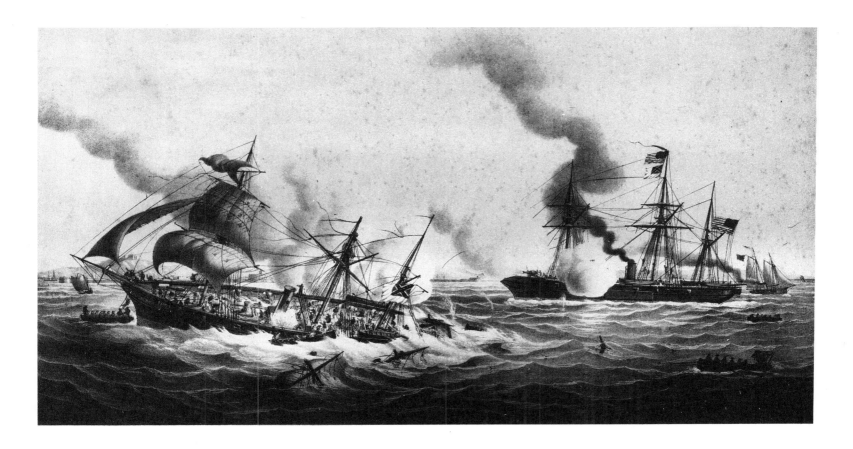

JULES BARBEY D'AUREVILLY

LE GAULOIS

"Manet, Marine Painter"

July 4, 1872

Among all the graphic artists, *only one* has conveyed to me a powerful feeling for Nature, and this man of whom I am about to talk is not, properly speaking, a landscape painter, nor is the picture a landscape. You will be a little astonished, just as I was. I am going to talk of Édouard Manet and his picture *The Battle of the Kearsage and the Alabama*. According to some, Monsieur Édouard Manet has no talent. He is a systematic and deliberate dauber, who has latterly been pitilessly *ridiculed*, which doesn't mean that he *is* ridiculous – no! not by any means! According to others he is a man of genius (no less!) who, like all geniuses – the nobility of Art and Science – knows everything without having to be taught. As far as I am concerned, I know only one picture among the works of Manet that is at all original – *The Spanish Dancer* (but too Chinese for me, for I am not Chinese enough to like it very much). But what I like more than all the pictures, what appeals to me straight away, is the man, the artist and thinker, who tramples commonplace ideas under foot and who, sword in hand, rises above them to take the initiative.

Besides, men of *good* repute, whose praises have been sung to me all my life, have prejudiced me in favour of men of *bad* repute, and I can willingly disregard the insults and insolent jibes in which these latter are rolled like peeled peaches in sugar, and can judge for myself which of them is in fact an imposter and which of them is sometimes good. Finally, a last reason for favouring Monsieur Manet! Among those who expected much from this young painter – from the outset of his career – was Baudelaire; and in

The American Civil War: the naval battle 9 miles off Cherbourg between the "Kearsage" and the "Alabama", 19 June 1864. Lithograph (Photo Roger-Viollet).

Jules Barbey d'Aurévilly (1808–89), poet, novelist, critic and dandy. The battle between the two ships, the Union Kearsage *and the Confederate* Alabama, *an incident in the American Civil War, took place off Cherbourg on 19 June 1864. This sea battle inspired Manet's first attempts to paint a current event. (Colourplate 21.)*

COLOURPLATE 10

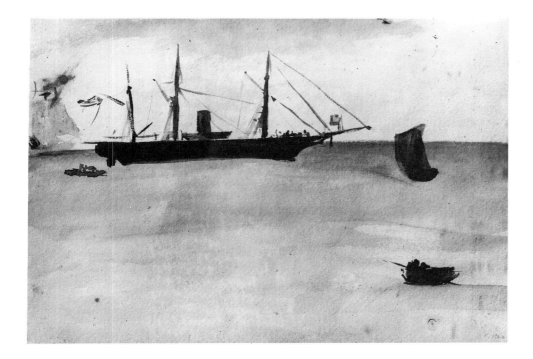

The "Kearsage" at Boulogne. 1864.
Watercolour, 10 × 13"
(25.5 × 33.5 cm). Musée des
Beaux-Arts, Dijon.

matters artistic, Baudelaire *is* somebody. He had a profound vision, *super-* and *sub*-acute, almost like a somnambulist. . . . He could ·see. His aesthetic works, full of conceptions inspired by painting, give a fine idea of his ability as an art critic, which he would have become had death not intervened. He loved courage, and Monsieur Manet did not frighten him. What would he have said had he lived to see *The Battle of the Kearsage and the Alabama*? I do not know – but the fact remains that I, who can divine less clearly than Monsieur Baudelaire a man's future ability and power, was moved by this picture of *The Battle of the Kearsage and the Alabama* in a way which I never believed Monsieur Manet capable of inspiring. I had a feeling of Nature and landscape . . . very simple and bold. How can I believe I owed this to Monsieur Manet? If there is any man who can be called civilized in this advanced and "gamey" (as they say of partridges) civilization, if there is anyone who is refined and fastidious in these days, when all Panurge's sheep are drowning themselves in universal vulgarity, if in this flock of sheep there is one man who wants to escape from this ocean of obsolete ideas – if there is anyone skilled and cunning in the world of art, then that man is Monsieur Manet. His picture (a picture of war and boarding parties, planned and executed with all the skill of a man who by hook or by crook is trying to escape from the commonplace which is swamping us) contains everything that is most natural and primitive within the scope of any paintbrush since the world began. All this has been expressed by Monsieur Manet in his picture of the *Kearsage* and the *Alabama*.

A less adroit man than Monsieur Manet would have placed his fighting vessels in the foreground in order better to fix the attention of the spectator on the fight itself; but Monsieur Manet has done as Stendhal did in his *Battle of Waterloo*, which is seen from the rear, by a small group of persons, far from the battlefield. He has done as did Chateaubriand, who, several leagues away from the battle, received the impressions of this terrible Waterloo from the trembling of the earth shaken by a cannon; and even like Byron, who breaks into the gaiety and music of a ball in Brussels with the first sound of cannon coming from afar. . . .

Monsieur Manet has thrown back his ships to the horizon. He has had the happy idea of making distance diminish them in size. But the sea which surges all around, the sea which stretches right up to the frame of his picture, tells sufficient of the fight itself. . . . One gets an idea of the

RIGHT *Marine.* 1864/5. Etching and aquatint, 5½ × 8"
(13.1 × 18 cm). Yale University Art Gallery (Lent by Walter Bareiss).

Stendhal (Marie-Henri Beyle) (1783–1843). The Battle of Waterloo *is a significant episode in his novel* La Chartreuse de Parme (The Charterhouse of Parma).

George Gordon, Sixth Baron Byron (1788–1824).

fight from the billows – from the mighty swell, torn from the depths – of these surging waters. I am of the sea. I was brought up in sea spray. As a Norman of Scandinavian stock, I have the blood of pirates and fishermen in my veins. I was carried away on the waves of Monsieur Manet's sea; I recognized that this was something I knew.

It is marvellously observed and understood. Above all, this picture by Monsieur Manet is a magnificent seascape. Here is a sublime landscape in the highest meaning of the word, not one of those landscapes of everlasting empurpled clearings in the woods as evening draws on, nor the everlasting "glimpse" of water reflecting trees upside-down, no! this is a vision of the infinite sea surging beneath the lost and almost imperceptible ships on the horizon! The sea which should be nothing but a detail, an adjunct, a background to Monsieur Manet's picture, becomes, because it has been so successfully rendered, the principal theme, the main interest and life of the picture.

One day, the famous Turner painted a landscape of atmosphere, nothing but atmosphere – a sky empty of everything but light and colour. Monsieur Manet might well have painted the sea alone, with its green and turgid billows, stronger than the men who fight and cannonade each other on the surface, whose bullets fall into the insatiable abyss of the waters!

Very fine – that – both in execution and idea! Monsieur Manet, in spite of this adorable and execrable civilization which corrupts us, may become a painter of Great Mother Nature! . . . He has acted like the Doge of Venice. He has cast a ring into the sea, and I swear to you that the ring is golden.

Joseph Mallord William Turner (1775–1851).

A reference to the ritual whereby the Doge of Venice weds the sea by throwing a ring into the Lagoon.

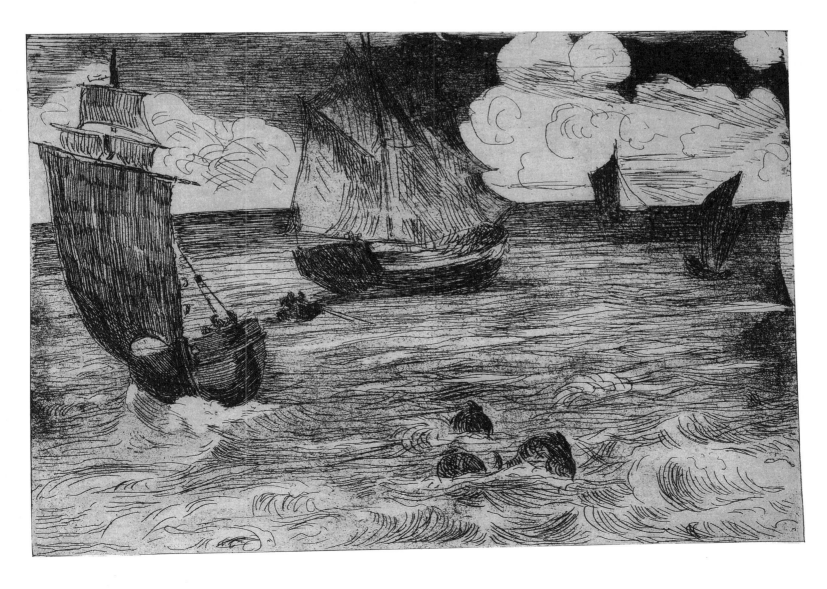

FERVACQUES
LE FIGARO
A Visit to Manet's Studio in the Rue de St Pétersbourg
December 25, 1873

Fervacques, pseudonym of Léon Duchemin (1840–76), novelist, journalist and art critic for Échos de Paris *and* Le Figaro.

Visited Manet's studio. As soon as we enter, the artist hurries towards us, smiling and affable, holding out a large, friendly, open hand. We go into the entrance hall. A huge panelled room, lined with old blackened oak, with a ceiling of small beams alternating with sombre coffering. A pure, sweet, very even light falls through the windows overlooking the place de l'Europe. The railway runs nearby, sending plumes of white smoke billowing through the air. The ground, constantly shaken, quivers beneath one's feet and shudders like the deck of a vessel at sea. In the distance one can see as far as the rue de Rome, with its pretty *rez-de-chaussée* apartments with their gardens, and its majestic houses. Then, on the rising boulevard des Batignolles, a dark, deep hollow: it is the tunnel which, like a dark mysterious mouth, swallows up the trains as they enter its rounded vaulting with a piercing whistle.

Manet's studio was in the rue de Saint-Pétersbourg (now Leningrad) near the Gare Saint-Lazare (Colourplate 61).

See pages 106–7.

On the walls hang some of the painter's works. Firstly, the famous *Luncheon on the Grass* rejected by the jury who, foolishly, have failed to understand that it showed, not a nude woman, but a woman undressed, which is something quite different. Then, paintings exhibited at different periods: *The Music Lesson, The Balcony,* the beautiful *Olympia,* with her negress and her strange black cat, undoubtedly a close relation of Hoffmann's famous Mürr. Then a *Seascape,* the sketch of two women seated in open fields, with a nearby village, a portrait of a woman and an exquisite *Polichinelle,* in a very jaunty pose.

COLOURPLATE 18

COLOURPLATES 50, 46, 14

While we were admiring this painting, so viciously attacked and yet so full of talent, Manet does a water-colour of another polichinelle who is posing in the middle of the studio, in his delightful traditional costume. . . .

See pages 134–5 and Colourplate 70

But let us come to the works that have not yet been seen. There is something quite remarkable on the easel, placed at the foot of the oak staircase leading to the gallery used, in days gone by, for firing practice, when this magnificent studio was an armoury. Incidentally, this loggia, of carved oak, is highly picturesque, framed with its gold fillets and its crimson satin curtains. It is as though this fragile, mysterious rampart might open up at any moment to reveal the head of some Mona Lisa or Rubens figure with its vermilion-tinted flesh, dressed in floral green and gold brocade, a diadem of pearls in its hair, smiling the beatific smile of the masterpiece which has been looking down upon you over the centuries, disdainful and motionless, in its eternal, unfailing beauty.

This canvas, which is intended for Faure, shows the corridor of the Opera on the night of a masked ball. Here is an exact description of the painting. Between the massive columns, the walls of the boxes against which the swells stand out flat as espaliered trees, and the entrances to the foyer separated by the legendary panels of red velvet, a sea of black evening suits, brightened here and there by a Pierrette or a *débardeuse* [woman in traditional fancy-dress stevedore costume], sways without making any headway. Discreet dominoes, their faces masked by their fourfold beard of lace, circulate amidst this sea of humanity, jostled, close-pressed, touched by a thousand prying hands. The poor creatures run the gauntlet of this perilous stretch, leaving here and there a fragment of lace, a branch of the white lilac that forms their bouquets, yellowing under the noxious exhalations of the gas lighting and the sour smell of humanity which wafts in dense, heavy eructations.

COLOURPLATE 64
For another description of this work see page 271.

ABOVE RIGHT *The Rue Mosnier.* 1878. Drawing, 11 × 17¼" (27.8 × 44 cm). Courtesy, The Art Institute of Chicago (Given by Alice H. Patterson in Memory of Tiffany Blake). The Rue Mosnier (since 1884 the Rue de Berne) runs parallel with the tracks of the St-Lazare station. Manet's studio looked down the Rue Mosnier.

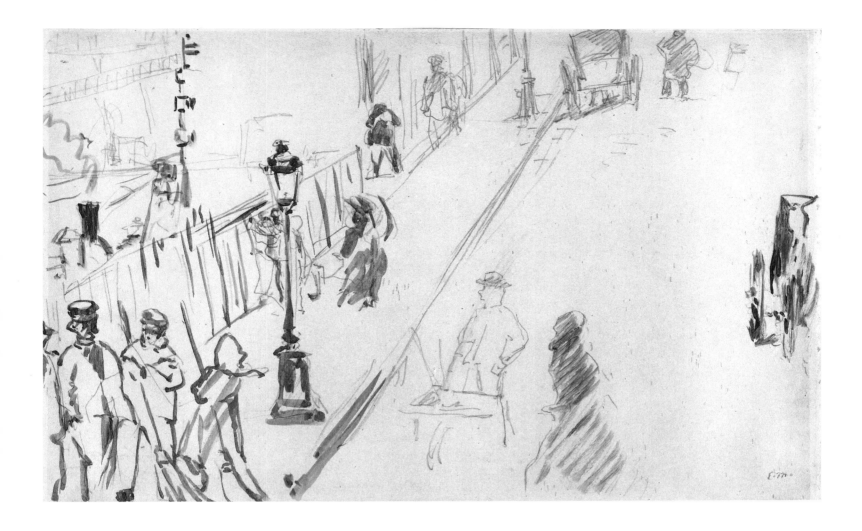

Groups form in the most various of attitudes. A brazen-faced gavroche, a gutter bloom which has grown up between two paving stones, yet lovely as the purest of antique statues – a mystery both unexplained and inexplicable – a young girl, her dress so low-cut as to challenge the sixth commandment, trousered with a scrap of red velvet the size of a man's hand, with a lot of buttons, admittedly, and sporting a cap angled at forty-five degrees over her mop of powdered hair, is holding her own against a group of white-tied scoffers. They are all there, eyes bright with the truffles and Burgundy of the dinners they have eaten, moist-lipped, satyr-eyed, rings on their fingers and thick gold chains in their waistcoats. Their hats are tipped insouciantly backwards in a conquering fashion: clearly, they are wealthy; their pockets are full of gold louis and they are there to enjoy themselves. This they are doing. They would take liberties with their sister if she passed that way.

Their adversary senses it. She meets their gaze, proudly, determined to retort loudly and firmly, combining Rabelais with Hervé and Gavarni with Molière. Neither prudent nor prudish, this descendent of the upstart Mère Angot will yield only to copper-bottomed reasoning and, in the meanwhile, crash, bang, spicy words pour from her delicate "kisser" like pearls from the silken body of the enchanted pug in the fairy tale. You can lip-read what she is "giving out," as the slang phrase has it. One can guess at the doubtful tropes borrowed from the repertoire of Vadé, her astounding flights of fancy, her hectoring tirades, which these young men, bloated with politics and favourable investments, swallow blissfully as though utterly satiated, their eyelids and palates stung with its peppery flavour.

Perhaps all this is not to be found in this painting; perhaps it is about something quite other. At all events, it is a most excellent work, direct, yet thought out and admirably rendered. We shall see, at the next Salon, if the public shares my view.

Photograph of Manet (from Manet's photograph album). Bibliothèque Nationale, Paris.

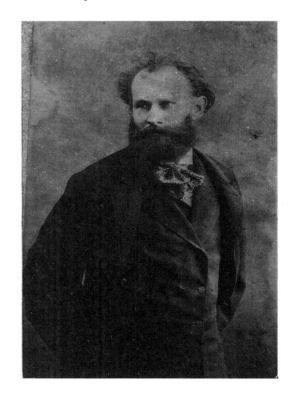

STÉPHANE MALLARMÉ

LA RENAISSANCE LITTÉRAIRE ET ARTISTIQUE

"The Painting Jury of 1874 and Manet"

April 12, 1874

Stéphane Mallarmé (1842–98), French poet. Manet and Mallarmé had known each other for about a year in 1874. Manet wrote a letter of thanks for this article: "If I had a few champions like you, I could just laugh off the jury."

All those in whom the approach of the Salon arouses a degree of curiosity, and the collectors who turn their gaze towards new studios, have learned very suddenly, during these last days, that the Painting Jury has rejected two out of three paintings sent in by M Manet.

For some, even among the general public, the disappointment of not being able, this year, to study the complete manifestation of an exceptional talent, is great; and the dyed-in-the-wool enemies of new ambitions have simply to exclaim: "Why did they not reject the whole lot?"

I myself share the feelings of the former, and align myself absolutely with the exclamations of the others.

If one wishes to spare the visitors to the Salon the spectacle of a type of painting which will trouble them on occasions (as does any revelation whose message is still unclear) and to preserve them from the danger of allowing themselves to be gradually won over by certain blazing qualities, one must, indubitably, have the courage fully and absolutely to misuse a power which was conferred with quite another aim. Why invoke those deeply rooted (and briefly forgotten) habits of dictating to the public's taste only by halves, or indeed two-thirds? (Perhaps, through them, Art may be saved, like everything else.)

Nonetheless, to the surprise of none but the members of the jury, one might argue that the case is in fact more down-to-earth and that two of the canvases presented by the painter have such faults, compared to the third, that their acceptance was impossible. Such, despite the apparent absurdity implied by these words, is, indeed, the conclusion presented to the public by the recently pronounced verdict. No systematic exclusion, as you see! Why, a degree of judgement is even being exercised.

Personally, by virtue of the mere fact that these lines are appearing in some publication which is concerned with art, I would fear humiliating these Gentlemen; they are a group of people who are primarily skilled painters rather than blundering men, simply exercising deception, and out of some sense of deference, I prefer to indict the bad faith they have brought to the use of a mandate which has fallen into their hands rather than their technical perspicacity. Something awkward, were this not true, emerges from one of these accusations: the second, as I know, can be dodged with a smile – why not provoke this smile?

As far as the execution no less than the conception of his paintings is concerned, M Manet does indeed constitute a danger for an Academy (and unfortunately, in our society, this is what any closed official assembly becomes). The simplification brought about by a seer's gaze (so positive is it!) to bear upon certain procedures of painting, whose chief wrong is to conceal the origin of this art made of colours and of unguents, may seduce the foolish who are tempted by an appearance of facility. As for the public, stopped in its tracks before the direct reproduction of its many-sided personality, will it never again tear its gaze from this perverse mirror, nor cast it once more upon the allegorical magnificence of those landscape-deepened ceilings or panels, on to ideal and sublime Art? What if the Modern were to prove prejudicial to the Eternal?

Such, manifestly, is the opinion of the majority of the painters who make up the jury, infantile in one case, puerile in the other, and not totally misplaced (with regard to a thousand other matters) except if they wish to cause it to intrude, in any way at all, into their judgements. How, and on what pretext, can one now proceed from this theory to practice?

Three paintings were presented by the indomitable intruder: *The Masked Ball at the Opera*, *The Swallows* and *The Railway*. Of the three, one, *The Masked Ball*, of primary importance in the painter's work and marking as it were a culminating point from which to sum up many an earlier essay, was, indeed, the work least likely to be exhibited to universal acclaim; the second, *The Swallows*, which is very remarkable to the amateur's eye and blessed with a serene power of seduction, might be passed off as less significant. To reject the latter along with the former was thus the idea: not to concentrate all the rigour on the more extreme work, but to strike the lesser offender with an even-handed severity. Since the deepest wisdom cannot foresee everything and as its best-laid plans may always go awry, there remained the third painting, itself deceptively important and rich in pointers for those who truly like to look. I believe that this painting, which slipped through the net of the schemes and ruses of the Salon organizers, actually holds another surprise in store for them, when what there is to say about is has been said by those concerned with certain matters, notably connected with pure craftsmanship.

COLOURPLATES 64, 71, 61

This is the business of the report which will be given here at the Salon itself: as for the two rejected works, which tomorrow will return to those galleries where their place awaits them, they should be discussed, not with the Jury which, if need be, would spoon-feed me with my likes and dislikes, but before the public which lacks any basis on which to ground its convictions.

What were the dangers in embarking on the bold undertaking of rendering a scene from a ball at the Opera? Essentially, the jarring boldness of costumes which are not real clothes, and the confused gesturing, which is not that of any time or place, and offers plastic art no repertoire of genuinely human attitudes. Thus all that the masks do in the painting is to break up the threatened monotony of the background of black suits by a few touches of fresh nosegays; and they are sufficiently unobtrusive for one to see this solemn stationary parade of lobby promenaders as just a gathering designed to give the mood of a modern crowd, which could not be painted without the odd bright note to cheer it. The aesthetics are unimpeachable and the treatment of the scene, which the demands of uniform contemporary dress make so very difficult, can simply arouse nothing other than astonishment at the delicious range to be found in the blacks: dress-coats and dominoes, hats and velvet masques, cloth, satin and silk. The eye scarcely senses the need for the bright touches added by the fancy dress: it registers them only when drawn and held at first by the pure charm of the grave and harmonious colour imparted by a group *formed almost entirely of men*. Hence there is nothing disorderly and scandalous as to the painting itself, nothing which as it were demands to step out of the frame; but, on the contrary, the admirable attempt to use the pure means demanded of this art, to fill it with the whole vision of the contemporary world.

As to *The Swallows*, I accord the most superficial of criticism one single objection, which I shall quash in a moment. Here we have two women seated on the grass of one of those dunes so typical of northern France, stretching to the closed-in horizon behind which one senses the sea, so vast is the space around the two figures. And from this space come the swallows which give the painting its title. There is an immediate impression of being in the open air; and indeed these women, utterly rapt in their day-dreaming or contemplation, are mere accessories in the composition, as the eye of the painter, caught purely by the harmony of their grey clothes and of a September afternoon, is bound to perceive them in such a vast space.

This painting, refused by the 1874 Salon jury, was probably painted while Manet was on holiday with his family at Berck-sur-Mer, during the summer of 1873. (See also Colourplate 58.)

I noted one reservation, made from the technical point of view by the kind of person who would take no account of certain preceding remarks: it consists, if you like, in saying, to use the colloquial expression, that "the painting is not sufficiently finished," or worked. For a long time now this idiocy seems to me to have been questioned by those who first proferred it. What is an "insufficiently finished" work when there is a consonance between its parts through which it holds together and which exerts a charm that is easily broken by any additional touch? Wishing to make myself entirely explicit, I could point out that, in any case, this criterion applied to the value of a painting, with no previous study of the quantity of the impression given, should, logically, lead to excess in the "finished" as in the slipshod: while, by a remarkable lack of consistency, one never observed judges inveighing against a canvas which is insignificant and at the same time meticulous to a nightmarish degree.

The public, cheated of its right to admiration or to mockery, now knows it all: all that remains is to formulate a question of general interest in its name, suggested by the whole saga.

The problem to be resolved once again, and with the same pointlessness as ever, is entirely contained in these words: what, in the double judgement given both by the jury and the public on the year's painting, is the task incumbent upon the jury, and what is that of the public?

The mere fact of the assembling of the outstanding talents of an epoch, each one necessarily possessing a very different originality, naturally means that the comparison between them hinges not on their originality, but on the pure talent, abstract and precise, contained in the work to be judged. All artists have a very neutral feeling of the artistic value (vague at times in the solitude of their work but reinforced in their contact with one another) discernible in everything where it is to be found: a precious commodity, and one whose contribution alone is asked of them in the present case. It is up to the public, who pay in glory and in cash, to decide whether the spirit in which a work of art has been conceived (backward-looking or modern) and its nature (rich or rarefied) – in a word, everything which concerns the public's instinct – is worthy of their money and their words. They are the masters on this point, and they can demand to see *everything there is*. Entrusted by the shadowy vote of the painters with the task of choosing the real paintings from among all those presented in a single setting, and to put them before us, the jury has simply to say: this is a painting, or indeed: this is not a painting. It cannot hide one away: as soon as certain tendencies, hitherto latent in the public, have found their artistic expression, or their beauty, in a painter, the one must make the acquaintance of the other; and not to introduce them is to compound a blunder with a lie and an injustice.

The present case is an example of such a blunder: and as such, it is sufficient to erase the grave words that logic has just put forward. Indeed, it offered the perfect opportunity for the stragglers of all schools which have enjoyed success during these last years, to show the one man who had tried to open a new way for it and for painting, that indeed an attachment to points of view that were old but had not yet perhaps yielded up all their secrets, was what was dearest to them, and not a total blindness to the present. They thought they had to close their eyes further: for no good reason. The day when the public, sorely tried, becomes utterly wearied, what can be done without the lure intended, in wise anticipation, to satisfy the legitimate taste for the new? The public, from whom nothing can be hidden, since everything emanates from it, will recognize itself, once again, in the accumulated and surviving work: and its detachment from the things of the past will, this time, be all the more absolute. To steal a few years' march on M Manet: what a pathetic policy!

As a result, this new master, who has been seen annually displaying the development of his style in such a thoughtful way and with such ill-understood sagacity, is becoming increasingly unpopular; whereas in fact he had a right to wait until the implications of his approach were understood, ultimately, by fastidious judges concerned with nothing other than talent. The jury has preferred to give the ridiculous impression, for another few days, that it was a shepherd of souls.

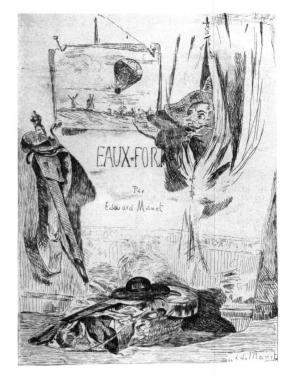

Frontispiece for an edition of etchings: *Polichinelle*. 1862. Etching, 10½ × 8¼″ (29.4 × 21 cm). New York Public Library (Astor, Lenox and Tilden Foundations).

Manet et Manebit, Manet's *ex-libris*. Engraving by F. Bracquemond. 1876. British Library.

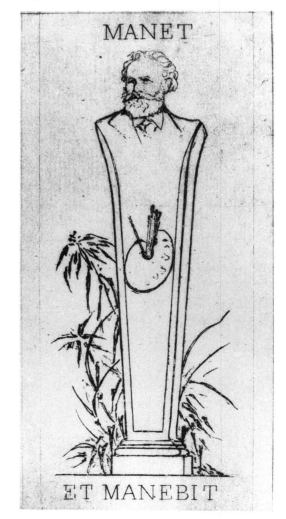

CHARLES CROS AND THÉODORE DE BANVILLE

Verses for "Polichinelle"

1874

He's ugly, riff-raff, drunk, with double humps,
Cares not a damn about society,
Policemen, ice-lipped death, propriety,
The devil. Yet we love him, for he thumps.

Hump-nosed, hump-backed, hump-trunked, a perfect blight,
He meets the law with cudgels, all ungloved.
He's most immoral. Why then is he loved?
We men perhaps prefer rough might to right.

Who will he light on now, our Mr Punch?
The watchman's throttled; all the devils fled;
Even grim death has been despatched to bed.
Hold – squint-eyed boredom's waiting for the crunch.

CHARLES CROS

Fearsomely pink, eyes glinting with the glare of Hell,
Brazen and drunk – divine – that's him, Polichinelle.

THÉODORE DE BANVILLE

A. POULET-MALASSIS

Letter to Manet

December 24, 1874

"Manet et manebit"

Dear Sir,
I called on you this morning – first of all to have the pleasure of shaking your hand, and secondly, because there is something I want to ask you.

Bracquemond has just finished your ex-libris, which I saw on the copper plate. I don't know whether he told you that it was I who had the idea for it. I found the subject and the motto without having to look very far. They consist of your bust with the device *manet et manebit*, which is a play on your name in Latin, and which means in that language, *it remains*, and in the future tense, *manebit, it will remain*.

I am going to publish a work on ex-libris. Will you allow me to include yours among them? It will be placed between those of Victor Hugo and the Messieurs Goncourt, designed by Gavarni.

As you know,
I am, yours ever,
A. Poulet Malassis

P.S. To my great satisfaction I have sold the Baudelaire to Monsieur Bruyas of Montpellier, and it is now included among the pictures presented to his native town by this great art-lover.

Manet's Polichinelle *lithograph (Colourplate 70) was based on a watercolour exhibited at the 1874 Salon. The artist organized a competition among his friends for verses to accompany the print. This was won by Théodore de Banville. A large edition of the print was planned for publication in June 1874, but the police stopped production, claiming that the print was a caricature of the President of the Republic, Marshal MacMahon.*

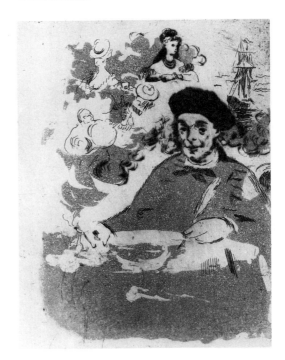

Frontispiece for an edition of *Les Ballades* by Théodore de Banville. 1874. Etching and aquatint, 9¼ × 6″ (23.6 × 15.7 cm). British Museum.

Paul-Auguste Poulet-Malassis (1825–78), publisher of Leconte de Lisle, Théodore de Banville and Baudelaire. Bankruptcy forced him to Belgium, but he eventually returned to France, where he specialized in the reprinting of rare books.

Victor-Marie Hugo (1802–85).
Édmond (1822–96) and Jules (1830–70) de Goncourt, brothers, novelists, critics and social commentators (see pages 214–15).
Paul Gavarni (Sulpice-Guillaume Chevalier) (1804–66), French lithographer and caricaturist.
The Portrait of Baudelaire *by Gustave Courbet was painted c. 1847. Alfred Bruyas (1821–77), son of a Montpellier financier, was the owner of one of the most important collections of contemporary art. He bequeathed his collection to the Musée Fabre, Montpellier.*

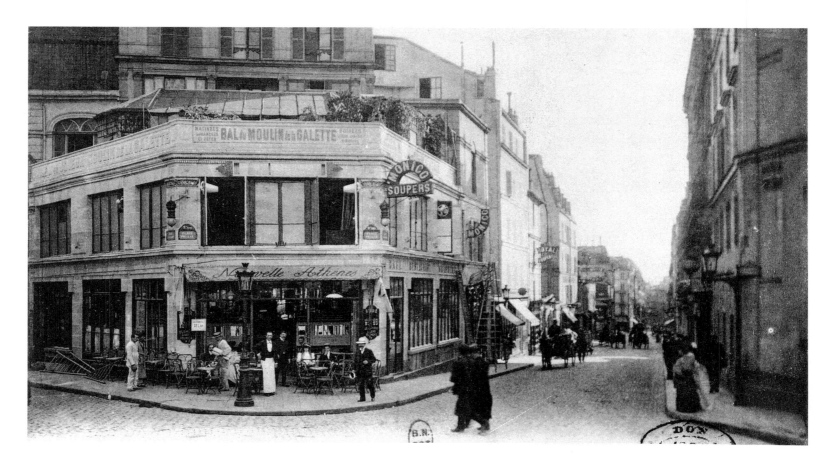

The Café de la Nouvelle-Athènes,
Rue Pigalle, Paris. Photograph.

CAMILLE DE SAINTE-CROIX

PORTRAITS D'HIER

"A Collegian and Manet, 1875"

December 15, 1909

I was a student in the second form of the Lycée Fontanes, and I was just rising fifteen years old.

One day when I arrived at school, a boy in my class handed me an imposing-looking envelope which had just been left with the caretaker of the rue du Havre. It was addressed to a young boy – me!

The school bell had not yet rung. I ran to my desk ahead of the class and teachers; then blushing with happy expectation, I split open the five seals which enclosed the letter. . . . It was just what I had been looking forward so much to for three whole days, without really daring to hope; it was Édouard Manet's reply to my present of a sonnet – a photograph of *A Good Glass of Beer*, with a signed dedication.

And this is how this marvellous piece of good luck came my way:

. . . . My parents were then living at the top of the rue des Martyrs, and my daily walk to and from school took me past the Place Clichy and the Trinité Quarter. In the summer I was able to see every day, after half past four, a group of young men sipping apéritifs on the terrace of the famous Café de la Nouvelle Athènes, in the centre of the Rond-Point Pigalle, all recognizable by the cut of their special jackets, flowing cravats and cloche hats. They were always gesticulating vigorously as they discussed the very latest ideas.

On these walks from the Lycée, my constant companion was a big lad, two years older than I, a day scholar in the philosophy class and nephew of a Montmartre sculptor.

*Camille de Sainte-Croix (1859–1915),
French writer and critic; an opponent of
General Boulanger.*

COLOURPLATE 54

He knew most of the painters of the Nouvelles Athènes from having met them while visiting his uncle's studio.

"They are 'Impressionists'," he explained to me.

This word, still in its infancy, was scarcely known in the lycées and I, being a curious little fellow, was already intrigued to know it and to know by sight these painters, who belonged to a set which was still only half-recognized.

My comrade quoted several names to me: Zandomeneghi, Caillebotte, Michel de la Haye, Paul Pouce, Paul Vogler, Hawkins, Jolibois known as "La Pomme," Forain, Flornoye, Pissarro, Lépine, etc., etc.

The catalogues of the annual Salons had not taught me to know a single one of these artists, who lived on the fringe of the Universal Exhibitions, and who disdained to chase after honours.

Their appearance pleased me no end, and without knowing anything about them, I instinctively imagined that they comprised the *élite* of artistic heroes, and found them marvellously attractive.

One Saturday evening, as we walked to and fro, idling away the eve of the holiday, my comrade suddenly pointed out to me a very smart gentleman, elegantly dressed in a blue jacket and bowler hat, and sporting a neatly trimmed beard.

This "gentleman," so perfectly bourgeois in appearance, so trim and tidy, had jumped out of a cab to join the group on the terrace, to shake hands here and there and exchange affectionate and rapid *bonjours*. Then, without sitting down, he returned to his carriage and disappeared round the corner of the rue Duperré.

Nothing remarkable about the appearance of this man who so quickly vanished! "*He* can't be one of them – an Impressionist – not that chap!" I exclaimed to my companion.

He drew himself up in a superior and condescending way.

"No, old boy! It's much more extraordinary than that. . . . That's Manet . . . Manet! Édouard Manet!"

This time, the better known name sounded a more familiar ring in my fourteen-year-old ears. I remembered a certain quarrel over him at home, between my parents and some friends, on the evening of the last private view at the Palais de l'Industrie.

To have seen, to have actually *seen* with my own eyes, a man who was so talked about – that was an event to be registered for ever in a school kid's mind!

The following Thursday, on my companion's recommendation, I found the opportunity to run over to a picture-dealer in the rue Le-Peletier, where a whole series of early Manet's were on sale.

There I saw *The Absinthe Drinker, The Spanish Singer* and *The Old Musician*. When I saw them I felt that painting would be something that I would come to love, if I could only see painting like this. That same evening, bubbling over with an enthusiasm which I kept to myself, I composed a few puerile verses in my room in the Lycée, and on the following day, risking a black mark for leaving school in the morning, I took my missive to Manet's concierge in the Quartier Europe. I did not expect too much; but contrary to all my expectations, what I have just now recounted came to pass. My little verses had amused the Master who compensated me for my schoolboy cheek by sending me, in the middle of class, a dedicated photograph with a charming little note inviting me to visit him on the following Thursday. When the skinny naïve little kid with an untidy mop of hair (me) was shown into the studio where Manet lived and worked in the rue de Saint-Pétersbourg (it was so modern and so uncluttered with bric-à-brac as to be almost British) this kindly man shook my hand, thus showing that he took me seriously and just because I was only fourteen years of age there was no occasion to tease me.

"Well, my boy, do you want to chuck up school? . . . Do you want to be a painter? . . . So soon?"

Federico Zandomeneghi (1841–1917), Italian painter, resident in Paris from 1874; Gustave Caillebotte (1848–94), French painter and art collector (see page 16); Paul Vogler (1852–1904), French landscape painter; Jean-Louis Forain (1852–1931), French painter and printmaker; Stanislaus Lépine (1835–92), landscape painter.

COLOURPLATES 2, 4, 9

"Oh, no . . . no. . . . I want . . . I just wanted . . . to meet you. . . . That's all."

"Ah, well and good but. . . ." and his gesture showed me that we hadn't really got much to say to each other. But then he thought again. "Wait a minute . . . stay a bit. Let's have a chat," and in a moment or two he was paying me the greatest attention. I suppose he no longer felt the need to lecture an obstinate kid and send him away disillusioned, with a flea in his ear, back to his school work and family.

In high spirits he spoke to me at length, as if he was speaking to an old friend. He spoke about the two words *art* and *study*, and what they should mean to someone growing up. Then, looking not unlike his self-portrait, *Manet with Palette* in the Pellerin Collection, in a yellow waistcoat and soft hat, he sat, in front of me, facing the light, while I remained standing. He presented to my keen gaze a high, smooth forehead, watchful eyes, deep-set beneath frowning eyebrows, a large, firm, straight nose, a delicate mouth under a bushy but well-tended moustache, and a long soft beard, parted in the middle. He held a pencil and sketch-pad in his hands and all the while he talked, he drew rapidly.

See page 251.

After talking a good hour, he offered me some little keepsake and said good-bye, inviting me – just like that – to come and see him the following Thursday morning, because my parents made no difficulties about letting me go out.

And that was all. I had had the courage to go there all right, but I didn't dare return.

Ten years later, a dear friend of my second youth, none other than that powerful and sensitive artist, Paul Pouce (who never had the opportunity of showing himself other than an incomparable sketcher), who was struck down by a cruel and violent illness just as his genius was reaching maturity (a few magnificent sketches hanging on the walls of friends' houses – Forain's, Dr. Duchastelet's, my own – are all that remains of his work), showed me a book of tiny sketches given to him by Édouard Manet, now dead, with whom, in company with Toulouse-Lautrec, he had worked – before both of them began haunting Forain's studio in the Faubourg Saint-Honoré.

Henri de Toulouse-Lautrec (1864–1901).

Now this book was the same sketch-book that the creator of *A Good Glass of Beer* was holding in his hands on that famous Thursday visit. Drawn in pencil I recognized myself, filling some twenty pages – quick sketches of me – at all angles – in my short jacket, sailor collar, with hair falling over my nose! I suddenly understood quite well why the Master had spoken to me so freely and intimately.

Photograph of Manet by Franck (from Manet's photograph album).

My precocious Parisian mug had interested him and it had seemed good enough to note down for some future composition. And it was to this end, no doubt, that he had entertained me so long with a thousand different things without me realizing it – so rapid and discreet was his pencilling. He had made me pose . . . pose in the fullest sense of the word.

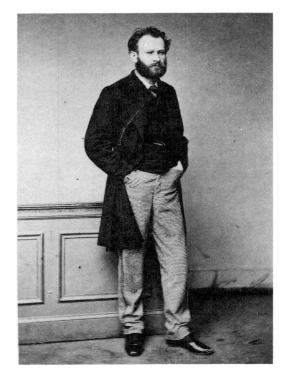

AMBROISE VOLLARD

RECOLLECTIONS OF A PICTURE DEALER

Manet and Venice

1936

Ambroise Vollard (1868–1939), French art dealer, born in St-Denis, Île de la Réunion. This account by the French painter Charles Toché, as recorded by Vollard, is the main source of information concerning Manet's trip to Venice in October 1875. The only known examples of Manet's Venetian paintings are the Grand Canal (Blue Venice) (Colourplate 69) and The Grand Canal, Venice, in a private collection.

One day at the Louvre I saw a visitor standing before Manet's *Olympia*, in whom I recognized the painter Charles Toché. I went up to him and reminded him that I had often heard him speak of his relations with Manet.

"How did you come to know him?" I asked.

"I was in Venice, eating an ice at the Café Florian, when the great painter, whose elegant figure was familiar to me, came and sat down near by. His wife was with him, and I was struck by her majestic bearing. Her sunshade fell down and I stooped to pick it up. Manet thanked me: 'I see you're a Frenchman. *Mon Dieu*, how this place bores me.' Madame Manet smiled at me. Her rosy childish face beamed from under an enormous hat. 'Édouard likes joking,' she said. 'He's playing the Parisian.'"

"M Toché, tell me about that famous picture of Manet's, *Grand Canal*."

"I shall not forget Manet's enthusiasm for that motif: the white marble staircase against the faded pink of the bricks of the façade, and the cadmium and greens of the basements. Oscillations of light and shade made by the passing barges in the rough water, that drew from him the exclamation, 'Champagne bottle-ends floating!' Through the row of gigantic twisted posts, blue and white, one saw the domes of the incomparable *Salute*, dear to Guardi. 'I shall put in a Gondola,' cried Manet, 'steered by a boatman in a pink shirt, with an orange scarf – one of those fine dark chaps like a Moor of Granada.' Some of the guests of the villa Medicis were listening to Manet from a neighbouring boat. At these words they sniggered. I heard the word 'pompier.'"

* * *

"When the picture was finished, I was really astounded. One could not imagine anything more true, better situated in the atmosphere. Replying to a remark of mine, 'It was not at school,' Manet said, 'that I learnt to construct a picture. On my first day at Couture's they gave me an antique to draw from. I turned it about in every direction. It seemed to me most interesting head downwards. Anyway, after two or three attempts I gave up trying to get anything out of the antique. But I learnt a great deal during my voyage to Brazil. I spent night after night watching the play of light and shade in the wake of the ship. During the day I watched the line of the horizon. That taught me how to plan out a sky.'"

"How did Manet paint? I remember Cézanne saying, 'Manet spatters his tones on to the canvas.'"

"That expresses it. It was not at all a linear process, but with rapid individual touches he scattered shadows, lights, reflections over the canvas with astonishing sureness, and his layout was made.

"I remember dining with him in a little restaurant opposite the Giudecca. The table was laid in an arbour covered with vines. A little opening in this arbour framed the lovely church of San Salvatore, whose pink tones contrasted with the glaucous green of the water and the black spindle-shapes of the gondolas. Manet observed and analysed the different colours taken on by each object as the light faded. He defined their values and told us how he would try to reproduce them, steeped in this ashy

Charles Toché (1851–1916) executed murals for the Château de Chenonceaux and the theatre at Nantes.

COLOURPLATE 69

Paul Cézanne (1839–1906).

twilight greyness. Suddenly he got up, and taking his paint-box and a little canvas, he ran down to the quay. There, with a few strokes of the brush, he set up the distant church."

"Any picture by Manet certainly suggests brush-strokes put down definitely, once for all."

"Wait a bit! That was what I thought before I had seen him at work. Then I discovered how he laboured, on the contrary, to obtain what he wanted. The *Grand Canal* itself was begun I know not how many times. The gondola and gondolier held him up an incredible time. 'It's the devil,' he said, 'to suggest that a hat is stuck firmly on a head, or that a boat is built of planks cut and fitted according to geometrical laws!'"

I could have listened all day to M Toché.

* * *

"In Venice I used to go and join him almost every day. The lagoons, the palaces, the old houses, scaled and mellowed by time, offered him an inexhaustible variety of subjects. But his preference was for out-of-the-way corners. I asked him if I might follow him in my gondola. 'As much as you like,' he told me. 'When I am working, I pay no attention to anything but my subject.' Now and then he would make a gesture of annoyance that set his boat rocking, and I would see his palette knife scraping away with ferocity. But all at once I would hear the refrain of a song, or a few notes whistled gaily. Then Manet would call out to me, 'I'm getting on, I'm getting on! When things are going well, I have to express my pleasure aloud.'"

"M Toché, how do you account for Manet, the bantering Parisian, the true *boulevardier*, having such a passion for Spain and Italy?"

"He liked Spain much the better of the two. 'Spain,' he said to me one day, 'is so simple, so grandiose, so dramatic with its stones and its green-black trees. Venice, when all is said, is merely scenery.'"

"But the great Venetian painters. . . ."

"One morning I was looking with him at the *Glory of Venice*, by Veronese, in the Ducal Palace. 'There's something about that that leaves one cold,' he said. 'So much useless effort, so much wasted space in it. Not a shadow of an emotion. I like the Carpaccios, they have the naïve grace of illuminations in missals. And I rank highest of all the Titians and Tintorettos of the *Scuola di San Rocco*. But I always come back, you know, to Velazquez and Goya.'"

"What did he think of Tiepolo?"

"Tiepolo irritated him. 'These Italians bore one after a time,' he would say, 'with their allegories and their *Gerusalemme Liberata* and *Orlando Furioso*, and all that noisy rubbish. A painter can say all he wants to with fruits or flowers, or even clouds.'

"I remember wandering with him round the stalls of the *Old Fish Market*, under the bridge of the Rialto. Manet was intoxicated by light. He bubbled over with delight at the sight of the enormous fish wth their silver bellies. 'That,' he cried 'is what I should have liked to paint if the Conseil Municipal of Paris had not refused my decorative scheme for the Hôtel de Ville. You know, I should like to be the St Francis of still-life.' Another time we went to the vegetable market. Manet, a slender figure in blue, his straw hat tilted to the back of his head, went striding over the heaps of provisions and vegetables. He stopped suddenly before a row of pumpkins, the kind that grows only on the shores of the Brenta. 'Turks' heads in turbans!' he cried. 'Trophies from the victories of Lepanto and Corfu!'

"When Manet had been working hard, he would set out, by way of relaxation, to 'discover' Venice. Madame Manet would accompany him, and they would wander through the most tortuous of the little streets, or, taking the first gondola that came, explore the narrow *canaletti*. Manet was mad on old tumble-down houses, with rags hanging from the windows, catching the light. He would stop to look at the handsome shock-headed

See page 166. This letter is usually dated 1879.

girls, bare-necked, in their flowered gowns, who sat at their doors stringing beads from Murano or knitting stockings of vivid colours. In the fishing quarter, at San Pietro di Castello, he would stop before the great piles topped with enormous eel-pots made of withies, that the light turned to amethyst. He marvelled at the children, burnt golden by the sun, shaking off their fleas on the crumbling steps of the old staircases and quarrelling among themselves, their faces smeared with polenta and water-melon. The afternoon would end up with visits to the second-hand dealers, in whose miserable booths there was no hint of the sumptuous antique shops that were to arise on the same sites fifty years later. Nothing delighted him so much as to ferret out an old piece of lace, a finely worked jewel, a valuable engraving."

* * *

"What a relaxation Venice must have been for Manet, after the busy life of Paris!"

"In Venice he thought of nothing but painting. What a number of plans he made that were never to be realized! There was that Sunday in September, for instance, when I accompanied him to Mestre, where regattas were being held in the lagoon. Each racing gondola, with its rowers clad in blue and white, seemed a fold of an immense serpent. Lying on the cushions of our boat, a rug over his knees, one hand dragging in the water, Manet, from under his wife's parasol, described to us the plan of a picture he would like to paint of this regatta. Manet, who was considered an extravagant innovator at the École des Beaux-Arts, had thought out this composition according to such classical rules that the statement he made of it to us would, I fancy, have delighted Poussin. I noted down with the greatest care the incomparable lesson that I had just heard.*

"This must be one of the last things Manet enjoyed in Venice. Not long afterwards he came to my room early one morning, and I was struck by his dejected air.

"'I have been recalled to Paris,' he told me. 'My life here was too pleasant, I suppose. Who knows what fresh worries await me over there?' I accompanied my delightful new friends to the station. On the way, Manet gazed once more, intently, at the Grand Canal, the rose-coloured palaces, the old weathered houses, the gigantic piles looking like bag-wigs as they emerged from the slight fog. Up to the moment when he got into the train, Manet said not a word."

"But you saw him again in Paris?"

"I did not come back to France till four years later. Then I went to see him in his studio in the rue de St-Pétersbourg. Everything there was of a monkish simplicity – not a useless piece of furniture, not a knick-knack, but everywhere the most brilliant studies on the walls and easels. At the end of the room, on the mantelpiece, a plaster cat, with a pipe in its mouth."

"Had not Manet another studio in the rue d'Amsterdam?"

"Yes, a most picturesque one, in a sunny courtyard. You came in by a vestibule whose walls were smothered in a profusion of sketches. On a number of little tables there were bunches of flowers arranged in water-bottles or ordinary tumblers. The well-known portrait of Antonin Proust stood on an easel. Studies of women in light-coloured dresses, with big hats on their heads, were ranged along the wooden staircase, painted red, which led to the studio proper. Sheets of paper, covered with strokes of charcoal or pastel, covered the floor. On the walls were some big pictures half begun. A horsewoman's black hat standing out from the white canvas, a horse's head with an anxious eye, a pink sunshade, and so forth. Like certain sketches by Velazquez and Goya, these gave me a sensation of vibration and of life that the finished picture does not always produce."

"Did you see Manet during the last years of his life?"

"A few weeks before his death I went to the rue d'Amsterdam. I found the great artist alone, sad and ill. 'I am working,' he said, 'because one must live.' When I assured him that all lovers of painting believed in him as much as ever, 'Splendid!' he replied. 'But alas! can faith without works be considered a sincere faith? It is true that my tailor admires me! And then there is Faure. How they slated me for the portrait I did of him as Hamlet! They said the left leg was too short. But when a figure is rushing forward, how can the two legs be like those of an infantryman standing at attention? And the sloping floor? By Jove, I'd like to know what the official drawing-masters would do to give the illusion of Hamlet running towards the spectators.' Manet had risen. He shrugged his shoulders, rammed his flat-brimmed hat on his head, and said to me, with a smile that drew up the corners of his moustache, 'Let's drop all that! We'll go and have something at Tortoni's.' He felt one of his pockets. 'Good!' he said, 'I have my sketch-book. There's always something to jot down in the street. Look here.' And he showed me a charming study of legs, pinned to the wall. 'A waiter was opening a syphon the other day, at the café. A little woman was going by. Instinctively she picked up her skirt.'"

*This is the note, which M Toché kindly allowed me to copy:

I. With a scene like this, so disconcerting and so complicated, I must first select the characteristic episode, delimit my picture by an imaginary frame. The most salient things here are the masts with their multi-coloured bunting, the green, white and red of the Italian flag, the dark, undulating line of the barges laden with spectators, and the arrow-like line of the black-and-white gondolas fading away into the distance, with, at the top of the picture, the line of the water, the goal set for the races and the ethereal islands.

II. I shall first try to distinguish the different values as they build themselves up logically according to their several planes in the atmosphere.

III. The lagoon, mirror of the sky, is the parvis of the barges and their passengers, of the masts, pennants, etc. It has its own colour – tints borrowed from the sky, the clouds, the crowd and the other objects reflected in it. There can be no question of wire-drawn lines in a moving thing such as this, but only of values which, rightly observed, will constitute the real volume, the unquestionable design.

IV. The gondolas, the various barges with their mainly sombre colouring, and their reflections, constitute the foundation I shall lay on my parvis of the water.

V. The figures, seated or gesticulating, dressed in dark or brilliant colours, their parasols, their kerchiefs, their hats, form the crenelations, of differing values, which will provide the necessary foil and give their true character to the planes and the gondolas which I shall see through them.

VI. The crowd, the competitors, the flags, the masts, will be built up into a mosaic of bright colours. I must try to catch the instantaneousness of the gestures, the shiver of the flags, the rocking of the masts.

VII. On the horizon, far up, the Islands. . . . The sails in the furthest distance will be merely hinted at in their delicate, accurate colouring.

VIII. Lastly, the sky, like an immense glittering canopy, will envelop the whole scene, playing its light over figures and objects.

IX. The painting must be light and direct. No tricks; and you will pray the God of good and honest painters to come to your aid.

ADOLPHE TABARANT

MANET, HISTOIRE CATALOGRAPHIQUE

Manet's 1876 Studio Exhibition

1931

Adolphe Tabarant (1863–1950), French art historian and author of two catalogues raisonnés of Manet's work: Manet: Histoire catalographique, *Paris 1931,* and Manet et ses oeuvres, *Paris 1947. The Tabarant archives are now in the Pierpont Morgan Library, New York. Manet's studio exhibition took place in the two weeks preceding the opening of the official Salon.*

Washing and *The Artist* were brutally rejected by the Jury of the 1876 Salon. "We have given Manet ten years to mend his ways. He is not doing so. Rejected!" declared one of the jury, applauded by all his colleagues except two, unexpectedly: Bonnat and Henner. Refusing any revision, Manet immediately withdrew his canvases and decided to call upon the public by having an exhibition of the rejected works in his own studio, in rue de St-Pétersbourg. The news immediately spread through Paris. One night, as the *Evènement* of April 16, 1876 put it, the daubers of the Nouvelle Athènes placed a large sign below the windows of Manet's studio bearing this inscription: *In competition with the Jury.*

Invitations to the exhibition were worded as follows: "*Be true to yourself and let others say what they will.*

"M Manet invites M . . . to do him the honour of coming to see the paintings rejected by the 1876 Jury, which will be exhibited in his studio, from April 15 – May 1, from 10–5, 4, rue de St-Pétersbourg, on the ground floor."

Invitations were sent out. Everyone was allowed into the famous studio. The papers (which were generally hostile) having given this exhibition the best possible publicity, the whole of Paris flocked to see it, and there was a positive crush at certain times of the day. Two policemen stood at the door. Paper was placed on a table in the ante-room, so that the visitors could, if they wanted, sign their names and, if the occasion arose, note down their comments. Among the first signatures were those of Ch Chaplin, Marcellin Pellet, the deputy for the Gard; Philippe Burty, Ernest Adam, Castagnary, Charles Bigot, Théodore de Banville, H Second, Théodore Duret, Th de Langeac, André Gill, Carrier-Belleuse, François and Leopold Flameng, Emile Bergerat, Robert de Liry, Régamey, Armand Silvestre, Paul de Saint-Victor, Camille Farcy, Emmanuel Gonzalès, Armand Gouzien. The lovely Méry Laurent came, brought by the painter Alphonse Hirsch. She did not yet know Manet. "But it's lovely," she exclaimed. Hidden behind a curtain, Manet heard her, and was delighted by this spontaneous tribute.

But soon the handful of paper was covered with signed or anonymous comments, or indeed ones bearing whimsical signatures, comments that were sometimes laudatory, sometimes offensive, sometimes preposterous, and worse.

PAGE 147, COLOURPLATE 76

Léon-Joseph Bonnat (1838(?)–1922), successful academic painter. He became a member of the Institut in 1881. He owned a large art collection.
Jean-Jacques Henner (1829–1905), painter. He had won the Prix de Rome in 1858, and a first-class medal at the Salon of 1878.

Charles Joseph Chaplin (1825–91), French painter and printmaker (see page 110); Théodore de Banville (1823–91) (see page 135); André Gill (1840–85), French caricaturist; Marie-Auguste Flameng (1843–93), French painter; Armand Silvestre (1837–1901), French author; Paul de Saint-Victor (1825–81), French critic; Alphonse Hirsch (1843–84), French painter. For Méry Laurent see page 289.

STÉPHANE MALLARMÉ

ART MONTHLY REVIEW

"The Impressionists and Édouard Manet"

September 1876

Without any preamble whatsoever, without even a word of explanation to the reader who may be ignorant of the meaning of the title which heads this article, I shall enter at once into its subject, reserving to myself either to draw my deductions, new from an art point of view, as the facts I relate present themselves or leave them to ooze out when and as they may.

Briefly, then, let us take a short glimpse backward on art history. Rarely do our annual exhibitions abound with novelty, and some few years back such years of abundance were still more rare; but about 1860 a sudden and a lasting light shone forth when Courbet began to exhibit his works. These then in some degree coincided with that movement which had appeared in literature, and which obtained the name of Realism; that is to say, it sought to impress itself upon the mind by the lively depiction of things as they appeared to be, and vigorously excluded all meddlesome imagination. It was a great movement, equal in intensity to that of the Romantic school, just then expiring under the hands of· the landscape painters, or to that later one whence issued the bold decorative effects of Henri Regnault, and it then moved on many a new and contemporaneous path. But in the midst of this, there began to appear, sometimes perchance on the walls of the Salon, but far more frequently and certainly on those of the galleries of the rejected, curious and singular paintings – laughable to the many, it is true, from their very faults, but nevertheless very disquieting to the true and reflective critic, who could not refrain from asking himself what manner of man is this? and what the strange doctrine he preaches? For it was evident that the preacher had a meaning; he was persistent in his reiteration, unique in his persistency, and his works were signed by the then new and unknown name of EDOUARD MANET. There was also at that time, alas! that it should have to be written in the past tense, an enlightened amateur, one who loved all arts and lived for one of them. These strange pictures at once won his sympathy; an instinctive and poetic foresight made him love them; and this before their prompt succession and the sufficient exposition of the principles they inculcated had revealed their meaning to the thoughtful few of the public many. But this enlightened amateur died too soon to see these, and before his favourite painter had won a public name.

That amateur was our last poet, Charles Baudelaire.

Following in appreciative turn came the then coming novelist Emile Zola. With that insight into the future which distinguishes his own works, he recognized the light that had arisen, albeit that he was yet too young to then define that which we today call Naturalism, to follow the quest, not merely of that reality which impresses itself in its abstract form on all, but of that absolute and important sentiment which Nature herself impresses on those who have voluntarily abandoned conventionalism.

In 1867 a special exhibition of the works of Manet and some few of his followers, gave to the then nameless school of recent painting which thus grew up, the semblance of a party, and party strife grew high. The struggle with this resolute intruder was preached as a crusade from the rostrum of each school. For several years a firm and implacable front was formed against its advance; until at length vanquished by its good faith and persistency, the jury recognized the name of Manet, welcomed it, and so far recovered from its ridiculous fears, that it reasoned and found it must

The original French text of Mallarmé's essay does not survive. About one month after the appearance of this article, Manet began work on his portrait of Mallarmé (Colourplate 78).

Henri Regnault (1843–71), French painter.

Alfred Le Petit, *Édouard Manet: King of the Impressionists.* Caricature in *Les Contemporains,* 16 June 1876.

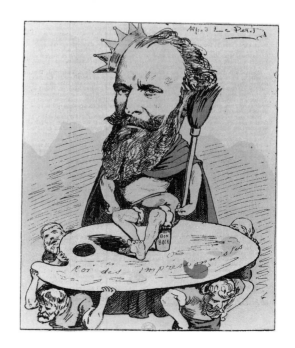

either declare him a self-created sovereign pontiff, charged by his own faith with the cure of souls, or condemn him as a heretic and a public danger.

The latter of these alternatives being nowadays definitively adopted, the public exhibition of Manet's works has of late taken place in his own studio. Yet, and notwithstanding all this, and in spite of concurrent Salons, the public rushed with lively curiosity and eagerness to the Boulevard des Italiens and the galleries of Durand-Ruel in 1874 and 1876, to see the works of those then styled the Intransigeants, now the Impressionists. And what found they there? A collection of pictures of strange aspect, at first view giving the ordinary impression of the motive which made them, but over beyond this, a peculiar quality outside mere Realism. And here occurs one of those unexpected crises which appear in art. Let us study it in its present condition and its future prospects, and with some attempt to develop its idea.

Manet, when he casts away the cares of art and chats with a friend between the lights in his studio, expresses himself with brilliancy. Then it is that he tells them what he means by Painting; what new destinies are yet in store for it; what it is, and how that it is from an irrepressible instinct that he paints, and that he paints as he does. Each time he begins a picture, says he, he plunges headlong into it, and feels like a man who knows that his surest plan to learn to swim safely is, dangerous as it may seem, to throw himself into the water. One of his habitual aphorisms then is that no one should paint a landscape and a figure by the same process, with the same knowledge, or in the same fashion; nor what is more, even two landscapes or two figures. Each work should be a new creation of the mind. The hand, it is true, will conserve some of its acquired secrets of manipulation, but the eye should forget all else it has seen, and learn anew from the lesson before it. It should abstract itself from memory, seeing only that which it looks upon, and that as for the first time; and the hand should become an impersonal abstraction guided only by the will, oblivious of all previous cunning. As for the artist himself, his personal feeling, his peculiar tastes, are for the time absorbed, ignored, or set aside for the enjoyment of his personal life. Such a result as this cannot be attained all at once. To reach it the master must pass through many phases ere this self-isolation can be acquired, and this new evolution of art be learnt; and I, who have occupied myself a good deal in its study, can count but two who have gained it.

Wearied by the technicalities of the school in which under Couture, he studied, Manet, when he recognized the inanity of all he was taught, determined either not to paint at all or to paint entirely from without himself. Yet, in his self-sought insulation, two masters – masters of the past – appeared to him, and befriended him in his revolt. Velazquez, and the painters of the Flemish school, particularly impressed themselves upon him, and the wonderful atmosphere which enshrouds the compositions of the grand old Spaniard, and the brilliant tones which glow from the canvases of his northern compeers, won the student's admiration, thus presenting to him two art aspects which he has since made himself the master of, and can mingle as he pleases. It is precisely these two aspects which reveal the truth, and give paintings based upon them living reality instead of rendering them the baseless fabric of abstracted and obscure dreams. These have been the tentatives of Manet, and curiously, it was to the foreigner and the past that he turned for friendly counsel in remedying the evils of his country and his time. And yet truth bids me say that Manet had no pressing need for this; an incomparable copyist, he could have found his game close to hand had he chosen his quarry there; but he sought something more than this, and fresh things are not found all at once; freshness, indeed, frequently consists – and this is especially the case in these critical days – in a co-ordination of widely scattered elements.

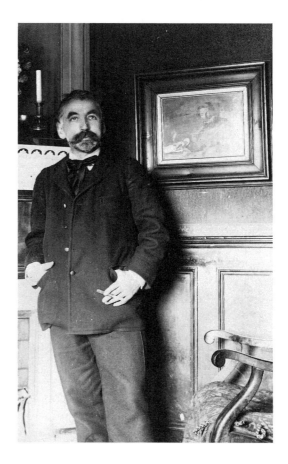

Photograph of Stéphane Mallarmé next to his portrait by Manet.

Photograph of Manet by J.M. Lopez.

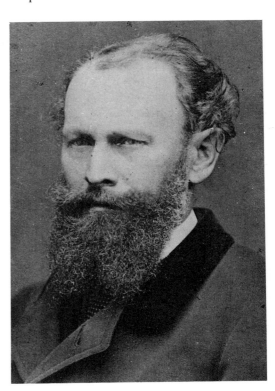

The pictures in which this reversion to the traditions of the old masters of the north and south are found constitute Manet's first manner. Now the old writers on art expressed by the word "manner," rather the lavish blossoming of genius during one of its intellectual seasons than the fact fathered, found, or sought out by the painter himself. But that in which the painter declares most his views is the choice of his subjects. Literature often departs from its current path to seek for the aspirations of an epoch of the past, and to modernize them for its own purpose, and in painting Manet followed a similarly divergent course, seeking the truth, and loving it when found, because being true it was so strange, especially when compared with old and worn-out ideals of it. Welcomed on his outset, as we have said, by Baudelaire, Manet fell under the influence of the moment, and, to illustrate him at this period, let us take one of his first works, *Olympia*; that wan, wasted courtesan, showing to the public, for the first time, the non-traditional, unconventional nude. The bouquet, yet enclosed in its paper envelope, the gloomy cat (apparently suggested by one of the prose poems of the author of the *Fleurs du Mal*) and all the surrounding accessories, were truthful, but not immoral – that is, in the ordinary and foolish sense of the word – but they were undoubtedly intellectually perverse in their tendency. Rarely has any modern work been more applauded by some few, or more deeply damned by the many, than was that of this innovator.

If our humble opinion can have any influence in this impartial history of the work of the chief of the new school of painting, I would say that the transition period in it is by no means to be regretted. Its parallel is found in literature, when our sympathies are suddenly awakened by some new imagery presented to us; and this is what I like in Manet's work. It surprised us all as something long hidden but suddenly revealed. Captivating and repulsive at the same time, eccentric and new, such types as he gave us were needed in our ambient life. In them, strange though they were, there was nothing vague, general, conventional or hackneyed. Often they attracted attention by something peculiar in the physiognomy of his subject, half hiding or sacrificing to those new laws of space and light he set himself to inculcate, some minor details which others would have seized upon.

Bye and bye, if he continues to paint long enough, and to educate the public eye – as yet veiled by conventionality – if that public will then consent to see the true beauties of the people, healthy and solid as they are, the graces which exist in the bourgeoisie will then be recognized and taken as worthy models in art, and then will come the time of peace. As yet it is but one of struggle – a struggle to render those truths in nature which for her are eternal, but which are as yet for the multitude but new.

The reproach which superficial people formulate against Manet, that whereas once he painted ugliness now he paints vulgarity, falls harmlessly to the ground, when we recognize the fact that he paints the truth, and recollect those difficulties he encountered on his way to seek it, and how he conquered them. *Luncheon on the Grass, The Execution of the Emperor Maximilian, A Table Corner, People at the Window, A Good Glass of Beer, A Corner of the Masked Ball, The Railway* and the two *Boaters* – these are the pictures which step by step have marked each round in the ladder scaled by this bold innovator, and which have led him to the point achieved in his truly marvellous work, this year refused by the Salon, but exhibited to the public by itself, entitled *Doing the Washing* – a work which marks a date in a lifetime perhaps, but certainly one in the history of art.

The whole of the series we have just above enumerated with here and there an exception, demonstrate the painter's aim very exactly; and this aim was not to make a momentary escapade or sensation, but by steadily endeavouring to impress upon his work a natural and general law, to seek out a type rather than a personality, and to flood it with light and air; and such air! air which despotically dominates over all else. And before

RIGHT *Doing the Washing*. 1874. 57 × 45¼″ (145 × 115 cm). © The Barnes Foundation, Merion Station, Pennsylvania.

COLOURPLATE 14

COLOURPLATES 18, 36, 54, 64, 61, 65, 66

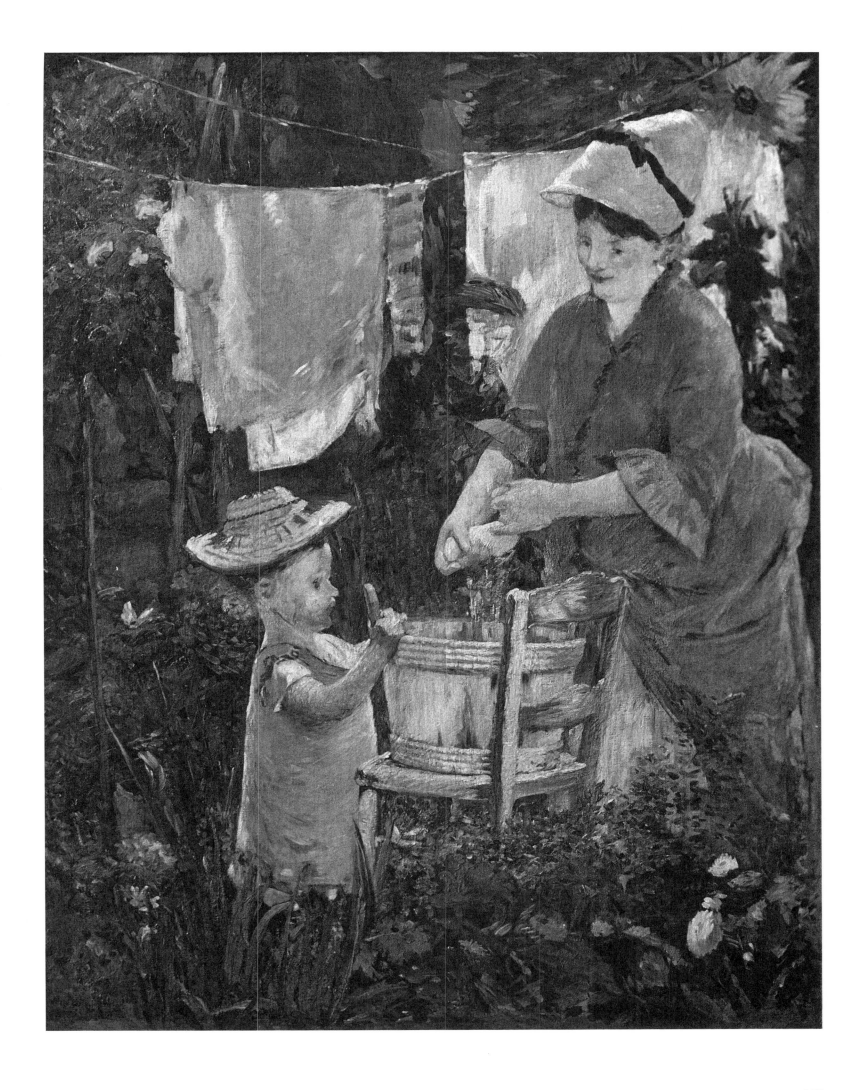

attempting to analyse this celebrated picture I should like to comment somewhat on that truism of tomorrow, that paradox of today, which in studio slang is called "the theory of open air" or at least on that which it becomes with the authoritative evidence of the later efforts of Manet. But here is first of all an objection to overcome. Why is it needful to represent the open air of gardens, shore or street, when it must be owned that the chief part of modern existence is passed within doors? There are many answers; among these I hold the first, that in the atmosphere of any interior, bare or furnished, the reflected lights are mixed and broken and too often discolour the flesh tints. For instance I would remind you of a painting in the Salon of 1873 which our painter justly called a *Rêverie*. There a young woman reclines on a divan exhaling all the lassitude of summer time; the jalousies of her room are almost closed, the dreamer's face is dim with shadow, but a vague, deadened daylight suffuses her figure and her muslin dress. This work is altogether exceptional and sympathetic.

Woman is by our civilization consecrated to night, unless she escapes from it sometimes to those open air afternoons by the seaside or in an arbour, affectionated by moderns. Yet I think the artist would be in the wrong to present her among the artificial glories of candle-light or gas, as at that time the only object of art would be the woman herself, set off by the immediate atmosphere, theatrical and active, even beautiful, but utterly inartistic. Those persons much accustomed, whether from the habit of their calling or purely from taste, to fix on a mental canvas the beautiful remembrance of woman, even when thus seen amid the glare of night in the world or at the theatre, must have remarked that some mysterious process despoils the noble phantom of the artificial prestige cast by candelabra or footlights, before she is admitted fresh and simple to the number of every day haunters of the imagination. (Yet I must own that but few of those whom I have consulted on this obscure and delicate point are of my opinion.) The complexion, the special beauty which springs from the very source of life, changes with artificial lights, and it is probably from the desire to preserve this grace in all its integrity, that painting – which concerns itself more about this flesh-pollen than any other human attraction – insists on the mental operation to which I have lately alluded, and demands daylight – that is space with the transparence of air alone. The natural light of day penetrating into and influencing all things, although itself invisible, reigns also on this typical picture called *Washing*, which we will study next, it being a complete and final repertory of all current ideas and the means of their execution.

Some fresh but even-coloured foliage – that of a town garden – holds imprisoned a flood of summer morning air. Here a young woman, dressed in blue, washes some linen, several pieces of which are already drying; a child coming out from the flowers looks at its mother – that is all the subject. This picture is life-size, though this scale is somewhat lower in the middle distance, the painter wisely recognizing the artificial requirements forced upon him by the arbitrarily fixed point of view imposed on the spectator. It is deluged with air. Everywhere the luminous and transparent atmosphere struggles with the figures, the dresses and the foliage, and seems to take to itself some of their substance and solidity; whilst their contours, consumed by the hidden sun and wasted by space, tremble, melt and evaporate into the surrounding atmosphere, which plunders reality from the figures, yet seems to do so in order to preserve their truthful aspect. Air reigns supreme and real, as if it held an enchanted life conferred by the witchery of art; a life neither personal nor sentient, but itself subjected to the phenomena thus called up by the science and shown to our astonished eyes, with its perpetual metamorphosis and its invisible action rendered invisible. And how? By this fusion or by this struggle ever continued between surface and space, between colour and air. Open air: – that is the beginning and end of the question we are now studying.

Aesthetically it is answered by the simple fact that there in open air alone can the flesh tints of a model keep their true qualities, being nearly equally lighted on all sides. On the other hand if one paints the real or artificial half-light in use in the schools, it is this feature or that feature on which the light strikes and forces into undue relief, according to an easy means for a painter to dispose a face to suit his own fancy and return to bygone styles.

The search after truth, peculiar to modern artists, which enables them to see nature and reproduce her, such as she appears to just and pure eyes, must lead them to adopt air almost exclusively as their medium, or at all events to habituate themselves to work in it freely and without restraint: there should at least be in the revival of such a medium, if nothing more, an incentive to a new manner of painting. This is the result of our reasoning, and the end I wish to establish. As no artist has on his palette a transparent and neutral colour answering to open air, the desired effect can only be obtained by lightness or heaviness of touch, or by the regulation of tone. Now Manet and his school use simple colour, fresh, or lightly laid on, and their results appear to have been attained at the first stroke, that the ever-present light blends with and vivifies all things. As to the details of the picture, nothing should be absolutely fixed in order that we may feel that the bright gleam which lights the picture, or the diaphanous shadow which veils it, are only seen in passing, and just when the spectator beholds the represented subject, which being composed of a harmony of reflected and ever-changing lights, cannot be supposed always to look the same, but palpitates with movement, light and life.

But will not this atmosphere – which an artifice of the painter extends over the whole of the object painted – vanish, when the completely finished work is as a repainted picture? If we could find no other way to indicate the presence of air than the partial or repeated application of colour as usually employed, doubtless the representation would be as fleeting as the effect represented, but from the first conception of the work, the space intended to contain the atmosphere has been indicated, so that when this is filled by the represented air, it is as unchangeable as the other parts of the picture. Then composition (to borrow once more the slang of the studio) must play a considerable part in the aesthetics of a master of the Impressionists? No; certainly not; as a rule the grouping of modern persons does not suggest it, and for this reason our painter is pleased to dispense with it, and at the same time to avoid both affectation and style. Nevertheless he must find something on which to establish his picture, though it be but for a minute – for the one thing needful is the time required by the spectator to see and admire the representation with that promptitude which just suffices for the connection of its truth. If we turn to natural perspective (not that utterly and artificially classic science which makes our eyes the dupes of a civilized education, but rather that artistic perspective which we learn from the extreme East – Japan for example) – and look at the sea-pieces of Manet, where the water at the horizon rises to the height of the frame, which alone interrupts it, we feel a new delight at the recovery of a long obliterated truth.

The secret of this is found in an absolutely new science, and in the manner of cutting down the pictures, and which gives to the frame all the charm of a merely fanciful boundary, such as that which is embraced at one glance of a scene framed in by the hands, or at least all of it found worthy to preserve. This is the picture, and the function of the frame is to isolate it; though I am aware that this is running counter to prejudice. For instance, what need is there to represent this arm, this hat, or that river bank, if they belong to someone or something exterior to the picture; the one thing to be attained is that the spectator accustomed among a crowd or in nature to isolate one bit which pleases him, though at the same time incapable of entirely forgetting the adjured details which unite the part to the whole, shall not miss in the work of art one of his habitual enjoyments, and whilst recognizing that he is before a painting half believes he sees the mirage of some natural scene. Some will probably object that all of these means have been more or less employed in the past, that dexterity – though not pushed far – of cutting the canvas off so as to produce an illusion – perspective almost conforming to the exotic usage of barbarians – the light touch and fresh tones uniform and equal, or variously trembling with shifting lights – all these ruses and expedients in art have been found more than once in the English school, and elsewhere. But the assemblage for the first time of all these relative processes for an end, visible and suitable to the artistic expression of the needs of our times, this is no inconsiderable achievement in the cause of art, especially since a mighty will has pushed these means to their uttermost limits.

But the chief charm and true characteristic of one of the most singular men of the age is, that Manet (who is a visitor to the principal galleries both French and foreign, and an erudite student of painting) seems to ignore all that has been done in art by others, and draws from his own inner consciousness all his effects of simplification, the whole revealed by effects of light incontestably novel. This is the supreme originality of a painter by whom originality is doubly forsworn, who seeks to lose his personality in nature herself, or in the gaze of a multitude until then ignorant of her charms.

Without making a catalogue of the already very considerable number of Manet's works, it has been necessary to mark the successive order of his pictures, each one of them an exponent of some different effort, yet all connected by the self-same theory; valuable also as illustrating the career of the head of the school of Impressionists, or rather the initiator of the only effective movement in this direction; and as showing how he has patiently mastered the idea of which he is at present in full possession. The absence of all personal obtrusion in the manner of this painter's inter-pretation of nature, permits the critic to dwell so long as he pleases on his pictures without appearing to be too exclusively occupied by one man; yet we must be careful to remember that each work of a genius, singular because he abjures singularity, is an artistic production, unique of its kind, recognizable at first sight among all the schools of all ages. And can such a painter have pupils? Yes, and worthy ones; notably Mademoiselle Eva Gonzalès, who to a just understanding of the master's standpoint unites qualities of youthfulness and grace all her own.

But his influence as from friend to friend is wider spread than that which the master exercises over the pupil, and sways all the painters of the day; for even the manner of those artists most strongly opposed in idea to his theory is in some degree determined by his practice. There is indeed no painter of consequence who during the last few years has not adopted or pondered over some one of the theories advanced by the Impressionists, and notably that of the open air, which influences all modern artistic thought. Some come near us and remain our neighbours; others, like M Fantin-Latour and the late M Chintreuil, painters without any common point of resemblance, while working out their own ideas have little by little attained to results often analogous to those of the Impressionists, thus creating between his school and that of academic painting a healthy, evident, true and conjunctive branch of art, at present upheld even by the generality of art lovers. But the Impressionists themselves, those whom cosy studio chats and an amicable interchange of idea have enabled to push together towards new and unexpected horizons, and fresh-formed truths, such as MM Claude Monet, Sisley and Pizzaro [*sic*], paint wondrously alike; indeed a rather superficial observer at a pure and simple exhibition of Impressionism would take all their works to be those of one man – and that man, Manet. Rarely have three workers wrought so much alike, and the reason of the similitude is simple enough, for they each endeavour to suppress individuality for the benefit of nature. Nevertheless the visitor would proceed from this first impression, which is quite right as a synthesis, to perceiving that each artist has some favourite piece of

Antoine Chintreuil (1814–73).

Alfred Sisley (1839–99).

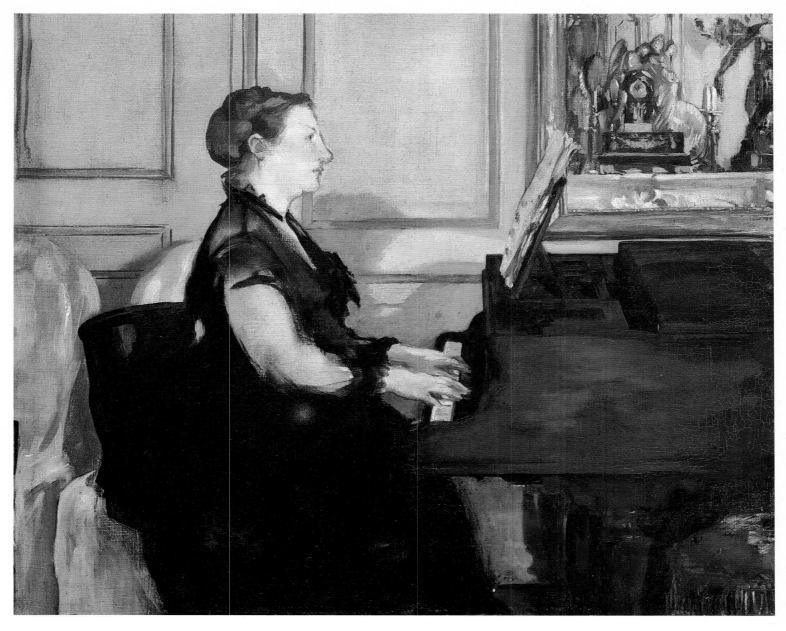

COLOURPLATE 38. *Madame Manet at the Piano*. 1867–8. 15 × 18¼″ (38 × 46.5 cm).
Musée d'Orsay, Paris.

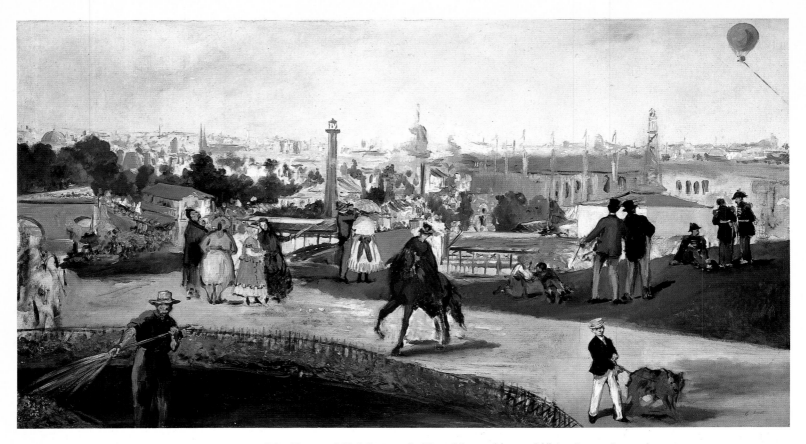

COLOURPLATE 39. *The Universal Exhibition of 1867*. 1867. 42½ × 77¼″ (108 × 196.5 cm).
Nasjonalgalleriet, Oslo.

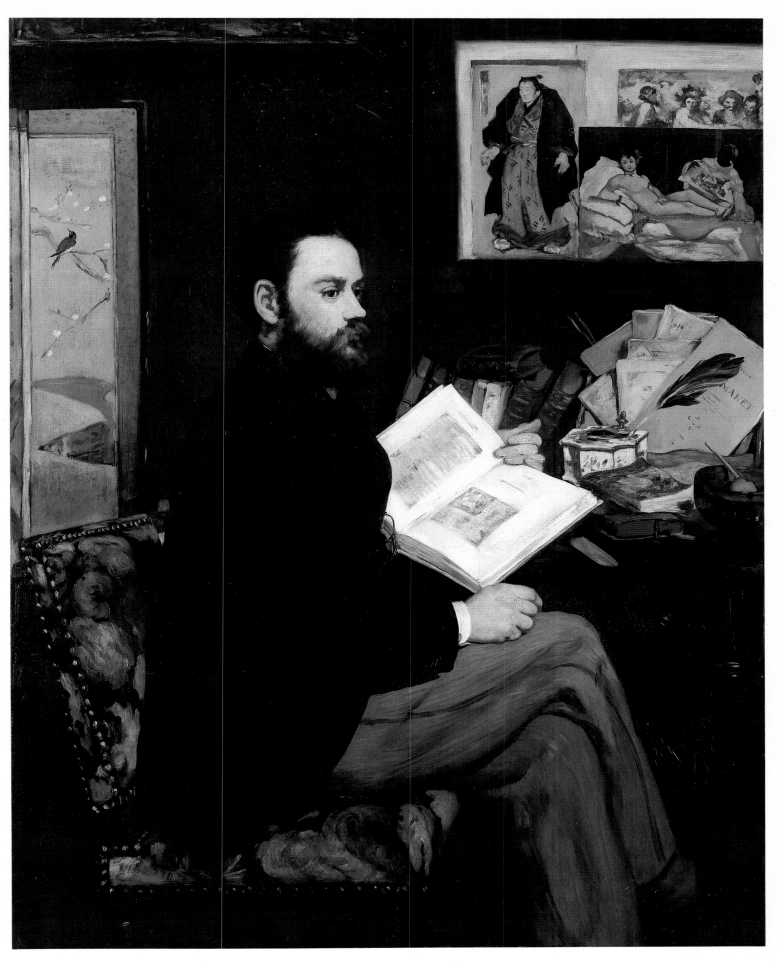

COLOURPLATE 40. *Portrait of Émile Zola*. 1868. 57½ × 45″ (146 × 114 cm).
Musée d'Orsay, Paris.

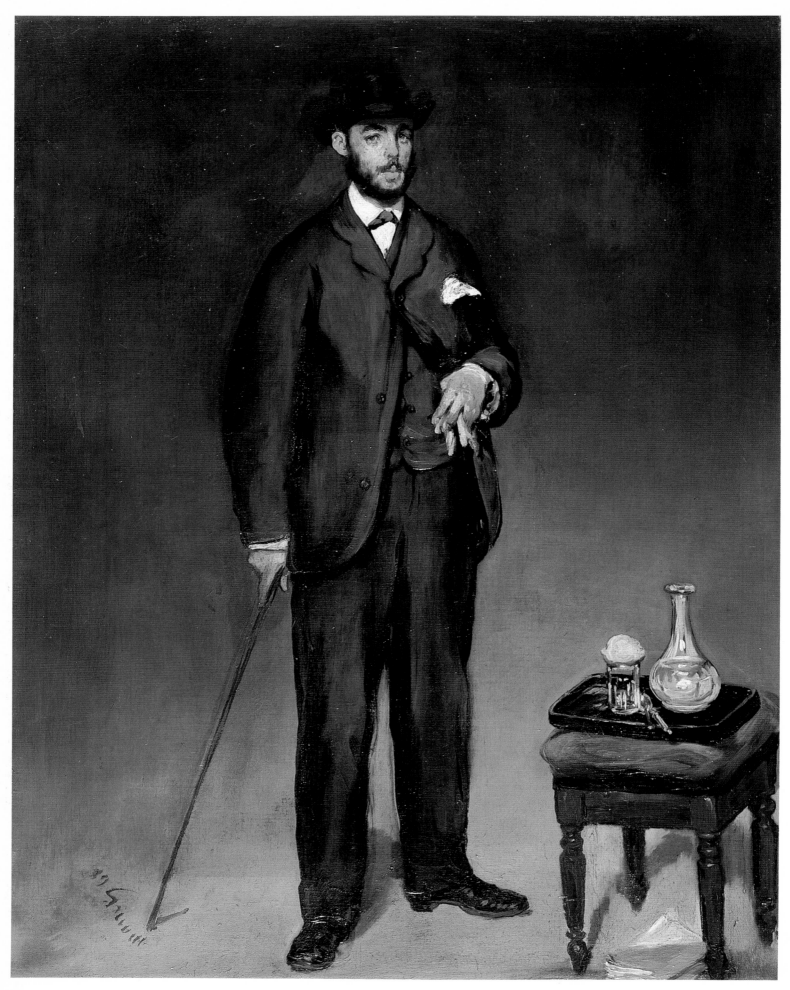

COLOURPLATE 41. *Portrait of Théodore Duret*. 1868. 17 × 13¾″ (43 × 35 cm).
Musée des Beaux-Arts de la Ville de Paris, Petit-Palais, Paris.

154

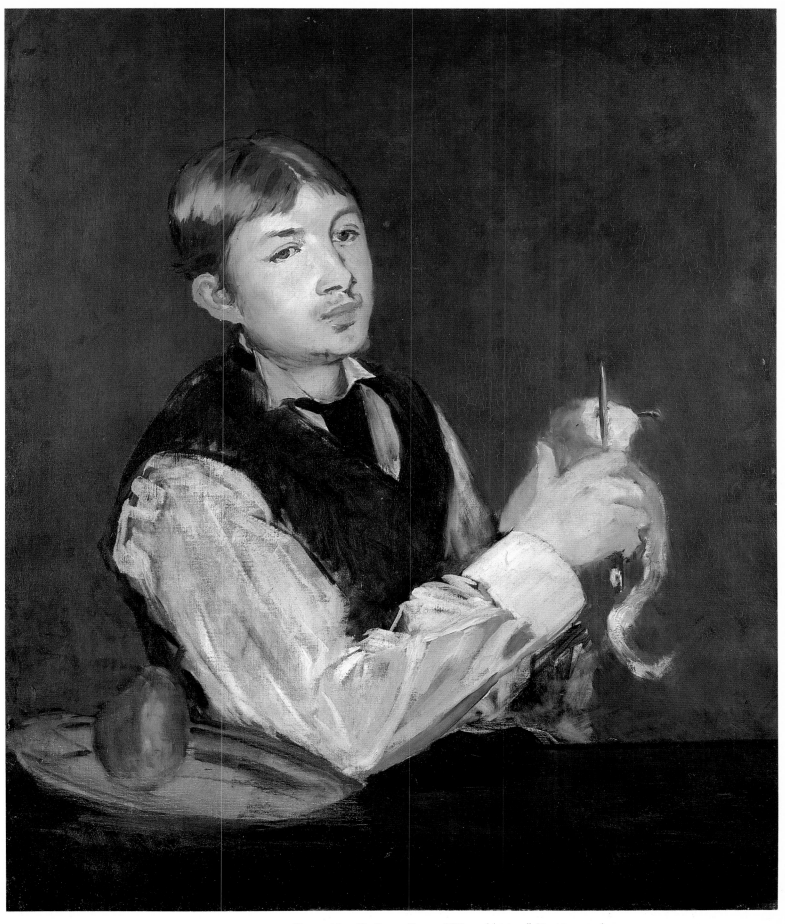

COLOURPLATE 42. *Young Man Peeling a Pear.* 1868. 33½ × 29″ (85 × 74 cm).
National Museum, Stockholm.

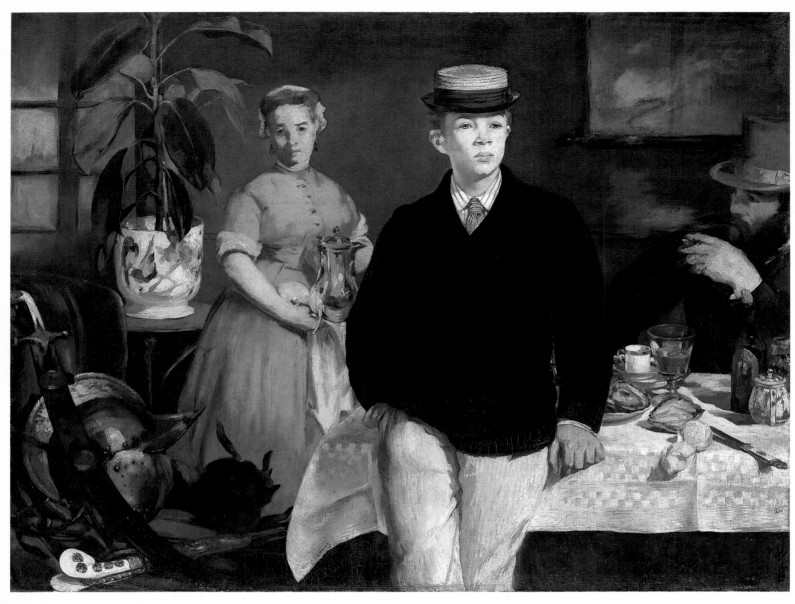

COLOURPLATE 43. *Luncheon in the Studio*. 1868. 46½ × 60½″ (118 × 154 cm).
Neue Pinakothek, Munich.

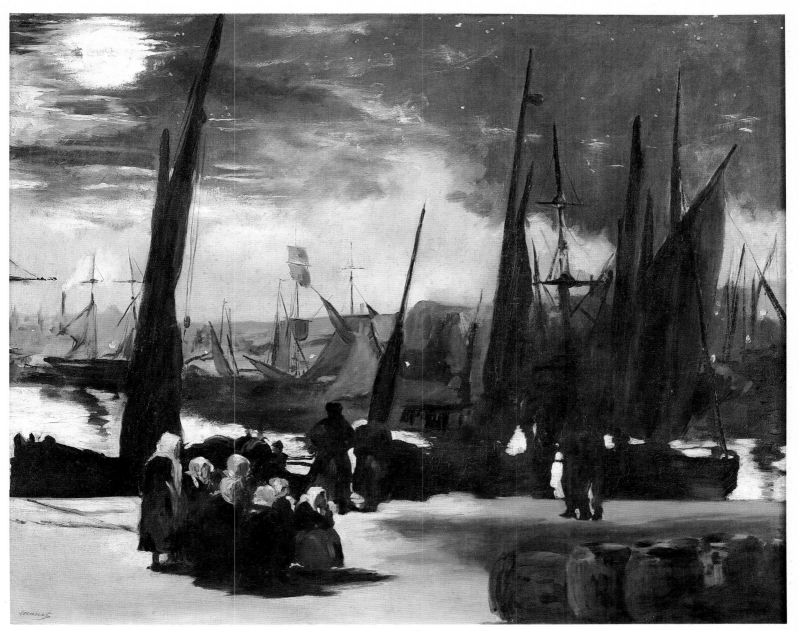

COLOURPLATE 44. *Moonlight over Boulogne Harbour.* 1869. 32¼ × 39¾″ (82 × 101 cm).
Musée d'Orsay, Paris.

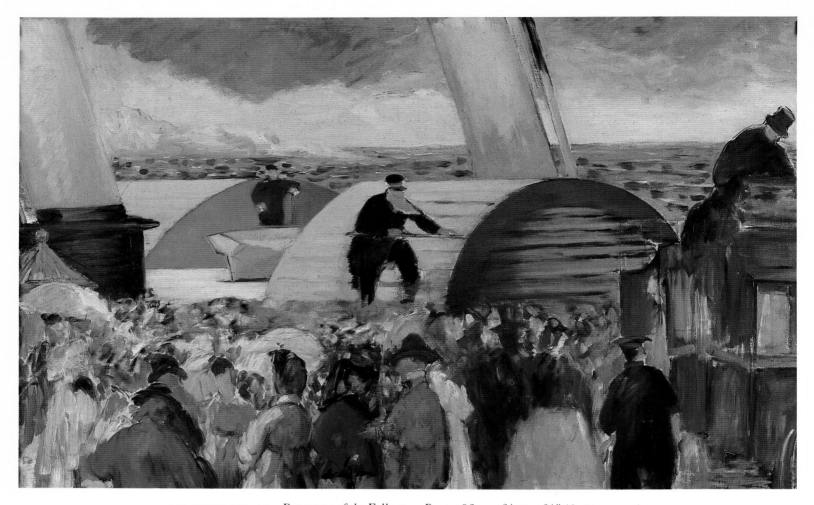

COLOURPLATE 45. *Departure of the Folkestone Boat.* 1869. 24¾ × 39¾" (63 × 101 cm).
Oskar Reinhart Collection, Winterthur.

execution analogous to the subject accepted rather than chosen by him, and this acceptation fostered by reason of the country of his birth or residence, for these artists as a rule find their subjects close to home, within an easy walk, or in their own gardens.

Claude Monet loves water, and it is his especial gift to portray its mobility and transparency, be it sea or river, grey and monotonous, or coloured by the sky. I have never seen a boat poised more lightly on the water than in his pictures, or a veil more mobile and light than his moving atmosphere. It is in truth a marvel. Sisley seizes the passing moments of the day; watches a fugitive cloud and seems to paint it in its flight; on his canvas the live air moves and the leaves yet thrill and tremble. He loves best to paint them in spring, "when the young leves on the lyte wode, waxen al with wille," or when red and gold and russet-green the last few fall in autumn; for then space and light are one, and the breeze stirring the foliage prevents it from becoming an opaque mass, too heavy for such an impression of mobility and life. On the other hand, Pizzaro [*sic*], the eldest of the three, loves the thick shade of summer woods and the green earth, and does not fear the solidity which sometimes serves to render the atmosphere visible as a luminous haze saturated with sunlight. It is not rare for one of these three to steal a march on Manet, who suddenly perceiving their anticipated or explained tendency, sums up all their ideas in one powerful and masterly work. For them, rather are the subtle and delicate changes of nature, the many variations undergone in some long morning or afternoon by a thicket of trees on the water's side.

The most successful work of these three painters is distinguished by a sure yet wonderfully rapid execution. Unfortunately the picture buyer, though intelligent enough to perceive in these transcripts from nature much more than a mere revel of execution, since in these instantaneous and voluntary pictures all is harmonious, and were spoiled by a touch more or less, is the dupe of this real or apparent promptitude of labour, and though he pays for these paintings a price a thousand times inferior to their real value, yet is disturbed by the afterthought that such light productions might be multiplied *ad infinitum*; a merely commercial misunderstanding from which, doubtless, these artists will have still to suffer. Manet has been more fortunate, and receives an adequate price for his work. As thorough Impressionists, these painters (excepting M Claude Monet, who treats it superbly) do not usually attempt the natural size of their subjects, neither do they take them from scenes of private life, but are before everything landscape painters, and restrict their pictures to that size easiest to look at, and with shut eye preserve the remembrance of.

With these, some other artists, whose originality has distanced them from other contemporary painters, frequently, and as a rule, exhibit their paintings, and share in most of the art theories I have reviewed here. These are Degas, Mademoiselle Berthe Morisot, (now Madame Eugène Manet,) and Renoir, to whom I should like to join Whistler, who is so well appreciated in France, both by critics and the world of amateurs, had he not chosen England as a field of his success.

The muslin drapery that forms a luminous, ever-moving atmosphere round the semi-nakedness of the young ballet dancers; the bold, yet profoundly complicated attitudes of these creatures, thus accomplishing one of the at once natural and yet modern functions of women, have enchanted M Degas, who can, nevertheless, be as delighted with the charms of those little washerwomen, who fresh and fair, though poverty-stricken, and clad but in a camisole and petticoat, bend their slender bodies at the hour of work. No voluptuousness there, no sentimentality here; the wise and intuitive artist does not care to explore the trite and hackneyed view of his subject. A master of drawing, he has sought delicate lines and movements exquisite or grotesque, and of a strange new beauty, if I dare employ towards his works an abstract term, which he himself will never employ in his daily conversation.

More given to render, and very succinctly, the aspect of things, but with a new charm infused into it by feminine vision, Mademoiselle Berthe Morisot seizes wonderfully the familiar presence of a woman of the world, or a child in the pure atmosphere of the sea-shore, or green lawn. Here a charming couple enjoy all the limpidity of hours where elegance has become artless; and there how pure an atmosphere veils this woman standing out of doors, or that one who reclines under the shade of an umbrella thrown among the grasses and frail flowers which a little girl in a clean dress is busy gathering. The airy foreground, even the furthermost outlines of sea and sky, have the perfection of an actual vision, and that couple yonder, the least details of whose pose is so well painted that one could recognize them by that alone, even if their faces, seen under the shady straw hats, did not prove them to be portrait sketches, give their own characteristics to the place they enliven by their visit. The air of preoccupation, of mundane care or secret sorrows, so generally character-istic of the modern artist's sketches from contemporary life, were never more notably absent than here; one feels that the graceful lady and child are in perfect ignorance, that the pose unconsciously adopted to gratify an innate sense of beauty is perpetuated in this charming water-colour.

The shifting shimmer of gleam and shadow which the changing reflected lights, themselves influenced by every neighbouring thing, cast upon each advancing or departing figure, and the fleeting combinations in which these dissimilar reflections form one harmony or many, such are the favourite effects of Renoir – nor can we wonder that this infinite complexity of execution induces him to seek more hazardous success in things widely opposed to nature. A box at the theatre, its gaily dressed inmates, the women with their flesh tints heightened and displayed by rouge and rice powder, a complication of effects of light – the more so when this scene is fantastically illuminated by an incongruous daylight. Such are the subjects he delights in.

All these various attempts and efforts (sometimes pushed yet farther by the intrepid M de Césane [sic] are united in the common bond of Impressionism. Incontestably honour is due to these who have brought to the service of art an extraordinary and quasi-original newness of vision, undeterred by a confused and hesitating age. If sometimes they have gone too far in the search of a novel and audacious subjects, or have misapplied a freshly discovered principle, it is but another canvas turned to the wall; and as a set off to such an accident they have attained a praiseworthy result, to make us understand when looking on the most accustomed objects the delight that we should experience could we but see them for the first time.

If we try to recall some of the heads of our argument and to draw from them possible conclusions, we must first affirm that Impressionism is the principal and real movement of contemporary painting. The only one? No; since the other great talents have been devoted to illustrate some particular phrase or period of bygone art; among these we must class such artists as Moreau, Puvis de Chavannes, etc.

At a time when the romantic tradition of the first half of the century only lingers among a few surviving masters of that time, the transition from the old imaginative artist and dreamer to the energetic modern worker is found in Impressionism.

The participation of a hitherto ignored people in the political life of France is a social fact that will honour the whole of the close of the nineteenth century. A parallel is found in artistic matters, the way being prepared by an evolution which the public with rare prescience dubbed, from its first appearance, Intransigeant, which in Political language means radical and democratic.

The noble visionaries of other times, whose works are the semblance of worldly things seen by unworldly eyes, (not the actual representations of real objects) appear as kings and gods in the far dream-ages of mankind;

Gustave Moreau (1826–98), Symbolist painter.

recluses to whom were given the genius of a dominion over an ignorant multitude. But today the multitude demands to see with its own eyes; and if our latter-day art is less glorious, intense and rich, it is not without the compensation of truth, simplicity and childlike charm.

At that critical hour for the human race when nature desires to work for herself, she requires certain lovers of hers – new and impersonal men placed directly in communion with the sentiment of their time – to loose the restraint of education, to let hand and eye do what they will, and thus through them, reveal herself.

For the mere pleasure of doing so? Certainly not, but to express herself, calm, naked, habitual, to those newcomers of tomorrow, of which each one will consent to be an unknown unit in the mighty numbers of an universal suffrage, and to place in their power a newer and more succinct means of observing her.

Such, to those who can see in this the representative art of a period which cannot isolate itself from the equally characteristic politics and industry, must seem the meaning of the manner of painting which we have discussed here, and which although marking a general phase of art has manifested itself particularly in France.

Now in conclusion I must hastily re-enter the domain of aesthetics, and I trust we shall thoroughly have considered our subject when I have shown the relation of the present crisis – the appearance of the Impressionists – to the actual principles of painting – a point of great importance.

In extremely civilized epochs the following necessity becomes a matter of course, the development of art and thought having nearly reached their far limits – art and thought are obliged to retrace their own footsteps, and to return to their ideal source, which never coincides with their real beginnings. English Preraphaelitism, if I do not mistake, returned to the primitive simplicity of mediaeval ages. The scope and aim (not proclaimed by authority of dogmas, yet not the less clear), of Manet and his followers is that painting shall be steeped again in its cause, and its relation to nature. But what, except to decorate the ceilings of saloons and palaces with a crowd of idealized types in magnificent foreshortening, what can be the aim of a painter before everyday nature? To imitate her? Then his best effort can never equal the original with the inestimable advantages of life and space. – "Ah no! this fair face, that green landscape, will grow old and wither, but I shall have them always, true as nature, fair as remembrance, and imperishably my own; or the better to satisfy my creative artistic instinct, that which I preserve through the power of Impressionism is not the material portion which already exists, superior to any mere representation of it, but the delight of having recreated nature touch by touch. I leave the massive and tangible solidity to its fitter exponent, sculpture. I content myself with reflecting on the clear and durable mirror of painting, that which perpetually lives yet dies every moment, which only exists by the will of Idea, yet constitutes in my domain the only authentic and certain merit of nature – the Aspect. It is through her that when rudely thrown at the close of an epoch of dreams in the front of reality, I have taken from it only that which properly belongs to my art, an original and exact perception which distinguishes for itself the things it perceives with the steadfast gaze of a vision restored to its simplest perfection."

ANTONIN PROUST

ÉDOUARD MANET: SOUVENIRS

Manet and Stéphane Mallarmé

1913

Manet had friendships which largely consoled him for these rebuffs. I am speaking here of his friendship with Stéphane Mallarmé, who was shy and modest. Armed with the sublime instrument of poetry, a lover of fine prose, passionate about the rhyming harmony of pure diction, Mallarmé pursued his dream – the training of an imagination which delighted in everything, without being satisfied with anything.

The first time I saw him was in Manet's studio. At that moment, he had the full beauty of youth. His eyes were large, his straight nose stood out above a thick moustache which his lips underlined with a light stroke. He had a prominent forehead beneath a shock of hair. His beard tapered to a sharp point, rising above a dark cravat rolled around his neck.

There was talk of the poems of Edgar Poe, which he had translated; Manet was working on the illustrations. Mallarmé's voice was slow, resonant. Word followed word, chosen with great care for the right tone. His gestures were broad.

Lettered in the best sense of the word, passionate about philology, he revelled in evoking the pagan world, in reconstituting vanished Olympias, and he loved to cast his thought in classical sobriety, but with such a personal turn that a single one of his pages, when one can understand it, says more than volumes produced by the fecundity which finds such favour in our age.

He was supremely kind. As is well known, he taught English at the Collège Rollin, then at the Lycée Condorcet. Previously, he had done the same at the lycée in Avignon, after having taught in Tournon. During his stay in Provence, he was asked by the magistrates of Aix to act as interpreter for a clergyman who had been arrested for vagrancy. What had

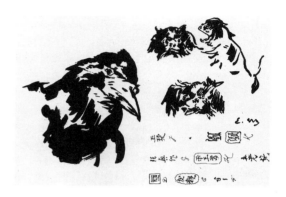

Manet probably met Stéphane Mallarmé in 1873, the year of the poet's arrival in Paris. (See also pages 132 and 144.)

Like Charles Baudelaire, whom he greatly admired, Mallarmé translated a number of the works of the American writer Edgar Allan Poe. The Raven, *the poem for which Manet had produced lithographic illustrations, was published in 1875. Mallarmé and Manet also worked on a projected publication of* Annabel Lee.

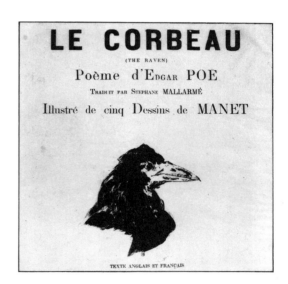

The Raven. 1875. Title-sheet for Stéphane Mallarmé's translation of Edgar Allan Poe's poem. Transfer lithograph?, 6¼ × 6″ (16.2 × 15.2 cm).

TOP *Bust of a Raven and Small Dogs.* 1875. From *The Raven.* Transfer lithograph?, 10 × 12½″ (25 × 32 cm).

LEFT *Under the Lamp.* 1875. From *The Raven.* Transfer lithograph?, 10¾ × 15″ (27.3 × 37.8 cm).

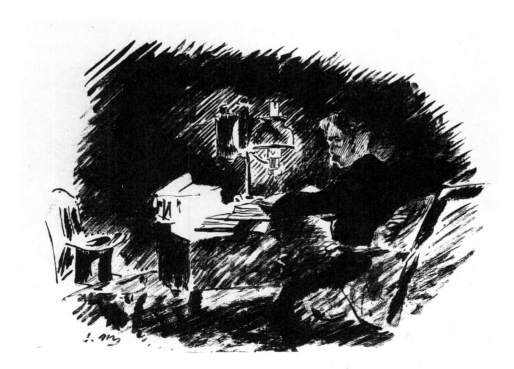

this clergyman done? He had committed the crime of embarking on French soil not knowing a word of our language.

Fleeced by hotel owners – the language of money is at everyone's disposal – he had arrived in Aix completely penniless. But the countryside was beautiful, the nights star-filled, he had decided to take up his abode in the open air, which is prohibited by the customs of civilized nations. He waited patiently for his family, whom he had alerted, to send the necessary subsidy. Questioned, then arrested by the uncomprehending police, he had appeared before judges who were as ignorant of English as the police. These judges asked Mallarmé whether he would get them out of difficulty. He gladly agreed.

"It is impossible," he said, "to conceive of anyone more unworldly and at the same time more inept than my client, but his answers were imbued with such a tone of honesty that I began to plead his case like a born lawyer. He was acquitted and released. I took him into my home and succeeded, not without difficulty, in getting him to accept the loan he needed.

"He promptly paid me back on his return to London, and every year, on the anniversary of what I call my 'counsel's speech,' I received a gift of flowers. One year, the flowers did not arrive, the anniversary passed over in silence. That saddened me."

A volume would not suffice to list all the good actions this superior being has scattered on his way, with apostolic simplicity and discretion. Furthermore, when Stéphane Mallarmé allowed himself such confidences, it was in the intimate circle of his friends.

He was very fond of Manet. Here is a letter he wrote to him from his beloved retreat at Valvins, whence he liked to go to Fontainebleau to pay homage to Primaticcio's women, whose tapering legs and eloquent foreshortenings he loved.

My dear Manet,

For days now I have been wanting to hear from you, but laziness and the old confidence I used to have in your health delayed my letters. The information I got from rue de St-Pétersbourg two or three days after your departure, which seemed to me to occur in excellent conditions, immediately reassured me vis-à-vis the absurd piece of news of a relapse, which appeared in various papers. I didn't even want to write to you, so as not to have seemed to have believed it all for a moment.

How have you been these last two months? I'd love a word from you. Is the fresh air doing you more good than last year? Are you working away quietly? Already I can see several vivid garden scenes on the easels, on my first visit to the studio.

Nothing new here. I cover several sheets of paper in the morning and slip into the yawl or drop anchor during the inevitable afternoon bad weather. . . . In a word, the usual old Valvins, from which I shall bring back a store of strength and freshness of spirit.

Thinking of you who had done so the other year, I re-read Jean-Jacques Rousseau's *Confessions*. Yes, it's a wonderful book.

My dear friend, there's our usual bit of chit-chat, with the advantage that I am not rushing off to teach; and the disadvantage that I am not seeing you.

Your friend,
Stéphane Mallarmé

Monday (I'm not dating my letter, not daring to consult the calendar and know that I have so few good days left.)

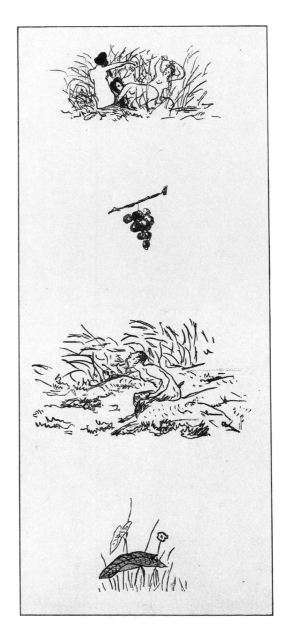

Afternoon of a Faun. 1876. Wood engraving for an edition of the poem by Stéphane Mallarmé. British Museum.

Rousseau's Confessions, *written between 1767 and 1770, were published posthumously in 1782.*

ÉMILE ZOLA

VIESTNIK EUROPI

"Paris Letter"

June 14–16, 1879

Zola's review of the 1879 Paris Salon was published in Russian translation in Viestnik Europi. *Both the* Revue politique et littéraire *and* Le Figaro *published one paragraph of the review in French, mistakenly substituting Manet's name for that of Monet. Zola immediately wrote a placatory letter to Manet, who admitted to having been deeply hurt by the criticisms he had read in the French extracts of the review. Zola's essay seems to mark a growing disenchantment with the work of Manet and the Impressionists.*

The Impressionists have introduced *plein air* painting, the study of the changing effects of nature according to the myriad conditions of time of day and weather. Among them it is believed that Courbet's fine methods can produce only magnificent pictures painted in the studio. They push the analysis of nature further, to the decomposition of light, to the study of the air in movement, of the nuances of colour, the random vibrations of light and shade, all the optical phenomena which make a horizon so mobile and difficult to render. It is hard to grasp the revolutionary implications of the mere fact of painting in the open, when one must reckon with the flow of the air, instead of shutting oneself up in a studio where a cold, well-balanced light comes in through a north-facing window. It is the final blow for classical and romantic painting and, what is more, it signifies the Realistic movement, launched by Courbet, freed from the shackles of craftsmanship and seeking the truth in the myriad effects of the play of light.

I have not named Édouard Manet, who was the leader of the group of Impressionist painters. His pictures are exhibited at the Salon. He carried on the movement after Courbet, thanks to his perceptive eye, so expert at discerning the right tones. His long struggle against public bafflement is explained by the difficulty he finds in execution – I mean that his hand is not the equal of his eye. He has not been able to forge himself a technique; he has remained the enthusiastic novice who always sees exactly what is going on in nature but who is not confident of being able to translate his impressions in a thorough and definitive fashion. That is why, when he starts out, one never knows how he will reach his goal, nor indeed if he will reach it at all. He works blind. When a painting succeeds, it is outstanding: absolutely true, and of a rare skilfulness; but he does sometimes lose his way – and then his canvases are flawed and uneven. In a word, for fifteen years now we have seen no painter more subjective. If his technique equalled the soundness of his perceptions, he would be the greatest painter of the second half of the nineteenth century.

Actually, all the Impressionist painters sin through technical inadequacy. In the arts as in literature, form alone supports new ideas and new methods. To be a talented man, one has to realize what is alive within one, otherwise one is just a pioneer. The Impressionists, in my view, are just that. At one point they had placed great hope in Monet; but he seems exhausted by over-rapid production; he is content with the approximate; he does not study nature with the passion of a true creator. All these artists are too easily satisfied. Wrongly, they disdain the solidity of works pondered upon at length; this is why one may fear that they are merely pointing the way to the great artist of the future whom the world is waiting for.

It is true that clearing the ground for the future is already honorable, providing one happens to have found the right way. Thus there is nothing more characteristic than the influence of the Impressionist painters – rejected each year by the Jury – when it is exercised upon those painters with deft techniques who are conspicuous in the Salon each year.

Therefore, let us examine the official exhibition from this point of view. This year's winners, namely the painters upon which the critics concentrate, and which attract the public, are Bastien-Lepage, Duez, Gervex; these gifted artists owe their success to the application of the naturalist method in their painting. . . .

This will be my conclusion, since it is pointless to list new names and prolong this discussion of the Salon. I have wanted simply to use certain examples to show that the triumph of Naturalism is making increasing headway in painting as in literature. Today success crowns those particular young painters who have broken with the establishment and who appear as innovators vis-à-vis those masters who have outlived their day. The way is clear for the painter of genius.

The French painters Jules Bastien-Lepage (1848–84), Ernest-Ange Duez (1843–96) and Henri Gervex (1852–1929).

J.K. HUYSMANS

L'ART MODERNE

"Salon Review of 1879"

1883

Joris-Karl Huysmans (1848–1917), novelist and critic. During the 1870s and early 1880s, as a disciple of Émile Zola, Huysmans was preoccupied with Realist depictions of modern life. His novel À Rebours (Against Nature), *published in 1884, was to establish his reputation as a "decadent" writer.*

This year Manet has had his two canvases accepted. One, entitled the *Conservatory*, represents a woman seated on a green bench, listening to a gentleman who leans over the back of the bench; on all sides are tall plants, and on the left some red flowers. The woman, a bit awkward and thoughtful, is dressed in a gown which seems made with great strokes, rapidly – yes indeed, go to see it – and superbly executed; the man, bare-headed, the light playing over his forehead, sparkling here and there, touching the hands boldly drawn in a few strokes, holds a cigar. Posed this way, in a casual conversation, the woman is truly beautiful; she is a lively flirt. The air moves, the figures are marvellously projected in this green envelope which surrounds them. This is a most attractive modern work, a battle engaged and won against the academic conventions of sunlight, which is never studied from nature.

In the Conservatory (Colourplate 96) is a double portrait of two of Manet's friends, M and Mme Jules Guillemet, owners of a shop on the rue du Faubourg Saint-Honoré. Mme Guillemet, an American, was renowned for her elegant attire.

His other canvas, *Boating*, is just as unusual. The bright blue water continues to exasperate a number of people. Water isn't that colour? I beg your pardon, it is, at certain times, just as it has green and grey hues, just as it contains lavender, and slate-grey and light-buff reflections at other times. One must make up one's own mind to look about. And there lies one of the great errors of contemporary landscape painters who, coming upon a river with a preconceived formula, do not establish between it, the sky reflected in it, the position of the banks which border it, the time and season as they are at the moment they are painting, the necessary accord which nature always establishes. Manet has never, thank heavens, known those prejudices stupidly maintained in the academies. He paints, by abbreviations, nature as it is and as he sees it. The woman, dressed in blue, seated in a boat cut off by the frame as in certain Japanese prints, is well placed, in broad daylight, and her figure energetically stands out against the oarsman dressed in white, against the vivid blue of the water. These are indeed pictures the like of which, alas, we shall rarely find in this tedious Salon.

Manet painted Boating (Colourplate 66) *at Argenteuil during the family summer holiday in 1874 at Gennevilliers. Manet and Claude Monet saw much of each other during this two-month period.*

Stop, *In the Conservatory*. Caricature in *Le Journal Amusant*, 24 May 1879. British Library.

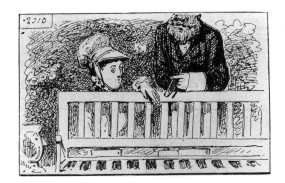

ÉDOUARD MANET

Letter to the Prefect of the Seine

1879

Monsieur le Préfet,

I have the honour to submit for your approval the following project for the decoration of the Municipal Council Chamber of the new Hôtel de Ville of Paris:

To paint a series of pictures representing *The Guts of Paris* (if I may use the expression so popular today and which illustrates my idea very well) with the different guilds [*corporations*] in their own surroundings – the public and commercial life of today, I would include the Paris markets, the Paris railways, Paris bridges, Paris tunnels, Paris race courses and public gardens.

For the ceiling there would be a gallery, around which would be shown, in appropriate action, all the men alive today who have contributed in a civic capacity to the grandeur and richness of Paris.

Please accept, etc.
Édouard Manet,
artist-painter, born in Paris,
77 rue d'Amsterdam

Manet's letter proposed a decorative scheme for the new Paris town hall (the earlier building had been destroyed during the Commune). Le Ventre de Paris was also the title of one of Zola's novels (1873), set in Les Halles, the great provision market of Paris.

CHARLES CROS

"Transition"

1879

Charles Cros (1842–88), poet and inventor, friend of Nina de Callias (see page 286). Cros dedicated his poem Transition to Manet. His La Fleuve, illustrated with eight etchings by Manet, had been published in 1874.

TO ÉDOUARD MANET

The wind, mild harbinger of spring's assault,
Casts a green mist of buds among the boughs.
The boisterous wind, the sun, the lull it brought,
Woods black on skyline, snow in whitened strips,
Alternate. Nature's seventeen again.
A young girl, fidgety, swinging her hips,
Laughs, cries, as sudden whim allows.

Springtime not yet, but winter springtime kissed.
Your soul, beloved, has these mingled hours.
The branches, black, are full of a green mist.
Harsh words and sorry ones, like sun and showers,
Cease on your lips, half-opened eglantine,
As I kiss them. So do the sudden showers
Melt, and the green's enamelled with gay flowers.

Your poutings, at my kisses, change to laughter,
As snow, pale lingerer, melts quite away
In sun's triumphant warmth. And briefly after,
Your eyes, which darted me a panther's ray,
Are gentle. Dearest, your anger's borne aloft
Just as the cold snow-laden wind has dropped.
The evening, and your cheek, are flushed and soft.

Under the Arch of the Bridge. 1874.
From *The River* by Charles Cros.
Etching and aquatint, 4½ × 6"
(11.6 × 15.5 cm).

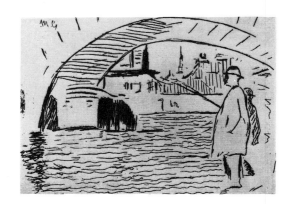

COMTE GASTON DE BEAUPLAN

Letter to Manet on "Maximilian"

1879

*Gaston de Beauplan, theatre manager.
The exhibition of Manet's painting* The
Execution of Maximilian *(Colourplate
36) in New York and Boston was organized
by the singer Émilie Ambre and her manager.
Plans to take the painting to Chicago were
cancelled due to lack of public interest.*

Clarendon-hotel, New York
November 30, [1879]

Monsieur Manet,
Last Saturday night, my dear friend, we had the press reception.
Everything went well, and we should be very pleased. A young man from
Alsace, whom I had met during the voyage, had agreed to join me, and
gave most intelligent assistance with receiving my guests. The light was
very good, the room well-arranged, the buffet tempting: and the painting,
well-varnished, seen to great effect. Of 120 invitations sent, I had about
fifty guests. Some reporters will probably come on Monday or Tuesday.
Everyone stayed at great length to admire the work. The general
impression was one of astonishment and admiration. . . . The effect
produced must have been great indeed for these journalists (who *all*
wanted chiefly to know the dimensions of the painting) to have stayed so
long in admiring it from all points of view. Three American painters,

*The Execution of the Emperor
Maximilian.* 1867. 77⅛ × 102¼″
(196 × 259.8 cm). Courtesy,
Museum of Fine Arts, Boston
(Gift of Mr and Mrs Frank Gair
Macomber). This is the first of
the series of Maximilian
canvases; the others are in the
National Gallery, London, Ny
Carlsberg Glyptotek,
Copenhagen and the Kunsthalle,
Mannheim (Colourplate 36). See
page 103.

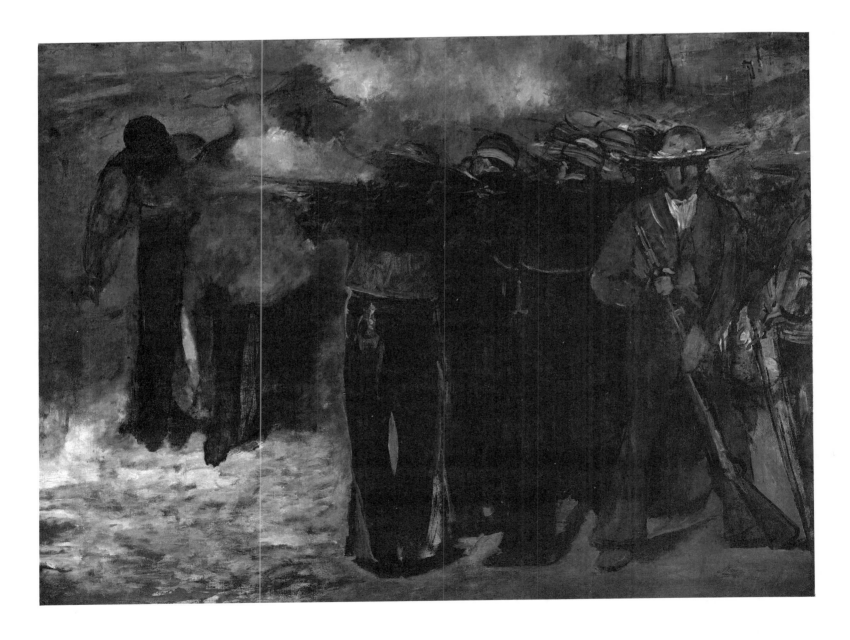

whom the critic on the *Herald* had suggested I invite, were ardent admirers and promised me they would speak highly of the interest and excellence of the painting everywhere. "How casually it is painted," they kept saying. . . . In a word, an excellent, an exquisite evening. This morning, Sunday, 500 posters are to be put up. It is preferable to put them up more frequently, and fewer at a time. The invitation with your portrait was very well-received, and at the door everyone asked if they could keep the letter. I will send you some, which you can keep as a souvenir.

Today I am very pleased that things started off so well, and you will immediately realize the importance of all this. I am leaving for Boston, Chicago etc. for a fortnight on December 30. This week, I will send you an account of the expenses. They are as low as possible, and indeed I am amazed at having done so well for so small an outlay.

Yours sincerely,
G de Beauplan

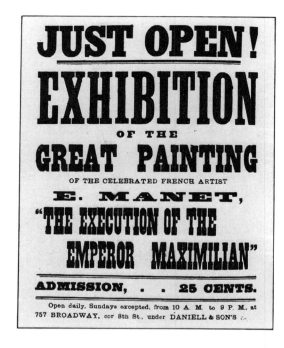

Handbill for the exhibition of Manet's *The Execution of the Emperor Maximilian* in America, 1879–80.

ANTONIN PROUST

ÉDOUARD MANET: SOUVENIRS

Manet's Views on State Acquisition of his Work

1913

While Manet was painting my portrait, I had indeed talked to him of my plan to get one of his pictures into the Luxembourg.

"I don't want to get into museums piecemeal," he had replied. "I want to get in all at once, or not at all."

I alluded to the concept of small beginnings.

"Quite so," he had retorted, "but the truth is that they should have a wall for each artist in museums, with space between the frames and a proper setting. Whereas the hanging is inept, the general arrangement absurd and the decoration of the rooms ridiculous. It's mutual destruction. If I can't be given a wall, I'd prefer nothing."

"But the *Boy with a Sword* alone created a minor revolution in the United States."

"That may be, but I would prefer nothing."

When I was at the Ministry of Arts, I had made a further attempt. I had just bought the Courbets which are in the Louvre, the *Stags Fighting*, the *Man with a Leather Belt* and *The Wounded Man*. The budget for the acquisition of works of art being exhausted for 1881 and the same budget being in part spoken for for 1882, the government would normally have had to ask the Chamber for a supplementary grant just before the Courbet sale. I did not think that I should do this for fear of over-exciting the auction rooms, but I gave instructions to the State representative not to exceed the total of the sum, in these auctions, which was still available for the 1882 budget. However, anticipating the possibility of the price exceeding the sum available, I had recourse to the good offices of a friend, Henri Hecht, to put himself at our service to acquire the works which the State had earmarked, and to hand them over to it at a later date, should Parliament approve the acquisitions made.

Proust served as Minister of Fine Arts under the prime ministership of Léon Gambetta from November 1881 to January 1882 and was instrumental in the awarding of the Légion d'honneur to Manet in December 1881. Proust's portrait (Colourplate 104) is dated 1880. (See also page 169.)

COLOURPLATE 6

See page 126.

I suggested to Manet that I should act for him as I had acted for Courbet.

He refused.

"There would be uproar among your colleagues. Don't forget, Courbet is a classic painter in comparison with me, and just remember how this classic painter was received in the Chamber. It has changed its tune since, I admit. But as much cannot be said for the curators of the Louvre, can it? They thrust the Courbets into badly lit rooms, and hung them too high up. As Gambetta wittily put it, you were virtually forced to trail your Courbets round in a caravan to keep within your budget, just as Emilie Ambre took my *Maximilian* across America.

See page 167.

"And then, I'm in no hurry. There was a time when I was; but no longer. I've become patient, philosophical; I'll wait, or at least my work will wait, because the attacks I've been the butt of have broken something vital within me. People just can't imagine what it's like to be constantly insulted. It sickens you and destroys you.

"Siredey has just reproached you for not having had one of my paintings bought by the State. Let's not say another word about it, do you mind? But you must promise me one thing, and that is, never to let me get into a museum piecemeal, at least without a fight. Can you see me in the Louvre with a single painting, *Olympia* or *Père Lathuille*? My work wouldn't be seen as a whole, and I want it to be seen whole."

See John House, "Seeing Manet Whole", Art in America, *November 1983, no. 10 (pp. 178–88).*
COLOURPLATES 14, 91

ÉDOUARD MANET

Letter to Antonin Proust

1880

My dear friend,

Your picture has been on exhibition in the Salon for the last three weeks – badly hung near a door, on a divided panel, and even worse criticized. But it seems to be my lot to be slanged and I accept it philosophically.

However, you have no idea how difficult it is, my dear friend, to place a single figure on a canvas, and to concentrate all the interest on that one and only figure without its becoming lifeless and unsubstantial. Compared with this, it's child's play to paint two figures together who act as foils to each other.

Ah! that portrait with the hat, in which I'm told everything was blue. All right! I'm ready for them. Personally, I can't see it – later, after I'm gone, it will be admitted that I did observe things accurately with a clear mind.

Your portrait is painted with the utmost sincerity possible. I remember, as if it were only yesterday, the quick and simple way I treated the glove you're holding in your bare hand and how, when you said to me at that moment, "*Please*, not another stroke," I felt in complete sympathy with you and could have hugged you.

Oh, how I hope that later on, there will not be some stupid idea of hanging this picture in a public collection. I've always disliked intensely this idea of crowding works of art together so that you can't even see daylight between them, in the way novelties are displayed in fashionable shops. Anyway, "He who lives will see," – it's in the hands of fate.

The portrait of Antonin Proust (Colourplate 104) exhibited at the Salon of 1880 was one of several depictions by Manet of his friend. Proust, who claimed that Manet had executed most of the work of the Salon portrait in a single sitting, kept the picture until his death.

The portrait is now in the Toledo Museum of Art, Ohio, USA.

RENÉ MENARD

L'ART

Salon Review

1881

René Joseph Menard (1827–87), French painter and critic, pupil of Troyon and Théodore Rousseau. He exhibited at the Salon until 1866.

The commotion which occurs at each Salon over the name of Manet has been increased this year by an official award which some consider a very tardy and entirely inadequate reparation, while others are tempted to see in it an incomprehensible bit of mystification. In any case this award satisfies no one and takes first place among the complaints which have arisen on all sides against the decisions of the jury in regard to the awards. Manet is not a newcomer, and those who are satisfied to laugh over the brutality of his technique only give proof to a very superficial acquaintance with artistic matters. This painter has a doctrine, he carries a banner, he is the leader of a school. And when I say that he is the leader of a school, I do not mean that he teaches art to young people who have come to put themselves under his direction; I know very well that he does nothing of the sort. But I insist that his painting disturbs even the artists who slander it most, and that after shrugging his shoulders before a work which he has qualified as detestable, more than one painter has said to himself, "This man knows neither how to draw nor paint, but he has a manner of seeing nature which is not without charm." I am absolutely sure that Manet has exercised and still exercises a very real influence on contemporary painting.

Does this mean that Manet is a man whose talent is destined to compel recognition and to triumph one day over all the reservations of public opinion? I should not dare to maintain that, for I have followed this artist since his beginnings and I do not know a single work of his which can hold its place beside those of the masters. To uphold for twenty years a doctrine which still endures in spite of the very poor reception which it has everywhere received is assuredly a sign of strength, but never to formulate it in a decisive work is at the same time a proof of weakness. This is Manet's position. As a revolutionary his banner proclaims his courage, but each of his works is a new witness of impotence. I shall not mention his portrait of Rochefort, destitute of any character as drawing, but his *Lion Hunter* has indeed the right to arrest our attention, since a jury of artists signals him out for impossible attention, and the lion which he has killed never resembled any real beast whatsoever. The absence of drawing is a fault which one must concede to Manet since he is accustomed to it, but the colour of a painting lives only in the concord of hues which vibrate in unison, and here all the colours are out of tune. The face itself is accurate enough in colour but it swears in this place, and the violet colour of the ground can, at worst, be found in nature but never with such intensity. In the portrait of Antonin Proust in the last Salon, in *A Good Glass of Beer*, and in several other works by Manet, the painter's audacity depended less on accurate resemblance. Now that is precisely what is lacking here, and Manet, whose talent has always been very uneven, has certainly not raised himself this year to the height of his previous exhibitions. I don't complain at all about the medal which has been awarded him, but I deeply regret that he has not had it sooner, because it would perhaps have been applied to works infinitely more meritorious.

Manet won a second-class medal at the Salon for his Portrait of M Henri Rochefort *(Colourplate 111). This placed him* hors concours — *he would no longer have to submit his entries to the jury in order to be exhibited at the Salon.*

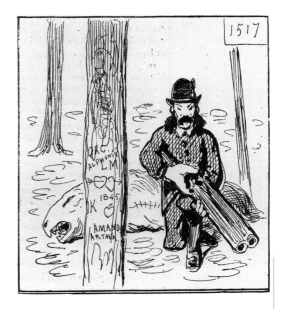

Stop, *M. Pertuiset asks God's and Man's Forgiveness for Having Fired at an Old Stuffed Skin.* Caricature in *Le Journal Amusant,* 28 May 1881. COLOURPLATE 110

A Good Glass of Beer (Le Bon Bock) *(Colourplate 54) enjoyed an enormous success at the Salon of 1873. The lithographer Bellot, who had modelled for the picture, went on to found an association called "du Bon Bock".*

H. GUÉRARD

LE CARILLON

Manet's Decoration by the State

July 16, 1881

The recent but inadequate medal awarded by a liberal-minded Jury to the painter Manet, has offered critics an opportunity for new discussion in connection with which the stale old bourgeois clichés have been wheeled out yet again. There was a lot of indignation, but even more applause and, overall, discussion could be summed up by a total of praise for the brilliant talent of this courageous man.

One objection, however, loomed alarming and irrefutable (or at least so his adversaries thought): the famous objection concerning *plein air*. Oh what faith has been invested therein: that Manet had invented *plein air* painting! So what were Millet and Corot doing? Well, just a little more than the other landscapists who didn't have their talent. *Plein air* painting does not necessarily result from simply painting in the open, though of course you have to be out of doors to do *plein air* painting. Real *plein air* painting, that of Manet, is a new art which requires particular execution, observation, sense of hearing; in a word, it is a new art formula.

Plein air painting does not consist simply of painting a tree, even outside; by that count, Diaz would have been a *plein air* painter; and I do not believe that he was. The interest of this famous *plein air* painting which exercises so many people, is life, the human figure in all its modernity, moving in an outdoor atmosphere, with the intense effects and values, the unequivocal contours which, by simplifying them, invest people and objects with real light and sun.

It is in this sense that Manet is its *first* exponent, its master; and to mention only a few examples of his considerable work, *Doing the Washing, The Boaters, At Père Lathuille's, The Battle of the Kearsage and the Alabama, Querétaro*, these are the pictures whose equivalents in modern painting I seek in vain, because they are conscientiously observed and frankly expressed.

What continues to make Manet a master of whom the French school will be proud, is the absolute modernity of all his subjects; the determination with which he always moves forward will cause him ever to be seen as the painter who has best represented the life of our time.

Besides, it is not so much the open and intensely luminous mood of Manet's paintings which shocks observers at the Salon, as the mass of drab, vague and neutral things which surround them. It is just that the public eye, accustomed for centuries to a conventional and very prudent art, is not yet accustomed to the dazzle of the truth, though it will become so.

Another problem may be added to that of *plein air*, and it lies in the exact observation of the settings in which the scenes represented occur, for instance: many of those artists who do not work from photographs have been quite content to adopt the habit of using models to pose for their soldiers, working men and peasants, and put marquis's clothing on people who might just be entitled to wear a livery. All this without realizing that the models so posing have neither the posture nor the appearance of the types they are representing, whence the ensuing falseness, a falseness to which one becomes accustomed. And if someone sincere like M Manet extends conscientiousness as far as making a waiter pose as a waiter, or doing Rochefort's portrait from Rochefort himself, people cry out that it is scandalous or shabby; in that case they have not seen the famous pamphleteer.

Henri Guérard (1846–97), printmaker. Guérard exhibited prints at the Salon during the decade of the 1870s and was known for his experiments with coloured prints. He married Eva Gonzalès in 1879.

Narcisse-Virgile Diaz de la Peña (1808–76), French painter and lithographer, member of the Barbizon School.

PAGE 147, COLOURPLATES 66, 91, 21

Querétaro is a reference to Manet's Execution of Maximilian *(Colourplate 36) (see page 103).*

Henri Rochefort (1830–1913) had gained notoriety under the Second Empire as a pamphleteer and critic of Napoleon III and the Imperial régime. One of his most famous witticisms was: "There are 25 million French subjects, not counting subjects of complaint". Rochefort was deported in 1873 as a result of his support for the Commune, but escaped from the prison colony in New Caledonia in 1874. His escape provided Manet with the subject for two paintings executed in 1880–81 (Colourplate 112).

Would it not be better to admit that all faultfinding with a man of Manet's quality is in vain, and that nothing in the world can stand in the way of the imminent success and glorification of so rigorously personal a talent, one so inevitably true?

Would it not be better to admit that most of his detractors are the last survivors of a school at bay who, knowing the story of the famous *assiette au beurre* still cling to it, knowing well that they will founder when their powerful adversary's hour of triumph arrives?

GEORGES JEANNIOT

LA GRANDE REVUE

Two Visits to Manet's Studio

August 10, 1907

During a convalescent leave, I had got to know the publisher Georges Charpentier; I was a regular contributor to his illustrated journal *La Vie Moderne*. But the moment came when I had to rejoin my regiment and leave Paris. Some days before my departure, I said to Charpentier, who knew Manet, that I would very much like him to introduce me to him. "Why don't you just go round yourself? Manet's a charming man; he takes *La Vie Moderne*, he's seen your drawings and he'll be delighted to meet you." The next day, I went to ring on the door of Manet's studio in the rue d'Amsterdam. A voice called out "Come in!" Manet was standing, in front of his easel, painting some flowers. Very moved, I nonetheless managed to tell him who I was and what led me there. I had brought with me three painted canvases, I asked him if he would be good enough to give me some advice. He watched me, smiling, while I untied my package. "So, it's you who does the drawings in *La Vie Moderne*?" he said. "Yes." "Then try to do them in brush and Indian ink; your composition would benefit, just the light and shade. But the public might not be too pleased, and after all a review is produced to be sold; how annoying that this reproduction cannot render the half-tones." I then placed a life-sized bust of a soldier with red epaulettes on the ground against the easel. After having looked at it for a few seconds, Manet turned and said, still smiling: "I say, you're in the business too." I was flooded with joy. "Don't you ever think of resigning?" "I have no personal fortune." "You enjoy it a lot, don't you?" "Yes; but above all since I saw your painting." "Oh heavens! Then you have a treat in store!" And I talked to him of those paintings of his which I knew." "So, you like them?" "Yes, and I have just one regret; I'm leaving the day after tomorrow and I don't know when I'll be able to see you again." "When you do, I'll always be delighted." I took up my canvases, he held out his hand, and I left him. I had no idea that this man, so full of life, goodness and good humour, was soon to fall prey to a frightful disease, and die. I took away with me an indelible memory of my visit; I felt full of courage; his welcome had heartened me, particularly when I compared it, in its kindly simplicity, with that of a certain pundit whose studio I had had the misguided idea of trying to enter, one year earlier, during a stay in Paris. My admiration for Manet the artist was now compounded by a respectful devotion. Manet's character was at one with his painting, his eye was clear and frank, his speech simple and full of original observations; he expressed his ideas rapidly and often elliptically. He was a man of imagination. The reputation he has gained as a revolutionary does not strike me as according with reality. For half his life, Manet had copied the masters. He did so, admittedly, with imagination. Then, nourished upon the marrow

The expression "assiette au beurre" (usually translated as "cushy number") referred to the source of profits and favours, with particular reference to political parties who were in power and abusing this position.

Georges Jeanniot (1848–1934), artist and illustrator. Jeanniot worked for the magazine La Vie Moderne, *and met Manet in the early 1880s.*

Georges Charpentier, publisher of Flaubert, Zola and the Goncourt brothers. M and Mme Charpentier, renowned for their literary and political salon, were early supporters of Manet and the Impressionist painters.

Manet died after the amputation of his left leg due to gangrene, generally thought to be the result of syphilis.

RIGHT *Bar at the Folies-Bergère.* 1881. Oil sketch for exhibited work. 18½ × 22″ (47 × 56 cm). Stedelijk Museum, Amsterdam.

which only tradition contains, he looked at nature and applied what these masters had taught him . . . .

When I returned to Paris, in January 1882, the first visit I paid was to Manet. He was then painting *The Bar at the Folies-Bergère* and the model, a pretty girl, was posing behind a table laden with food and bottles. He recognized me immediately, held out his hand and said: "It's most irritating, forgive me, I have to remain seated, I've got a bad foot. Do sit down."

I took a chair behind him and watched him work. Although he painted his pictures from the model, Manet did not copy nature at all; I became aware of his magisterial simplifications; the head of his woman had a sense of depth, but this modelling was not obtained with the means that nature offered him. Everything was abridged; the tones were clearer, the colours more vivid, the values closer, the tones more varied. The result was complete harmony, tender and limpid. Someone came in, and I recognized my childhood friend, doctor Albert Robin. There was talk of Chaplin. "You know he was very talented," said Manet, painting the gilded wrapping of a champagne bottle with little strokes; "very talented," he repeated. "He knows about a woman's smile, and that's very rare." "Yes, I

COLOURPLATE 117

Albert Robin (1847–1928), physician and art collector; friend of Manet, Mallarmé and Méry Laurent.

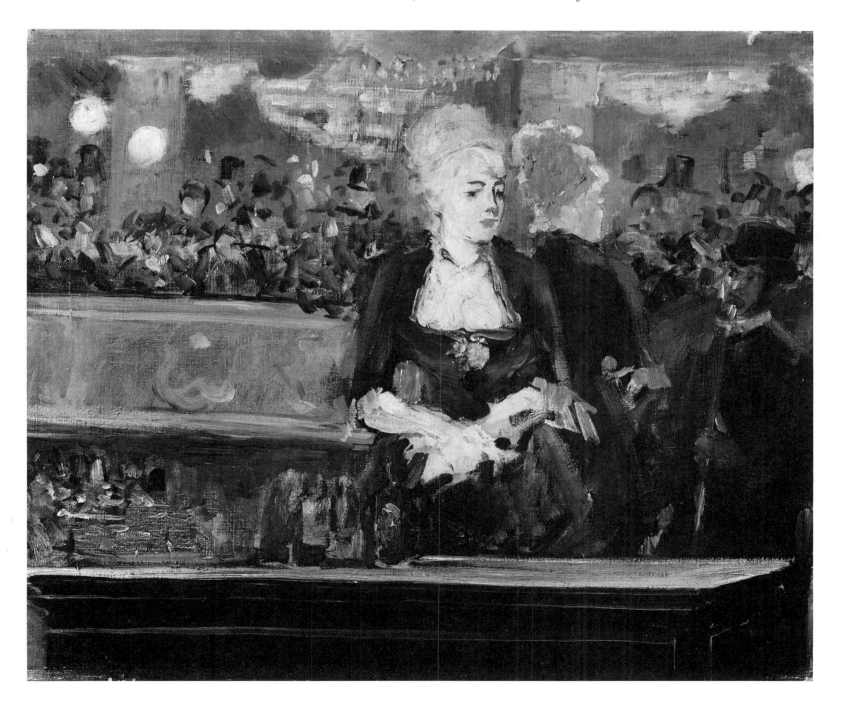

know; some people complain that his painting is over-polished; they are wrong, it's very broadly painted, and the colour is wonderfully handled, too."

Other people came and Manet stopped painting to go and sit on the divan against the right-hand wall. It was then that I saw how illness had ravaged him; he walked with a stick and seemed to tremble; but he was cheerful and talked of his imminent recovery. I went back to see him during my stay in Paris. He said things such as the following: "In art, conciseness is both a necessity and a luxury; a concise man provokes thought, a wordy man provokes boredom; always move towards conciseness. In the figure, look for the main light and the main shadow, the rest will come of itself: often, it amounts to very little. Then cultivate your memory; for nature will never give you anything except information – nature is like a parapet to stop you falling into the commonplace. You have to remain master all the time, and do what you like. No 'impositions.' That's the worst thing. By the way, since you like my work, have a look in there," and he pointed to a door. I opened it and found myself in a junk room, where there was a whole pile of paintings. I saw *Olympia, Doing the Washing, At Père Lathuille's, Dead Christ with Angels, Argenteuil.* I was drawn by *At Père Lathuille's,* which was the best lit. I had seen it in the Salon of 1860 and it had stayed in my mind as the most extraordinary representation of a Paris restaurant. Baudelaire wrote:

"Scents, sounds and colours answer one another."

White cloths, cool greenery, sparkling glasses, light air, delicate smells, all qualities which give these places in Paris a quintessence which the provincial or foreigner senses with delight before he becomes accustomed to them. These pleasures, which each address themselves to a sense and which, together ravish all of them at the same moment, form a large part of the attraction of this exquisite town. Before the *Père Lathuille* I had a sort of retrospective shock at everything Paris had enabled me to sample by way of agreeable surprises and choice delights. In my mind the colours, juxtaposed by a deeply perceptive observer, corresponded to the scents, the subtleties and diverse music that Paris offers her lovers, often free; I stood in front of that painting, thinking of the mysterious lures of a supremely subtle painting, and goodness knows how long I would have stayed there had I not heard Manet's voice calling me. I left the room piled high with those spurned masterpieces, and came back to him. I told him as best I could what his painting made me feel and I had the joy of seeing his eyes, whose vivacity had been spared by illness, light up again with an emotion which remains one of the most precious memories of my life.

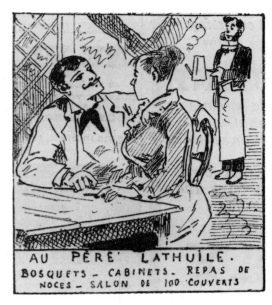

At Père Lathuille's. Caricature in *Le Charivari,* 1 May 1880 (see Colourplate 91).

A reference to Baudelaire's poem "Correspondances" first published in Les Fleurs du Mal *in 1857.*

J.K. HUYSMANS

L'ART MODERNE

The Bar at the Folies-Bergère

1883

COLOURPLATE 117

Manet's *Bar at the Folies-Bergère* stupefies the onlookers who throng, exchanging baffled comments, to the sheer mirage of this painting.

Before us, standing, is a large girl in a low-cut blue dress, cut off below the waist by a counter on which are stacked champagne bottles, phials of liqueurs, oranges, flowers and glasses. Behind her is a mirror which shows us both the woman's reflected back, and a man seen full-face talking to her; further away, behind or rather beside this couple, we see the whole of

Huysmans had written a vivid description of the Folies-Bergère, Les Folies-Bergère en 1879 *(1880), reprinted in* Croquis parisiens, *Paris 1886.* The Bar at the Folies-Bergère, *exhibited in 1882, was Manet's last major Salon painting.*

174

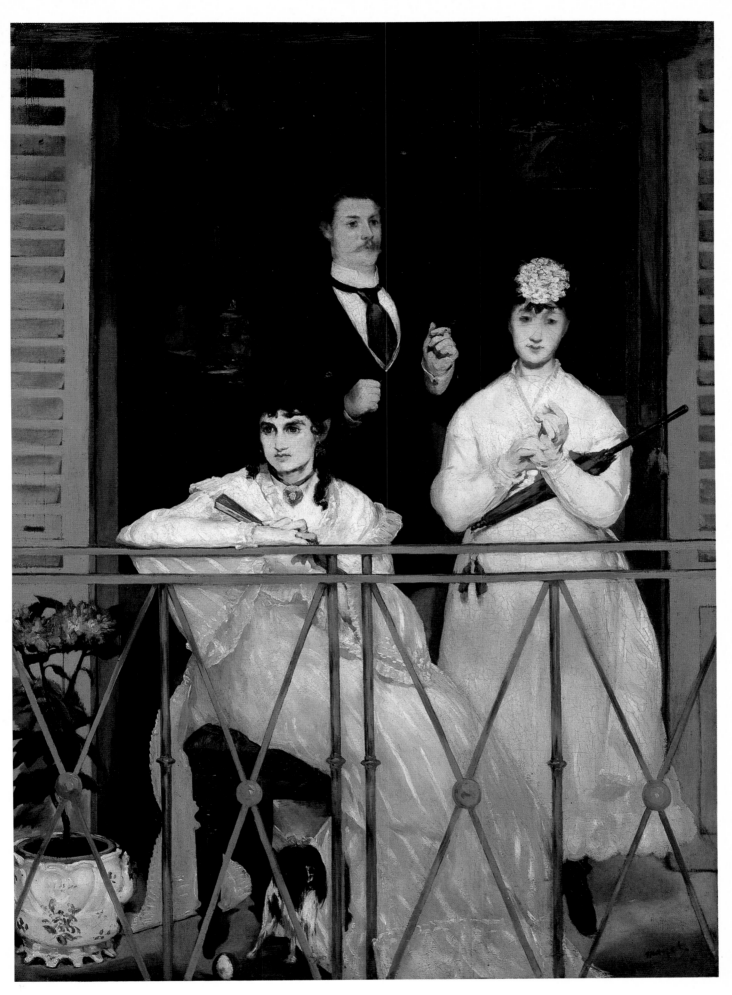

COLOURPLATE 46. *The Balcony*. 1868–9. 66½ × 49¼″ (169 × 125 cm).
Musée d'Orsay, Paris.

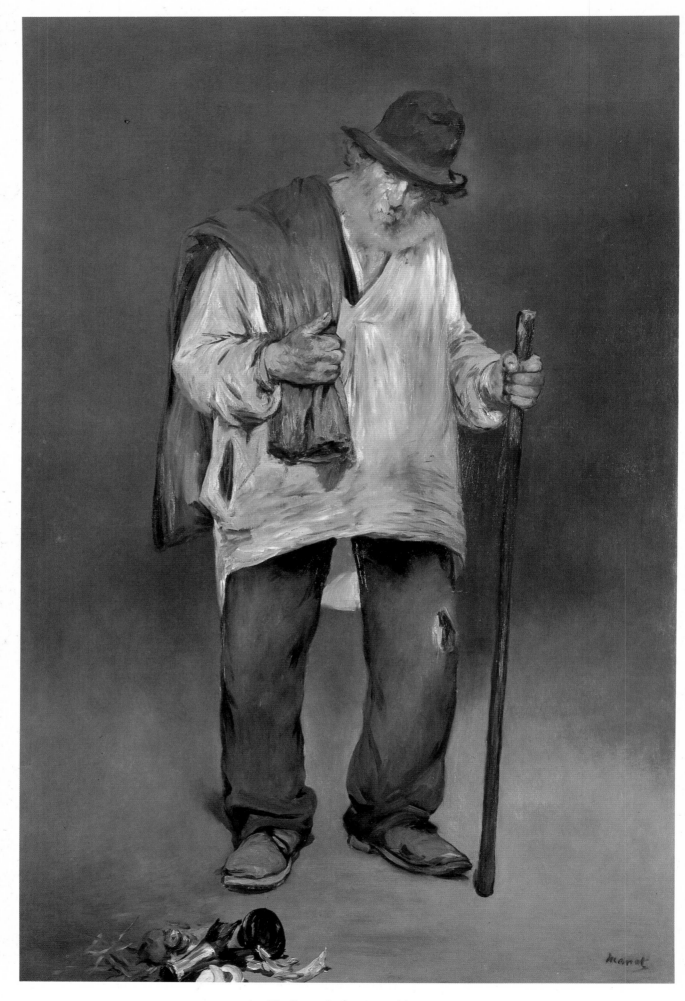

COLOURPLATE 47. *The Ragpicker*. 1869. 76¾ × 51¼″ (195 × 130 cm).
Norton Simon Foundation, Los Angeles.

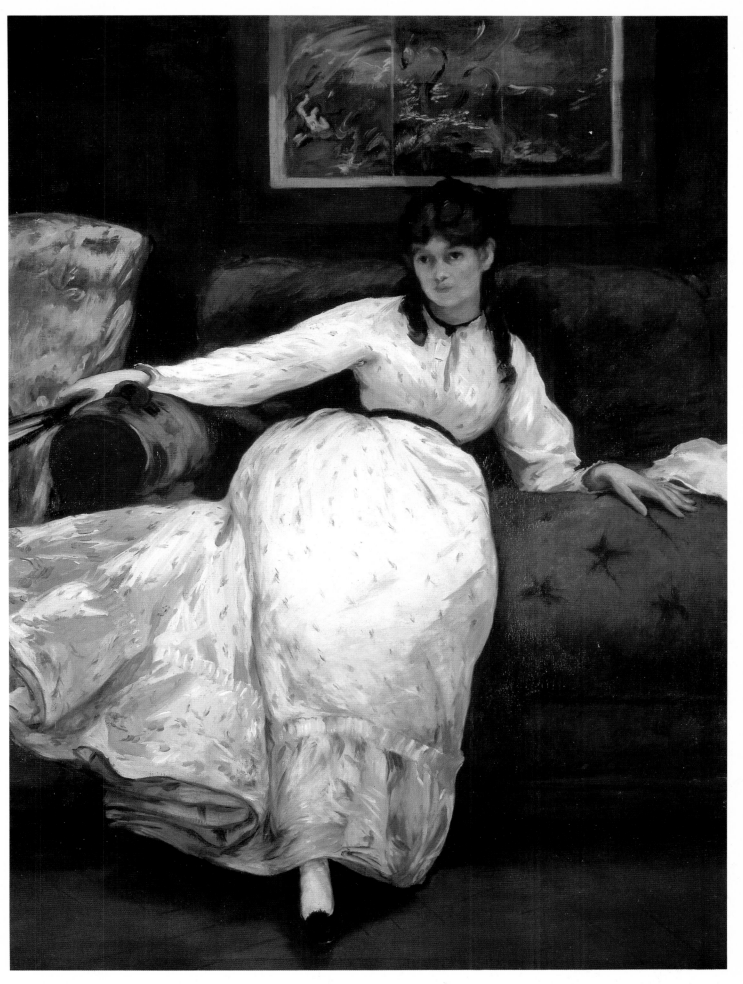

COLOURPLATE 48. *Repose: Portrait of Berthe Morisot*. 1870. 58¼ × 43¾" (148 × 113 cm).
Museum of Art, Rhode Island School of Design, Providence, Rhode Island (Bequest of the Estate of
Mrs Edith Stuyvesant Vanderbilt Gerry).

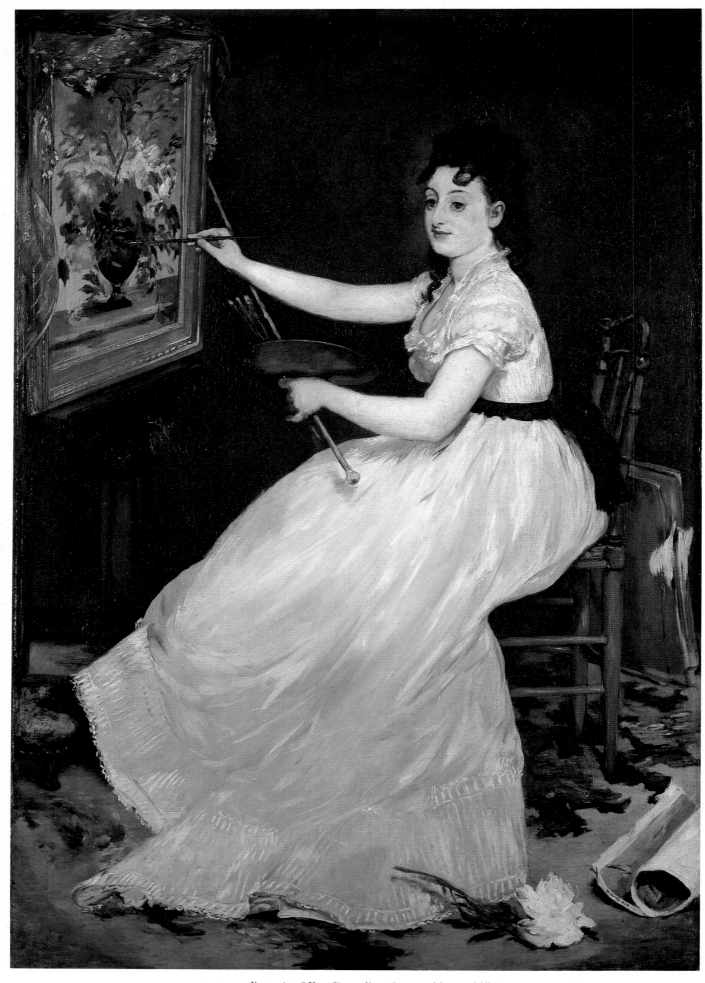

COLOURPLATE 49. *Portrait of Eva Gonzalès*. 1870. 75¼ × 52¼″ (191 × 133 cm).
National Gallery, London.

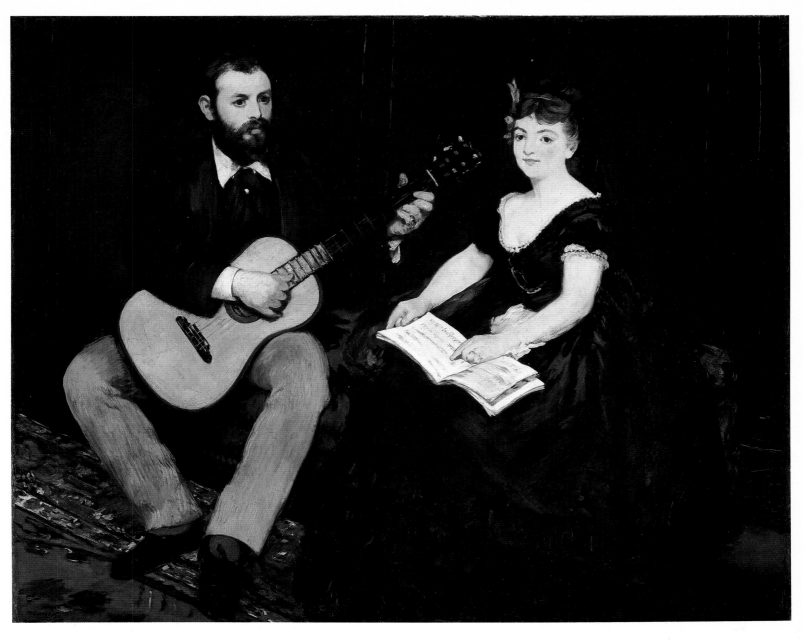

COLOURPLATE 50. *The Music Lesson*. 1870. 55½ × 68⅛″ (141.1 × 173.1 cm).
Courtesy, Museum of Fine Arts, Boston (Anonymous Centennial Gift in Memory of Charles Deering).

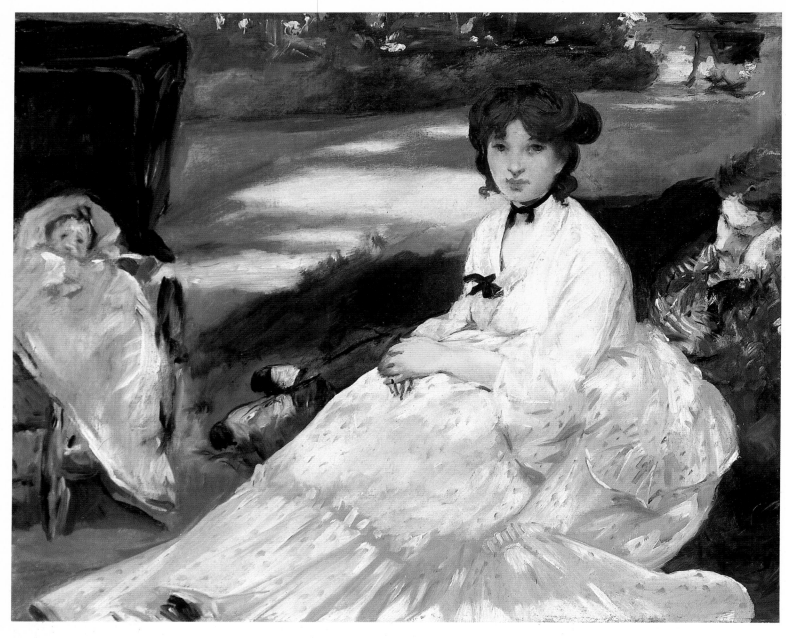

COLOURPLATE 51. *In the Garden.* 1870. 17 × 21½″ (43 × 55 cm).
Shelburne Museum, Shelburne, Vermont.

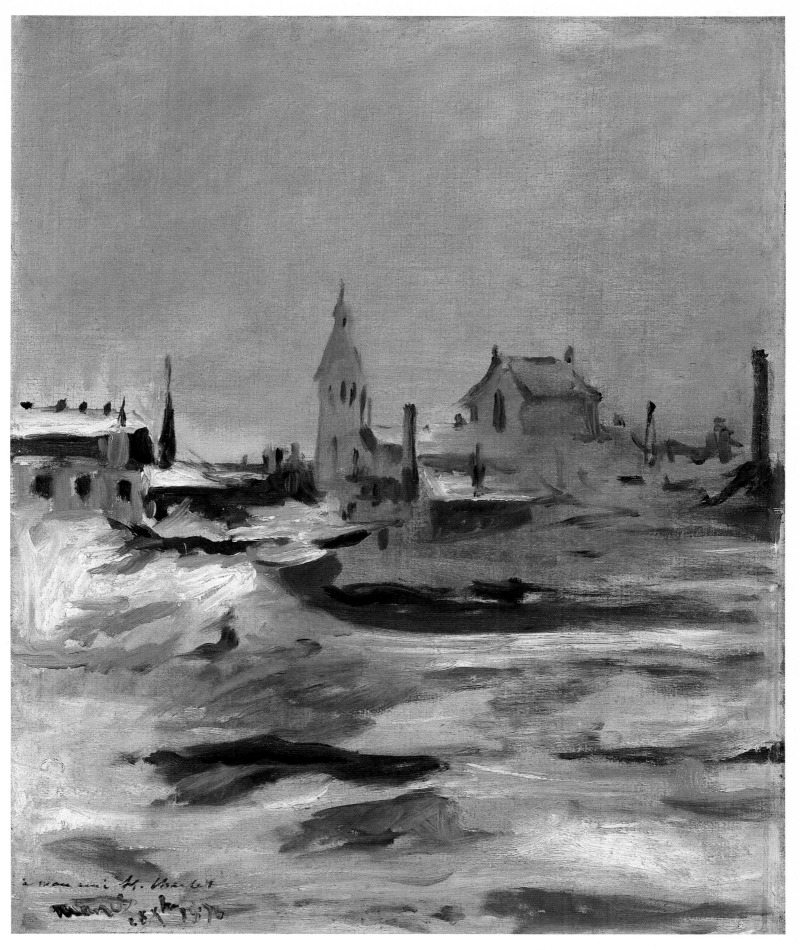

COLOURPLATE 52. *Snowy Landscape at Montrouge.* 1870. 24 × 19¾" (61 × 50 cm).
National Museum of Wales, Cardiff.

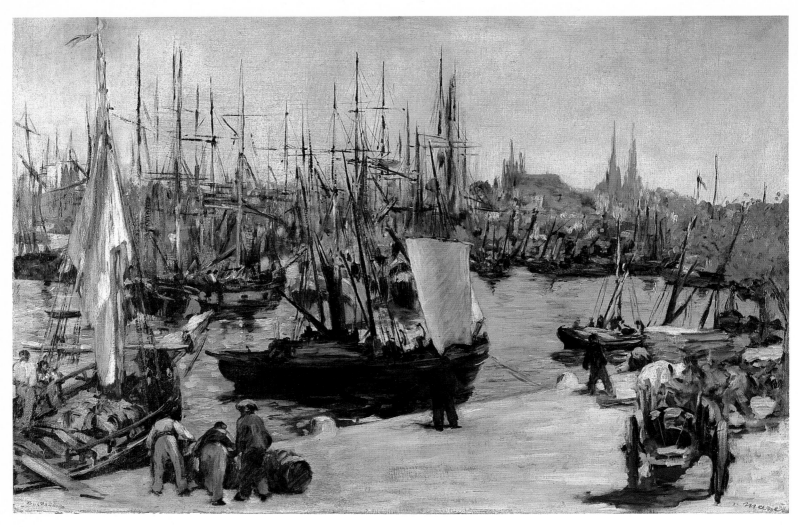

COLOURPLATE 53. *The Port of Bordeaux*. 1871. 25½ × 39¼″ (65 × 100 cm).
Private Collection, Switzerland.

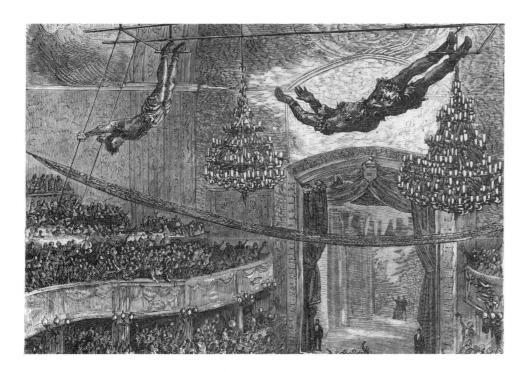

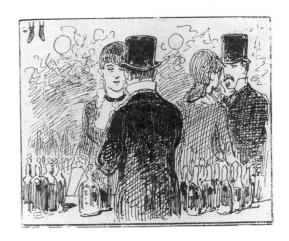

the Folies and, in a corner up above, the leek-green boots of an acrobat standing on her trapeze.

The subject is modern indeed and Manet's idea of thus putting the figure of his woman in her setting, is ingenious; but what does this lighting mean? Is this gaslight, electric light? Come now, this is a sort of *plein air* painting, bathed in daylight! From then on, everything falls apart – the Folies-Bergère can exist only by night; understood and falsified in this way, it becomes absurd. It is indeed deplorable to see a man of M Manet's substance conforming to such subterfuges and, in a word, making paintings as conventional as those of the rest!

I regret this all the more in that, despite the chalky tones, Manet's bar is full of qualities, the woman is well portrayed, the crowd teems with life. Despite everything, this bar is certainly the most modern and most interesting painting this Salon contains.

GUSTAVE GEFFROY

LA JUSTICE

"Manet the Initiator"

May 3, 1883

It is the evening of the opening of the Salon. The crowd has scarcely departed, the doors are hardly closed, when it is learnt that Manet is dead. The artist had been suffering for many months and the news was not unexpected, but that made no difference; all who had known the man, all who had loved his work, were heart-broken on learning of his sad end.

A shadow was cast over the first day of the Salon – that festival of art and spring which all Parisians love to celebrate – by the strange coincidence of death, all unconsciously, striking down Manet on the anniversary of his battles, in the fullness of his time and talent, when success had at last come to him and a long line of works from his hand was still awaited.

The artist had brought about, quite naturally, an evolution in art, as do all original artists. For a long time he had refused to look at Nature through the eyes of art school teachers or in terms of the pictures of the Old Masters. He had learnt to draw – not the sort of drawing which is merely related to lines surrounding objects, but drawing which indicates subtleties of movement, which reproduces form, recession, action, the vibration of air: drawing which indicates a pose or an expression in a few summary lines. He composed for himself a luminous palette, made up of bold tones and light transparent half-tones. With these means to hand he confronted things and painted them as he saw them. To begin with it was stupefying: so accustomed had one become to see pictures painted in a light other than that out-of-doors.

Convention was an accepted thing: an indoor light shed on a landscape, trees with green-black foliage, dark figures, portraits painted in a cellar with a ray of electric light illuminating the face only – these things did not shock eyes accustomed to the compromises which for many people constitute art. Nobody wished to acknowledge that the pictures that are so admired in museums are covered with a golden patina put there by time, and that their colours are growing darker every day.

Astonishment was therefore intense on seeing pictures by this artist who did not paint trees and rivers under a studio light, but under the harsh light of afternoon. That is Manet's contribution and which will make his work endure.

Must we consider then that a new era was born with his appearance and regard his predecessors cheaply? Neither he, nor any of his defenders have ever entertained such an idea. Who would quibble, from the point of view of painting, over the mathematical way, so to speak, in which Delacroix applies the law of tone values? Who would deny the revolution made in landscape painting by Corot, that admirable painter of grey? But, also, what an injustice it would be to refuse Manet his place in the undefined evolution of art. With Corot, Jongkind, Degas and Claude Monet, he has added his own important contribution to truth. He has forced everyone who has not been too taken up with convention to think; he has shown the way to those who will come after him.

Just as so many great, sensitive artists of the past have done for the centuries in which they lived, he too wished to introduce into his art the society by which he was surrounded and to realize an intimate union between his work and the world into which he was born. From this moment he dismissed *Christs, Espadas*, history and mythology. He painted the reality that was under his eyes, the woman of his times, the manifestation of our pleasures, our occupations and dreams.

People who would never dream of protesting because Velazquez painted *The Spinners* and *The Drinkers*, or because Rembrandt painted a butcher's shop and *The Night Watch*, protest vehemently when confronted by the pictures in which Manet has represented aspects of modern life – as though the France of the nineteenth century was unworthy of being perpetuated for future generations. Manet, together with Courbet, must be honoured as one of the best artisans of this artistic movement, parallel with the literary movement started by Balzac and continued by Flaubert, the Goncourts and by Zola, who has at last given artistic expression to our times, customs and morals.

This is the role of Édouard Manet. This is the essential task which he has accomplished and for which he must always be honoured. Has he not imposed on us a new way of looking at things – this accurate observance of the luminous film of light which envelops everything, which triumphs today in private exhibitions and in the Salons, and which obtrudes itself even in the official studies and art schools patronized by the Academy and the State? A whole galaxy of able painters, recognized by everyone, employs these methods; are they not striding forward into that field opened up by this painter who was so ridiculed, who will be buried tomorrow? The others who will come after him and who will do better than he – would they have existed without him?

Johan Barthold Jongkind (1819–91), Dutch painter and printmaker.

Honoré de Balzac (1799–1850), best known for his series of novels entitled La Comédie Humaine; *Gustave Flaubert (1821–86).*

That Manet has had failures, that the modelling of the flesh of his portraits is weak, that he sometimes starts in too high a key in establishing his tone values, that he has not carried some of his pictures far enough, and that some of his drawing is faulty – this I admit. This is not the moment to discuss his very considerable output, picture by picture, to point out his errors and the qualities of his technique. His friends owe it to him to organize a complete exhibition of his works which will allow the wordy warfare to die down and truth to be established. Personally, I await the day with complete confidence.

What can be discussed today is not the importance of Manet's pictures in themselves – as museum or gallery pieces – but the importance of Manet's role as an "initiator" from the point of view of the history of Art; the importance of the consequences of the revolution which he has affected, the influence that he has exercised, and which he *will* continue to exercise, until another original artist appears on the scene to exasperate the public who will castigate him in the name of Manet, whose *Olympia* and *Luncheon on the Grass* will be, by that time, already in the Louvre.

COLOURPLATES 14, 18

JULES-CAMILLE DE POLIGNAC

Manet's Funeral

May 5, 1883

The hearse stands in front of the door – the centre of a vast black patch – friends of Manet, who have come to pay their final homage to the Master who breathes no more; people who wish to be seen; people who wish to see.

Everyone of consequence from Montmartre [*le Tout-Montmartre*] is there.

On the opposite pavement, passers-by, girls out buying their lunch, people who have come there to stare, necks outstretched and mouths agape – death's idlers.

The windows filled to bursting with people hanging out of casements like bunches of grapes – here a servant's white apron hastily put on, yellow chignons, brown hair, beards, dishevelled babies, stand out vividly against the pale houses painted in with a sweeping brush-stroke.

No sky; no sun. Pale clouds cast a soft grey light over the "picture of a street."

The funeral car jolts and slowly starts on its way, making a charcoal stroke across the light of day and pale pavement. This hearse however is a feast of colour – against the black pall, lilacs, violets, immortelles, cornflowers, pansies and roses explode like laughter in the glory of wreaths and the intoxication of flowers.

Behind, the crowd follows – a long ribbon of mourning unwound for Death.

Friends – Clemenceau, Antonin Proust, who will presently speak, Zola, who is one of the pall-bearers, Aurélien Scholl, Puvis de Chavannes, who, seen back-view, looks as though he were cut out of one of his own pictures; Degas, Pissarro, Renoir – "three Impressionists," Mallarmé, Jean Marras, Franc Lamy, the independent painter; Henry Ghys, the musician, etc., etc., men who have already achieved success, men to whom success will come tomorrow – all are there to follow the body of their valiant friend.

And they are five hundred strong.

They march slowly, slowly, through the streets.

The pall-bearers at Manet's funeral were Proust, Zola, Philippe Burty, Alfred Stevens, Théodore Duret and Claude Monet.
Aurélien Scholl (1833–1902), journalist.
Appears in Music in the Tuileries Gardens *(Colourplate 11).*
Pierre-Désiré Franc-Lamy (1855–1919), French painter.
Esprit-Charles-Henry Guys (1839–1908), piano teacher and composer.

The first time that I went to Manet's studio, he was working on a picture (which I believe now belongs to Faure) which represented a crowded corridor in the Old Opéra during a masked ball. . . .

Glances and lips, a thousand sighs, a thousand words, the chatter of women; rips, tarts and grass widows, pale loiterers idly gossiping under the brilliant lights, the feverish but weary high-life which is at its most boring when it amuses itself – all that was evoked in this canvas painted in immortal colours by the hand of a master.

Manet's fascinating head – pale golden blond, with delicately pure features, lit by lively blue eyes, a beard carefully trimmed to a point, was that of an artist of one's dreams.

But – he was bald.

"I lost my hair in the cause of art," he said, raising his painter's beret with a magnificent flourish and tapping his skull.

One day, in the new Opéra house, he made a delightful joke. Looking at the immense mirrors with which the foyer is faced, he remarked sadly, "Ah, you can see that Garnier [the architect] still has his own hair!"

The procession stops at the porch of the church of Saint-Louis d'Antin, where, in front of the high altar, resplendent with candles, a catafalque is standing.

Manet enters, followed by his family and a small number of friends, and immediately the choir burst into song – followed by the poignant solos of the office for the dead.

One should have seen him in the studio, this ex-sea pilot, with his rolling sailor's walk and captivating shrewd face, turning half-round to make some witty retort, with an urchin's gesture. He always caused a laugh with a little shrug of the shoulder, as hand in pocket and pipe in mouth, he twirled his tobacco pouch.

Manet was essentially a Parisian, witty, refined in his pleasures, and a lover of all that was elegant. He had at his command all the sallies and quick replies of a street Arab, even the accent – which did not prevent him when he chose, from behaving as the most correct of gentlemen.

Outside the church door, where most of the crowd had remained, groups formed and chatted.

"It wasn't much good chopping him up," a gentleman remarked.

The procession resumed once more its slow march. Boulevard Haussmann, rue La Boétie and rue Marbeuf, as far as the Trocadéro. Passy cemetery is a few steps further on.

Here the sky was washed clean, and the route seemed charming. After the long monotony of the streets, we were happy, in spite of our tiredness and sorrow, to see suddenly, through some gap, Paris, luminous under clear skies, extended before us, and to see in this Avenue du Trocadéro the two green lines of orderly trees silhouetted against the blue sky, and closer, the fresher patch of colour of young green leaves, and we were happy to see here and there a shaft of sunlight falling on Manet and ourselves.

Here we are at the cemetery, very simple and very pretty, and one or another of us is surprised into saying: "How very gay!"

On leaving the threshold, one passes to left and right two lawns, spread like green cloths dotted with little white flowers, very pleasing to the eye. Then before one's eyes the whole cemetery stands out against a grey and luminous sky – no funeral trees, no pompous, shriekingly white, new monuments.

Everything in this picture is perfectly in tone; it is a profound, sincere painting. The accents of the trees and stones, just as in an Impressionist painting seen five years later, melt into a whole, full of art and truth. This enclosure is permeated with light and emotion.

Manet will be well off there.

COLOURPLATE 64

Charles Garnier (1825–98), French architect and designer of the new Paris Opéra, built 1862–75.

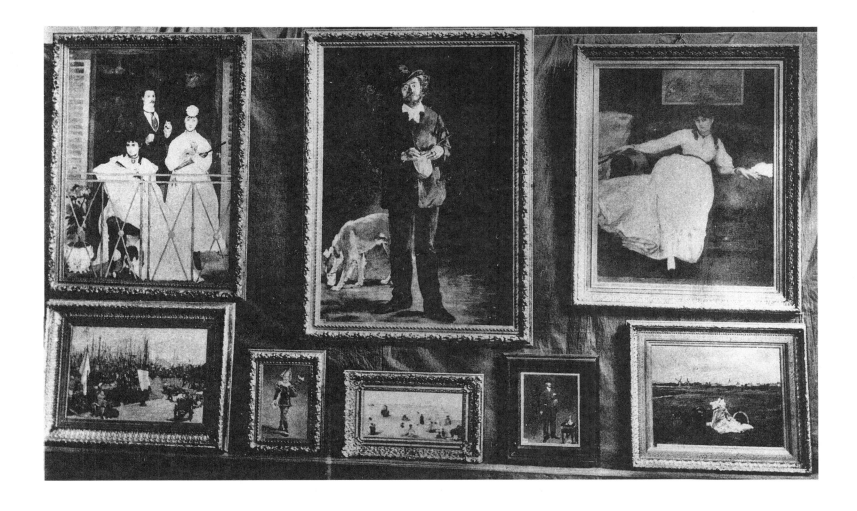

ÉMILE ZOLA

CATALOGUE OF POSTHUMOUS EXHIBITION OF MANET'S PAINTINGS

Manet's Influence

January 1884

Photograph of Manet's
posthumous exhibition at the
École des Beaux-Arts. 1884.
British Library.

*Zola's essay appeared in the catalogue of the
posthumous exhibition of Manet at the École
des Beaux-Arts. The exhibition had come
about largely through the influence of Antonin
Proust. Despite Zola's final tribute to his
friend, he did not contribute to the fund
organized by Monet in 1889 for the purchase
of* Olympia (Colourplate 14) *for the Louvre
(see also page 250).*

On the day after Manet's death, there was an abrupt apotheosis. All the Press bowed down declaring that a great painter had just died. Those who were still joking and quibbling about his work on the previous day, bared their heads and rendered public homage to the triumphant Master who lay finally in his coffin. For us, who had been faithful to him from the beginning, it was a sad victory. What of it! The eternal story repeats itself – the stupidity of the public kills people before putting up statues in their honour! All that we said fifteen years ago – all is now reiterated. Behind the hearse which bears our friend to the cemetery, our heart is softened and weeps at these belated praises which he can no longer hear.

But today, complete amends will have been made. An exhibition of the principal works of the artist has been organized with pious care. The faculty of the Ecole des Beaux-Arts has been kind enough to allow the use of its galleries, an act of intelligent liberalism for which it must be thanked, for there must still be some blockheads among them who will be offended by the entrée of Manet into the sanctuary of tradition.

Behold his work, come and judge for yourselves. We are certain of this last victory which will assign him definitely a place among the greatest masters of the second half of the century.

The masters, truth to tell, are judged as much by their influence as by their works – and it is principally on this that I lay stress, because it was quite impalpable. It would be necessary to write a history of our school of painting over the last twenty years to show the all-powerful role that Manet has played therein. He was one of the most energetic instigators of luminous painting (studied direct from Nature and executed in the full light of contemporary surroundings), who little by little has lured our salons away from their bituminous recipes, and cheered them with real sunshine. It is as a regenerator that I wish to portray him in these few, too short pages, whose sole merit is that they are written in all sincerity.

I got to know Manet in 1866. He was then thirty-three, and lived in a large, shabby studio in the Plaine Monceau. He was already in the middle of his struggles. Pictures exhibited at Martinet's, and especially those he sent to the Salon des Refusés had stirred up all the critics in revolt against him. People laughed uncomprehendingly. Unquestionably, this was the time when the painter was piling up pictures with the greatest confidence, always at work, determined to conquer Paris. His youth had been troubled, there had been quarrels with his father (a magistrate who was worried by painting), then a desperate journey to America, then lost years in Paris, a period spent in Couture's atelier, a slow and painful period of self-analysis. After that, he faced up to Nature honestly – he never had any other master. And all the while he remained a Parisian, in love with life, elegant and refined, who laughed a lot when the caricaturists represented him as a slovenly dauber.

In the following year, 1867, having been unable to gain admission to

A reference to Manet's journey to Brazil, 1848–9 (see pages 38–9).

Odalisque. 1868. Etching and aquatint, 4¾ × 7½″ (12 × 19.1 cm). British Museum.

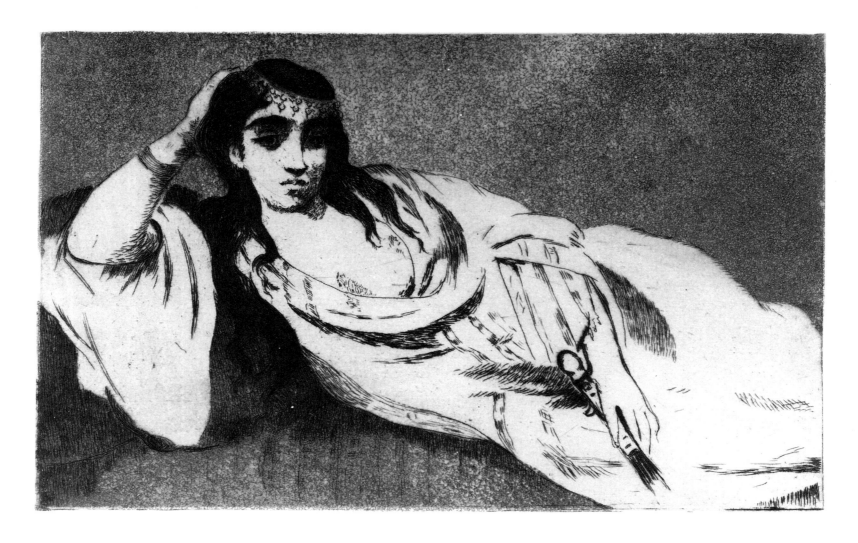

the Universal Exhibition, Manet arranged to have all his work assembled in a gallery which he had had built in the Avenue de l'Alma. His *oeuvre* was already considerable, and the artist's approach to out-of-doors painting, which he was to carry to such lengths later on, could be clearly noticed. The first pictures, *The Absinthe Drinker*, for example, still retained the influence of the "studio technique," with dark shadows arranged according to formula. Then came the successful canvases, *The Spanish Singer* which earned him an honourable mention, and *The Boy with a Sword*, a picture which was later used as an excuse to destroy his reputation. It was good and sound painting, without much individuality. But the artist, who should have stuck to this manner of painting had he wished to live happily, bemedalled and honoured, found to his cost that his temperament led him to make constant evolutions in his art; and, perhaps in spite of himself, he came to paint *Music in the Tuileries Gardens* (exhibited at the Galerie Martinet), the terrible *Luncheon on the Grass* and . . . *an Espada* and . . . *a Mayo*, exhibited in the Salon des Refusés in 1863. After that, the rupture was complete. He became engaged in a twenty years' battle, which only concluded by death.

COLOURPLATE 2

COLOURPLATES 4, 6

COLOURPLATES 11, 18, 31, 19

How strikingly new and original these pictures in the Avenue de l'Alma were! That exquisite *Olympia* lorded it in the middle of one wall, *Olympia* who, in the Salon of 1865, had succeeded in making Paris exasperated with the artist. There too one saw *The Fifer*, so gay in colour; *The Dead Toreador*, a fragment of a superb painting; *The Street Singer*, so absolutely right and delicate in tone; *Lola de Valence* – perhaps the gem of the whole exhibition, so charming in its strangeness! I won't mention the marine subjects, among which was the astonishingly realistic *Battle of the Kearsage and the Alabama*. I won't mention the still-life subjects, the salmon, rabbit and flowers, which even the adversaries of the painter declare to be first-rate, equal to the still-life paintings of the classical Old Masters of the French School.

COLOURPLATE 14

COLOURPLATES 32, 20, 13, 10

COLOURPLATE 21

COLOURPLATES 22, 23, 27

This private exhibition naturally made the critics furious with Manet. Insults and jibes abounded. He was as yet not seriously hurt by them, although a natural impatience began to unnerve him. This revolutionary painter, who adored the fashionable world, had always dreamed of the success that would one day be his in Paris, of the compliments of women, of the welcoming praise of salons, of a life of luxury in the midst of an admiring public. He left his dilapidated studio in the rue Guyot and rented a sort of very ornate gallery – an old fencing school, I believe – and took up work again, determined to conquer Paris by charm. But his temperament was always there to deny him the possibility of making concessions, and he was forced in spite of himself, into the path which he had opened. It was at this period that his painting began to become lighter. His desire to please ended with canvases which were more personal and more revolutionary than the old ones. If he worked less, his vision and the way he depicted things, on the other hand, became more highly developed. One may prefer the more muted tones and accuracy of his first manner, but it must be acknowledged that in his second manner, he reached that logical intensity of *plein air*, that definitive formula which was to have so great an influence on contemporary painting.

To begin with he was enchanted by a success – *A Good Glass of Beer* had been praised by everybody. Here was a return to the dexterous handling of *The Boy with a Sword*, only it was bathed in a fuller light. But he was not always master of his hand, he never employed any fixed method, always retaining the fresh *naïveté* of a student in the presence of Nature. When he started a picture he never knew how it was going to turn out.

COLOURPLATE 54

If Genius consists of unconscious reaction and a natural gift for seeing the truth, then he certainly had genius. Nor was he able to rediscover, no doubt in spite of efforts to the contrary, the happy balance of *A Good Glass of Beer*, in which his own original touch was tempered by a skill which disarmed public opinion.

One after the other, he painted *Doing the Washing, The Masked Ball at the Opera, The Boaters* – strongly individualistic canvases which I prefer, but which threw him back once more into the fray, so entirely different are they from the current methods of other painters.

PAGE 147, COLOURPLATES 64, 66

The evolution was complete. He had succeeded in producing light with his brush.

Then onwards, his talent was completely mature. He had once again changed residence. He produced, one after the other, in his studio in the rue d'Amsterdam, *The Café-Concert, Luncheon on the Grass, In the Conservatory* and yet more works, which are easily recognizable by their limpid quality and the transparency of the air which fills the canvas. From this period date also those admirable pastels – portraits of exquisite delicacy and colour.

COLOURPLATES 84, 96

COLOURPLATES 85, 86, 87, 89, 94, 107

He was taken ill, but he did not lose courage, and spent the spring in the country from which he brought back sketches of flowers and gardens and people lying on the grass.

When it became impossible for him to walk any longer, he seated himself once more before his easel and painted in this way until the last. Success had come to him, he had been decorated, everyone accorded him the place he merited in the art world of our time. He realized quite well, that if his position was not more publicly acclaimed, only a little effort was yet needed for it to be finally established. He was dreaming of the future, hoping to overcome his illness and finish his task, when death put an end to any resistance to his work and made him stand triumphant.

For us his role was filled. He had put the finishing touch to his work. The years that he might have lived would have only consolidated his conquests. In this rapid review it only remains to me to bring to your notice his portraits which are so contemporary in character – those of his father and mother, of Mademoiselle Eva Gonzalès, of Messieurs Antonin Proust, Rochefort, Théodore Duret, de Jouy and Emile Zola. I would also like to mention his old studies, those very interesting copies: *The Virgin with the Rabbit*, the portrait by Tintoretto, a head by Filippino Lippi, which prove how familiar this painter, who was accused of ignorance, was with the Old Masters. Finally, he has left some etchings which are both vigorous and delicate at the same time. Here is twenty-five years of work, battle and victory. This collection shows his whole range of work – how every day he cast away a little of the precepts of art schools, bringing his own vision to bear, by means so clear and obvious that today they have been adopted by all our successful painters.

COLOURPLATES 49, 104, 111, 41, 40
For de Jouy, see page 51.
Titian's Virgin with Rabbit *was painted c. 1530.*

I don't wish here to assume the job of a critic. I say what is. Manet's formula is quite simple. He just looked at Nature and his whole ideal was to force himself to record it truthfully and forcefully. "Composition" has disappeared. All that is left are familiar scenes – one or two figures, sometimes crowds, milling around – which he has captured at a glance. One sole rule guided him – the law of "values," the way someone or some object appears in light. His evolution sprang from that – it is light which forms the design just as much as colour. It is light which puts each thing in its proper place, which is the very life of the subject. Hence those exact tonal values of such singular intensity which routed a public accustomed to the traditional false tone values of art school painting. From that moment features became simplified and were treated as large masses in relation to the picture plain, which made the public burst their sides with laughter, accustomed as it was to seeing everything, down to the very last hairs of a beard, in the blackened backgrounds of historical painting. Nothing is more unbelievable, more exasperating than truth, when one's eyes have been blinded by centuries of lies.

It must be added that Manet's personality made this new formula even less acceptable for people who preferred the beaten track. I have mentioned his unconscious approach, his departure into the unknown, each time he placed his white canvas on his easel. Without nature he was powerless. It was necessary that the subject should pose, and then he could attack it as a copyist, without any tricks, without any recipe of any sort, sometimes with great ability, other times extracting from his clumsiness some delightful effects. Hence his elegant ruggedness, with which he is reproached – those unexpected lacunae which are to be found in his less successful works. His fingers did not always obey his eyes, which were marvellously acute. If he made mistakes, it was not because of lack of study, as has been claimed, because no painter has ever worked with such tenacity as he. It was simply that he was constitutionally made this way. He did as well as he could and could not paint in any other manner. But he had no *parti pris* – he really would have liked to please.

He gave up his whole life to his task, and none of us who knew him well ever dreamed of wishing him to be more balanced or more perfect, for had this been the case, he would certainly have lost most of his originality – that sharp light, that exact sense of values and that vibrant quality which distinguishes his pictures from all others.

Forget all ideas about "perfection" and the "absolute." Don't believe a thing is beautiful just because it is perfect according to certain physical and metaphysical precepts; a thing is beautiful because it lives, because it is human. Then you will savour the art of Manet to the full – this art which blossomed just at the hour when it had a message to impart and which it delivers with such originality. It is intelligent and witty, much more so than those clever "what-d'ye-call-its," now already consigned to the dust of store rooms, with which his work was compared in order to discredit him.

His art could only flourish in Paris – it has the pallor of our women by gaslight, it is the true daughter of an obstinate artist who loved society and who wore himself out conquering it.

If you wish to establish exactly the great place which Manet occupies in our Art, try to name some artists who have come after Ingres, Delacroix and Courbet. Ingres remains the champion of our dying Classical School. Delacroix glows throughout the whole Romantic period; then comes Courbet, a realist in his choice of subjects, but Classical in tone and workmanship, who borrowed a skilful technique from the Old Masters. Certainly, after those great names, I do not ignore certain gifted men who have left numerous *oeuvres*, but I am seeking an innovator, someone who has brought a new outlook to bear on life, who, above all, has modified profoundly the artistic outlook of the art schools, and I am obliged to return to Manet, this man who caused such a scandal, who was denigrated for so long and whose influence today is predominant.

The influence is undeniably there, affirming itself more and more at each new Salon. Remind yourself of what was being thought twenty years ago, remember those dark-hued Salons, where even studies of the nude remained obscure as though covered with dust. The big historical and mythological canvases were smeared with a coat of bitumen. There was no escape into the real living world, bathed in sunlight, except where here and there just one small canvas dared to make a hole in the blue sky.

Then little by little, we have seen the Salons lighten. Mahogany Romans and Greeks and porcelain nymphs have been disappearing from year to year, while the spate of modern subjects, taken from everyday life, grows higher, encroaching on the walls, which it lights up with its vivid colours. It was not only a new world – it was a new sort of painting, a tendency towards *plein air*, in which the law of tone values was respected, in which each figure is painted in light in its correct relation, and no longer treated "ideally" in conformity with traditional convention. I repeat, the evolution is complete. You only have to compare this year's Salon with that of 1863 for example, and you will appreciate the enormous strides which have taken place in the last twenty years; you will be aware of radical difference between these two periods.

Jean-Auguste-Dominique Ingres (1780–1867).

191

In 1863 Manet aroused the public to fury at the Salon des Refusés, in spite of the fact that he was leader of that movement. But now how many times one stops in front of bright pictures with clear colour, to exclaim, "Well, well! a Manet!" He is not a painter one can imitate without admitting it. But it is not the slavish imitators who are by any means the most characteristic – what must be carefully noted is the influence of the artist on the good contemporary painters. While he was being booed for his originality, to which he made absolutely no concessions, all the wily brothers of the brush were gathering crumbs from his table, borrowing from his recipe what the public could not stomach, dressing *plein air* with bourgeois sauce. I will mention no names, but what fortunes have been made, and what reputations built, on his foundations! He used to laugh a little bitterly sometimes, when he realized he was incapable of these pretty tricks. He was robbed to be served up as a dainty titbit to delighted amateurs, who would have quaked in front of a real Manet, but who swooned before the counterfeit Manets which were manufactured wholesale as goods from Paris.

Things came to such a point that even the Ecole des Beaux-Arts was seduced. The most intelligent of its students caught the infection and broke with the recipes as taught in the school, and threw themselves also into the study of *plein air*. Today, whether they admit it or not, all our young painters who are in the vanguard have submitted to Manet's influence, and if they pretend that this resemblance is merely fortuitous, it is none the less evident that he was the first to step out in this direction, thus pointing the way to others. His role as forerunner can no longer be denied by anybody. Since Courbet, he is the last "force" to reveal himself – by "force" I mean a fresh development in vision and interpretation.

That is what everybody will understand today, when they look at the 150 works which we have been able to collect together here. There is no more argument. We pay homage to the heroic effort of the Master and the great part which he has played in Art. Even those who don't entirely accept him, recognize the enormously important place he occupies. Time will succeed in classing him among the great workmen of this century who have given their life that truth might triumph.

PAUL MANTZ

LE TEMPS

"The Works of Manet"

January 16, 1884

Mantz became Director General of the Ministry of Fine Arts in 1882.

When in 1876 the Selection Committee of the Salon, bent on saving the country, turned down the pictures which Manet had submitted, the artist, who was a most correct and courteous "gentleman," invited the fashionable world to the rue de St-Pétersbourg to see the pictures which the jury had considered a danger to the public. This invitation, which I have preserved from a love of history, was in the form of a little card, decorated with a banderole on which was written in gold, *Faire vrai, laisser dire.*

That was his brave device. But these two phrases imposed on the man, who had thus emblazoned his shield, two very disproportionate obligations. When a painter introduces a new element into art, or perhaps one which is merely forgotten, it is highly probable that he will be misunderstood. Many artists, even great ones, have borne this cross. One could make a library from the collection of insults which were levelled at

Delacroix, Théodore Rousseau, Corot and poor Millet. All of them suffered. Manet, the revolutionary, conformed strictly to tradition in giving the public the right to laugh at him. He felt himself caught up in the struggle and became easily resigned to it. But as for the first part of the device, *Tell the truth (faire vrai)*, this was quite a different business. To achieve this ambition was beyond Manet's technical ability. In conjunction with his works, this device appears ironic. The artist has pursued one aspect of Nature but he has not thoroughly understood it; sometimes, he has even betrayed and slandered it. In some ways Manet is "chimerical." One is aware of the sharp division of opinion between the painter's friends and more dispassionate critics. For there is something strange about Manet's case: he is freely praised for qualities which he does not possess. He is considered one of the naturalist painters. He first delighted in searching for purely optical effects, sampling tone-values without asking himself whether they were correct or not, and, later, began to be seduced by the laws of harmonic contrast.

It is from this point of view that the works of Manet are interesting. Even when they do not seem to have "come off," and that is more often than not, they present problems of colour. That is already something, because there are a lot of honest painters in the world, who have never given a thought to these questions.

Manet's history is known, but even if it has been told elsewhere, fresh light is thrown on it by the exhibition organized in the galleries of the Ecole des Beaux-Arts. The catalogue has been arranged in a sufficiently accurate chronological order to be instructive. By following the order of dates, one can appreciate the different phases which Manet's talent passed through from beginning to end. One can see quite well that the artist was uneasy, almost repentant, and that he would have liked to have been excused for the first violence of youth, by means of certain *délicatesses* achieved at great cost.

In 1850, when he was about seventeen, Manet made a trip to Brazil in compliance with the wishes of his family. This was not a voyage for art's sake and from the point of view of painting, the profit obtained from it was negligible. On his return he made two journeys which were important in another way. He visited Holland and Italy. Perhaps he was too young to understand this double lesson, which, however, bore fruit. One could say that Manet was seduced by the creations of the Primitives. A copy, a fairly fine copy moreover, can be found at the Ecole des Beaux-Arts of Filippino Lippi's portrait of a young man in the Uffizi in Florence. It was a happy inspiration that led Manet to ask advice of Filippino because, to begin with, one should learn to know and love the fifteenth century and the painters who do not lie. Holland also seems to have interested Manet. It was here that he learned to know Franz Hals (then so poorly represented in the Louvre) and was able to study his vigorous workmanship and whip-lash technique.

The lessons of these Masters were unfortunately contradicted by the lessons Manet was taught in Couture's atelier. It is said that he worked there several years – he must have wasted his time. The studio of the painter of *Romans of the Decadence* was the temple of chic and artificial methods. Manet, whose innocence should have been respected, there learnt the odd thing, that to draw a figure with a brush and separate it from its surrounding background, one must put a black line round it! He was simple enough to accept this doctrine and was poisoned by it all his youth. Even in his famous *Olympia*, painted about 1863 (although it only appeared in the Salon in 1865) a trace of this primitive error is still visible. The unpleasing figure of this wretched little woman is enclosed in a contour which might have been drawn in soot. This is not in the least the way that light fixes the boundaries of a body. Manet certainly never saw anything like this in Nature. But the evidence of those far-off days – and his works, too – are there to show that Manet started to paint in blacks. It

Théodore Rousseau (1812–67), French painter and member of the Barbizon School.

COLOURPLATE 14

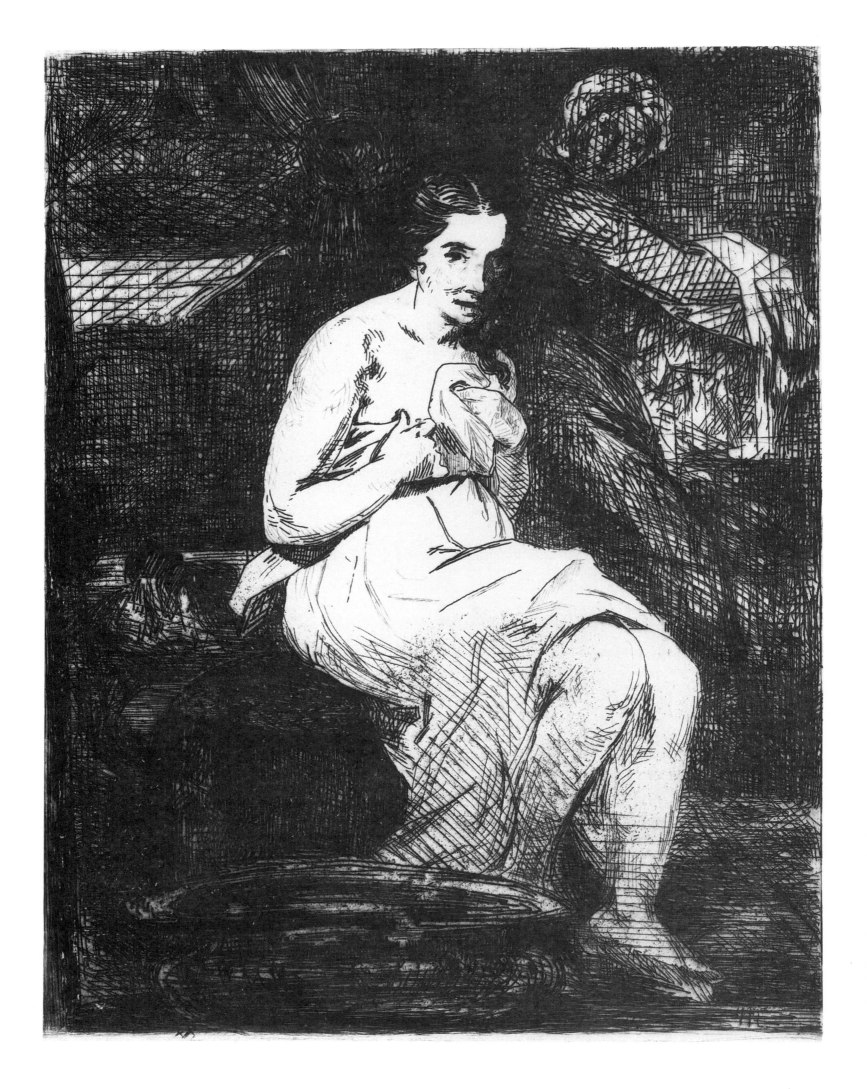

194

was not without difficulty that he decided to follow the poet's advice and cleanse himself – not with ambrosia like Mercury – but with light.

To begin with Manet was a sombre painter. He lived underground. *The Absinthe Drinker* is dated 1860. This is a studio figure, a figure that stifles in airless surroundings. No contrast, no relief, no realism! Strange; this toper is a purely subjective vision – one might say that at that time Manet had not yet opened the window on Nature and life. Surely, for a man like Manet, this is a strange point of departure.

But this poor fare was intolerable. Manet emerged from his cellar where he had been momentarily locked in. He saw clearly that his *Absinthe Drinker* was poorly done, and he appreciated that free and vigorous brushwork (whatever the mystics might say) played a role of capital importance. He looked for the "accent of touch" and with a deliberate hand painted *The Spanish Singer* of the 1861 Salon, and also soon afterwards, *The Boy with a Sword* which we are sorry not to see at the Ecole des Beaux-Arts.

The Spanish Singer had a success. "Caramba!" exclaimed Théophile Gautier, "here's a guitarrero who hasn't just stepped out of the Opéra Comique and who would not look too good as an illustration to a romance." What the dear critic was admiring in this beginner's picture, was the beauty of the impasto and the boldness of brushwork. This was everybody's opinion at a time when official opinion was supporting the doubtful charms of certain neo-Classicists, whose way of painting was mean and dry, or, like poor Hamon's, melted into a pale fog. In *The Spanish Singer* and in *The Boy with a Sword* there was a hint, not of Velazquez as people freely said, but of Franz Hals, that great swash-buckler. I don't want to discuss here the colour, but the way in which the paint is spread on the canvas. By painting in this manner, Manet, who up to now had had so little experience, could claim forever-glorious ancestors. To somewhat vague form, he applied determined, decisive brush strokes. The figures, true, are still studio products. They stand out from dark or arbitrary backgrounds, in made-up surroundings, and in an unbreathable atmosphere. As art, this was crude but dashing enough.

At this moment, an evolution began to take place in Manet's art which *The Absinthe Drinker* in no way foreshadowed. He was about to open that window which had been so hermetically sealed during his years of apprenticeship. His eye was more sensitive; he looked more closely at Nature and saw better. For his own edification, he devoted himself to a very worthwhile job – an unusually instructive study. Manet laid out a white table-cloth, and on this table-cloth he placed dishes, kitchen utensils, victuals – all the intimate things that even the most ethereal of men need twice a day. Manet then began to copy consciously what he saw. This was good drill for hand and eye. In this type of painting, to which he often returned, Manet has produced some excellent canvases, in which the tone relationships have been carefully studied – if not in their delicate transparency, at least in their particular coloration. This table-cloth, which constituted the dominant note in his still-life pictures, taught Manet a great lesson and gave him freedom; for now on, one notices that "white" was no longer forbidden to this painter of "blacks."

All this came about without too much fuss. The social order did not as yet feel threatened; but the tumult was about to break out; it was to be terrible and unending. The real advent of Manet took place in the middle of a storm. The Salon of 1863 was being prepared. Under the influence of the new rays which were beginning to shine on him, Manet painted three pictures to which he attached great importance, which were to demonstrate – only too perceptibly, alas – this unforeseen transformation. He wanted to show the people of Paris *Bathing* (which today is known as *Luncheon on the Grass*), *Portrait of a Young Man in the Costume of a Mayo* and *Portrait of Mlle V . . . in the Costume of an Espada*. These pictures were regarded as offensive. They were all rejected by the jury.

COLOURPLATE 2

COLOURPLATES 4, 6

Gautier's remark continued: "Velázquez would have greeted him with a friendly wink, and Goya would have asked him for a light for his papelito. . . ."

COLOURPLATES 18, 19, 12

OPPOSITE *The Toilette.* 1862. Etching, 11 × 8¾" (28.4 × 22.3 cm).

We have always deplored this abuse of power. It does not conform to the rights of the individual and serves no purpose. I maintain that there was not sufficient reason for the jury to have taken such extreme action as far as these pictures were concerned – there was, in fact, in these "doubtful" paintings something to be admired – clear tone.

Manet's three pictures were exhibited in the Salon des Refusés. There was a considerable fuss over them. All the same, in spite of the inevitable protests which his methods provoked, and which still provoke, the artist, in the eyes of those who did not lose their heads, seemed to be worth studying. In spite of all his ugliness, for which he will never be forgiven, he turned the modern palette into a sort of flower, not unknown, but too long forgotten. He arrived on the scene, with clear and rosy colours, at a time when Courbet, robust and ponderous, was a celebrity. This Guercino from the Franche-Comté had allowed his feet to drag through the mud of the Bolognese school. Many of his associates liked this deplorable "gravy" but demanded a bright painter. Perhaps in these three pictures in the Salon des Refusés there was perceptible the beginning of a protest and the possibility of hope.

For those who know a little history, it is unnecessary to point out that these clear, light tonal values were by no means a new invention. One no longer "invents," all one does is to "resuscitate." Clear tone is one of the religions of the past. In the fifteenth century Roger Van der Weyden, Memling and Piero della Francesca found a way of expressing everything by painting pale faces, practically without a shadow. A hundred years later, many portrait painters were continuing to paint in this honest way. Holbein sometimes, Janet always. The admirable portrait of the Duc d'Alençon in the Saint Petersburg Museum, the work of an unknown Frenchman, has the delicate freshness of a Persian rose. Fresh tones used to be appreciated, and were appreciated for a long time. It was the decadent schools, Bologna in particular, which incarcerated the poor painter in a cellar full of rusty, sooty colours. The mistakes of the Carracci will never be punished. It was left to Rubens, the pupil of Phoebus, to rouse the sleeping colours in dens of black shadow. After having been compromised for a little while by his association with Caravaggio, Rubens rendered to the art of painting the joys of his flowing brush. On that day, the world was saved. Almost the whole of the eighteenth century sailed under a rosy pennant. At least that is the lesson we learn from history. Manet never discovered an America – he merely returned to the traditions of the past. But the manipulation of clear colours implies a perfect dexterity with one's tools, an exquisite delicacy of touch. Manet was neither strong nor supple enough to put into practice the principles which he had restored. There was a contradiction between the man and the artist. This fine fellow who was so distinguished in appearance and so gentle in manner, had a brush tipped with unconscious harshness. He was afraid of appearing insipid and so became increasingly and unnecessarily brutal. An adventurous jeweller when he had discovered a delicate colour, he set it in surroundings of tawdry vulgarity. Monsieur Émile Zola was right every time – *Luncheon on the Grass* **is** a terrible picture.

It is terrible and it is cruel. It is not that the subject is indecent, as the members of the jury thought in 1863. A young naked woman, lunching in the company of two fully dressed men is something which one can see every day, if not in real life, in the Venetian School of painting. When Giorgioni painted his *Concert*, in which the nude woman is so happily related to the empurpled gentleman, he did not upset the modesty of the *gardes champêtres* of Castelfranco. Manet was inspired by entirely legitimate motives. But the scene has a certain harshness which is hard on the eyes of the passer-by. Perhaps all this should be explained. When at some future date – still some way off – professors of aesthetics organize conferences on Manet, they will say that as far as colour is concerned – and that was the principal thing with which he was preoccupied – this so-called "natural-

See page 189.

The reference to Giorgione's "concert" probably relates to the Concert Champêtre *in the Louvre. This work has been attributed to both Giorgione and Titian.*

ist" painter spent the first half of his life practising a cult of systematic exaggeration. Manet could see perfectly well that there was an interval between tones of greater or lesser intensity, between tones impregnated, to a greater or lesser degree, with light. But after measuring this interval, he doubles or trebles it to obtain more striking or more strident contrasts. He believes in imitating the courage of the poppy which bravely installs itself in the midst of green grass, but he forgets that if the poppy has effrontery, it is also neighbourly, and when kissed by light, its red petals and the neighbouring verdure exchange courtesies – I mean reflections – which are like caresses, and which render the harshness of the scene harmonious.

Manet suppresses these liaisons, these friendships, which link objects together without restricting their individuality. In *Luncheon on the Grass* he practises a crude theory of brusque and sharp contrasts; he does not believe in making colours harmonize in the pervading atmosphere.

The savagery of this manner frightened away many respectable people, even those who had been converted to the cult of clear tones by a walk in the country or into the fifteenth century. Manet was not slow to perceive that he had struck too hard. He understood that after all harmony perhaps was not an invention of Hell, and he began to add a little music to his palette. *The Dead Man*, exhibited in the Salon of 1864 COLOURPLATE 20 under another title, revealed a perceptible progress in the artist's work. There is nothing outrageous about this figure, in which some beautiful dark passages – a colourist's dark tones – may be noted. It is executed more freely while still remaining strong and bold. At the same time Manet discovered a certain piquant grey which was to stand him in very good stead. This grey, too often neglected until now, was to serve as a means of uniting colours together which hitherto had been segregated. It was in this sombre key that Manet painted *Reading*, a picture which does not offend COLOURPLATE 25 the eye and at which the artist's admirers scarcely cast a glance. One knows that these greys, variegated in the intensity of their warmth and heightened with pink, were used later in *A Good Glass of Beer*, the only COLOURPLATE 54 picture by Manet ever truly to be accepted by the public, and which made some uncompromising people believe that its author was capable of all possible manner of treachery and was secretly putting up for the Academy.

This period, characterized by the study of grey, marks a curious moment in the evolution of Manet's vision. His painting becomes more delicate, although it still excludes completely the appearance of things as they are out of doors. In 1866, this grey colour is used as a background for various figures – *The Fifer* for example – which for several years passed as a COLOURPLATE 32 classic and definitive type. This picture represents a young musician, not too well drawn, painted in lively colours, among which the red of the trousers sings out boldly. He is set against a monochrome grey background. No ground, no air, no perspective. The wretched fellow is stuck against an imaginary wall.

The idea that there is real atmosphere behind bodies or that they are surrounded by air does not enter Manet's head. He remains faithful to the system of the "cut-outs." He remains faithful to the good old makers of playing cards. *The Fifer*, an amusing specimen of primitive illustration, is like a Jack of Diamonds, stuck on a door.

It is obvious that the evolution in art which was begun by Manet was held up by initial doubts. He was already thirty-two years of age, and was still confining himself to researches into the handling of paint and colour; he had not yet made contact with true light. What a waste of time!

How many years spent in fighting against the memories of dark paint! We regret that we cannot fix exactly the moment when Manet began precisely to conceive the idea of an "out-of-doors" atmosphere.

There seems to be a lacuna here in the exhibition at the Ecole des Beaux-Arts, but by digging into the past we can still gain a vivid impression of what our contemporaries thought, when, in the spring of 1867, Manet made himself into his own selection committee and exhibited all the paintings he had made up to that date. . . .

By putting all his works under his own personal roof, Manet was copying the example of Courbet – the only time that he ever imitated him. This exhibtion was scoffed at, but quite wrongly, because it showed that the artist was not condemned for ever to crude painting. Here, together with his former violent pictures, were flower pieces, fruit and glimpses of landscape – there were also some marine subjects.

I feel strongly that the change that was to take place in Manet's work, was due to the influence of the magnificent views of the sea which had so captured his imagination. His *Steamboat, Seaview* and *The Battle of the Kearsage and the Alabama* were on view at this private view of 1867. He did not study the sea in his studio. In order to paint his marine subjects, their author had to measure his strength against the horizon and the wind. The sea which he had already crossed, had a ready appeal for him – it owned no master and was free. From a purely nautical point of view I do not know whether his combat between the two American ships has verisimilitude – but "likeness" was never one of Manet's worries. He observed colour, and during his sea trips he discovered an intense strong blue. He never forgot this deep vigorous blue; he loved it so much that he used it sometimes even out of place. I am referring here to a picture – *Argenteuil* – which belongs to Manet's last manner, and which as a human document is absolutely characteristic. This painting has already been commented on apropos of the Salon of 1875, but we must return to it because it cancels out Manet, the instinctive painter, and substitutes Manet the scientific painter. A man and woman are seated in a canoe in sunshine. It is the light of full summer. The torrid hot season and the sunshine has turned them to gold. Their faces and arms are painted orange with a touch of brown. Manet wished to emphasize the flesh tints of these figures, and then recalled what he had learned in textbooks. So, anxious to achieve harmony, by the use of complimentary colours, he introduced blue into the background against which the figures are set, and then, delighted with the result, he wanted to enhance the brown tones even more and so forced up the azure tones. He forgot all about Argenteuil and geography and turned the Seine into a deliciously blue Mediterranean Sea. The harmonious contrast of the two colours is interesting, but the intellectual accident is even more so. It proves conclusively that Manet is anything but a "realist." He seeks to relate tones rather than express the actual resemblance of things about him – when the "truth" bothers him, it is suppressed.

This quest for well-thought-out contrasts characterizes Manet's last manner. Why, in *The Bar at the Folies-Bergère*, is the doll sitting [sic] at the counter, selling oranges? Merely because she is wearing a blue dress, and because Manet knows the colour of the paper on which stall-holders display their "fine oranges" in the streets. But this quest has sometimes led the artist into adventurous paths; he is certainly unaccountable and tends to exaggerate when he tries to analyse the colour of shadows. There are some disquieting blues in *At Père Lathuille's*, and an accumulation of unnecessary ugliness. One is also familiar with the violet with which Monsieur Pertuiset has thought fit to surround himself in order to bring down his prey. This is all very odd – and quite different from *Luncheon on the Grass* and the old work; for now, at the end of his life, Manet was substituting studies in harmony for his former savage manner, and he seems to be asking to be forgiven for having assaulted one's senses with his sharp multi-coloured contrasts. *In The Conservatory* and *Jeanne* both leave an impression on the eye of deliberate repose. But *plein air* of which we all have spoken so much is scarcely apparent in these two pictures. The figures appear to be stuck on painted paper backgrounds, and no breath of air disturbs the foliage.

COLOURPLATE 21

COLOURPLATE 65

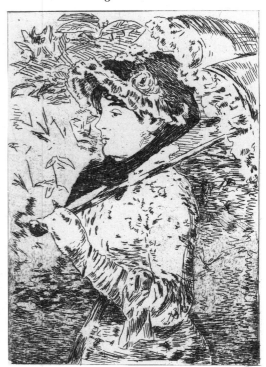

Jeanne: Spring. 1882. Etching and aquatint, 6 × 4¼″ (15.4 × 10.7 cm).

COLOURPLATE 91

COLOURPLATE 110

COLOURPLATE 96

198

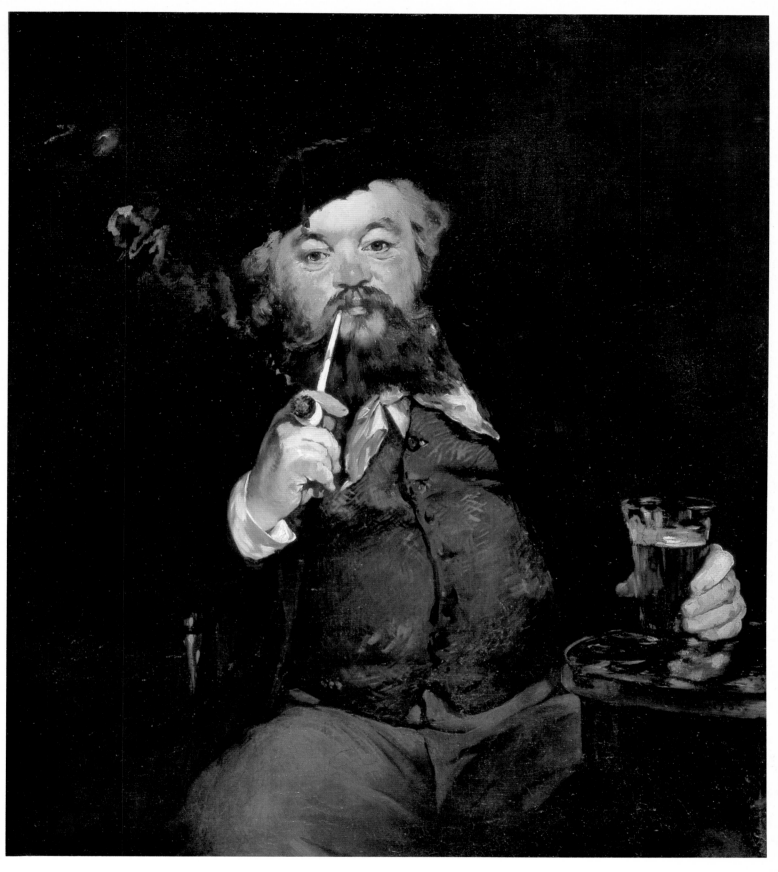

COLOURPLATE 54. *A Good Glass of Beer (Le Bon Bock)*. 1873. 37¼ × 32¾″ (94 × 83 cm).
Philadelphia Museum of Art (The Mr and Mrs Carroll S. Tyson Collection).

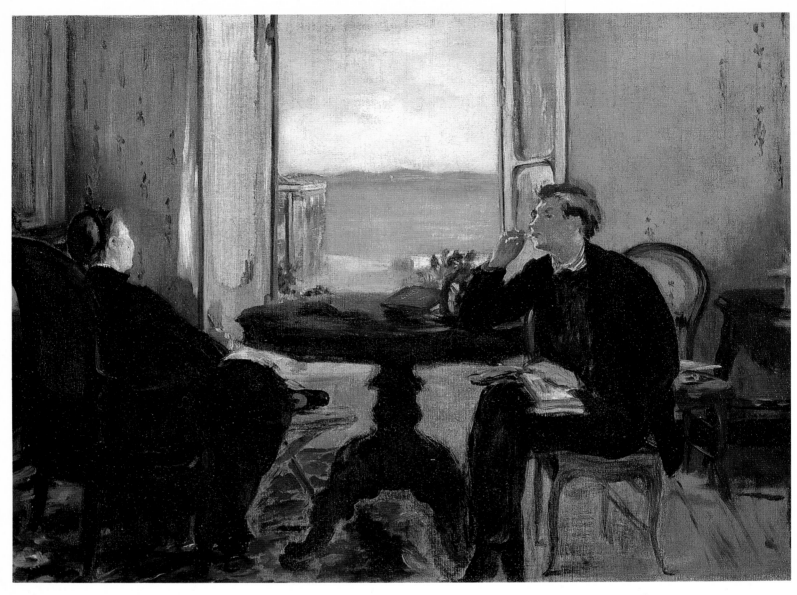

COLOURPLATE 55. *Interior at Arcachon*. 1871. 15½ × 21⅛″ (39.4 × 53.7 cm).
Sterling and Francine Clark Art Institute, Williamstown, Mass.

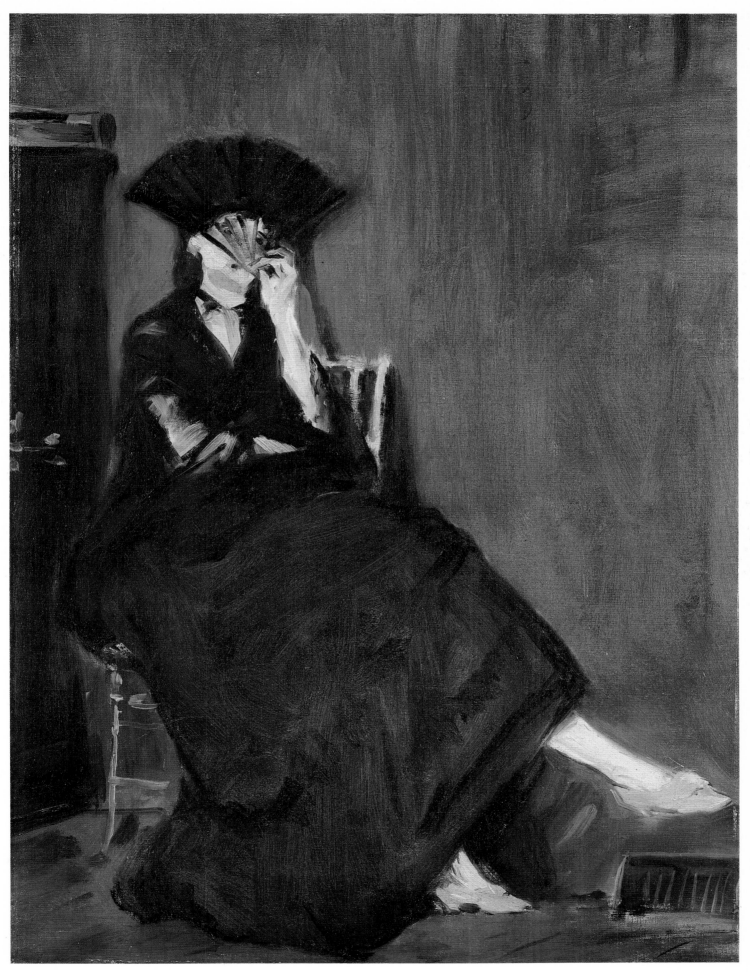

COLOURPLATE 56. *Berthe Morisot with a Fan.* 1872. 23½ × 17¾″ (60 × 45 cm).
Musée d'Orsay, Paris.

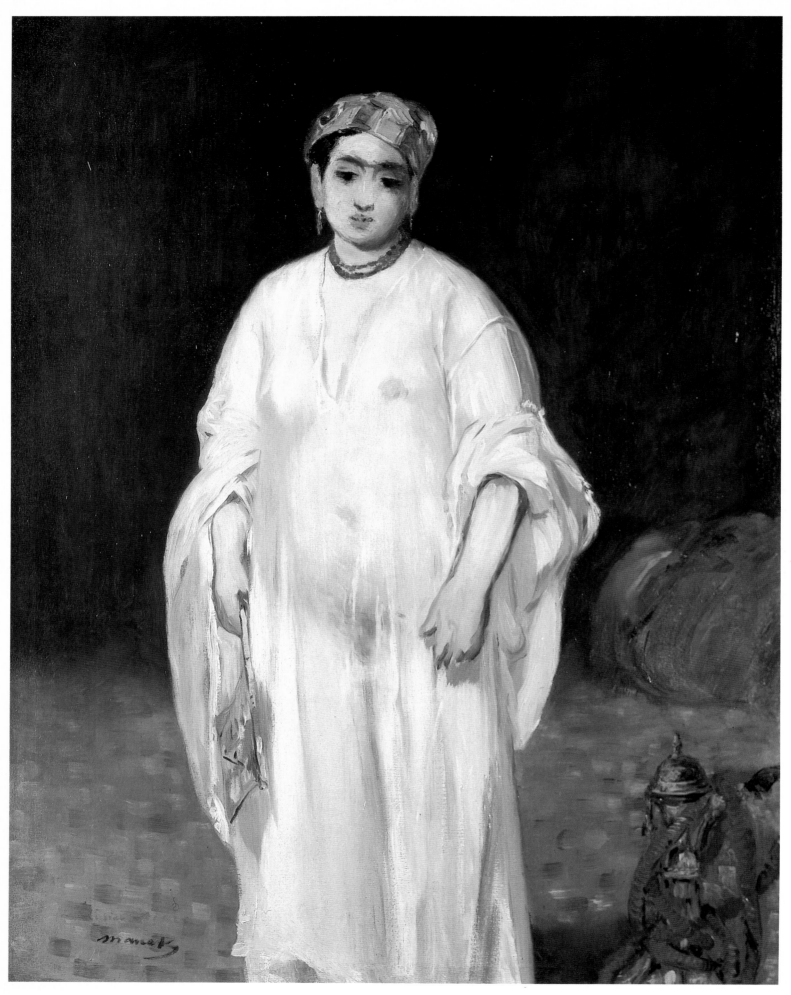

COLOURPLATE 57. *Young Woman in Oriental Costume*. c. 1871. 36¼ × 28¾″ (92 × 73 cm).
Foundation E.G. Bührle Collection, Zurich.

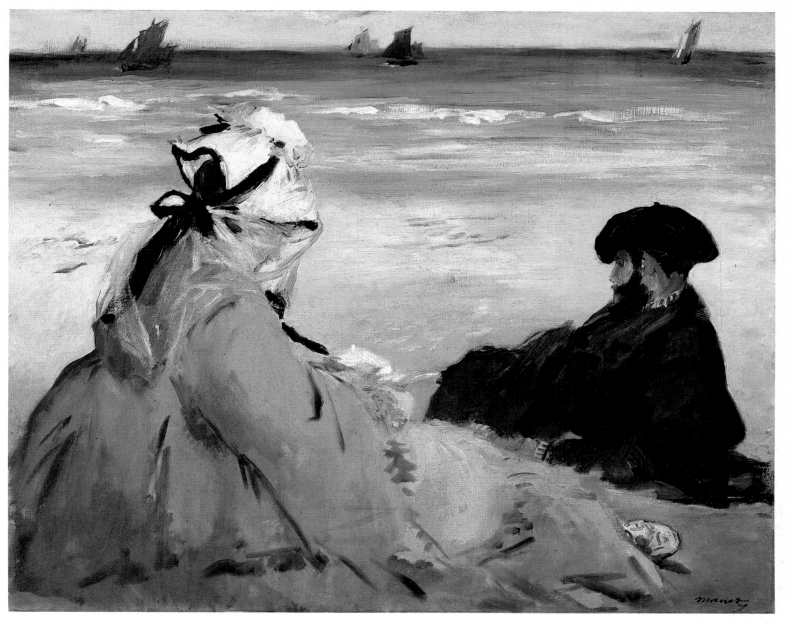

COLOURPLATE 58. *On the Beach*. 1873. 23½ × 18″ (59.6 × 73.2 cm).
Musée d'Orsay, Paris.

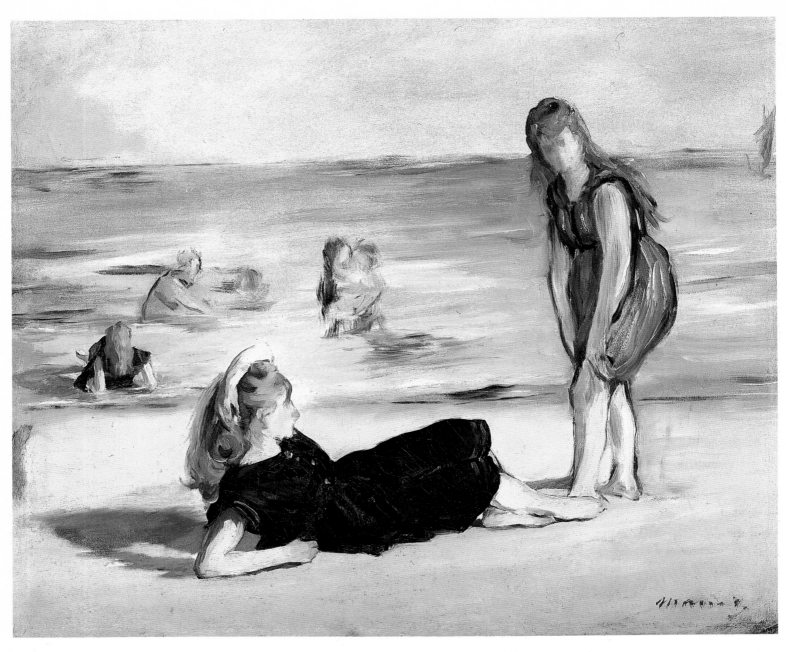

COLOURPLATE 59. *Women on the Beach*. 1873. 15 × 17¼″ (38 × 44 cm).
Detroit Institute of Arts (Bequest of Robert H. Tannahill).

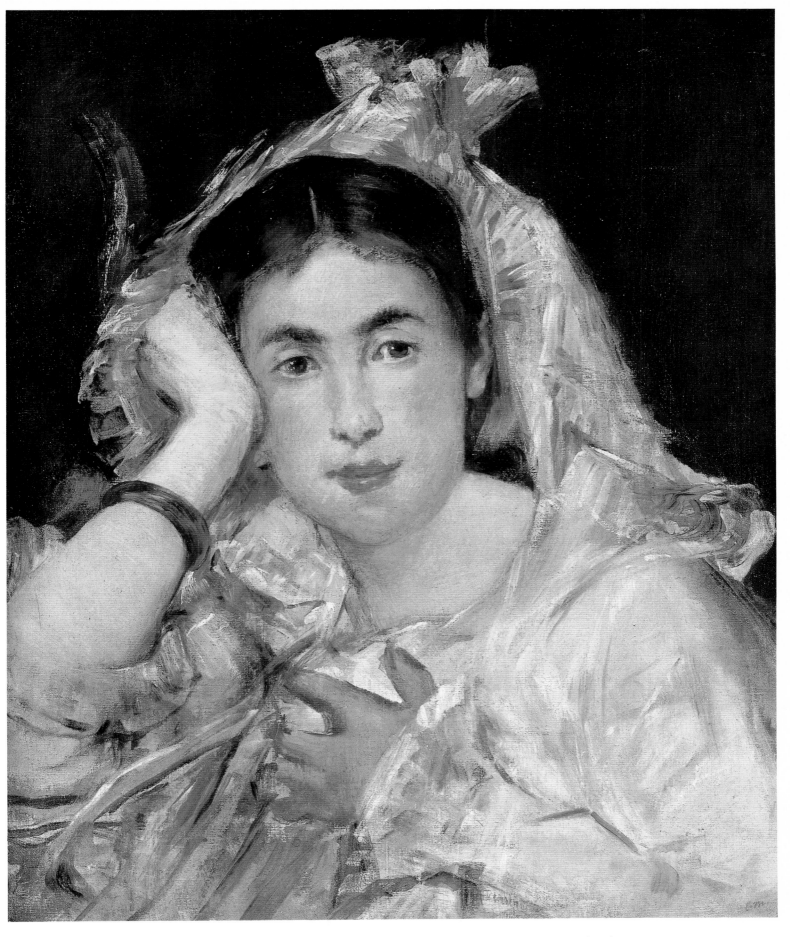

COLOURPLATE 60. *Portrait of Marguerite de Conflans*. 1873. 22 × 18″ (56 × 46 cm).
Oskar Reinhart Collection, Winterthur.

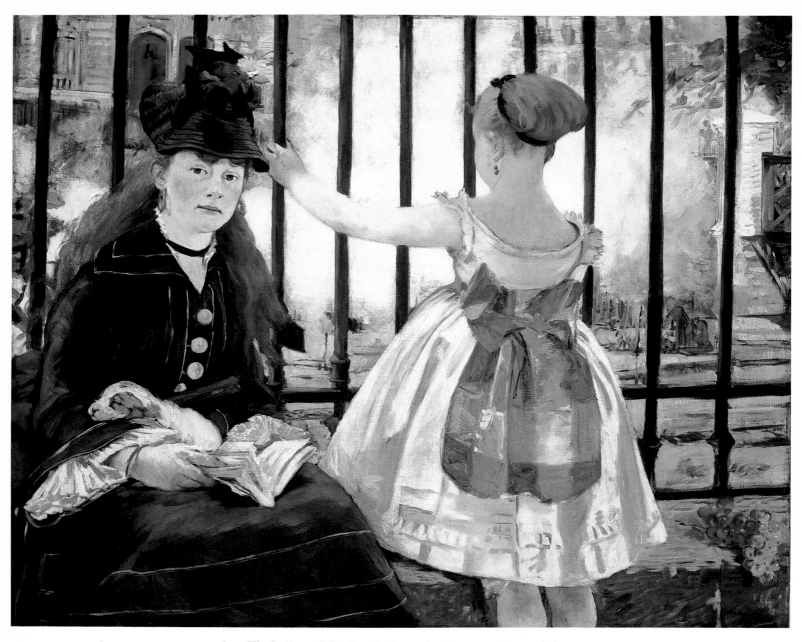

COLOURPLATE 61. *The Railway (The Gare St-Lazare)*. 1872–3. 36¾ × 45⅛″ (93.3 × 114.5 cm).
National Gallery of Art, Washington D.C. (Gift of Horace Havemeyer in Memory of his Mother,
Louisine W. Havemeyer).

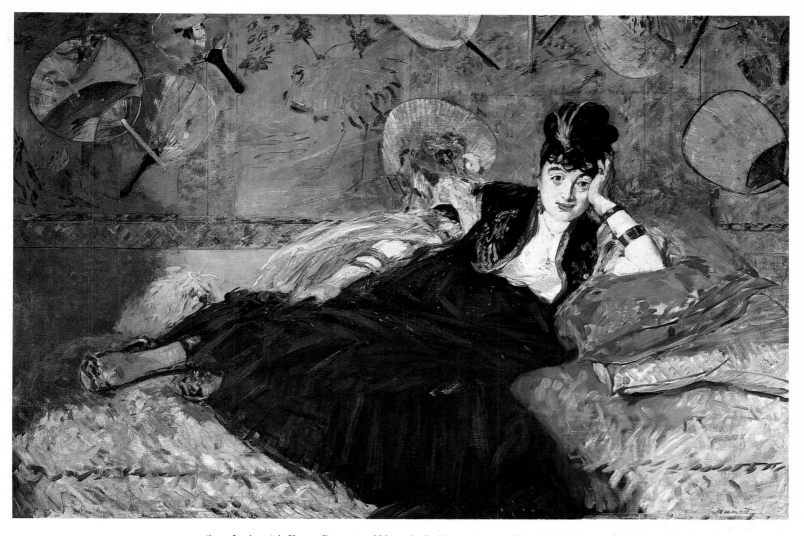

COLOURPLATE 62. *Lady with Fans: Portrait of Nina de Callias.* 1873. 44¾ × 65½″ (113.5 × 166.5 cm).
Musée d'Orsay, Paris.

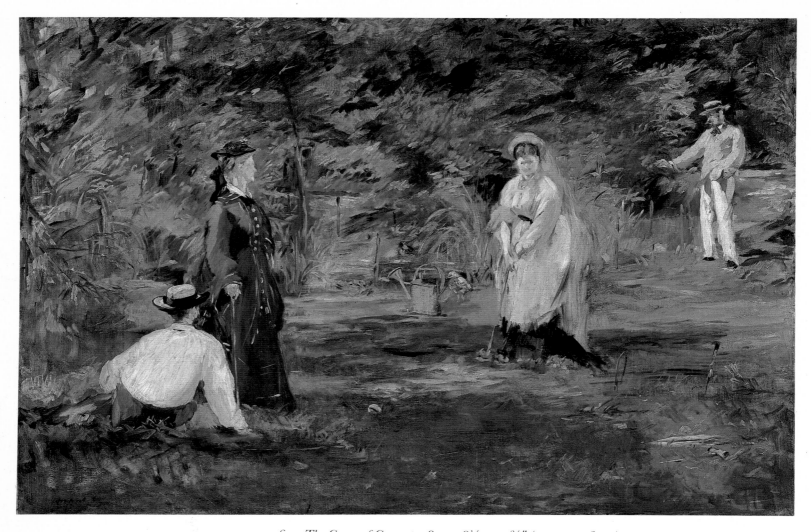

COLOURPLATE 63. *The Game of Croquet.* 1873. 28½ × 41¾″ (72.5 × 106cm).
Städelsches Kunstinstitut, Frankfurt.

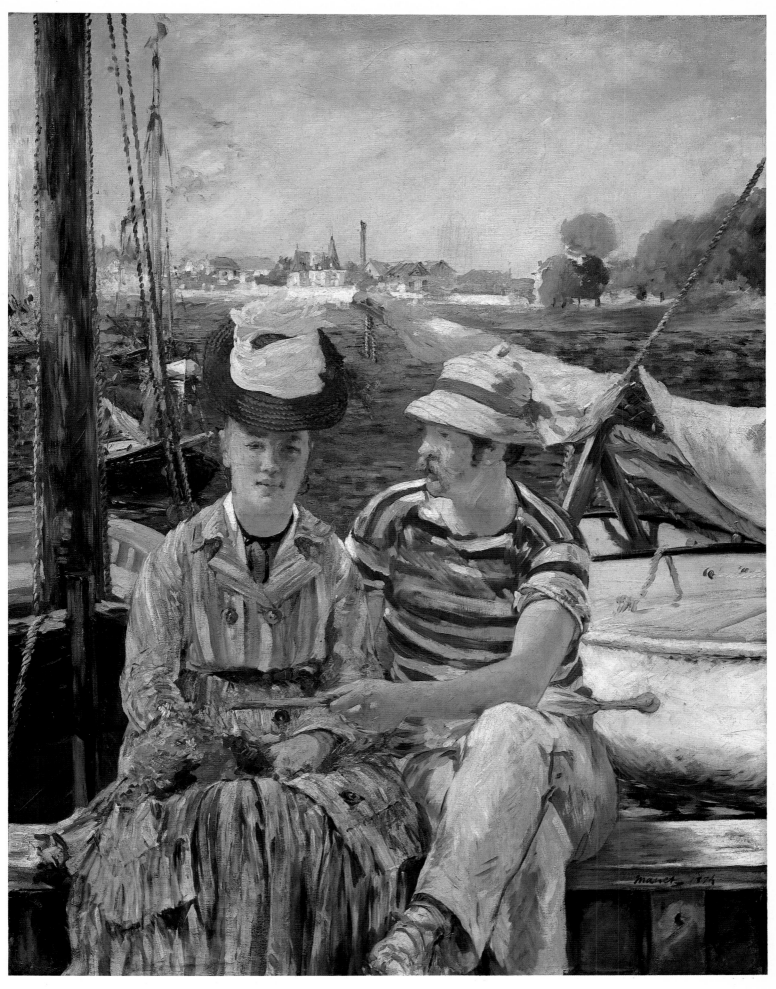

COLOURPLATE 65. *Argenteuil*. 1874. 58½ × 45¼″ (149 × 115 cm).
Musée des Beaux-Arts, Tournai.

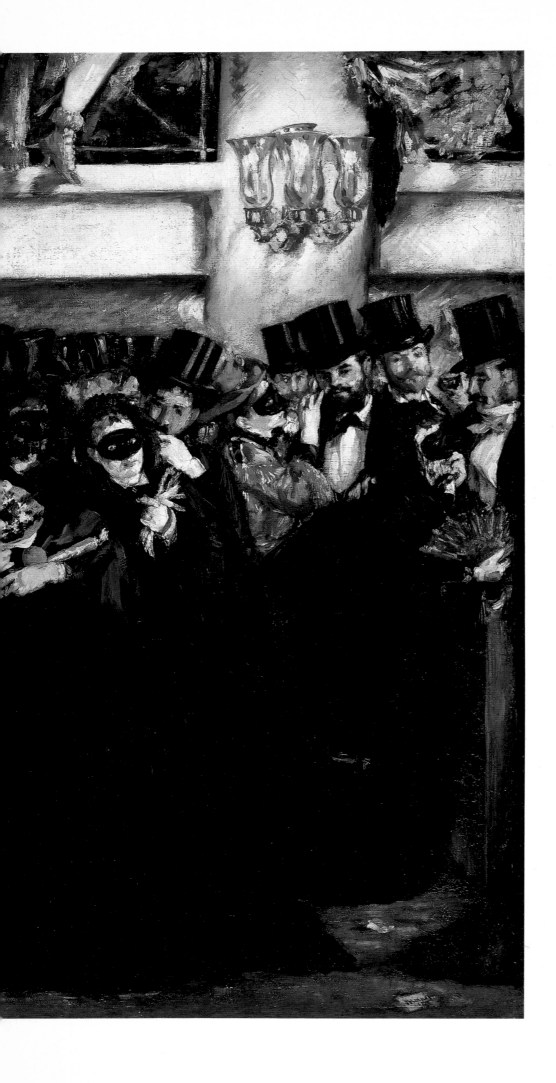

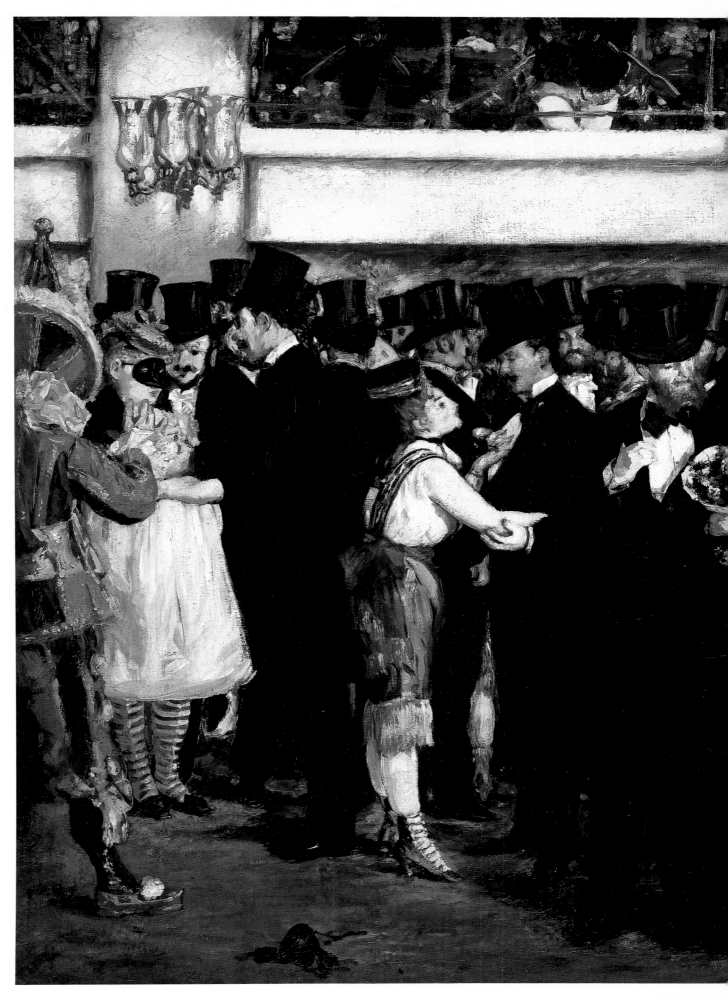

COLOURPLATE 64. *Masked Ball at the Opéra.* 1873–4. 23¼ × 28½″ (59 × 72.5 cm).
National Gallery of Art, Washington D.C. (Gift of Mrs Horace Havemeyer in Memory of her
Mother-in-Law, Louisine W. Havemeyer).

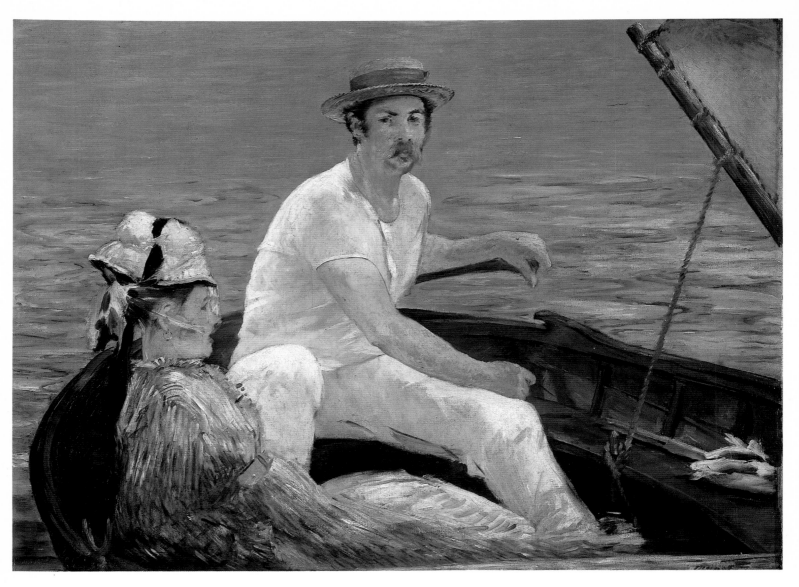

COLOURPLATE 66. *Boating*. 1874. 38¼ × 51¼″ (97 × 130 cm).
Metropolitan Museum of Art, New York (Bequest of Mrs H.O. Havemeyer, 1929. The H.O.
Havemeyer Collection).

During these last years Manet, who would have liked to please, found a more delicate means than the brush to express the subtle character of his discoveries. He took to using pastel and showed a happy dexterity in the use of chalk. The works on exhibition at the Ecole des Beaux-Arts are not much more than rough sketches for subjects, but in these pinky-greys and pale ash colours there are the beginnings of a rare delicacy.

What is the significance of Manet's art? I don't understand why it is that people are pleased to regard a collection consisting of imperfectly developed ideas as something so significant. If the representation of human life, with its attendant joys and miseries, counts for anything in painting, then Manet's work, looked at from the point of view of motif, has very little to tell us. Except for the beer drinker, enjoying his pint and smoking, and *Lola de Valence*, whose graceful bearing evokes memories of Spain, the actors whom he places on the stage, are mostly dumb. They pose immobile – don't ask them to show any feeling, or to express an opinion. They share the calm of a still-life group. They are examples of painting in which the sole interest lies in the technical questions they raise. This absence of conscious charm is evident in many works – with the exception of the pastels, where a *morbidezza* softens the form – chiefly because Manet was an indifferent painter of flesh. This is a grave accusation to make in a biography of a "naturalist" painter. The faces which the artist portrays are for the most part masks painted in more or less pale colours, but are only very mediocre as far as vivacity is concerned. To love the little blue serving girl in the Folies-Bergère we must learn to grow fond of cardboard women. Our hearts reject such a thought.

COLOURPLATE 10

Astonishingly, happy brushwork, frequent mistakes, a doubtful respect for the human figure and a strange contempt for feminine beauty are not sufficient in themselves to play a part in the history of painting. But Manet had something more. With him everything is subservient to the problem of colour and light. That was his main preoccupation which will remain the most interesting aspect of his work. It is a pleasure to see him struggling against the sombre tones of his early period and then to see clear, fresh flesh tints among examples of his savage manner; and then to see little by little how he accepted the idea of using delicate greys and how he finally replaced these experiments, which temperamentally he was not always able to carry off, by carefully considered colours which were strong, complementary and vibrant, or delicately related.

The future will tell whether these essays (which are only too often unsuccessful because of exaggeration or because – and the friends of Manet have admitted this – his mind was not always master of his hand) will take their place in the history of art. Manet chose for himself a thorny path which was far from attractive. His approach to painting is violent and for this reason the value of the lessons to be learnt from it is considerably lessened. However he served a purpose, and will do so later. He has reduced the *cuisiniers* of Bologna to silence. In his happiest moments he had a real understanding of light. From this point of view he was ahead of his times. Manet *suspected* how clear tones might be achieved, others will *state* it. We only see in him a "beginning." Manet is like a false dawn, still surrounded by night.

JACQUES DE BIEZ

ÉDOUARD MANET. CONFÉRENCE FAITE À LA SALLE DES CAPUCINES

Manet's Realism

January 22, 1884

As I understand it, Manet is a less powerful analyst than the author of the Rougon-Macquart. If he is working with the living document, he does not slash at it with sabre cuts. Zola persists, tries again, delves and delves once more into all the unexplored corners. Less deep than his critic, Manet has an attitude of delicate tenderness which is quite unlike the general tone of Emile Zola's novels. If we were to have to find a true equivalent for him in the world of letters, we would perhaps have to look to the Goncourts when they write of life in the eighteenth century. Like them, he proceeds using a delicate, elegant, vivid, brilliant (and very French) type of synthesis of the external aspects of the aristocratic France of the last century.

The quintessential French spirit is of this temper, it is clear and moves rapidly over the surface of things. It is quick-witted. It understands immediately. No need to insist too much, that wearies it. Any superfluity of explanatory details stuns it, numbs it. To a German who might proffer twenty volumes of notes to explain Molière, it replies that it can't abide the slogging approach, and that it learns far more from going to see a performance of *Le Misanthrope*.

In order to know what Manet might have done had he been a man of letters, one might turn to this delicious picture of an omnibus in *Manette Salomon*, "that contraption which gives the impression of moving forward and yet is constantly stopping," which is in fact given by a painter, Coriolis. Here everything is written in terms of light, of shifting patches of colour, glimpses of passing forms, shadows, waves, touches, which are as it were the plastic expression of things seen.

". . . I had finished spelling out those lowering advertisements, the Etoile candle, Collas benzene. I was staring dully at houses, streets, shadowy masses, things lit up, gas jets, shop windows, a little pink woman's shoe in a watch on a glass shelf, little things, nothing really, just whatever passed by. . . . I had reached a point where I was mechanically following the endless flow of shadows of people as they passed across the shutters of closed shops . . . a series of silhouettes. . . . Opposite me I had a man with glasses who was doggedly trying to read a newspaper . . . there were always reflections in his glasses. . . .

"Have *you* noticed how mysteriously pretty women look, at night, in carriages? . . . They seem to have something shadowy, ghostly, mask-like about them . . . a veiled look, a voluptuous appearance, things one can guess at and not clearly see, a vague hue, a night smile, with lights falling on their features, all those half-reflections which swim beneath their hats, the great touches of black they have in their eyes, their very skirts, so full of shadows. . . . This is how she appeared . . . elegant and eyes lowered. . . . The light of the lantern shone on her forehead (which had the silkiness of ivory) . . . and cast a sprinkling of light on to the roots of her hair, which looked like floss in sunlight. . . . Three touches of brightness, on the line of the nose, on a cheek-bone, on a chin tip . . . then, total eclipse . . . she has turned her back to the lantern. . . . Her face opposite me is an intense patch of darkness. . . . Nothing now except a shaft of light on a corner of her temple and a tip of her ear where a little diamond button glints

Jacques de Biez (1852–1915), journalist, historian and art critic. De Biez's lecture was delivered in Paris at the Salle des Capucines to coincide with the posthumous showing of Manet's work at the École des Beaux-Arts.

The generic title of the cycle of twenty novels written 1871–83 by Émile Zola. Zola described the series as the "natural and social history of a family at the time of the Second Empire".

Molière (Jean-Baptiste Poquelin) (c. 1622–73). Le Misanthrope *was written in 1666.*

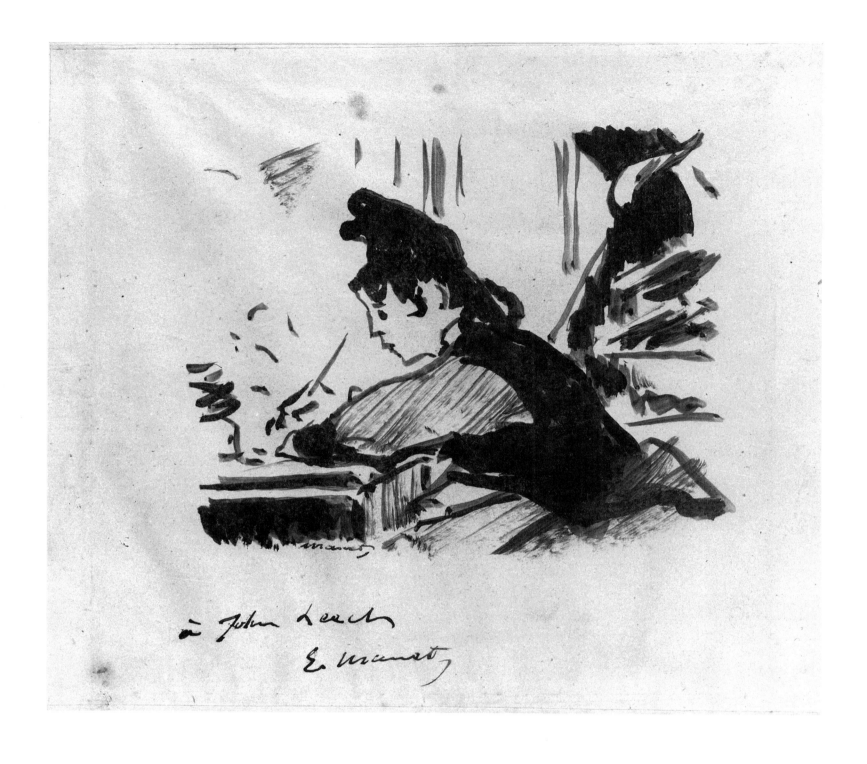

fiercely. . . . The Carousel, the embankment, the Seine, a bridge with plaster sculptures on the parapet . . . then dark streets with glimpses of laundry women working by candlelight . . ."

Compare this style, which I regard as close to that of Manet, with Zola's turn of phrase, which often has the weightiness, the heaviness of a lead being crushed. Here the line is less evident, less heavy to the eye. It lightens under the rattle of the words, almost disappears, just as Manet's line fades as the patch of light takes flight. To tell the truth, I find nothing in the Goncourts' work of the magisterial realism of *l'Assommoir* and *La Curée*. Their realism as they describe both our century and the previous one offers the eye and the taste a savour and harmony of artistic elegance, distinction and scepticism, full of reminiscences of La Tour's pastels, with their bright velvety touches, very similar to the glowing, mellow downiness of those of Manet.

Woman Writing. 1862–4. Pen and black ink, 6 × 6¼″ (15.2 × 15.9 cm). Sterling and Francine Clark Art Institute, Williamstown, Mass.

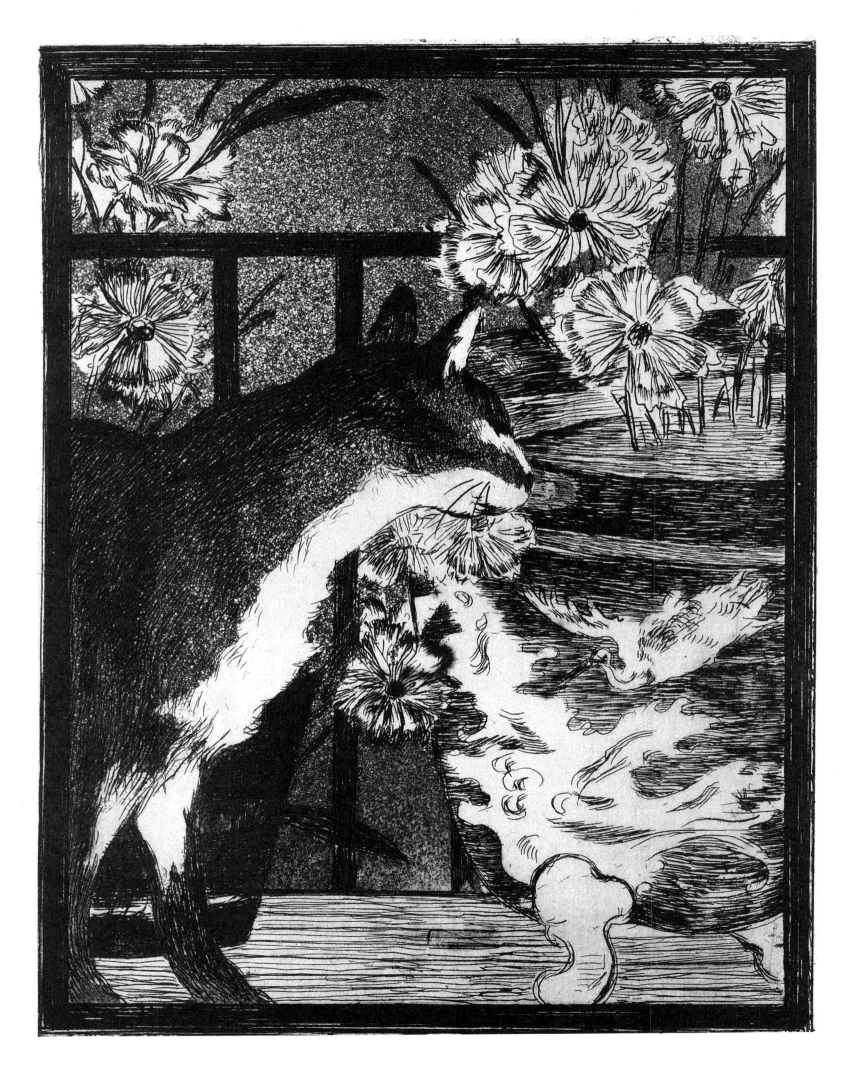

JACQUES DE BIEZ

ÉDOUARD MANET. CONFÉRENCE FAITE À LA SALLE DES CAPUCINES

Manet as Portrait Painter

January 22, 1884

Manet coarse! Never! He was much too much of an artist! He was subjective, living within his own world like all superior beings, convinced that there is a thousand times more art in judging and admiring things in accordance with one's own convictions than in looking and judging in accordance with those of others, champions of some random theorizing; what appealed to him above all in the outside world was what he put into it of himself. His art pleased him, charmed him, enchanted him, by virtue of what he had put into it of his innermost substance. What he liked in others, was what he found in them of himself, and the feeling, emotion, friendship and devotion he extended to them.

If this attitude is not the very essence of art, what is it? Clearly, it bespeaks empathy of some sort. Unless, of course, you prefer to see it as a human equivalent of the strange, mysterious egoism of the cat, the most artistic of animals because it is the most independent.

Look carefully at this fireside beast. Follow it in its solitary ramblings, walking on silent paws, stopping in corners, leaping expertly on to shelves among saucers and glasses, contemplating man with its bright sphinx-like gaze. What is it thinking of while it surveys you? Make no mistake, it is thinking of itself. Itself which it sees in you, less endearing, less supple, less mindful of the eloquence of silence; and also less careful of your dignity and less watchful of your pride. You men forgive. And after having invented confession, so demeaning and humiliating to the character, you set the seal upon your ignominy by dreaming up absolution.

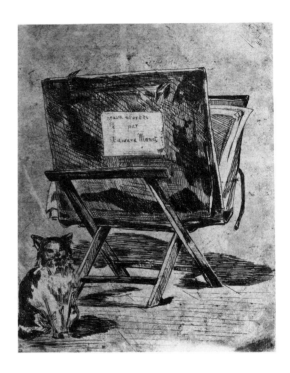

Cat and Portfolio. Frontispiece for an edition of etchings. 1862. Etching, 10½ × 7½" (27 × 19 cm). New York Public Library (Astor, Lenox and Tilden Foundations).

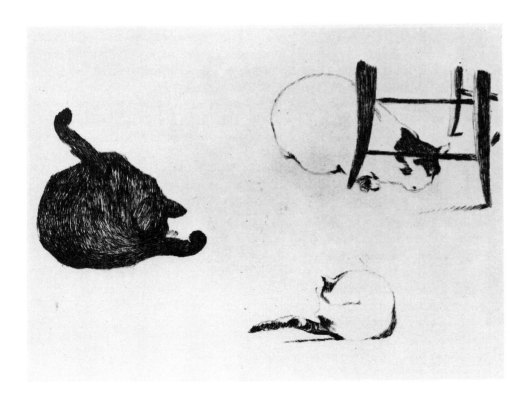

OPPOSITE *Cat and Flowers.* 1869. Etching and aquatint for Champfleury's book *The Cats,* 6½ × 5" (16.5 × 12.7 cm).

LEFT *The Cats.* 1869. Etching, 4½ × 7½" (11.5 × 18.8 cm).

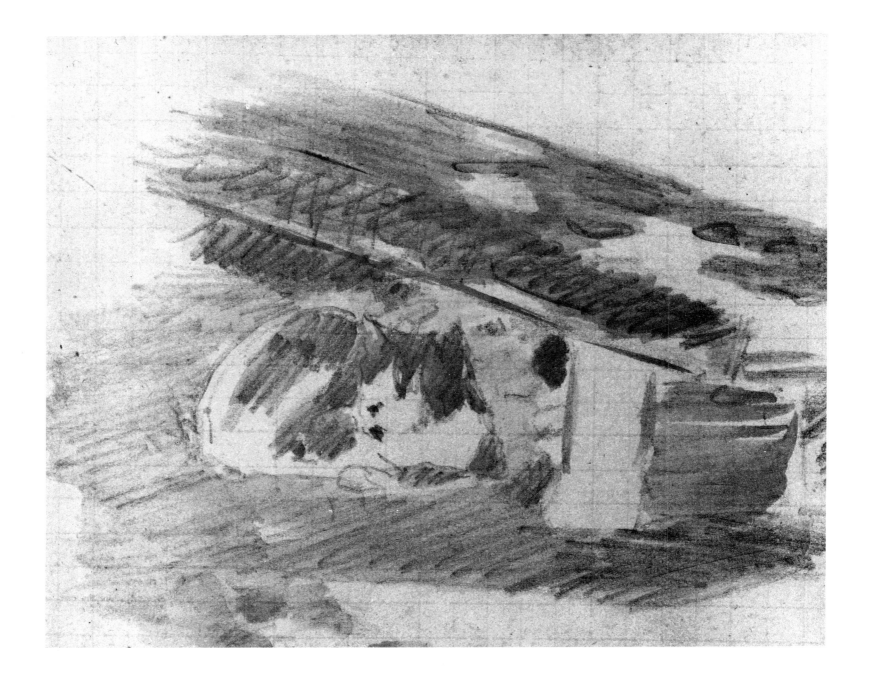

Forgiveness, forgetting the injury or the fault, these are weaknesses alien to the nobility of the cat, a domestic animal in the *domus* sense of the word, but nothing to do with being tamed, domesticated. The cat turns its back upon people who have done it harm. It despises them. They are weak, they attack. The cat, which is strong, never opens hostilities. The tooth and nail are its weapons, defensive weapons. All Manet's "bons mots," and they are many, are defensive. When a cat loves someone, it is for ever. Look how Manet spoke of his friends: once a cat has earned affection, it is for ever. Look how Manet's friends continue to plead his cause and battle for it after his death.

Fantin-Latour's portrait captures the feline quality of this artist who so loved Edgar Poe's amazing cats. As elegant as a cat, the most elegant of animals. His face is as gay and smiling as the face of a lovely cat. Even his wavy hair and beard suggest the subtle blonde colouring of a cat.

Manet, coarse? Come now. Look how he treats his pictures of flowers and portraits of women. Not conventionally beautiful, not prettified through obedience to some foolish partiality. Pretty with all the prettiness of their woman's nature, charming with all the loveliness of their sex, and that is all, without affectation, without disguise, as they are when they are most truly themselves and have much of the woman in them.

Cat under a Bench. 1875/82. Pencil and ink wash on squared paper, 4¾ × 4¾" (12 × 12 cm). Bibliothèque Littéraire Jacques Doucet, Paris. This is thought to be Mallarmé's cat.

His brush moves softly over their transparent and lustrous feminine skin, light and penetrating as a caress. The exquisite little faces of these parisiennes, with their noses so often tipped towards some titbit, carry the mark of the artist's thought with an apt variety, a liveliness of feeling and a nimbleness of touch which soothes and reassures. Have no fear. He will make no scratch-marks. The pink and whiteness of those apple cheeks will not be darkened with the red of blood. Cat does not scratch female cat – for her he has a velvet paw.

These portraits of modern French women in their depiction of tender glowing complexions, in their spontaneous quality and their impression of incompleteness, seem to emit a disturbing perfume. There is no sign of any coarse speck of face powder. Manet will not have the slightest "dot" of it on his palette. But one feels one can sense it. One can scent it, as it were. And its heady vapour rises to your nostrils. Those pastels! Their beauty is truly so fresh, their scent so alluring, that you are tempted to kiss them. And suddenly you bury your nose in them, so likely does it seem that they must smell sweet!

All this is written and painted with an exquisite sense of the sex which had "vapours" under Louis XV and which now, in our day, is left only with its nerves. One more illusion torn from us by steely fingered science – odious science, which cuts and dries and dares to let its nails wander scissor-fashion over the very softness of our homage to women, freezing its moisture at a breath.

Now let us look at the portraits of men. Manet proceeds in quite a different way.

Gentle with female cats, hard on the males, the painter treats his fellow men with broader touches, the angles are sharper, the light spreads more violently, with a harsher grip, and the contrasts proclaim the harmony of opposition more loudly.

Here there are clawmarks. The character has to be seized and emphasized from a closer viewpoint.

Since female grace, and tenderness towards it, is no longer what is required, since the velvet of a woman's skin does not have to figure in this male form, we are going to see a different approach. Brusquely Manet returns to the cult of the picturesque through the study of character.

Take the portrait of M Antonin Proust. He is seen, in all his pale blondeness and distinction, in the indolent and slightly relaxed pose of the orator who is concentrating on what he is saying, and listening to the murmur of his unhurried, carefully measured sentences rolling along in the half-tones of a muted solo.

Then there is Rochefort. Here, everything mocks and flares. Raillery seems to stream upwards through his hair, rising in order to mock indiscriminately at those in power.

Look at the composition of this portrait of Henri Rochefort. It is very like the model. The painting is dominated by a patch of light. In places it almost does away with the underlying anatomy, it is so vibrant and incisive. In this it is very similar to the pamphleteer's famous "bons mots" – those ink-blot words, leaving indelible scars, for which Henri Rochefort has a special gift, those sallies which burn to the advantage of their own brightness, gnawing at the design of the sentence which bears them, as they eat away at the skin of the people they affect.

Note, in these portraits, how the painter is concerned above all with the head. Whether in his own or in those of his friends Théodore Duret or Marcellin Desboutin (all three full-length), the legs are visually insignificant. They are summarily dealt with, thrust into any old trousers. This artist who, as Mantz has said, is "anything you like except a brutal realist," has an astonishing sense of essential character. It is the head he looks at above all in a man, a man who looks at himself with increasing disdain the lower he looks.

Louis XV (1710–74), king of France 1715–74.

COLOURPLATES 104, 111, 41, 76

Stop, *M. Rochefort, Furious at Having Embraced Nana ...* Caricature in *Le Journal Amusant,* 11 June 1881. (See Colourplate 111.)

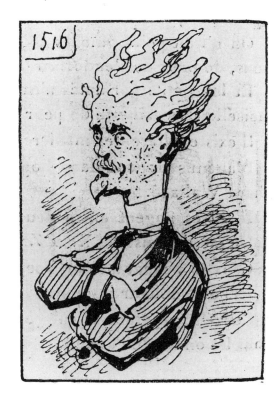

JACQUES DE BIEZ

ÉDOUARD MANET. CONFÉRENCE FAITE À LA SALLE DES CAPUCINES

Manet as Precursor

January 22, 1884

Today, Manet has found his place. His influence is no longer disputed. And his usefulness is recognized. "He has been useful," M Paul Mantz has written, "and he may be useful later on. He has reduced the last Bolognese 'confectioners' to silence; at his best, he had a vision of the music of light. In this sense, he moved forwards."

He never dreamt of attaining the pedantic halo of leader of a school. Those who doggedly persist in so crowning him today do so purely to discredit him. It is an excellent means of so doing. It denies Manet a title he does not claim, since he has done nothing to deserve it.

An artist to the depths of his being, an artist even in his failings, even in his incompleteness, wholly concerned with himself, absorbed in writing his impressions in the shifting sky of his emotions, he lived only to bring forth the idea he had within him, the idea of light, the idea of the rebirth of French art through clarity in painting. Utterly coherent in his incongruity, with a talent that was all unevenness, unexpectedness and exaggeration born of spontaneity, his whole being was in his art.

Those who persist in cloaking Manet with the grand title of leader of a school are turning their backs on good faith. Manet's considerable influence on his time should not be seen as papal sway. He never wore a triple crown. And he had no throne whence to preach or bless his faithful.

The influence of Manet's genius derives quite simply from the fact that he brought to his time a right, ripe idea which fitted into place. Genius is superior to reason in that genius is the supreme blossoming of instinct. And Manet's reform, it should be stressed, is utterly instinctive. If everyone seized upon it the moment it appeared, this was because the idea was in the air. . . .

Manet leaves no school. Manet leaves an art, an art which is a delicate synthesis of light, and characterized by a clear, very French concern with externals.

Manet never had pupils in the strict sense of the word. Manet had disciples. People do not imitate him, they benefit from him. Manet was not the kind of painter people walk behind. Some have already overtaken him. That is because Manet is a precursor. He paved the way. It is up to others to follow it and progress along it in the ways suggested by his work. Having accomplished this task, he died.

Dying with his mission fully triumphant, he has as much a right to the Louvre as his predecessors. He has more of a right to the Louvre than Courbet, who has just entered it. More, because of the results. Courbet, all in all, was just a skilful decadent master whose selfish glory will benefit him alone. Manet, as creator and renewer, worked for the future. By delving back to the light of the primitives, and once again steeping French art in the fresh and limpid sources of its origins, he has given us genuine guarantees against decline.

A reference to the seventeenth-century school of Bolognese painters and their later followers; probably implies academic painters.

PAUL EUDEL

LE FIGARO

"The Sale of Manet's Work"

February 5, 1884

After waiting a month at the Ecole des Beaux-Arts and two days at an exhibition at the Hôtel Drouot, a sale took place yesterday of the pictures left by poor Manet, whose death after terrible suffering has so deeply affected us.

As a man he was sympathetic, intelligent and hard-working. The painter had his enthusiastic admirers and bitter opponents. No one has been more praised by his own coterie, no one more vilified by the critics.

"*Sera-t-il dieu, table ou cuvette?*" That's the question that's being asked in the art world and which does not yet seem to be quite decided.

"Pure masterpieces!" exclaim some. "A continuation of Goya and Velazquez!" – "Baudelaire interpreted!"

"Abominable daubs! Caricatures rightly ridiculed!" shrieked the Academicians.

"Manet is like a false dawn, still surrounded by night," writes Paul Mantz in *Le Temps*.

"It is shameful," Edmond About states categorically.

"It's admirable," Fourcaud riposts.

"*Manebit!* He will last," Edmond Bazire concludes in a recent book on Manet.

What's to be done about it?

Such varied appreciations from so many good and authoritative persons worry and embarrass me. . . .

I am as perplexed as Buridan's ass. [I am torn in two directions at once.] I will be decidedly careful to abstain from taking sides in this conflict of ideas. My mind is not made up. I will keep out of it. But in order to avoid giving just a dry list of names in this review (which is *not* an appreciation) I will try, in my capacity as a collector, to give in passing some of the contradictory opinions that have been expressed by critics on each picture. My readers will in this way understand my embarrassment and I think they will share it with me.

It is two o'clock. All artistic Paris, including the Batignolles School, as the Institute contemptuously calls it, is at the Hôtel Drouot. The gallery is filled with noise: the apostles of *plein air* pour out their enthusiasm to the public.

"There will be a change of opinion," they loudly proclaim, "just as in the case of Courbet. The State will buy. His absence leaves a gap in the Louvre."

Whatever else it may be, it is a solemn hour for the memory of Manet. It is a question neither of praise nor attack. That costs nothing. It is no longer the painter who has any say – it is money – and it is money that often says the last word as far as a painter's reputation is concerned.

The setting is as simple as could be. For the purpose, Galleries 8 and 9 have been thrown into one. The principal pictures decorate the walls. The desk is in the centre. Messieurs Chevallier and Robert Le Sueur preside. They are assisted by two auctioneers, Daire and Broust. Standing beside his colleague Georges Rett, Monsieur Durand-Ruel introduces the pictures.

There is some preliminary skirmishing, advance guard action. It is only a question of drawings and they don't want to waste their powder. *The Spaniard*, who looks terribly like my President Emmanuel Gonzalès, is

Paul Eudel (1837–1911), art collector and author of Collections et Collectionneurs (1885), Champfleury (1891) and Mes Souvenirs (1896).

One hundred and sixty-nine works by Manet were exhibited at the Hôtel Drouot on February 2 and 3. The sale took place over two days, February 4 to 5, the works sold making a total of 116,637 francs. This is the account of sales on February 4. The following day Olympia was sold to Léon Leenhoff for 10,000 francs, Autumn to J.B. Faure for 10,000, At Père Lathuille's to Théodore Duret for 8,000 and the Balcony for 3,000 to the painter Gustave Caillebotte (Colourplates 14, 113, 91, 46).

See page 213.

Édmond-François-Valentin About (1828–85), writer, journalist and art critic. He founded Le XIXe Siècle in 1871 and was elected a member of the Academie française in 1884.

Jean Buridan (c.1297–c.1385), philosopher and rector of Paris University in the fourteenth century. Buridan is often credited as author of the fable which compares the human will, unable to act between two equally balanced motives, to an ass dying of hunger between two equal and equidistant bundles of hay.

Louis-Jean Emmanuel Gonzalès (1815–87), French novelist, President of the Société des Gens de Lettres, and father of Eva Gonzalès.

knocked down for 50 francs. I strongly suspect that the President posed for it. An *Odalisque* falls to Monsieur Bernstein for 85 francs. *The Cats' Rendezvous*, which served as a poster for my old friend Champfleury, fetches 200 francs, and the engraving of *Polichinelle*, for which my colleague, Chincholle, paid 15 francs, goes up to 265 francs, although the couplet by the brilliant and strange author of *Odes Funambulesques* is not printed underneath it. . . .

Jules Champfleury (1821–89), French author and critic. Manet provided illustrations to Champfleury's Les Chats — Histoire, Moeurs, Observations, Anecdotes *(see pages 13, 216).*

We now come to the water-colours.

The copy of Velazquez's *Infanta* fetches 150 francs.

La Posada, done in the house of Alfred Stevens, 300 francs, and the two pictures of flowers, *Iris des Toits*, 140 and 180 francs respectively.

Then come the pastels, a procession of Parisiennes, which according to Jules Claretie, have a peculiar clarity and vitality.

Jules Claretie, art critic. Prince Jérôme Napoléon (1784–1860), king of Westphalia 1807–13, brother of Napoleon I. Patron of the arts under the Second Empire.

The portrait of Dr Matern, one of Prince Napoléon's doctors (*Male Portrait* in the catalogue) goes up to 380 francs, and the *Nude Woman*, 550 francs. The model, *Jeanne on the Beach*, seen in perspective – something which nobody had the courage to do before Manet – fetches 1,500 francs. Albert Hecht buys successively a *Profile of a Woman* (310 francs), *Viennese Woman*, well-known in the Parisian fashionable world (650 francs), and *Young Girl*, whose eyes sparkle like carriage lamps in the darkness (420 francs).

COLOURPLATES 107, 87

Man in a Round Hat, who is none other than the most charming of editors, my good friend Georges Charpentier (according to my neighbour), rises rapidly to 1,050 francs under the reiterated bids of Monsieur Bernstein.

COLOURPLATE 86

After this curtain-raiser, the main play begins without an interval, as Monsieur Chevalier speedily gets down to business. He holds the gavel in a nervous hand, and conducts the bidding with great rapidity, bringing out his words like hammer blows on an anvil. Johann Strauss, conducting the infernal galop in the *Bal de l'Opéra*, was never more passionate or stormy [*maestria*, ie like the mistral]. The bids shoot out from all sides like a spray of fireworks. It's a really fine battle! I have seen many others, but I am pleased to have been present at this one.

The commissionaires bring in *The Music Lesson*, which is none other than the portrait of Zacharie Astruc, painter, sculptor, and man of letters, who plucks a guitar.

COLOURPLATE 50

Now I efface myself and hand over to the critics.

"Those who turned away in derision today might well recognize the courage of this incomparable artist." – René Maizeroy, *Le Réveil*, January 12, 1884.

This is *Argenteuil*! The picture is well-known. I will not photograph it. Monsieur Rudolphe Leenhoff, a fine upstanding fellow in a boating costume, faces the public in the company of a lady. They are treated life-size. Manet never wanted to part with it. Here is what they said about it in the Press. I transcribe without comment, as promised: "This painting cancels out Manet the instructive painter, and substitutes Manet the scientific painter." – Paul Mantz, *Le Temps*, January 10, 1884. ". . . In the background a jelly-like Argenteuil on an indigo river. The master is at the stage of a twenty-year-old student." – Jean Rousseau, *Le Figaro*, May 2, 1875. Durand-Ruel asks 15,000 for the picture, which Monsieur Leenhoff, Manet's brother-in-law, takes back for 12,500.

COLOURPLATE 65

We now come to *Hamlet*, who, sword in hand, wishes to avenge his father. At this juncture, everyone present turns towards Faure, of whom this is a portrait. This is what the famous baritone himself said about its author: "I am not an exclusive admirer of Manet. I abandoned him to his exaggerations." – *L'Evénement*, January 6, 1884. As for Cham, he made a caricature with this legend: "Hamlet having gone mad, has his portrait painted by Manet." Durand-Ruel, at 3,500 francs, is the purchaser of this picture.

COLOURPLATE 80

The Bar at the Folies-Bergère. A barmaid, with a hair-style *à la chienne*, surrounded by flagons of champagne, with a mirror behind her, in which is reflected a gentleman at whom she is making eyes.

COLOURPLATE 117

Is it a success? Is it a set-back? This picture priced at 10,000 francs when it was exhibited in 1882, sells to Monsieur Chabrier for the sum of 5,850 francs.

"It is the most harmonious picture that Manet has produced." – Fourcaud, *Le Gaulois*, May 4, 1882.

Skating. The two models, Victorine and Henriette Hauser, in the foreground, with an outline of the engraver, Henri Guérard. 1,670 francs. Again to Monsieur Chabrier.

COLOURPLATE 77

The Waitress. This is one-half of a picture which was called *Brasserie de Reichschoffen*. In it you can see friend Guérard and Ellen Andrée. The other half is at Marseilles. One of my friends said of it: "Manet has just entered posterity." – Gaston Goetschy, *Le Clairon*, January 6. Bought by Durand-Ruel for 2,500 francs. For whom?

COLOURPLATE 90
See note to Manet's Reichshoffen project, page 126.

Nana, in blue corset and short skirt is "making up" in front of a small cheval glass, while the Comte Muffat looks on. "It is a marvel of shameless elegance." – Edmond Bazire. Bought by Dr Robin, the historian, for 3,000 francs.

COLOURPLATE 79

And his enthusiastic admirers continue to buy, swept along by the persuasive manner of the auctioneer. I have difficulty in following in my catalogue the pictures which are carried past me in procession. The sketch for *The Balcony*, acquired for 580 francs by the painter Sargent; *The Masked Ball at the Opera* for 380 francs, acquired by Albert Hecht; *The Young Girl in a Cape* for 550 francs, by the landscape painter Grandsire; the portrait of a child for 350 francs by Monsieur Revillon; a *Woman's Head* by Monsieur de Jouy, and the sketch, *Woman in Pink* bought by Faure, and which prompted Théophile Gautier to say: "This head is smooth and ugly." – *Le Moniteur*, March 11, 1868. And Pierre Véron: "Monsieur Manet's talent is prodigious. Can you imagine, his model was entrancing!"

John Singer Sargent (1856–1925), American portrait painter. He went to Paris in 1874 to study painting but moved permanently to London in 1885.

Then *The Bullfight*, again bought by Monsieur Hecht, whose attention I would like to draw to this appreciation written by the Academician, newly elected last week: "A wooden torero killed by a rat." – Edmond About.

COLOURPLATE 29

But I was about to forget the purchase made by my colleague Henri d'Ideville of *An Interior* for 210 francs, and that of the painter Roll of *Singer in a Café-concert*, painted in the style of Guys, for 500 francs; also *Study of a Racetrack*, bought by the Impressionist painter Caillebotte for 200 francs, and the two dozen *Oysters* for which Michel Lévy paid 305 francs; *Peaches* for which Faure paid 780 francs, and the picture of the escape of Rochefort and Olivier Pain from the island of Nouméa, which in the midst of much commotion, was sold to Manet's sincere and devoted friend, the aforesaid Monsieur Albert Hecht, for 640 francs.

Photograph of the actress Ellen Andrée by Nadar.

Time is pressing and I will stop here at the end of this first day's sale, when the total sum for eighty lots has reached the figure of 72,000 francs. "Manet has been vindicated." So say his friends as they leave.

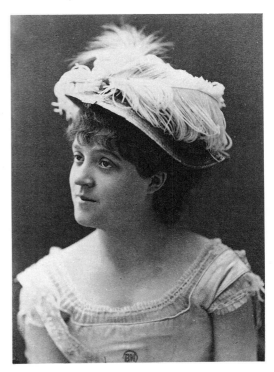

Letters to her Sister, Edma

See page 109.

1884

"Do you know that the exhibition of the works of Édouard Manet opens at the Beaux-Arts on January 5? Mme Riesener asked me very seriously whether you would not come to Paris to see it. I think that it will be a great success, that all this painting so fresh, so vital, will electrify the Palais des Beaux-Arts, which is accustomed to dead art. It will be the revenge for so many rebuffs, but a revenge that the poor boy obtains only in his grave."

* * *

"Here I am again. I am sending you the catalogue, not of the exhibition at the Beaux-Arts but of the auction at the Hôtel Drouot. Do you want to buy any pictures? I am sure that at this question your husband will jump out of his chair and you will think me a little crazy; but it is certain that it is with such ideas of wisdom and extreme caution that one misses all good opportunities. In the old days, it would never have occurred to father or mother to use a 1,000 franc or even a 500 franc note for a purchase of this kind, but today Faure is offered 20,000 francs, which he refuses, for *The Dead Man*, which he bought for 1,000, and [*illegible*] for the *Masked Ball at the Opera*; as a good speculator he is waiting till their value increases further.

COLOURPLATES 20, 64

"I want to buy some if I can; I have even the ambition to own a large one, counting on the inheritance from Maman Manet.

"I have marked with a cross those of the smaller ones which I like best. All the heads in pastel are pretty but I think they will be sold relatively high. If you answer me on this matter be sure to indicate the catalogue numbers. I think you must leave a margin of 500 to 1,500. If you do not think this idea is absurd, answer me.

"I am negotiating to sell my *Boy with Cherries* by Édouard; it is a relatively average piece but it had enormous success at the exhibition. I am asking 5,000 francs for it and I will get it. I have bought for 1,700 francs a little corner of the garden which is a jewel, one of the prettiest things he ever did. I also have a magnificent sketch of Mme Manet in the garden.

COLOURPLATE I

"I have nothing in which to wrap the catalogue today; you won't receive it till tomorrow. I think that everything would sell at extremely high prices if we were not in the midst of a depression. Don't mention my buying projects to anyone for if they were known they could be harmful to the auction." . . .

"It's all over, and it was a fiasco. Following the victory at the Beaux-Arts the auction was a complete failure. I got for you, for 620 francs, the picture of the departure of the steamboat. It is not a nocturne; it is a daytime scene, with a crowd swarming on the dock. It is a very pretty piece. If you want it tell me right away; I shall have it packed for you; if not, I shall keep it to resell at a profit, not that I do not like it enormously, but in this rout the brothers thought they had better step in, and we spent 20,000 francs. It is true that I have three big pieces, *Doing the Washing, Madame de Callias*, and *The Young Girl in the Garden*, and some small ones – a singer at a café concert, two pastels, a torso of a woman, and some oysters. It was certainly more advantageous to buy the smaller canvases rather than the big ones, but the former were bringing relatively high prices whereas the large ones would have gone for nothing if we had not intervened. Anyway I am brokenhearted. The only consolation is that everything has fallen into the hands of connoisseurs, of artists.

PAGE 147, COLOURPLATES 62, 105

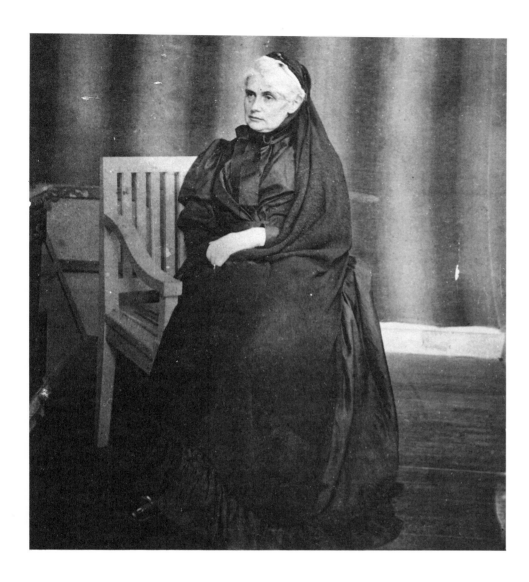

Photograph of Berthe Morisot.

"In all, the auction brought 110,000 francs, whereas we were counting on 200,000 at the least. Times are bad, that is certain, but no matter, it is a severe blow. Did you see, in the studio, *Madame de Callias*, a woman in black reclining on a sofa with Japanese fans hung in the background? It is a marvel that will go to the Louvre.

"As for *Washing*, you know it. *The Young Girl*, a girl sitting under rose bushes, is just as large, but much less finished.

"Anyway, here I am with a whole gallery, our future inheritance from Madame Manet has been eaten into, but no matter, one can only laugh.

"Answer me about the picture of the boat; do exactly as you please." . . .

"I shall show the picture to Adolphe; he will take it if he likes it and leave it if he does not, but I cannot exchange any with him for I have given all the small ones to Gustave; moreover, only the still-life was not high-priced, and you had written me that 600 francs was your maximum. As the days go by we are resigning ourselves to the result of the auction. We take into consideration the fact that times are bad, that people are reluctant to spend money, that those who bought the pictures represented an elite – not because of their well-lined pockets but at least because of their good taste – and that they all now value their pictures almost as they value their own lives and will never part from them except for their weight in gold; and all this gives us hope for a more complete vindication in the future. I am sure that you will be enthusiastic about *Madame de Callias*; I am in love with it, I think that I prefer it to *Doing the Washing*. At all events I shall not let it go except to the Louvre, and if this does not come to pass in my lifetime, it will in Bibi's."

JOSEPH PÉLADAN

L'ARTISTE

"Manet's Methods"

February 1884

*Joséphin Péladan (1859–1918), French
writer and playwright. His* Le Vice
Suprême *was published in 1884. He was
involved in the late nineteenth-century revival
of Rosicrucianism.*

According to aesthetes, all that the Pharisees despise is good. Isn't it
delectable to see Manet stupefying the die-hards in their own sanctuary,
setting up his excellent pastiches and his brave *crépons* within the very
walls wherein Meissonier and Gérôme taught? Even though poor Manet,
who was afflicted with friends even more stupid than his enemies, was no
more than an excuse for Monsieur About to flourish his badge of office as
protector of the bourgeoisie [*sortir son écharpe de commissaire de la bourgeoisie*];
or for Mr Reporter of *L'Intransigeant* to become art critic, or for the painter
of *The Cockfight* to assume a grotesque cock's comb [*de se crêter en grotesque*];
or for Meisonnier, the scarab of style, to rattle his elytrons; or for the
bourgeois to belch stupidities; or for the Institut to receive a slap which
brought a flush to its pale face; even though he was no more than the
jawbone of an ass with whom to smite the Philistines – Manet is welcome,
very welcome indeed. I salute him as a seeker of truth, I salute him
ceremoniously as the vanquished are saluted in *The Surrender of Breda* [by
Velazquez]. No, Monsieur Gérôme, if the *Folies-Prudhomme* was suitable
for your own exhibitions of bourgeois anecdotes, then the Folies-Bergère is
not fit to be shown in the Manet exhibition. Ethics demand that it should
be exhibited in the same place as you are to be found. The unfortunate
Manet is the *Mene, Mene, Tekel Upharsin* of the Fine Arts, his is the ghostly
hand that wrote your fate; Manet is your castigation. *You* are responsible
for the *crépons* of this erring man. Why instead of shuffling in the well-trod
footsteps of Delaroche, have you not learnt from Piero della Francesca and
Fra Angelico? Courbet would not then have become a Guercino [*n'eût pas
guerchiné*] and Manet would not have made *crépons*. You sent Manet flying
in search of light and the letter, which is rightly attributed to you, proves
what resentment was felt by the Gerontes of the Institut, whose incompe-
tent emissary you were.

*Jean-Louis-Ernest Meissonier (1815–91),
French painter best known for his military
and historical subjects; Jean-Léon Gérôme
(1824–1904), academic painter, one of the
leading opponents of the acceptance of the
Caillebotte bequest of Impressionist pictures
by the Luxembourg Museum in 1894.*

   "I have tried to present the people and things of my times, and also the
pure sky of the Primitives. I have demanded light of Spain and Holland,
and even of Japan, because, in the rue Bonaparte, they only teach one how
to cook up Bolognese recipes. I did not find what I needed, but I have at
least brought light back into the painting of my times. Duez, Nittis and
Gervex have been formed by me. A Columbus without an America, I
have, however, managed to produce Vespuccis – and how many of them
there are! I have a right to the walls of the Ecole des Beaux-Arts, because,
after Courbet, I was the most influential *professor* of the second half of the
century. As for my failures, I ask only that they should be judged in one
way: one has the more right to esteem – the gallant sailor who goes down
with his ship, or the slippered bourgeois who sits at ease over his
conservative stove?"

   That is what you could have read, for a whole month, on the walls of
the Salle Melpomène. . . .

   I suspect Monsieur Gérôme prefers himself to Hals or Goya. I also
suspect him of knowing little about the history of art, since half of Manet's
canvases are servile copies of the old Masters. *The Dead Man*, for example,
is a copy of *Dead Orlando* by Velazquez in the Prado.

   The only differences lie in the head and the seventeenth-century velvet
costume, revealing the end of a cuirasse. Manet has copied the position of
the body and the hand and all the tonal values, even to the black edge of

*Péladan's usage of this word is obscure; it
could refer to a textile, a kind of rough paper
or a plaster cast.*
*Gerontes were old men or elderly comic figures
in classical comedy. The Institute of France,
formed in 1795, was composed of a group of
men distinguished in the arts, sciences and
letters. The Academy constituted the fine arts
section of the Institute; Academicians served
on Salon juries as well as controlling the
curriculum at the École des Beaux-Arts.
Giuseppe de Nittis (1846–84), Italian painter
resident in France. A friend of Degas.*

Orlando Muerto, *now known as* Dead
Soldier, *formerly hung in the Pourtalès
Collection, Paris (see page 55). It is now in
the National Gallery, London, and is thought
to be Neapolitan. Manet would probably have
known it from a reproduction published in
1863. His* Dead Man *is Colourplate 20.*

the finger-nails. No critic has remarked on this flagrant pastiche, not even Monsieur Gérôme, whose standards of taste must be so upset by his own painting that he cannot appreciate Manet's *The Desserts*, which is as good as the finest Chardin, or *The Pike*, which is as good as *The Skate* which the painter of *The Blessing* sent to the Academy as his diploma piece. What a strange confusion of contemporary skill. A metaphysician who despises the *bodegones* ought to tell the "party members" that as a still-life painter, Manet has no equal; Manet's brush is a lance, and I will not pluck the *crépon* that floats from it like a flag of challenge to the bourgeoisie of the Academy. . . . I am ashamed of this day and age, ashamed to see how fame is distributed. Mediocrities of all arms and bourgeois of every calibre are triumphant. Soon, the Institute will be nothing more than a Sanhedrin for lawyers.

"Lend a hand to all scorners of the bourgeoisie," says the aesthete.

No sooner do I visualize Manet as a horripilator [*sic*] of the bourgeoisie and the insulter of the Academy, than I isolate the man from his times and look only at his pictures and assess their intrinsic value. Then I see straight away that here is a man without any sort of originality or sensibility.

* * *

Manet is merely a painter, and a painter of fragments – devoid of ideas, imagination, emotion, poetry or powers of draughtsmanship. He is incapable of composing a picture. All that one must look for in his work is the way it is rendered and his pursuit of clear skies. Only a technician can judge it and enjoy it. Not having danced to the piper's tune in the salons of the Empress and not having had my Salons influenced by Chenavard . . . not belonging to any particular popular coterie such as *La Revue du XIXe Siècle*, I am able to study with care these works, which Lawyer About regards as so much rubbish, appalling rubbish. To crown as a complete fool this hater of crowns, seems to me to be merely an act of gratuitous irresponsibility perpetrated for the delectation of the readers of the *L'Artiste*. This being the case, I dismiss the ladies and journalists and assume a pedant's gown.

Manet's so-called originality (to speak the language of Strauss-Diaforius) has seven formative influences: Couture, Courbet, Velazquez, Goya, Frans Hals, Piero della Francesca and *crépons*. These formative influences (to continue in the Prussian's style) must be examined under four headings: colour, tone value, brushwork and light. Breaking away from the Bolognese cellar, Manet burst into sunshine. His progression is constant. As his work advances, his colours become more localized, the tone values more pronounced, the brush-strokes sharper and the light more clear. A Parisian, that is to say, a man without a background, a man without that feeling for the land which gives such savour to an *oeuvre*, Manet, the pupil of the Abbé Poiloux at Vaugirard, and later of the Collège Rollin, uttered the cry of Giorgione at the age of seventeen (according to Monsieur Zola) which upset his family so much, that behold him, a cadet, bound for Rio de Janeiro! On his return from Brazil (which can hardly be considered the *Alma Parens* of painters), he visited Italy, Holland and Spain. On exhibition is his sketch of *Portrait of a Young Man*, after Filippino Lippi in the Uffizi, but it was more probably the pictures of a Fra Angelico of a Piero della Francesca that inspired him with a love of pure colour and which was to be his downfall at the same time as his glory. To this influence we owe the lighting in *The Luncheon on the Grass, Argenteuil* and the modelling in *The Railway*. In Holland he saw nothing but Hals, and the bravura of his brushwork.

When Manet comes to remember the clear tones of Della Francesca and the bravura of Hals, he mixes up the two techniques with unutterable contempt, and devotes himself, like a descendent of Greco, to painting in a lunatic fashion, in order *not* to resemble Titian. In Spain he copied

Jean-Baptiste-Siméon Chardin (1699–1779), French painter.

COLOURPLATES 18, 65, 61

Velazquez and appropriated to himself his blacks and greys – the blacks of *The Dead Man*. But Goya, that so uneven and so modern painter, teaches the lessons he had learnt in Italy – the clear tones which he had learnt from Tiepolo – the first of the Decadents to discover a little bit of the clarity of tone of the Primitives. On his return to Paris, Manet entered Couture's school and spent six years there. Those who have been through this school speak of it with horror. Can you imagine Félicien Rops, that great realist, learning to spread a coat of black paint on red drapery and then wiping it down with his hand, in order to obtain an effect of age? Puvis de Chavannes told me how one day when the skies were grey and the model looked pale, the flesh took on a silvery tone, and as he was trying to obtain this effect, Couture passed by, and seizing a brush, began to tone down the flesh colour with a dirty yellow in accordance with a recipe laid down by the "dirty school of painting". . . .

The exhibition opens with a canvas of 1859 – *The Boy with Cherries* in the manner of Caravaggio, with a good rich impasto. If Manet had continued to paint in this way, Lawyer About, whose [critical] essay occupies the first two columns of the *XIXe Siècle*, would have accorded him the same esteem as he does to Monsieur Prudhomme, to Sarcey and to himself. The Musée Reattu at Arles possesses a red "phiz" by Caravaggio which seems to be the father of this ruddy rascal. In the following year, Couture's pupil became preoccupied with Courbet. *Monsieur and Madame Manet* – Monsieur, firmly seated, holding his head (capped with a black beret) very straight; Madame, plunging a hand into a basket of coloured wool – are treated very solidly. But the form, which is very strongly modelled, is achieved here by means of hard browns in a generally sooty atmosphere. Another picture, made entirely to Couture's prescription, is *The Absinthe Drinker*, painted throughout in the brown gravy and motive-less reds and dirty yellows which will soon be eliminated from Manet's palette when his brush makes a hole in this dark cellar. I am probably the first to make a sharp distinction between *contemporaneity* and what is called *genre*, which I despise as a manifestation of bourgeois taste in art.

Apart from the picturesque subjects borrowed from contemporary Spain, Manet has the merit of not despising his own period as does a Gérôme. This vagabond in a stove-pipe hat, wrapped in a musty old cloak, with a glass of absinthe by his side, sketching with the point of his toe an uncertain, weaving dance step, in the first stages of drunken exhilaration, is Monsieur About's contemporary, something which should please them both. The second essay in *contemporaneity* – *Music in the Tuileries Gardens* – is so grotesque and so completely lacking in style, that it misfires.

Half Murillo in the sky, half Velazquez in the head, *The Boy with a Dog* is the eternal flea-ridden Spanish rascal, and when Manet copies, he never trifles with the subject, only with the colour and tone values. It is really difficult and tiresome to follow all the mutations of influences in Manet's work. Thus *The Reclining Figure*, the first work which is incontestably Manet, is executed in the colours of Hals with the brushwork of Goya. . . . At the foot of the green bench (on which he is seated) is a bird, which would make that "market-gardener" painter, Monsieur Philippe Rousseau, cry with vexation.

The Boy with a Sword, an excellent canvas, belongs also to this period. Here too is *The Street Singer* of 1861 – a charming study in grey, set off by the pretty yellow of the paper and the colour of the cherries. The canvas is imbued with a melancholy grace.

If I had the time to look up the names of the jury of 1863, I would dub them all imbeciles. Of the three pictures which he submitted to the jury, *Portrait of a Young Man in the Costume of a Mayo* is the most inoffensive and least interesting; it has the common fault of much of Manet's work in that its background and foreground are too vague and unconvincing. As for *Bathing* and *Portrait of Mlle V . . . in the Costume of an Espada*, these are two masterpieces, and the idiotic jury should never have turned them down.

COLOURPLATE 1

COLOURPLATE 2

COLOURPLATE 11

COLOURPLATE 7

COLOURPLATE 17

COLOURPLATES 6, 13

COLOURPLATE 19

COLOURPLATES 18, 12

* * *

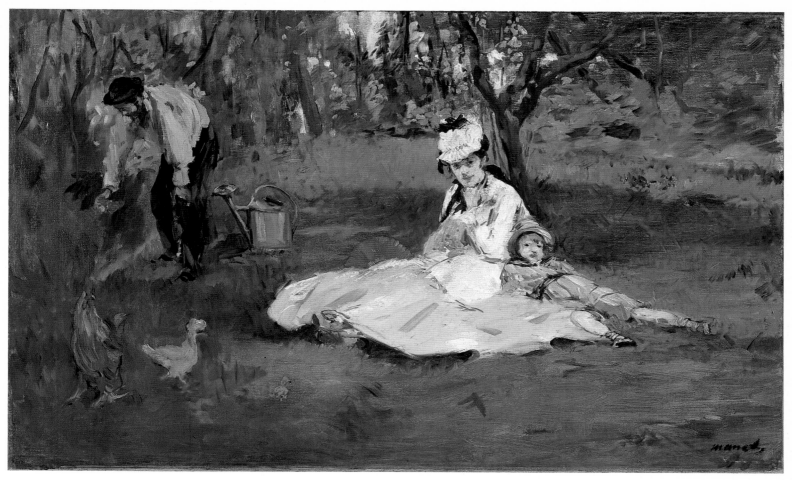

COLOURPLATE 67. *The Monet Family in the Garden.* 1874. 24 × 39¼″ (61 × 99.7 cm).
Metropolitan Museum of Art, New York (Bequest of Joan Whitney Payson, 1975).

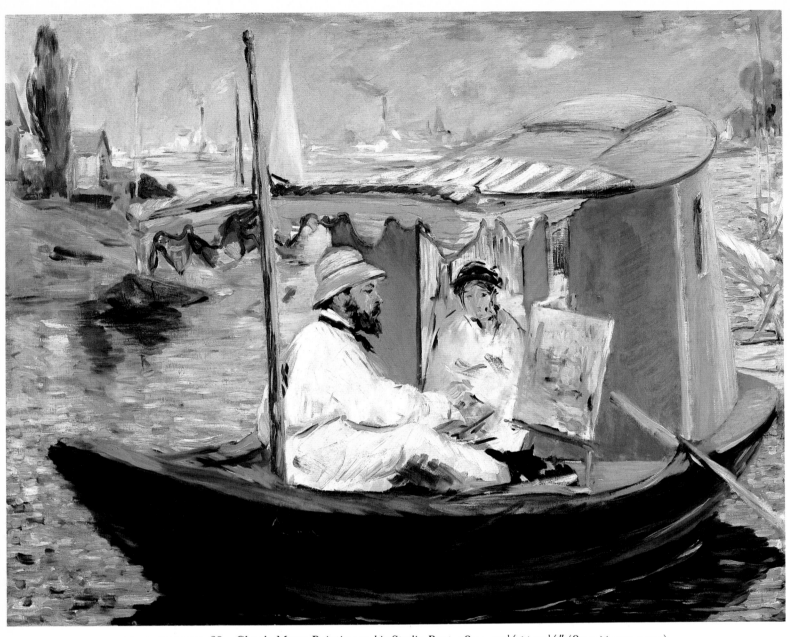

COLOURPLATE 68. *Claude Monet Painting on his Studio Boat.* 1874. 32½ × 39½″ (82.5 × 100.5 cm). Neue Pinakothek, Munich.

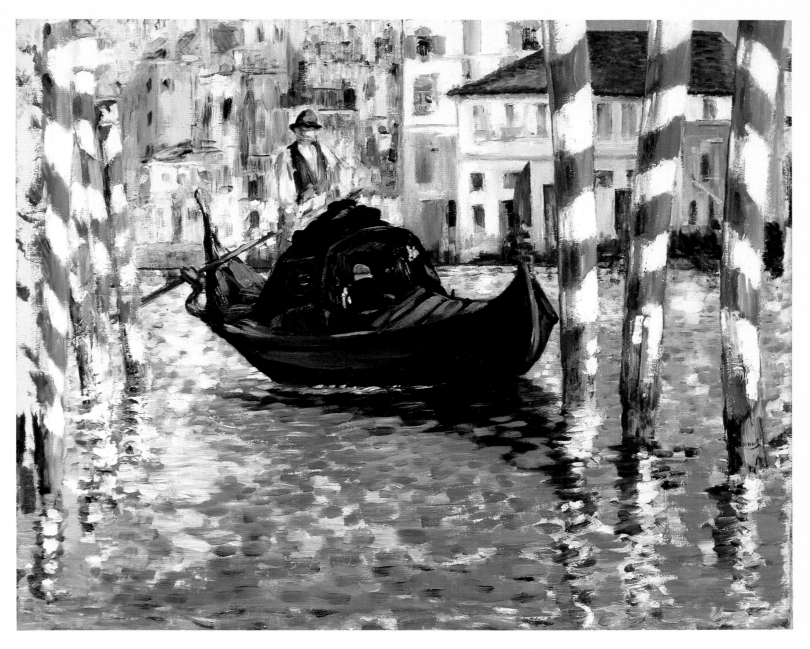

COLOURPLATE 69. *The Grand Canal, Venice (Blue Venice)*. 1875. 22¾ × 28″ (58 × 71 cm).
Shelburne Museum, Shelburne, Vermont.

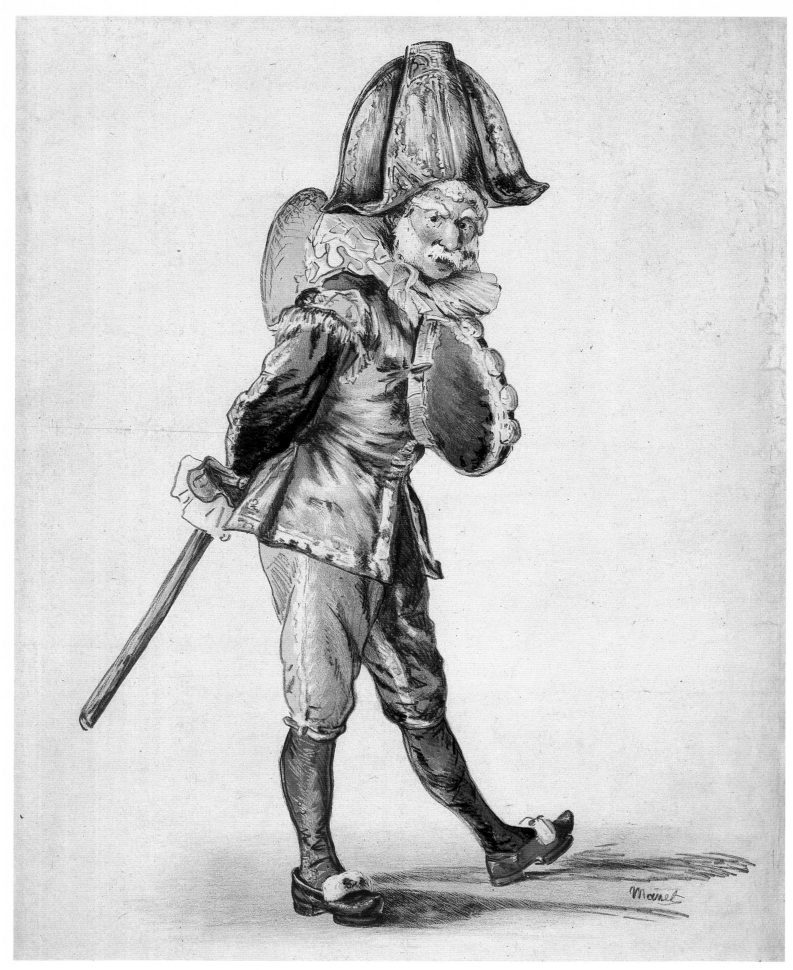

COLOURPLATE 70. *Polichinelle*. 1874. Colour lithograph, 18¼ × 13¼″ (46.3 × 33.7 cm).
British Museum (Department of Prints and Drawings).

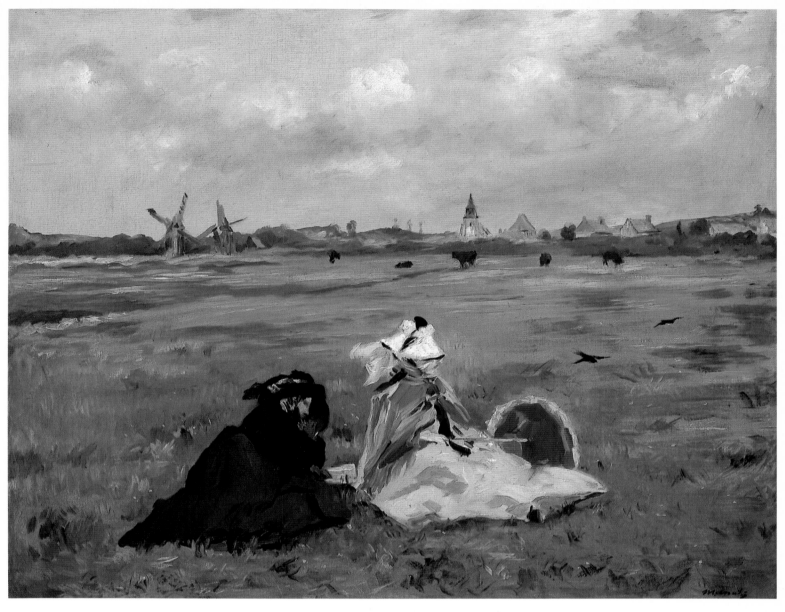

COLOURPLATE 71. *The Swallows*. 1874. 25½ × 32″ (65 × 81 cm).
Foundation E.G. Bührle Collection, Zurich.

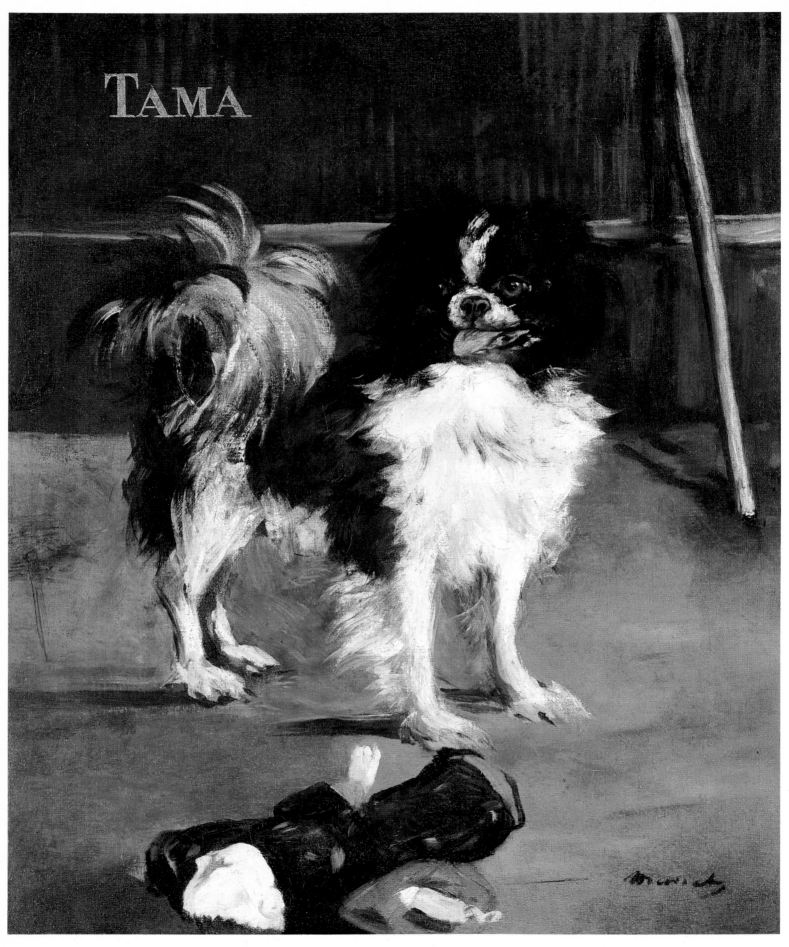

COLOURPLATE 72. *Tama, the Japanese Dog.* c. 1875. 24 × 19½″ (60 × 50 cm).
Mr and Mrs Paul Mellon Collection, Upperville, Virginia.

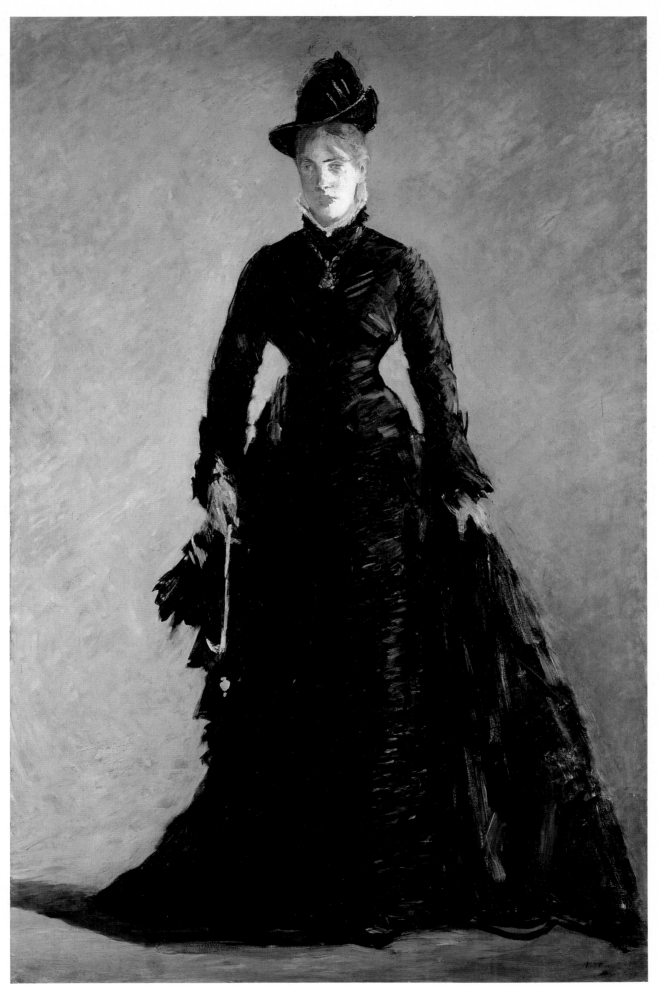

COLOURPLATE 73. *The Parisienne*. 1875. 74¾ × 48½″ (190 × 123 cm).
National Museum, Stockholm.

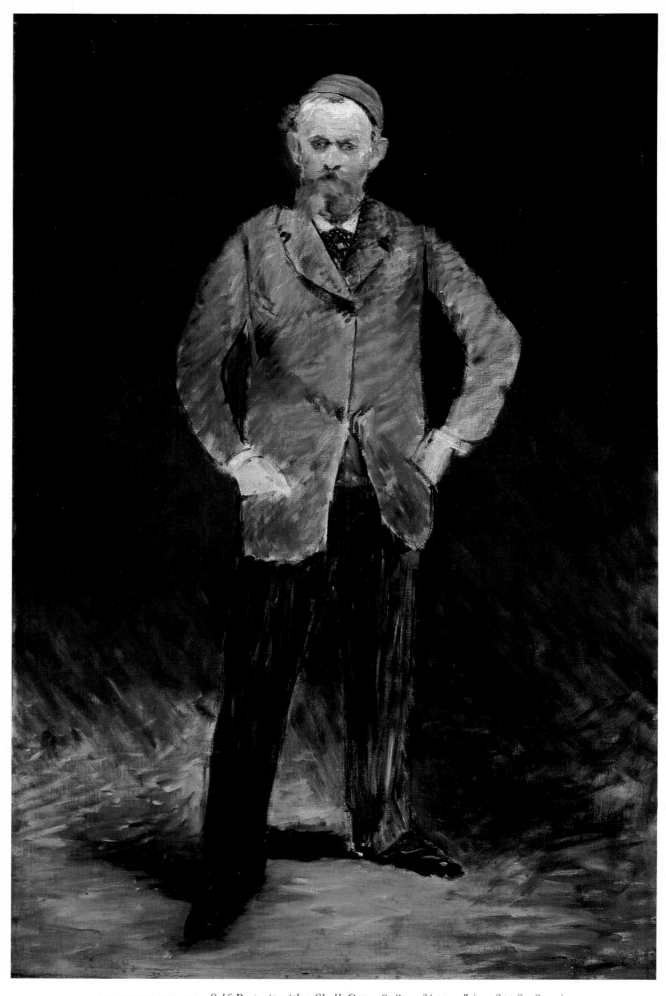

COLOURPLATE 74. *Self-Portrait with a Skull-Cap.* 1878. 37¾ × 25″ (95.6 × 63.6 cm).
Bridgestone Museum of Art, Tokyo.

The modesty of the atheists veils itself in hypocrisy and turns away (like the *Vergognosa* in the Campo Santo) from *Bathing*, just because a nude woman is seated between two clothed men. If this scene was being enacted in a room, it would be "smut," but, by setting it in the middle of the country Manet is taking the same liberties as Giorgione in his *Concert Champêtre*. These young men are in jackets, instead of doublets; they have delicate features which would look well above a doublet, and that is all one asks of them. As for the nude woman, who is resting her elbows on her knee and turning towards the spectator, she is infinitely more chaste than Phryne before the Areopagus, or the nudes of Monsieur Laurens in Sainte-Geneviève. This picture, which must be bought by the Luxembourg, if not by the Louvre, seems to me, together with *Mlle V . . . an Espada*, the best of the works in the first manner. *Bathing* has only one fault – it is a Courbet and *not* a Manet. The landscape and two students belong to the Master of Ornans; but the nude bathing girl who turns her pretty and delightful face towards us, belongs entirely to Manet. No pastiche is noticeable here. It is so personal, that it would be mean to find reminders here of other painters. The brilliant flesh tints – firm, matt and tasty (*savoureuse*) – lightly modelled à la Pietro [*sic*], and the adorable pretty colour of the cape give a general impression of suppleness and harmony, and of a, so to speak, hermaphrodite charm.

I regard that *Espada*, that *matadoress*, as the pearl of all the *oeuvre*, the picture which the Government ought to acquire to hang in the Louvre beside the fuliginous *Burial at Ornans*, in order to show by this juxtaposition how if the wily Guercino from the Franche-Comté was responsible for making a new contribution to landscape painting, in figure painting he never departed from the colours and modelling of the Bolognese school. . . .

Gautier saluted *The Spanish Singer* with an Andalusian oath. It would be interesting to find out what he said about the unusual *Spanish Dancer* [*Lola de Valence*] – a first-rate realistic painting, with exquisite colouring and tonal values. Here is another picture for the Louvre, more Spanish than Monsieur Worms. . . . Cabanal has never painted such a bold figure or one so expressive, or one with such beautiful, faithful fresh colour. To the Louvre with this, along with *Mlle l'Espada* and *Bathing*!

In 1867, *L'Artiste* (which was also called *La Revue de Paris*) published a long essay on Édouard Manet by Monsieur Zola. The author of the Rougon-Macquart series – a complete ass as far as painting is concerned and the most inerudite of writers – has had the audacity to entitle his article, *A New Way of Painting*. No one but an ignoramus would dare make such a sweeping statement. The article which had the praiseworthy intention of vindicating Manet from the blackguardism of the Institut, has the hallmark of utter incompetence. As a proof of this I cannot do better than quote the following piece of stupidity, which shows how deadly ignorant friends can be: "In 1865 he [Manet] exhibited his masterpiece, *Olympia*. I say 'masterpiece' and I do not withdraw the word. I believe that this picture is the artist's real flesh and blood and he will never repeat it. It is the complete expression of his temperament; it contains everything, and nothing but what he is. It will endure as the most characteristic of examples of his talent, the highest point in his art, and measure of his strength."

Monsieur Zola knows no better than the journalists and students who think themselves art critics. A model of bad painting, *Olympia* will not stand up to even a cursory examination. *Bathing* is an excellent canvas, distantly derived from Giorgione's *Concert Champêtre*. *Olympia* who is nothing but the wife of Olympus, is a caricature of the sleeping Venus of the Tribune. I pass over the ugliness of the form and only criticize the execution. The pink rose of the ear is clumsily placed, the hand turned over on the stomach is ungainly, the flesh tints are earthy and unconvincing, the modelling is achieved by filthy shadows, and to crown everything,

A reference to Gustave Courbet.

See page 195.

COLOURPLATE 10

Alexandre Cabanel (1824–89), French painter much admired by Napoleon III.

COLOURPLATE 14

the contour is contained by a dirty line. In addition to the mahogany bedstead, the sheets, painted with too much blue, look unnatural. The Negress's head is killed by the sombre green of the curtain. Ugly enough to draw howls from Hoffmann's cat, which is introduced into the picture, *Olympia* is so badly painted that it would gladden the heart of Monsieur Gérôme. Such is the masterpiece discovered by Monsieur Zola – that constant reiterator of documentary science and *posteriori* [*sic*] who wishes to have his personal study on analytical evidence, and who bravely announces to the world *a new way of painting*, without even being able to distinguish between Giotto and Van Orley. No, indeed, *Olympia* has no claims to be anything but a painting by a clumsy pupil of Couture.

* * *

In 1864, we find the famous *Dead Man*, and I am surprised that Monsieur Paul Mantz, one of the four or five competent critics of today, regards this picture as an original work. If Monsieur Paul Mantz cares to recall it, there is, in the Museum of Madrid, a *Dead Orlando*, lying in the same posture, with the same hand on his wound. The finger-nails of this hand are rimmed with black which Manet has not omitted in his copy. The beautiful blacks with which Manet is credited, belong to the *Orlando*, who is clad in black, with just a bit of cuirasse showing and a pennant at his side. *The Dead Man*, therefore, is an actual copy of colours, tonal values, lighting and brushwork. *The Philosophers*, which belong to the 1865 period, are throwbacks to the Bolognese school (apart from the light painting of the heads); the foreground and background are lost in unoriginal chiaroscuro. In *Boy Blowing Soap Bubbles* and also in the painting in which he is drinking from a pitcher, we begin to find what might be called the "grey series," derivative of Velazquez. *Reading* is an excellent canvas and the best of what Monsieur About would call "sensible painting." *A Good Glass of Beer*, the only work by the artist which had a real success, reveals strangely faulty craftsmanship. When one paints in *pastosità*, leaving a rough surface with no glazing, the brush must be employed in a logical way and must embrace not only the form but also the outline. One can study the question of "sense of touch" in the works of Hals and Rembrandt. Take for example a detail from Rembrandt's *Man in a Fur Cap*. Here we see that the impasto, laid on unerringly and precisely, in conformity with the drawing, in no way detracts from the impression of spontaneity. In Hal's paintings we can even follow the marks made by the hairs of the brush, and we do not find the perpetual haphazard brushstrokes which, in Manet's paintings, carry the colour over the outline, like one sees in cheap and too hastily printed chromo-lithographs. Another of Manet's technical faults, which arises from a lack of control of his brush, is the way the contours appear to be flattened. Nothing turns the corner, nothing is solid. *The Fifer* would have difficulty in showing us the seat of his trousers. His ruddy face, indeed, is modelled in clear strong tones, but the body is nothing more than a silhouette, something cut out and stuck on grey paper. *Matador Saluting*, a remarkable fragment, continues this series of vague backgrounds and imaginary foregrounds, but the action, the stamping feet and the treatment of the features, are only to be praised.

The Battle of the Kearsage and the Alabama is to be counted among the finest marine paintings of the French school. Monsieur d'Aurevilly, who knows the sea and loves it like the Rollos from whom he is descended, has given us a remarkable description of it.

Moonlight over Boulogne Harbour and *The Jetty* are also excellent marine pictures, and Manet will always be honoured for having painted the sea incomparably well. *His* portraits of her majesty [the sea] seem to me much more creditable than all Monsieur Winterhalter's, that rascal from Gotha.

Here Manet's first manner ends – these constant mutations of influence – from which he was to struggle free, to work intuitively in pursuit of pure clarity of tone.

* * *

COLOURPLATE 37

COLOURPLATES 25, 54

COLOURPLATE 32

COLOURPLATE 21

COLOURPLATE 44

Franz Xaver Winterhalter (1805–73), German portrait painter.

238

Manet . . . has followed the example of all the Primitives, who without exception employed diffused light. But Manet seriously compromised his case and made it impossible by not taking into account the co-existence of coloured light and white light. He rejected aerial perspective, which is purely a question of optics, and which quite simply is this: Atmosphere exists, that is to say, there is a space between an object and the background. Now there is only one way to observe this law. The foreground must be broadly treated, the figure must be very clear-cut, and the background more indistinct. Manet, whose eye was spoilt after 1870, eschewed all atmosphere, modelling and design. He relied on the use of lovely splashes of colour, and produced barely finished sketches instead of pictures. But it must be admitted, in extenuation, that if Manet was guilty of such faults in his pneumatic [sic] painting, which we call *plein air* (no doubt because he was denied the possibility of seeing the relative values of tones), he did employ his crazy brush to record nothing but the contemporary scene.

This requires courage and meant a renunciation of popular success, and deserves all credit.

An unusual little canvas represents a corner of the Grand Canal at Venice. Water and sky are indigo; the white mooring posts are garlanded with blue stripes. This symphony in blue major is neither absurd nor untrue to life. I have seen Venetian afternoons of just such a colour; but Manet has exaggerated an impression to an almost chimerical degree. Behind these efforts by this unfortunate man, who had fallen in love with clarity, one is aware of his search for light and of his exceptional idealism. All the so-called "naturalist" painters are *"farceurs."* Courbet belongs to the school of Bologna, Zola is a clumsy exaggerator [*un boeuf qui voit les pavés à l'état de tours Saint-Jacques*] and Manet is a chimerical colourist.

COLOURPLATE 69

There can never be such a thing as "naturalist" painting, because it is forbidden to man to reproduce nature. Let the hermit of Médan storm and rage, but I defy him to show me one single picture, or painting – whether beautiful or ugly is no consequence – which in one way or another conforms to Nature. . . . Man cannot escape from his natural inclination, which is to create gods or monsters and nothing else.

The Game of Croquet [sic] is an example of Manet's lack of appreciation of tone values. The women's dresses, which should stand out sharply, are lost in the foliage of the background. *Racing* is a pretty sketch which could be turned into a picture. The maid who serves the "tough" in a smock, and indeed the "tough" himself, make one want to exclaim: "That's just like it!" to Monsieur Camescasse. . . .

COLOURPLATE 63

COLOURPLATE 28

The tart in pink slumped over her plum is strikingly realistic, and the rosy colour of her dress is unbelievably felicitous. Many people have stopped in front of *The Bar* and have felt doubts about the lighting, which has a bluish quality like the light out-of-doors, and also concerning the reflection in the mirror. While admitting that *The Bar* is full of defects, it must be said that bits of the picture, especially the blue dress, are excellent. . . .

COLOURPLATES 83, 117

It is an odd thing that Manet, this lover of light, should have had a passion for blue instead of red and yellow, which are much more brilliant and warm colours. *Argenteuil* is a "madly blue" picture. This hideous boating lady and her ugly companion *sub Jove crudo* are very odd, and the exaggeratedly indigo sea behind them, is even odder. Here we have, in the highest degree, a perfect example of an isochromatic [sic] painting which instead of soothing the optic nerve only irritates it.

COLOURPLATE 65

At Père Lathuille's does possess a little atmosphere. The distance between the table and the background is more or less accurately observed, but it cannot possibly be said that the young man's cravat and the flesh tints of the woman are in any way related. The cravat jumps out of the picture like the well-known red toque in the painting by Valentino in the Vatican Gallery. In the painting *The Boaters*, the tone of the sea is

COLOURPLATE 91

COLOURPLATE 66

accurately observed, but how can the hands of the yachtsman be justified? – they are just blobs of paint with no drawing. Patches of paint, however nice, cannot take the place of form, and *Doing the Washing* is so full of bad brushwork and such discordant tonal values that the only criticism one could make about it would have to be either medical or ophthalmic.

PAGE 147

The Railway – a nurse-maid and a little girl – is singularly good as far as flesh tints are concerned – identical with Piero della Francesca's. The form is modelled independently of lighting; it is form seen under a diffused, white light.

COLOURPLATE 61

A bright and charming little picture – the sort to annoy Monsieur Meissonier – is Manet's *Polichinelle*.

"Effronté, saoul, divin, c'est lui Polichinelle!" as Banville said. One of these adjectives applies to Manet. He is drunk [*saoul*] with light, and rarely sober. But it is unnecessary to add that a ray of light shines forth from these failures which has been shared by painters like Diaz, Gervex, and de Nittis.

Manet could have been an excellent landscape artist, rather than a figure painter. In the four views of his garden, which are on exhibition, the defects in his last works are replaced by some fine quality of painting.

As a portrait painter he has left us, besides the portrait of Zola (a solid and well-enough executed work) and the slipshod violet-coloured Pertuiset, an astonishing *rittrato* of Maître Desboutin. The subject suits Manet's rough manner of painting so well, that the canvas is imbued with life and tremendous *bonhomie*. Another portrait is of Monsieur Antonin Proust, who has the honour of being the only elegant frock-coated figure to please the eye in modern painting. The colour is excellent and everything here is done famously – Monsieur Bonnat would do well to study it. Among the pastels is a portrait of a delicious young girl, which one would like to hang in one's home. Its charm could not be excelled. The other numerous pastels of women are all "rubbed in" with delicate and delightful velvety colours.

COLOURPLATES 40, 110, 76, 104

Casting a glance over the whole of this exhibition which comprises a complete résumé of all Manet's *oeuvre*, you will find nothing painted in the first manner which is really outstanding (the picturesque Spanish subjects excepted) apart from *Bathing*. The second manner is a lesson in light and consists of pictures which have not "come off." As for the still-life paintings, they don't count. It is his contemporary approach which gives Manet's work its character. His flesh painting may be criticized, but there is no doubt that he has understood exceptionally well the woman of today, whether she be a lady or a street-walker. Apart from the young girl in muslin, seated on a sofa, who is full of grace, all his women – especially the woman in black, lolling on cushions – whether they are painted in oils or pastel, express forcibly the hopeless stupidity of contemporary woman, chaste or otherwise.

M. Manet Studying the Beauties of Nature. Caricature in *Le Charivari*, 25 April 1880.

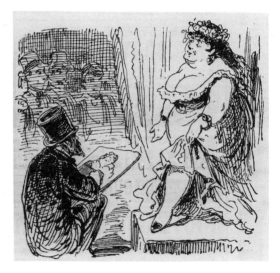

But by observing the fair sex of today as just so many patches of colour, this unimaginative painter has seen them with the eye of a philosopher, and Manet's work will disclose the fatuity of our Anadyomenes to the Goncourts of tomorrow who, three centuries hence, will reconstruct our ridiculous way of life.

Manet's pictures are usually no more than sketches – but what *are* his sketches? After seeing the exhibition at the Ecole des Beaux-Arts, the show at the Hôtel Drouot was most instructive. Here there were some indescribable and unspeakable concoctions. I firmly believe that when Manet became preoccupied with light and original colour schemes, he lost some of his previous technical ability. *The Café-Concert* is enough to make a dog howl – a child making blobs on canvas could have done better. As for drawing – it is simply non-existent. Manet doesn't even know how to copy. His study of the group of noblemen by Velazquez in the Louvre verges on the ridiculous. He had converted these proud hidalgos into country bumpkins.

COLOURPLATE 84

* * *

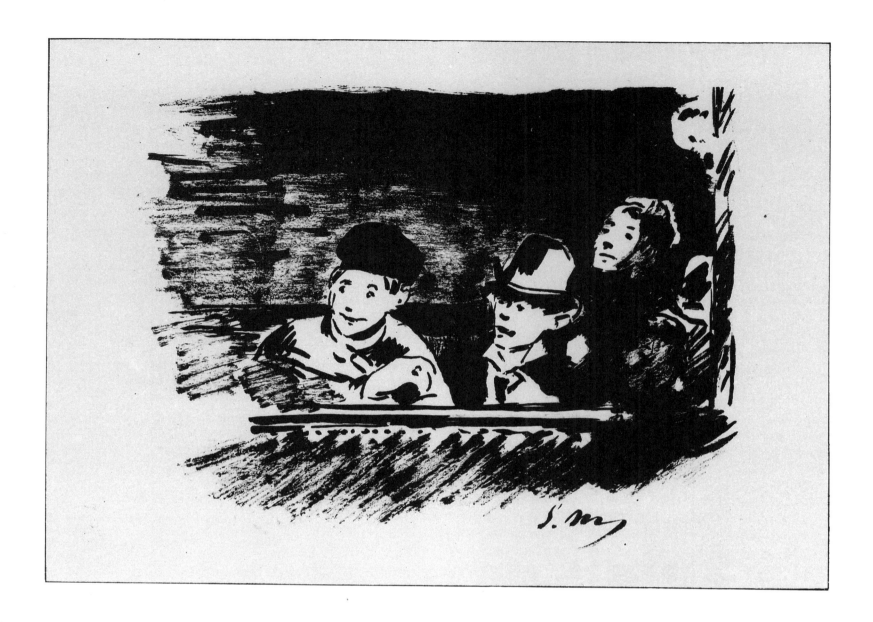

In the "Gods". 1880. Transfer
lithograph, 9¾ × 13¼"
(24.5 × 34 cm).

As an artist Manet did his duty – to discover a personal technique and
to devote himself to the portrayal of the contemporary scene. In sordid
business or on the Stock Exchange only worldly success breeds respect.

It would be unfair to pretend that financial success and the good
opinion of the man-in-the-street could never have come to the painter of
The Boy with Cherries. He had only to continue to work away quietly in this
technique and shut himself up with *bodegone*, like Philippe Rousseau or
Vollon. But he loved art more than creature comforts. He never signed
any degrading contract with a Goupil or a Petit. He never descended to
painting fashionable pictures to please the ladies. He pursued an ideal of
"clarity," which had already been realized by Fra Angelico, but which he
was never to reach. Compared with Courbet he painted very few "gallery"
pictures, but he showed incomparably greater originality. The Guercino
from the Franche-Comté introduces his own personality into Bolognese
scenes, but he still paints in the manner of the Carracci. Manet's work
echoes the cry of Goethe: "Let there be light. . . ."

At the same time as the pictures by the painter of *Bathing* were on sale
at the Hôtel Drouot, there were also on sale a number of exquisite
canvases – all derivative of Manet – by Hawkins. And in every gallery,
what a lot of followers there are of this man, who was treated as a mere
dauber by stupid journalists!

After Courbet, Manet must be considered as the greatest teacher of the
second half of the century. (Yes, Lawyer About, you *have* read me
correctly!) He "illuminated" the whole of contemporary art. *Manebit.*

Parisian art dealers.

EDMOND BAZIRE

MANET

Manet as Pastellist

See page 300.

1884

The prodigious activity of this lively temperament demanded still further
outlets. Manet made miniatures, which are owned by his family, and also
ceramics. A porcelain service dates from the beginning of his career, and
in the last years of his life he decorated several dozen exquisitely tasteful
plates. Have I mentioned the water-colours and drawings? This was a
form of relaxation; he poured out sketches, sometimes comic, such as the
Singers in a Café-concert, captured in two rapid strokes, sometimes dense and
serious, like the intimate drawing of Courbet or the Bazaine done at
Trianon.

But his passion was pastels. He did not, in truth, use the coloured
crayons to perpetuate the dainty tradition of most pastellists. He did not
work tightly, and proceeded by broad touches, even brutal on occasion.
He brought fire to this gentle technique, one often taken up by young
women; pastel did not seem to him necessarily an etiolated medium, he
saw it as embracing the whole range of colours, which was there to be
used. Not because he felt unequal to transitional shades, that is, nuances,
but because he was eager to infuse life and blood into his figures. Take that
of the Englishman Moore – admirable, surely, concise and synthetic,
summing up all England at a stroke. Or the woman, veiled in gauze,
moving by like a fay in a cloud, a deliciously insubstantial apparition. Or
the daring study of a nude, treated by a draughtsman of the first order,
even though this draughtsman has not omitted, as a consummate
colourist, to render the mellow tones and soft folds of the flesh. Manet,
ordinarily, did not pay meticulous attention to detail: hence the doubts
about certain very highly worked pieces attributed to him. But he readily
retouched incomplete studies. He reddened lips, brightened eyes, toned
down a touch of lightness, caused a shadow to blaze. Vigorously.
Inspiredly. At a stroke. Once, having strayed among a group of serene
young damsels who were wiling away their untroubled leisure by engaging
in the essentially domestic diversion of the pastel, he found qualities
scattered here and there in the work submitted to him. But there was an
absence of those tiny touches which are enough to lift a banal work into
something that is interesting, if not outstanding. He opened the box where
the serried ranks of crayons lay well-ordered and, one after another,
crushed them on to the ingenious and sensitive works of which the gentle
company was so proud. Terrible anguish evinced by the spectators of this
massacre. No doubt some novel effects were being obtained; the original
banality was vanishing; the lion's claws were out; but, at the same time,
the box was emptying. What devastation! And Manet, sensing these
intimate sufferings made reparation for the crime committed by offering
his victims both the amended study and his own box, to replace the
ravaged original.

The list of his pastels is interminable. Having seen a hundred, you feel
sure that you have seen them all; not so; you learn that twenty have eluded
you, and having made good this omission, that there are ten more
elsewhere; then more are announced. The multiple models have multiplied, and for a single one who was sitting facing the interpreter, there are
three, four, six interpretations. I know this unquenchable fecundity is
sometimes cause for complaint. From the unproductive.

*In April 1883 Manet wrote to the artist
Francis Defeuille asking for lessons in
miniature painting. None of the miniatures or
ceramics mentioned here appear to have
survived.*

COLOURPLATES 85–87, 89, 94, 107, 119

See page 252 and Colourplate 101.

Portrait of Madame Zola. 1879.
Pastel, 20½ × 17¼″ (52 × 44 cm).
Musée d'Orsay, Paris.

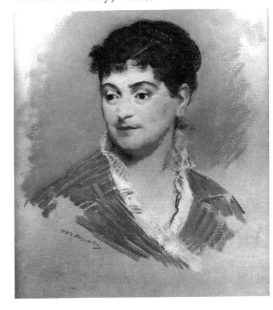

GEORGES JEANNIOT

LA GRANDE REVUE

J.S. Sargent's Visit to Manet's Widow

See pages 251 and 309.

August 10, 1907

One June afternoon in 1885 I was in Sargent's studio – Sargent professed the greatest admiration for Manet – when they began to speak of his death, of the care that Mme Manet had lavished on her husband, her devotion to his memory and her retirement to her property at Gennevilliers, where she lived out her mourning among the paintings that had been bought back at auction.

Sargent was intending to leave Paris to go and settle in London; but he said that before leaving he would like to see this little house where these paintings were kept. It was agreed that we would take the tram for Gennevilliers. When we arrived, there was no one there; we left again very put out, when a woman in black passed nearby. "I think that is Mme Manet," I said to Sargent. Retracing our steps, we approached her; it was she.

Her apartment consisted of several rooms whose walls were covered in paintings. Above the piano was *Olympia*, very much in evidence, and other paintings and pastels formed an admirable ensemble. Sad in the midst of her memories, Mme Manet went from one to the other, speaking to us of her dead beloved. She recounted his life of hard work, perpetual struggle and bitterness, in simple, heart-rending tones. If only the wretched jokers who had exercised their heavy-handed wit at the expense of this great artist, if the critics who had distilled the poison of their incompetence upon him for so many years, had been able to hear this woman, so full of faith and grief, I am sure they would have ceased their laughter and their criticism! As we were asking Mme Manet if she were not thinking of parting with some pictures, she answered us, her eyes full of tears: "That would be like having to sell my children!" Sargent and I left quite upset, and returned to Paris in silence.

COLOURPLATE 14

ÉMILE ZOLA

L'OEUVRE

The Salon des Refusés

1886

It had struck twelve, and Claude was working at his picture when there was a loud, familiar knock at the door. With an instinctive yet involuntary impulse, the artist slipped the sketch of Christine's head, by the aid of which he was remodelling the principal figure of his picture, into a portfolio. After which he decided to open the door.

"You, Pierre!" he exclaimed, "already!"

Pierre Sandoz, a friend of his boyhood, was about twenty-two, very dark, with a round and determined head, a square nose, and gentle eyes, set in energetic features, girt round with a sprouting beard.

L'Oeuvre (The Masterpiece) *was one of Zola's* Rougon-Macquart *series. The hero of the novel, Claude Lantier, is based partly on Manet and partly on Paul Cézanne. For the reading public of 1886, the fictionalized account of the 1863 Salon des Refusés, with its undisguised reference to* Luncheon on the Grass, *linked Claude closely with Manet. The book has been interpreted as an expression of Zola's disillusionment with the art of his contemporaries and friends. (See also Robert J. Niess,* Zola, Cézanne and Manet — A Study of L'Oeuvre, *Ann Arbor, University of Michigan Press, 1968.)*

"I breakfasted earlier than usual," he answered, "in order to give you a long sitting. The devil! you are getting on with it."

He had stationed himself in front of the picture, and he added almost immediately: "Hallo! you have altered the character of your woman's features!"

Then came a long pause; they both kept staring at the canvas. It measured about sixteen feet by ten, and was entirely painted over, though little of the work has gone beyond the roughing-out. This roughing-out, hastily dashed off, was superb in its violence and ardent vitality of colour. A flood of sunlight streamed into a forest clearing, with thick walls of verdure; to the left stretched a dark glade with a small luminous speck in the far distance. On the grass, amidst all the summer vegetation, lay a nude woman with one arm supporting her head, and though her eyes were closed she smiled amidst the golden shower that fell around her. In the background, two other women, one fair, and the other dark, wrestled playfully, setting light flesh tints amidst all the green leaves. And, as the painter had wanted something dark by way of contrast in the foreground, he had contented himself with seating there a gentleman, dressed in a black velveteen jacket. This gentleman had his back turned and the only part of his flesh that one saw was his left hand, with which he was supporting himself on the grass.

"The woman promises well," said Sandoz, at last; "but, dash it, there will be a lot of work in all this."

Claude, with his eyes blazing in front of his picture, made a gesture of confidence. "I've lots of time from now till the Salon. One can get through a great deal of work in six months. And perhaps this time I'll be able to prove that I am not a brute."

* * *

"Ah, to be able to see and paint everything," exclaimed Claude, after a long interval. "To have miles upon miles of walls to cover, to decorate the railway stations, the markets, the municipal offices, everything that will be built, when architects are no longer idiots. Only strong heads and strong muscles will be wanted, for there will be no lack of subjects. Life such as it runs about the streets, the life of the rich and the poor, in the market places, on the racecourses, on the boulevards, in the populous alleys; and every trade being plied, and every passion portrayed in full daylight, and the peasants, too, and the beasts of the fields and the landscapes – ah! you'll see it all, unless I am a downright brute. My very hands are itching to do it. Yes! the whole of modern life! Frescoes as high as the Pantheon! A series of canvases big enough to burst the Louvre!" . . .

See page 166, Manet's letter.

Claude, who had stepped back as far as the wall, remained leaning against it, and gazing at his work. Seeing which, Sandoz, overcome by fatigue, left the couch and joined him. Then both looked at the picture without saying a word. The gentleman in the velveteen jacket was entirely roughed in. His hand, more advanced than the rest, furnished a pretty fresh patch of flesh colour amid the grass, and the dark coat stood out so vigorously that the little silhouettes in the background, the two little women wrestling in the sunlight, seemed to have retreated further into the luminous quivering of the glade. The principal figure, the recumbent woman, as yet scarcely more than outlined, floated about like some aerial creature seen in dreams, some eagerly desired Eve springing from the earth, with her features vaguely smiling and her eyelids closed.

"Well, now, what are you going to call it?" asked Sandoz.

"*The Open Air*," replied Claude, somewhat curtly.

The title sounded rather technical to the writer, who, in spite of himself, was sometimes tempted to introduce literature into pictorial art.

"*The Open Air!* that doesn't suggest anything."

"There is no occasion for it to suggest anything. Some women and a man are reposing in a forest in the sunlight. Does not that suffice? Don't fret, there's enough in it to make a masterpiece."

He threw back his head and muttered between his teeth: "Dash it all! it's very black still. I can't get Delacroix out of my eye, do what I will. And then the hand, that's Courbet's manner. Everyone of us dabs his brush into the romantic sauce now and then. We had too much of it in our youth, we floundered in it up to our very chins. We need a jolly good wash to get clear of it."

* * *

There was a knock at the door, and Dubuche came in. He was a stout young fellow, dark, with regular but heavy features, close-cropped hair, and moustaches already full-blown. He shook hands with both his friends, and stopped before the picture, looking nonplussed. In reality that harum-scarum style of painting upset him, such was the even balance of his nature, such his reverence as a steady student for the established formulas of art; and it was only his feeling of friendship which, as a rule, prevented him from criticizing. But this time his whole being revolted visibly.

"Well, what's the matter? Doesn't it suit you?" asked Sandoz who was watching him.

"Yes, oh yes, it's very well painted – but –"

"Well, spit it out. What is it that ruffles you?"

"Not much, only the gentleman is fully dressed, and the women are not. People have never seen anything like that before."

This sufficed to make both the others wild. Why, were there not a hundred pictures in the Louvre composed in precisely the same way? Hadn't all Paris and all the painters and tourists of the world seen them? And besides, if people had never seen anything like it, they would see it now. After all, they didn't care a fig for the public!

Not in the least disconcerted by these violent replies, Dubuche repeated quietly: "The public won't understand – the public will think it indecorous – and so it is!"

"You wretched *bourgeois* philistine!" exclaimed Claude, exasperated. "They are making a famous idiot of you at the School of Arts. You weren't such a fool formerly."

These were the current amenities of his two friends since Dubuche had attended the School of Arts. He thereupon beat a retreat, rather afraid of the turn the dispute was taking, and saved himself by belabouring the painters of the School. Certainly his friends were right in one respect, the School painters were real idiots. . . .

But Claude had mechanically taken up a brush and set to work again. Beside the gentleman in the velveteen jacket the figure of the recumbent woman seemed to be fading away. Feverish and impatient, he traced a bold outline round her so as to bring her forward.

"Are you coming?"

"In a minute; hang it, what's the hurry? Just let me set this right, and I'll be with you."

Sandoz shook his head and then remarked very quietly, lest he should still further annoy him: "You do wrong to worry yourself like that, old man. Yes, you are knocked up, and have had nothing to eat, and you'll only spoil your work, as you did the other day."

But the painter waved him off with a peevish gesture. It was the old story – he did not know when to leave off; he intoxicated himself with work in his craving for an immediate result, in order to prove to himself that he held his masterpiece at last. Doubts had just driven him to despair in the midst of his delight at having terminated a successful sitting. Had he done right, after all, in making the velveteen jacket so prominent, and would he not afterwards fail to secure the brilliancy which he wished the female figure to show? Rather than remain in suspense he would have dropped down dead on the spot.

* * *

For two long hours he stood to his work with such manly energy that he finished right off a superb roughing out of the whole figure. Never before had he felt such enthusiasm in his art. It seemed to him as if he were in the presence of some saint; and at times he wondered at the transfiguration of Christine's face, whose somewhat massive jaws seemed to have receded beneath the gentle placidity which her brow and cheeks displayed. During those two hours she did not stir, she did not speak, but from time to time she opened her clear eyes, fixing them on some vague, distant point, and remaining thus for a moment, then closing them again, and relapsing into the lifelessness of fine marble, with the mysterious fixed smile required by the pose.

* * *

On May 15, a Friday, Claude, who had returned at three o'clock in the morning from Sandoz's, was still asleep at nine, when Madame Joseph brought him up a large bouquet of white lilac which a commissionaire had just left downstairs. He understood at once. Christine had wished to be beforehand in celebrating the success of his painting. For this was a great day for him, the opening day of the "Salon of the Rejected," which was first instituted that year, and at which his pictures – refused by the hanging committee of the official Salon – was to be exhibited. . . .

On the previous night he had promised Dubuche and Sandoz to call for them at the latter's place at eight o'clock, in order that they might all three go together to the Palais de l'Industrie, where they would find the rest of the band.

* * *

A few carriages, very few at that early hour, were ascending the avenue, while a stream of bewildered, bustling people, suggesting a swarm of ants, plunged into the huge archway of the Palais de l'Industrie.

When they were inside, Claude shivered slightly while crossing the gigantic vestibule, which was as cold as a cellar, with a damp pavement which resounded beneath one's feet, like the flagstones of a church. He glanced right and left at the two monumental stairways, and asked contemptuously: "I say, are we going through their dirty Salon?"

"Oh! no, dash it!" answered Sandoz. "Let's cut through the garden. The western staircase over there leads to 'the Rejected.'"

Then they passed disdainfully between the two little tables of the catalogue vendors. Between the huge red velvet curtains and beyond a shady porch appeared the garden, roofed in with glass. At that time of day it was almost deserted; there were only some people at the buffet under the clock, a throng of people lunching. The crowd was in the galleries on the first floor, and the white statues alone edged the yellow-sanded pathways which with stretches of crude colour intersected the green lawns. There was a whole nation of motionless marble there steeped in the diffuse light falling from the glazed roof on high. Looking southwards, some holland screens barred half of the nave, which showed ambery in the sunlight and was speckled at both ends by the dazzling blue and crimson of stained-glass windows. Just a few visitors, tired already, occupied the brand-new chairs and seats, shiny with fresh paint; while the flights of sparrows, who dwelt above, among the iron girders, swooped down, quite at home, raking up the sand and twittering as they pursued each other.

Claude and Sandoz made a show of walking very quickly without giving a glance around them. A stiff classical bronze statue, a Minerva by a member of the Institute, had exasperated them at the very door. But as they hastened past a seemingly endless line of busts, they recognized Bongrand, who, all alone, was going slowly round a colossal, overflowing, recumbent figure, which had been placed in the middle of the path. With his hands behind his back, quite absorbed, he bent his wrinkled face every now and then over the plaster.

A reference to the Salon des Refusés. The Salon jury of 1863 had refused over 4,000 works; there was such an outcry over this that the Emperor Napoleon III decreed that a "Salon des Refusés" be held in the galleries next to the official Salon. Many painters withdrew their submissions, not wishing to be exhibited in such a context, but the Refusés contained well over 600 works.

"Hallo, it's you?" he said, as they held out their hands to him. "I was just looking at our friend Mahoudeau's figure, which they have at least had the intelligence to admit, and to put in a good position." Then, breaking off: "Have you been upstairs?" he asked.

"No, we have just come in," said Claude.

Thereupon Bongrand began to talk warmly about the Salon of the Rejected. He, who belonged to the Institute, but who lived apart from his colleagues, made very merry over the affair; the everlasting discontent of painters; the campaign conducted by petty newspapers like *The Drummer*; the protestations, the constant complaints that had at last disturbed the Emperor, and the artistic *coup d'état* carried out by that silent dreamer, for this Salon of the Rejected was entirely his work. Then the great painter alluded to all the hubbub caused by the flinging of such a paving-stone into that frog's pond, the official art world.

"No," he continued, "you can have no idea of the rage and indignation among the members of the hanging committee. And remember I'm distrusted, they generally keep quiet when I'm there. But they are all furious with the realists. It was to them that they systematically closed the doors of the temple; it is on account of them that the Emperor has allowed the public to revise their verdict; and finally it is they, the realists, who triumph. Ah! I hear some nice things said; I wouldn't give a high price for your skins, youngsters."

He laughed his big, joyous laugh, stretching out his arms the while as if to embrace all the youthfulness that he divined rising around him.

"Your disciples are growing," said Claude, simply.

But Bongrand, becoming embarrassed, silenced him with a wave of his hand. He himself had not sent anything for exhibition, and the prodigious mass of work amidst which he found himself – those pictures, those statues, all those proofs of creative effort – filled him with regret. It was not jealousy, for there lived not a more upright and better soul; but as a result of self-examination, a gnawing fear of impotence, an unavowed dread haunted him.

"And at 'the Rejected,'" asked Sandoz; "how goes it there?"

"Superb; you'll see."

Then turning towards Claude, and keeping both the young man's hands in his own. "You, my good fellow, you are a trump. Listen! they say I am clever: well, I'd give ten years of my life to have painted that big hussy of yours."

Praise like that, coming from such lips, moved the young painter to tears. Victory had come at last, then? He failed to find a word of thanks, and abruptly changed the conversation, wishing to hide his emotion.

"That good fellow Mahoudeau!" he said, "why, his figure's capital! He has a deuced fine temperament, hasn't he?"

Sandoz and Claude had begun to walk round the plaster figure. Bongrand replied with a smile.

"Yes, yes; there's too much fulness and massiveness in parts. But just look at the articulations, they are delicate and really pretty. Come, good-bye, I must leave you. I'm going to sit down a while. My legs are bending under me."

Claude had raised his head to listen. A tremendous uproar, an incessant crashing that had not struck him at first, careered through the air; it was like the din of a tempest beating against a cliff, the rumbling of an untiring assault, dashing forward from endless space.

"Hallo, what's that?" he muttered.

"That," said Bongrand, as he walked away, "that's the crowd upstairs in the galleries."

And the two young fellows, having crossed the garden, then went up to the Salon of the Rejected.

It had been installed in first-rate syle. The officially received pictures were not lodged more sumptuously: lofty hangings of old tapestry at the doors; "the line" set off with green baize; seats of crimson velvet; white linen screens under the large sky-lights of the roof. And all along the suite of galleries the first impression was the same – there were the same gilt frames, the same bright colours on the canvases. But there was a special kind of cheerfulness, a sparkle of youth which one did not altogether realize at first. The crowd, already compact, increased every minute, for the official Salon was being deserted. People came stung by curiosity, impelled by a desire to judge the judges, and, above all, full of the conviction that they were going to see some very diverting things. It was very hot; a fine dust arose from the flooring; and certainly, towards four o'clock people would stifle there.

* * *

Claude, whose spirits had revived amidst that martial odour, grew animated and pugnacious as he listened to the laughter of the public. He looked as defiant, indeed, as if he had heard bullets whizzing past him. Sufficiently discreet at the entrance to the galleries, the laughter became more boisterous, more unrestrained, as they advanced. In the third room the women ceased concealing their smiles behind their handkerchiefs, while the men openly held their sides the better to ease themselves. It was the contagious hilarity of people who had come to amuse themselves, and who were growing gradually excited, bursting out at a mere trifle, diverted as much by the good things as by the bad. Folks laughed less before Chaîne's Christ than before the back view of the nude woman, who seemed to them very comical indeed. The *Lady in White* also stupefied people and drew them together; folks nudged each other and went into hysterics almost; there was always a grinning group in front of it. Each canvas thus had its particular kind of success; people hailed each other from a distance to point out something funny, and witticisms flew from mouth to mouth; to such a degree indeed that, as Claude entered the fourth gallery, lashed into fury by the tempest of laughter that was raging there as well, he all but slapped the face of an old lady whose chuckles exasperated him.

"What idiots!" he said, turning his back towards his friends. "One feels inclined to throw a lot of masterpieces at their heads. . . ."

But of a sudden Jory stood before them. His fair handsome face absolutely beamed. He cut his way through the crowd, gesticulated, and exulted, as if over a personal victory. And the moment he perceived Claude, he shouted:

"Here you are at last! I have been looking for you this hour. A success, old fellow, oh! a success –"

"What success?"

"Why, the success of your picture. Come, I must show it you. You'll see, it's stunning."

Claude grew pale. A great joy choked him, while he pretended to receive the news with composure. Bongrand's words came back to him. He began to believe that he possessed genius.

"Hallo, how are you?" continued Jory, shaking hands with the others.

And, without more ado, he, Fagerolles and Gagnière surrounded Irma, who smiled on them in a good-natured way.

"Perhaps you'll tell us where the picture is," said Sandoz, impatiently. "Take us to it."

Jory assumed the lead, followed by the band. They had to fight their way into the last gallery. But Claude, who brought up the rear, still heard the laughter that rose on the air, a swelling clamour, the roll of a tide near its full. And as he finally entered the room, he beheld a vast, swarming, closely packed crowd pressing eagerly in front of his picture. All the laughter arose, spread, and ended there. And it was his picture that was being laughed at.

"Eh!" repeated Jory, triumphantly, "there's a success for you."

A reference to J.A.M. Whistler's (1834–1903) painting Symphony in White No. 1: The White Girl, *1862 (National Gallery, Washington D.C.).*

Gagnière, intimidated, as ashamed as if he himself had been slapped, muttered: "Too much of a success – I should prefer something different."

"What a fool you are," replied Jory, in a burst of exalted conviction. "That's what I call success. Does it matter a curse if they laugh? We have made our mark; tomorrow every paper will talk about us."

"The idiots," was all that Sandoz could gasp, choking with grief. . . .

But Claude did not stir. An icy chill had come over him. For a moment his heart had almost ceased to beat, so cruel had been the disappointment. And with his eyes enlarged, attracted and fixed by a resistless force, he looked at his picture. He was surprised, and scarcely recognized it; it certainly was not such as it had seemed to be in his studio. It had grown yellow beneath the livid light of the linen screens; it seemed, moreover, to have become smaller; coarser and more laboured also; and whether it was the effect of the light in which it now hung, or the contrast of the works beside it, at all events he now at the first glance saw all its defects, after having remained blind to them, as it were, for months. With a few strokes of the brush he, in thought, altered the whole of it, deepened the distances, set a badly drawn limb right, and modified a tone. Decidedly, the gentleman in the velveteen jacket was worth nothing at all, he was altogether pasty and badly seated; the only really good bit of work about him was his hand. In the background the two little wrestlers – the fair and the dark one – had remained too sketchy, and lacked substance; they were amusing only to an artist's eye. But he was pleased with the trees, with the sunny glade; and the nude woman – the woman lying on the grass appeared to him superior to his own powers, as if someone else had painted her, and as if he had never yet beheld her in such resplendency of life.

He turned to Sandoz, and said simply:

"They do right to laugh; it's incomplete. Never mind, the woman is all right!" . . .

His friend wished to take him away, but he became obstinate, and drew nearer instead. Now that he had judged his work, he listened and looked at the crowd. The explosion continued – culminated in an ascending scale of mad laughter. No sooner had visitors crossed the threshold than he saw their jaws part, their eyes grow small, their entire faces expand; and he heard the tempestuous puffing of the fat men, the rusty grating jeers of the lean ones, amidst all the shrill, flute-like laughter of the women. Opposite him, against the hand-rails, some young fellows went into contortions, as if somebody had been tickling them. One lady had flung herself on a seat, stifling and trying to regain breath with her handkerchief over her mouth. Rumours of this picture, which was so very, very funny, must have been spreading, for there was a rush from the four corners of the Salon, bands of people arrived, jostling each other, and all eagerness to share the fun. "Where is it?" "Over there." "Oh, what a joke!" And the witticisms fell thicker than elsewhere. It was especially the subject that caused merriment; people failed to understand it, thought it insane, comical enough to make one ill with laughter. "You see the lady feels too hot, while the gentleman has put on his velveteen jacket for fear of catching cold." "Not at all; she is already blue; the gentleman has pulled her out of a pond, and he is resting at a distance, holding his nose." "I tell you it's a young ladies' school out for a ramble. Look at the two playing at leap-frog." "Hallo! washing day; the flesh is blue; the trees are blue; he's dipped his picture in the blueing tub!"

Those who did not laugh flew into a rage: that bluish tinge, that novel rendering of light seemed an insult to them. Some old gentlemen shook their sticks. Was art to be outraged like this? One grave individual went away very wroth, saying to his wife that he did not like practical jokes. But another, a punctilious little man, having looked in the catalogue for the title of the work, in order to tell his daughter, read out the words, "*In the Open Air*," whereupon there came a formidable renewal of the clamour, hisses and shouts, and what not else besides. The title sped about; it was repeated, commented on. "*In the Open Air*! ah, yes, the open air, the nude woman in the air, everything in the air, tra la la laire." The affair was becoming a scandal. The crowd still increased. People's faces grew red with congestion in the growing heat. Each had the stupidly gaping mouth of the ignoramus who judges painting, and between them they indulged in all the asinine ideas, all the preposterous reflections, all the stupid spiteful jeers that the sight of an original work can possibly elicit from *bourgeois* imbecility.

CAMILLE DE SAINTE-CROIX

PORTRAITS D'HIER

Manet's "Olympia" in the Louvre

See page 30.

December 15, 1909

In 1890, having learned that Mme Manet had found a buyer in America for *Olympia* for a considerable sum, the American painter Sargent hastened to inform Manet's friends and make them understand that it was crucial that this French masterpiece should remain French. A subscription fund was set up, with the following as subscribers: MM Braquemond, Philippe Burty, Albert Besnard, Maurice Bouchor, Felix Bouchor, de Bellio, Jean Beraud, Beroudt, Marcel Bernstein, Bing, Leon Béclard, Edmond Bazire, Jacques Blanche, Boldini, Blot, Bourdin, Paul Bonnetain, Brandon, Cazin, Eugène Carrière, Jules Chéret, Emmanuel Chabrier, Clapisson, Gustave Caillebotte, Carriès, Degas, Desboutin, Dalou, Carolus Duran, Ducq, Durand-Ruel, Dauphin, Armand Dayot, Jean Dolent, Théodore Duret, Fantin-Latour, Auguste Flameng, Guérard, Mme Guérard Gonzalès, Paul Gallimard, Gervex, Gustave Geffroy, Guillemet, J-K Huysmans, Maurice Hamel, Harrison, Hellen, Jeanniot, Frantz Jourdain, Roger Jourdain, Lhermitte, Lerolle, Leclanché, Lautrec, Sutter-Laumann, Stéphane Mallarmé, Octave Mirbeau, Roger Marx, Moreau-Nélaton, Alexandre Millerand, Claude Monet, Marius Michel, Louis Mullem, Oppenheim, Puvis de Chavannes, Antonin Proust, Camille Pelletan, Camille Pissarro, Portier, Georges Petit, Rodin, Ribot, Raffaelli, Ary Renan, Roll, Robin, H Rouart, E Rops, A de la Rochefoucauld, J Sargent, Scey-Montbéliard, Thornley, de Villegroy, Von Cutsen.

Olympia was offered to the State by these subscribers and placed, on November 17, 1890, with the consent of M Bourgeois, the minister of education – and at the insistence of M Camille Pelletan – in the Luxembourg Museum. It stayed there, in isolation, among the works of official art, until 1894. At that date, the Impressionist painter Caillebotte died, bequeathing his collection to the State. His bequest was accepted: it was made up exclusively of Impressionist painters. Thus Manet found himself surrounded, henceforth, by the revolutionary avant-garde – Degas, Renoir, Claude Monet, Pissarro, Cézanne, Caillebotte and Sisley. And *Olympia* had *The Balcony* as a pendant in the State Museum, since it had been in the triumphant collection.

Lastly, in 1907, the coming to power of M Clemenceau, Prime Minister and minister of home affairs, was marked by an unforgettable gesture. Under his influence, MM Briand, minister of education, and Dujardin-Beaumetz, under secretary of State for the fine arts, took *Olympia* out of the Luxembourg and placed it in the Louvre.

It was Sargent who informed Claude Monet of the impending sale in late 1888. Monet initiated a public subscription and offered the sum collected (19,415 francs) to Suzanne Manet in March 1890.

Mme. Guérard Gonzalès, i.e. Eva Gonzalès.

Georges Clemenceau (1841–1929), physician, politician and journalist. Clemenceau met Claude Monet in the 1860s and was to become an enthusiastic supporter of the artist. In 1870 Clemenceau became mayor of Montmartre, the XVIIIth arrondissement of Paris, and in 1875 president of the Paris Municipal Council. With Camille Pelletan he founded the republican journal La Justice. *He was premier from 1906 to 1909 and from 1917 to 1920. (Colourplate 98.)*
Monet and Gustave Geffroy had intervened with Clemenceau to persuade him to issue the order to Dujardin-Beaumetz.

It is there now, in a place of honour, in the large room devoted to nineteenth-century French painting, as a pendant to Ingres' *Odalisque*. Thus it has attained the final victory of a national eclecticism which places the most classic work of the most magisterial of the classic masters on an equal footing with the most revolutionary painting by the most extreme of revolutionary masters.

JULIE MANET

JOURNAL

1893-99

Julie Manet (1878–1966), daughter of Berthe Morisot and Eugène Manet.

SUNDAY JANUARY 29

We go with Jeanne to see the Pellerin collection. I understand nothing of this man who knows nothing of painting and yet seems to worship my uncle Édouard's talent, and who owns some superb works of his: *Léon Leenhoff in Velvet in Front of a Table* covered with a quantity of wonderfully painted things, *Nana*, the woman dressed in Spanish dress lying on a couch, which I did not know and which is marvellous, what a painting! then *Skating*, *The Bar*, *The Artist*, which I like less, a *Nude Woman* with which Pellerin is enchanted and which is indeed lovely, but the background is of a black which I find surprising, then sketches, minor things, an *homme suicidé* impressively realistic, *Portrait of Eva Gonzalès* and a little Spaniard with her, all done in four brushstrokes, some charming pastels and a sketch of Mother, seen in profile with a violet hat and fur coat, which is utterly like her, I would like to own that canvas. Of Mother's, we see the portrait of *Lucie Léon Dressed in Blue at the Piano* which is truly ravishing and individual, then *Maurecourt* and a *Woman in Pink Reclining* with her back to the light, in pastel, giving an astonishing impression of light. Pellerin also owns the lovely *Woman and Child*, by M Renoir, and a pretty little landscape by Sisley, several by Monet, including a charming *plein air* of the banks of the Seine. We return full of enthusiasms for this collection which shows the work of my uncle Édouard to such advantage. What a great painter, what reality in his canvases and how he captures movement. I do nothing but think about this beautiful painting, so full of simplicity; in fact, simplicity is the prime condition of beauty. . . .

Auguste Pellerin (1852–1929), margarine manufacturer, owned a large art collection, including many works by Cézanne. In 1897 Pellerin bought a number of Manet drawings from Antonin Proust. In 1910 he sold several works by Manet to the dealers Bernheim-Jeune, Paul Cassirer and Durand-Ruel.

COLOURPLATES 43, 79, 17, 77, 117, 76, 49

TUESDAY JANUARY 31

When we are talking of the Pellerin collection, Mme Renoir tells us that the Bs have repainted a picture by my uncle that they sold to M Pellerin for 100,000 francs. Paule and I have no hesitation in thinking that it must have been the background of the *Nude Women* which has been redone.

TUESDAY FEBRUARY 7

To aunt Suzanne's to whom I talk about P's retouched picture so that she will give me permission to bring a lawsuit, for I find it unacceptable that I should allow the works of my uncle to be thus spoiled; but I came away beside myself, there is simply nothing to be done, aunt Suzanne wrote on the back of the picture that she recognized it as being by her husband after having hesitated, noticing that there had been a bit of retouching: "I could not say that it was not by my husband," she told me with her Dutch nonchalance, "because the women were by him!" I tell her roundly that she should not have signed, I get a bit carried away, I think she feels I am

A reference to the gallery Bernheim-Jeune, owned by Josse Bernheim (1870–1941) and his twin brother Gaston (1870–1953), sons of the dealer Alexandre Bernheim, and directed for many years by Félix Fenéon. Bernheim-Jeune dealt primarily with Impressionist works.

meddling in matters that do not concern me, and she is very calm and tells me that it is always like that with sketches; it is true that her own brother has repainted several of my uncle's canvases. So that is what happened; these crafty Bs have covered themselves by arranging to get aunt S's signature before the painting was completely repainted. There is nothing one can do with people like that. Aunt Suzanne believes that P is working in collusion with them. I don't know, in that case he would be well-covered. . . .

I tell M Renoir that I had met P who had invited me to see his new Manets which were totally unknown: "Even Manet had never seen them, is what you should have replied," said M Renoir.

GEORGE MOORE

MODERN PAINTING

Manet Paints Moore's Portrait

1898

George Moore (1852–1933), Irish critic and novelist. Moore arrived in Paris in March 1873 to study art. He probably met Manet in 1878 or 1879. (See Colourplate 101, page 264 and page 337.)

Being a fresh-complexioned, fair-haired young man, the type most suited to Manet's palette, he at once asked me to sit. His first intention was to paint me in a café; he had met me in a café, and he thought he could realize his impression of me in the first surrounding he had seen me in.

The portrait did not come right; ultimately it was destroyed; but it gave me every opportunity of studying Manet's method of painting. Strictly speaking, he had no method; painting with him was a pure instinct. Painting was one of the ways his nature manifested itself in everything that concerned him – in his large plain studio, full of light as a conservatory; in his simple, scrupulous clothes, and yet with a touch of the dandy about them; in decisive speech, quick, hearty and informed with a manly and sincere understanding of life. Never was an artist's inner nature in more direct conformity with his work. There were no circumlocutions in Manet's nature, there were none in his art.

The colour of my hair never gave me a thought until Manet began to paint it. Then the blonde gold that came up under his brush filled me with admiration, and I was astonished when, a few days after, I saw him scrape off the rough paint and prepare to start afresh.

"Are you going to get a new canvas?"

"No; this will do very well."

"But you can't paint yellow ochre on yellow ochre without getting it dirty?"

"Yes, I think I can. You go and sit down."

Half an hour after, he had entirely repainted the hair, and without losing anything of its brightness. He painted it again and again; every time it came out brighter and fresher, and the painting never seemed to lose anything in quality. That this portrait cost him infinite labour and was eventually destroyed matters nothing; my point is merely that he could paint yellow over yellow without getting the colour muddy. One day, seeing that I was in difficulties with a black, he took a brush from my hand, and it seemed to have hardly touched the canvas when the ugly heaviness of my tiresome black began to disappear. There came into it grey and shimmering lights, the shadows filled up with air, and silk seemed to float and rustle. There was no method – there was no trick; he merely painted. My palette was the same to him as his own; he did not

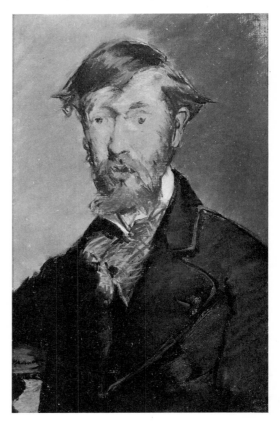

Portrait of George Moore. 1879. Pastel, 21¾ × 13⅞" (55.2 × 35.5 cm). Metropolitan Museum of Art, New York (Bequest of Mrs H.O. Havemeyer, 1929. The H.O. Havemeyer Collection).

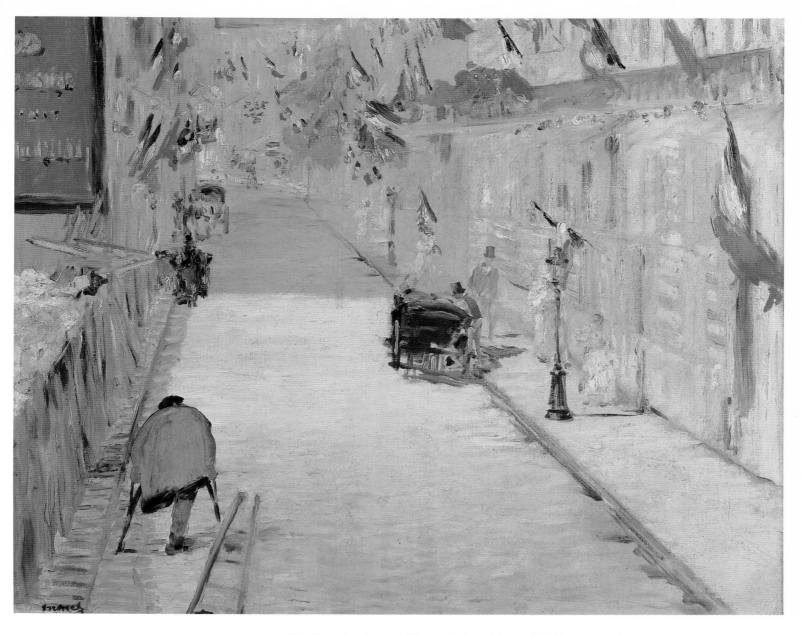

COLOURPLATE 75. *The Rue Mosnier with Flags.* 1878. 25½ × 31½″ (65 × 81 cm).
Mr and Mrs Paul Mellon Collection, Upperville, Virginia.

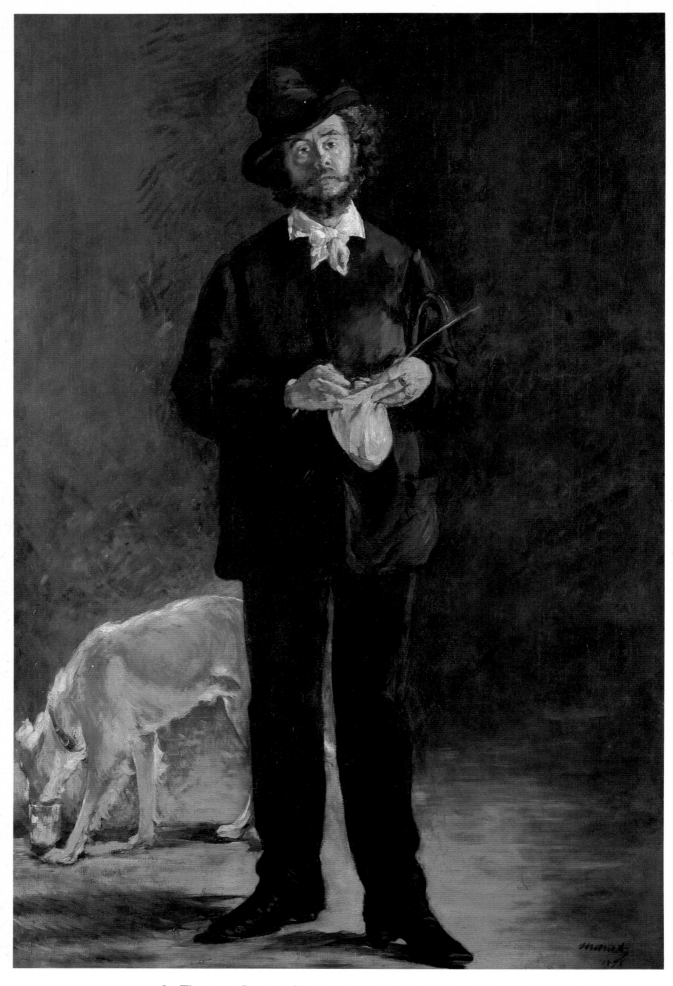

COLOURPLATE 76. *The Artist: Portrait of Marcellin Desboutin.* 1875. 75½ × 50¼″ (192 × 128 cm).
Museu de Arte, São Paulo, Brazil (Photo Luiz Hossaka).

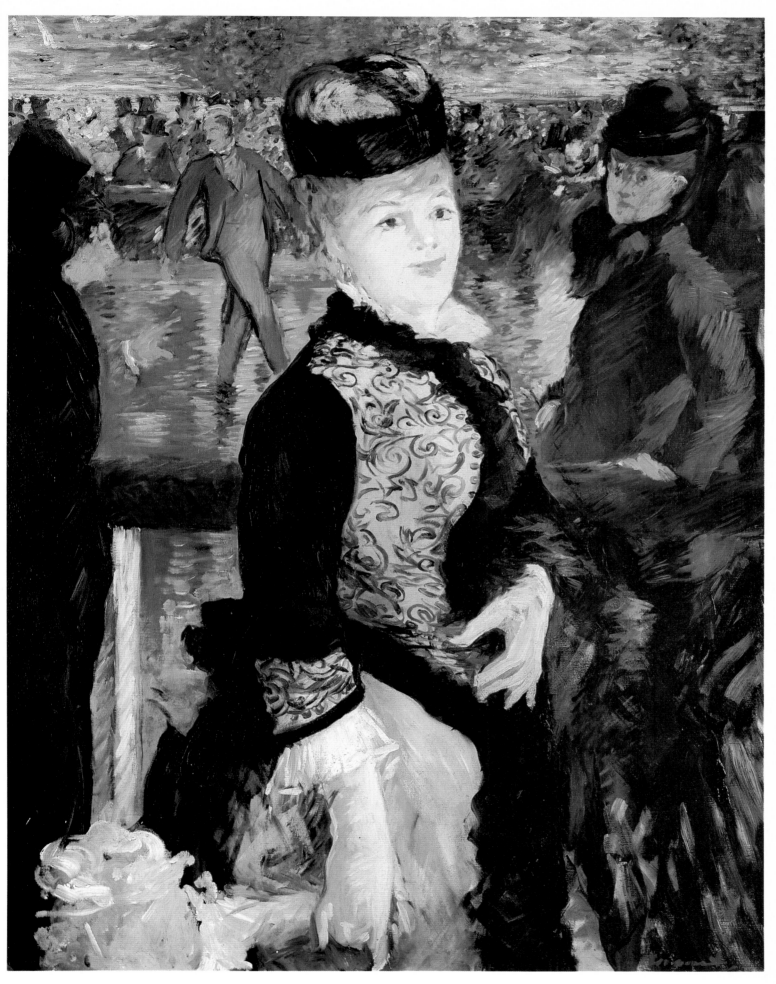

COLOURPLATE 77. *The Skating Rink*. 1877. 36¼ × 28″ (92 × 71.6 cm).
Fogg Art Museum, Cambridge, Mass. (Bequest of Maurice Wertheim).

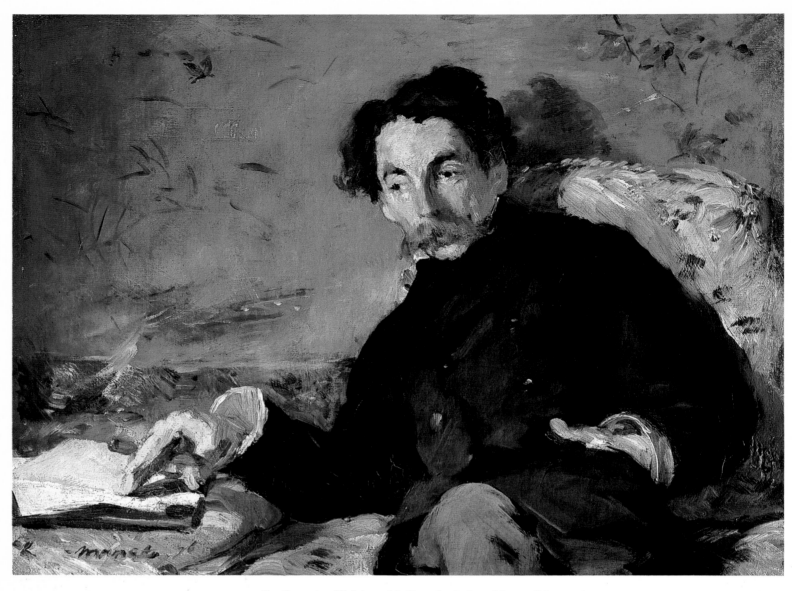

COLOURPLATE 78. *Portrait of Stéphane Mallarmé.* 1876. 10¾ × 14″ (27.5 × 36 cm).
Musée d'Orsay, Paris.

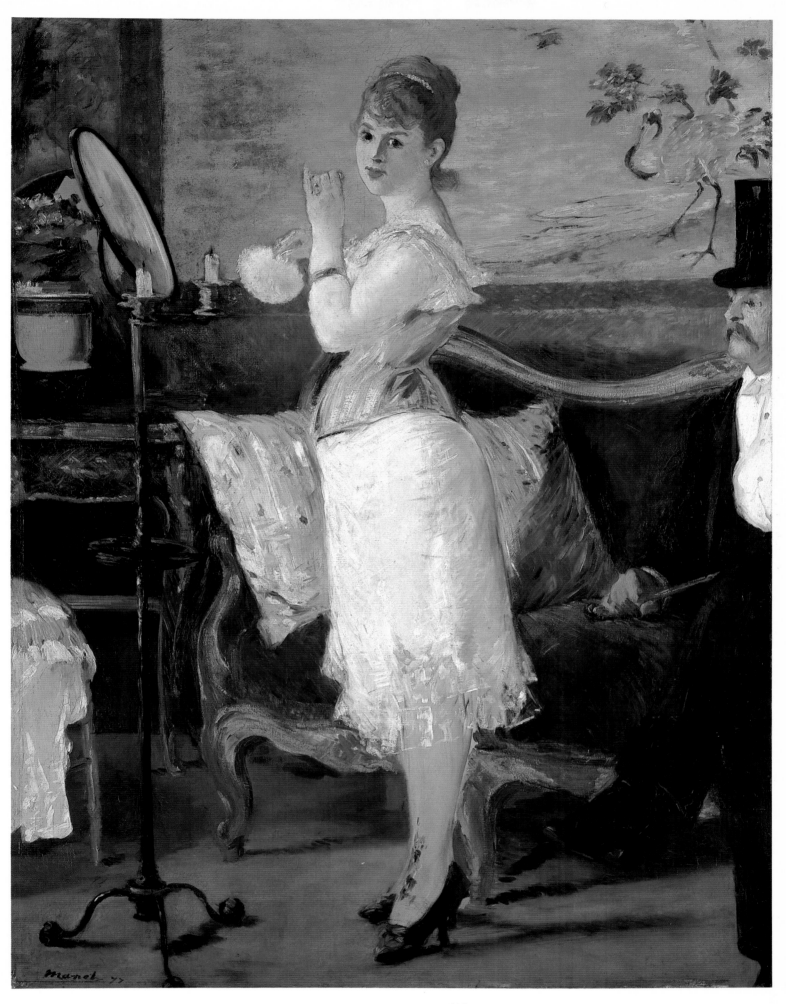

COLOURPLATE 79. *Nana*. 1877. 59 × 45¾″ (150 × 116 cm).
Kunsthalle, Hamburg.

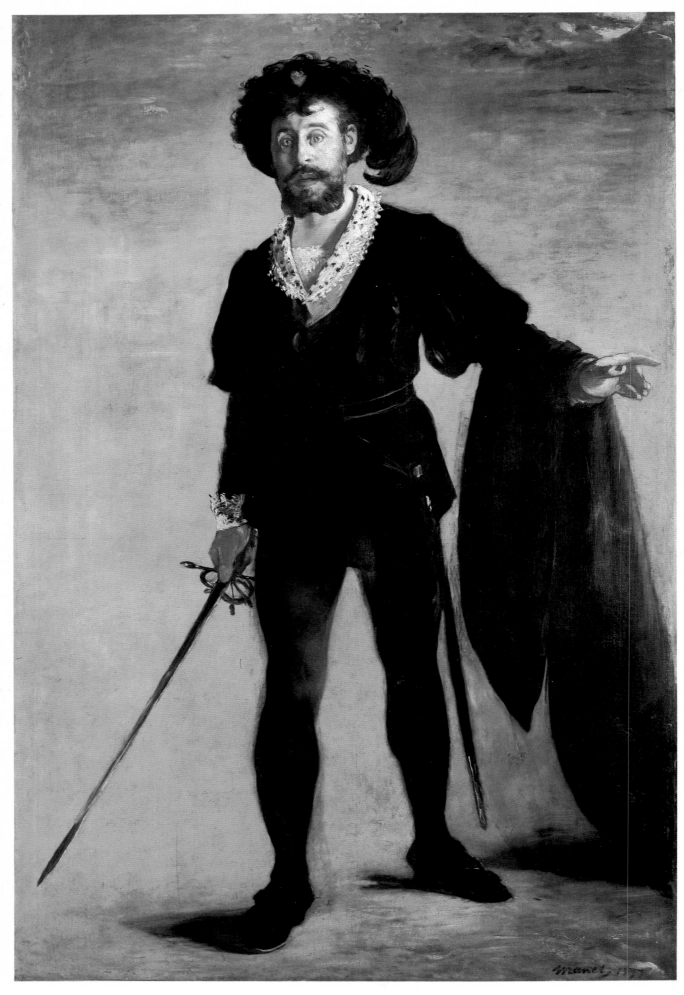

COLOURPLATE 80. *Portrait of Faure in the Role of Hamlet.* 1877. 77 × 51″ (196 × 130 cm).
Folkwang Museum, Essen.

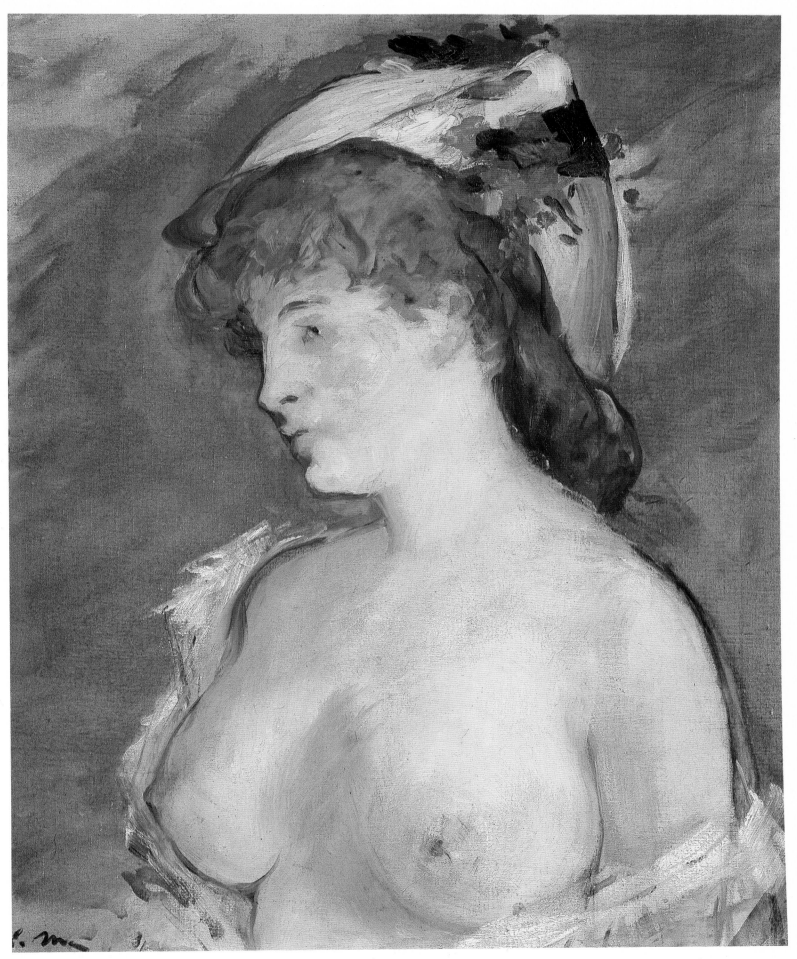

COLOURPLATE 81. *Blonde Girl with Naked Breasts*. 1878. 24½ × 20½″ (62.5 × 52 cm).
Musée d'Orsay, Paris.

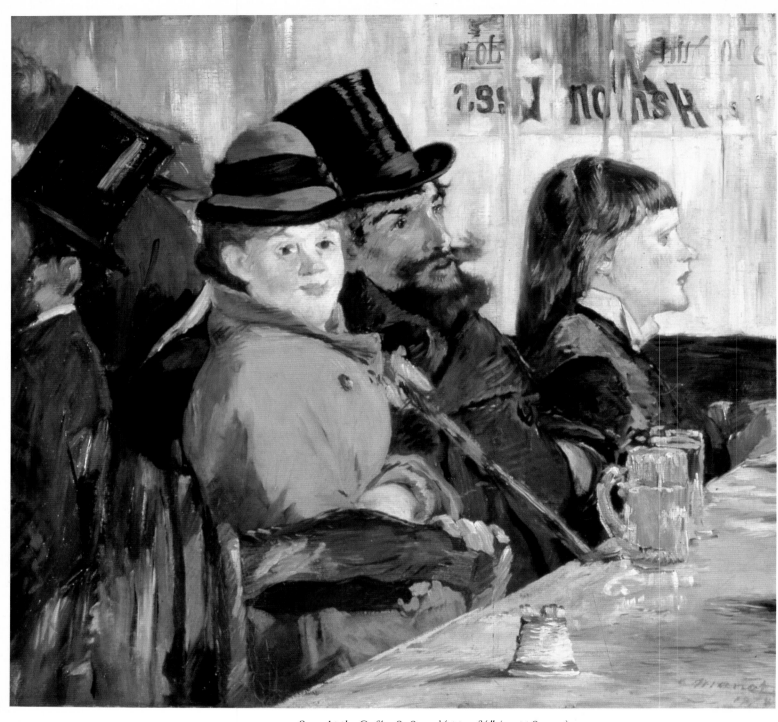

COLOURPLATE 82. *At the Café*. 1878. 30¼ × 32¾″ (77 × 83 cm).
Oskar Reinhart Collection, Winterthur.

prepare his palette; his colour did not exist on his palette before he put it on the canvas; but working under the immediate dictation of his eye, he snatched the tints instinctively, without premeditation. Ah! that marvellous hand, those thick fingers holding the brush so firmly – somewhat heavily; how malleable, how obedient, that most rebellious material, oil-colour, was to his touch. He did with it what he liked. I believe he could rub a picture over with Prussian blue without experiencing any inconvenience; half an hour after the colour would be fine and beautiful.

And never did this mysterious power which produces what artists know as "quality" exist in greater abundance in any fingers than it did in the slow, thick fingers of Édouard Manet: never since the world began; not in Velazquez, not in Hals, not in Rubens, not in Titian. As an artist Manet could not compare with the least among these illustrious painters; but as a manipulator of oil-colour he never was and never will be excelled. Manet was born a painter as absolutely as any man that ever lived, so absolutely that a very high and lucid intelligence never for a moment came between him and the desire to put anything into his picture except good painting. I remember his saying to me, "I also tried to write, but I did not succeed; I never could do anything but paint." And what a splendid thing for an artist to be able to say. The real meaning of his words did not reach me till years after; perhaps I even thought at the time that he was disappointed that he could not write. I know now what was passing in his mind: *Je ne me suis pas trompé de métier*. How many of us can say as much? Go round a picture gallery, and of how many pictures, ancient or modern, can you stand before and say, *Voilà un homme qui ne s'est pas trompé de métier?*

Perhaps above all men of our generation Manet made the least mistake in his choice of a trade. Let those who doubt go and look at the beautiful picture of Boulogne Pier, now on view in Mr Van Wesselingh's gallery, 26 Old Bond Street. The wooden pier goes right across the canvas; all the wood piers are drawn, there is no attempt to hide or attenuate their regularity. Why should Manet attenuate when he could fill the interspaces with the soft lapping of such exquisite blue sea water. Above the piers there is the ugly yellow-painted rail. But why alter the colour when he could keep it in such exquisite value? On the canvas it is beautiful. In the middle of the pier there is a mast and a sail which does duty for an awning; perhaps it is only a marine decoration. A few loungers are on the pier – men and women in grey clothes. Why introduce reds and blues when he was sure of being able to set the little figures in their places, to draw them so firmly, and relieve the grey monotony with such beauty of execution? It would be vain to invent when so exquisite an execution is always at hand to relieve and to transform. Mr Whistler would have chosen to look at the pier from a more fanciful point of view. Degas would have taken an odd corner; he would have cut the composition strangely, and commented on the humanity of the pier. But Manet just painted it without circumlocutions of any kind. The subject was void of pictorial relief. There was not even a blue space in the sky, nor yet a dark cloud. He took it as it was – a white sky, full of an inner radiance, two sailing-boats floating in mist of heat, one in shadow, the other in light. Vandervelde would seem trivial and precious beside painting so firm, so manly, so free from trick, so beautifully logical, and so unerring.

ANTONIN PROUST

THE STUDIO

"The Art of Édouard Manet"

January 1901

"Be true" – that was his formula. At Boulogne, where he painted his admirable *Fishermen's Wives in Moonlight*, he was so scrupulous in this respect that he absolutely refused to touch his canvas with the brush when he could not find the scene exactly as it was the night before. This was the period of what has been called his "third manner." His work had taken definite shape, and there was nothing left to give any reminder of this or that great master.

From 1869-79 he produced a long succession of drawings, pastels, paintings and studies, among them being *A Good Glass of Beer*, which was done just to show his imitators that when he chose he, too, could tickle the public fancy. For this the critics applauded him; but the vials of their wrath were once more outpoured when he exhibited his *Doing the Washing* and his *Railway*, with its vivid whiteness.

After a number of portraits come *Polichinelle, In the Conservatory*, another set of etchings, the illustrations to Edgar Allan Poe, etc., etc. Life and light everywhere. The effect is seen on every palette. No one can escape his influence, from Paul Baudry, of the Institute, down to the most insignificant Impressionist. But it was useless for them to borrow Manet's "manner" – it was his *manner of seeing* they lacked, and that was not to be acquired!

Manet cared little for all this, and when they told him he couldn't draw, he would say, with a shrug of his shoulders, "I don't draw silly lines as they are taught in the schools; but I challenge any of the illustrious professors teaching there to obtain an effect of light; they cannot do it. I defy them to do it. What do they know of atmosphere, of the mobile light which envelops everything around in its dazzling splendour? Ask this of the people who stick a face on a canvas just as one sticks a butterfly in a case." And, referring to a portrait by a fashionable painter, he would exclaim, "I can see he has painted an overcoat – an excellent, well-cut overcoat. But where are the lungs? The model does not breathe beneath his clothes; he has no body; he is simply a tailor's figure."

Nowadays, everyone admits that Manet rendered a great service to art by insisting on the necessity of observation, by discarding mere imitation of things already achieved, and by concentrating his powers, not on the past, but on the present.

Manet has been reproached for having painted his women in an ugly light. Nothing could be more unjust. His portrait of Eva Gonzalès is something more than the faithful presentment of a beautiful woman. The pose is perfect in its grace, and the movement is as happy as can be; while it suffices to name the exquisite pictures of Mlle Demarsy, Mme Valtini, Méry Laurent and Mlle Lemonnier to disprove the charge entirely. There is a sense of distinction in these portraits such as few artists have achieved and none have surpassed.

When, soon after Manet's death in April, 1883, his works were displayed at the Ecole des Beaux-Arts, the public was shocked to find – as at the Pont de l'Alma exhibition in 1867 – that a large number of his pictures had never got beyond the rough state. Yet the non-completion of all these works is entirely to the credit of the artist. Never would he allow himself to finish a picture unless he could do it as he had begun – from nature direct. Such was his intense respect for what he had actually seen;

Proust's articles on Manet were expanded and reissued as Édouard Manet, Souvenirs *in 1913.*

COLOURPLATE 44

COLOURPLATE 54

PAGE 147
COLOURPLATE 61
COLOURPLATE 96

Paul Baudry (1828–86), French painter.

COLOURPLATE 49

Mlle Isabelle Lemonnier, one of Manet's favourite models and sister-in-law of Georges Charpentier (Colourplates 94, 97, 103).

and this shows a degree of scrupulousness not too often met with among artists. One of the weaknesses of Corot and of Millet consisted in their habit of completing their canvases in the studio. A day will come when the truth of Manet's doctrine will be admitted. "Do nothing," said he, "without consulting Nature." Whether there be truth or not in the old definition that "art is man *plus* Nature" – *homo additus naturae* – certain it is, Nature must be there. Not even the most faithful memory can take its place. Such was Manet's oft-expressed opinion.

From 1860-83 Manet made daily progress, for the simple reason that he was constantly trying fresh experiments; and though to this day there are those who refuse to recognize the splendid merit of most of his works, there will come a time when even the slightest sketch by this truly great artist will be sought for and analysed as containing a lesson in its every line.

As a striking instance of that high intuition which has made Manet one of the most notable artistic figures of this century, let me mention his much-abused picture of the fight between the *Kearsage and the Alabama*. Ridicule was cast upon it; yet is there a picture, old or new, in which the sea has been reproduced so amply? And what a delight it is for those who are capable of enjoying painting *as* painting, and of separating it from all rhetorical prejudices and all the pretentious reflections of literature!

Chatting with me one night in his studio in the rue d'Amsterdam, Manet began to talk of all the adverse criticisms with which for twenty years he had been assailed whenever he had exhibited, whether in the

COLOURPLATE 21

The Beautiful Pole. 1878/81.
Transfer lithograph, 11¼ × 10½"
(28.5 × 26.5 cm). Bibliothèque
Nationale, Paris.

Salon, or in the building erected at his expense in 1867 at the end of the Pont de l'Alma, or in the Rue de St-Pétersbourg Gallery. It was in 1882, Manet was already suffering from the disease which was to carry him off in the following year. "This war to the knife," said he, "has done me much harm. I have suffered from it greatly, but it has whipped me up. I would not wish that any artist should be praised and beslavered at the outset, for that means the annihilation of his personality." Then he added, with a smile, "The fools! They were for ever telling me my work was unequal; that was the highest praise they could bestow. Yet, it was always my ambition to rise – not to remain on a certain level, not to remake one day what I had made the day before, but to be inspired again and again by a new aspect of things, to strike frequently a fresh note. Ah! I'm before my time. A hundred years hence people will be happier, for their sight will be clearer than ours today."

A long silence followed, and as we parted, Manet said to me, as he often said, "You know, my work must be seen in its entirety. If I should vanish, I beg you not to let me go bit by bit into the public collections, for people would judge me ill."

See page 169.

My friend died in the following year. A few months after his death we organized a complete exhibition of his works in the Ecole des Beaux-Arts. A few years later (in 1889) I was able to repeat the display at the Champ de Mars, and then, as in 1883, it was truly an apotheosis.

At the Exposition Universelle of 1889, where fifteen of Manet's works were shown.

GEORGE MOORE

REMINISCENCES OF THE IMPRESSIONIST PAINTERS

Moore's anecdotal writings on French painters were instrumental in making French art known to a British audience.

Manet

1906

The work of the great artist is himself, and, being one of the greatest painters that ever lived, Manet's art was all Manet; one cannot think of Manet's painting without thinking of the man himself. The last time I saw Monet was at the dinner in the Café Royal, and, after talking of many things, suddenly, without any transition, Monet said, speaking out of a dream, "How like Manet was to his painting," and I answered delighted, for it is always exciting to talk about Manet: "Yes, how like. That blonde, amusing face, the clear eyes that saw simply, truly and quickly;" and having said so much, my thoughts went back to the time when the glass door of the café grated upon the sanded floor, and Manet entered. Though by birth and by education essentially Parisian, there was something in his appearance and manner of speaking that often suggested an Englishman. Perhaps it was his dress – his clean-cut clothes and figure. That figure! Those square shoulders that swaggered as he went across the room, and the thin waist; the face, the beard, and the nose, satyr-like shall I say? No, for I would evoke an idea of beauty of line united to that of intellectual expression – frank words, frank passion in his convictions, loyal and simple phrases, clear as well water, sometimes a little hard, sometimes as they flowed away bitter, but at the fountain head sweet and full of light.

I should emphasize Manet's courage, for without courage there cannot be art. We have all heard the phrase, "I should not like to think like that," and whosoever feels that he would not like to think out to its end every thought that may happen to come into his mind I would dissuade from art if I could. Manet's art is the most courageous ever seen. One looks in vain for those subterfuges that we find in every other painter. What he saw he stated candidly, almost innocently, and what he did not see he passed over. Never in his life did he stop to worry over a piece of drawing that did not interest him because it was possible that somebody might notice the omission. It was part of his genius to omit what did not interest him. I remember a young man whom Manet thought well of – a frequent visitor to the studio – and one day he brought his sister with him – not an ill-looking girl, no better and no worse than another, a little commonplace, that was all. Manet was affable, and charming; he showed his pictures, he talked volubly, but next day when the young man arrived and asked Manet what he thought of his sister, Manet said, extending his arm (the gesture was habitual to him): "The last girl in the world I should have thought was your sister." The young man protested, saying Manet had seen his sister dressed to her disadvantage – she was wearing a thick woollen dress, for there was snow on the ground. Manet shook his head. "I have not to look twice; I am in the habit of judging things." These were his words, or very nearly, and I think this anecdote throws a light upon Manet's painting. He saw quickly and clearly, and he stated what he saw candidly, almost innocently.

* * *

Interior of a Café. 1869. Pen and black ink, 11½ × 15½″ (29.5 × 39.5 cm). Fogg Art Museum, Harvard University, Cambridge, Mass. (Meta and Paul J. Sachs Bequest).

The word "unashamed" perhaps explains Manet's art better than any other. It is essentially unashamed, and in speaking of him one must never be afraid to repeat the word "unashamed." Manet was born in what is known as refined society, he was a rich man, in dress and appearance he was an aristocrat; but to be aristocratic in art one must avoid polite society. Manet was obliged for the sake of his genius to separate himself from his class; he was obliged to spend his evenings in the café of the Nouvelle Athènes, and his friends were artists; however poor and miserable, if they were artists they were welcome in Manet's studio. We have often heard artists laughed at for wearing long hair, for not speaking as ambassadors speak, but how superficial is this criticism when the essence of art is to separate, to repudiate all conventions, to be ashamed of nothing but to be ashamed. The price one pays for shamelessness, for truth, sincerity, personality is public neglect. During the years that I knew Manet he never sold a picture. Some years earlier Durand-Ruel bought 2,000 pounds worth of his pictures but as these remained on his hands he bought no more. You will wonder why, in a city like Paris, he did not find support. Support means money, and monied men do not appreciate shamelessness in art. In many ways Paris is more like the rest of the world than we think, and the monied man in Paris like the monied man in London admires pictures in proportion as they resemble other pictures; those who like pictures in proportion as they differ from others are rare.

After Manet's death his friends made some little stir, there was a sale, and then the prices sank again, sank almost to nothing, and it seemed as if the world would never appreciate Manet. There was a time, fifteen or sixteen years ago, when Manet's pictures could have been bought for twenty, thirty, forty or fifty pounds a piece. I remember saying to Albert Wolff some years after Manet's death – it was at Tortoni's, the celebrated café is now gone: "How is it," I said, "that Degas and Whistler and Monet have come into their inheritance, but there is no sign of recognition of Manet's art!" Wolff was the art critic of *Le Figaro*, and understood painting as well as another. He answered: "Put that hope aside, the time will never come when people will care for Manet's painting." I can recall the feeling of depression that this pronouncement caused me, and how I went away asking myself if the most beautiful painting the world had ever seen was destined to remain the most unpopular. That was fifteen years ago. We are

Moore exaggerates Manet's lack of sales; the artist had a number of patrons during his lifetime (see page 126).

Albert Wolff (1835–91).

The Café Tortoni. 1889. Illustration for *Harper's* Magazine. Bibliothèque Nationale, Paris (Cabinet des Estampes).

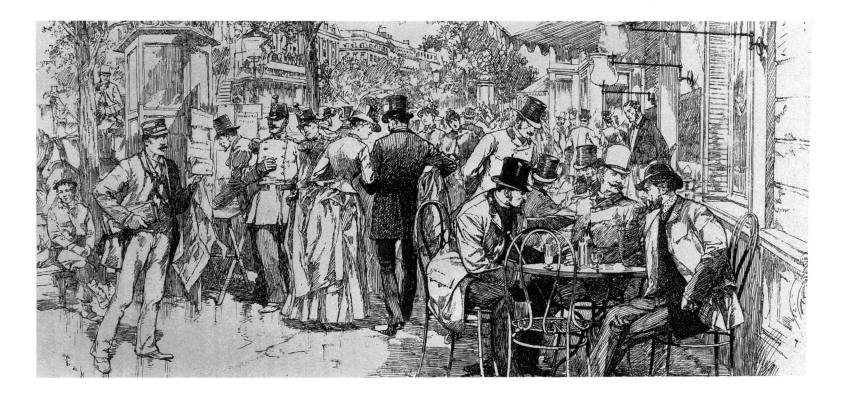

impatient for the triumph of the things we love, and it took fifteen years for the light of Manet's genius to reach Ireland.

I have been asked which of the two pictures hanging in this room it would be better to buy for the Gallery of Modern Art, *The Old Musician* or the portrait of Mademoiselle Gonzalès. Mr Lane himself put this question to me, and I answered: "I am afraid whichever you choose you will regret you had not chosen the other." The picture of the *Old Musician* is a Spanish Manet, it was painted after Manet had seen Goya, but it is as obviously a Manet as the portrait of Mademoiselle Gonzalès. To anyone who knows Manet's work it possesses all the qualities which we associate with Manet; the eye that sees clearly and quickly is as apparent in one picture as in the other. Manet saw Nature rapidly, and in full contour, and before he began to paint all those people were seated and standing in his mind's eye as they are on the canvas. The painting is as unashamed as Whitman; Manet is a sort of Whitman in paint. Look at that girl's foot – it is stated without either fear of offending or desire of pleasing anybody, and was not that Whitman's attitude of mind? Mademoiselle Gonzalès' rounded white arm is even more courageously stated, for it is entirely without sexual appeal, and I am afraid the picture will to many people seem vulgar for that very reason. In the Spanish picture Manet is disguised a little, so little that one hesitates to admit it; but one should never hesitate about saying anything – the larger picture is Manet and Goya, whereas the portrait is Manet and nothing but Manet. That portrait is an article of faith. It says: "Be not

COLOURPLATE 9
Sir Hugh Lane (1875–1915), the Irish collector of Old Masters and Impressionist art. Lane took advice from Steer, Sickert and Yeats, as well as Moore, in making his purchases. He had bought Music in the Tuileries Gardens *(Colourplate 11) from Durand-Ruel for 100,000 francs in 1906. This picture, as well as the* Portrait of Eva Gonzalès *(Colourplate 49), were bequeathed to the National Gallery, London, after Lane died in the sinking of the liner* Lusitania.

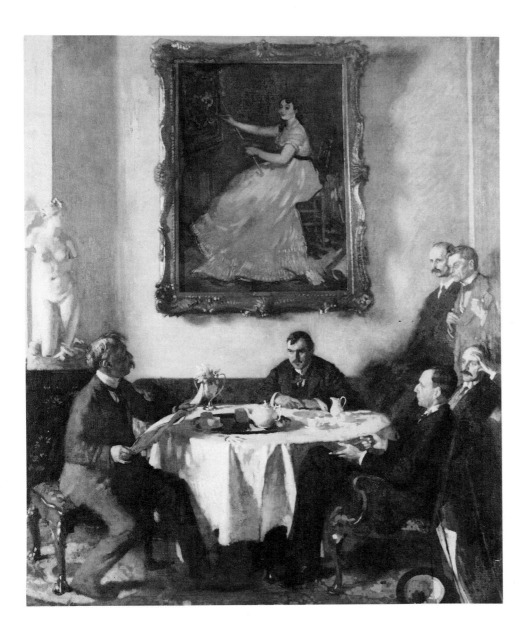

Sir William Orpen (1878–1931), *Homage to Manet.* 1909. 64⅛ × 51³⁄₁₆″ (162.9 × 130 cm). City Art Gallery, Manchester, England. The painting represents George Moore, Philip Wilson Steer, D.S. MacColl, Walter Richard Sickert, Henry Tonks and Sir Hugh Lane.

267

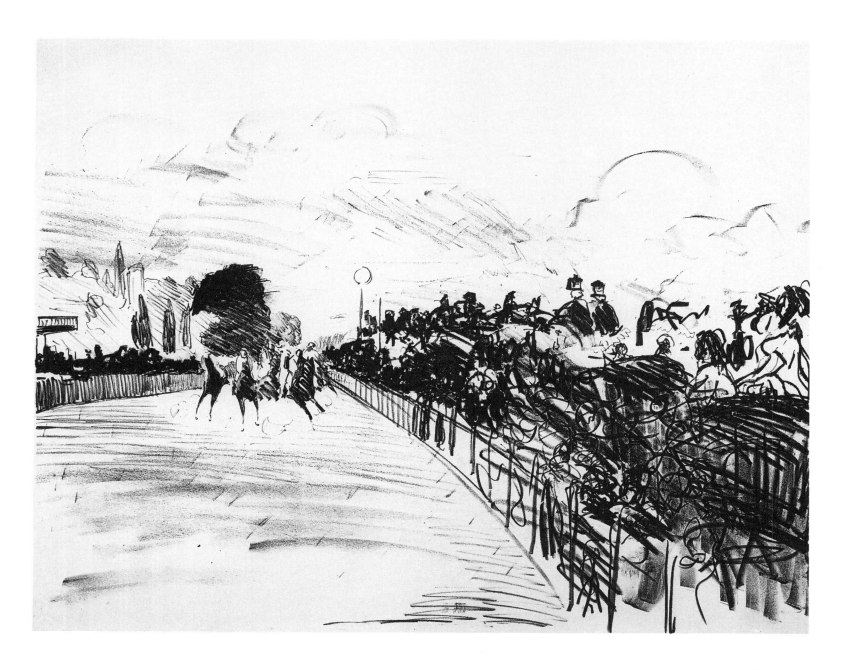

The Races. 1865. Lithograph, 14¼ × 20″ (36.5 × 51 cm). British Museum.

ashamed of anything, but to be ashamed." Never did Manet paint more unashamedly. There are Manets that I like more, but the portrait of Mademoiselle Gonzalès is what Dublin needs. In Dublin everyone is afraid to confess himself. Is it not clear that whosoever paints like that confesses himself unashamed; he who admires that picture is already half free – the shackles are broken, and will fall presently. Therefore I hope it will be Mademoiselle Gonzalès that will be purchased, for it will perhaps help to bring about the crisis we are longing for – that spiritual crisis when men shall begin once more to think out life for themselves, when men shall return to nature naked and unashamed.

* * *

The glass door of the café grates upon the sand again. It is Degas, a round-shouldered man in a suit of pepper and salt. There is nothing very trenchantly French about him either, except the large necktie. His eyes are small, his words are sharp, ironical, cynical. Manet and Degas are the leaders of the Impressionistic school, but their friendship has been jarred by the inevitable rivalry. "Degas was painting *Semiramis* when I was painting *Modern Paris*," says Manet. "Manet is in despair because he cannot paint atrocious pictures like Duran and be fêted and decorated; he is an artist not by inclination but by force, he is a galley slave chained to the oar," says Degas. And their methods of work are quite different.

Émile-Auguste Carolus-Duran (1837–1917), best known as a portrait painter. Together with Meissonier and Puvis de Chavannes, he founded the Société Nationale des Beaux-Arts. He was a friend of Manet, who executed his portrait in 1876. This work (unfinished, Rouart/Wildenstein I 245) is now in the Barber Institute of Fine Arts, Birmingham. Carolus-Duran was a member of the Salon jury which awarded Manet a second-class medal in 1891.

Manet paints his whole picture from nature, trusting to his instinct to lead him aright through the devious labyrinth of selection. But his instinct never fails him, there is a vision in his eyes which he calls nature, and which he paints unconsciously as he digests his food, thinking and declaring vehemently that the artist should not seek a synthesis, but should paint merely what he sees. This extraordinary oneness of nature and artistic vision does not exist in Degas, and even his portraits are composed from drawings and notes.

*   *   *

I think that Degas was more typical of his time than was Manet. Looking at a picture by Degas we think, "Yes, that was how we thought in the seventies and in the eighties." Manet desired modernity as earnestly as Degas, but his genius saved him from the ideas that were of his time. Manet was a pure painter, and it mattered nothing to him whether he painted a religious subject – angels watching by the side of the Dead Christ – or yachting at Argenteuil. Manet was an instinct, Degas an intellectuality, and his originality is according to the prescription of Edgar Poe, who held that one is original by saying, "I will not do a certain thing because it has been done before." So the day came when Degas put *Semiramis* aside for a ballet girl. *Semiramis* had been painted, the ballet girl in pink tights, clumsy shoes and bunched skirts, looking unnatural as a cockatoo, had not. And it was Degas who introduced the acrobat into art, and the *repasseuse* [laundress]. His portrait of Manet on the sofa listening to Madame Manet playing the piano is one of the most intellectual pieces of painting ever done in the world; its intellectuality reminds one of Leonardo da Vinci, for, like Degas, Leonardo painted by intellect rather than by instinct.

*   *   *

Manet said to me once, "I tried to write but I couldn't write," and I thought he spoke apologetically, whereas his words were a boast. "He who paints as I paint could never think of doing anything else," was what was in his mind, and if Manet had lived till he was a hundred he would have painted to the last. But Degas, being merely a man of intellect, wearied of painting; he turned to modelling for relaxation, and he has collected pictures. His collection is the most interesting in Paris, for it represents the taste of one man. His chief admirations are Delacroix and Ingres and Manet, especially Ingres. There was a time when he knew everyone who owned an Ingres, and it is said that the *concierges* used to keep him informed as to the health of the owners of certain pictures, and hearing of an appendicitis that might prove fatal, or a bad attack of influenza, Degas at once flapped his wings and went away like a vulture. One day I met him in the rue Mauberge. "I've got it," he said, and he was surprised when I asked him what he had got: great egoists always take it for granted that everyone is thinking of what they are doing. "Why, the *Jupiter*, of course the *Jupiter*," and he took me to see the picture – not a very good Ingres, I thought – good, of course, but somewhat tedious – a Jupiter with beetling brows, and a thunderbolt in his hand. But next to it was a pear, and I knew that pear, just a speckled pear painted on six inches of canvas; it used to hang in Manet's studio, six inches of canvas nailed to the wall, and I said to Degas, "I think, after all, I like the pear better than *Jupiter*;" and Degas said, "I put it there, for a pear painted like that would overthrow any god."

*   *   *

[Monet] began by imitating Manet, and Manet ended by imitating Monet. They were great friends. Manet painted Monet and Madame Monet in their garden, and Monet painted Manet and Madame Manet in the same garden; they exchanged pictures, but after a quarrel each

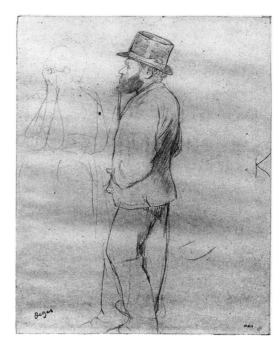

Edgar Degas, *Manet at the Races*. c. 1867/72. Pencil, 12⅝ × 9⅝" (32 × 24 cm). Metropolitan Museum of Art, New York (Rogers Fund, 1918).

Jupiter and Thetis, *painted in 1811.*

Still-life of Pear, *1880, private collection, Rouart/Wildenstein 355. For Degas as collector, see pages 311–12.*

COLOURPLATE 67

269

returned the other his picture. Monet's picture of Manet and his wife I never saw, but Manet's picture of Monet and Madame Monet belongs to a very wealthy merchant, a Monsieur Pellerin, who has the finest collection of Manet's and Cézanne's in the world.

* * *

Among the Impressionist painters there was an English, I should say an American, Mary Casat. She did not come to the Nouvelle Athènes it is true, but she lived on the Boulevard Extérieur; her studio was within a minute's walk of the Place Pigale, and we used to see her every day. Her art was derived from Degas as Madame Morisot's art was derived from Manet. Madame Morisot, or I should say Berthe Morisot, was Manet's sister-in-law, and I remember him saying to me once, "My sister-in-law would not have existed without me; she did nothing but carry my art across her fan."

Mary Cassatt (1845–1926), American painter resident in Paris. She exhibited at four of the eight Impressionist exhibitions. She was instrumental in helping to sell Impressionist works to American collectors (see also pages 320–40).

ROGER FRY

"Manet and the Post-Impressionists"

1910

Roger Fry (1866–1934), British painter and critic. Fry had directed the Metropolitan Museum of Art in New York from 1905 to 1910. Organizing the exhibition Manet and the Post-Impressionists *at the Grafton Galleries, London (November 1910–January 1911), was an important aspect of Fry's promotion of French art in Britain. Nine works by Manet were exhibited, including the* Bar at the Folies-Bergère *(Colourplate 117).*

The artists who felt most the restraints which the Impressionist attitude towards nature imposed upon them, naturally looked to the mysterious and isolated figure of Cézanne as their deliverer. Cézanne himself had come into contact with Manet and his art is derived directly from him. Manet, it is true, is also regarded as the father of Impressionism. To him Impressionism owes much of its power, interest and importance. He was a revolutionary in the sense that he refused to accept the pictorial convention of his time. He went back to seventeenth-century Spain for his inspiration. Instead of accepting the convention of light and shade falling upon objects from the side, he chose what seemed an impossibly difficult method of painting, that of representing them with light falling full upon them. This led to a very great change in the method of modelling, and to a simplification of planes in his pictures which resulted in something closely akin to simple linear designs. He adopted, too, hitherto unknown oppositions of colour. In fact he endeavoured to get rid of chiaroscuro.

Regarded as a hopeless revolutionary, he was naturally drawn to other young artists, who found themselves in the same predicament; and through his connection with them and with Monet he gradually changed his severe, closely constructed style for one in which the shifting, elusive aspects of nature were accentuated. In this way he became one of the Impressionists and in his turn influenced them. Cézanne, however, seized upon precisely that side of Manet which Monet and the other Impressionists ignored. Cézanne, when rendering the novel aspects of nature to which Impressionism was drawing attention, aimed first at a design which should produce the coherent, architectural effect of the masterpieces of primitive art. Because Cézanne thus showed how it was possible to pass from the complexity of the appearance of things to the geometrical simplicity which design demands, his art has appealed enormously to later designers.

JULIUS MEIER-GRAEFE

ÉDOUARD MANET

The Masked Ball at the Opera

1912

Julius Meier-Graefe (1867–1935), German art historian. Meier-Graefe wrote extensively on later nineteenth-century French art. (See also page 130.)

COLOURPLATE 64

With the *Masked Ball at the Opera* Manet produced a pendant to *Music in the Tuileries Gardens* painted twelve years previously and, like the earlier work, it was an incisive comment on contemporary life. All the figures are portraits of members of his own circle, who like him, relished the joys of Parisian life – composers, writers, men of the world and demi-mondaines. In the same way as Menzel, Manet had asked his acquaintances to pose in evening dress in his studio. In some instances, as in the case of Théodore Duret, the viewer can only make out a glimpse of the individual amidst the crowd, but this fragment is so accurately conveyed that it suggests the whole person. The entire picture is composed in this manner: fragments suggesting the whole. The rich colours of the costumes alternate with the black of the tailcoats and dominoes. Above the multitude of faces so expressive of the mood of the gathering, a zigzag line of gleaming top hats is framed by the strong horizontal line of the balcony behind which can be discerned the movement of dark legs and silk-clad thighs. An immediate impression of frenetic activity – and at the same time much more than an immediate impression. In this painting Manet attempted a new form of composition which he, no doubt, had been seeking previously in the *Balcony*. The vivid life of this meat market forms dense and imposing masses which move to the rhythm of hidden music. The barely concealed lust of the men, the false modesty of the flirtatious women, suggestive looks, groping hands, coarse gestures, conveying all the nuances of urban life – all form the components of a style. Based on contemporary life, this style was virtually unknown before Manet's time and, initially, it was regarded as being merely the portrayal of a particular world as had been the novels of the Romantic writer Zola. Guys had foreshadowed the possibility of this style, possibly also Menzel, as in his *Théâtre Gymnase*. In Manet's small picture, the style seems to attain its definitive form, but this kind of composition risks monotony. It is nothing other than an all-encompassing vision, capable of discerning the ideal in the particular.

Manet had worked for a long time on this picture. It led on to several others which are, more or less, related to it. The figure of Polichinelle, cut off by the left-hand frame in *The Masked Ball at the Opera*, repeatedly occurs in sketches and paintings before eventually appearing in a different pose in Manet's most popular lithograph for which Banville composed his witty couplet.

See Linda Nochlin, "A Thoroughly Modern Masked Ball", Art in America, *November 1983, No. 10 (pp. 188–202).*

Adolphe Menzel (1815–1905), German painter.

Émile Zola developed a form of literary realism known as Naturalism.

See page 135.

ANTONIN PROUST

ÉDOUARD MANET: SOUVENIRS

Manet's Attitude to Women's Clothes

1913

From that moment on, he began to feel the ravages of the illness which was to cause his death. Physical suffering affected his mood and paralysed his work. He was harsh on those of his friends he was closest to. Without believing himself ill, he conscientiously followed a course of showers prescribed by Dr Siredey at the Beni-Barde establishment. "When the Beni-Barde ladies see me going down the steps of the pool laughing," he would say smilingly, "I'll be in the clear, and that will be quite shortly."

Yet when he felt more restricted in his movements, he would indulge in bitter reflections, though such moods were short-lived. The mere sight of a flower was enough to bring back all his gaiety. "I'd like to paint them all," he would exclaim.

He spent a day in ecstasy contemplating some material that Mme Derot was unrolling. The next day, it was the hats of a well-known milliner, Mme Virot, which filled him with enthusiasm. He wanted to design a costume for Jeanne, who subsequently took on the stage name Mlle Demarsy, and who was the model for the exquisite canvas *Spring*. Going into Mme Virot's apartment and seeing her leaning on the mantelpiece wearing a *fichu* à la Marie-Antoinette, an arrangement of lace showing off the whiteness of her hair: "Good grief, madame," he exclaimed, "what a stylish way to go to the scaffold."

But then one day he had a sudden bout of irritation at Mme Virot's. Seeing him leaning on a cane, someone offered him a chair:

"I have no need of a chair," he said, "I am not a cripple."

Truth to tell, he was in pain, but his pride refused to allow him to accept the fact.

Coming back to the rue d'Amsterdam, he continued to wax lyrical about the things he had seen at Mme Virot's. Then, cheerfully:

"The idea of making me out to be a legless cripple in front of all those women!" Ah, women. Yesterday I met a woman on the pont d'Europe. She was walking as only Parisiennes know how to walk, but with an added jauntiness. I would paint her from memory, because there are things that remain engraved in my mind. In fact, I could make you an illustration of the festivities Gambetta gave at the Palais Bourbon."

While so saying, he sketched an outline of a woman on a canvas prepared for a pastel. Then suddenly he rubbed it out. "That's not it at all. There's no doubt about it, one can't do anything without nature."

"But what you said about how impressions persist is so true," I pointed out to him, "that when Corot came to make a study of the port of la Rochelle, where he was living with his friend, the banker Théophile Babut, on his return, after having worked *en plein air*, he painted what he had seen on the panels of the dining-room without any recourse to his studies."

"Yes, that's fine for landscape, but a figure from memory, never. Ah, talking of figures, I'm going to do one when I've finished *Spring*. I'm going to do *Autumn*, using Méry Laurent. I went to talk about it with her yesterday. She has had a pelisse made. What a garment, my friend, all tawny brown with an old gold lining. I was stupefied. I left Méry Laurent saying: 'When this pelisse is worn out, you must leave it to me.' She promised me, it will make a marvellous background for something I'm thinking of."

Manet's interest in feminine attire was shared by Stéphane Mallarmé, who wrote a fashion column under the name of "Miss Satin".

Seated Woman in Profile. c. 1874. Ink on squared paper. British Museum (Department of Prints and Drawings).

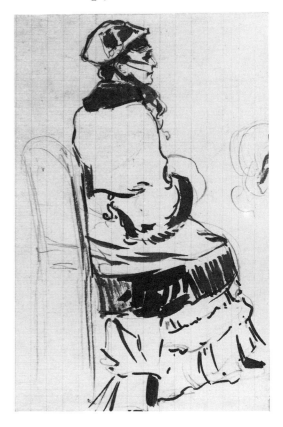

Léon Gambetta (1838–82), Republican politician, elected to the Assembly as a member for Marseilles in 1869. As Minister of the Interior and War, he became renowned for his energetic resistance during the Franco–Prussian War. In November 1881 he became Prime Minister for nine weeks.

COLOURPLATE 113

272

THÉODORE DURET

LA RENAISSANCE DE L'ART FRANÇAIS ET DES INDUSTRIES DE LUXE

"The Portraits Painted by Manet and Rejected by Their Sitters"

July 1918

For sitters' accounts of Manet's portrait techniques, see pages 98, 101 and 252.

There have always been men who have known how to paint portraits: initially in such a way as to please the rich, who wanted their features reproduced, then, later, to please their relatives, friends and acquaintances and, lastly to please the public, at exhibitions.

The execution of portraits of this kind is usually traditional. The men who do such portrait painting have adequate skills and techniques. They know how to give their models an engaging physiognomy, by painting them according to the current formulae and accepted rules of draughtsmanship. They are careful not to accentuate their features when they are of a distinctive character and have particularities which may be considered as ugly. However, they try to impart a degree of individuality to the features painted in this manner, so that it may be said that their portraits are good likenesses.

The men who specialize in this sort of work also manage to endear themselves to their sitters through the choice of traditional poses, the addition of certain props and, above all, when painting a woman, by clothing them in fashionable costumes. Many are those who have found, find and will find success and fortune in portrait painting.

There is another sort of man who paints portraits in a different way. This is the artist who is an original by temperament, who has his own way of seeing things, a way from which he could not stray, who also has a technique, a personal method which he applies to the execution of his work, without deviating, as being the only one which enables him to fix his vision in all its power. Manet being one of these, let us now look at the reception given to his portraits.

He has long aroused general approbation. The rich, who want portraits in accordance with their own taste, would thus not dream of commissioning him to paint their portraits. Nonetheless, he has executed many portraits, but in a disinterested way, without being paid for them. These were portraits of friends or acquaintances. In such circumstances he was able to give rein to his originality, and to endow the portraits with the exceptional character typical of all his work.

One of his first portraits, dating from 1860, was that of a young woman, a family friend. He had painted her standing, life-size. She was not, apparently, pretty. Allowing himself to follow his natural bent, he had had to emphasize certain physiognomic peculiarities. Nonetheless, when she saw herself on canvas, as portrayed, she began to cry – Manet himself told me this – left the studio with her husband and never wanted to see the painting again.

In 1868, for the Salon, Manet painted a portrait of the actor Rouvière playing the part of Hamlet. The Jury rejected it.

COLOURPLATE 30

In 1881 Manet succeeded in getting the Salon to accept the portrait of Henri Rochefort, a head and bust in his best manner. The portrait is now in the Hamburg museum. Attracted by his striking physiognomy, Manet had asked Rochefort to agree to have his portrait painted. He had not for a

COLOURPLATE 111

moment thought of gaining any profit from it. When the work was finished, he offered it to the sitter and would have been delighted for him to accept it. But Rochefort, who has only ever liked dry, lifeless, highly finished painting, found it displeasing. He did not want it, and refused. As things turned out, he was wrong.

Albert Wolff was at the time a well-known columnist and critic on *Le Figaro*. He spent his time, like many others, commending to public admiration the sort of mediocrities who will leave nothing behind them and whose names are subsequently forgotten. And when, by chance, he found in Manet and the Impressionists that rare breed that creates and invents, he had nothing but disdain for them. Yet having made Manet's acquaintance, he had gone to see him in his studio. Manet had suggested that he paint his portrait. He had accepted. Then Manet had sat him in a bentwood rocking-chair. The pose involved certain difficulties, entailing lengthy sittings, which would have led others to reject it. But Manet never worried about such things. After conceiving a composition, whatever it was, he set to work.

So he had begun to paint Wolff and, in accordance with his bold technique, he had proceeded by scattering patches of colour over the canvas, returning to each part anew and, through gradual additions, bringing the whole together to a point of completion he judged suitable. However, he immediately concentrated on the important point, the head, and from the moment it was sketched in, had given it a distinctive character.

Now Wolff was hideously ugly and naturally Manet, in his portrait, had caught this instantly, perfectly, but giving it a certain style. Wolff should have admired the work, which made something artistic, something of a higher order, of his ugliness, which was known to all. He could understand only the type of painting which attempts to attenuate unusual forms and to modify those features normally regarded as ugly. So he went all over town saying that, as he had always thought, Manet was nothing but an incomplete, fumbling artist and that, after several sittings, his portrait was still a mere sketch, approached in vain from various viewpoints etc. etc. In reality it was the inherent ugliness of his face which he did not like.

Manet, to whom these comments were reported, was very displeased. The portrait was dropped. Indeed it was left unfinished. But as it stands it reveals the master. Only a man who knew all the resources of his art could have sketched on canvas so living, so superbly expressive a head.

Found after Manet's death in his studio, the portrait was handed over to Wolff by the family. It was part of the Wolff sale after his death. But Wolff must have put it away somewhere, in some corner, without it ever coming to anyone's attention, because the expert who was supposed to inventory it did not believe it to be a work of Manet's. Not knowing what to think, he entered it in the sale catalogue under the heading: *in the style of Manet*.

Faure, the best-known singer at the Opéra, the public's favourite baritone, collected pictures. He had been introduced to Manet as a possible buyer by Durand-Ruel, and he used to visit Manet in his studio.

In 1877, he asked him to paint his portrait. He posed as Hamlet, a part he was then playing successfully in the opera of that name by Ambroise Thomas. He is shown standing, thrusting forward, a sword in his hand. It would be impossible to imagine a better likeness, if one conceives a likeness as necessarily the synthesis of the features of a model. But what emerges from the work is the image of a virtuoso, singing rather characterless music, with the stage make-up of an Opéra singer. With his superior eye, Manet had thus caught the true appearance of his model.

This sort of resemblance did not please Faure. When he had asked Manet to paint his portrait to add to those of his works he already owned, he had intended, as a wealthy man, to pay him for it; when it was finished

COLOURPLATE 80
Ambroise Thomas (1811–96), French composer who became director of the Paris Conservatoire. His Hamlet *was written in 1868.*

and put into the 1877 Salon, he declared himself dissatisfied and refused to take it.

Despite everything, Faure still wanted his portrait painted by Manet. He thus asked him for a portrait in contemporary dress, a head and bust in place of the one in which he was depicted as Hamlet. Faure then posed, seated, and Manet began to paint. But into this new portrait he put more or less the same expression he had put into the other. He could not do otherwise, that was what he saw.

After some time, Faure would get up, pass in front of Manet and examine his work. "But my dear chap," he would say, "what a head you've given me. You should alter the features, change that outline, etc." Manet needed money; this portrait was a godsend, and was to be exceptionally well paid. So he had to make every effort to please.

Faure would go and sit down again. Manet would set to work again. Still the same expression. The portrait was begun anew unsuccessfully on several canvases. Finally Manet had to give up, exasperated by the comments of his model.

About the time when Manet was struggling with the portrait of Faure, he was beginning the one of M Clemenceau, then deputy for the XVIII arrondissement of Paris. The portrait was executed on two canvases. On the one, it has remained a mere sketch, on the other it has been taken further. Since its model was not at all taken with it, it was not completed.

Manet accentuated the character of his models' physiognomies. As a true artist, he overlooked details. He made a synthesis of the features of a face and rendered its true expression. Now men in general think themselves handsome or impressive, they are unable to see themselves as they are. When their appearance is shown them without artifice, they are naturally displeased. In painting his portraits, Manet not only accentuated those features which, through their singularity or ugliness, led him to produce a result then judged disagreeable, he also emphasised all expression and thus, when the expression happened to be of the kind likely to please the model and the public, he would, unusually, attain success. This was the case with the portrait of the engraver Belot in *A Good Glass of Beer*, at the Salon of 1873. Belot had a beaming expression, and emerged as engaging and likeable.

A Good Glass of Beer received more or less universal praise and earned its author a resounding success, destined to remain unique. But Manet was to experience a degree of favour with several other of his portraits. One such, at the Salon of 1880, was that of Antonin Proust. Proust was a man of the world, elegantly turned out, nonchalant in gait. These points were captured in the painting and delighted the public.

Even better received, in the Salon of 1882, was the portrait of a young girl, Jeanne, who was pretty enough but without any particular expression. The portrait was thus in a sense in the genre of those ordinary works which everyone likes. Thus after *A Good Glass of Beer*, this was destined to be the portrait most favourably received by the public.

The lack of success that Manet, as an original artist, first met with in his portraits should not be thought of as a piece of bad luck typical of him alone. For a long time the other originals of his age, Courbet and Rodin, fared little better. If one were to recount the circumstances in which they executed their portraits, and the receptions they were given at first, one would see that the treatment they received from their models and from the public differed little from that meted out to Manet.

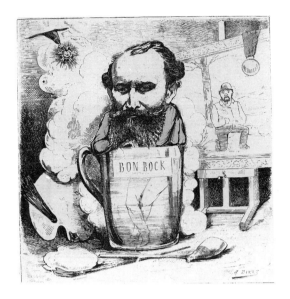

G. Darre, *Édouard Manet – Le Bon Bock*. Caricature in *Le Carillon*, 6 July 1881.

COLOURPLATE 54

COLOURPLATE 104

See page 198.

J.E. BLANCHE

PROPOS DE PEINTRE

"Some Notes on Manet – for George Moore"

1921

Jacques-Émile Blanche (1861–1941), French painter, best known for his portraits of society and literary figures. He also wrote reminiscences, and his biography of Manet appeared in 1924.

Manet's face is well known – a handsome, fair-haired, graceful man, elegant in a blue Lavallière cravat with white spots. A stockbroker? A clubman? Yes, charming, witty, engaging, smiling. His slightly husky voice was seductive, his speech had the accent of the Paris urchin.

Lavallière, a term used during the Third Republic to describe a man's silk scarf worn loosely knotted with long hanging ends; probably named after the Duchesse de la Vallière who was Louis XIV's mistress.

The fact that he was an artist threw his nearest and dearest into confusion – they loved him, but didn't really admire him and didn't know what attitude to adopt when they had to express themselves on his account, not taking the painting seriously. M Degas, who has since often repeated: "We didn't know he was so gifted!" talked of his work with malicious irony. "He's better known than Garibaldi, damn it all." He was too well known, and this was unforgivable, even on the lofty peaks where M Degas built his eyrie.

Manet himself was on a lower plane, more modest, more human, as sensitive to criticism as the next man, ambitious for medals and decorations. He very much wanted to paint portraits of pretty women, and to please. Of another artist painting works like his own, Manet might have talked as his friends talked of him.

A sitting: Mlle Suzette Lemaire is posing for a pastel; Manet is labouring, bending forward, turning towards the little mirror he keeps to his left where the mirror image of the young girl's pretty face is reflected. Manet wants to prove to Mme Madeleine Lemaire that he can rival Chaplin, the master portrait-painter of these ladies. He believes himself to be prettifying, flattering, he selects the choicest pinks, blends the pastel colours. He rubs out, begins again: the modelling is becoming more and more uneven, black predominates, ringing the contours. "It's a crow," says Aurélien Scholl. "You're hard on women."

Two pastels of Suzette Lemaire survive (Rouart/Wildenstein II 42 and 43). Manet had been introduced to Suzette Lemaire, the daughter of the watercolour artist Madeleine Lemaire, by Charles Éphrussi in 1880.

* * *

The second studio in the rue de St-Pétersbourg was the centre of great political gatherings. It had a north light, it was cold and unremarkable, at the end of a courtyard inhabited by numerous other artists; beside it was that of Henry Duprey, the cheerful military painter, who played the trumpet and the drum and amused everyone with his rowdy, sentimental barrack-room behaviour. In front of Manet's door were a few flowerpots and green tubs with laurel-bushes, as on the terraces of the restaurants of the time. There was a lot of coming and going between neighbours, but after the sitting everyone would meet in Manet's studio.

I can see him leaning on a cane, keeping his balance with difficulty on his rubber soles. He was proud of his neat feet, in their "English boots;" he often wore a Norfolk jacket with tucks and a belt, like an English sportsman. He disliked the "Bohemian" look. In a corner, to the right of the entrance, sunk deep in a red divan, were the usual crowd, Albert Wolff, Aurélien Scholl and a host of men-about-town and demi-mondaines. Charles Ephrussi and several Jewish financiers were beginning to buy his pastels, not that they judged Manet's painting worthy to figure alongside the gouaches of Gustave Moreau, or genuine Louis XV panelling; but people liked Manet and anyway, you never knew what the future held, after all. They could but try! . . .

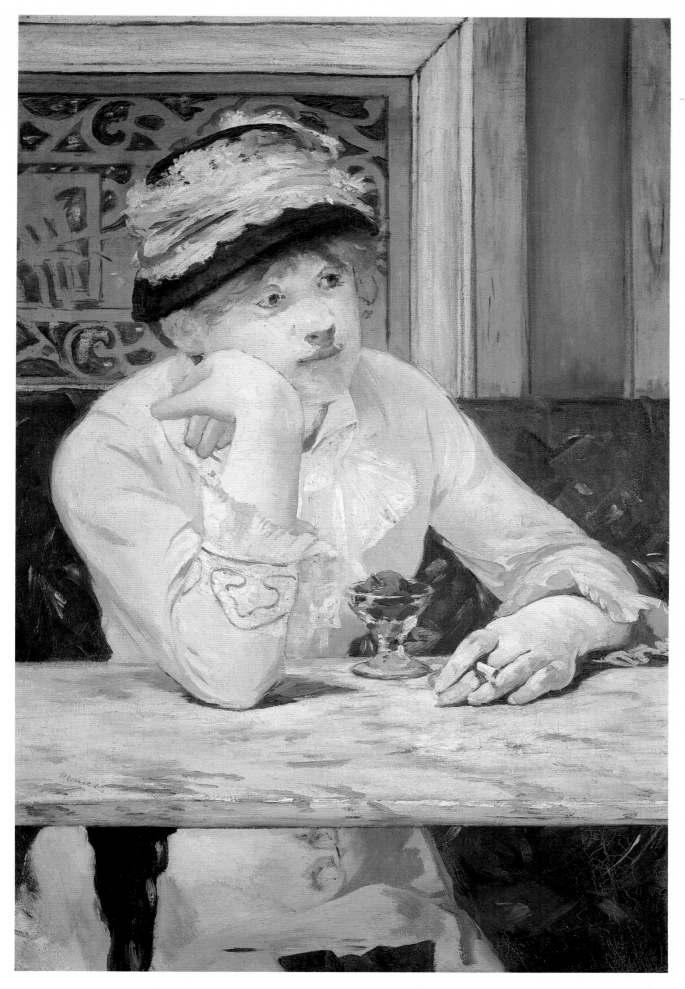

COLOURPLATE 83. *The Plum.* 1878. 29 × 19¾″ (73.6 × 50.2 cm).
National Gallery of Art, Washington D.C. (Mr and Mrs Paul Mellon Collection).

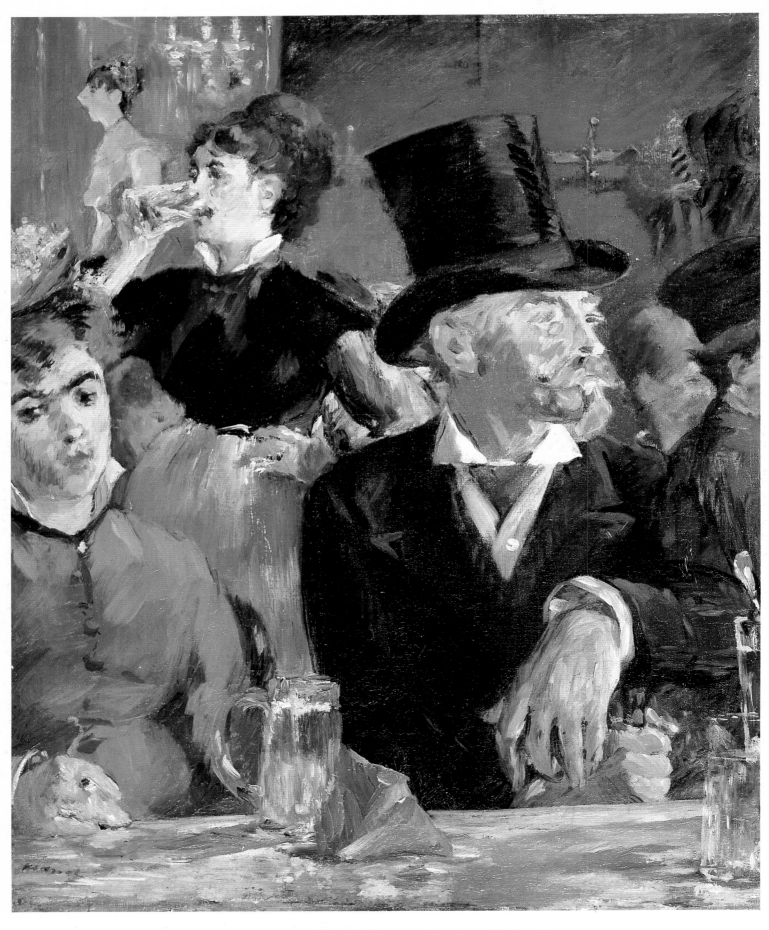

COLOURPLATE 84. *The Café-Concert.* 1878. 18 × 15″ (46 × 38 cm).
Walters Art Gallery, Baltimore, Maryland.

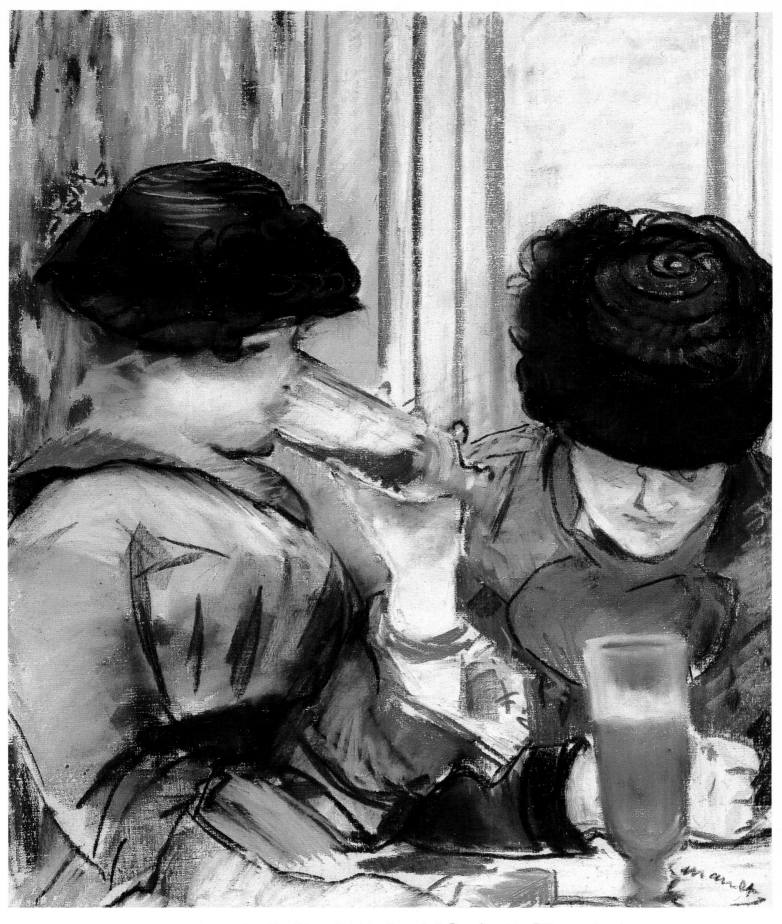

COLOURPLATE 85. *Two Women Drinking Beer*. 1878. Pastel, 24 × 20″ (61 × 50.8 cm).
Burrell Collection, Glasgow.

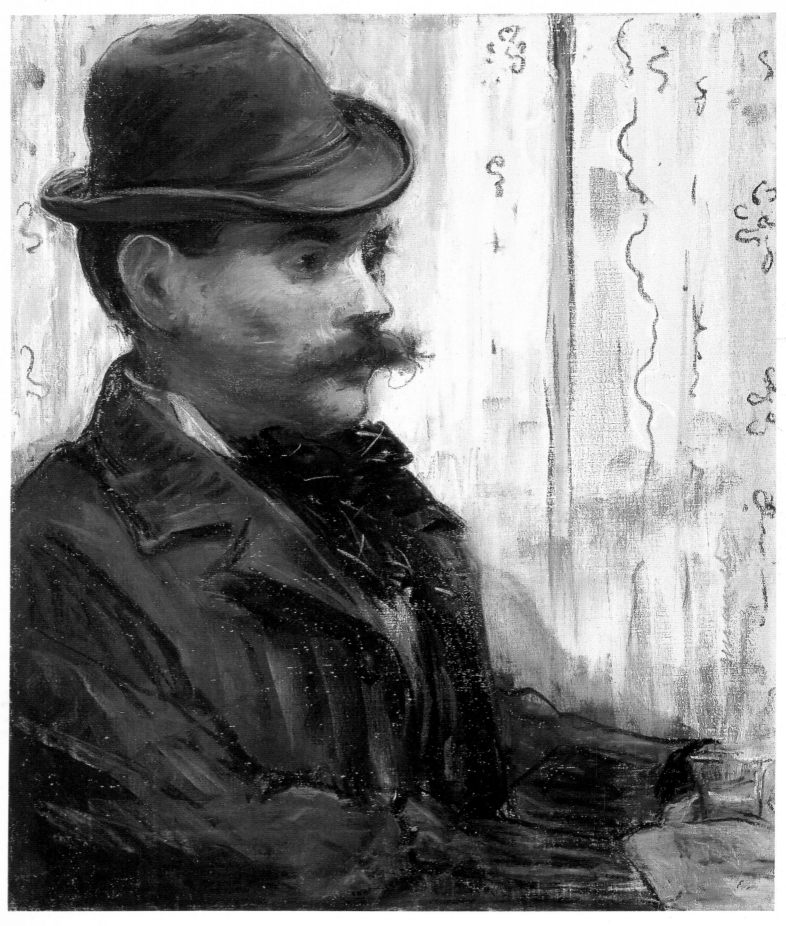

COLOURPLATE 86. *Man in a Round Hat*. 1878. Pastel, 21½ × 17¾″ (54.7 × 45.2 cm).
© Art Institute of Chicago (Gift of Kate L. Brewster, 1950).

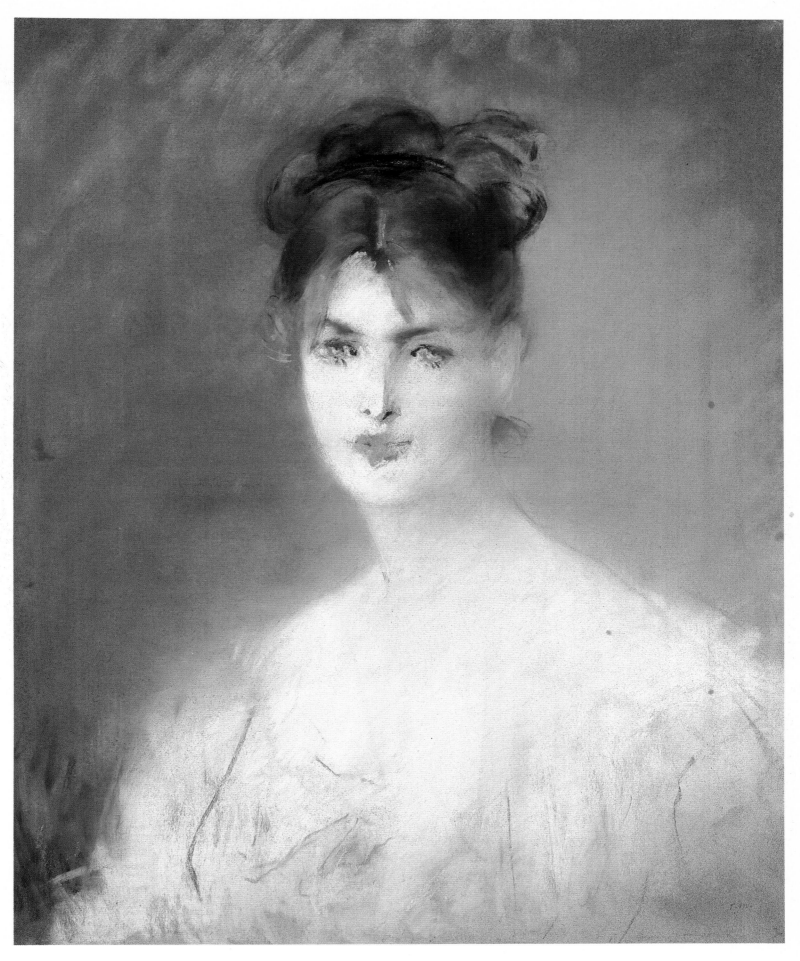

COLOURPLATE 87. *Young Blonde Woman with Blue Eyes*. 1878. Pastel, 24 × 19¾″ (61 × 50 cm).
Louvre, Paris (Cabinet des Dessins).

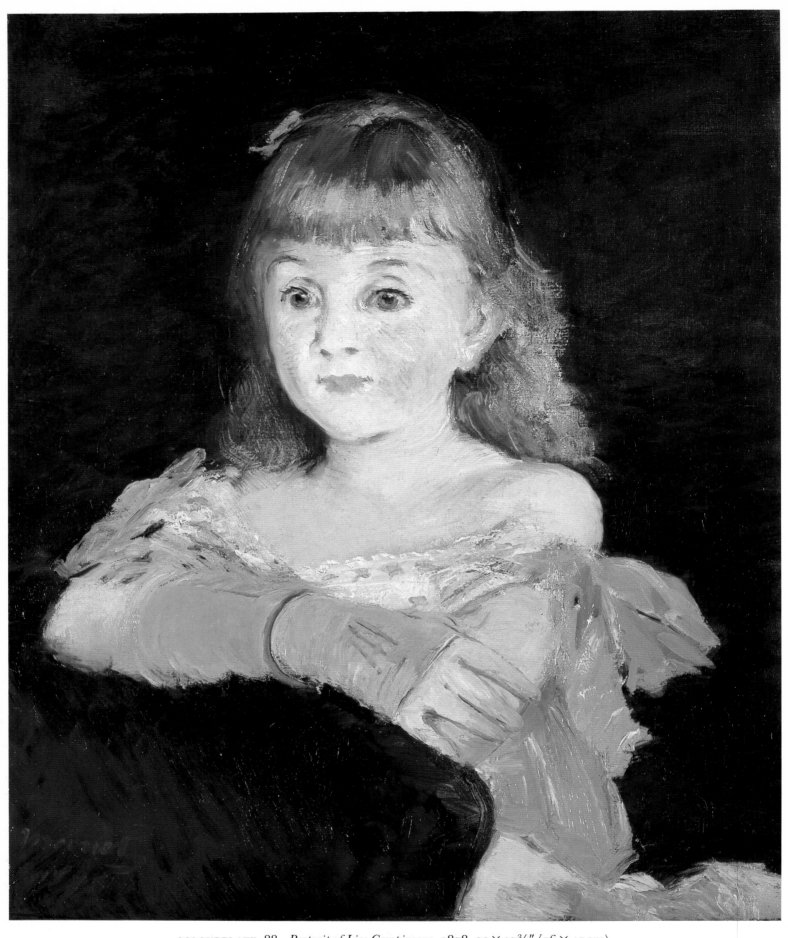

COLOURPLATE 88. *Portrait of Lise Campineano.* 1878. 22 × 17¾″ (56 × 45 cm).
Nelson Gallery-Atkins Museum, Kansas City, Missouri (Nelson Fund).

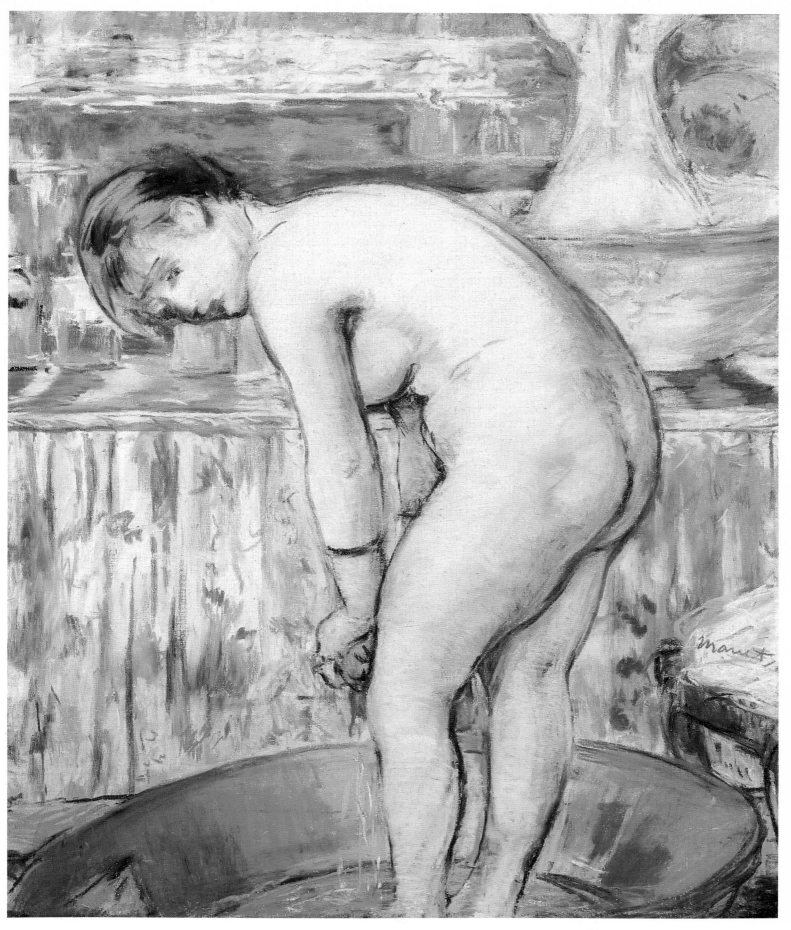

COLOURPLATE 89. *Woman in a Tub*. 1879. Pastel, 21¾ × 17¾″ (55 × 45 cm).
Louvre, Paris (Cabinet des Dessins).

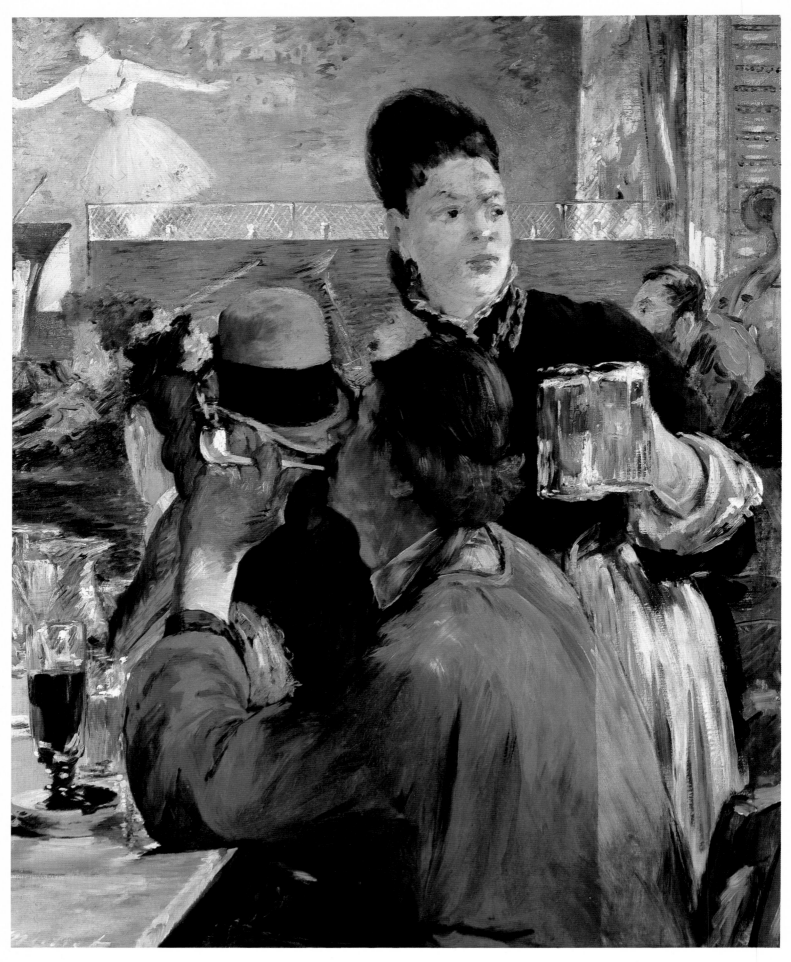

COLOURPLATE 90. *Corner in a Café-Concert (The Waitress)*. 1877–9. 38½ × 31″ (98 × 79 cm).
National Gallery, London.

Emmanuel Chabrier would utter witticisms. Manet adored puns, which are now so out-of-fashion. Towards five o'clock, one could barely find room anywhere near the artist. A waiter would serve small glasses of beer and apéritifs on a little round iron table, a prop often found in Manet's works. The habitués would come up from the boulevard to keep their friend company, now that he could no longer go down to the café de Bade.

One day, Manet said to me:

"Bring a brioche, I want to see you paint one: still-life is the touchstone of the painter."

I still have the little canvas I dashed off under his gaze and which seemed to please him.

"The lucky brute paints a brioche like nobody's business."

The canvas is dated October 27, 1881, 77 rue de St-Pétersbourg.

ADOLPHE TABARANT

MANET, HISTOIRE CATALOGRAPHIQUE

Victorine Meurent

1931

The woman who posed for this picture was called Victorine-Louise Meurend (or Meurent). From 1862-74, with long intervening lapses, for she had a will of her own, she was Manet's favourite model. Théodore Duret said that Manet, having met her by chance in a crowd in a room in the Palais de Justice, "had been struck by her original and distinctive appearance." She was scarcely twenty, yet looked easily twenty-five, so grave was her cast of feature. It is true that if her profile was rather hard, her full face belied this expression, with its lively, lovely eyes and fresh, smiling mouth. Then she had the sinewy body of the typical Parisienne, delicate in every one of its details, remarkable for the harmonious line and firmness of the breasts. Where did she spring from? She was not unknown on the Left Bank. A book of notes and sketches by Manet, dated 1861-62, contains the following entry: *Louise Meuran, rue Maître-Albert 17*. It was clearly she, who called herself sometimes Louise, sometimes Victorine. We might mention in passing that it was in rue Maître-Albert that Manet had his copperplates etched when he was beginning to work in this medium. Her early youth must have been that of so many working-class girls, who are ill-resigned to poverty and who know themselves to be beautiful. She immediately agreed to pose for Manet, distant though the rue Maître-Albert, between place Maubert and the quai de la Tournelle, was from his studio in the rue Guyot. In her he found the ideal model, that is, punctual, patient, discrete, taciturn, and above all not too coarse in her bearing, for the painter who was to scandalize the establishment pushed the aloofness he owed to his haute-bourgeois origins to the point of dandyism. He found artistic disarray utterly distasteful.

She modelled first for the *Street Singer*, then posed in an espada costume, then finally, undressing, she was the nude seated figure in the *Luncheon on the Grass* (second version). In 1863 she was *Olympia* (Salon of 1865), in 1866 the *Woman with a Parrot* and the *Guitarist* (which she played reasonably well). Then seven years went by. Victorine reappears in 1873 in the studio on the rue de St-Pétersbourg, where she posed for the young

Victorine Louise Meurent was born in 1844, and probably first met Manet when she was eighteen. By this time she was already a professional model, posing in the studio of Thomas Couture. She also sat for Alfred Stevens.

COLOURPLATES 13, 12, 18, 14, 33, 35

woman in the *Railway* and one of the figures in the *Game of Croquet at Paris*. There her relations with Manet ended; in 1862 he had done an admirable portrait of her. She had been seized with the ambition to paint in her turn. She asked advice, not of Manet, not of Alfred Stevens, who was interested in her around that time, but of the little-known Etienne Leroy, who lived in rue Turgot. She was then living in no. 1 Boulevard de Clichy, at the corner of the rue des Martyrs. She soon felt sufficiently sure of herself to exhibit at the Salon, whose Jury forgave her. In 1876 she submitted her own portrait and subsequently historical and anecdotal subjects. (In 1879, *A Sixteenth-Century Citizen of Nuremburg*). She then lived at 21, rue Bréda. Then she had various adventures. She left for America. When she came back, Manet was dead. At the Salon of 1885 she exhibited another painting, *Palm Sunday*. But she was no longer in the limelight. She took up her guitar again and played in the taverns of Paris and the surrounding districts (she had lodgings at Asnières). That was the end. She soon took to drink. A painting by Norbert Geonette, dated 1890, part of the Arsène Alexandre collection, shows her slumped on a chair, against a table on which stands a monkey dressed in red. In her right hand she holds her guitar, in her left, she clutches the neck of a bottle.

COLOURPLATES 61, 63

Étienne Leroy (b. 1828), French painter.

The Alexandre collection was established by Arsène Alexandre (1859–1937), critic, art historian and collector.

ADOLPHE TABARANT

MANET, HISTOIRE CATALOGRAPHIQUE

Nina de Callias

1931

Nina de Callias, known as Nina de Villard, lived separated from her husband, Hector de Callias, the author of *Mirages Parisiens* and sub-editor at *Le Figaro*. For more than fifteen years, from 1868-84, first in 17 rue Chaptal, then in a little hotel in the rue des Moines, at Batignolles, every riotous Parisian intellect and humorist, politician, man of letters, artist and bohemian passed through her salon. "Let's go to Nina's," the life-and-soul of some tipsy group would suggest. And they would pour on to an omnibus and go to Nina's, knowing that their hostess was unfailingly affable, endlessly cordial. Then they would begin to drink. People would play the piano, recite poetry, indulge in a thousand antics which would finish only at dawn, while the sun was beginning to parade its glory across the animation that was Paris.

The habitués included Paul Verlaine, Stéphane Mallarmé, the three Cros brothers, Jean Richepin, Catulle Mendès, Desboutin, Villiers de l'Isle-Adam, Jean de Cabanes, known as Cabaner, Paul Alexis, Maurice Rollinat, Edmond Bazin, Marie Kryzinska, Edmond Lepelletier, Emile Goudeau, Edouard Manet – who, himself, came as a neighbour, amused by the extraordinary colourfulness of this insane set-up. But who, in fact, was this Nina de Villard?

The daughter of a Lyon lawyer, her real name was Marie-Anne Gaillard. She had been born in Montmartre, in 1845. She lived with her mother, née Villard, on an income of 20,000 francs or so which made up her paternal inheritance. An outstanding musician, a piano virtuoso, smitten with everything which smacked of art or literature, priding herself on being a full-blown artist, she could conceive of no existence finer than her own, devoted to musicians, poets and painters. And she had a heart of gold. Mendès himself, who wrote a cruel book about this extravagant

Nina de Callias possessed an independent income and was known as a brilliant hostess. Manet had been introduced to her by Charles Cros (see page 166). Cros' poem (page 288) about Manet's portrait of Nina (Colourplate 62) appeared in the March 1874 issue of the Revue du Monde Nouveau, *accompanied by a woodcut after Manet depicting Nina in street dress and hat.*

Paul Verlaine (1844–96); Jean Richepin (1849–1926), French poet and dramatist; Catulle Mendès (1842–1909), poet, dramatist, novelist and literary critic; Jean de Cabanes, French art collector; Paul Alexis (1847–1901), French novelist and dramatist, friend of Zola.

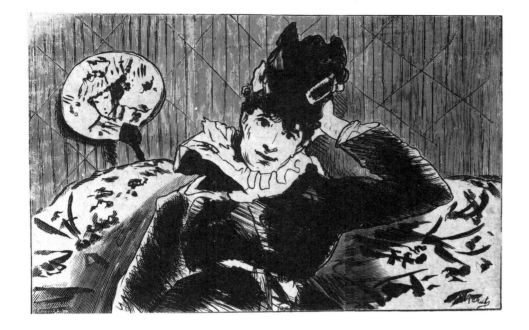

The Parisienne (Madame de Callias). 1874. Wood engraving from a drawing by Manet, 4 × 6″ (10 × 15.3 cm). Bibliothèque Nationale, Paris.

circle, *La Maison de la Vieille*, is forced to admit that Nina's kindness knew no bounds. This is how Bazire describes her: "She had a very high forehead, very big eyes, a very pale complexion, slender waist and tiny mouth. But what we painters have not been able to show was her kindness of heart, her brightness of soul, her loftiness of spirit." And Goudeau: "She was an attractive person, small in stature, with very expressive black eyes, magnificent ebony hair and a milk-white complexion." And Lepelletier, who saw the salon of the rue Chaptal as a forerunner of *Le Chat Noir*: "In 1868, she was a small, plump, lively woman, slightly hysterical, very prepossessing, and who left behind her a (justified) reputation for eccentricity, excess and unbridled hospitality." Elsewhere: "What a strange little fay, that little Nina, so mad, so full of laughter, so appealing, and of whom we all have the fondest memories." Yet Verlaine qualified her as "not very kind," probably out of a desire to tease, in the first quatrain of a sonnet he wrote in the visitors' book belonging to his hospitable hostess:

> Eyes all around her head,
> As Murger said.
> Not very kind. A sprite from Hell
> With a laugh like a bell.

Verlaine spent a lot of time in the rue Chaptal, but little at the rue des Moines. He wrote to Lepelletier in 1869: "I'm dining in the district Ninacum with Sivrot (Ch. de Sivry) and Gros Carolus." And Rollinat described the house, to which he attributed a "Circe-like seductiveness," adding: "After a dinner which went on late into the night, a côterie of rebellious young intellects, whipped up by alcohol, gave themselves over to all manner of intellectual debauchery, all manner of verbal clowning, in the over-excitement produced by a pretty woman, a slightly crazy muse." It should be said that Edmond de Goncourt (v. VII of his *Journal*) depicts Rollinat as a "curious product of this Callias circle, this hot-house of intellectual unhinging, which has created so many oddities, eccentrics, true madmen."

It was Manet who asked her to pose for him. She accepted, flattered. The poet Charles Cros, who acted as a sort of informal secretary for her, and with whom she collaborated on the second publication of the *Parnasse contemporain*, was present at the sittings. On the spot he wrote the following sonnet, dedicated to Manet, and which could act as an epigraph for the *Lady with Fans*:

She's frivolous – you put her at her ease
By talk of theatres, evenings of mirth,
Yourself as sailor, life on the high seas,
Heavy blue waters clawing at the earth.

Around her neck that strawberry you flung;
Velvet surrounding nonchalance so smooth,
Curls on her forehead hieroglyphs hung,
Those eyes, whose wicked glint your stories soothe.

Those features, that rich ease, and then those tones
(You were, I think, one of the Mirlitons)
Form on the canvas in a few brushstrokes.

Rising regretfully from where she sat,
"Oh, lovely," murmurs Nina, sighing – just –
"Out of my tiger he has made a cat."

This sonnet appeared in the first number of the short-lived review, *Le Monde Nouveau*, – which ran from March to May 1874 – whose editor was Charles Cros. Prunaire's wood-engraving was also reproduced there.

We said earlier that Nina lived separated from her husband, Hector de Callias. Shortly after this portrait was painted, Manet received the following letter:

"My dear friend,

Forgive me for speaking to you of a little matter that concerns me. Mme Nina Gaillard has had her portrait painted by you, which is her perfect right, on condition that the said portrait should not leave her house, or your studio.

I see in a number of the *Gaulois*, already dating back some time, that she had had this canvas announced as being a portrait of Mme de Callias. Your opinion of me is sufficiently high for you not to believe that I shall lend myself to such whims. For a long time now an arrangement has existed, through her notary, between this woman and myself, in which it was agreed that she might bear any name she chose, except my own.

Since you see her, and I do not have her address, kindly remind her of this agreement, to which I hold absolutely. Tell her too that any infringement in this connection would lead me immediately to take the most energetic measures against her: this is something that I owe myself, my family, and everyone else. You do understand, do you not?

A brief acknowledgement c/o *Le Figaro* would please me, if that is not too much trouble.

Yours sincerely,
Hector de Callias"

Manet responded very directly to this request: he apologized for not having managed to intervene with Nina, but he gave Hector de Callias, who thanked him in another letter, the categorical assurance that the portrait would not leave his studio. Nor did this happen

Nina died on July 22, 1884. Death, at the very least, spared her what she feared above all: decrepitude. According to Lepelletier, she was "a poor little doll" when she was laid in her coffin. She left sheaves of verses which, slightly edited, under the title of *Feuillets parisiens*, were published in 1885 under the supervision of Charles Cros, who dedicated *Le Coffret de Santal* to her. She herself had written a delightfully artless will:

I would not wish my resting place
In any gloomy cemetery;
I'd rather in a hot-house lie,
Where artists come and visit me.

Let mass be sung in Notre Dame,
Because it's Victor Hugo's church.
Let draperies be bright as day,
And someone on the piano play.

The *Lady with Fans* was buried at Montmartre Cemetery.

ADOLPHE TABARANT

MANET, HISTOIRE CATALOGRAPHIQUE

Méry Laurent

1931

It is Méry Laurent who is depicted here, this symbolic face in *Autumn* (though a face still very young) which, with the *Spring* posed for in the previous year by Jeanne de Marsy, was to be the second of the four paintings through which Manet intended to represent the seasons. Méry Laurent was one of the most captivating beauties of the late Empire and beginning of the Republic. In 1867, at a performance of *La Belle Hélène*, she appeared in the guise of Venus, and the well-known American dentist Thomas Evans immediately fell in love with her. He made her his mistress and appeared with her everywhere, though she was then only sixteen and a half. She soon became one of the women most in the public eye in the capital. We have already said that she came to Manet's studio, in the rue de St-Pétersbourg, with the painter Hirsch, for the special showing of *Washing* and *The Artist*, in April 1876. She had links with a number of artists and men of letters, including Stéphane Mallarmé. Having had a house built at 9 Boulevard Lannes, in 1894, she had her architect carve these verses by Mallarmé, which were subsequently effaced, on a stone of the façade:

> Tilted to the joy that waters it,
> So that nothing bitter inhabits it,
> Méry is a charming rose
> From a royal garden.

She died on November 26, 1900. Antonin Proust wrote to Manet's widow: "Mme Méry Laurent died very suddenly at four o'clock. She leaves her heirs several paintings and pastels by Manet, the sketch of the *Execution of the Emperor Maximilian*, a picture of pears, a portrait in oil and two portraits in pastel." She bequeathed the *Execution of the Emperor Maximilian* to Victor Margueritte, and her portrait, an allegory of autumn, to the Museum in Nancy.

George Moore devoted two striking pages to her: "If she were not dead, I would stop at her little lilac-shaded house. On the wall hangs her portrait by Manet, with the toque she wore at the time. What a masterly touch! How exquisitely the pearls are painted. And, as I think about the painter's admirable craft, I remember his studio. I see a large, beautiful

COLOURPLATE 113

Marie Laurent was the stage name of Anne-Rose Louviot (1849–1900). She left the provinces for Paris at the age of sixteen, working first at the Gaîté, then at the Variétés theatres. Dr Thomas Evans, dentist to Emperor Napoleon III, became her protector, and it is supposedly his American pronunciation of her name that resulted in "Méry". In the last years of her life, she came to know Marcel Proust, and formed one of the models for his character Odette Swann.
The operetta La Belle Hélène, *produced in 1864, was composed by Jacques Offenbach (1819–80).*

PAGE 147, COLOURPLATE 76

Photograph of Méry Laurent.

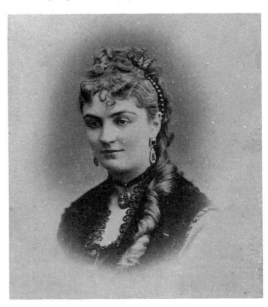

woman entering it, for all the world like a tea-rose: Méry Laurent. The daughter of a peasant and mistress of all the great men of the time, or perhaps I should say all the distinguished men. I used to call her *Toute la Lyre* [the whole gamut, the name of a collection of poems by Victor Hugo].

"The last time I saw her, we talked of Manet. She told me that each year she would take the first lilacs to his grave. Is there today, I wonder, any one of her numerous lovers who finds a free moment to put flowers on *her* grave? What remains unforgettable about her was her pleasure in life, her desire to give back to life all the pleasure it gave her, and her awareness of this desire. Evans, the well-known dentist, gave her an income of 50,000 francs, and he was no little put out, one evening, when he met Manet on the staircase. So, as to rid herself of the American, she had invited him to dinner, intending to plead a migraine, excuse herself and lie down. . . . So she did. No sooner had the guest left than she took off her peignoir, which covered her ball dress, and signalled with her handkerchief to Manet who was mounting guard at the street corner. They go down together, and whom do they meet? The dentist, who has forgotten his notebook. He was so upset at meeting his beautiful, and faithless, mistress that he sulked for three days. His anger mattered little to Méry, for another lover also paid her an income of 50,000 livres and thus, backed by 100,000 livres, she devoted herself to love and conversation with her friends – writers, musicians and painters."

Photograph of Méry Laurent with Mallarmé and Manet. 1872.

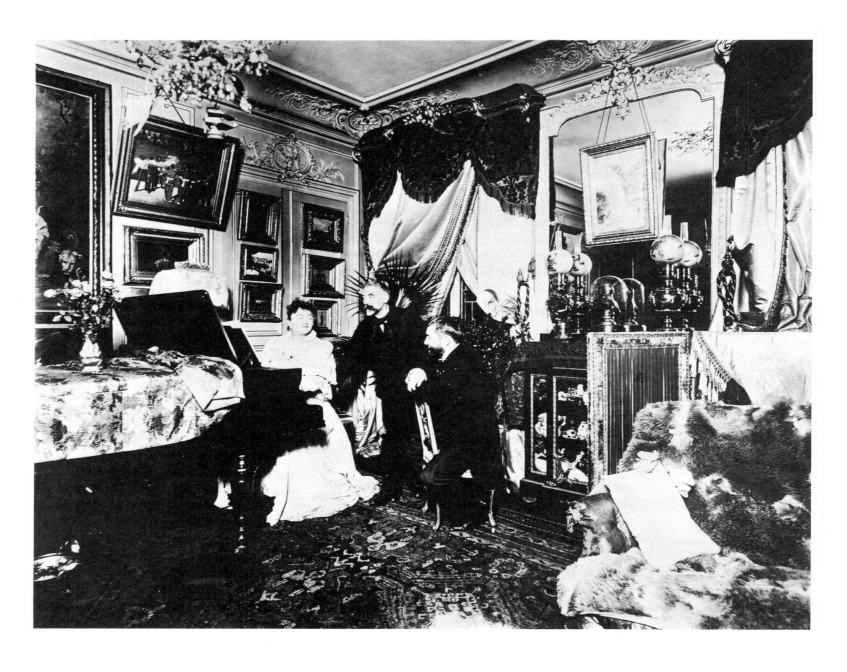

L'INTRANSIGEANT

"Édouard Manet as seen by Henri Matisse"

Henri Matisse (1869–1954).

January 25, 1932

Yesterday was the hundredth anniversary of the birth of Manet. Preparations are under way to celebrate the events with some major exhibitions of the work of the great painter who aroused the habitual wrath of the official critics of his time, as inevitably happens with all true creative work, and the incomprehension of some of its foremost writers, as also happens to some of the best literary men of all ages.

We have recently been talking of this event with Matisse. Here are a few of his thoughts as he expressed them to me.

Manet was the first painter to translate his sensations immediately, thus freeing his instinct. He was the first to *act through reflex*, and thus simplify the painter's craft.

To do this he had to eliminate everything which had come to him through education, retaining only what came to him from himself.

One example of the way he simplified his craft was that instead of doing some often fairly lengthy preparatory work to obtain a transparent tone, he applied his colour all at one time and realized the equivalent of this transparency by means of accurate and precise relationships.

Manet was as direct as it is possible to be. He abandoned the old subjects which could have hindered the simplicity of his craft, and expressed only those things that touched his senses directly.

His romantic nature drew him towards Spain. Thus instead of repeating yet again the legend of Orpheus torn apart by the Maenads, as Michelangelo had done, he painted *Dead Toreador*. (The painting is one of his finest. I saw it in Philadelphia in the Widener collection, in the midst of a magnificent collection of works of all ages, including those of Rembrandt and Rubens, and it dazzled me by the magisterial way it equalled its neighbours.)

COLOURPLATE 20

Thus one may be able to change one's methods at a stroke while feelings retain a continuity which may sometimes develop, but only gradually.

The *Olympia* belongs to Manet's transition period. If in certain ways this famous painting contains some pointers for the future, it remains very faithful to the traditional painting of the great masters. It is not, possibly for this reason, one of his best canvases.

COLOURPLATE 14

Manet was open to all influences, and at one single time. At the end of his life he was overtly influenced by Claude Monet. A victim of his own sincerity, he was aware of it himself. There is a *Garden on the Outskirts of Paris*, executed in separate touches, which resembles a Monet or a Sisley. This painting has neither the depth of colour habitual to Manet nor the finesse of Monet. When Monet mingles tones, the colour is never murky or dirty. When Manet uses his own methods, his colour is limpid too. In this attempt at a landscape the colour, being neither truly of the one or the other, appears rather mediocre.

A great painter is one who creates personal and enduring signs plastically to express the object of his vision. This Manet did.

PAUL VALÉRY

DEGAS MANET MORISOT

"The Triumph of Manet"

1932

Paul-Ambroise Valéry (1871–1945), French poet, essayist and critic. During the 1890s, Valéry was much influenced by the Symbolist poets; he is often referred to as the protégé of Mallarmé. He married Jeannie Gobillard, Berthe Morisot's niece.

If allegories were in fashion, and some painter chose to create a *Triumph of Manet*, it might well occur to him to surround the figure of the great artist with a concourse of the famous colleagues who acclaimed his gifts, upheld his enterprise, and followed him on the way to fame – though as a group they cannot in any way be compared or confined to a "School."

Around Manet would appear the likenesses of Degas, Monet, Bazille, Renoir, as well as the unique and elegant figure of Berthe Morisot; all with their own vision, their own different methods, and character; and all different from the master.

Monet, with his singular visual sensibility, the relentless analyst of light, and virtual master of the spectrum; Degas, with his dominant intellect, his austere pursuit of *form* (and even grace) by way of a rigorous and implacable self-criticism (which left ample room for criticism of others) and endless meditation on the essentials and the resources of his art; Renoir, with his sensual delight in the natural, the painter of women and fruits: these men had nothing in common, except their belief in Manet and a passion for painting.

Nothing could be more unusual or a surer sign of greatness than the ability to dominate temperaments so various, bring together men so independent, so diverse from each other in instinct, ideas and inner convictions, so jealous of what they felt to be distinctive and unique in themselves; and all so remarkable. On one point alone did their dissonance resolve into splendid and perfect harmony; up to the end they were in agreement about the painter of *Olympia*.

But the composition of this academic triumph would require the placing of another group of famous men – more divided from each other perhaps than the former, but no less united in their love for Manet's art, in their equal zeal and passion to defend it and enhance its fame.

This would be a group of *writers*, including no doubt Champfleury, Gautier, Duranty, Huysmans . . . but above all, Charles Baudelaire, Emile Zola, Stéphane Mallarmé.

As a critic, Baudelaire was never wrong. I mean that, over the past seventy years, despite a dozen changes in aesthetic notions, all those whom he appreciated, whose talent or genius he noted, have continually grown in value. In the case of Poe, Delacroix, Daumier, Corot, Courbet – perhaps even Guys – in the case of Wagner, and finally in that of Manet, all whom he admired are still admired.

Honoré Daumier (1808–79), French caricaturist, painter and sculptor.

With that sensuous logic which was peculiar to him, he divined and directed the coming change in taste which, toward the end of the nineteenth century, was to be that of the most distinguished minds. He either foreshadowed or founded a system of values which is only now ceasing to be "modern." Perhaps an age feels itself to be "modern" when it finds it can admit equally a whole host of doctrines, tendencies and "truths" all different from each other if not totally contradictory, all existing simultaneously and actively in the same individuals. Such an age consequently appears more "comprehensive" or more "aware" than an age more or less dominated by a single ideal, a single faith, a single style.

In the list of names I have quoted, which gives a systematic definition of Baudelaire's tastes, there are to be found both romanticism and realism, logical gifts and mystical tendencies, "nature" poetry and poetry based on history or myth, as well as the poetry of the moment, all represented by artists of the first rank.

In Manet, Baudelaire must have sensed a certain division between the picturesque romanticism which was dying out, and the realism which resulted from it as by an elementary reflex, easily taking its place, as if by a reaction of mental distaste and weariness.

Just as the eye replies with a "green" to a too prolonged and insistent "red," so, in the arts, an overindulgence in fantasy is compensated for by a regime of "truth." Which is no reason why one side should insult the other; nor why one side should consider itself bolder, and the other consider itself infinitely wiser.

Manet, with his fondness for the picturesquely exotic, still paying tribute to the toreador, the guitar and the mantilla, though already half won over to everyday objects, to models found in the street, must have seemed to Baudelaire like a close reflection of his own problem: the crucial condition, for an artist, of being subject to several opposing temptations and actually capable of expressing himself in a variety of admirable styles.

We need only glance through the slender collection of *Les Fleurs du Mal*, noting the significant and as it were concentrated variety of subjects in the poems, and compare it with the variety of subjects to be remarked in the list of Manet's works, to decide on a reasonably obvious affinity between the preoccupations of the poet and the painter.

There cannot but be a profound kinship between a man who can write "Bénédiction," "Les Tableaux parisiens," "Les Bijoux," and "Le Vin des chiffonniers," and a man who in turn paints a *Dead Christ with Angels*, an *Olympia*, a *Lola* and an *Absinthe Drinker*.

COLOURPLATES 24, 14, 10, 2

A few further remarks confirm the resemblance. Both were born into the same environment of the old Paris *bourgeoisie*, and both display the same rare combination of a refined elegance in matters of taste with a singular strength of will in their work.

Furthermore: they were both equally contemptuous of any effects not arrived at by conscious clarity, and the full possession of the resources of their craft; it is this quality which defines *purity*, in painting as in poetry. They have no mind to speculate on "sentiment" or introduce "ideas," until the "sensation" has been skilfully and subtly organized. In fact, what they aimed at and reached was the supreme quality in art – *charm*, a term which I use here in all its force.

That is what I think of when I recall the delicious line – a line that seemed equivocal to the evil-minded, and a scandal to the Law – the famous *bijou rose et noir* which was Baudelaire's tribute to *Lola de Valence*. A mysterious jewel, it seems to me less appropriate to the strong and stocky *danseuse* in her rich and heavy Spanish petticoat, standing superbly in wait behind the scenes, ready, with all her supple sureness of muscle, for the signal that will release the vigour, rhythm and syncopated violence of her dance, than to the cold and naked *Olympia*, that monster of banal sensuality, ministered to by a negress.

Olympia shocks, inspires a sacred horror; she dominates and triumphs. A scandalous idol, she has all the force of a public exposure of one of society's wretched hypocrisies. Her empty head is separated from her essential being by a thin band of black velvet. Impurity personified – whose function demands the frank and placid absence of any sense of shame – is isolated by that pure and perfect stroke. A bestial Vestal of absolute nudity, she invokes a dream of all the primitive barbarity and ritual animality which lurks and lingers in the ways and workings of prostitution in the life of a great city.

Perhaps that is why the Realist movement was so ardent in the cause of Manet. The aim of the Naturalists was to present life and everything human just as it was – a purpose and programme not without ingenuousness; but their positive merit, it seems to me, was to have found (or rather to have introduced) *poetry*, and sometimes the highest poetry, in things or themes which until then had been considered base or insignificant. But in the world of the arts there is no subject or material which the artist's handiwork cannot ennoble or debase, render disgusting or delightful. We have Boileau's word for it! . . .

Emile Zola, whose characteristic vehemence so easily became violence, was therefore supporting a very different kind of artist from himself, a man whose vigour – sometimes approaching brutality in his art – and whose bold vision were nevertheless part of a temperament imbued with elegance and with all the spirit of lighthearted liberty still in the air of Paris. As for doctrines and theories, Manet the sceptic, the detached Parisian, believed only in good painting.

His own, accordingly, won over to him some incomparable minds. It might be a source of great pride to him that Zola and Mallarmé, at the two literary extremes, were both so enamoured of his work.

Of these, the former believed, in all simplicity, in things as they are: nothing was too solid, too heavy or too strong for him: or, from a literary point of view, too explicit. He was convinced of the ability of prose to *render* – almost to recreate – the earth and human beings, cities and organisms, habits and passions, flesh and machines. Confident of the *total effect* of the mass of detail, of the sheer number of pages and volumes, he was eager to wield, through the novel, an influence on society, the law and the mob; and this anxiety to reach an aim quite other than that of entertainment, the aim of exciting the masses, led him to invest his criticism with the sarcasm, bitterness and threats which are the usual property of political activity – or what is taken for such. Zola, in short, was one of those artists who commit themselves to mass opinion, and appeal to statistics. Of his tremendous undertaking, a few admirable fragments remain.

The other, Stéphane Mallarmé, was in every way his opposite: the essence of choice. But relentlessly to choose one's language and forms means, in the end, to be excessively choice of readers. Deeply preoccupied with perfection, devoid of any childish trust in the favours of the crowd, he wrote next to nothing; and that for the few, his equals. So far from wishing to *re-create beings and things* in terms of writing and studious description, his idea was that poetry should *consume* them, his dream was that their only conceivable function and end would be to be used up by poetry. The world, to his thinking, was made to end in a fine book; absolute poetry was to be its apotheosis.

Because of the violence of its terms, I am unable to report here a conversation that took place fifty years ago, in Goncourt's Grenier, between Zola and Mallarmé. Courtesy and crudity appeared as the terms of their disparity.

The *Triumph of Manet* thus brings together (and did so, even in the painter's lifetime) the utmost variety of genius, even to the point of total antagonism between some of those who loved him and furthered his cause. Whilst what Zola, for example, saw and admired in Manet's painting was the real presence of things, the strong and living grasp of the "truth," what most pleased Mallarmé was the marvellous sensuous and intellectual transposition which the painting achieved. And besides, he found Manet himself infinitely charming.

I must add that in Zola's works, he valued (as the intensely refined critic that he was) certain powerfully poetic qualities, a sort of intoxicating insistence. Witness the delightful lines he wrote about *Nana*, that supremely carnal creation of the great novelist, whom the great painter, for his part, wanted to paint. . . .

Diverse as they were, the lovers of his painting were unanimous in claiming that his place was among the *masters*, among those whose skill and supremacy endow the things of their time, the flowers of a day, the ephemeral fashions, the flesh, the momentary glances, with a sort of life that outlasts numbers of centuries – with a contemplative value and significance comparable to those of a sacred text. Many a generation will profit by *their* way of looking at and handling the world of the senses, by the individual science of the hand and eye with which they transformed the act of seeing into a thing seen.

I neither intend, nor have I the capacity, to seek out the essence of Manet's art, the mystery of his influence, nor – a capital problem – to analyse what he emphasizes and what he leaves out on the canvas. Aesthetics are not my forte; and then, *how is one to talk about colours?* It might reasonably be left to the blind to discuss them, just as we all discuss metaphysics; but those who have eyes know just how irrelevant words are to what they see.

Nevertheless I must try to isolate one particular impression.

There is nothing of Manet's which I would place higher than a certain portrait he painted of Berthe Morisot, in 1872.

The figure is painted against the clear and neutral background of a grey curtain, and slightly smaller than life-size. What struck me before all else was the *black* – the absolute black of the little mourning hat, along with its tie strings as they mingle among the locks of chestnut hair with rosy gleams of light on them; it is a black that could only be Manet's.

Attached to the hat is a wide fold of black ribbon, coming over the left ear, then surrounding and sitting oddly on the neck; a short black mantle round the shoulder parts to reveal slightly the clear skin in the opening of a white linen collar.

These startling passages of intense black enclose and emphasize a face whose too large, dark eyes have an absent-minded, almost a distant expression. The painting is fluid, coming easily, obediently to the supple brush stroke; and the shadows on the face are so transparent, the lights so delicate, that it makes me think of the tender and precious moulding of that head of a young woman, by Vermeer, in the Hague Museum.

But here the painting has been carried out with greater promptness, freedom and immediacy. The modern painter works quickly, acting on the impression before it fades.

What with those overpowering blacks, the cool simplicity of the background, the pale or rosy luminosity of the flesh, the odd silhouette of the hat, which was "young" and "the latest fashion," the confusion of curls, tie strings and ribbon to each side of the face; the face itself with its great eyes whose vague fixity suggests the profoundest abstraction, a sort of *presence in absence* – the total effect adds up to a singular impression of . . . *poetry*, a term whose application I must at once try to clarify.

Many a fine painting has no necessary suggestion of poetry. There are many masterpieces that have no overtones.

It can even happen that the poet comes late to birth in a man who, until then, was simply a great painter: Rembrandt, for instance, after attaining perfection in his early works, rises, later on, to the sublime level, to the point where art itself grows imperceptible, and is forgotten: having attained its supreme object without any apparent transition, its success absorbs, dismisses or consumes the sense of wonder, the question of how it was done. In the same way, music can sometimes so enchant us that the very existence of the sounds is forgotten.

And now I can say why the portrait I was speaking of is a *poem*. With the strange colour harmonies, and their inconsistent tones; with that contrast between the ephemeral and fussy detail of the old-fashioned coiffure and a something almost tragic in the expression of the face, Manet has contrived to infuse his work with overtones, adding an element of mystery to his firm craftsmanship. He has matched the physical likeness of his sitter with the one and only harmony that might convey a singular personality, thus boldly transfixing the distinct and abstract charm of Berthe Morisot.

ROGER FRY

CHARACTERISTICS OF FRENCH ART

The Influence of the Impressionists on Manet's Art

1932

For a later account of the supposedly detrimental influence of the Impressionists on Manet's work, see pages 340–3.

Manet was so personal and original that it is difficult to place him in the sequence of nineteenth-century art. Had Impressionism come directly out of Courbet there would have been nothing to wonder at, but that it should have been fathered on Manet is almost paradoxical. For Manet, without being the least archaistic, found his natural expression in that art of the seventeenth century that grew out of Caravaggio's peculiar manner of illuminating his figures. Manet's specific feeling was for figures seen under a strong light against a dark background. The figures are lighted from directly behind the artist's head, so that there is scarcely any shadow on the figure except at the edges. These conditions satisfied his personal predilection for large, suavely rounded contours and his feeling for certain harmonies of pale yellowish whites and faded rose.

Within this rather peculiar frame his vision was intense and his mastery of means astonishing. For in spite of the handicap imposed by his flat illumination he was able to give full relief to his figures by the vigour and subtlety of his modelling and by the rich density and fullness of his impasto.

In these early works Manet attains to a rare distinction of style. His forms are expressed with the utmost breadth and simplicity but in all their solid reality, and his colour shows the same aristocratic distinction and restraint. The portrait of his parents seems to me one of the most distinguished portraits of the nineteenth century. But that distinction, that air of nobility, which it achieves, is not the result of any *parti pris*. It comes unconsciously out of Manet's honesty and sympathy of vision and his frank and vigorous directness of statement.

Manet's pictures of this early period are actually less Impressionist than Velazquez's – they take less account of the changes in local colour due to reflection from different sources of light. Indeed, he simplifies in the direction of frank statement of local colour. Without any deliberate intention he strikes an almost archaic note, he almost foretells the new Byzantinism which came with the Post-Impressionist reaction. It was rather his position in face of the bourgeois sentiment of the day that forced him to become the standard-bearer of the Impressionist revolt.

I need not repeat to you the story of the *Luncheon on the Grass* and the *Olympia* and the veritable man-hunt they provoked. The papers howled with rage; wherever he was recognized he was a marked man. This refined gentleman, who belonged to the most cultured circles of the professional class, was really believed by the public to be an almost inhuman monster of depravity, because he had painted two pictures which repeated two favourite themes of the old masters. The effect of this on so sensitive a nature was violent.

COLOURPLATES 18, 14

* * *

I only tell you this to show what these artists had to face. With the great public of today, chastened as it has been by experience, it may even be an advantage for an artist to provoke a mild man-hunt as the quickest and surest advertisement for his art. But the great philistine public of the last century was far more redoubtable. In any case, Manet, though he never ceased to protest that he was no revolutionary, found himself involuntarily in the vanguard of the Impressionist revolt. There was, perhaps, just this much excuse for the misunderstanding that he was in the habit, at times, of leaving the first summary statement of a scene in which he had succeeded in realizing the essentials by his brilliant shorthand. Such statements had of course been frequently made in the past. Corot's portrait of Daumier, for instance, is almost as summary – and Manet's sketches show no evidence of the Impressionist conception of atmospheric colour and tone. They are in a deliberately restricted, not to say artificial, colour scheme which disregards completely atmospheric inflections of local colour. But in any case he found himself surrounded and acclaimed by the young Impressionists; and the result was deplorable. He tried to learn the new vision which they proclaimed. No doubt he learned it more or less successfully, but it was never his natural reaction to vision and, in abandoning that, he lost his finest individual qualities, his suave and dignified contours, his broad handling and his precious colour harmonies. His handling became abrupt and staccato, he could no longer get the lighting he preferred, because he was forced to paint out of doors in a full blaze of even light. His pictures became vulgarly brilliant and harshly accented. If it be not blasphemy to say so, one of his still-lifes at Burlington House might almost have been from the hand of the late Mr Sargent.

It is a sad story. The bitterness of his enemies threw him into the arms of his friends, and his friends achieved his ruin.

In his great composition of the *Bar at the Folies-Bergère*, however, he made, at the end of his life, an heroic and almost successful attempt to recapture something of the suavity of contour and the distinction of his early work, and with that he regained something of the specific quality of his colour, its fine reticence and consistency.

COLOURPLATE 117

PAUL JAMOT AND
GEORGES WILDENSTEIN

MANET

Berthe Morisot and Eva Gonzalès

1932

Paul Jamot (1863–1939), art historian and museum curator. From 1933 to 1936 he was head curator of paintings at the Louvre. Georges Wildenstein (1892–1963), art historian and art dealer; son of Nathan Wildenstein (1851–1934), who founded the famous Paris art gallery bearing his name.

Among Manet's female friendships, there were two which must be seen apart for the character of the person, as well as the feelings involved. These were two young girls who became his pupils, who worked with him, for whom he had a particular tenderness and who then married: Berthe Morisot and Eva Gonzalès. They entered Manet's life in quick succession. He was thirty-five or thirty-six. It was in 1869 that Mlle Gonzalès, the daughter of a novelist who was rather fashionable at the time (Emmanuel Gonzalès, who became secretary to the Société des Gens de Lettres) made the acquaintance, as a pupil, of the painter of the *Luncheon on the Grass* and *The Fifer*. She was twenty, and her Spanish origins had bequeathed her a dark beauty of a kind well calculated to appeal to Manet. She had those wide-open, wide-set eyes, in a matt-white complexion, which he loved. That same year she posed for two pictures by her master. The following year, he painted the famous portrait of his pupil . . . and over which he took such pains. It is hard to believe that he did not have a hand in the *Box at the Italiens* which dates from 1879, which is Eva Gonzalès' masterpiece

COLOURPLATE 49

and which bears a strange resemblance to many an authentic work of Manet's. But oddly enough, it is not of what Manet was painting in 1879 that one thinks. By then five years had passed since Manet had rallied unreservedly to *peinture claire*. Eva Gonzalès remained faithful to the Manet she had known ten years earlier, at the time of *Luncheon in The Studio* and *The Balcony*. Thus one might say that her attitude vis-à-vis her master was very different from the one we see in Berthe Morisot. A stronger personality, despite her admiration for Manet, she did not give up her independence; her own initiatives even contributed to Manet's development, while one feels that Eva Gonzalès would rather have held her master back, had she had the power to do so. But who knows what would have become of her had she not died prematurely, at thirty-four, shortly after marrying the engraver Henri Guérard?

Manet made the acquaintance of the Morisot family in 1868. A high-ranking civil servant at the Cour des Comptes, Tiburce Morisot, had a son to whom he had given his own name and three daughters of whom the oldest, Yves, was then already married. The two others, Edma and Berthe, were studying painting. But Edma's marriage to a naval officer was soon to put an end to her artistic career, while Berthe bore the signs of a vocation that nothing could interrupt. Both before and after her marriage, she was an artist, probably the most exquisitely original of the women painters who have never been more numerous than in France over the last two centuries. Furthermore, this marriage did not cut her off from the world of the arts, since it made her the wife of Eugène Manet, and Edouard's sister-in-law. The two young women, after failing to be put off painting by their first master Chocarne, had worked under the intelligent guidance of the romantic Joseph Guichard, from Lyon. Then they had had the great honour of sometimes frequenting Corot's studio and receiving advice from this master, who never had any pupils in the strictest sense but who evinced much sympathy for these two talented young girls, Berthe in particular.

According to certain family memoirs, from 1860 onwards Berthe Morisot and her sister, who were assiduous visitors to the Louvre, both to listen to Guichard's lessons and to paint from the great masters, and who already knew Fantin-Latour and Braquemond (who, like them, were habitués of the Italian gallery) had noticed a young man who interpreted the classic masters with astonishing virtuosity. This was the time when Manet was doing his famous copy of the *Madonna of the White Rabbit* by Titian and faithfully reproducing Tintoretto's *Self-Portrait*. At the time Berthe Morisot was using Veronese as her model, copying the *Calvary* and *In the House of Simon*. It is not therefore over-hasty to conjecture that sympathetic words might have been exchanged, under the auspices of the great Venetians, between the two young ladies chaperoned by their excellent teacher and this Edouard Manet who was already, as he was always to be, a charming "enfant terrible," but also a witty and most distinguished man of the world.

However, seven or eight years passed before regular relations were established, and it was Fantin who acted as gentle intermediary between the two families. A letter from Manet to Fantin, which is very interesting from more than one point of view, shows us that on August 26, 1868 the acquaintance was a recent one: "I am of your opinion," writes Manet, "the misses Morisot are charming." Then, possibly to conceal a sympathy that might have seemed to arise too suddenly, he blusters, in a tone that is not in impeccable taste: "It is annoying that they are not men. However, as women, they could serve the cause of painting by each marrying an academician and sowing discord in the field of these dotards. But that would be asking a great deal of their devotion." Then the gentleman resurfaces, though one can guess at something quite other than coldness through the very correct formula he uses: "In the meantime, give them my respectful greetings."

Joseph-Benoît Guichard (1806–80), French Romantic painter.

Photograph of Eva Gonzalès (from Manet's photograph album). Bibliothèque Nationale, Paris.

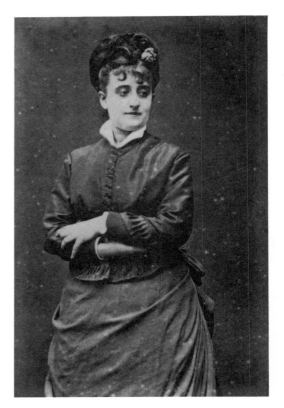

Indeed, he immediately became interested by the talent of Berthe, the younger of the "misses Morisot;" he instantly responded to the charm of her spirit and her whole person. In 1868 Berthe was no mere beginner. She had benefited considerably from her long sessions in the Louvre; she had profited no less from her visits to Corot's studio. We know of certain charming and intelligent copies she did from Corot; they are at least as good as her copies from Veronese. She did more. It is the spirit of Corot, subtly transposed through a feminine finesse and gentleness, which enlivens an *Oriental Port* or the little masterpiece called *Paris seen from the Trocadéro*. She had exhibited at the Salons of 1865, 1866 and 1867: her contribution to this last Salon was in fact the *View of Paris as seen from the Trocadéro*.

It should be said that her relationship with Manet was very much a mutual exchange. He gave her advice and, above all, set her an example. She became imbued with his spirit, but did not imitate him any more than she had imitated Corot. It would not even be difficult to find at least one case where the rôles were reversed. Manet's painting entitled *Universal Exhibition of 1867* is a view done almost exactly at the same spot where Berthe Morisot had stationed herself one year earlier. There is an obvious resemblance between the two paintings. It is more than probable that Manet had seen the canvas of the young girl with whom he was not yet on familiar terms at the Salon. It is no insult to one of the greatest painters of our time and of all time to say that, having borrowed the idea of a painting from a woman, he did no better than she. The pupil triumphs. Besides, Berthe Morisot's canvas is reminiscent of Corot rather than of Manet.

She went through the different experiences of her life as an artist in this way: first Corot, then Manet and, at the end, Renoir. These are the influences which appear in her work and she would never have thought to disavow them, but they did not harm her personality, they merely sustained and nourished her original gifts. Unlike other women, she never wanted to act the man, and strength was never her aim. She remained a woman in all things, and a woman of the world, through her taste, her innate distinction, and the lightness of a hand which, to use a phrase as witty as it is accurate, made a picture as a milliner makes a hat.

A discerning adviser, when needed, she was also Manet's devoted model. Everything he painted using her as a model is in his best vein. As a first trial, she figured, standing, in the large picture *The Balcony*, which was exhibited in the Salon of 1869 and which entered the Luxembourg through the Caillebotte bequest, then the Louvre. It is she who is seated in the foreground, holding a fan, her hand resting on the balcony railing, and the intense expression of her large eyes beneath the taut arc of her eyebrows casts light on a passage from the letter which I have already quoted. "His painting," wrote Berthe to her sister, Mme Pontillon, "produces, as always, the impression of a wild or even slightly unripe fruit. It is far from displeasing me." Following the almost unvarying custom with regard to portraits, particularly portraits of women, people had probably said to her: "How awful. M Manet really has not flattered you!" But she was too much of an artist to allow herself to be influenced by the comments of those who understood nothing of painting, and it is clear that she cannot have been too displeased with her portraitist: "I am more strange than ugly," she goes on. "Apparently the phrase 'femme fatale' has been going the rounds."

Shortly afterwards, in 1870, she inspired Manet to paint one of his most perfect canvases, perhaps the most beautiful of the female images he ever created. In a light, white dress, she is seated casually on a sofa, her bust thrown slightly backwards; the *contre-jour* adds mystery to her fine face, while her great black eyes seem engaged in a deep, almost painful *rêverie*. The canvas was called simply *Repose* when it was exhibited in the Salon in 1873; it bears this name in New York, in the Vanderbilt collection, one of whose gems it is. But it was in fact a portrait, an

COLOURPLATE 39

Portrait of Berthe Morisot. 1872. Lithograph, 7½ × 5¼″ (19 × 13.5 cm). British Museum.

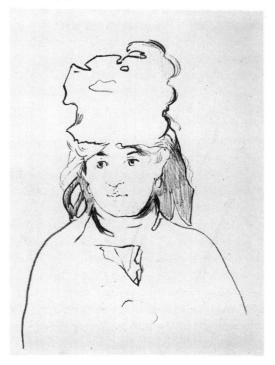

The Vanderbilt collection was formed by George Vanderbilt (1862–1914), an American art collector.

admirable portrait: it is impossible sufficiently to admire the supreme distinction of the bold casualness of the pose, the hint of shyness which shines through the worldly elegance and, diffused throughout the painting, a charm which had never hitherto made itself felt.

Apart from these two great works, countless portraits – busts, profile or full-face, with or without hat – perpetuate for us the features of this noble woman, all the subtleties of expression of those eyes and that face! Manet never wearied of portraying those eyes especially, with their large pupils, where he sensed such ardour and melancholy, trying to transmit their enigmatic allure. Even when he portrayed her dressed to go out, with a fashionable hat, a bunch of violets pinned to her corsage, with the pleasant and almost cheerful, or at least relaxed, air that one is expected to wear in the accomplishment of one's worldly duties, it is the large-eyed gaze, in the half-tone of the *contre-jour*, which makes the canvas more, and something other than, a charming portrait of a young woman, and gives it the mysterious magic of an apparition.

COLOURPLATES 46, 48, 56

PAUL JAMOT AND GEORGES WILDENSTEIN

MANET

Manet's Pastel Portraits of Women

See page 242.

1932

The woman, the modern woman, the Parisienne, is the main source of inspiration for Manet the pastellist. Mme Manet was succeeded by numerous models, mostly unpaid: family relations, women friends, artists, agreeable creatures from all walks of life, who needed no recommendation other than their kindness and their elegance, stream through his studio on rue d'Amsterdam. Two of them deserve special mention for their inexhaustible obligingness and the friendship Manet showed them: Mlle Isabelle Lemonnier, the sister of Mme Georges Charpentier, and Méry Laurent, witty and devoted, who, in the years of trial, lavished a thousand attentions and indulgences upon the artist. Manet relished this female company, he created vivid images of hats miniscule and immense, glistening bodices, lace, fur and fashion generally, in an always odd and seductive setting, for those with eyes to see; he registered eyes light and dark, bright and langorous, painted lips, faces coquettish and naïve.

He rendered all this in fifty pastels which are one of the most charming and original aspects of his work, sometimes with a frankness of touch which nonetheless does not exclude delicacy, sometimes crushing his coloured crayons into an intangible powder. Thus he expressed, at one and the same time, both what was within him, and the poetry of his time. It is, I believe, by giving a body and, if possible, a soul to his feminine ideal that a great painter mainly exercises his power of creation. It was inevitable that a man such as I have tried to portray Manet, an artist of his kind, should have had the need to surround himself by female grace, and also that he should have created models characterized by this grace. Large, wide eyes, somewhat wide-set, slightly surprised, a profile lacking any regularity, yet full of charm and distinction, full lips, delicately rimmed, a mouth unintentionally giving a hint of a childish, or humorous, pout. Such is Manet's heroine, one he always discovers afresh, to some degree, beneath the varying traits of his lovely women friends. No one has done more for the glory of the Parisienne of the 1880s. These young women who distracted him from his suffering and who had nothing to offer

Head of a Woman. 1880. Ink, 7¾ × 4½″ (19.7 × 11.8 cm). Staatliche Graphische Sammlung, Munich.

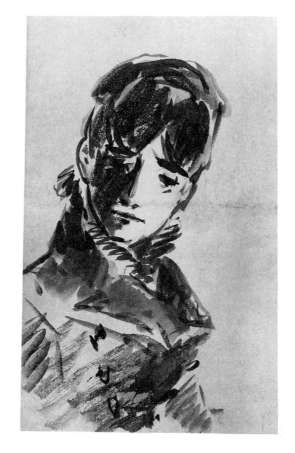

300

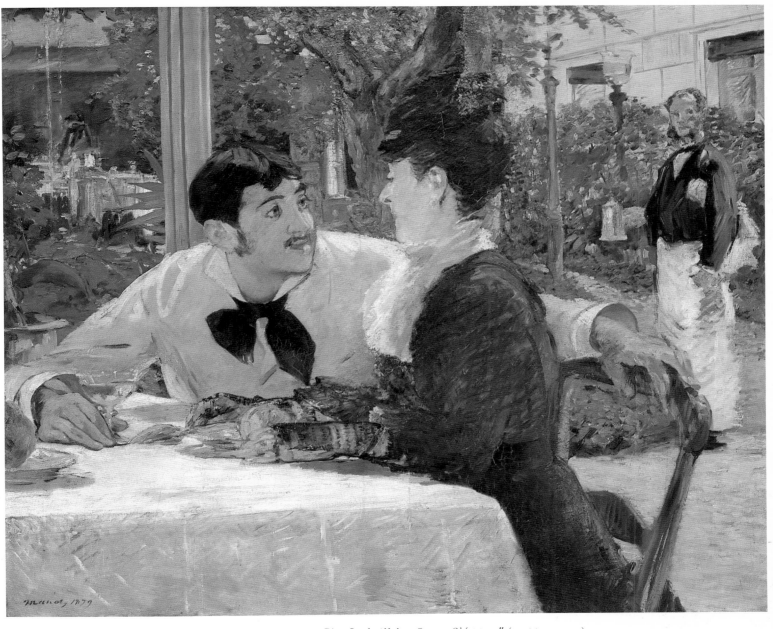

COLOURPLATE 91. *At Père Lathuille's*. 1879. 36¼ × 44″ (92 × 112 cm).
Musée des Beaux-Arts, Tournai.

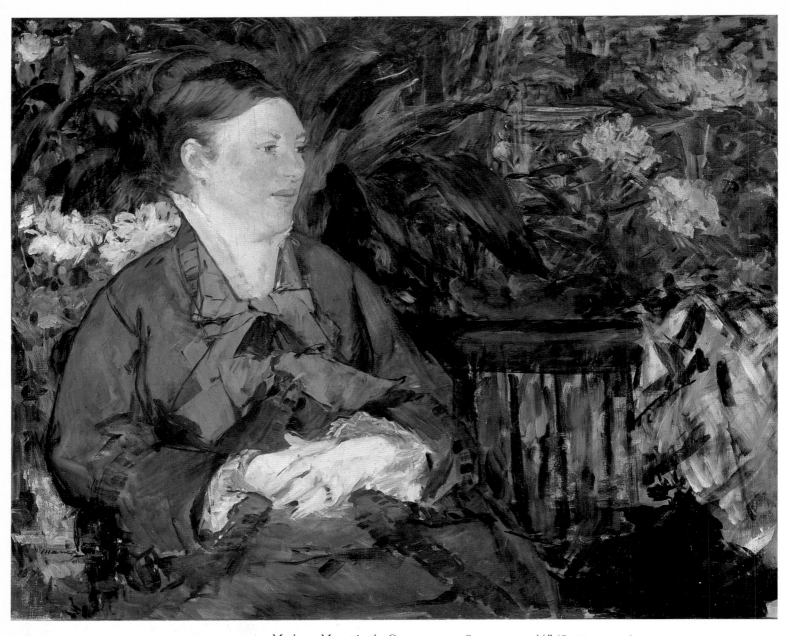

COLOURPLATE 92. *Madame Manet in the Conservatory*. 1879. 32 × 39¼″ (81 × 100 cm).
Nasjonalgalleriet, Oslo.

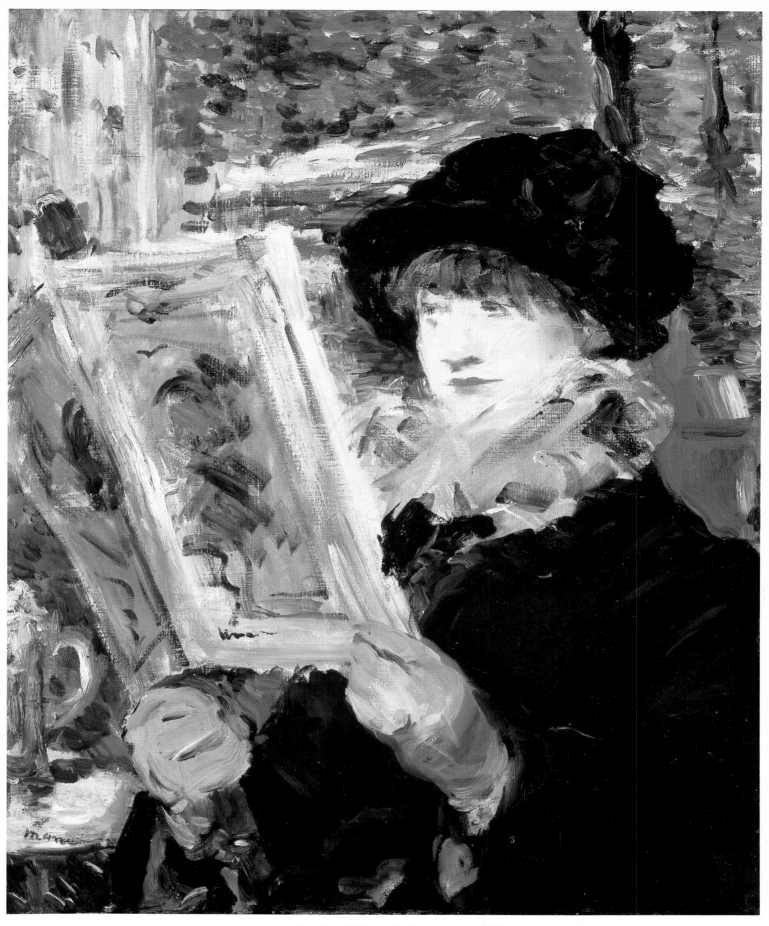

COLOURPLATE 93. *Reading* L'Illustré. 1879. 24 × 20″ (61.2 × 50.7 cm).
© The Art Institute of Chicago (Mr and Mrs Lewis Larned Coburn Memorial Collection).

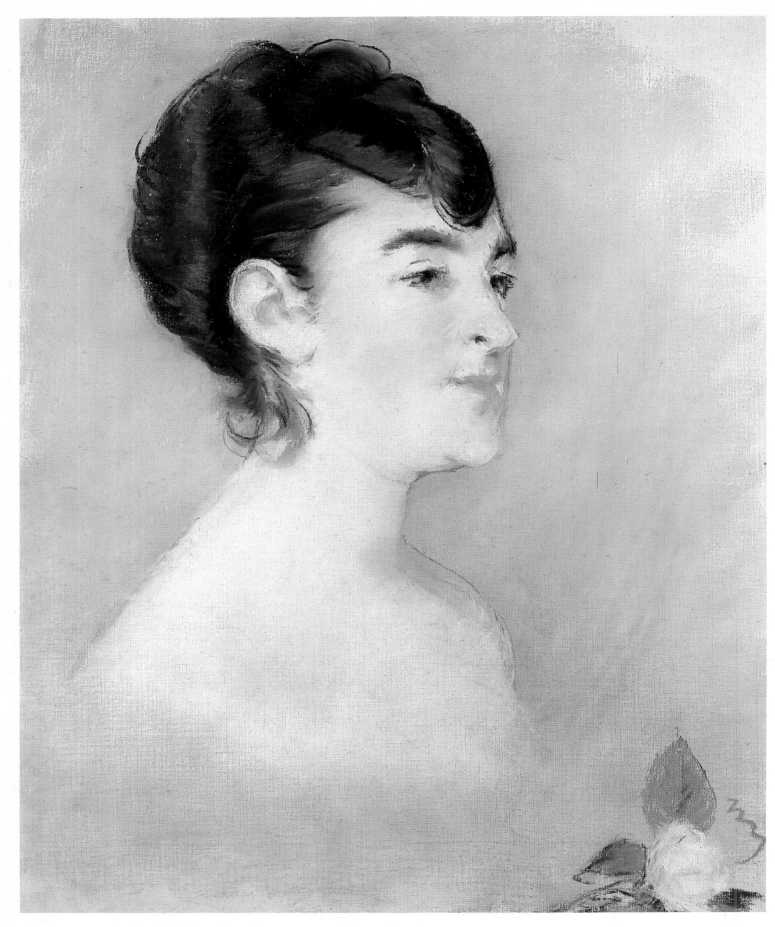

COLOURPLATE 94. *Portrait of Isabelle Lemonnier*. 1879. Pastel, 22 × 18¼″ (55.9 × 46.4 cm). Metropolitan Museum of Art, New York (Bequest of Mrs H.O. Havemeyer, 1929. The H.O. Havemeyer Collection).

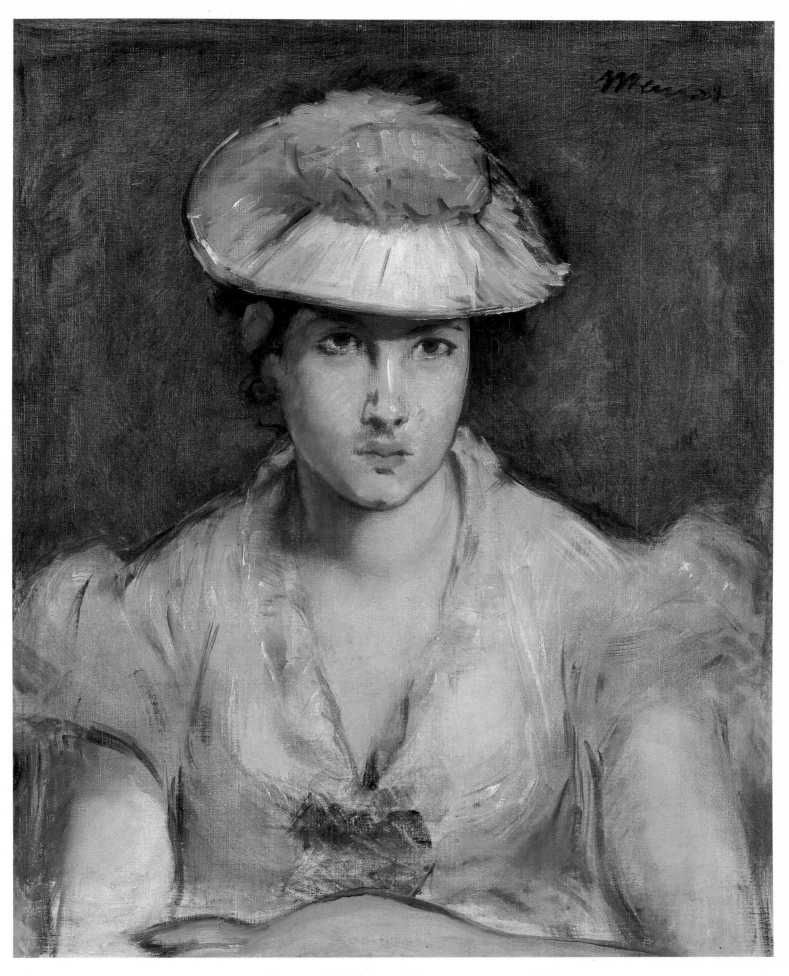

COLOURPLATE 95. *Portrait of Mlle Gauthier-Lathuille*. 1879. 24 × 19¾″ (61 × 50 cm).
Musée des Beaux-Arts, Lyon (Photo Studio Lontin).

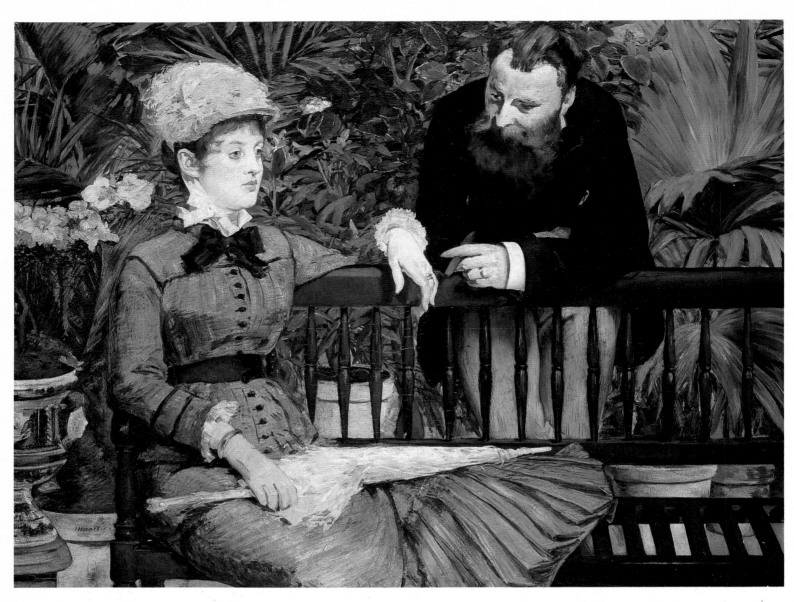

COLOURPLATE 96. *In the Conservatory.* 1879. 45¼ × 59″ (115 × 150 cm).
Staatliche Museen Preussischer Kulturbesitz, Nationalgalerie, Berlin (West).

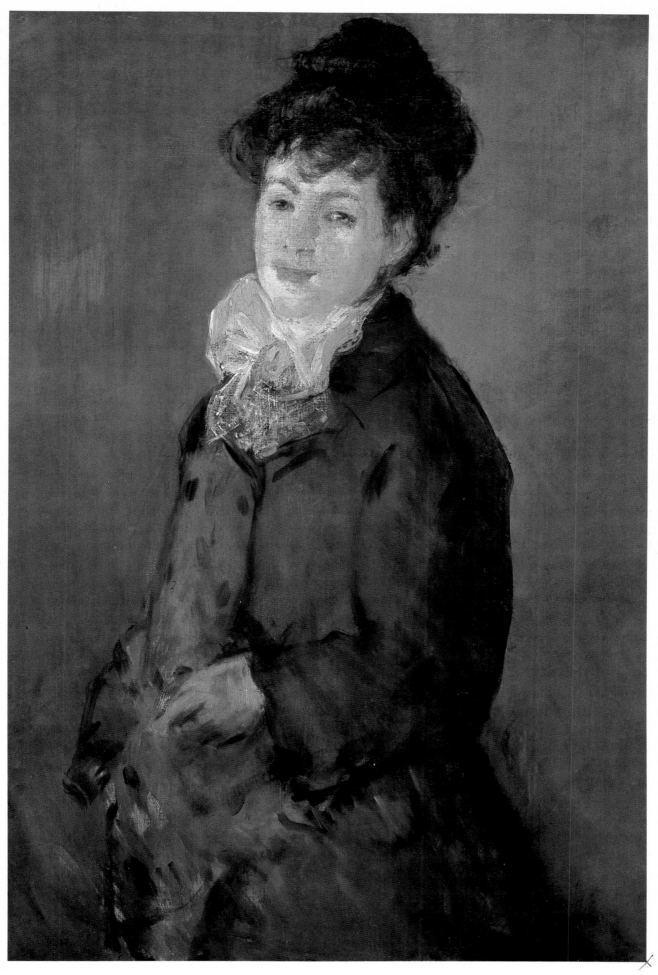

COLOURPLATE 97. *Portrait of Isabelle Lemonnier in a White Scarf.* 1879. 33¾ × 24¾″ (86 × 63 cm).
Ny Carlsberg Glyptotek, Copenhagen.

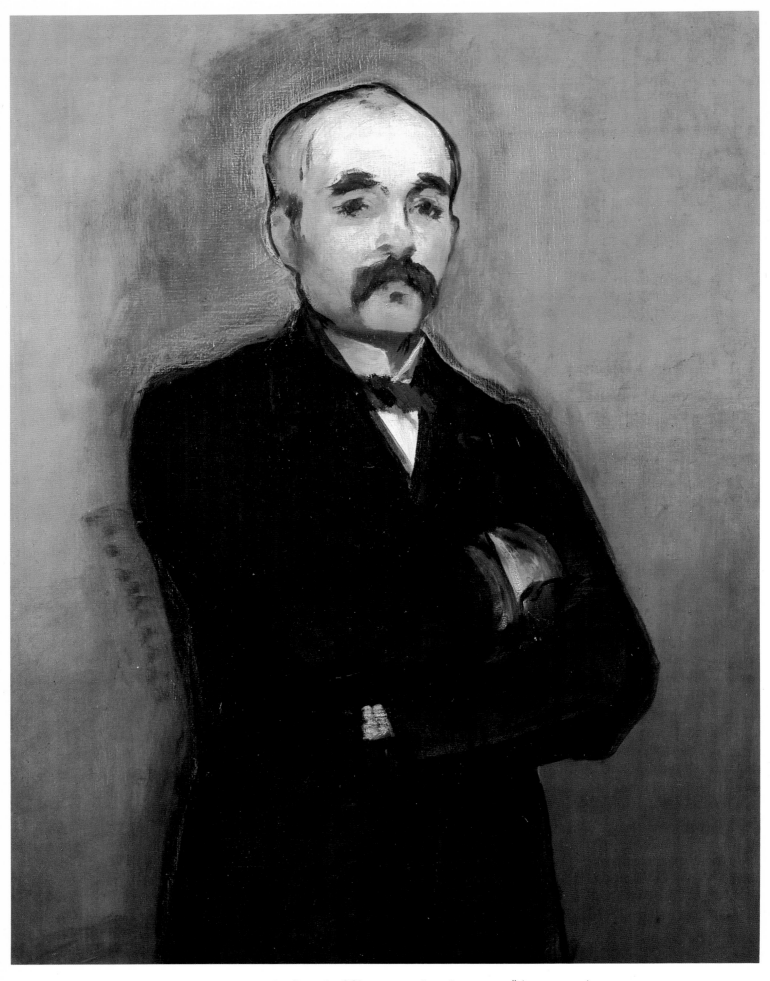

COLOURPLATE 98. *Portrait of Clemenceau.* 1879–80. 37 × 29″ (94 × 74 cm).
Musée d'Orsay, Paris.

him but pleasure, the consolation of their pretty outfits, their pretty eyes and their pretty smiles, have been well served. They are immortal. A single reproach might issue from their lips: "Why did you give us such ugly ears?" Why indeed did Manet, who could do anything with his brush, never proceed to the slight effort of finding an acceptable sort of abbreviatory hieroglyph? It is a small failing in a great artist! Might it not be said to be of the order of those mysterious danger signals which seem destined to humble the pride of genius and also somewhat to lessen the distance that separates great men from the common run of mortals? At all events, it does not detract from the beauty of the images Manet has left us of creatures who enjoyed the disquieting and intoxicating boon of life during his own time. It does not really impair the reputation of his gentle models. At most it might make us regret that Manet did not live in an age when women hid their ears. For women have always to change something in nature, they always feel the need to conceal, correct or distort features of what was given them at birth. The obliging victims of these attempts are now the ears, now the forehead, now the eyebrows, now even the eye itself. In Manet's time, women had not yet thought of shaving their eyebrows and replacing them by two strokes of the brush, but their eyebrows had been rendered invisible by their hairstyle, with the long fringe which completely covered their foreheads. Without reviewing the outcome of these bloodless revolutions, let us remind the reader that in the fifteenth century women found the means to hide both their foreheads and their hair, and to thrust their chins into nuns' veiling; though virtue was none the better protected thereby.

AMBROISE VOLLARD

RECOLLECTIONS OF A PICTURE DEALER

"At Madame Manet's"

1936

Vollard's premises were in the rue Lafitte, Paris. In 1895 he showed drawings by Manet, obtained from the artist's widow, at his first small exhibition. Concerning the fate of Manet's works after the artist's death, see Charles F. Stuckey, "Manet Revised: Whodunit?", Art in America, *November 1983 (pp. 158–78). See also pages 243 and 251.*

I went at once to Madame Manet's house, where I found a whole collection of drawings by the Master, which, as I discovered later, were known to quite a lot of people, only nobody had wanted them because they were merely sketches, and at that time things of that sort were not valued. I managed to buy up the despised collection; and I arranged a little show of them, which had a tremendous success with the artists and helped to give me a start.

After this visit to Mme Manet, I had occasion to see her again more than once. The first time I was there I met a very charming young man, in whom, however, I at first apprehended a competitor.

"My brother Leenhoff," said Mme Manet, introducing him.

When I left, he asked me when I should be coming again.

"Since you are interested even in the unimportant things," put in Mme Manet, "I'll tidy the house up a bit, and see if I can't find some of the stuff the dealers declared was unsaleable. I've left it all lying about; for since I put on weight it tires me to move about much. Leenhoff can help me to look for them. Only the other day he found quite a nice water-colour of my husband's on top of a cupboard. I managed to get rid of it through Portier."

I have spoken elsewhere of this strange dealer in the rue Lepic, whose dining-room did duty as show-room for the canvases that accumulated pretty well everywhere in the modest *entresol* he inhabited with his family. Many a time I saw, alongside a marvellous *Place Clichy* of Renoir's that wouldn't "go off," that masterpiece of Manet's – a picture of a man and woman standing beside a child's perambulator, in a public garden. And I shall always remember Portier's air of triumph when at last he was able to announce: "Things are on the move! I've found a purchaser for my Manet. Two thousand francs!"

Mme Manet told me that this picture had originally been given by Manet to the painter de Nittis, in exchange for one of his own. At Manet's death Mme de Nittis came to see his widow:

"My dear friend," she said, "in memory of my husband, I would like to have the picture back that he exchanged in the old days."

Mme Manet, whose tenderness for the memory of her husband was no less, was glad to accept, and the paintings were exchanged once more.

There were not only sketches left with the widow of the great painter. What a number of fine canvases the collectors had refused! I was reminded of this when, at the triumphant exhibition of Manet's works in 1932, I was present at the unpacking of one of the Master's pictures which had arrived by aeroplane, under the care of a "nurse" whose duty it was, while the exhibition lasted, to superintend the temperature of the layer of air between the canvas and the glass that protected it.

A famous picture of Manet's which was not treated with such care was one of the variants of the *Execution of the Emperor Maximilian*, as important as that which is the pride of the Mannheim museum. Mme Manet's brother considered this variant inferior because Maximilian, and the generals executed with him, did not appear to him as "finished" as in the other painting. The family feared that if they put both pictures up for sale at the same time, it might injure the chances of the more finished one, for which, as it was, they were unable to obtain 6,000 francs. So the replica, which was considered too cumbersome to be hung on the wall in Mme Manet's flat at Asnières, was taken off its stretcher, rolled up, and put away in the store-room, under a cupboard.

One day it occurred to Mme Manet's young brother that perhaps after all there was something to be done with this picture, considered unsaleable till then: the sergeant loading his rifle, for instance, shown by itself, might easily pass for a *sujet de genre*. The sergeant was immediately cut out and handed to Portier. What remained of the picture after this mutilation was all the less easy to market, that a line of cracks ran right across the bellies of the soldiers about to fire. Yet even reduced to these proportions, the *Execution of the Emperor Maximilian* was too voluminous to be thrown in the dustbin. Rolled up again, it was replaced under the cupboard, whence M Leenhoff fished it out once more to offer it to me. I remember Mme Manet's wistful expression when these remains were spread out before us:

"What a pity Édouard took all that trouble with it! What a lot of nice things he could have painted in the time!"

I concluded the bargain. But how was I to get the fragment to the repairer? I could not think of taking the omnibus with this sort of stove-pipe in my arms. I went for a cab. Seated inside it, with my Manet on my knees, I had to be perpetually on the look out to preserve it from the dangers of my journey, holding it upright like a church taper when my cab threatened to get wedged between two other vehicles. In this way I got safely to Chapuis's workshop – the picture-repairer who also worked for Degas.

When Chapuis had unrolled the picture, he said:

"But, M Vollard, surely this is the picture the *Sergeant* was taken from, that I re-stretched for M Degas? He was told the rest of the picture had been destroyed by accident. And you should have heard him on the subject of the legatees!"

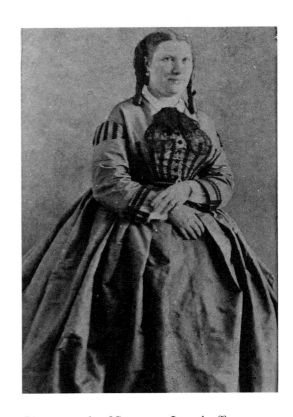

Photograph of Suzanne Leenhoff, Madame Manet (from Manet's photograph album). Bibliothèque Nationale, Paris.

When Degas saw the *Soldiers* in my shop, which he recognized at once as having belonged to the same canvas as his *Sergeant*, he was thunderstruck, and found no words to express his indignation but:

"The Family again! Beware of the Family!"

Then recovering himself, he took his stand between me and the picture, and with his hand on it by way of taking possession, he added:

"You're going to sell me that. And you'll go back to Mme Manet and tell her I want the legs of the sergeant that are missing from my bit, as well as what's missing from yours: the group formed by Maximilian and the generals. I'll give her something for it."

So I went back to M Leenhoff. When I told him the imperative errand I had been entrusted with, he shook his head.

"It looked so tattered," he said, "with the sergeant's legs dangling from it, that I thought it would be better without them, and without the head of Maximilian, which had been destroyed by the dampness of the wall. If I'd thought that a few scraps of torn and mouldy canvas could be of any value, I wouldn't have used them to light the fire with."

All I told Degas was that the missing pieces of the canvas had been destroyed by the dampness of the wall. But he repeated, "You see, Vollard, how one should beware of the Family."

And by way of protest he had the *Sergeant* and the fragment of the *Execution of the Emperor Maximilian* he had bought from me pasted on to a plain canvas, of the supposed size of the original picture, the blanks in the canvas representing the missing parts.

"The Family! Beware of the Family!" he would repeat incessantly, whenever he brought his visitors to look at this restoration.

I remember that on one such occasion, someone asked injudiciously:

"But, M Degas, didn't Manet himself cut up the portrait you did of him and his wife?"

Said Degas sharply:

"What business have you, sir, to criticize Manet? Yes, it's quite true, Manet thought his wife didn't fit into the picture; as a matter of fact he was probably right. And I made a fool of myself over that affair, for, furious as I was at the time, I took down a little still-life that Manet had given me, and wrote to him: 'Monsieur, I am sending you back your *Plums*. . . .' Ah! What a lovely painting that was! It was a clever thing I did that day, and no mistake! When I had made it up with Manet, I asked him to give me back 'my' *Plums*, and he had sold it!"

At the sale held after Degas' death, the *Maximilian* was bought by the London National Gallery, and underwent a further transformation – the two fragments of which it was composed, and which Degas had pasted on to a single canvas, by way of protest, were taken apart again and framed separately.

The whitish streak caused by a crack across the middle of the *Firing Party* had meanwhile been deftly obliterated.

At the exhibition that preceded the sale, I saw a couple looking with curiosity at the *Maximilian* in its fragmentary state.

"They ought to have given you that picture to restore," said the woman.

The man nodded:

"When you think that from a single leg, which was all that remained of an Old Master after a fire, I was able to reconstitute a period picture: figures, costumes, atmosphere and everything – absolutely everything. . . ."

"Yes, and the customer thought his picture even finer than before. . . ."

At this same exhibition there was a copy of the *Olympia* done by Gauguin, which belonged to Degas' private collection. Among the crowd gathered round the picture were two women, one of whom, with a note of anger in her voice, exclaimed: "That's the sort of woman men desert us for."

This may be a reference to Manet's still-life Nuts in a Salad Bowl *of 1866 (Bührle Collection, Zurich, Rouart/Wildenstein 119). Manet apparently gave the picture to Degas after a dinner at which Manet had broken a salad bowl, but Degas returned the canvas following a disagreement between the two artists.*

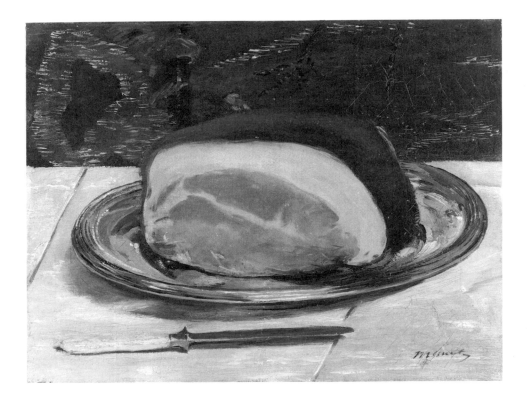

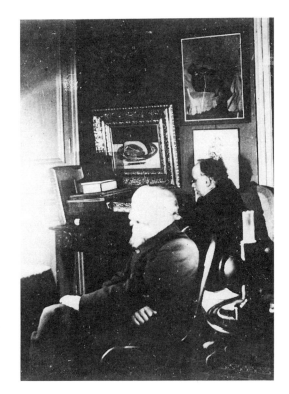

At this same sale of Degas' there were, among other works of Manet's, the *Ham* and a *Madame Manet* in white on a blue sofa – two outstanding pictures which, in 1894, that is to say, more than ten years after the painter's death, were still in the possession of his widow, awaiting a purchaser.

She also retained, at that time, a portrait of herself in a conservatory, and another portrait in which she was seated at the piano. This latter, I fancy, belongs to the Camondo collection. And I am leaving out many that were still to be admired in the little *pavillon* at Asnières, among others a portrait of Manet with a palette, another of Manet standing, and a woman, life-size. To these may be added everything that in those days was referred to as "sketches," things which today are the pride of the museums, such as the *Portrait of M Brun*, life-size, and the *Madame Manet* in pink, with a cat on her lap. Both these paintings were likewise bought at Degas' sale by the National Gallery.

I must also mention another wonderful sketch for the *Maximilian*, with life-size figures, now in the Boston Museum, which had also lain for a long time rolled up in a corner of the store-room at Mme Manet's. If this canvas escaped being cut up, it was doubtless because the figures were thought to be really too little "finished" for M Leenhoff to retail. Renoir, looking at this *Maximilian*, said:

"It's pure Goya. And yet Manet was never so much himself!"

Among the notable paintings at Mme Manet's there was also a sketch of Faure even more expressive, perhaps, than the finished picture. I remember too a study by Claude Monet of Manet painting in his garden. I wanted to buy this picture, but Mme Manet told me it was not for sale. Some time after, I noted that the place the picture had occupied was empty. Mme Manet had followed my glance:

"I was in need of money," she said. "A German came to see me and took a fancy to the picture. You can understand why I wouldn't sell it to you: I shouldn't have liked M Claude Monet to see his picture in a dealer's window. But to a foreigner, like that. . . ."

The days were yet to come when a picture could be sold in Berlin, bought back in Paris, sold again in New York, all in the space of a few weeks.

ABOVE LEFT *The Ham*. c. 1875/8. 12¾ × 16¼″ (32.4 × 41.2 cm). The Burrell Collection, Glasgow, Scotland.

ABOVE Photograph of Degas at home with Bartholomé. Manet's *Ham* hangs in the background.

I had almost forgotten to mention one of the most important of Manet's works, which remained for a long while in the possession of his widow: the *Gypsies en Voyage*. Mme Manet asked 5,000 francs for it, and could not find a purchaser. The wife of a *conseiller général* of the Seine, Mme L . . . had set her heart on the two children in the middle of the picture. She had several times made an offer for this fragment, which Mme Manet had rejected – without much conviction, the lady seemed to think, for she returned to the assault.

One day she said in my hearing:

"My dear Mme Manet, I've offered you so far 1,500 francs: I'll make it 2,000. Come, be reasonable! You're asking 5,000 for the whole thing, and I'm leaving you at least three-quarters of the picture!"

And taking Mme Manet's silence for consent, she seized a big pair of scissors which was lying on the table. Mme Manet, seeing the weapon aimed at the picture, sprang up with what alacrity her corpulence permitted:

"Don't you do that! You and your scissors! I should feel you were stabbing my husband himself!"

The Gypsies, *a large painting executed by Manet in 1862, survives as three fragments: Rouart/Wildenstein I 42, 43 and 44. For Manet's etching after the painting, see page 52.*

AMBROISE VOLLARD

EN ÉCOUTANT PARLER CÉZANNE, DEGAS ET RENOIR

Renoir's Recollections of Manet

1938

As well as writing his own memoirs, Recollections of a Picture Dealer, *1936 (see page 139), Vollard produced books on some of the artists he handled, for example* Cézanne *(1914),* Renoir *(1918) and* Degas *(1924). Vollard was also known for his publication of portfolios of artists' prints.*

Degas' remark to Manet is well known:

"I'll get to the Institut before you, Manet."

As is Manet's retort:

"Yes. Through draughtsmanship."

* * *

Me [Vollard]: "What were the relations between Manet and Courbet?"

Renoir: "Manet felt drawn to Courbet, whereas Courbet did not have much time for Manet's painting. It was quite natural that this should be so: Courbet was still in the mainstream. Manet ushered in a new era in painting. Or rather, it goes without saying that I am not naïve enough to claim that there are any absolutely new trends in the arts. In art, as in nature, what we are tempted to see as novelties are, basically, only a more or less modified continuation of the same. But this does not mean that the effect of the revolution of 1789 was not beginning to destroy all tradition. The disappearance of tradition in painting, as in the other arts, occurred only slowly, imperceptibly, and the most apparently revolutionary masters of the first half of the nineteenth century, Géricault, Ingres, Delacroix, Daumier, were still imbued with the old traditions. Courbet himself, with his leaden draughtsmanship. . . . While with Manet and our school, you had the coming of a generation of painters at a point when the work of destruction begun in 1789 was finished. Of course, some of these newcomers would have liked to renew links with a tradition whose immense benefits they unconsciously felt; but for that to happen, they had above all to learn the craft of painting, and when one is left to one's own devices, one has inevitably to start from the simple and proceed towards the complex just as, to read a book, you have to begin by learning the letters of the alphabet. So it is logical that, for us, the great goal was to paint as simply as possible; but it is also logical that the heirs of previous traditions – from men in whom those traditions, which they no longer understood, ended up by deteriorating into the commonplace and the vulgar, like Abel de Pujol, Gêrome, Cabanel etc., to painters like Courbet, Delacroix, Ingres – tended to become very disoriented in the face of what seemed to them 'images d'Epinal', crude, naïve painting. Yet Daumier made the remark, while visiting an exhibition of Manet's work:

'I don't like everything about Manet, but I do grant it this great quality: it takes us back to Lancelot' [a playing-card figure].

"And the very aspect that attracted Daumier had come between Courbet and Manet.

"'I'm not a member of the Institut,' Courbet used to say, 'but painting isn't a matter of creating playing cards.'"

Edgar Degas, *Édouard Manet and Madame Manet*. c. 1865. Kitakyushu Municipal Museum of Art, Japan.

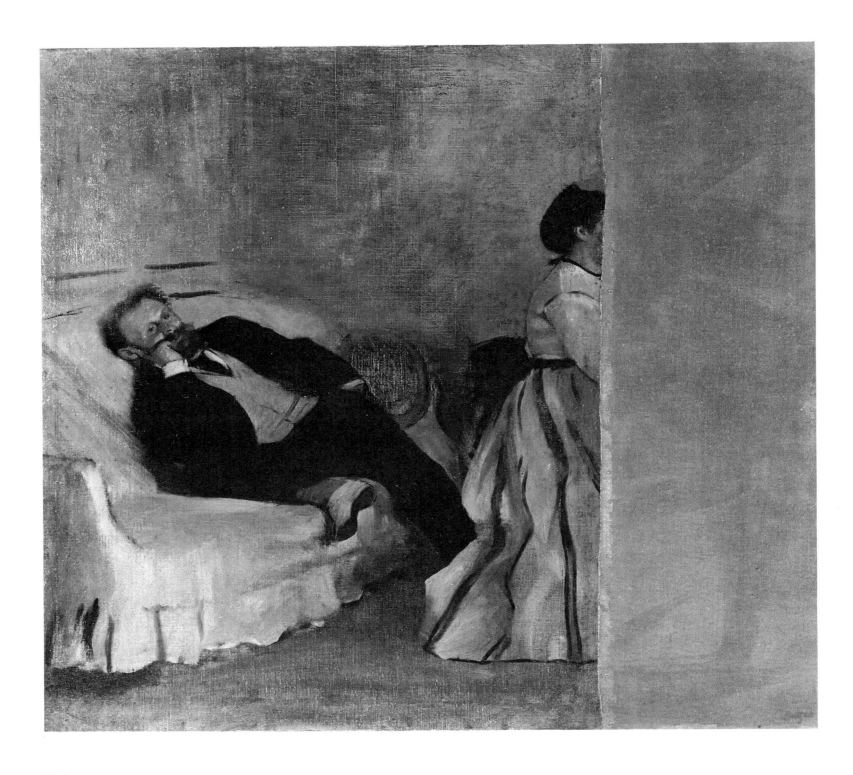

314

Me: "How did Manet, who loved Courbet, get anything out of Couture's teaching?"

Renoir: "It's not quite right to say that he did get anything out of it. He had gone to Couture because there were models. . . . In that spirit one might go even to someone like Robert-Fleury. . . ."

Me: "Robert-Fleury of whom people said to Manet: 'Come now, Manet, don't be so unpleasant . . . a man with one foot in the grave . . .' to which Manet replied: 'Yes . . . but in the meantime, he's got the other foot in the burnt Sienna.'"

Renoir: "Harmony can't have reigned for long between Couture and Manet. They parted with these words from master to pupil:

'Good-bye, young Daumier.'"

* * *

Me: "You haven't told me anything about the relations between Manet and Degas?"

Renoir: "They were very close. They admired each other as artists and enjoyed each other's company. Degas could sense the well-bred man and 'principled bourgeois' that he was himself behind Manet's somewhat worldly manner. But, like all close friendships, this one was not without its perpetual upsets, followed by reconciliations. During some quarrel Degas wrote to Manet: 'Monsieur, I am sending you back your *Plums* . . .' and Manet, for his part, returned to Degas the portrait he had just done of *M and Mme Manet*. In fact it was in this connection that they had their most serious disagreement. This picture showed Manet half-lying on a sofa and Mme Manet beside him at the piano. Manet, thinking he would look better alone, had coldly cut out Mme Manet, except for a piece of her skirt. You know how Degas likes anyone touching his work, and all the fuss he would make if anyone so much as replaced his special 'garden frames,' as Whistler called them, that he put his canvases in, by a gilded frame. . . .

"But Degas' picture must have inspired Manet with one of his own masterpieces: *Mme Manet at the piano*. Everyone knows how easily influenced Manet was: 'a pasticheur of genius' as he has been called. But when he let himself be swayed by his own feelings. . . . In a shop window, in rue Laffitte, I saw two *Women's Legs*, one of those little scraps of sketches that Manet did in the street: absolutely unique! . . .

"I have just told you that Degas recognized in Manet the bourgeois Parisian that he was himself. But there was another side to Manet, and one that was no less intriguing: a streak of mischievousness which always led him to try to mystify those he was dealing with."

Me: "Dujardin-Beaumetz told me a story of how a member of the Institut, meeting Manet in Guillemet's studio, informed Manet that he was working on a study of modern painters, and asked him to say something about Couture. . . .

"So Manet said: 'There was a time-honoured custom in the master's studio which struck me greatly. There was a flageolet there which the pupils used to put up their behinds. And when a visitor came to the studio, he was invariably told that tradition required that everyone who was admitted to Couture's studio should play that flageolet!'"

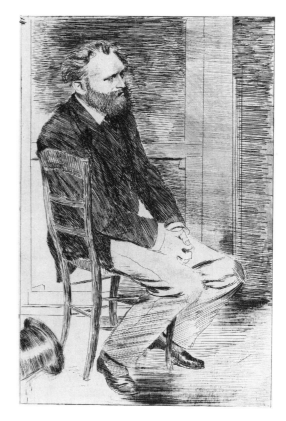

Edgar Degas, *Manet Seated, Turned to the Right*. 1864–5. Etching and drypoint. Detroit Institute of Arts (Founders' Society Purchase, General Membership Fund).

BELOW Photograph of Degas (from Manet's album). Bibliothèque Nationale, Paris.

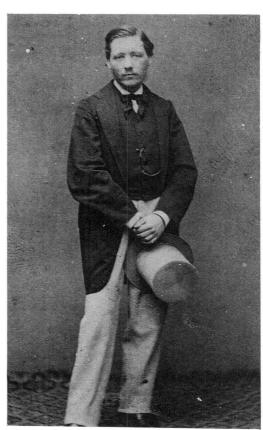

NILS GOSTA SANDBLAD

MANET: THREE STUDIES IN ARTISTIC CONCEPTION

Manet's *flâneur* Realism

1954

Nils Gosta Sandblad, Swedish art historian. Sandblad's study is an investigation of Manet's work of the 1860s.

Manet portrayed contemporary Paris with a fresh eye for the unified and the momentary, and his pictures assumed a new pictorial character of summariness and movement. This *flâneur* realism has its precedents in the engravings of the late eighteenth and early nineteenth centuries. Outside the stricter confines of art, the illustrated newspapers helped to prepare the way for this kind of realism. Baudelaire became its literary spokesman. But only with Manet did the realism of the *flâneur* begin to play its role in the history of art. He himself remained faithful, in his choice of motif, to the ideal expressed in 1862, and after the Spanish journey of 1865 also returned to the pictorial style he had employed in the earlier period. But this is not enough. The visits of Bazille and Monet to the exhibition where *Music in the Tuileries Gardens* was being shown for the first time, instituted a contact which was to be of significance to a whole generation of artists. Manet's *flâneur* realism is one of the most important starting points for the Impressionism of the 1870s and 1880s, and in the history of this movement the Gardens of the Tuileries play the part of a resting place on the way to *La Grenouillère, Le Moulin de la Galette* and *Gare St. Lazare.*

During the *Olympia* period, Manet became preoccupied with the cultivation of formal qualities in a work of art, a development which was facilitated by his attitude of unconcerned stroller. His intentions in this respect were only partly fulfilled by the Impressionists. But when, about 1890, the linear surface-style established itself conclusively, his paintings from the heroic years around 1863 began to arouse new interest. How marked this interest was, becomes clear if one considers the parts played by successive admirers. Cézanne's intermediary role is far too complicated to be treated in this short survey. But it may be pointed out that if it was the leading Impressionist – Monet – who, in 1890, secured for *Olympia* a place in the Luxembourg museum, it was the leading synthetist – Gauguin, on his way to Tahiti – who first copied the famous painting, and the leading fauvist – Matisse – who displayed the greatest comprehension in adopting its formal peculiarities. For what else is the large picture which Matisse called *Luxe, Calme, Volupté,* after a line of Baudelaire's verse – a picture strict in its conduct of line and its concentration on surface values – what else is this if not a paraphrase, profoundly experienced, of the painting in which Manet, in 1863, striving for an almost equally strict and consistent technique of surface-painting, showed his serving maid handing a bouquet to an indifferent mistress?

Therefore, in the apparent desire to break the centuries-long traditions of realism, Manet's painting from the 1860s foreshadowed not so much Impressionism as far more recent movements. In spite of this, the artist was not so far removed from the older style of painting, the painting of a prescribed subject, as has often been claimed. We have seen how willingly he made room in his painting, even when it was most strictly dominated by form, for striking observations, playful allusions to this or that source, and sometimes for strongly emotional elements. This is worth bearing in mind in the discussion which is being conducted with such eagerness just now, on the precedents and growth of modern art. Right up to Picasso and his followers, artists from different camps have carried out the experiments with pure painting which Manet introduced in the 1860s, under the protests of the Parisian salon public. But, like him, they have not given up their right to be affected by a Querétaro.

La Grenouillère *(1869) and* Le Moulin de la Galette *(1876) were painted by Renoir.*

Querétaro refers to the Execution of Emperor Maximilian *(see page 103).*

GEORGES BATAILLE

MANET

"Manet's Secret"

1955

Georges Bataille (1897–1962), French art historian, philosopher, novelist and political economist.

One of the most surprising aspects of Manet's new painting was precisely its close connection with dress and costume. In fact, as I see it, costume and painting have developed along parallel lines. At least this is true of masculine dress which, as it gradually lost the majesty that had distinguished it in the seventeenth century, grew more and more vulgar. It had once been elegant, eloquent, colourful, but fashion relentlessly stilled its eloquence, dimmed its colours. Today men have altogether lost the polish once conferred on them by an inherent sense of dignity and by dress befitting that dignity. Men have chosen – a little reluctantly – to accept the more realistic standards of democratic equality and, finally, to repudiate a majesty presumptuously bestowed by high birth and religious orders. Today even the wealthy man, however elegant his dress, abstains from the ostentation that might differentiate him from his fellows. It is not too much to say that in his very sobriety he defers to a supreme convention which aspires to the absence of convention, and in effect successfully attains that end.

This unobtrusiveness and sobriety – which many men today go to great lengths to observe – did not gain the upper hand without a struggle, and even then were all too often accompanied by hypocrisy and misgivings. From the start, the new trend was openly resisted. At first the bourgeoisie would have none of a world democratically reduced to *what it was*, and man reduced to plain and simple humanity. It is often harder than it seems for us to forego that idealization of man associated with qualities we call noble, royal, divine. These words carried vital meaning so long as they had a solid basis in political reality. But with the triumph of the bourgeoisie that reality had ceased to exist. The bourgeoisie thereafter confined them to the realm of art, where it was thought that, undisturbed, they could go on as before upholding the values of a glorious past, whose forms were sacred. Art was not to be harried or impeded by the changes the bourgeoisie had brought about in government, social life, costume and so forth; on the contrary, its lofty realm of divine and noble forms stood intact – all those forms harmoniously, majestically ordered there as they had once been ordered in a now abolished but well-remembered past. Art was only art by virtue of ignoring what we *see*, what we *are*, in the interests of a theatrical imagination parading before the eye such ghosts of a bygone splendour as might console us for the present banality of the world. In the studios the master's byword was not to copy the model as it might really appear. . . .

All his life Manet personally respected that particular notion of elegance which stipulated sobriety in dress. He eschewed those aristocratic fashions which, by the mid-nineteenth century, lingered on as mere uncouthness and pretence in the bourgeoisie. He wanted to, and did, belong to his own time, and dressed and painted accordingly, rejecting outright the anachronisms that screened off reality behind a façade of fiction. Courbet before him had resolutely shown things as they really are, with a gusto that still amazes us. The density and fine vital energy of Courbet's art are undeniable, but his realism had not yet been stripped of eloquence; his art pleads nobly, eloquently, for the truth of things and this nobility is the one relic of a dead past to which Courbet clung. His eloquence, needless to say, had nothing in common with the turgid, highflown, bare-faced lying of conventional art. But it was not yet the laconic elegance, the economy of statement that we do not find till Manet stepped forward – till the day, that is, when the subject, treated with indifference, became a mere pretext for the picture itself.

What is more, stripped to essentials, Manet's sober elegance almost immediately struck a note of utter integrity by virtue not simply of its indifference to the subject, but of the active self-assurance with which it expressed that indifference. Manet's was *supreme indifference*, effortless and stinging; it scandalized but never deigned to take any notice of the shock it produced. Scandal merely for scandal's sake would have been inelegant, a breach of sobriety. His sobriety was the more complete and efficacious in moving from a passive to an active state. This active, resolute sobriety was the source of Manet's supreme elegance.

There is a seeming contradiction here. I said that the working principle of this elegance was indifference. The stuff indifference is made of – we might say its intensity – is necessarily manifested when it enters actively into play. It often happens that indifference is revealed as a vital force, or the vehicle of a force, otherwise held in check, which finds an outlet through indifference. In Manet's case the pleasure of painting – nothing less than a passion with him – fused with that indifference to subject matter which opposed him to the mythological world in which Raphael and Titian had felt at home. With Manet the exultation in his sober powers went hand in hand with the sober delights of destroying what was no longer viable in art. Thanks to his technical virtuosity he could work in the silence of complete freedom and, by the same token, in the silence of rigorous, unsparing destruction. *Olympia* was the height of elegance in that both its rarefied colour scheme and the negation of a convention-bound world were carried to the same pitch of intensity. Conventions were meaningless here since the subject, whose meaning was cancelled out, was no more than a pretext for the act – the *gamble* – of painting.

COLOURPLATE 14

Indifference to the subject distinguishes not only Manet's approach to painting, but that of the Impressionists and, with few exceptions, of all modern painters. Monet once said that he would have liked to come into the world blind, and then regain his eyesight, so as to see forms and colours independently of the objects and uses to which, by force of habit, we relate them. But in the work of Monet and his friends we do not find the passion for silencing that which is naturally moved to speak, and for stripping that which convention clothes. This operation, seen at work in *Olympia*, where its forthright precision is almost magical in effect, makes for Manet's unique charm and distinguishes him from his successors. It gives *Olympia* the pre-eminence that led his friends, in 1889, to purchase it from his widow and offer it to the Louvre, and so strongly did Manet's friends feel about the matter that they grew indignant at the lone dissent of Antonin Proust, who felt *Argenteuil* to be a better picture. But the operation had reached its climax in *Olympia*; there could be no denying that. And if Manet's contribution to the new painting were to be summed up in a single picture, that picture could only be *Olympia*. His friends unhesitatingly singled out the same picture singled out by his enemies for opposite reasons.

COLOURPLATE 65

I have pointed to a similar operation – of silencing the rhetorical forms of old and stripping them of their conventional baggage – in *The Execution of the Emperor Maximilian*, in which, perhaps, it is "brought off" less perfectly, but no less plainly than in *Olympia* and *Luncheon on the Grass*; its principles were laid down, at least to a point, in *Music in the Tuileries Gardens*. In each, instead of the theatrical forms expected of him, Manet offered up the starkness of "what we see." And each time it so happened that the public's frustrated expectation only redoubled the effect of shocked surprise produced by the picture. That frustrated expectation was one thing, the beauty and daring of Manet's colour contrasts another; the former amplified the latter, and it is in the former and not, as Malraux would

COLOURPLATE 36
COLOURPLATES 18, 11

André Malraux (1901–76).

318

have it, in "the green of *The Balcony*" or in "the pink patch of *Olympia*" that there resides "the contribution, not necessarily superior, but totally different that Manet made." Malraux is perhaps open to blame for not having stressed the magic workings of the strange, half-hidden operation to which I refer. He grasped the decisive steps taken by Manet, with whom modern painting and its indifference to the subject begin, but he fails to bring out the basic contrast between Manet's attitude and the indifference of the Impressionists towards the subject. He fails to define what gives *Olympia* – which in itself is no finer a picture than several other Manets – its value *as an operation*.

Olympia reveals Manet's secret. Nowhere else is it so patently revealed; but once we see it here we find traces of it in nearly all his works. Manet afterwards did his level best to repeat what he had brought off so successfully in *Olympia*; in his *Portrait of Zacharie Astruc* he even reverted to the background partition he had taken over from Titian's *Venus of Urbino*. Elsewhere he resorted to other devices whose purpose was always the same; to frustrate conventional expectations. I think it is safe to say that, in *A L'Ombre Des Jeunes Filles En Fleur*, Marcel Proust's analysis of Elstir's mannerisms and style really applies to Manet. Elstir himself is not Manet, whom Proust could hardly have known personally as he was only a twelve-year-old boy at the time of Manet's death. But Elstir is not far removed from Manet. Proust spoke of "the period . . . in which Elstir's personality had not yet fully emerged and still drew inspiration from Manet." This is true in the sense that the character of Elstir in the novel is patterned to some extent after Manet as he was in real life. Proust tacitly admits as much when he says that "Zola wrote a study on Elstir," and again when he specified that, in addition to his Balbec seascapes, Elstir painted *A Bunch of Asparagus*. These seascapes are anything but imaginary; they are those Manet painted at Boulogne, Berck and elsewhere. The gist of what Proust had to say about them is that where we should expect to see land, the painter shows us water, and then shows land where we should expect to see the water. "One of the most frequently recurring metaphors in the seascapes he had near him at the time was precisely his way of likening shore to sea and thereby abolishing all distinction between them. It was his way of drawing this comparison, repeating it implicitly and

COLOURPLATE 46

COLOURPLATE 26

Marcel Proust (1871–1922). À L'Ombre des Jeunes Filles en Fleur *is one of the series of novels* À La Recherche du Temps Perdu.

On the Beach at Boulogne. 1869. Virginia Museum (Gift of Mr and Mrs Paul Mellon).

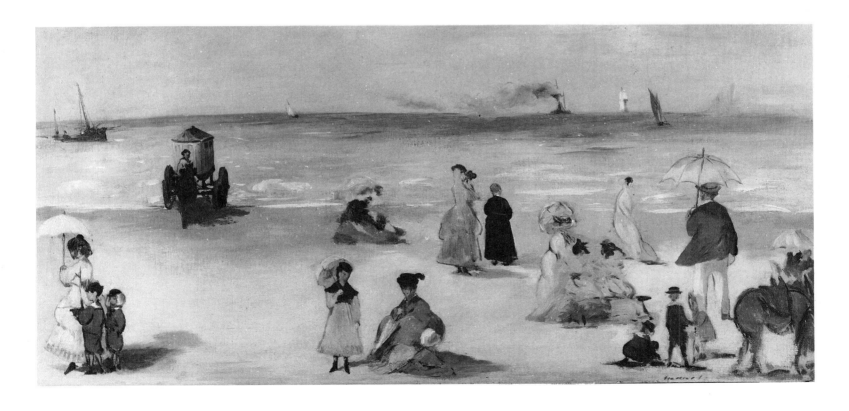

unwearyingly throughout a given canvas, that imparted to it that power-ful, many-sided unity, the source, though not always clearly recognized as such, of the enthusiasm Elstir's painting aroused in certain art-lovers." What Proust is driving at is the unity of visual effect the spectator enjoys as he moves smoothly and easily from one aspect of the subject to another. When Proust alludes to a ship as "some citified, earth-built thing," to what other painting to these words more aptly apply than to Manet's *Departure of the Folkestone Boat*? This knack of producing the unusual and unexpected by abolishing habitual distinctions between unlike things had an even larger significance for Proust, who wrote: "It sometimes happened in Paris that, from my room, I overheard a dispute, almost a riot, which I went on listening to until I had identified the cause of the uproar, for example a carriage, whose shrill, discordant clamour my ears had really heard, but which until then I had not acknowledged, knowing in my mind that wheels do not produce such sounds." In the writer's mind, as in the painter's, the same transition occurred, the prosaic responses of the mind melting away into sense impressions; both men found this phenomenon far richer, far more inspiring than the inevitable reverse transition from sensibility back to intelligence, and both, whether by instinct or calcula-tion, practised a subtle artistic wizardry that enabled them to recapture all the innocence and freshness of the original impression. We see its effects in *Women on the Beach*, in which the immensity of the figures relegates the sea to insignificance. Or in *Interior at Arcachon*, in which the sea, visible through the open window, overwhelms the room itself.

COLOURPLATE 45

COLOURPLATES 59, 55

This disproportion of the picture elements is absent from the general run of Impressionist paintings. Unquestionably it was Manet whom Proust had in mind when he described the process. In writing about it he carried it even further than Manet had, since he was expressing not so much what Manet had actually done as the conceptions of the post-Impressionist and above all post-Manet painter he himself, Proust, potentially was.

LOUISINE W. HAVEMEYER

SIXTEEN TO SIXTY: MEMOIRS OF A COLLECTOR

On Collecting Manet

1961

Louisine Havemeyer (1855–1929), American collector. The Havemeyers' great fortune derived from sugar refining; Louisine and her husband Henry (1847–1907) were among the most energetic collectors of Manet's work after the artist's death. Mrs Havemeyer's large bequest of French later nineteenth-century paintings entered the Metropolitan Museum of Art, New York, in 1929. For a biography of the Havemeyers see Frances Weitzenhoffer, The Havemeyers: Impressionism Comes to America, *1986.*

One must turn over a new page in the history of art if one wishes to know anything of the painter Manet, that apostle of light and air. Gay, debonair, fearless, lightly carrying the opprobrium of "Impressionist" upon his shoulders, he sauntered along the Boulevards, answering the jests which were flung at him from the habitués of the cafés as he passed by, with a repartee or a prophecy which caused his merry critics to tip back their chairs lest their sides be oppressed by the laughter he evoked. He tripped lightly through his span of life, threw magic juice into the eyes of his derogators and said with Puck when he found he was not understood: "Oh, what fools these mortals be." Like the light-footed Harlequin, he rapped right and left at the art world of Paris, took its breath away; and when the art world would strike back, it heard only the echo of his laughter. He had already disappeared to paint another picture which would set those stupid Bottoms by the ears, those dull bellowsmakers who had no more idea of his art than Shakespeare's tinkers and tailors had of Pyramus and Thisbe. Like those they could not have told his art-lantern from a moon.

Manet's portrait by Fantin-Latour shows us a rather effeminate face with merry blue eyes and a sensitive smiling mouth, and anyone who understands physiognomies cannot look upon that delicate nose with its flaring nostrils without knowing that its possessor was artistically endowed to the highest degree.

Manet felt the fire within, and realizing the folly of the modern studio life for him, he started forth to see things for himself and to paint nature as he saw it, brilliant with life, gay with colour. This magician of the brush loved to startle Paris with his legerdemain. Paris never could tell what would come out of that wonderful studio, come forth from under the prestidigitator's silk handkerchief or out of his silk hat. One day would appear a canvas as big as ambition could stretch it and Paris stood aghast before *Luncheon on the Grass*. The Parisian public turned their thumbs down, held their hands before their faces, while the conservative Dogberrys filled the reviews with stupid appreciations meant to be stinging criticisms, and then hurried to the clubs to enjoy the bons mots and the jests the new creation called forth. Manet laughed and shrugged his shoulders. "My fête is at Bougival, yours is in Italy," he said to his critics. "Go to the Salle Carrée, go look at your Giorgione and admire his fifteenth century fête, mine is of today and I can wait for my public."

He kept his critics waiting for his academic, that painter's crux by which he must stand or fall. They thought they would catch him at the bridge, but lo, when Manet brought it forth and stood at the bridge with single sword to defend it, there wasn't a Gracchus or a Roman who dared attack him. What could they say of it? Nay, what could they think of it? Was that a nude, an academic? Surely, no. For never had they seen one like it. Yet who in the wide world or in Paris would have dared present such a composition or would have courted such difficulties in the doing, as Manet did when he painted his *Olympia*? A nude woman lies upon a white sheet, a black cat is at her feet, a Negress leans over her couch and offers her a bunch of brilliant flowers wrapped in white paper such as one sees in the Parisian flower market. Never before had a painter put a nude in contrast with such blacks and whites! Who but Manet could have done it? The critics gnashed their teeth at the problem he offered. "It can't be done," they cried, "it is not art." "Why not?" said Manet who enjoyed the fun. "There are Negresses, and black cats, and flowers in white paper, and nudes on sheets." And he added, snapping his fingers: "I have done it, it is my academic, and what is more, one day it will hang in the Louvre." It hangs there today and fate with mocking irony has placed it as a pendant to the academic and conservative Ingres. Thus Manet left his critics stampeded at the bridge and quietly returned to his studio to prepare a fresh surprise for them.

This was Manet the modern, who was to fill a new page in art's history with a long list of remarkable works.

Strange to say, I never met him. I recall that when I was a very young girl I went to see Miss Cassatt at Marly-le-Roi. Her villa joined Manet's home and his fatal malady made him very ill at that time. After luncheon we walked over to his villa to ask after him. Mme Morisot met us at the gate and at Miss Cassatt's inquiry sadly shook her head, saying that she feared the worst. Mme Morisot walked back to our villa with us and I recall that she was a charming, intelligent woman, and that she and Miss Cassatt were very friendly and talked of art matters, and spoke of the pity of young American girls wasting their time in the Parisian studios. "It would be far better," said Mme Morisot, "if they would go to some city where there were a few good pictures, like Nantes for instance, or Lille, and study quietly there." That is all I remember of the conversation for Mme Morisot left us hurriedly to return to poor Manet.

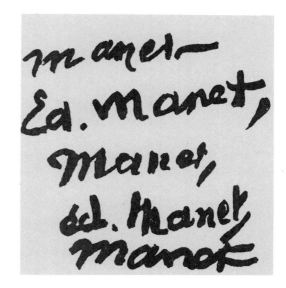

Photograph of Manet's signatures (Photo Roger-Viollet).

COLOURPLATE 14

I think it was in 1883 that I was in Paris when two of Manet's works were exhibited at the Salon. They were *Portrait of M Pertuiset the Lion Hunter* and the portrait of Rochefort, the editor of *La Lanterne*. I saw these pictures many times and always regretted that I did not understand French better, for if I had been able to catch the meaning of the phrases and jokes that filled my notebook each afternoon with witty remarks and observations, which, in view of Manet's place in art today, would be interesting to my readers. There was always a crowd before these two pictures, there was tittering, elbow nudging and shoulder shrugging with much laughter and vociferous exclamations of "Ah, ah" and "Ma foi" and "Oh, lá, lá." The public made frank fun of the lion hunter but the portrait of Rochefort came in for the largest share of ridicule. One day I saw a young man, a student probably, draw his companion away saying: "You must not go near it, don't you see his face is just about breaking out with smallpox." . . .

COLOURPLATES 110, 111

One picture which set all the wiseacres' heads awagging was *The Masked Ball at the Opera* which soon entered our collection. Was there ever such a picture! Surely Manet had never drawn anything so incomprehensible out of his magician's hat before. Hat! Why the whole picture was hats. Hats ad infinitum! High hats, low hats, black hats, silk hats, queer hats, hats such as Parisians wore with dress suits to the Opéra, hats with strings, hats open, hats shut, hats in the hand, hats on the head, hats tilted, tipped, tossed, thrown upon the head, hats on straight, hats on crooked, hats on the crown, hats on the ear, hats on the forehead, hats down over the eyes, hats at one angle, hats at another. The foyer of the Opéra was just a sea of hats. They filled the vestibule, they lined the stairway. Men in hats crowded the entrance of the Opéra and mingled with women in dominoes and with the soubrettes in bright costumes. And the background, what could the critics say of that? "May the saints of the Academy forgive him," they cried. Never had art or artists from the days of Phidias down produced such a background – the marble of the great stairway. Yes, just some marble, toned by the lights from the dome above with a yellow lustre, impossible to describe, that was the background and it threw the mass of hats into relief. A woman's leg ending in a pretty shoe was thrown over the marble stairway to let us know that the frolic was going on above as well as in the scene before us.

COLOURPLATE 64

How the critics whistled and hissed, packed the reviews with articles upon the virtues of the old school and the villainies of the new one, found the masked ball (which they attended night after night) indecent and a menace to society, and all because they saw it for the first time represented to the life. . . .

The Masked Ball at the Opera fell to our share of Manet's works. We bought it in 1894 and the purchase of it marked one of those dramatic occasions, when two amateurs clash in the transaction. Our purchase of *The Masked Ball at the Opera* was a disappointment to Count Camondo who desired to see the picture in his collection, which is now in the Louvre; just as his buying Degas's *Pédicure* (a marvel of a picture) was a disappointment to us – a rare happening, but one which does occur in the art world.

See page 312.

I learned that in order to paint his *Masked Ball at the Opera* Manet had spent a winter in studying black hats. He invited acquaintances to come to his studio in order that he might make a study of their hats. He would drop in at a fellow artist's studio and ask to be allowed to make a sketch of his hat. Friend Goncourt came in for a little chat and was immediately pressed into service and requested to keep his hat on. Duret's hat was painted, the family hat was painted. Manet's own hat served as a model. And you may be sure that when Fantin-Latour painted his friend's portrait which now hangs in the Art Institute of Chicago, Manet wore a high hat.

I hung *The Masked Ball at the Opera* in my gallery for a time, but I found that there were many of Puck's foolish mortals still posing as art amateurs in America. I took it down and hung it in my own apartment, where I have studied and enjoyed it, hour after hour, year after year, until I have learned to consider it one of Manet's best if not his greatest work.

Everyone who knows Manet's works, knows what a great painter of still-life he was and it is a curious fact that we, who probably own more of his figure pieces than any other collector, should have selected a still-life as our first example of the artist. To be a great collector one must be open to conviction and the following anecdote will show you how Mr Havemeyer began collecting Manets with a still-life and ended with the *Gare St. Lazare* and *Dead Christ with Angels*. One morning, I think the year was 1889, Mr Havemeyer as he bade me good morning, said: "I think I will stop in with Mr Colman and see the Durand-Ruel exhibition at the Academy. They have some Impressionist pictures there, they will probably shock Mr Colman." "Not at all," I said, "you will probably be intensely interested and if you find any Manets there, be sure and buy me one." My husband said he did not think there was any likelihood of his buying a Manet, but when he returned in the afternoon and greeted me, he said quietly: "I saw the exhibition this morning. There were two Manets in it, one a boy with a sword and the other a still-life. The still-life was very fine and I bought it for you, but I confess the *Boy with a Sword* was too much for me." "I must see it," I answered, and then, an unusual thing for me to do, I asked the price of the *Boy with a Sword*. "Oh I think they asked $3,500 for it," answered Mr Havemeyer carelessly. I add that as a dainty bit for a new *Memorials of Christie's* of modern sales, or for the amusement of the amateurs who will go on buying Manets at varying prices for many years to come. Often did Mr Havemeyer refer to our mistake in not buying the *Boy with a Sword*. It was at first a little difficult to understand Manet's method of modelling in light, but my husband learnt quickly to appreciate him, and the rapidity with which he collected many of his greatest works is the best proof I can offer of my husband's intelligence. The *Boy with a Sword* now belongs to the Metropolitan Museum of Art and is considered one of the finest pictures in the gallery.

We began very modestly, buying some of Manet's smaller pictures first. One is an *Interior*, with Mme Manet seated by a table and a young boy, her nephew I believe, seated near her. Manet must have taken his family to some watering place, for the large window is open and one has a beautiful view of the distant sea. It is full of atmosphere, very harmonious and not at all difficult to understand. He evidently had gone away from Paris and forgotten his critics for a time, or he may have been just "resting on his oars," "keeping his hand in" as painters say, while his mind was busy with some important work. The other one, no larger than the first, shows an enchanting bit of garden where Manet's brother-in-law has thrown himself upon the grass, and seated close beside him is his wife dressed in the favourite white; they are watching the baby carriage which is placed in the shadows of the trees. It is a picture full of charm and sentiment, of home life and refinement, executed with admirable skill and showing Manet's mastery of light and shade. Mr Havemeyer, who was feeling his way, also bought a flower piece, some roses in a glass vase. The colour is cool and transparent and the delicate petals tremble and quiver; one has fallen off and lies beside the vase. It is a little bit of art such as an amateur prizes as a precious thing and would not part with ever.

Nevertheless, to collect Manet, the great Manet, Manet the magician, one must not consider dimensions, must not measure canvas by the rule, but must take whatever comes forth from his workshop, must accept the creations of the master. Miss Cassatt and I helped Mr Havemeyer through the ordeal of deciding upon a large Manet by just buying the "big one" for him ourselves. On a wintry morning, during one of her very rare visits to America, Miss Cassatt and I were taking a walk together and as we passed the Durand-Ruel gallery she suggested we should drop in and see if they had received any new pictures. After greeting us, M Joseph

COLOURPLATES 61, 2, 3/4

COLOURPLATE 6

COLOURPLATE 55

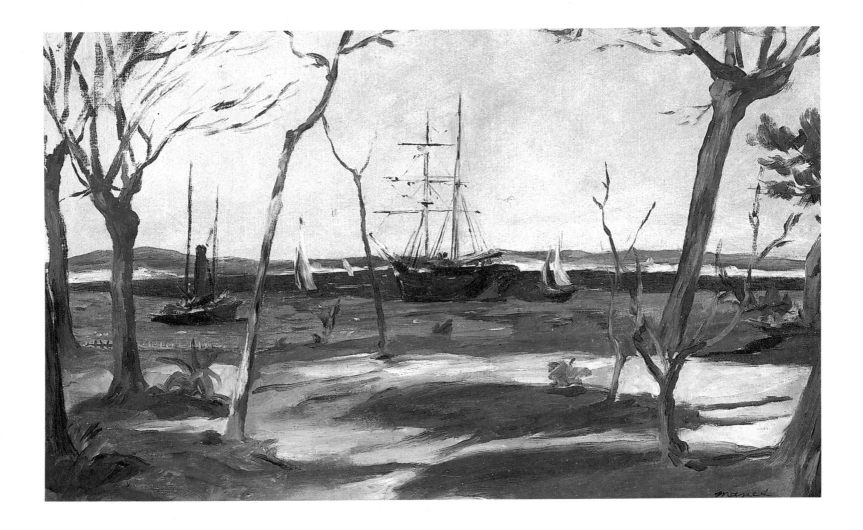

made a remark to Miss Cassatt which I did not hear, but I heard her exclaim: "What! He returned that Manet *Seascape* to buy a Whistler. Mercy sakes, what is art coming to?" and turning to me she added, "Horace W. has returned his Manet *Seascape*. Do let us go see it, for you will surely want it."

We went into the gallery and there hung Manet's *Alabama*, a superb picture which I carefully examined while Miss Cassatt related to us the exciting and interesting details about Manet's painting of the picture. "Manet was very much excited over the *Alabama* affair," she said, "and actually went to Cherbourg to paint this picture. He had scarcely finished it when the battle with the *Kearsage* took place just outside the harbour. Manet witnessed the battle and he told me it was one of the most exciting moments of his life. He had never seen a naval contest and it was a great experience for him to see the attack and sinking of the *Alabama*." With a characteristic gesture she continued, "Look at that water! Did you ever see anything so solid? You feel the weight of the ocean in it. You must buy it, my dear, Mr Havemeyer must not lose it."

I did buy it, and rather elated with my purchase, I said something that had been on my mind for many a long day. I pointed to Manet's *Espada* – the bullfighter stands in the ring holding his sword, covered with the red cape, in his hand and doffs his cap, probably to the royal family, before attacking the bull. "I think we ought to buy that picture," I said.

"Why don't you?" quietly rejoined Miss Cassatt.

"I fear Mr Havemeyer would think it too big," I answered.

"Don't be foolish," said Miss Cassatt, "It is just the size Manet wanted it, and that ought to suffice for Mr Havemeyer; besides, it is a splendid Manet, and I am sure he will like it if you buy it."

"Very well," I said, "I will buy it, and now let us go home and tell him."

The Bay of Arcachon. 1871. Foundation E.G. Bührle Collection, Zurich.

COLOURPLATE 21

COLOURPLATE 31

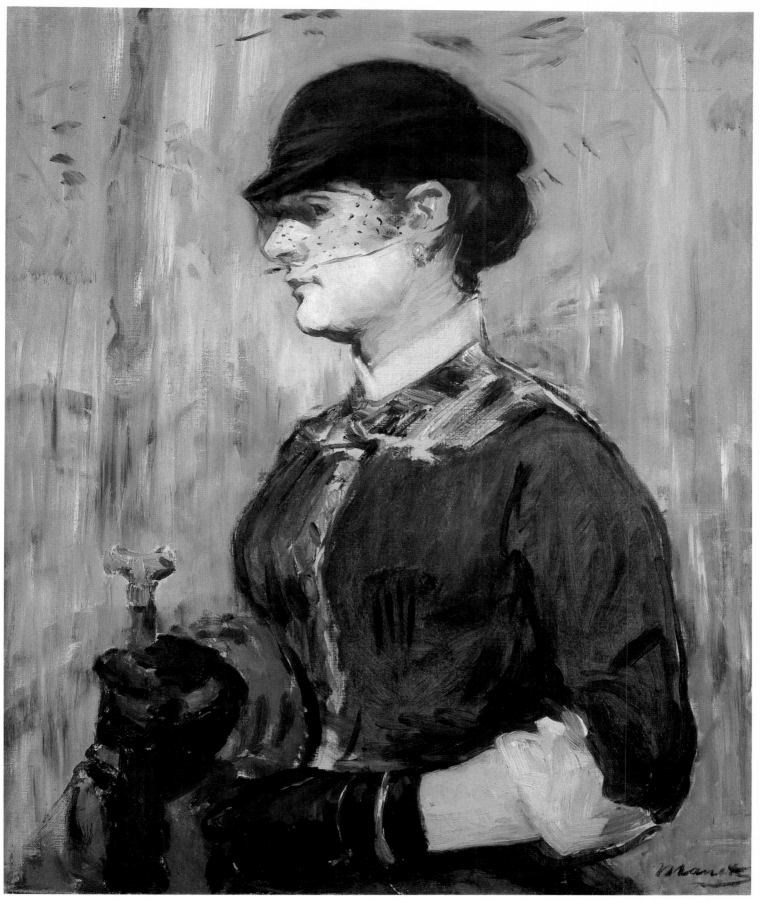

COLOURPLATE 99. *Young Woman in a Round Hat.* 1879. 22 × 18½″ (56 × 47 cm).
The Henry and Rose Pearlman Foundation, New York (Photo Metropolitan Museum).

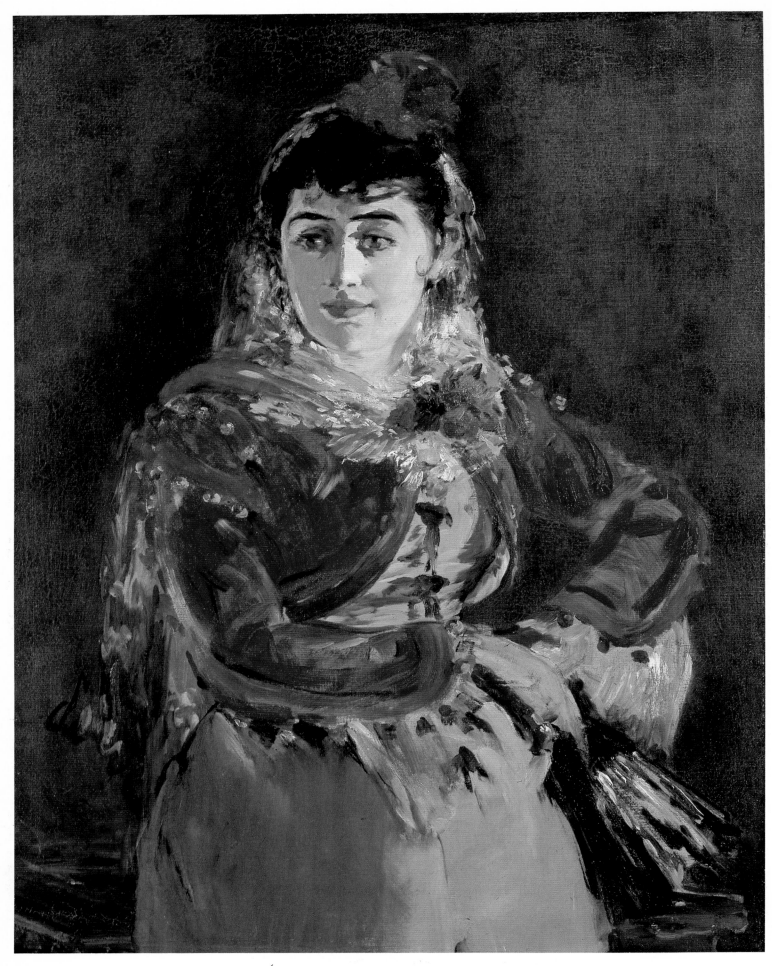

COLOURPLATE 100. *Émilie Ambre in the Role of Carmen.* 1879–80. 36 × 29″ (95 × 75 cm).
Philadelphia Museum of Art, Philadelphia (Given by Edgar Scott).

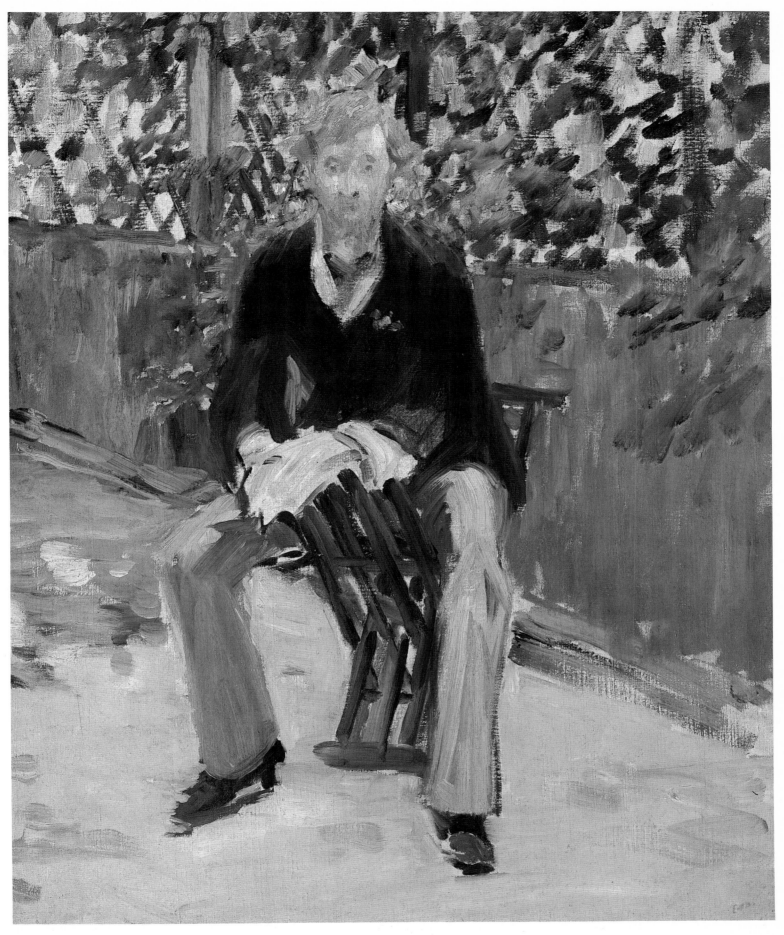

COLOURPLATE 101. *Portrait of George Moore*. 1879. 21½ × 17¾″ (55 × 46 cm).
Mr and Mrs Paul Mellon Collection, Upperville, Virginia.

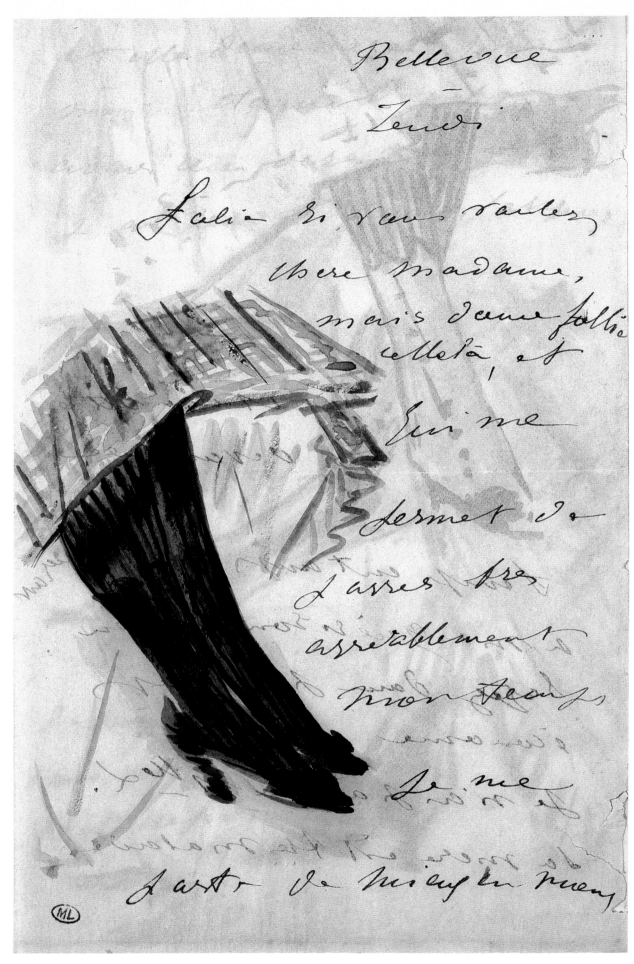

COLOURPLATE 102. *Sketches of Women's Legs*. 1880. Watercolour, in a Letter to Madame Guillemet,
page size 7¾ × 5″ (20 × 12.5 cm).
Louvre, Paris (Cabinet des Dessins).

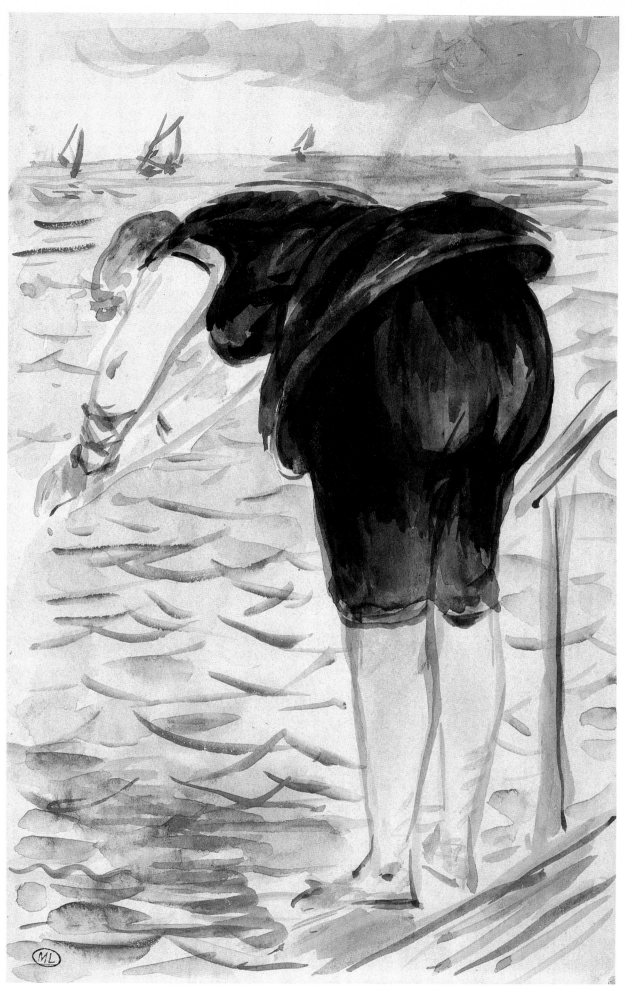

COLOURPLATE 103. *Isabelle Diving.* 1880. Watercolour in Letter, page size 7¾ × 5″ (20 × 12.5 cm).
Louvre, Paris (Cabinet des Dessins).

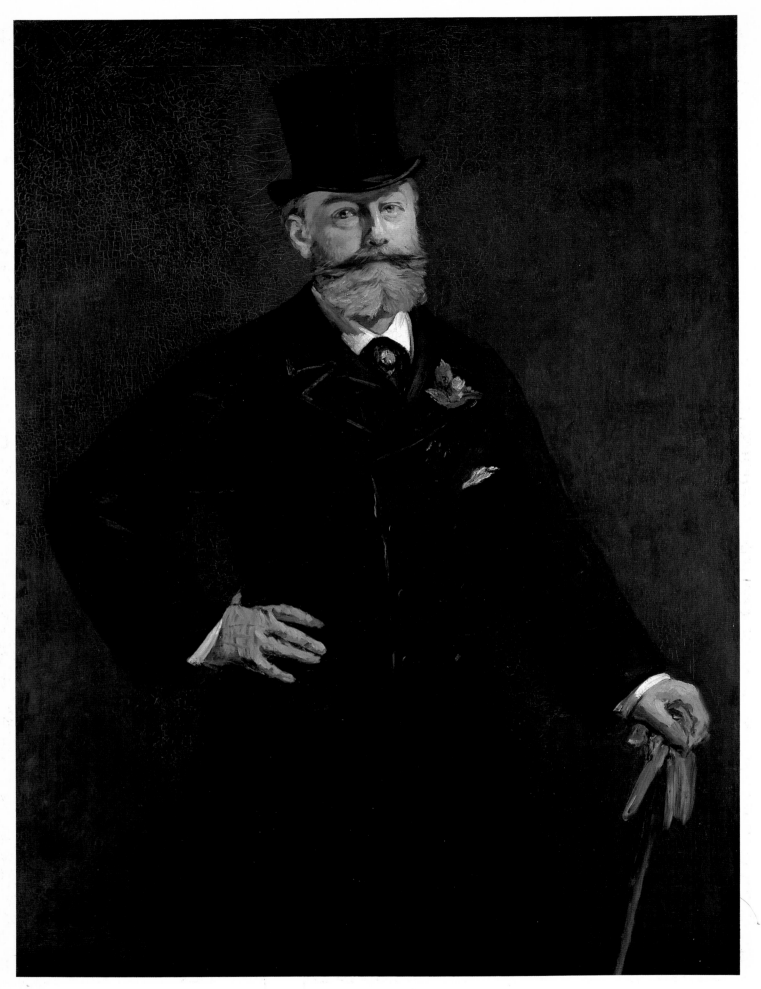

COLOURPLATE 104. *Portrait of Antonin Proust.* 1880. 51½ × 38″ (131 × 97 cm).
Toledo Museum of Art, Ohio.

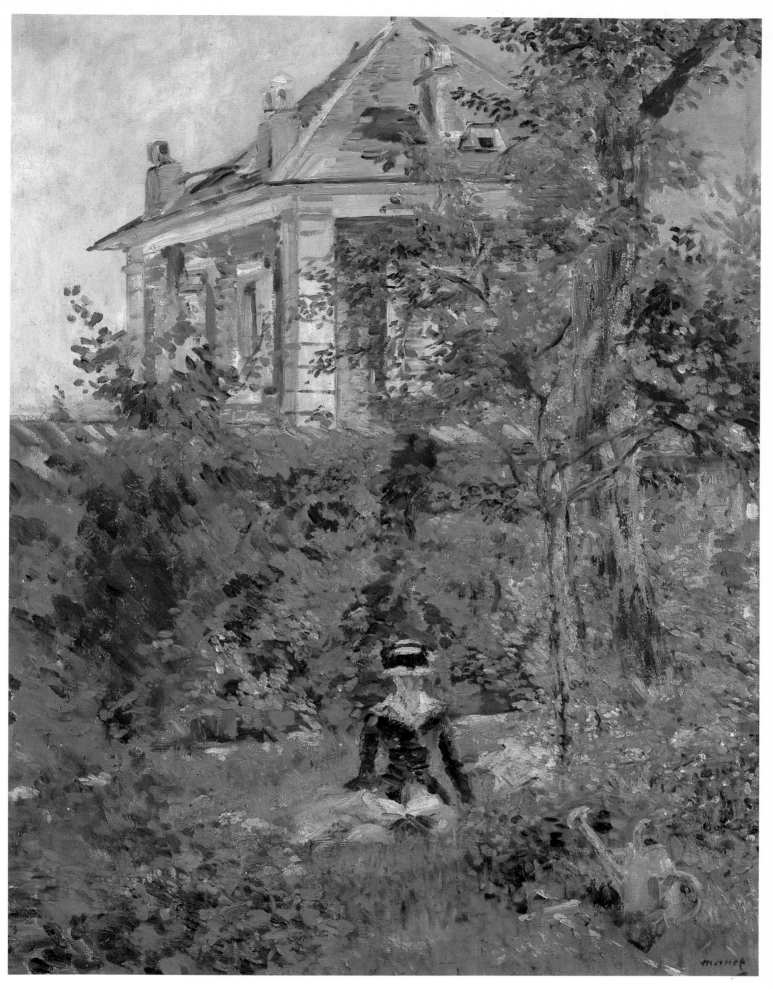

COLOURPLATE 105. *A Corner of the Garden at Bellevue (Young Girl in the Garden)*. 1880. 36¼ × 27½″
(92 × 70 cm).
Foundation E.G. Bührle Collection, Zurich.

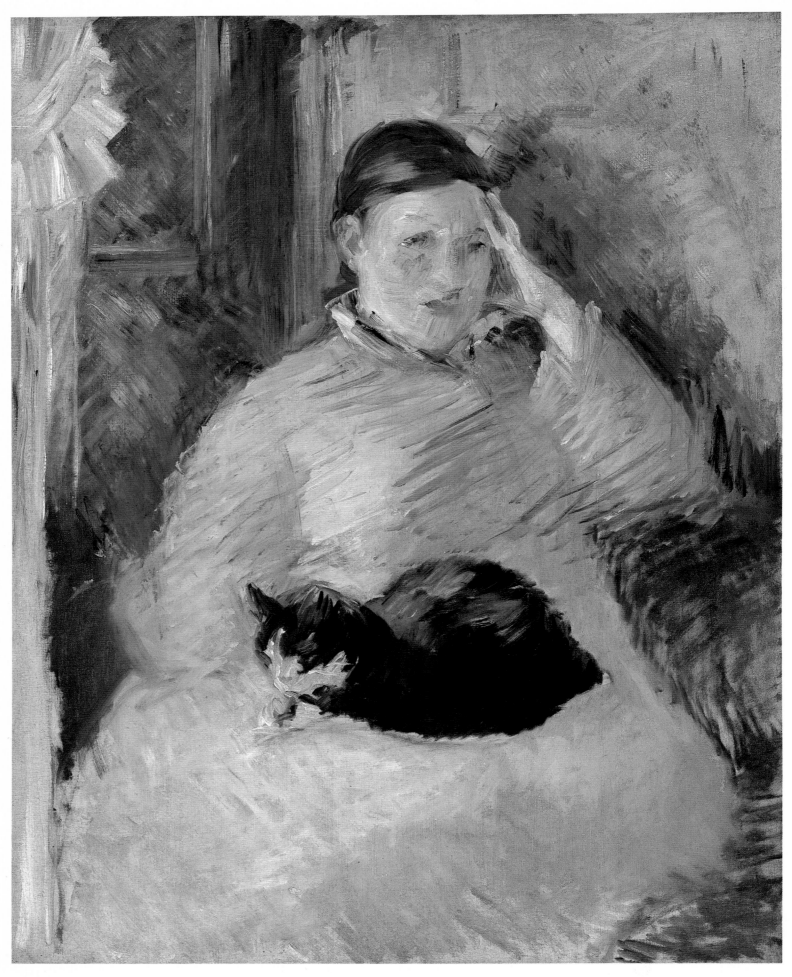

COLOURPLATE 106. *Portrait of Madame Manet (Woman with a Cat)*. 1880. 35¾ × 28¾″ (91 × 73 cm)
Tate Gallery, London.

I think we enjoyed "telling Mr Havemeyer" what we had done quite as much as we had enjoyed buying the pictures. I made a little bow and, imitating his manner, repeated the words he always said when he presented a picture to me. "Mr Havemeyer," I said, "Manet's *Bullfighter* is yours." He smiled so genially at us that Miss Cassatt said to me quickly: "What did I tell you?"

But Mr Havemeyer, not understanding what she meant, said to me: "It no doubt is a very fine picture, but now, my dear, it is up to you to hang it." Hanging it meant a lot of work which I enjoyed, but I was obliged to change many pictures.

When my husband saw how well the big Manet looked in our gallery it was not long before he bought Manet's *Majo*, a life-sized figure in a Spanish costume of the province of Catalonia. He has a pale face and brilliant black eyes; he leans upon a staff and a gorgeous red scarf is thrown over his arm. It is a strong portrait, done in Manet's most characteristic manner, and it makes a worthy pendant to the *Bullfighter*.

COLOURPLATE 12

Shortly after, Mr Havemeyer bought the most important of our large Manets. *Mlle V . . . in the Costume of an Espada.* It was painted after Manet's return from Spain, where he undoubtedly studied Velazquez, and, I believe, determined to paint a large picture of a bullfight, which project was never completely realized but to which we owe both our *Bullfighter* and *Mlle V.* This picture of Mlle V. is one of the greatest and most difficult things Manet ever did. I hesitate to describe it, for I recognize my inability to give you an adequate idea of the beauty of the picture. Mlle V. stands in the middle of the arena holding in her hand a sword over which is thrown the traditional red rag, which Manet has made as lovely a bit of colour as ever left his palette. It is well that Manet left the bull out of the picture, for were he as ferocious as any that ever came from the Andalusian hills, he would probably have crouched at the feet of this graceful *espada* and would have licked the hand of his beautiful executioner, even when she waved the bit of coloured silk which Goya never surpassed. A picador on horseback and three toreadors stand in a distant part of the arena, and give us a hint that our magician has been to the Prado and has learned more sleight of hand from the Spanish wizard of Philip's reign who painted *The Surrender of Breda* and who revealed to Manet some of the wonders of his art.

But why should I go on? I cannot with words make you see the beauties of Manet's pictures nor feel his art – only, if ever it be possible, I advise you to see and study Manet for yourself. There is a Manet you can see, for it is now in the Munich gallery. I think it is called *Luncheon in the Studio*. For many years it hung upon the walls of our gallery until one day – for some reason I never understood – Mr Havemeyer asked me if I objected to his returning it to the Durand-Ruels. I never questioned my husband's decisions, and I acquiesced, of course. Manet's still-life in the

COLOURPLATE 43

View of Arcachon in 1869.
Engraving.

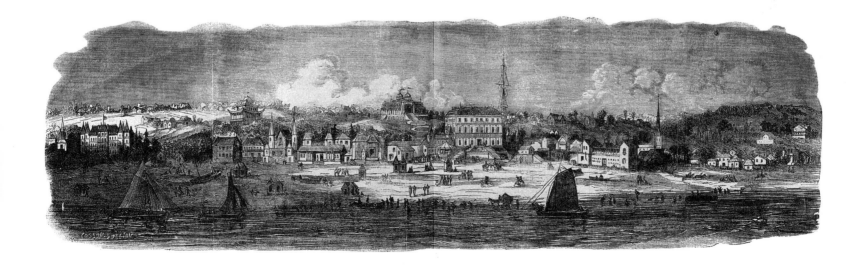

picture, and the boy with the black jacket and straw hat were lost to us forever; there was certainly nothing wrong with the black velvet jacket, but I often wished the young man in the straw hat could have been more intelligent and have made a more interesting central figure!

We soon bought another *Seascape* painted just after Manet's *Argenteuil*, COLOURPLATES 66, 65 now in the gallery in Brussels. Miss Cassatt calls it "the last word in painting" and told me that after having worked long and laboriously over the *Argenteuil* (which is about the same subject, a man in a sailing boat) Manet was keyed up with the effort and training of the other picture and accomplished this one in a couple of days; did it in a white heat, like the race horse who makes a sudden dash and wins by a length, scarcely realizing the effort it has cost him. A still more striking illustration of this concentration of an artist's powers through which he produces the chef d'oeuvre on which his fame will rest, is our *Blue Venice*, a picture which Mr COLOURPLATE 69 Havemeyer bought for me from M Durand-Ruel's private collection. In writing of this picture I must again quote Miss Cassatt who knew Manet so well and to whom he could speak of his work and its difficulties with the frankness of a fellow artist. She congratulated us when we bought this picture saying she considered it one of Manet's most brilliant works; it was so full of light and atmosphere and expressed the very soul and spirit of Venice.

"Manet told me," she said, "that he had been a long time in Venice. I believe he spent the winter there and he was thoroughly discouraged and depressed at his inability to paint anything to his satisfaction. He had just decided to give it up and return home to Paris. On his last afternoon in Venice, he took a fairly small canvas and went out on the Grand Canal just to make a sketch to recall his visit; he told me he was so pleased with the result of his afternoon's work that he decided to remain over a day and finish it. My dear," concluded Miss Cassatt, "that is the way Manet happened to paint your Venice."

Happened! Was not that a misleading word for Miss Cassatt to use? Happened! Oh no! a picture like my *Blue Venice* does not happen, it is created, created by the slow and painful struggle of production. From the moment Manet arrived in Venice every stroke he made, every touch of colour he put upon his canvas, helped to create my *Blue Venice*. Through every hour of discouragement it was incubating in the cells of his brain, and being nourished by his heartbeats and by the echoes of his sighs. Disappointment forcing him back to Paris! Oh no! it was forcing him to take that bit of canvas on that last afternoon and to go out on to the lagoon and to paint that masterpiece that had matured in his brain and was ready to come forth. He fastened his gondola to the big blue and white posts which give the name to my picture, and painted Venice as he saw it in that brilliant sparkling sunlight during the last few hours of his sojourn in the bewildering city. I think I see him painting there, wrapped in his work, forgetting how modern he is, sinking back into the centuries past as he paints the lagoons and the palaces of long ago. I think of him as he works, picturing to himself Venice in her grand old days when doges held their court in the Ducal Palace and encouraged their sculptors and painters to adorn the piazzas and the churches, giving orders for them to paint the fair women of that fair city. Who knows but that this living French modern may have evoked the shade of that modern of long ago, the shade of Veronese himself? Manet may have allowed the "father of Impressionism" in renaissance Venice to have a look over his shoulder as the blue posts and the bright waters grew upon his canvas. Surely they had much to say to each other, this patriarch of realism and the magician of the boulevards.

"Do those posts look thus to you, Father Paul?" queries the modern. "Aye, my son," answers the great Venetian, "paint them as you see them and others will learn through your eyes. I had trouble enough in my day and criticism too, mind you." Upon hearing that, the modern drops his brushes, and turning to the venerable shade says quickly: "Critics! Father

Paul, did you have critics? and in Venice long ago? Did they sit in the cafés of the piazza and cast jests at you as you passed by?" "Fie! my son" answers the shade reproachfully, "you a painter! – and mind critics! Go your way and think naught of them. A fool can criticize, it takes knowledge to appreciate," and he laughs in his shadowy beard as he adds, "I too had my critics." "But," persists the modern, thinking bitterly of the boulevards and his tormentors, "I painted a picture of a *Ball* once and painted many men in high hats, high crowns to the hats just as I saw them there myself. I did not think them strange, but you should have heard the critics!"

"I have heard them, young man," says the venerable shade. "I hear them still," and he gives a sly chuckle as he thinks of the past and continues, "there was a young man in my day who painted some Venetian ladies on the upper terraces of their palaces, whither they had gone to bleach their hair; and they wore hats without crowns, for how could they bleach their hair if the crowns remained? But the critics! Santa Maria, the critics! This young man's name was Carpaccio; did you ever hear of him or of his work?" "Yes," rejoins the modern, "we all know him, and of that picture. A critic! – think of it! a critic – calls it 'the greatest picture in the world.'" "Ha! ha! ho! ho!" laughs Father Paul, "a critic says that! a critic thinks of it; then they have learned something in 400 years, those critics; and of me, do they say aught of me?" "Oh surely, Father Paul," rejoins Manet, as flushed with enthusiasm he works more rapidly than before, "they call you the father of the modern school."

The shade of the great master gazes earnestly for a moment at the painter and his work, and then with a sigh he gently closes his eyes, and as he vanishes, Manet hears the words: "Modern! there is no modern, art is life! art is light!"

All this I seemed to see and hear as I looked at my *Blue Venice*; indeed it would take many pages to tell you the delight that picture has given me. It is just a view of the lagoon with the blue and white posts conspicuous before the palace he paints; but it satisfies you that it is the Venice you saw, the Venice you know, the Venice you would paint; and what can art do more? It inspired me once to answer a guest who asked me if I would not prefer a string of pearls to a picture. "No," I said hastily, "I prefer to have something made by a man than to have something made by an oyster." If it was a good rejoinder, I take no credit for it; it was my *Blue Venice* that fairly put the words into my mouth.

As I am not writing a biography of Manet, nor a history of his art, but am just jotting down as they occur to me, the recollections of how we acquired so many of Manet's important works, it would be almost impossible and it is not necessary for me to mention them in chronological order, for in the course of our collecting we bought early works late and late works early.

I recall that one beautiful autumn morning when Mr Havemeyer and I were enjoying the few remaining days of a visit to Paris, Miss Cassatt entered the salon and said to me: "How would you like to have a portrait of Clemenceau by Manet?"

"Let us see it, " I answered, "can we?"

"Certainly," she said, "I saw Clemenceau yesterday and he wants to sell his portrait. He says he does not like it, but I rather think he is hard up and wants some money. He really asks very little for it, only 10,000 francs. The picture is not completely finished, as you may imagine, with the combination of two such men as Clemenceau and Manet. Manet did not finish the still-life in the picture, but he had forty sittings for Clemenceau's portrait and I think it is a very fine and interesting picture."

COLOURPLATE 98

"Very well," I said, and looked at my husband who acquiesced.

We were soon at Clemenceau's home, a pretty villa out of the whirl of Paris, with an attractive garden, whence we found the fearless statesman on whose broad shoulders had fallen the burden of premiership and who carried it as intrepidly as anyone since the days of Gambetta. It was shortly before the *Agadir* incident, when Clemenceau firmly encouraged the French president to *tenir tête* with Germany, while gracefully offering "to relinquish his portfolio if he did not." At that time Clemenceau was not very grey and he still resembled his portrait; Manet had painted a very forceful Clemenceau. His black eyes look determinedly from underneath his heavy eyebrows, and his head, round and hard, appears ready to strike any other head, however round and however hard that other head might be. His arms are lightly crossed upon his chest and he plainly says: "Yes this is my attitude, what is yours?" A vigorous, middle-aged, keen, defiant Clemenceau, justly conscious of his own worth, enjoying his power, admiring his own ability, and a little, just a little, proud of his wit.

We became friendly at once. I learned that in his struggling days, when he was at odds with the French government, he had sought a home in America and had taught French for many years in a school not over a mile from our Connecticut home. He told me he did not like the portrait. "I sat for Manet many, many times," he said, "but he could never make it like me," and he took hold of the frameless portrait and swung it around to show it to us.

"I don't care for it, and would be glad to get rid of it," he continued. I thought it would be as well for the portrait to be rid of him, for he switched it about so indifferently it was a wonder he had not put a hole in it, or ruined it entirely. "Manet never finished it," said Clemenceau to Mr Havemeyer, "and yet I gave him forty sittings! just think of it, forty sittings for one portrait!" He said it contemptuously as if he could decide the fate of nations in far less time, and turning the frameless canvas with its face to the wall he said: "I shall never hang it anyway." . . .

We bought it for 10,000 francs, the price at which Clemenceau said he would sell it.

Acting upon Miss Cassatt's advice I took another stretcher and folded back that part of the canvas on which Manet had indicated the table and the still-life. This was very easy to do as the picture was oblong. No one will ever know, perhaps, unless they read these lines or someone else writes a record of the fact, that almost half of the original canvas of the Clemenceau portrait is neatly folded behind the stretcher, nor, furthermore, will they understand that it is hidden there because a great statesman and a greater painter after forty sittings could neither of them yield, and the tug of personalities prevented them from co-operating in an effort to produce a great work of art. The blood of our century beats faster and hotter than it did when Holbein painted. Our portrait of *Jean de Carondelet* which is so calm and poised, so firm and reposeful, shows the difference of temperament of the different centuries.

Besides the Clemenceau, we bought a woman's portrait in oil by Manet. It is not quite life-size, her hair is undone, she leans her cheek upon her hand and looks directly at you out of the canvas. Alas, she is not beautiful, but could Manet that master of realism make her beautiful when she was in truth ugly? Oh no, but he painted her with all his superb technique, in broad brush-strokes and with his beautiful brilliant colouring. It is a painters' portrait and is always admired by them. I have even heard it extolled as being better than *The Lady with the Parasol* which was formerly in the Faure Collection in Paris.

Manet, as well as Degas, knew the value of pastel as a medium for portrait painting. He knew what light and life it gave to flesh, and his works in pastel are among his best. Mr Havemeyer bought several of Manet's pastel portraits. One is of Guys, the caricaturist who did interesting aquarelles of many French types and who was a great friend of Manet. Later we bought many of Guy's aquarelles and drawings. Mr Havemeyer bought a portrait of *Mlle Lemonnier* which many consider Manet's greatest achievement in pastel, and indeed it seems to defy art to go further, for if he had blown those chalks on he could not have done it with a lighter touch or with greater freedom. The face is in profile, with full red lips and black hair in which is a deep red rose, and Manet has

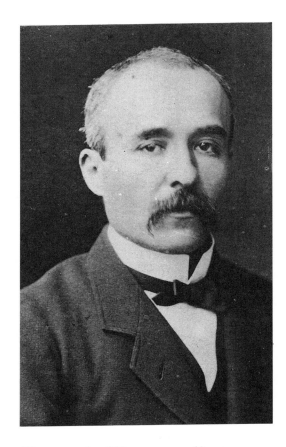

Photograph of Clemenceau (from Manet's photograph album). Bibliothèque Nationale, Paris.

COLOURPLATE 94

made her so alive that the white throat seems to palpitate and the blood to circulate freely and the breath to dilate in the nostrils. I became accustomed to the exclamations of admiration as visitors saw the portrait for the first time. By the side of this portrait hung another of Manet's pastels, the portrait of a beautiful blonde, her hair carefully arranged and with an elaborate costume of the time. Her elegance had evidently impressed Manet and it was most carefully done and highly finished, "pushed" as the painters say. It was much talked of in its day, and Madame clung to her beautiful portrait; it was only in her old age that she decided to sell it and it came into our possession. Our third and last woman's portrait is that of a young girl with a retroussé nose and with a pretty tipped bonnet, that carries out the line of the dainty nose, on her head. She is perky and jaunty in her pretty clothes. You feel she took pleasure in posing for her portrait and was quite satisfied as the youthful face developed under Manet's brilliant pastels. I admire it very much for it is full of fire and life and youthful insouciance.

By far the best known and the most amusing of all our Manet pastels is the portrait of George Moore, a one time dilettante artist and an all time writer on art. He is best known in England as an art critic but it is of his portrait I would speak. There was a French dealer with an unpretentious gallery near Montmartre, where we often went to see some of the greatest pictures of the day. Pottier was a favourite with the so-called Impressionists and we bought from him many of our important pictures. One day he came to our hotel and it was easy to see he had something important to suggest. With Miss Cassatt, we started forth to see pictures, going to a small apartment here, or a smaller one there. The owners would take down some of the finest examples of modern art and sell them to us, not so much for the price, for they were usually well-to-do, but for the love of collecting, in order to have money in hand so that at the next exposition or the next opportunity they might be able to make new purchases and again astonish their neighbours with their judgement in art. I think it was on that very afternoon that Pottier took us to see the *Stonebreakers* which Mr Havemeyer tried to buy; but its owner, a blacksmith, did not care to sell. I recall that we went to the home of a dentist and bought two superb Degas's and as we left the apartment Pottier said to us that he knew of a very fine portrait by Manet which he thought might be bought, but that it would be very dear – very dear, he repeated, evidently fearful of the price the owner might ask for his picture. "It is a wonderful portrait," he said, "a wonderful portrait of a very ugly man."

"Whose portrait is it?" asked Mr Havemeyer.

"George Moore's," answered Pottier.

"George Moore!" exclaimed Miss Cassatt. "Can Manet's *George Moore* be had? Let us see it by all means," and while we drove to a distant part of Paris, into one of its pretty suburbs filled with homelike villas, Miss Cassatt told us of George Moore and of Manet's painting the portrait.

"George Moore," she said, "painted a little, he went to his friends, he even boasted to me, that Manet had invited him to come to work in his studio. I was surprised at Manet's doing such a thing, but when I saw the portrait I understood it all. While George Moore was studying in Manet's studio, Manet was studying George Moore and painting a portrait of him, and it was one of the finest portraits he ever did. He did George Moore for all time," said Miss Cassatt. "Of course, George Moore did not like it and said horrid things about it to me. I suppose George Moore sold it?" she asked turning to Pottier.

"Yes, it is here," answered Pottier as we drew up before an attractive house. "I think the parties will sell," he added in a low voice as we were ushered into the apartment, "but at a price."

We entered and among other fine pictures we saw George Moore's portrait. He certainly was not handsome, but all Manet's art was in it: it was the very epitome of characterization, the *ne plus ultra* of elimination.

There was nothing upon the canvas but just the body and soul of George Moore laid bare, divested of all his self-complacency, of all his effort to produce effect. It could be none other but George Moore, for it suggested no other human being you had ever seen or could conjure up. No one ever had such hair; no eyes looked like his as they sought to see the hair above and dispute the superior right of the eyebrows; nose, mouth and chin fitted into the amusing oval. That was what we saw – a few features revealing to us all there was to know of George Moore. The jacket could be his only, no other would have worn it, and so was the cravat, it belonged to him just as much as did his hair or his eyes. With a vision as penetrating as Velazquez's, Manet had taken the features of George Moore and trans-fixed them forever upon canvas, using a little coloured powder mixed with transcendent art. We looked at it long and silently, then Mr Havemeyer turned suddenly toward Pottier and said:

"You say it is dear? How much do they ask for it?"

"10,000 francs," replied Pottier with a doleful shake of his head.

"We will take it," said Mr Havemeyer decidedly, and the affair was concluded.

If it is any consolation, George Moore may know that his portrait attracted more attention than any Manet in our gallery. I grew accustomed to the exclamations I would hear as soon as visitors saw it. "Is that the *George Moore* by Manet?" cautiously asked the amateur who had heard of it "somewhere." "That is Manet's *George Moore*," remarked the critic, who had heard much of it. "*George Moore!*" ejaculated the painter who knew it well. "Hello! Manet's *George Moore* as I live," said the Frenchman almost to himself as he looked at it. Manet's genius had even enveloped the canvas, for he made every observer throw more light upon the character of his portrait, through the tone of his voice or by the exclamations he made. I never met, I never saw George Moore, but I learned many things about him from the remarks of those who knew him well. The echo of raillery and laughter in the casual observations made me certain that Manet's portrait was considered a huge joke on George Moore; what was amusing was that he had sold it and it would forever be on view, and George Moore would have to abide by it as a portrait of himself. Would the portrait live through George Moore, or George Moore through the portrait? That was the question that caused a laugh whenever it was raised; would it be George Moore's Manet or Manet's *George Moore*? If ever I made a catalogue, should the name of George Moore be in big black letters and Manet's name in little diamond, or should Manet have the black letters and the name of George Moore be in little script? What shall I do? Will George Moore come to my gallery some day and give me his opinion of Manet and the relative merits of painter and sitter? Or will the great Judge, who sits with his hourglass in his hand in the court of courts, pass judgement upon it and determine which name shall outlive the other?

* * *

With *George Moore* ends the list of our Manet pastels, and to complete the list of oils I have only to mention two more paintings well known to anyone acquainted with Manet's works: his *Dead Christ with Angels* and his *Gare St. Lazare*. I persuaded Mr Havemeyer to buy the *Dead Christ with Angels* because it went begging both here and abroad. I have said it and I repeat it, it went begging, and let the public galleries explain it if they can, for if ever there was a museum Manet, it seems to me it is his *Dead Christ with Angels*. Long afterward the Louvre bought Manet's *Olympia*, which had I been a little more persistent, they would have lost; at that time Manet's *Dead Christ* was no longer in the market. When my husband bought it, I knew it was not suitable for our gallery but I felt if it once left our shores it would never return to America, so to please me Mr

Havemeyer bought it, saying as he gave it to me: "I really do not know what you will do with it." I hung it in various places in our home, but I found it crushed everything beside it and crushed me as well. Finally I concluded it would be impossible to live with that mighty picture, to look day after day upon the Christ supported by these pitying angels, to gaze upon the Redeemer offering the sacrifice of Gethsemane for the salvation of mankind. For several years I put it away, but after my husband's death, when Manet was better understood, I sent it to the Metropolitan Museum, where it hangs beside the Manet Mr Havemeyer saw and rejected because it was "too much for him," the splendid *Boy with a Sword*.

The *Gare St. Lazare* Mr Havemeyer bought to please himself, for the painter had become an open book to my husband and he recognized the *Gare St. Lazare* as one of Manet's finest achievements, the ripened fruit after many years of growth, when, as Frenchmen say, he had "found his way." Although he still clings to his straight and narrow path, he has a complete grasp of his method, he knows his technique and models in light as few have ever done before him; he has that greatest of all qualities in a painter, a marvellous vision that reveals to him nature as she is and places him among the great names of all times. We see in the *Gare St. Lazare* a very rift in nature. It is as realistic as any picture Manet ever painted. A little child, a very human little girl, returning from the park on a warm afternoon is attracted, as children always are, by the mysterious steam engine that blows shrill whistles from nowhere and rings bells without human hands. She peers through the railings of the gare St. Lazare to see the black smoke that trails above the tracks and disappears under the bridge beyond. Too interested to feel tired, she stands lightly against the rail and is unconscious that her mother, probably fatigued with her afternoon in the Tuileries, has sunk upon the stone curb of the railing and rests there, quietly waiting with her dog upon her arm. We see only the back of the child; her dress is not pretty, her hair is not fluffy but is drawn up on the top of her head and held back from her temples by a black comb; her little hands grasp the iron rails and she does not care a fig for anyone, will not even turn her head that we may see her face, nor pose in the pretty way children are supposed to do when sitting for their portraits. She is just a natural little girl, doing just what a little girl naturally would do when she found herself beside the big gare St. Lazare where the trains were rushing in and out – she looks and looks and looks. You say, and many others say: "That is not a painting! How could anyone in their senses paint a child and turn her back towards us?" Probably no one else, in or out of his senses, but Manet could, and thereby he proves that he had more sense than others. He had the sense of fine perception, the sense of reasoning vision which saw the results, and the conviction that he could express it. He concentrated all his art, all his ability, on that which he wished to paint and was still able – what a gift to a painter – to eliminate all unnecessary details. No wonder he was so little understood by his contemporaries, who failing to understand made bold to jeer, while Manet putting his hands in his pockets nonchalantly walked the boulevards, listening to tattling critics and occasionally permitting himself the consolation of repeating to them: "Nevertheless, some day it will hang in the Louvre."

You ask me how we could have bought such a portrait? How we could have disregarded the silk stockings, the satin slippers, the best frock, the tortured hair, or the pretty bow? And again you ask, is that a portrait, what is the attraction in it, what made us want to possess it? What caused us to forgive Manet that we should never see the child's face? You ask why we paid for iron rails and steam engines we barely see? You tell us that the child is not even pretty and that the mother is positively ugly – only Manet's model in another dress – that even the doggie is unattractive, and you long to know why we put so much money into such a picture, when we might have had a gorgeous academic, an imposing English portrait, or some splendid Eastern scene, for the same price.

I answer art, art, art. It is there appealing to you, as it appealed to us. You must feel it. You must hear the voice calling to you, you must respond to the vibrations Manet felt, which made his heart throb and filled his brain, which stirred his emotions and sharpened his vision as he put his brush upon the canvas. Art, art, art, I say; you must try to see with Manet's eyes and comprehend how he can make a chef d'oeuvre out of a homely story, or how others make a great symphony out of a simple melody. When Beethoven lifts our very souls on the wings of his compositions, we are not concerned about his chords and their resolutions, and care little whether the wood and wind are blown or beaten or whether the violins are held against the shoulders or grasped between the knees. We are listening to the message, and art is the interpreter. The *Gare St. Lazare* appeals to our inherent love of truth, and we look at the picture again and again because it might be our child, nay, it might even be ourselves when we were children, clinging to those rails and looking with the same interest on the busy scene below. It tells us of childhood – of all childhood – not only in Paris by the gare St. Lazare, but of any city where children exist and railway stations can be seen. And then the execution of it! Where in art will you find a curve like the one which outlines the dress upon the child's shoulders, or see such light as that which creeps up to the yellow hair and models the lovely neck? Look at the pose of the head, the movement of the arm, the way the flesh of the little hand is pressed against the iron rail, see how atmosphere and light envelop the two figures and give distance to the scene below. Finally, notice the colour! Did you ever see anything more beautiful and harmonious? Notice all these things and many more and do not ask me why we bought the *Gare St. Lazare* – the picture of a little girl who refuses to be seen and turns her back upon us. We bought it because we thought it a great picture and one of Manet's best. I cannot look upon it, without thinking of the lines of another great modern:

> But each for the joy of the working, and each,
>   in his separate star.
> Shall draw the Thing as he sees It for the God
>   of Things as They are.

CLEMENT GREENBERG

ART FORUM

"Manet as an artist exceptional in his inconsistency"

January 1967

Clement Greenberg (b. 1909), American critic and art historian, perhaps best known for his writings on American Abstract Expressionism during the 1950s and 1960s. For Manet's response to nineteenth-century accusations of "inconsistency" see page 264.

Manet is far from being the only master who doesn't develop in a straight line, with one step following the other in readily intelligible order. Nor is he the only master whose total body of work doesn't make a coherent impression. But he is exceptional in his *inconsistency*. I don't mean the inconsistency of his quality. He is uneven, but less so than Renoir or Monet. I mean the inconsistency of his approach and of his direction. That is what struck me particularly at the large Manet show in the Philadelphia Museum of Art.

In one and the same year, 1862, Manet painted a picture like *Young Woman Reclining in Spanish Costume* and a picture like *Gypsy with a Cigarette*; the first, with its undulations of plum and silvery little gleams of bright

COLOURPLATES 17, 8

color, is a masterpiece; the showy brushing and illustrativeness of the second anticipate present-day magazine art. So in its own way does *Emilie Ambre in the Role of Carmen* of 1879-80, with its overdone highlights. But all three of these pictures are *well* painted. *Portrait of a Man* (1860), though it has real character, and *Angelina* (1865) are not; it is hard to believe that their spindly drawing and opaque modelling came from the same hand that did the beautifully sleek *Dead Torero* of 1864; they seem much more related to the black paintings Cézanne was doing in those same years. The only other places where I can see Manet having equal trouble with his drawing are in some of his backgrounds of the same period and in his etchings (he did not handle an etching needle with the same ease that he did a brush or pencil).

COLOURPLATE 100

COLOURPLATE 20

Elsewhere, Manet's inconsistency has much more to do with what I would call, for lack of a better word, his orientation than with his taste or manner of painting. It is not that he dealt with a tremendous variety of subjects or tried different paint techniques. It is that he so often changed his notion of what a picture should be: built-up, put-together, and "composed," or random and informal, studied or spontaneous, intimate and subdued or grand and imposing. All through the 1860s he kept one eye on the Old Masters, but it was an eye that wavered. *Déjeuner sur L'Herbe* (1863), though its layout comes from Florence, goes toward Venice; *Olympia* (likewise 1863), with an arrangement that comes from Venice, goes toward Florence.

COLOURPLATES 18, 14

Yet Manet's best years were just those, the 1860s, in which he was most inconsistent. After the middle of the 1870s his approach becomes a little more settled, to some extent no doubt under the influence of the Impressionists. But it was no gain. His handling turned lighter and fluffier; he did some wonderful things with this handling, new things, but many of them represent a lowering of level. The pastel *Man with a Round Hat* and the very thinly painted *Young Woman* (both dating from around 1879) are perfect in their different ways but they, too, predict some of the banal and slick art of later times.

COLOURPLATE 86

Manet's case makes it quite clear that consistency is not an artistic virtue in itself. It did not keep him, any more than his prodigious skill with the brush did, from creating great works of art that are not *tours de force* and have nothing to do with virtuosity. Nevertheless, his inconsistency does seem to offer an obstacle to many people. They find it difficult to get his art into clear focus. It's their own fault, of course, more than it is Manet's. One looks at one picture at a time, one looks at single works, not at a whole *oeuvre*. Or rather, one should.

Manet's inconsistency can be attributed more to his plight as the first modernist painter than to his temperament. The question of what you were supposed to paint, and with what intentions, was still wide open when he came on the scene. He was not the one to settle it – that was left to the Impressionists, who took their cue from Corot more than from anyone else. Unlike Corot, Manet had conventional ambitions and wanted to shine in the Salons. He painted in the new and startling way that he did simply – and yet not so simply – because he wanted to get away from the "stews and gravies" (his own words) of orthodox painting in his time, with the black, brown, and grey murk of its close shading and shadowy backgrounds. He filled his own pictures with blacks, greys, and browns, but the blacks were usually local colors, and he gave the greys that he shaded with, and the occasional browns, a particularity and clarity like that of local color. That is, they no longer remained neutral. Manet was able to achieve this because of the new, syncopated kind of shading-modeling that he adopted. This kind of shading was not entirely new; there were precedents, among them the very recent one of photography. In frontally lit photographs especially, the shading becomes compact and patch-like because it skips so many of the intermediate gradations of light-and-dark value that the sculpturally oriented painting of the Renaissance tradition contrived to see. By being juxtaposed more abruptly, without gradual transitions and blurrings, the different shading tones of grey or brown are allowed to come through as particularized colors in their own right. This has the effect, in turn, of letting the local colors that the greys or browns shade come through more purely – which means more flatly. For the sake of luminousness Manet was willing to accept this flatness (Courbet reproached him for it by saying that *Olympia* looked like a playing card – the "Queen of Spades coming out of her bath"). The Pre-Raphaelites, too, had wanted to do brighter pictures, but were unwilling to accept flatness, and so they had imposed detailed shading on their heightened color, imitating the Quattrocento Italians. But whereas the latter could get away with it because in their time and place they could get away with anything that served to increase the sculptural realism of their art, the Pre-Raphaelites could not. Their timidity in the face of the tradition of sculptural illusion led them into what proved to be a blunder of taste more than anything else. (A decade separated the beginnings of Pre-Raphaelitism [1848] from Manet's own beginnings, but the difference between them in artistic culture seems more like an aeon.)

Manet learned a lot about syncopated modeling from his teacher, the much-maligned Couture (who had an influence on Homer and Eakins as well). Couture had his own glimmer of the new, and there are unconventionally sharp contrasts of light and dark, black and white in his more informal paintings. But he acted on his glimmer half-heartedly, confining its expression to his smallest and least ambitious works. Manet himself seems to have been harassed by the question of the difference between ambitious and unambitious efforts. During the first years of his artistic maturity he continued to believe, apparently, that a "machine," a picture big enough in size and complicated enough in subject and composition, was what a painter had to prove himself with. But composition in the accepted sense posed a strong illusion of relief or else of quasi-theatrical space. Both of these were denied to him by his flat handling. He had trouble always in managing the transition from foreground to middle- and background when the foreground was occupied by one or more figures of any size. (That its background falls away hurts *Déjeuner sur L'Herbe* which would have profited by having its canvas cut down at the top and sides.)

All through the 1860s it was as though each picture (save for the still lifes and the seascapes) confronted Manet with a new problem. It was as though he could accumulate nothing from experience. But this, precisely, worked to keep his art so fresh during that time. Each painting was a one-time thing, a new start, and by the same token completely individual. Nothing could have been more different from the way in which most of the Impressionists, and Cézanne and Van Gogh too, went from one day to the next in their work. Their pictures tended to take their places in a sequence, like so many steps in the solution of a single set of problems. This by no means renders their art inferior to Manet's but it does tend to make their pictures less markedly individual among themselves, less markedly individual in the context, that is, of the given artist's *oeuvre*. (This is the way it is, too, with the Classical Cubist works of Picasso, Leger, and Braque; but it is not that way, for the most part, with Matisse's paintings.)

Manet's still lifes and seascapes show a greater consistency of approach, as well as a steadier level of quality, than anything else in the total body of his works in oil. When it came to dealing with fruit and flowers and fish his qualms about composing disappeared. Actually, he handled still life a little more traditionally than he did other kinds of subject; or rather the absence of close modeling was less conspicuous within a small compass than within a large one. And in his seascapes the very nature of the subject relieved him automatically of "problems of composition" by offering him the simplicity of a single broad plane tilted against the vertical one of the sky and punctuated by relatively few three-dimensional objects. (It was the same, for that matter, with an

The American painters Winslow Homer (1836–1910) and Thomas Eakins (1844–1916).

Vincent van Gogh (1853–90).

Pablo Picasso (1881–1973).
Fernand Léger (1881–1955).

outdoor subject that contained a large enough expanse of greensward.)
Manet could have played it safe by confining himself to still lifes and
seascapes. But had he done so he would have amounted to no more than a
superior Fantin-Latour or Boudin. That would still have been a lot; it
would in fact have been immense, but it wouldn't have been enough to
compensate for the non-existence of paintings like *Olympia*, the *Luncheon* of
1868-9, *The Fifer* of 1866, the *Bon Bock* of 1873, the *Bar at the Folies-Bergère* of
1882, and more than a few others. . . .

Eugène Boudin (1825–1908), French painter.

COLOURPLATES 32, 54, 117

HANS HAACKE

MANET-PROJEKT '74

1974

*Hans Haacke (b. 1936), German artist. The
"Manet–Projekt '74" consisted of ten panels
of German text, nine of which included a
portrait of the person under discussion.*

PROJEKT '74 was an exhibition billed as representing "aspects of international art at the beginning of the seventies." It was staged in the summer of
1974 by the Wallraf-Richartz-Museum in Cologne (now Wallraf-Richartz-
Museum/Museum Ludwig), on the occasion of its 150th anniversary. The
exhibition reportedly cost more than $300,000. It was promoted with the
slogan, "Art Remains Art." The Cologne Kunsthalle (like the museum, a
city institution) and the local Kunstverein (a private institution with sub-
sidies from the city) joined the Wallraf-Richartz-Museum in presenting this
exhibition.

Invited to participate in the exhibition, Haacke submitted a general
outline for a new work:

Manet's Bunch of Asparagus *of 1880, collection Wallraf-Richartz-Museum, is on a
studio easel in an approx. 6 × 8 meter room of* PROJEKT *'74. Panels on the walls
present the social and economic position of the persons who have owned the painting over
the years and the prices paid for it.*

Dr. Evelyn Weiss, the modern art curator of the Wallraf-Richartz-
Museum (1986, senior curator and deputy director of the Museum
Ludwig) and one of six members of the *PROJEKT '74* organizing team,
responded that this plan was "one of the best projects submitted," but that
it could not be executed in the exhibition or printed in the catalogue.

This decision was reached in what was described as a "democratic vote"
by the organizing team; the vote was three to three. Voting for the work's
exhibition were Dr. Evelyn Weiss; Dr. Manfred Schneckenburger, then
director of the Kunsthalle (organizer of *Documenta* in 1977 and 1987); and
Dr. Wulf Herzongenrath, director of the Kunstverein. The votes against
the work were cast by Dr. Horst Keller, director of the Wallraf-Richartz-
Museum (now retired); Dr. Albert Schug, the museum's librarian; and Dr.
Dieter Ronte, the personal aide of Prof. Dr. Gert von der Osten, who was
head of all Cologne municipal museums and co-director of the Wallraf-
Richartz-Museum until his retirement in 1975 (Ronte is the director of the
Museum of Modern Art, Vienna, since 1979). With the exception of the
director of the private Kunstverein, all team members were subordinates
of Prof. von der Osten.

Dr. Keller objected to listing Hermann J. Abs' nineteen positions on
boards of directors. Information about his social and economic standing
was provided in the work because, in his capacity as chairman, he represented the Wallraf-Richartz-Kuratorium (Association of the Friends of the
Museum), when it acquired the Manet painting. In a letter to the artist, Dr.

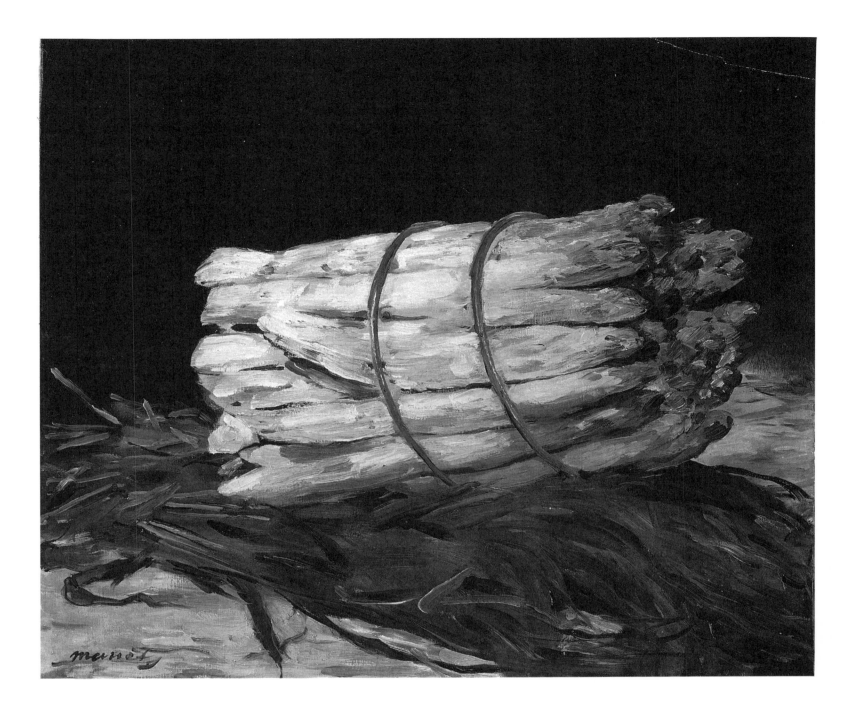

Keller elaborated on his position. After explaining that the museum, although financially carried by the city and the state, depends on private donations for major acquisitions, he continued:

It would mean giving an absolutely inadequate evaluation of the spiritual initiative of a man if one were to relate in any way the host of offices he holds in totally different walks of life with such an idealistic engagement . . . A grateful museum, however, and a grateful city, or one ready to be moved to gratefulness, must protect initiatives of such an extraordinary character from any other interpretation which might later throw even the slightest shadow on it . . .

He also remarked,

A museum knows nothing about economic power; it does indeed, however, know something about spiritual power.

Dr. Keller and Prof. von der Osten never saw or showed any interest in seeing the work before they rejected it. Instead, on July 4, the day of the press opening of *PROJEKT '74*, Manet-*PROJEKT '74* went on exhibition at Galerie Paul Maenz in Cologne, with a full-size colour reproduction in place of the original *Bunch of Asparagus*.

A Bunch of Asparagus. c. 1880. 17¼ × 21¼″ (44 × 54 cm). Wallraf-Richartz Museum, Cologne.

Daniel Buren incorporated in his own work in *PROJEKT '74* a scaled-down facsimile of *Manet-PROJEKT '74*, which Haacke had provided at his request. He also attached to it a poster entitled, "Art Remains Politics" – referring to the exhibition's official slogan, "Art Remains Art" – with an excerpt from "Limites Critiques," an essay Buren had written in 1970:

. . . Art, whatever else it may be, is exclusively political. What is called for is the analysis of formal and cultural limits (and not one or the other) within which art exists and struggles. These limits are many and of different intensities. Although the prevailing ideology and the associated artists try in every way to camouflage them, and although it is too early – the conditions are not met – to blow them up, the time has come to unveil them.

On the morning after the opening, Prof. von der Osten had those parts of Buren's work which had been provided by Haacke (including a colour reproduction of the Manet still life) pasted over with double layers of white paper.

Several artists, among them Antonio Diaz, Frank Gillette, and Newton and Helen Harrison, temporarily or permanently closed down their works in protest. Carl Andre, Robert Filliou, and Sol LeWitt had previously withdrawn from the exhibition, after hearing that *Manet-PROJEKT '74* would not be admitted.

In response to a question by Prof. Carl R. Baldwin, who was preparing an article on the incident for *Art in America*, Dr. Keller wrote in a letter of September 25, 1974: "In any event, it is not an uncommon practice for a museum to paste over an artist's work, when an artist has expressly disregarded an agreement previously reached with a museum . . ."

Hermann J. Abs, still an honorary president and member of the Deutsche Bank's advisory board, has lately represented German interests at international art auctions. In 1983, he successfully bid for an old German illuminated manuscript, the Gospels of Henry the Lion, at Sotheby Parke-Bernet in London. The manuscript was acquired by the German consortium for $11.7 million.

In 1982, Abs was appointed by Pope John Paul II to the advisory board of the Institute of Religious Works, the agency that manages the Vatican's finances. The appointment drew strong protests and an immediate call for Abs' resignation by the Simon Wiesenthal Center at Yeshiva University in Los Angeles.

Bunch of Asparagus 1880 PAINTED BY ÉDOUARD MANET

Lived from 1832 to 1883 in Paris. Descendant of a well-to-do Catholic family of the French bourgeoisie. Father, Auguste Manet, lawyer, chief of personnel at Ministry of Justice, later judge (*magistrat*) at the Cour d'appel de Paris (court of appeals). Republican. Knight of the Legion of Honor. Grandfather, Clément Manet, mayor of Gennevilliers, on the Seine, near Paris. Family owns 133-acre farm there. Mother, Eugénie-Désirée Fournier, daughter of French diplomat who managed the election of Marshall Bernadotte to the Swedish throne. Charles XIV of Sweden, her godfather. Her brother, Clément Fournier, colonel in the artillery. Resigned during revolution, 1848. Two brothers of Manet in the civil service.

Manet attends renowned Collège Rollin (with Antonin Proust, later politician and writer). Goes to sea for a short while, contrary to his father's wish for law studies. Fails entrance exam for École Navale (Naval Academy). 1850–56, studies art in private atelier of Thomas Couture, a successful salon painter. Travels to Italy, Germany, Austria, Switzerland, Belgium, Holland, Spain.

Financially independent of the sale of his paintings. Lives in richly furnished Parisian houses, with servants. Exhibits since 1861 at the Salon and in private art galleries with uneven success. 1863, participation in the

"Salon des Refusés" (Salon of the Rejected). Paintings are attacked by establishment critics for their offenses against convention. Support from Zola, Mallarmé and Bertaud.

After the death of his father in 1863, marries Suzanne Leenhoff. She is his former piano teacher, daughter of a Dutch musician. Her son, Léon-Edouard Köella, born 1852, is Manet's illegitimate child; adopted by Manet.

1867, in protest against conservative jury, exhibits fifty paintings in a pavilion specially constructed at his own expense for 18,000 francs on the grounds of the Marquis de Pomereu, near the Exposition Universelle in Paris. Followers among younger, especially impressionist artists.

As a national guardsman, participates in the defense of Paris during the Franco-Prussian War, 1870. Messenger for the regimental staff. During the Paris Commune with his family in southern France. Antiroyalist. Admirer of the Republican Léon Gambetta, the future prime minister.

1871, the art dealer Durand-Ruel, a friend of impressionist painting, buys a great number of his works. Meets with the approval of circles of Parisian society that are open to artistic innovation. Numerous commissions of portraits. Wins second-class medal at the Salon, 1881. At the suggestion of Antonin Proust, appointed Knight of the Legion of Honor.

During his fatal illness, treated by former physician of Napoleon III.

1883, memorial exhibition at the École des Beaux-Arts, Paris. Preface to catalogue by Émile Zola. Proceeds of sales for heirs, 116,637 francs.

Bunch of Asparagus 1880 FOR 800 FRANCS ACQUIRED BY CHARLES ÉPHRUSSI

Born 1849 in Odessa, dies 1905 in Paris. Descendant of Jewish family of bankers with banks in Odessa, Vienna, Paris. Family relations to French high finance (Baron de Reinach, Baron de Rothschild).

Studies in Odessa and Vienna. 1871, moves to Paris.

Own banking activities. Art historical writings about Albrecht Dürer, Jacopo de Barbarij, Paul Baudry, etc. 1875, works for *Gazette des Beaux-Arts*; 1885, co-owner; 1894, publisher.

Member of numerous cultural committees and salons of Parisian society. With Gustave Dreyfus, the Comtesse Greffulhe, and Princess Mathilde, organizes art exhibitions and concerts of the works of Richard Wagner, among others. Second model for Marcel Proust's Swann.

Collector of works from the Renaissance, the eighteenth century, and contemporary painters, plus works by Albrecht Dürer and East Asian art. Instead of paying Manet 800 francs for *Bunch of Asparagus* as agreed upon, he pays 1000 francs. To show his gratitude, Manet sends him the still life of a single asparagus (1880, oil on canvas, 6½ × 8½″, Paris, Musée de l'Impressionisme) with a note: "Your bunch was one short."

Knight (1881), officer (1903) in the Legion of Honor.

Bunch of Asparagus BETWEEN 1900 AND 1902 ACQUIRED BY ALEXANDRE ROSENBERG

Born about 1850 in Pressburg (Bratislava), dies 1913 in Paris. Descendant of a Jewish family from Bohemia.

Emigrates to Paris at the age of nine. 1870, founds a firm dealing with antiques and fine art.

1878, marries Mathilde Jellineck of a Viennese family. They have three sons and one daughter.

After his death in 1913, continuation of the firm by his youngest son, Paul, born 1881 in Paris. Specialization in the art of the nineteenth and twentieth centuries. 1940, moves to New York. At present, Paul Rosenberg & Co. in New York, headed by Alexandre Rosenberg, a grandson.

Bunch of Asparagus AS OF UNKNOWN DATE OWNED BY OR ON CONSIGNMENT WITH PAUL CASSIRER

Born 1871 in Görlitz, commits suicide 1926 in Berlin. Descendant of well-to-do Jewish family. Father, Louis Cassirer, with two sons, founder of firm Dr. Cassirer & Co., Kabelwerke (cable factory) in Berlin. Brother, Prof. Richard Cassirer, neurologist in Berlin. Cousin, Prof. Ernst Cassirer, renowned philosopher.

Studies art history in Munich. One of the editors of *Simplizissimus*. Own writings.

1898, with his cousin, Bruno Cassirer, founder of publishing house and art gallery in Berlin. 1901, partnership dissolved. Continues Kunstsalon Paul Cassirer (gallery), Victoriastrasse 35, in wealthy section of Berlin.

Opponent, along with "Berliner Sezession" (association of artists), of official art of the court. Despite the kaiser's indignation, supports French Impressionism through publications and art dealing. Close relation to Parisian art dealer Durand-Ruel. Promotes German painters Trübner, Liebermann, Corinth, and Slevogt.

1908, founds publishing house, Paul Cassirer, for art publications, fiction, and poetry. Publishes work of literary expressionism. 1910, foundation of bimonthly magazine *Pan*, and *Pan*-Society for the promotion of dramatic works, among them works by Wedekind.

From his first marriage, one daughter and one son (commits suicide during World War I). Second marriage to actress Tilla Durieux.

1914, army volunteer. Awarded Iron Cross at Ypres. Becomes pacifist. Temporarily imprisoned (accused of having illegally sold French paintings). Escapes to Switzerland and stays in Bern and Zurich until the end of the war. Assists Harry Graf Kessler with French contacts for negotiations with France on behalf of Ludendorff. Publishes pacifist writings with Max Rascher.

After revolution of 1918, in Berlin, member of USPD (leftist faction of Social Democratic Party). Publishes socialist books, by Kautzky and Bernstein, among others.

Motives for suicide, 1926, probably related to conflict with Tilla Durieux. Continuation of Kunstsalon Paul Cassirer in Amsterdam, Zurich, and London by Dr. Walter Feilchenfeldt and Dr. Grete Ring, a niece of Max Liebermann.

Bunch of Asparagus FOR REICHSMARK 24,300 — ACQUIRED BY MAX LIEBERMANN

Painter. Lived from 1847 to 1935 in Berlin. Descendant of a Jewish family of industrialists. Father, Louis Liebermann, textile industrialist in Berlin. Also owns Eisengiesserei Wilhelmshütte (iron foundry) in Sprottau, Silesia. Mother, Philipine Haller, daughter of Berlin jeweler (founder of firm Haller & Rathenau). Brother, Felix Liebermann, well-known historian. Cousin, Walther Rathenau, industrialist (AEG), foreign minister of German Reich (murdered 1922).

Liebermann attends renowned Friedrich-Werdersches Gymnasium in Berlin, together with sons of Bismarck. Art studies in private Atelier Steffeck, Berlin, and at the Art Academy of Weimar. Works several years in Paris, Holland, Munich. Voluntary medic during Franco-Prussian War, 1870–71. Marries Martha Marckwald, 1884. Moves back to Berlin. 1885, birth of daughter Käthe Liebermann. Inherits father's mansion at Pariser Platz 7 (Brandenburg Gate), 1894.

Builds summer residence at Wannsee, Grosse Seestrasse 27 (since 1971, club-house of Deutscher Unterwasserclub e.V.). Financially independent of the sale of his works.

1897, major one-man exhibition at the Berliner Akademie der Künste. Great Gold Medal. His paintings, influenced by realism and French impressionism, indignantly rejected by Kaiser Wilhelm II. Paints genre scenes, urban landscapes, beach and garden scenes, society portraits, and portraits of artists, scientists, and politicians. Exhibition and sale through Kunstsalon Paul Cassirer in Berlin. Works in public collections, e.g., Wallraf-Richartz-Museum, Cologne.

Awarded honorary title of Professor, 1897. President of the "Berliner Sezession" (association of artists against art of the kaiser's court), 1898–1911; resignation due to opposition from younger artists. Member (1898), in the senate (1912), president of the Prussian Academy of Arts, 1920. Resignation, 1933. Honorary doctorate, University of Berlin. Honorary citizen of Berlin. Knight of the French Legion of Honor. Order of the Oranje-Nassau. Knight of the German Order pour le mérite and other decorations.

Owns works by Cézanne, Daumier, Degas, Manet, Monet, Renoir. Deposits his collection with Kunsthaus Zürich, 1933.

1933, dismissed from all offices by Nazis. Forbidden to exhibit. Removal of his paintings from public collections. Dies 1937 in Berlin. His wife, Martha Liebermann, commits suicide, 1943, to avoid arrest.

Bunch of Asparagus INHERITED BY KÄTHE RIEZLER

Born 1885 in Berlin, dies 1951 in New York. Daughter of the painter Max Liebermann and his wife Martha Marckwald.

Marries Kurt Riezler (Ph.D.), 1915, in Berlin. 1917, birth of their daughter Maria Riezler.

Dr. Kurt Riezler, born 1882 in Munich. Son of a businessman. Classical Greek studies at the University of Munich.

1905, dissertation: "The Second Book of Pseudo-Aristotelian Economics."

1906, enters Foreign Service in Berlin. Second secretary, later minister. Worked on the staff of Chancellor von Bethmann-Hollweg. 1919–20, head of the office of President Friedrich Ebert of the German Reich.

1913, under the pseudonym J.J. Ruedorffer, publication of "Prolegomena for a Theory of Politics"; 1914, "Basic Traits of World Politics of the Present." Later publications on the philosophy of history, political theory, and aesthetics.

1927, professor, vice-president, and chairman of the board of Goethe University in Frankfurt-am-Main.

1933, dismissed by Nazis.

Family returns to Berlin, moves into Max Liebermann's house, Pariser Platz 7. 1935. Inherits his art collection, which Liebermann had deposited with the Kunsthaus Zürich for protection.

1938, emigration of family to New York. Collection follows.

1939, Dr. Kurt Riezler becomes professor of philosophy at the New School for Social Research in New York, a university founded by emigrants. Visiting professor at the University of Chicago and Columbia University in New York. Käthe Riezler dies in 1951. Dr. Riezler retires 1952, dies in Munich, 1956.

Bunch of Asparagus INHERITED BY MARIA WHITE

Born 1917 in Berlin. Daughter of Prof. Dr. Kurt Riezler and Käthe Liebermann. Emigrates with her parents to New York in 1938.

Marries Howard Burton White.

Howard B. White, born 1912 in Montclair, N.J. Studies 1934–38 at the New School for Social Research in New York, where Dr. Kurt Riezler teaches.

1941, Rockefeller fellowship. Ph.D. Science, 1943, from New School.

Teaches at Lehigh University and Coe College. At present, Professor for Political and Social Science on the graduate faculty of the New School for Social Research. Teaches political philosophy.

Publications: *Peace Among the Willows: The Political Philosophy of Francis*

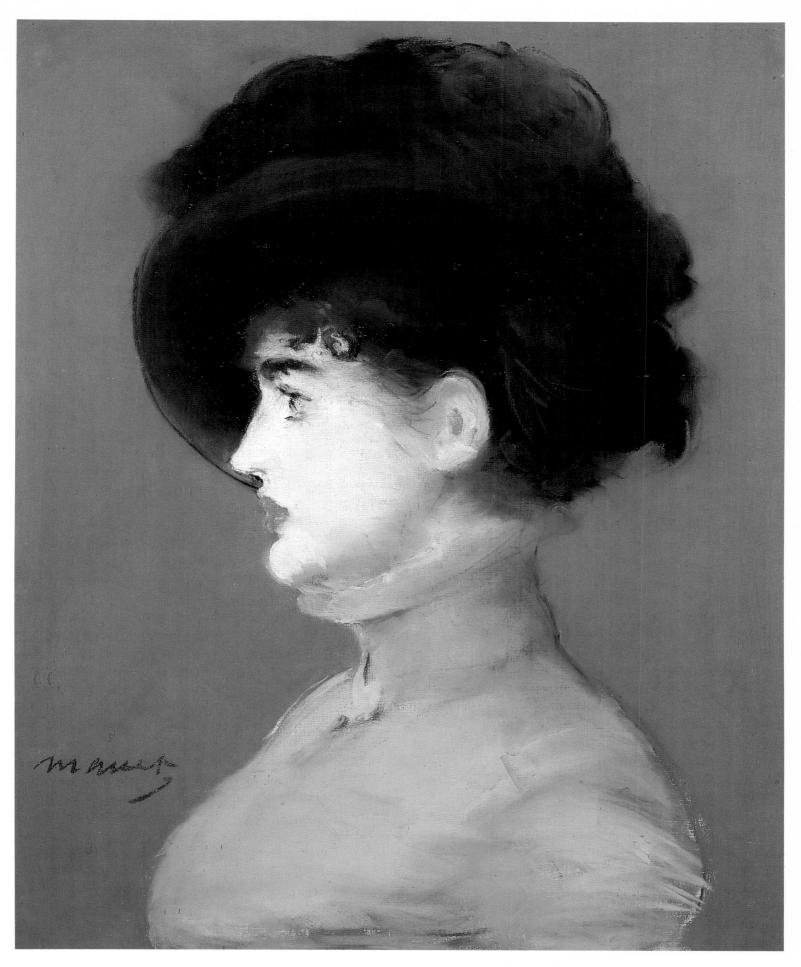

COLOURPLATE 107. *Portrait of Irma Brunner*. 1880. Pastel, 21¼ × 18″ (54 × 46 cm).
Louvre, Paris (Cabinet des Dessins).

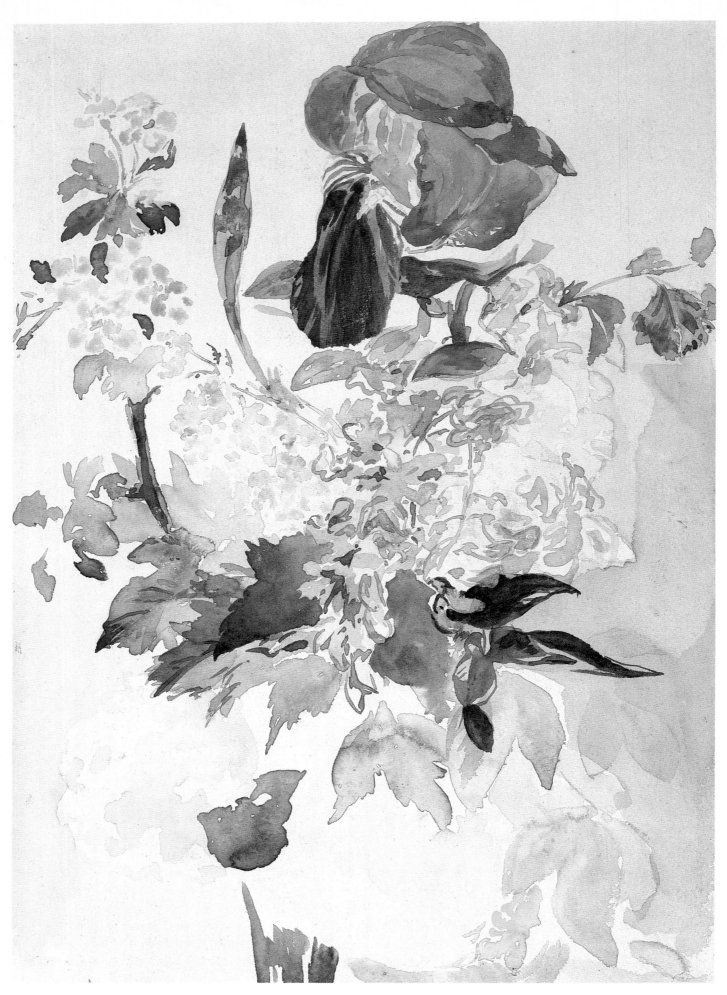

COLOURPLATE 108. *Flowers*. 1880. Watercolour on stationery paper, 13¾ × 10″ (35.1 × 25.6 cm).
Graphische Sammlung der Albertina, Vienna.

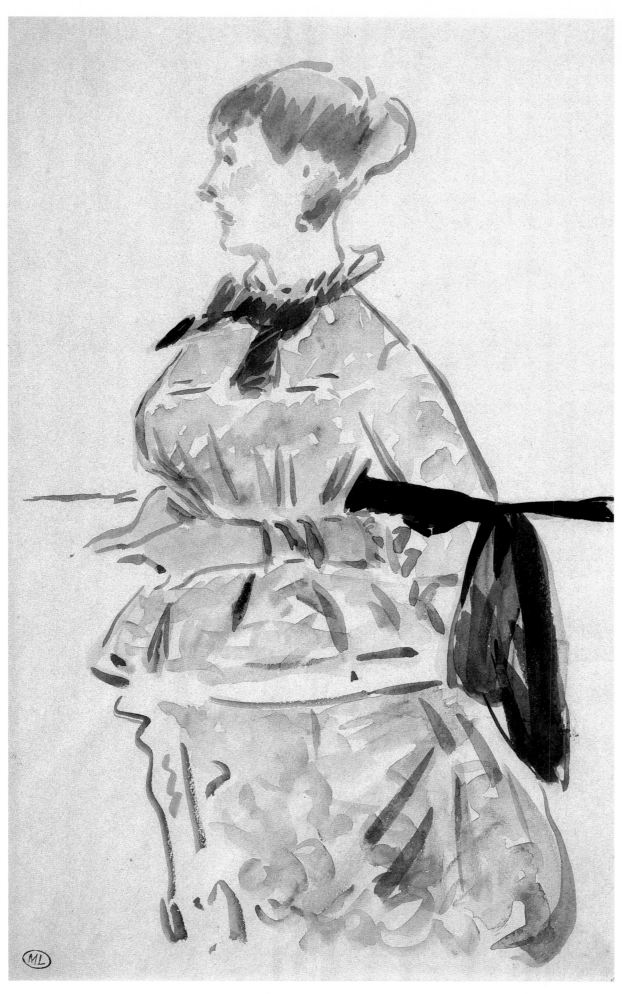

COLOURPLATE 109. *Portrait of Isabelle with Umbrella.* 1880. Watercolour in Letter,
page size 7¾ × 5″ (20 × 12.5 cm).
Louvre, Paris (Cabinet des Dessins).

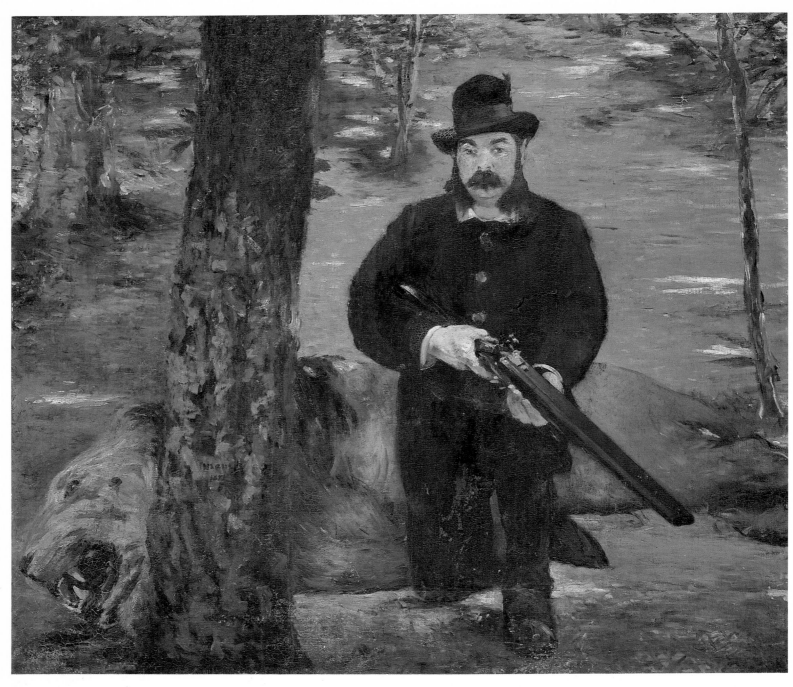

COLOURPLATE 110. *M. Pertuiset, the Lion-Hunter*. 1881. 59 × 67″ (150 × 170 cm).
Museu de Arte, São Paulo, Brazil (Photo Luiz Hossaka).

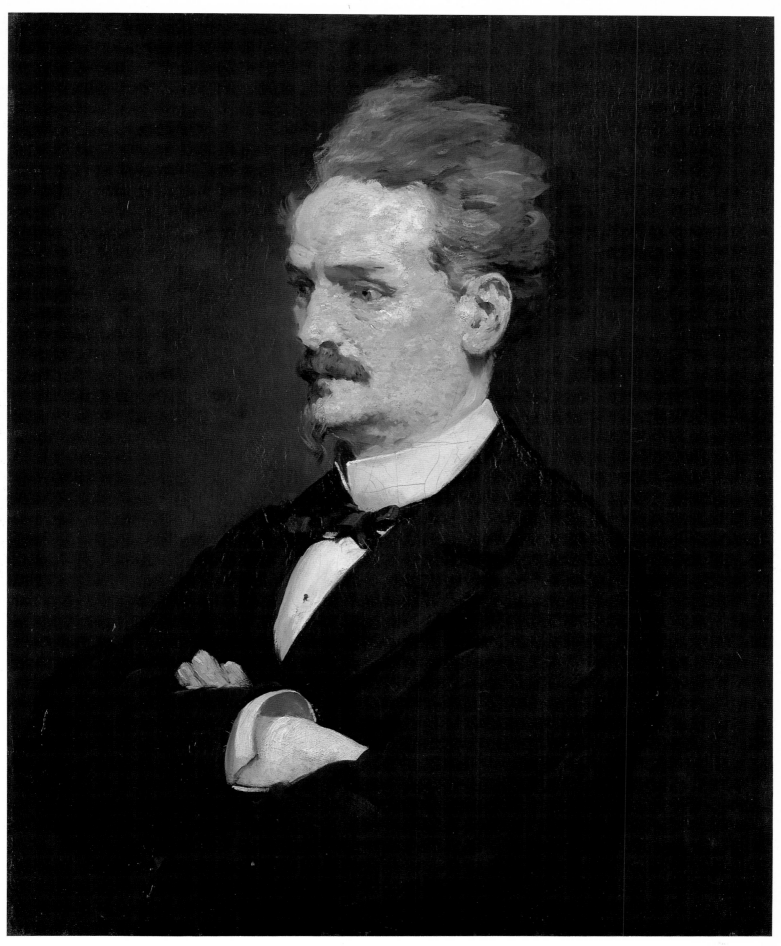

COLOURPLATE III. *Portrait of Rochefort*. 1881. 32 × 26″ (81 × 66 cm).
Kunsthalle, Hamburg.

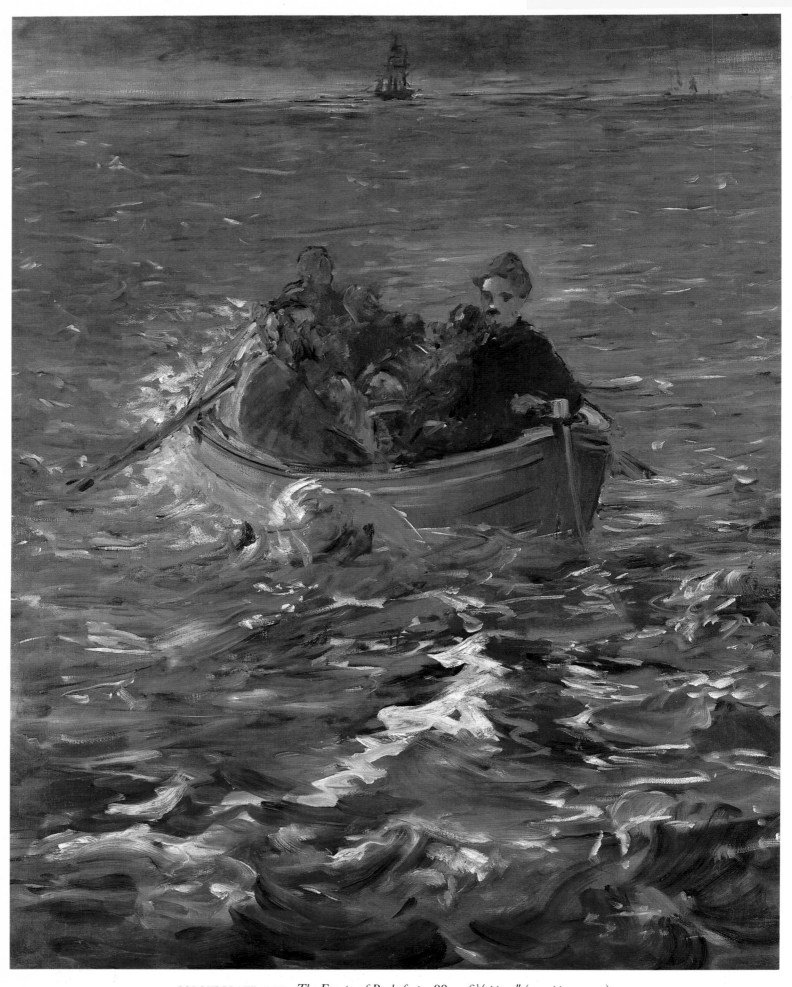

COLOURPLATE 112. *The Escape of Rochefort.* 1881. 56¼ × 45″ (143 × 114 cm).
Kunsthaus, Zurich.

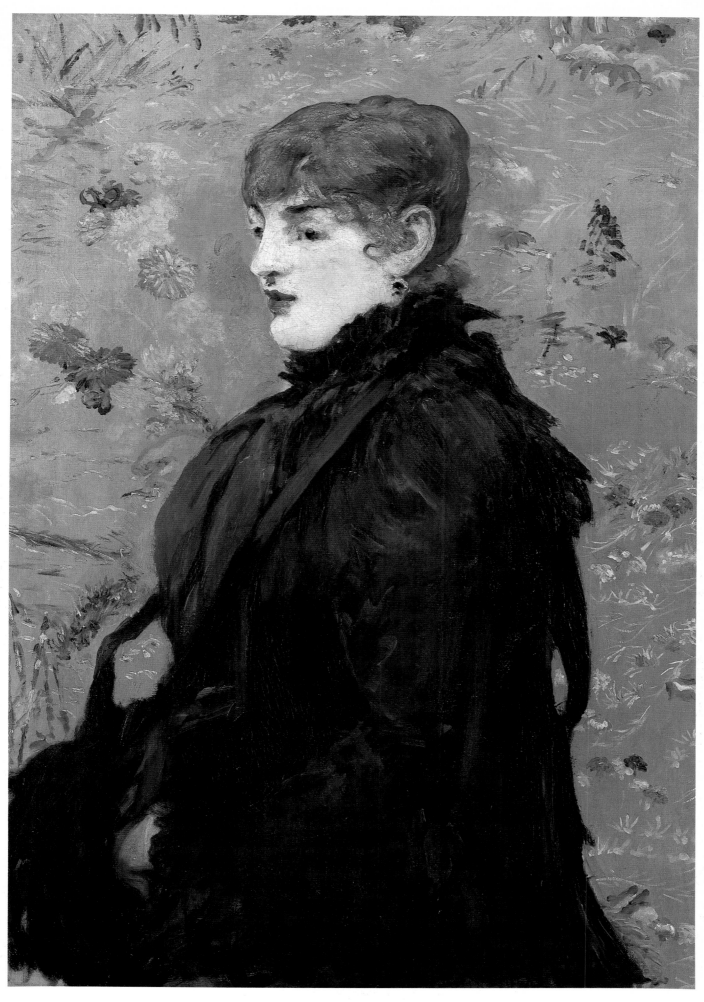

COLOURPLATE 113. *Autumn.* 1882. 28¾ × 20″ (73 × 51 cm).
Musée des Beaux-Arts, Nancy.

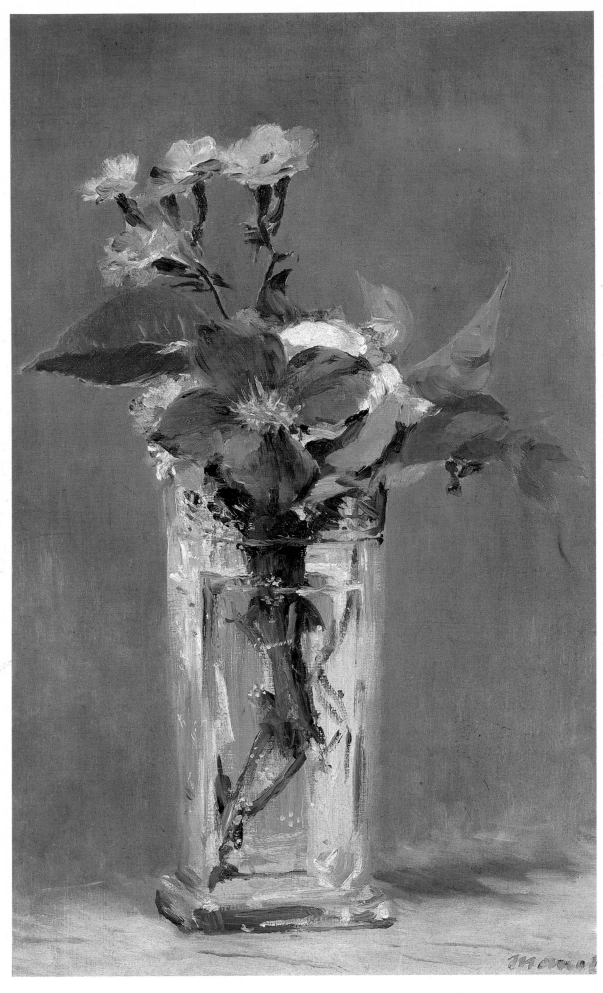

COLOURPLATE 114. *Pinks and Clematis in a Crystal Vase.* 1882. 22 × 14″ (56 × 35.5 cm).
Musée d'Orsay, Paris.

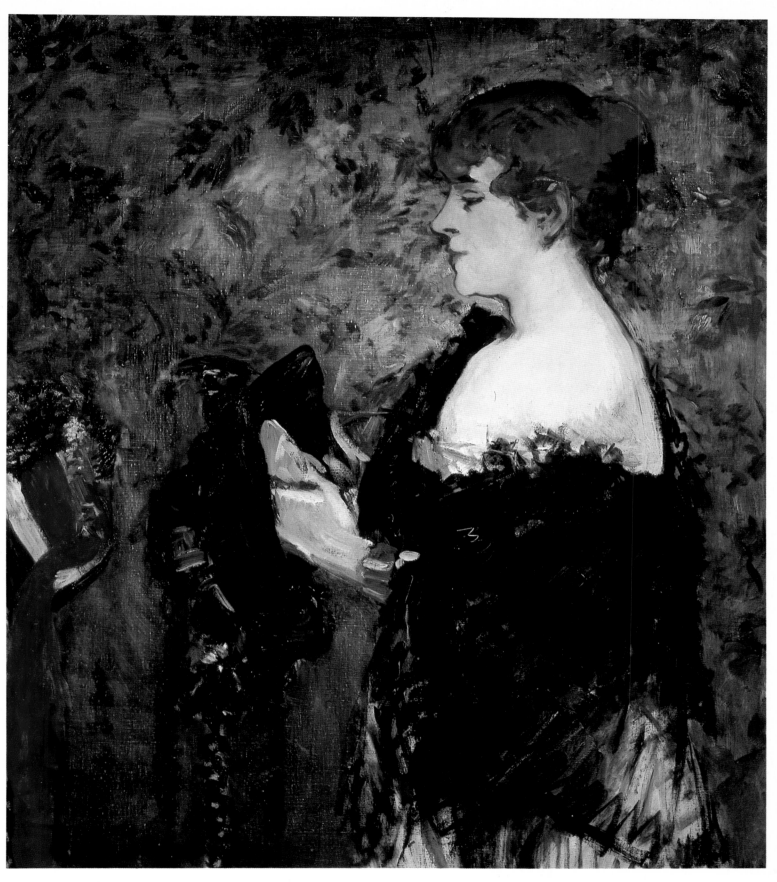

COLOURPLATE 115. *At the Milliner's*. 1881. 33½ × 29″ (85 × 74 cm).
The Fine Arts Museums of San Francisco (Mildred Anna Williams Collection).

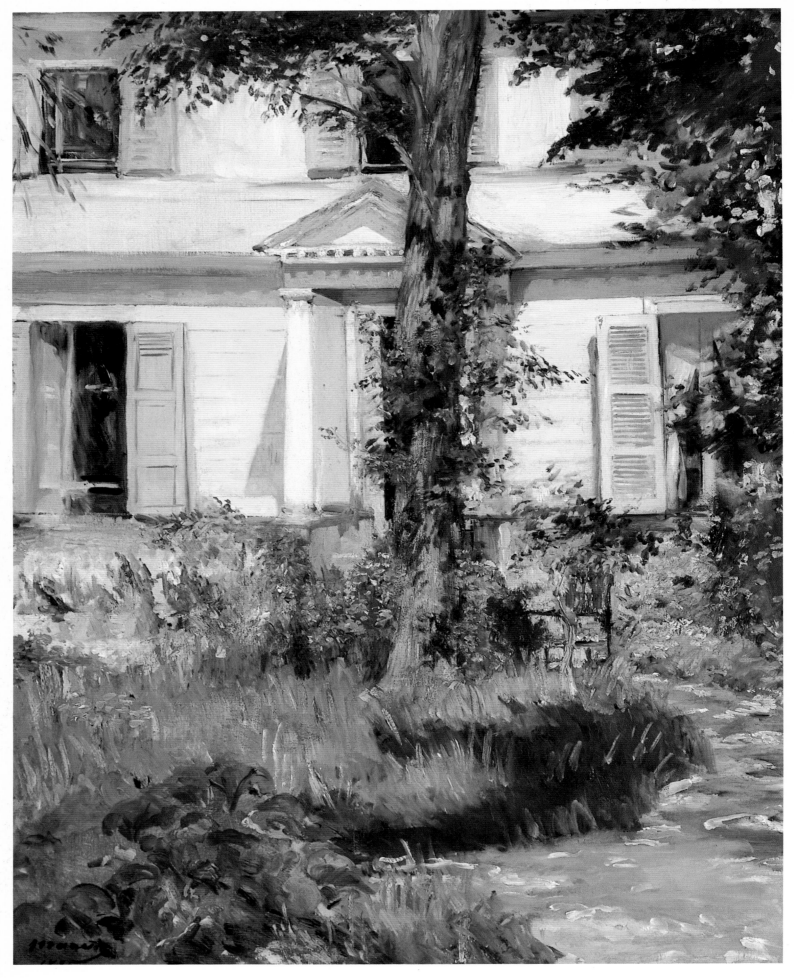

COLOURPLATE 116. *House at Rueil*. 1882. 36¼ × 28¾″ (92 × 73 cm).
National Gallery of Victoria, Melbourne.

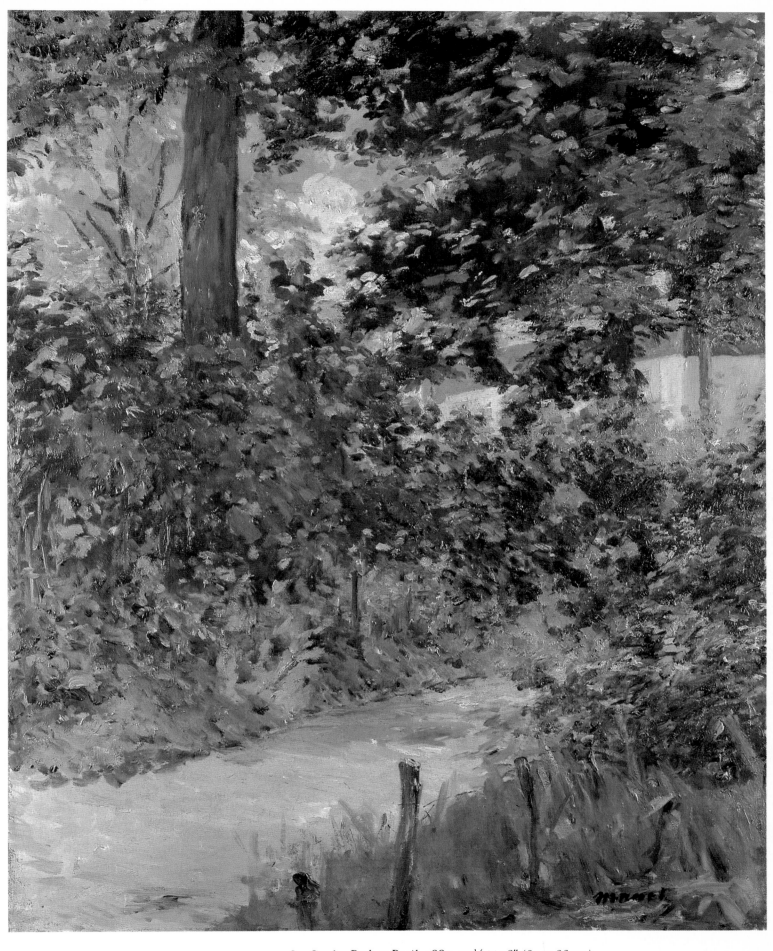

COLOURPLATE 118. *Garden Path at Rueil.* 1882. 32¼ × 26″ (82 × 66 cm).
Kunstmuseum, Bern.

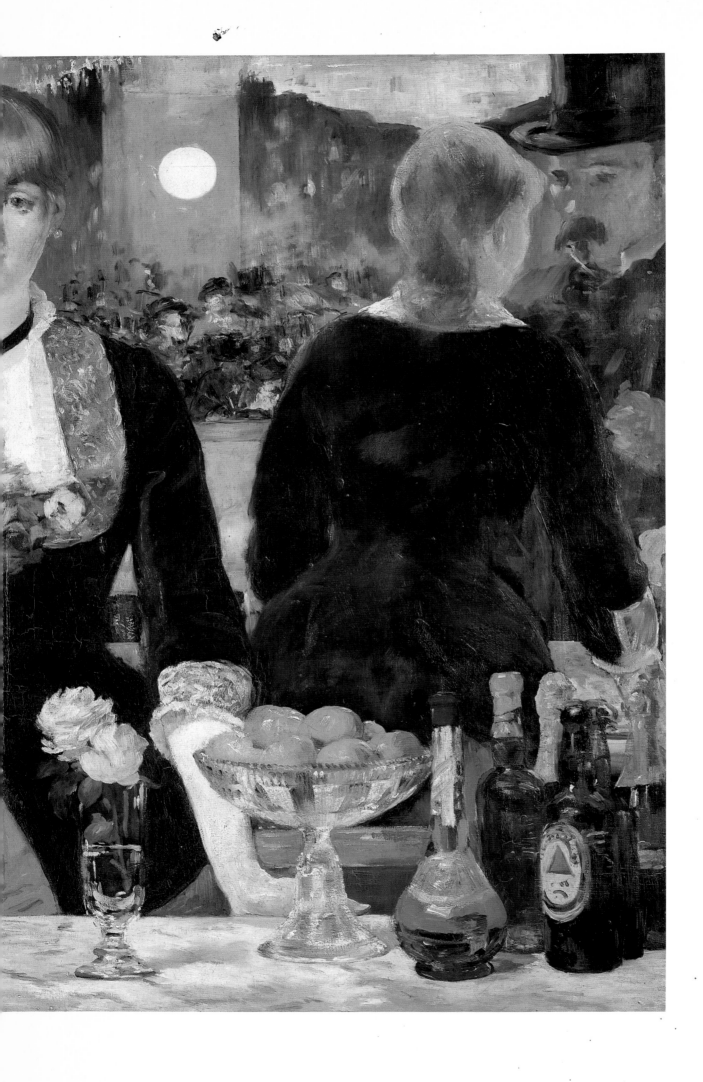

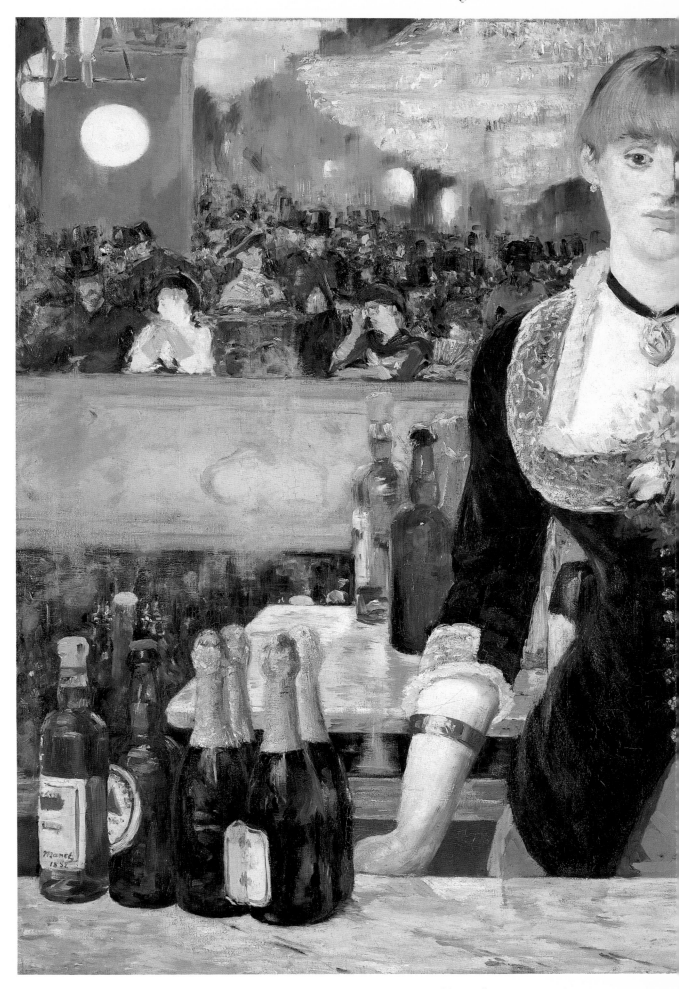

COLOURPLATE 117. *Bar at the Folies-Bergère*. 1881–2. 37¾ × 51″ (96 × 130 cm).
Courtauld Institute Galleries, London (Courtauld Collection).

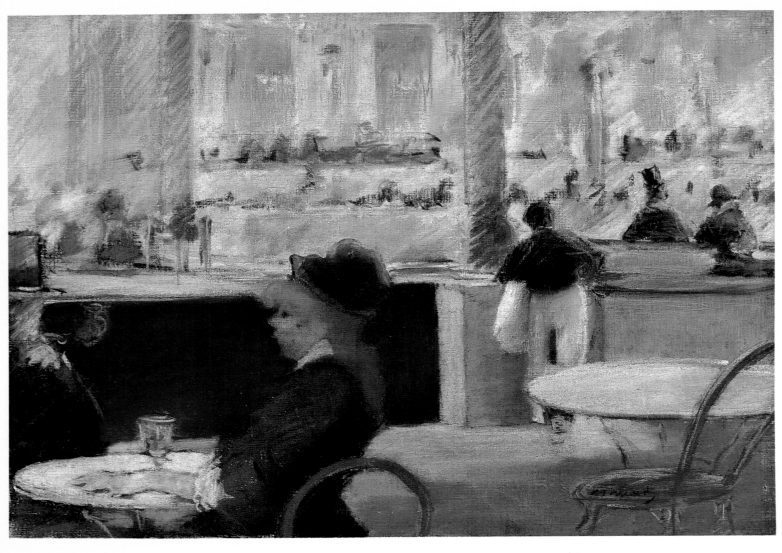

COLOURPLATE 119. *Café on the Place du Théâtre-Français.* 1881. Pastel, 12¾ × 18″ (32.4 × 45.7 cm).
Art Gallery and Museum, Glasgow.

Bacon, The Hague, 1968, and *Copp'd Hills Toward Heaven: Shakespeare and the Classical Polity,* The Hague, 1968, among others.

Maria and Howard B. White live in Northport, N.Y. They have two children.

Bunch of Asparagus 1968, BY WAY OF MRS MARIANNE FEILCHENFELDT, ZURICH, FOR 1,360,000 DEUTSCHEMARKS ($260,000) ACQUIRED BY THE WALLRAF-RICHARTZ-KURATORIUM AND THE CITY OF COLOGNE

Handed over to the Wallraf-Richartz-Museum as a permanent loan by Hermann J. Abs, chairman of the Kuratorium (friends of the Museum), on April 18, 1968, in memory of Konrad Adenauer.

Wallraf-Richartz-Kuratorium und Förderer-Gesellschaft e.V. Executive Committee and trustees: Hermann J. Abs, Prof. Dr. Kurt Hansen, Dr. Günter Henle, Prof. Dr. Ernst Schneider, Prof. Dr. Otto H. Förster, Prof. Dr. Gert von der Osten (managing director).

Trustees: Prof. Dr. Viktor Achter, Dr. Max Adenauer, Fritz Berg, Dr. Walther Berndorff, Theo Burauen, Prof. Dr. Fritz Burgbacher, Dr. Fritz Butschkau, Dr. Felix Eckhardt, Mrs Gisela Fitting, Prof. Dr. Kurt Forberg, Walter Franz, Dr. Hans Gerling, Dr. Herbert Girardet, Dr. Paul Gülker, Iwan D. Herstatt, Raymund Jörg, Eugen Gottlieb von Langen, Viktor Langen, Dr. Peter Ludwig, Prof. Dr. Heinz Mohnen, Cai Graf zu Rantzau, Karl Gustav Ratjen, Dr. Hans Reuter, Dr. Hans-Günther Sohl, Dr. Werner Schulz, Dr. Nikolaus Graf Strasoldo, Christoph Vowinckel, Otto Wolff von Amerongen.

Bunch of Asparagus ACQUIRED THROUGH THE INITIATIVE OF THE CHAIRMAN OF THE WALLRAF-RICHARTZ-KURATORIUM (FRIENDS OF THE MUSEUM) HERMANN J. ABS

Born Bonn 1901. Descendant of a well-to-do Catholic family. Father, Dr. Josef Abs, attorney and judge (*Justizrat*), co-owner of Hubertus Braunkohlen AG, Brüggen, Erft (brown coal mining company). Mother, Katharina Lückerath.

Passes final exam, 1919, at Realgymnasium Bonn. Studies one semester law, University of Bonn. Bank training at Bankhaus Delbrück von der Heydt & Co., Cologne. Gains experience in international banking in Amsterdam, London, Paris, the United States.

Marries Inez Schnitzler, 1928. Her father related to Georg von Schnitzler of executive committee of I.G. Farben syndicate. Aunt married to Baron Alfred Neven du Mont. Sister married to Georg Graf von der Goltz. Birth of two children, Thomas and Marion Abs. Member of Zentrumspartei (Catholic Party). 1929, on the staff, with power of attorney, of Bankhaus Delbrück, Schickler & Co., Berlin. 1935–37, one of five partners of the bank.

1937, on the board of directors and member of the executive committee of the Deutsche Bank in Berlin. Chief of its foreign division. 1939, appointed member of advisory council of the Deutsche Reichsbank by Walther Funk, minister of economics of the Reich. Member of committees of the Reichsbank, Reichsgruppe Industrie, Reichsgruppe Banken, Reichswirtschaftskammer, and Arbeitskreis of the minister of economics. 1944, represented on over fifty boards of directors. Membership in associations for the advancement of German economic interests abroad.

1946, for six weeks in British prison. Cleared by Allied denazification board and placed in category 5 (exonerated of active support of Nazi regime).

1948, participated in foundation of Kreditanstalt für Wiederaufbau (Credit Institute for Reconstruction). Extensive involvement in economic planning of West German federal government. Economic advisor to Chancellor Konrad Adenauer. 1951–53, head of German delegation to London conference to negotiate German war debts. Advisory role during negotiations with Israel at Conference on Jewish Material Claims in The Hague. 1954, member of CDU (Christian Democratic Party).

1952, on board of directors of Süddeutsche Bank AG. 1957–67, president of Deutsche Bank AG. Since 1967, chairman of the board.

Honorary chairman of the board of directors: Deutsche Überseeische Bank, Hamburg; Pittler Maschinenfabrik AG, Langen (Hesse).

Chairman of the board of directors: Dahlbusch Verwaltungs-AG, Gelsenkirchen; Daimler Benz AG, Stuttgart-Untertürkheim; Deutsche Bank AG, Frankfurt; Deutsche Lufthansa AG, Köln; Philipp Holzmann AG, Frankfurt; Phoenix Gummiwerke AG, Hamburg-Harburg; RWE Elektrizitätswerk AG, Essen; Vereinigte Glanzstoff AG, Wuppertal-Elberfeld; Zellstoff-Fabrik Waldhof AG, Mannheim.

Honorary chairman: Salamander AG, Kornwestheim; Gebr. Stumm GmbH, Brambauer (Westf.); Süddeutsche Zucker-AG, Mannheim.

Vice-chairman of the board of directors: Badische Anilin- und Sodafabrik AG, Ludwigshafen; Siemens AG, Berlin-München.

Member of the board of directors: Metallgesellschaft AG, Frankfurt.

President of the supervisory board: Kreditanstalt für Wiederaufbau; Deutsche Bundesbahn.

Great Cross of the Order of Merit with Star of the Federal Republic of Germany, Papal Star with the Cross of the Commander, Great Cross of Isabella the Catholic of Spain, Cruzeiro do Sul of Brazil. Knight of the Order of the Holy Sepulcher. Honorary doctorates of the universities of Göttingen, Sofia, Tokyo and the Wirtschaftshochschule Mannheim.

Lives in Kronberg (Taunus), and on Bentgerhof near Remagen.

Bunch of Asparagus ACQUIRED WITH DONATIONS FROM

Hermann J. Abs, Frankfurt; Viktor Achter, Mönchengladbach; Agrippina Rückversicherungs AG, Köln; Allianz Versicherung AG, Köln; Heinrich Auer Mühlenwerke, Köln; Bankhaus Heinz Ansmann, Köln; Bankhaus Delbrück von der Heydt & Co., Köln; Bankhaus Sal. Oppenheim Jr. & Cie., Köln; Bankhaus C.G. Trinkaus, Düsseldorf; Dr. Walther Berndorff, Köln; Firma Felix Böttcher, Köln; Robert Bosch GmbH, Köln; Central Krankenversicherungs AG, Köln; Colonia Versicherungs-Gruppe, Köln; Commerzbank AG, Düsseldorf; Concordia Lebensversicherungs AG, Köln; Daimler Benz AG, Stuttgart-Untertürkheim; Demag AG, Duisburg; Deutsch-Atlantische Telegraphenges., Köln; Deutsche Bank AG, Frankfurt; Deutsche Centralbodenkredit AG, Köln; Deutsche Continental-Gas-Ges., Düsseldorf; Deutsche Krankenversicherungs AG, Köln; Deutsche Libby-Owens-Ges. AG, Gelsenkirchen; Deutsche Solvay-Werke GmbH, Solingen-Ohligs; Dortmunder Union-Brauerei, Dortmund; Dresdner Bank AG, Düsseldorf; Farbenfabriken Bayer AG, Leverkusen; Gisela Fitting, Köln; Autohaus Jacob Fleischhauer KG, Köln; Glanzstoff AG, Wuppertal; Graf Rüdiger von der Goltz, Düsseldorf; Dr. Paul Gülker, Köln; Gottfried Hagen AG, Köln; Hein. Lehmann & Co. AG, Düsseldorf; Hilgers AG, Rheinbrohl; Hoesch AG, Dortmund; Helmut Horten GmbH, Düsseldorf; Hubertus Brauerei GmbH, Köln; Karstadt-Peters GmbH, Köln; Kaufhalle GmbH, Köln; Kaufhof AG, Köln; Kleinwanzlebener Saatzucht AG, Einbeck; Klöckner Werke AG, Duisburg; Kölnische Lebens- und Sachvers. AG, Köln; Viktor Langen, Düsseldorf-Meerbusch; Margarine Union AG, Hamburg; Mauser-Werke GmbH, Köln; Josef Mayr KG, Hagen; Michel Brennstoffhandel GmbH, Düsseldorf; Gert von der Osten, Köln; Kurt Pauli, Lövenich; Pfeifer & Langen, Köln; Preussag AG, Hannover; William Prym Werke AG, Stolberg; Karl-Gustav Ratjen, Königstein (Taunus); Dr. Hans Reuter, Duisburg; Rheinische-Westf. Bodenkreditbank, Köln; Rhein.-Westf. Isolatorenwerke GmbH, Siegburg; Rhein.-Westf. Kalkwerke AG, Dornap; Sachtleben AG, Köln; Servais-Werke AG, Witterschlick; Siemag Siegener Maschinenbau GmbH, Dahlbruch; Dr. F.E. Shinnar, Tel-Ganim (Israel);

T. J. CLARK

THE PAINTING OF MODERN LIFE

"A Bar at the Folies-Bergère"

1985

T.J. Clark, British art historian, author of The Absolute Bourgeois: Artists and Politics in France 1848–51 *and* Image of the People: Gustave Courbet and the 1848 Revolution.

COLOURPLATE 117

That the adjective "popular," applied to persons, manners or entertainment in the later nineteenth century, came to mean too many, too indefinite things. The word's elusiveness derived from its being used for ideological purposes, to suggest kinds of identity and contact between the classes – ways they belonged together and had interests in common – which did not exist in their everyday life or organized social practice, but seemed to in the spectacle. There was a sense in which the *nouvelles couches sociales* were nothing in our period, or very little, without the place allotted to them in "popular culture" – which is not to say that they lacked a determinate economic position, only that it was not yet clear, to them or anyone, what it was. Popular culture provided the petit-bourgeois aficionado with two forms of illusory "class:" an identity with those below him, or at least with certain images of their life; and a difference from them which hinged on his skill – his privileged place – as consumer of those same images. Painting was mostly a complaisant spectator of this spectacle, perfecting the petit bourgeois's view of things and leaving behind the best picture we have of what it amounted to. But there are certain canvases which suggest the unease and duplicity involved in this attaining to a new class; something of the kind is claimed in this chapter for Manet's last painting, *The Bar at the Folies-Bergère*.

* * *

Behind the girl is a mirror. One can make out the yellow moulding of its frame on either side of the barmaid's wrists, and take in the general haze and dazzle on the glass – the illusion being strongest towards the left, where white paint obscures the distant balcony, or over the heads of the crowd at the right. A mirror it palpably is: one has only to notice the edge of the marble counter reflected in it, or the back view of the bottle of pink liqueur, for the illusion to be inescapable. And is there not even the reflection of the central white rose in its wineglass, wedged in between the second barmaid and her client, hard against the picture's right-hand edge?

But as soon as the general grounds for such a reading have been established – and I take it that most viewers discover them fairly soon –

the difficulties in sustaining it begin. If that *is* a mirror behind the barmaid, then what exactly is being reflected in it? If it is a mirror, then the second young woman, towards the right, must be the mirror image of the one who looks out towards us. She must be, and she cannot be. There are clearly things about her which are meant to suggest that she is the same person seen from the rear. And yet how could the barmaid's reflection be there, so far towards the right? Does it mean – it must mean – that the mirror's whole surface is somehow arranged at an angle to our vision, quite a sharp angle, in fact, going back from right to left? Again, that could almost be so; and yet one look at the plain straight edge of the mirror's gilt frame, and the line of the counter just above it in the glass, puts paid to the possibility; and this leaves aside the more general problem of how this slanting mirror would fit in with the picture's overall formal logic.

For that overall logic is strict and emphatic. Every main thing in the picture is presented frontally, face on to the viewer, layer after layer aligned to the lower edge, where the frame itself cuts the marble. And the mirror is seemingly a main part of that arrangement: it is one more flat surface taking its place among the rest. Are we being invited, then, to insert into this orderly sequence of spaces *another* space altogether, a quite contrary diagonal? We surely cannot do it, by and large – or not in a way we can keep in being, and make part of a reasonably coherent picture; that tilted mirror will not stay in place, it keeps lining up again parallel to the bar and the balcony; the reflection at the right escapes from the person it belongs to.

This last is not simply a matter of inconsistent spaces, I think; it also derives from the painter's rather careful mismatching of the front and back views of his barmaid subject. Looking out at us, the woman is symmetrical, upright, immaculate, composed; looking in at him, the man in the mirror, she seems to lean forward a little too much, too close, while the unbroken oval of her head sprouts stray wisps of hair. She looks a bit plumper than she ought to; the pose she adopts is more stolid and deferential. And thus the critics' descriptions come back to mind: the *jolie vendeuse*, the *marchande de consolation, bien campée dans un mouvement naturel*, exchanging clichés with her serious admirer. The critics have a point, of course: the girl in the mirror does seem to be part of some such facile narrative, or could easily be made so. But that cannot be said of the "real" barmaid, who stands at the centre, returning our gaze with such evenness, such seeming lack of emotion or even interest.

And then, of course – final uncertainty – there is the gentleman in the mirror, standing in the top right-hand corner, clutching a gold-knobbed cane, wearing a top hat, a wing collar, and a drooping moustache. Who is this unfortunate, precisely? Where is he? Where does he stand in relation to her, in relation to us?

I wrote just now "looking out at us . . . looking in at him;" but the problem the picture presents is that the barmaid must be doing both at once, that *we* must be where *he* is. But we cannot be; not, anyway, if we are to remain what that easy "we" implies, in the discourse of looking – the single viewer of the painting in question; ourselves, myself; the subject for whom the picture exists and makes sense, who stands and sees a determinate world. "We" are at the centre; he is squeezed out to the edge of things, cut off by the picture frame. His transaction with the barmaid cannot, surely, set the tone for ours.

I suppose most viewers believe that the tone will be set properly, if at all, by the expression on the barmaid's face. And presumably those viewers do some work to make the face take on an expression that seems plausible given the circumstances, and compatible with the general air of deadpan. (I am leaving aside the inveterate modernist here, who no doubt sees at once that the face is nothing but that of painting itself, the presence of the signifier, the absence of the signified, etc.) It is perfectly possible, in fact, to imagine the barmaid's face as belonging to a definite state of mind or set of feelings: that of patience perhaps, or boredom and tiredness, or self-containment. We might even have it be "inexpressive," in the sense of the word that implies there is something being deliberately kept back, or that some mistake has been made about how best to signal what one is feeling. But the problem is that all these descriptions fit so easily and so lightly, and none cancels out or dominates the rest; so that I think the viewer ends up by accepting – or at least by recognizing – that no one relation with this face and pose and way of looking will ever quite seem the right one. In any case, we resist the suggestion that everything depends on the man with the cane and his ordering the next round. "We" are not looking from where he looks: we do not believe that all we are seeing is the professional impassivity of a barmaid or a prostitute. (It might be possible to dismiss this as a kind of sentimental wish for complexity on our part, were it not for the way the more general perplexities of the picture chime in with the viewer's sense of the face as ambiguous. Or, to put it another way: if this *is* the professional look of a prostitute, then surely the picture divests that look of any simplicity: it suggests that expressions have complex circumstances and are best understood as constructions – rather fragile constructions – in their own right.)

What I have been describing up to now is a texture of uncertainties. Some of them may have struck the reader as a bit hectic and contrived, and some not; the point in following them thus far is to suggest how easily doubts about looking accumulate in front of *The Bar at the Folies-Bergère*, doubts of various kinds, all reinforcing one another. What begins as a series of limited questions about relationships in space is likely to end as scepticism about relationship in general. Little by little we lose our imagined location, and because of that – as part of that – our first imaginary exchange of glances with the person in the picture is made to appear the peculiar thing it is. Here too, in the matter of persons and looks, we begin to struggle for a reading, become aware of contradictory cues, and feel obliged to include in the transaction the various things which may or may not be there in the mirror. And we cannot do it: the equation fails to add up. We cannot or will not take the place of the gentleman in the top hat, but there is no other place to occupy, it seems; we are left in a kind of suspended relation – to the barmaid, to ourselves as viewers, to the picture itself as a possible unity.

There seems little doubt that the structure which gives rise to these uncertainties was devised by the artist with conscious care. We have an oil sketch in which Manet put down his first general idea for *The Bar*, and it serves to show how easily things might have been sorted out and put in order if that had been what Manet had wanted. He might have given us, as he did in the sketch, a readable, eye-catching relation between the barmaid and man in the mirror; the more or less blousy *dame de comptoir* dwarfing the eager buyer of drinks. He might have put the barmaid and her reflection together, back to back, with the mirror established between them. He could have pushed the counter back in space and marked out its edges and sides; he could have put the barmaid safely behind it, and taken away her peculiar symmetry and her absolute, outward stare. But of course he did not: he seems to have worked instead to discover and exacerbate inconsistencies in his subject, teasing out the anomalies, letting in the blanks, having them dictate the picture's order.

And so the further question occurs, as to *why* the mirror was treated in this peculiar way. What does the mirror do in Manet's painting? Why is it placed as it is? What is the viewer supposed to make of the distance opened up between the objects and their reflections, and the suggestion that one belongs to the other only incompletely? These are partly questions about Manet's possible working procedures, about how it happened that the glass and reflections took this form in the process of painting. And partly they feel for possible intentions: kinds of matching, most probably sensed by the painter only indirectly, between a formal arrangement of this type and the actual subject, the bar and the barmaid. Both questions are speculative, given the evidence we have, and the answers I offer are therefore meant to be tentative. But at least they proceed from what seems to me the plausible hypothesis (on which this book as a whole is based) that inconsistencies so carefully contrived must have been felt to be somehow appropriate to the social forms the painter had chosen to show.

A mirror is a surface on which a segment of the surrounding world appears, directly it seems, in two dimensions; as such it has often been taken as a good metaphor for painting. Is that perhaps the way it is meant in *The Bar*? The great room, the lights, the crowd, the trapeze, the elusive atmosphere – the mirror fixes and flattens them all, before the painter begins. There is literally nothing behind the barmaid but glass, on which the world already takes place in miniature, much as it will on canvas. But in order for the mirror to have that connotation – for it to be read as a simple, factual surface calling to mind the plainness with which painting puts down the world of appearance – it would not do for the glass to be pictured at an angle. The mirror must repeat the picture's literal surface: it must be the same surface, only farther back. The thing it must *not* do is act on the matters of visual fact it shows; it must not *do* things to them. There is a plain fact of vision somewhere, and an equally plain one of painting; the mirror is there to show that each can be true to the other: it guarantees the orderly unfolding of the real world to the eye, band after band – counter, frame, counter, balcony, pillars – until the picture stops.

The mirror must therefore be frontal and plain, and the things that appear in it be laid out in a measured rhythm. And yet it is clear that some of those things will not be allowed to appear too safely attached to the objects and persons whose likenesses they are. I think that this happens . . . as a result of Manet's attitude towards the Folies-Bergère – towards modern life in Paris, if you like. It seems to me also that a degree of conflict exists between that attitude and the beliefs about painting and vision – the metaphysic of plainness and immediacy – just outlined. That Manet held both sets of beliefs is incontestable, and the tension between them was never more visible than in his last big painting.

It is a picture of a woman in a café-concert, selling drinks and oranges, and most probably for sale herself – or believed to be so by some of her customers. Those customers, we know, were a motley crew, *le plus drôle de mélange qui soit dans Paris*, and therefore peculiarly hard to make out. The elements involved in making sense of the situation were as follows: that the entertainments provided were popular, the general decor pretentious and glittering, the women loose, and the men engaged in a quite serious game of class. The face that the barmaid presents to this spectacle is, we might think, the only one possible. It is the face of fashion, first of all, made up to agree with others quite like it, the hair just hiding the eyebrows and leaving the ears free, the cheeks pale with powder, the lips not overdone this season, the pearls the right size. Fashion is a good and necessary disguise: it is hard to be sure of anything else about the barmaid, in particular what class she might belong to. She does not seem, as the critics hinted in their choice of language in 1882, to be firmly part of the bourgoisie; and that fact is the key to her modernity, in Alexis's smug sense; it is part of her appeal. The face she wears is the face of the popular, as previously defined, but also of a fierce, imperfect resistance to any such ascription. It is a face whose character derives from its not being bourgeois, and having that fact almost be hidden. For if one could not be bourgeois – if that status was always pushed just a little out of reach – then at least one could prevent oneself from being anything else: fashion and reserve would keep one's face from *any* identity, from identity in general. The look which results is a special one: public, outward, "blasé" in Simmel's sense, impassive, not bored, not tired, not disdainful, not quite

Georg Simmel, German sociologist.

focused on anything. Expression is its enemy, the mistake it concentrates on avoiding at all costs; for to express oneself would be to have one's class be legible.

The Bar is surely concerned to picture that kind of effacement, but also the actual social circumstances in which it took place and which made it obligatory. The painting delights in flatness in general, wherever it occurs, and no doubt it aims to show us what a face looks like when it too becomes two-dimensional – when that is the way it presents itself to the world. But it offers at the same time a form of explanation for that state of affairs, a form built into the picture's visual structure. The explanation consists, if I can put it this way, in the "actual social circumstances" barely appearing to be any such thing – to be either actual or social – to us or the actors involved in them. A curious balance must thus be struck. The circumstances must all be *there* in the picture, but somehow not quite convincingly. They must be seen to apply to the barmaid, but at one remove, as if they came to her – to us – as things slightly insubstantial, not wholly real.

That is why they are placed in a mirror and only half attached to the figure in front of it. For if the barmaid were *in* the mirror – part of the glamour of lights and performances, directly addressed by the man with the cane – she would be given back the actual social circumstances which are precisely what she does not have. And equally, if the mirror were all paradox and instability, its angle turning the room around and opening it up, then the gap between the woman and her reflection would lack the peculiar tension it has. It is important that even the Folies-Bergère appears in the picture as almost real, almost orderly, only just interrupted by the glass. For there is a definite set of class relations here to which the barmaid belongs; it is only her way of belonging to them that is the problem. The world that Manet offers as "modern" – and the same is true of *Olympia* or *Argenteuil, The Boaters* – is not simply made up of edges and uncertainties. It is plain as well as paradoxical, fixed as well as shifting; it lacks an order, as opposed to proclaiming the end of order as the great new thing.

I do not think, in other words, that the barmaid is carried away into the odd spaces and displacements I have spent my time describing; she is not dispersed by them. Even the word "ambiguous" will not quite do if we are aiming to describe her place in the picture and her relation to the life in the mirror. . . . It does not seem to me that she is animated by her alienation; she is posed and composed and confined by it; it is felt as a kind of fierceness and flawlessness with which she seals herself against her surroundings. She is *detached*: that is the best description. She looks out steadily at something or somebody, the various things which constrain and determine her, and finds that they all float by "with the same specific gravity in the constantly moving stream of money." The customer evidently thinks she is one more such object which money can buy, and in a sense it is part of her duties to maintain the illusion. Doing so is a full-time job.

SANDER L. GILMAN

CRITICAL INQUIRY

"Black Bodies, White Bodies"

Autumn 1985

Sander L. Gilman, Professor of Humane Studies and Psychiatry (History) at Cornell University, co-editor with J.E. Chamberlain of Degeneration, *1985. Gilman's essay is an indication of continuing preoccupation with the complex imagery of* Olympia.

. . . In the course of the nineteenth century, the female Hottentot comes to represent the black female *in nuce*, and the prostitute to represent the sexualized woman. Both of these categories represent the creation of classes which correspondingly represent very specific qualities. While the number of terms describing the various categories of the prostitute expanded substantially during the nineteenth century, all were used to label the sexualized woman. Likewise, while many groups of African blacks were known to Europeans in the nineteenth century, the Hottentot remained representative of the essence of the black, especially the black female. Both concepts fulfilled an iconographic function in the perception and the representation of the world. How these two concepts were associated provides a case study for the investigation of patterns of conventions, without any limitation on the "value" of one pattern over another.

Let us begin with one of the classic works of nineteenth-century art, a work which records the idea of both the sexualized woman and the black woman. Edouard Manet's *Olympia*, painted in 1862-63 and first exhibited in the Salon of 1865, assumes a key position in documenting the merger of these two images. The conventional wisdom concerning Manet's painting states that the model, Victorine Meurent, is "obviously naked rather than conventionally nude," and that her pose is heavily indebted to classical models such as Titian's *Venus of Urbino* (1538), Francisco Goya's *Naked Maja* (1800), and Eugène Delacroix's *Odalisque* (1847), as well as other works by Manet's contemporaries, such as Gustave Courbet. George Needham has shown quite convincingly that Manet was also using a convention of early erotic photography in having the central figure directly confront the observer. The black female attendant, based on a black model called Laura, has been seen as a reflex of both the classic black servant figure present in the visual arts of the eighteenth century as well as a representation of Baudelaire's *Vénus Noire*. Let us juxtapose the *Olympia*, with all its aesthetic and artistic analogies and parallels, to a work by Manet which Georges Bataille, among others, has seen as a modern "genre scene" – the *Nana* of 1877. Unlike Olympia, Nana is modern, a creature of present-day Paris, according to a contemporary. But like Olympia, Nana was perceived as a sexualized female and is so represented. Yet in moving from a work with an evident aesthetic provenance, as understood by Manet's contemporaries, to one which was influenced by the former and yet was seen by its contemporaries as modern, certain major shifts in the iconography of the sexualized woman take place, not the least of which is the apparent disappearance of the black female.

The figure of the black servant in European art is ubiquitous. Richard Strauss knew this when he had Hugo von Hofmannsthal conclude their conscious evocation of the eighteenth century, *Der Rosenkavalier* (1911), with the mute return of the little black servant to reclaim the Marschallin's forgotten gloves. But Hofmannsthal was also aware that one of the black servant's central functions in the visual arts of the eighteenth and nineteenth centuries was to sexualize the society in which he or she is found. The forgotten gloves, for instance, mark the end of the relationship between Octavian, the Knight of the Rose, and the Marschallin: the illicit nature of their sexual relationship, which opens the opera, is thereby

COLOURPLATE 14

See the study of this model (Rouart/ Wildenstein I 68), 1863.

COLOURPLATE 79

Hugo van Hofmannsthal (1874–1929), Austrian poet, dramatist and essayist, collaborating with Richard Strauss on the libretti of some of his operas.

linked to the appearance of the figure of the black servant, which closes the opera. When one turns to the narrative art of the eighteenth century – for example, to William Hogarth's two great cycles, *A Rake's Progress* (1733-34) and *A Harlot's Progress* (1731) – it is not very surprising that, as in the Strauss opera some two centuries later, the figures of the black servants mark the presence of illicit sexual activity. Furthermore, as in Hofmannsthal's libretto, they appear in the opposite sex to the central figure. In the second plate of *A Harlot's Progress*, we see Moll Hackabout as the mistress of a Jewish merchant, the first stage of her decline as a sexualized female; also present is a young, black male servant. In the third stage of Tom Rakewell's collapse, we find him in a notorious brothel, the Rose Tavern in Covent Garden. The entire picture is full of references to illicit sexual activity, all portrayed negatively; present as well is the figure of a young female black servant.

The association of the black with concupiscence reaches back into the Middle Ages. The twelfth-century Jewish traveller Benjamin of Tudela wrote that

> at Seba on the river Pishon . . . is a people . . . who, like animals, eat of the herbs that grow on the banks of the Nile and in the fields. They go about naked and have not the intelligence of ordinary men. They cohabit with their sisters and anyone they can find. . . . And these are the Black slaves, the sons of Ham.

By the eighteenth century, the sexuality of the black, both male and female, becomes an icon for deviant sexuality in general; as we have seen, the black figure appears almost always paired with a white figure of the opposite sex. By the nineteenth century, as in the *Olympia* . . . the central female figure is associated with a black figure in such a way as to imply their sexual similarity. The association of figures of the same sex stresses the special status of female sexuality.

* * *

Here [in *Olympia*] the linkage between two female figures, one black and one white, represents not the perversities of human sexuality in a corrupt society, such as the black servants signify in Hogarth; rather, it represents the internalization of this perversity in one specific aspect of human society, the sexualized female, in the perception of late nineteenth-century Europe.

In the nineteenth century, the prostitute is perceived as the essential sexualized female. She is perceived as the embodiment of sexuality and of all that is associated with sexuality – disease as well as passion. Within the large and detailed literature concerning prostitution written during the nineteenth century (most of which documents the need for legal controls and draws on the medical model as perceived by public health officials), the physiognomy and physiology of the prostitute are analysed in detail. We can begin with the most widely read early nineteenth-century work on prostitution, that of A.J.B. Parent-Duchatelet, who provides a documentation of the anthropology of the prostitute in his study of prostitution in Paris (1836). Alain Corbin has shown how Parent-Duchatelet's use of the public health model reduces the prostitute to yet another source of pollution, similar to the sewers of Paris. Likewise in Parent-Duchatelet's discussion of the physiognomy of the prostitute, he believes himself to be providing a descriptive presentation of the appearance of the prostitute. He presents his readers with a statistical description of the physical types of the prostitutes, the nature of their voices, the colour of their hair and eyes, their physical anomalies, and their sexual profile in relation to child-bearing and disease. Parent-Duchatelet's descriptions range from the detailed to the anecdotal. His discussion of the *embonpoint* of the prostitute begins his litany of external signs. Prostitutes have a "peculiar plumpness" which is attributed to "the great number of hot baths which the major part of these women take" – or perhaps to their lassitude, since they rise at ten or eleven in the morning, "leading an animal life." They are fat as prisoners are fat, from simple confinement.

* * *

Manet's *Olympia* stands exactly midway between the glorification and the condemnation of the sexualized female. She is the antithesis of the fat prostitute. Indeed, she was perceived as thin by her contemporaries, much in the style of the actual prostitutes of the 1860s. But Laura, the black servant, is presented as plump, which can be best seen in Manet's initial oil sketch of her done in 1862-63. Her presence in both the sketch and in the final painting emphasizes her face, for it is the physiognomy of the black which points to her own sexuality and to that of the white female presented to the viewer unclothed but with her genitalia demurely covered. The association is between these hidden genitalia and the signifier of the black. Both point to potential corruption of the male viewer by the female. This is made even more evident in that work which art historians have stressed as being heavily influenced by Manet's *Olympia*, his portrait *Nana*. Here the associations would have been quite clear to the contemporary viewer. First, the model for the painting was Henriette Hauser, called Citron, the mistress of the prince of Orange. Second, Manet places in the background of the painting a Japanese crane, for which the French word (*grue*) was a slang term for prostitute. He thus labels the figure as a sexualized female. Unlike the classical pose of the *Olympia*, Nana is presented being admired by a well-dressed man-about-town (a *flâneur*). She is not naked but partially clothed. What Manet can further draw upon is the entire vocabulary of signs which, by the late nineteenth century, were associated with the sexualized female. Nana is fulsome rather than thin. Here Manet employs the stigmata of fatness to characterize the prostitute. This convention becomes part of the visualization of the sexualized female even while the reality of the idealized sexualized female is that of a thin female.

* * *

The portrait of *Nana* is also embedded in a complex literary matrix which provides many of the signs needed to illustrate the function of the sexualized female as the sign of disease. The figure of Nana first appeared in Emile Zola's novel *L'Assommoir* (1877) in which she was presented as the offspring of the alcoholic couple who are the central figures of the novel. Her heredity assured the reader that she would eventually become a sexualized female – a prostitute – and, indeed, by the close of the novel she has run off with an older man, the owner of a button factory, and has begun her life as a sexualized female. Manet was captivated by the figure of Nana (as was the French reading public), and his portrait of her symbolically reflected her sexual encounters presented during the novel. Zola then decided to build the next novel in his Rougon-Macquart cycle about the figure of Nana as a sexualized female. Thus in Zola's *Nana* the reader is presented with Zola's reading of Manet's portrait of Nana. Indeed, Zola uses the portrait of the *flâneur* observing the half-dressed Nana as the centrepiece for a scene in the theatre in which Nana seduces the simple Count Muffat. Immediately before this meeting, Zola presents Nana's first success in the theatre (or, as the theatre director calls it, his brothel). She appears in a revue, unable to sing or dance, and becomes the butt of laughter until, in the second act of the revue, she appears unclothed on stage:

> Nana was in the nude: naked with a quiet audacity, certain of
> the omnipotence of her flesh. She was wrapped in a simple piece
> of gauze: her rounded shoulders, her Amazon's breasts of which
> the pink tips stood up rigidly like lances, her broad buttocks

which rolled in a voluptuous swaying motion, and her fair, fat hips: her whole body was in evidence, and could be seen under the light tissue with its foamy whiteness.

What Zola describes are the characteristics of the sexualized woman, the "primitive" hidden beneath the surface: "all of a sudden in the comely child the woman arose, disturbing, bringing the mad surge of her sex, inviting the unknown element of desire. Nana was still smiling: but it was the smile of a man-eater." Nana's atavistic sexuality, the sexuality of the Amazon, is destructive. The sign of this is her fleshliness. And it is this sign which reappears when she is observed by Muffat in her dressing room, the scene which Zola found in Manet's painting:

Then calmly, to reach her dressing table, she walked in her drawers through that group of gentlemen, who made way for her. She had large buttocks, her drawers ballooned, and with breast well forward she bowed to them, giving her delicate smile.

Nana's childlike face is but a mask which conceals the hidden disease buried within, the corruption of sexuality. Thus Zola concludes the novel by revealing the horror beneath the mask: Nana dies of the pox. (Zola's pun works in French as well as in English and is needed because of the rapidity of decay demanded by the moral implication of Zola's portrait. It would not do to have Nana die slowly over thirty years of tertiary syphilis. Smallpox, with its play on "the pox," works quickly and gives the same visual icon of decay.) Nana's death reveals her true nature:

Nana remained alone, her face looking up in the light from the candle. It was a charnel-house scene, a mass of tissue fluids and blood, a shovelful of putrid flesh thrown there on a cushion. The pustules had invaded the entire face with the pocks touching each other; and, dissolving and subsiding with the greyish look of mud, there seemed to be already an earthy mouldiness on the shapeless muscosity, in which the features were no longer discernible. An eye, the left one, had completely subsided in a soft mass of purulence; the other, half open, was sinking like a collapsing hole. The nose was still suppurating. A whole reddish crust was peeling off one cheek and invaded the mouth, distorting it into a loathsome grimace. And on that horrible and grotesque mask, the hair, that beautiful head of hair still preserving its blaze of sunlight, flowed down in a golden trickle. Venus was decomposing. It seems as though the virus she had absorbed from the gutters and from the tacitly permitted carrion of humanity, that baneful ferment with which she had poisoned a people, had now risen to her face and putrefied it.

The decaying visage is the visible sign of the diseased genitalia through which the sexualized female corrupts an entire nation of warriors and leads them to the collapse of the French Army and the resultant German victory at Sedan. The image is an old one, it is *Frau Welt*, Madam World, who masks her corruption, the disease of being a woman, through her beauty. . . . But it is yet more, for in death Nana begins to revert to the blackness of the earth, to assume the horrible grotesque countenance perceived as belonging to the world of the black, the world of the "primitive," the world of disease. Nana is, like Olympia, in the words of Paul Valéry, "pre-eminently unclean."

It is this uncleanliness, this disease, which forms the final link between two images of women, the black and the prostitute.

INDEX

(Numbers in italics refer to the page numbers of the illustrations)